DOC HOLLIDAY

Yours Truly
J. H. Halliday

DOC HOLLIDAY

THE LIFE AND LEGEND

Gary L. Roberts

WILEY

John Wiley & Sons, Inc.

Frontispiece: John Henry "Doc" Holliday, Prescott, Arizona, circa 1879; photograph by D. F. Mitchell.

This book is printed on acid-free paper. ∞

Copyright © 2006 by Gary L. Roberts. All rights reserved

Published by John Wiley & Sons, Inc., Hoboken, New Jersey
Published simultaneously in Canada

Photos courtesy of: frontispiece, pp. 16, 52, 66, 126 (middle), 286, 376, Craig Fouts; pp. 13, 23, 51, 63, 401, Robert G. McCubbin; pp. 18, 59, Constance Knowles McKellar; p. 29, Susan McKey Thomas; p. 37, Regina Rapier; p. 42, Mrs. Fred Arnold Martin Sr. and Charles C. Martin; p. 43, Albert S. Pendleton Jr.; p. 47, Sarah Cranford Bradford; p. 49, University of Pennsylvania School of Dentistry; p. 54, *History of Dentistry in Georgia,* Georgia Dental Association, 1962; p. 57, Angeline Delegal; p. 71, Buffalo Bill Museum, Cody, Wyoming; pp. 91, 162, Kansas State Historical Society, Topeka, Kansas; p. 93, Bob Boze Bell; p. 93 (inset), William B. Secrest; pp. 96, 126 (left, right) Arizona Historical Society, Tucson, Arizona; p. 98, Holliday Day House Museum, Fayetteville, Georgia; p. 129, Carl Chafin Collection; p. 151, New York Historical Society; pp. 190, 208, paul johnson; p. 217, Utah State Historical Society, Salt Lake City, Utah; p. 236, Jack Burrows; p. 253, Peter Brand; pp. 288, 342 (inset), from a woodcut in the *National Police Gazette;* pp. 342, 371, Western History Collection, Denver Public Library, Denver, Colorado; p. 346, Regina Andrus; p. 361, Kathryn Gardner; p. 393, Dr. A. W. Bork

For general information about our other products and services, please contact our Customer Care Department within the United States at (800) 762-2974, outside the United States at (317) 572-3993 or fax (317) 572-4002.

Wiley also publishes its books in a variety of electronic formats. Some content that appears in print may not be available in electronic books. For more information about Wiley products, visit our web site at www.wiley.com.

Library of Congress Cataloging-in-Publication Data:

Roberts, Gary L., date.
   Doc Holliday : the life and legend / Gary L. Roberts.
      p.   cm.
   Includes bibliographical references and index.
   ISBN-13 978-0-471-26291-6 (cloth : alk. paper)
   ISBN-10 0-471-26291-9 (cloth : alk. paper)
      1. Holliday, John Henry, 1851–1887. 2. Outlaws—West (U.S.)—Biography.
   3. Gamblers—West (U.S.)—Biography. 4. Frontier and pioneer life—West (U.S.)
   5. Dentists—West (U.S.)—Biography. 6. West (U.S.)—Biography. I. Title.

   F594.H74R63 2006
   364.152'3'092-dc22
                                                                2005022233

Printed in the United States of America
10 9 8 7 6 5 4 3 2 1

For
Susan McKey Thomas,
John Henry Holliday's cousin,
a true Southern lady in the finest sense of the term
and the inspiration for this book.

CONTENTS

ACKNOWLEDGMENTS

A book such as this is built on the generosity of others. Teachers, scholars, researchers, artists, and encouragers (many of whom never realized the role they played) influenced both this work's conception and explication while instilling a profound sense of humility in me. Countless individuals shaped not only my knowledge of and enthusiasm for this story but also the worldview and sense of history that gave it form and meaning. Regretfully, I cannot acknowledge or even remember all of them, but I am profoundly grateful to each.

My greatest debt is to Susan McKey Thomas, the granddaughter of John Henry Holliday's uncle, William Harrison McKey. Her encouragement and willingness to share the results of her own prodigious research made this book possible. She has been my mentor, my collaborator, and my friend. Long before I met Susie, though, the seed that spawned this book had already been planted in the living room of the late Alva McKey of Valdosta, Georgia, a first cousin of John Henry Holliday's. "Miss Alva" made Doc Holliday human for me that afternoon long ago; Susie revived my interest and challenged me to tell his story.

Other members of John Henry's family helped as well, some directly, some through collaboration with others: Edward R. Holliday, J. William F. Holliday, Robert Lee Holliday, Angeline De La Gal, Cathy E'Dalgo, J. C. E'Dalgo, Morgan De Lancey McGee, J. D. McKey, John McKey, Martha Wiseman McKey, Constance Knowles McKellar, Mac McKellar, Carolyn Holliday Manley, Catharine Holliday Neuhoff, Regina Rapier, Karen Holliday Tanner, I. H. Tillman, and Mrs. Clyde McKey White.

Casey Tefertiller, whose landmark *Wyatt Earp: The Life behind the Legend* set a new standard for students of frontier violence and its accompanying myths, encouraged me to make an old dream a reality, and provided advice and materials from his own research to help make it happen. Jeffrey J. Morey, a close student of Wyatt Earp and the Tombstone troubles, shared his own research and insights in ways that proved essential to the evolution of this book. Victoria Wilcox was generous to a fault with the fruits of her own research (especially relating to the Holliday family) as well as her unique and challenging perspectives on critical issues that helped me to see old questions in new ways. Robert F. Palmquist, a Tucson attorney and close student of Tombstone's colorful history, provided sage advice both on the substance of this story and on the peculiarities of the nineteenth-century legal system. Dr. David O. Moline, a dental surgeon and a historian of dental practice, shared critical information based on his own interest in Doc Holliday. The late Robert N. Mullin tutored me in this field for years with rare balance and perception. Without this half dozen, this book would never have been written.

Other researchers took the time to share unselfishly from their own important research in ways that provided new information that modified or informed my understanding. Regina Andrus, John Boessenecker, Arthur W. Bork, Peter Brand, Jack Burrows, Woody Campbell, Bob Cash, Paul Cool, Bruce Dettman, Bill Dunn, Mark Dworkin, Marcus A. Gottschalk, Teresa Green, Chuck Hornung, Roger Jay, Paul L. Johnson, Scott Johnson, Shirley Ayn Linder, William B. Shillingberg, Emma Walling, and Roy Young made critical contributions of this kind.

I have also benefited from the work of Doc Holliday's previous biographers—John Myers Myers, Patricia Jahns, Albert Pendleton Jr., Sylvia D. Lynch, Ben T. Traywick, Bob Boze Bell, and Karen Holliday Tanner—whose works blazed the trail for my quest for understanding and raised new questions that I might otherwise have missed.

Several private collectors—Carl Chafin, Craig Fouts, Robert G. McCubbin, Kevin J. Mulkins, and C. Lee Simmons—made it possible for me to examine documents that I could not have seen otherwise.

Other individuals, living and dead, who have contributed to this work include Rita Ackerman, Robin Andrews, Scott Anderson, Lynn R. Bailey, Allen Barra, Dr. Ernest Beerstecher, Verner Lee Bell, Mary Billings-McVicar, Peter Blodgett, Mark Boardman, Patrick A. Bowmaster, Jim Bradshaw, Donaly Brice, Richard Maxwell Brown, Tom Bryant, Neal Carmony, Robert J. Chandler, Peter Christoph, Ann Collier, Wayne Collier, Sharon Cunningham, Donald O. Davis, Joe

Davis, Robert K. De Arment, Jack DeMattos, Jim Dunham, Joan Farmer, Timothy W. Fattig, Steve Gatto, Tom Gaumer, Treese Hellstrom, Cindy Hines, Dr. L. C. Holtzendorff, Billy Johnson, Troy Kelly, Larry Knuth, E. Dixon Larson, Jennifer Lewis, Joe Lineburger, Randy Lish, Larry Martin, Gary McClelland, Nyle H. Miller, Carolyn Mitchell, Jan Morrison, Roger Myers, Bruce Olds, Clay Parker, Chuck Parsons, Chris Penn, Roger Peterson, Nancy Pope, Pamela Potter, Cyn Poweleit, S. J. Reidhead, Max Roberts, John Rose, Rod Rothrock, Clark Secrest, Larry G. Shaver, Keith Sladic, Chuck Smith, Jean Smith, Joseph W. Snell, Russell Street, John D. Tanner, Ben Tingenot, Kenneth Vail, Lawrence Vivian, Mark Warren, Jeff Wheat, Erik Wright, and Ronald Yeomans.

In my youth I was tutored patiently in the history of Western violence by a remarkable group of historians, book collectors, writers, researchers, and a few direct links to the Western past who shaped my approach to the field. They are gone now, but they were giants to me, and acknowledging them is both appropriate and necessary because of my great debt to them. In addition to Bob Mullin, Ramon F. Adams, Henry Allen (aka Will Henry and Clay Fisher), Ed Bartholomew, William R. Cox, J. Frank Dobie, Jefferson C. Dykes, John D. Gilchriese, Waldo E. Koop, Ethel Macia, Nyle H. Miller, Philip J. Rasch, C. L. Sonnichsen, Zoe A. Tilghman, and Opie Vermillion fed the vision that made this book possible.

The tyranny of space has forced me to confine my acknowledgments of numerous institutions, both public and private, to the extensive notes appended to this volume. I hope that the staffs of these institutions, past and present—literally dozens of people—who so generously helped me across the years will understand. I do not take lightly my debt to them or the places where they work, or have worked.

I am especially grateful to my editor, Hana Lane, and my production editor, Lisa Burstiner, whose patience, direction, and toughness made this dream become a reality.

Finally, I would like to thank my family and friends, especially my stepdaughter, LeahAnn Driscoll, who with one bright smile reminds me that there is a future as well as a past.

I can only hope that the results are worthy of the effort of all of these people—and more—on my behalf.

PROLOGUE

THE MEASURE OF A MAN

There's no such thing as a normal life, Wyatt. There's just life. Now get on with it.

— Doc Holliday to Wyatt Earp, *Tombstone* (1993)

At ten o'clock on the morning of November 8, 1887, at Glenwood Springs, Colorado, a slight, frail man of thirty-six succumbed to the effects of chronic pulmonary tuberculosis. In his last days, John Henry Holliday, his hair silvered and his gaunt form bent and worn from the ravages of his disease, hardly seemed the stuff of legend, although in the words of the local paper, "the fortitude and patience he displayed in his last two months of life, made many friends."[1] But when the *Denver Republican* noted his passing, the measure of the man came clearer: "Doc Holliday is dead. Few men have been better known to a certain class of sporting people, and few men of his character had more friends or stronger companions. He represented a class of men who are disappearing in the new West. He had the reputation of being a bunco man, desperado, and bad-man generally, yet he was a very mild-mannered man, was genial and companionable, and had many excellent qualities."[2]

This somewhat gentle assessment of the career of Doc Holliday underscored a problem that has plagued his biographers across the years since his death. The man was already obscured by his reputation before he was laid to rest in Glenwood Springs. He would be variously described as a Byronic aristocrat embittered by illness, the black sheep of a fine Southern family, a cynical and deadly killer, and a quarrelsome and profligate drunkard, but despite periodic rumors of personal

1

correspondence and other papers that might throw light onto his values and attitudes, Doc Holliday remains more myth than man.

Opinions always varied. Wyatt Earp (through his ghostwriter in 1896) described him as a "mad, merry scamp with heart of gold and nerves of steel; who . . . stood at my elbow in many a battle to the death." Earp's ghostwriter produced a vivid and compelling portrait of Doc—although he had him hail from the wrong state: "He was a dentist, but he preferred to be a gambler. He was a Virginian [actually a Georgian], but he preferred to be a frontiersman and a vagabond. He was a philosopher, but he preferred to be a wag. He was long, lean, an ash-blond and the quickest man with a six-shooter I ever knew."[3]

Bat Masterson was less kind, saying that Doc "had a mean disposition and an ungovernable temper, and under the influence of liquor was a dangerous man." Describing him as "a weakling who could not have whipped a healthy fifteen-year-old boy in a go-as-you-please fight," Masterson saw him as "hot headed and impetuous and very much given to both drinking and quarreling, and among men who did not fear him, [he] was very much disliked."[4]

Virgil Earp called him "gentlemanly," a "good dentist," and a "friendly man" and mused that Doc had been blamed for many things that could not be "traced up to his account."[5] The editor of the *Las Vegas (New Mexico) Daily Optic*—who was safely distant from Doc at the time—described him as a "shiftless bagged-legged character—a killer and a professional cut-throat and not a whit too refined to rob stages or even steal sheep."[6] A fellow Georgian who knew him as a young man and later dabbled in silver mining in Colorado said of him following his death, "He was a warm friend, and would fight as quick for one as he would for himself. He did not have a quarrelsome disposition, but managed to get into more difficulties than almost any man I ever saw."[7]

An unidentified newspaperman remarked about Doc in 1882, "Here is a man who, once a friend, is always a friend; once an enemy is always an enemy."[8] Ridgely Tilden, a correspondent for the *San Francisco Examiner* in 1882, wrote of him:

> Now comes Doc Holliday, as quarrelsome a man as God ever allowed to live on earth. A Georgian, well bred and educated, he happened in Kansas some years ago. Saving Wyatt Earp's life in Dodge City, Kansas, he earned his gratitude, and notwithstanding his many bad breaks since, has always found a friend in Wyatt. Doc Holliday is

responsible for all the killing, etc, in connection with what is known as the Earp-Clanton imbroglio in Arizona. He kicked up the fight, and Wyatt Earp and his brothers "stood in" with him on the score of gratitude.[9]

E. D. Cowen, a Denver newspaperman who met Holliday in 1882, provided yet another view:

> A person unfamiliar with Holliday's deeds . . . would pass him off as a specimen of human insignificance. Holliday was of medium stature and blonde complexion. He was small boned and of that generally slumped appearance common to sufferers from inherited pulmonary disease. The clenched setting of his firmly pointed lower jaw and the steadiness of his blue eyes were the only striking features of his pallid countenance. He was scrupulously neat and precise in his attire, though neither a lady's man nor a dandy. . . . [H]e was too deeply sincere to be voluble of speech and too earnest in his friendships to make a display of them.[10]

But Charles D. Reppy, John P. Clum's partner at the *Tombstone Epitaph*, said flatly, "Holliday was the most thoroughly equipped liar and smoothest scoundrel in the United States."[11]

In such fragments, tantalizing glimpses of truth doubtlessly appear, all the more intriguing because of the contradictory images they pose. Yet the measure of the man remains incomplete. The Doc Holliday of history is an individual seen almost entirely through the eyes of others. He remains, essentially, a man without a voice, a circumstance that makes him at once a compelling subject and a frustrating figure. He was a Southerner, a dentist, a gambler, and a consumptive who seemed to have no fear of death. He was Wyatt Earp's friend and stood with him at the most famous gunfight in the history of the American West. But those are all impersonal qualities and descriptive terms devoid of any true insight into character, personality, or motivation. They explain what he did, not who he was. They are so vague that they permit today, as in his own time, the diversity of opinion expressed by those quoted here.

Not a single sample of his writing that would provide insight into how he felt or what he believed appears to have survived.[12] In his lifetime he gave precious few interviews, and they are disappointing—except to the extent to which they reveal Doc's humor and studied disdain for the whole process of interview. He never stands clear as a historical figure in sharp relief. Perhaps that is his charm, the reason that in history books, novels, and motion pictures, though he would be unknown without his association with Wyatt Earp, Doc Holliday forever steals the show from the plodding, humorless, but always imposing Mr. Earp, who was clearly the central figure in the events that transpired in Tombstone, Arizona, during the troubled months of 1881 and 1882.

And so, curiously, for one so well known, Doc Holliday remains a mystery, a legend in the shadows. That is his charm and his frustration for would-be biographers. Biography is, after all, an arrogant, intrusive enterprise. It probes lives in all the places that people prefer to have left alone. Those who do it justify it usually because they find something compelling about a life or because they have a passion to bring down idols. In either case, biographers have purposes more complicated than simply "telling it like it really happened."

Biographers reveal much about themselves as well as about their subjects. None of them writes in a vacuum, nor should they, because biography—like all history—amounts to processing lives and events through third-party perceptions to gain the measure of a person and a time. Biographers inevitably see their subjects differently than the subjects saw themselves. No matter how honest, how forthright a subject is, distortions will come from what he or she says, or what he or she leaves out.

The truth of a life is more than a sum of the facts. A life is not merely about what a person does, but also about what a person thinks, feels, and values and how he or she affects the people and events around him or her, because ultimately what biographers and readers want to know is what a person's life *means*. And meaning involves more than how a person sees himself or herself or even what a person does. Meaning also involves how others see a person, and the perception of others is not always based on the truth of a life or even complete knowledge of it. So, then, approaching the life of a man like John Henry Holliday is complicated by the fact that the man behind the legend is obscured by conclusions and opinions that created the legend in the first place.

Without a body of letters or even reminiscences written by him that would serve as a corrective to the half-known life presented in the opinion-gripped contemporary press and the memories of men and women who saw him through the lenses of their own agendas and emotion-packed prejudices, John Henry Holliday tantalizes the biographer with unanswered questions. He did not have a frontierwide reputation until after his experiences at Tombstone in 1881 and 1882. Before then, his life did not always leave a clear trail. As a result, much of his life—even many of its most critical moments—are left to informed speculation and possibilities. This work, then, is not the final word on the life of Doc Holliday; it is, rather, an informed quest to understand the man and his legend that will point the way to further discoveries, raise new questions, and provide some answers in the search for meaning in the life of this brooding metaphor of the moral contradictions of life on the late nineteenth-century frontier.

CHILD OF THE
SOUTHERN FRONTIER

[T]o ignore the frontier and time in setting up a conception of the social state of the Old South is to abandon reality. For the history of the South throughout a very great part of the period from the opening of the nineteenth century to the Civil War . . . is mainly the history of the roll of frontier upon frontier—and on to the frontier beyond.

—W. J. Cash, *The Mind of the South*

The Old South is more an idea than a place or a time. In the popular mind it conjures up images of white-columned plantation houses surrounded by moss-bound oaks, magnolias, dogwoods, and azaleas in bloom, vast fields of cotton, gangs of slaves, and the full range of characters straight out of *Gone with the Wind*. Perhaps that is why it is almost irresistible to think of Doc Holliday as the scion of a plantation family or why one biographer could not resist characterizing him as "aristocracy's outlaw."[1] His story is infused with what might be called the Southern mystique as thoroughly and profoundly as it is with the legend of the last frontier. And so, the man behind the myth is both magnified and obscured by a double distortion.

Ironically, from the beginning John Henry Holliday was as much a child of the frontier as he was of the Old South. Indeed, he lived most of his youth on what was even then known as the Southern frontier. Georgia was the youngest of the original thirteen colonies, and although the young country of which it was part had pushed westward all the way to the Pacific Ocean by the time he was born, John Henry's childhood was spent in the red-clay country of Georgia only a few years distant from the time that the region was the domain of the Creek Nation. When the course of the Civil War persuaded his father that he should move his family beyond the reach of General William Tecumseh Sherman's armies, the young John Henry was transplanted into the piney woods and wiregrass of southwest Georgia, a thinly populated region of subsistence farmers and free grazers until the railroad gave it life and opened up economic opportunities in much the same way that the railroad generated the boomtowns of the last West.

Despite its ambitious claims, Georgia entered the nineteenth century still largely the homeland of the Creeks and the Cherokees. The tidewater region was already shifting its economic base from rice and indigo to the Sea Island cotton that would revitalize slavery and bring prosperity to the state, but the tidewater could not hold the burgeoning population. Restless settlers were pushing west along rivers into the interior, mindless of the claims of the natives and certain of their own "right" to be there.[2]

There was a Celtic edge on the invasion. Willful, sensate sorts, the Scots, the Irish, and the Scots-Irish generated a "Cracker" culture marked by fighting, drinking, gambling, fishing, hunting, idleness, and independence. They faced Georgia's frontier with the same leisurely attitudes of their Scottish and Irish forebears, and the open-range tradition they brought with them moved them into the interior before the agricultural potential was fully realized and created a values system at odds with the stern Yankee Puritanism and nascent capitalism that held sway to the north.[3]

At the heart of this Southern society was a fierce determination of its people to resist restrictions on their independence and movement. Their belligerence first manifested itself in their contest with the Indians. The Creeks did not call white Georgians *E-cun-nau-nux-ulgee* (People-greedily-grasping-after-land) for nothing.[4] Settlers assumed a right to go where they chose, and Georgia was perpetually a thorn in the side of not only the natives but federal Indian policy as well. In the nineteenth century, Georgia developed a liberal land lottery system for the distribution of land as an incentive to dispossession of the Indians, and in the first four decades of the 1800s, sixty-nine counties were created, while the population soared from 162,000 to 691,000.[5]

By November 1827, the last claims of the Creeks were ceded at the second Treaty of Indian Springs not far from where John Henry would be born, and Georgia turned its sights on the Cherokees as the last obstacle to Georgia's sovereignty over lands within its boundaries. The Cherokees attempted to avoid the fate of other tribes through acculturation. They sought to avoid being labeled as "savages" by adopting "civilized" ways. The Cherokees had a written constitution, their own alphabet, a newspaper, schools, an elected legislature, and a permanent capitol at New Echota. Georgia ignored constitutional restrictions on its powers to deal with the Indian tribes and declared on December 28, 1828, that the Cherokee Nation was part of Georgia and subject to its laws. Later, even after the U.S. Supreme Court took a hand in restraining its excesses, Georgia ignored court edicts as well as treaty rights and began the process of overrunning Cherokee lands and suppressing Cherokee laws. Following the discovery of gold in North Georgia in 1829 and the passage of the Indian Removal Act in 1830, the state ordered Cherokee lands to be surveyed in 1831, divided the region into ten new counties the following year, and gave away the land to whites in the Cherokee Lottery of 1833.[6]

Georgia then proceeded to confiscate Cherokee lands, occupy New Echota, and destroy Sequoya's newspaper, the *Cherokee Phoenix*, because of its opposition to removal. The federal government, rather than Georgia, eventually capitulated. Notwithstanding the Supreme Court's clear decisions in favor of the Cherokees, President Andrew Jackson refused to enforce the high court's rulings.[7] After the Georgians invaded Cherokee lands, tribal leaders appealed to Jackson directly, and he—wrongly—told them he could do nothing. When he failed to side with the Indians, the tribe divided into two factions: one accepting removal as the lesser of evils, the other determined to fight on.

Although the vast majority of Cherokees, led by John Ross, flatly opposed removal, federal authorities met with the treaty party led by Major Ridge at New Echota on December 19, 1835, and negotiated the sale of the Cherokee domain of eight million acres for $5 million, despite death threats against the treaty signers by the majority. When Ross's faction refused to migrate, the federal government sent General Winfield Scott to forcibly remove the remaining Cherokees. Eventually, thirteen thousand men, women, and children were rounded up and herded west to the Indian Territory on the Trail of Tears.[8]

The Holliday family was a beneficiary of that tragic story. John Henry's father, Henry Burroughs Holliday, was a self-made man—Andrew Jackson's "common man"—the kind of man nineteenth-century Americans celebrated.[9] His people were plain folk in the Old South. Henry's paternal great-grandfather, William Holliday, was one of three Scotch-Irish brothers who immigrated to America from Ireland sometime after 1750. He settled in the Laurens District of South Carolina, while his brothers, "objecting to settle in slave states," moved north, as Henry later recalled. William and his sons fought in the American Revolution with the "hero of Hornet's Nest," Elijah Clarke, and took their first lands in Wilkes County, Georgia, from bounties for that service.[10]

Later, William Jr., Henry's grandfather, returned to Laurens County, South Carolina. There, his son, Robert Alexander Holliday, met and later married Rebecca Burroughs, whose father had also fought with Elijah Clarke in the American Revolution. Henry Holliday was born to them on March 11, 1819, the first of eleven children.[11] After his father's death, Robert relocated to Anderson County, South Carolina, and in 1831 he followed opportunity into Georgia with his family and eight slaves. He opened a tavern on the road between Newnan and Decatur near Fayetteville and eventually bought an eight-hundred-acre farm in Fayette County, which was part of the old Creek Nation. Over the years, he enlarged his holdings and became a respected and well-known citizen.[12]

Like most white Georgians, emboldened by President Jackson's support of the state's position, the Hollidays saw the Cherokee removal as inevitable and right. The bulk of General Scott's force consisted of volunteers from Georgia, Tennessee, and North Carolina. On May 12, 1838, young Henry, still shy of twenty, enlisted in Fayetteville as a second lieutenant in Captain John D. Stell's company of the First Georgia Volunteers to help effect the final removal of the Cherokees from Georgia.[13] By May 26, 1838, Scott began operations. He urged the troops to act with humanity and mercy, but a contemporary observer reported that "[i]n most cases the humane injunctions of the commanding general were disregarded."[14]

It was disagreeable duty at best, taking men from their fields, women from the hearth, and children from play to push them at gunpoint to relocation centers, but many of the undisciplined and ill-trained militiamen seemed to enjoy the duty too much, taunting their captives and not allowing them time even to gather clothes and other items from their homes for the journey. A motley rabble followed behind the troops, burning homes and crops or moving into cabins to eat the food still cooking over the fires and to plunder the farms before the former owners were out of sight. Z. A. Zile, a Georgia militia officer who later served as a colonel in the Confederate army, would recall, "I fought through the civil war and have seen men shot to pieces and slaughtered by thousands, but the Cherokee removal was the cruelest work I ever knew."[15]

The Cherokees were held in makeshift stockades where sanitary conditions were awful and sickness and despair set in quickly. By June 18, General Charles Floyd of the Georgia militia reported to Governor George M. Troup that the only Cherokees left in Georgia were prisoners. General Scott now dismissed all troops save his regular army units, and the youthful Holliday, not yet twenty years old, was discharged with his company at New Echota on June 20. Having done his part to start the Cherokees west on their Trail of Tears, Henry received 160 acres of land in Pike County for his scant service and turned his thoughts to his own future.[16]

The rich red clay of the region was slowly freed from the forest by the sweat of white men and black men and turned under to become the new heart of Georgia's cotton belt. The luxuriant Sea Island cotton would not grow well there, but the cotton gin made short-staple cotton practical and profitable. These developments allowed cotton to flourish in the upcountry, but Georgia's economy was much more diverse than popular myth allows. Corn, wheat, oats, rice, tobacco, sweet potatoes, molasses, honey, butter, horses, mules, sheep, cattle, and swine completed a remarkably diverse agrarian way of life. White settlers poured into the new country of the piedmont, and early arrivals like the Hollidays made the most of their opportunities in the new country they had confiscated.[17] Henry settled at the new town of Griffin.

But if Henry Holliday was the product of the forces that glorified the common man in the "age of Jackson," his was also a society driven by notions of honor, manhood, family, and community. Henry could claim no genteel tradition. There is much in the myth of the Old South about class. Both the cavalier tradition and the Northern critique of

Southern life assume a rigid class system in the South similar to the class structure of Georgian England.[18]

Despite the pretensions of some, it was always largely a fiction in much of the Old South. This is not to say that there were no social distinctions, but that they have been misunderstood. In the first place, there were simply too many planters who wore white gloves to hide the calloused hands that betrayed their common origins and who shared values with the great bulk of ordinary Southerners. Outside of Virginia and a slender strip of tidewater through the Carolinas and Georgia, inherited wealth and position simply did not exist. The great heart of the Cotton Kingdom was frontier. There, rank, and even wealth, were not controlling factors in the measure of men. As was true on other frontiers, the great virtues and marks of distinction were more personal. Courage, strength, conviviality, ability with weapons, skill at cards, keeping one's word, a readiness to defend one's honor, and even the ability to hold one's liquor were just as important.[19]

Ironically, black slavery preserved a certain egalitarianism among whites. As W. J. Cash pointed out long ago, one of the oddities of the "peculiar institution" was that slavery served as a leveler that preserved independence and individualism and prevented the development of a rigid class system among whites. Middling and even poor whites were neither directly exploited by the Southern aristocracy nor dependent on it. The result, Cash noted, was "the almost complete disappearance of economic and social focus on the part of the masses. One simply did not have to get on in this world in order to achieve security, independence, or value in one's estimation and in that of one's fellows."[20]

For people like Henry Holliday, then, there was no real sense of social or economic limitation. His people were plain folk, and he lacked both the learning and piety of gentility. But Holliday nurtured the sense of honor, self-worth, magnanimity, and independence needed to forge a place for himself in the upcountry environment while he speculated in land and sought other economic opportunities. He acquired town lots and farmlands as the base for economic security, but, more important, he gained acceptance among his neighbors as a tough but fair-minded and honorable man.

Reputation was everything in the Old South. The opinion of others was a measure of inner worth. Virtue, honor, valor, and respect simply

Henry Burroughs Holliday, father of John Henry Holliday.

did not exist apart from the view of a man in the minds of other men. Some of the truculence for which Henry Holliday would be remembered by those who knew him doubtless arose from the aggressiveness and steadfastness that Southerners expected of leaders, but he also exhibited the attention to manners, courtesy, and hospitality that the social order demanded of community leaders. External, public factors established personal worth, and Henry made a place for himself in that milieu.

Making a place for oneself in the antebellum South was a different process from making a place for oneself in New England or other points north. It was less about capital success, sobriety, piety, class consciousness, and the Puritan work ethic than about sociability, honor, manliness, and loyalty to family and neighbors. It was a difference that puzzled Northerners, who dismissed Southerners as a profligate, lazy, and peculiarly violent species. Still, undeniably, Northerners were drawn to, if not charmed by, a warmhearted grace in their social intercourse that was lacking in the more sober, cautious, reasoned, and dignified Yankee ethic.[21]

Southerners assumed a harsh life, and fate was a part of it. They ordered life with a code of honor, a code rooted not so much in conscience as in pride. Honor imposed duties on every man. It called for self-restraint. It demanded courtesy toward others, even enemies, that sometimes struck outsiders as hypocrisy. And yet it allowed, even demanded, room to act impulsively to defend one's reputation and self-esteem. In the nineteenth century, especially among the middling and working classes, evangelical Christianity modified the foundations of the code for some to demand a higher standard of moral virtue with respect to such matters as fighting, drinking, and gambling, but Southern honor retained a distinctive character in which sociability and manliness were paramount and manifested, respectively, in loyalty to community and in personal independence.[22]

There was a martial air, what might even be called a warrior spirit, that prevailed in the South, and it fed the imagery of violence. Some observers attributed it to the dehumanizing impact of slavery, but recent historians credit the Celtic heritage and its peculiar notions of honor and individuality as the primary culprit.[23] Whatever the source, Southern individualism, independence, and codes of honor meant, practically, as Cash put it, that every Southerner regardless of station was prepared to "knock hell out of whoever dared to cross him."[24] Here was the origin of the brawling, dueling, and lynching that existed in the Old South to a greater degree than elsewhere, but here, too, was the harbinger of nobility, romanticism, and patriotism that made the Southerner a formidable fighting man in defense of family, community, and country.

In 1846, with the eruption of the Mexican War, Southerners flocked to the colors. Henry Holliday traveled to Columbus, Georgia, on the Chattahoochee River, with a company of men from Griffin who called themselves Fannin's Avengers, after the martyred Colonel James Fannin, a former Georgian whose command had been massacred in 1836 at Goliad during the Texas revolution. Holliday was commissioned a second lieutenant in Company I, and his company served in the regiment of Colonel Henry R. Jackson of Savannah.[25] They were soon bound for Mexico, where Jackson's regiment was in the thick of the fight with General Zachary Taylor at Monterrey and served with distinction at Veracruz and Jalapa under General Scott. Discharged at Jalapa on June 1, 1847, Henry Holliday continued to serve as a clerk in the army's Commissary Department for a time.[26]

When Holliday returned to Griffin, he revealed a side of himself that might not have shown itself easily through his rough exterior. He brought with him a Mexican boy named Francisco Hidalgo, who had been orphaned by the war, and took him into his household, though at the time Henry was still a bachelor.[27] That was about to change, however. Henry had his eye on Alice Jane McKey, the nineteen-year-old daughter of William Land McKey and Jane Cloud McKey, whose Indian Creek cotton plantation attested to the family's prominence and success. How and when they met is not evident from the record, but that Alice Jane responded to his courtship was a coup for Henry, ten years her senior, and evidence of his progress toward goals that satisfied his prospective in-laws as well as himself. Henry and Alice Jane were married on January 8, 1849, and the couple moved into a house on Tinsley Street north of the railroad tracks in Griffin.[28]

Alice Jane brought added respectability to Henry. Like the Hollidays, her parents had moved to Georgia from South Carolina. By 1849, they were well-known and respected citizens of Henry County. Her father was well-born himself, while her grandfather, Joseph Cloud, was a member of one of the wealthiest slaveholding and landholding families in the region, owning property for a distance of more than fifty miles from Stone Mountain to Griffin. Henry's acceptance by the McKeys was itself evidence of his growing reputation and success.[29]

Henry settled into married life at Griffin as a druggist and began to build a reasonably good life for his aristocratic wife and himself. He was soon a prominent citizen, noted as a hard-nosed businessman and a quick-tempered adversary. Griffin prospered, benefiting from a railroad line that ran from Atlanta to Macon and from the slaves who worked the surrounding cotton fields. It soon became a central point for shipping cotton. Its future seemed bright if not certain.[30] Henry grew with the town, speculating in land and eventually acquiring forty-six plots within the town limits and hundreds of acres in the county as well as potential railroad properties in other parts of the state.

By all accounts, Alice Jane was a refined, genteel, and pious woman, as befitted her background, a wife devoted to her husband and committed to charity and church. Reared a Methodist, she joined the Presbyterian church in Griffin to bring the family together in matters of faith, although she never personally embraced the doctrine of predestination. Henry had married well, and she gave him the kind of home that enhanced his social position as well as fostered the family Henry wanted.[31]

Alice Jane McKey Holliday and infant John
Henry Holliday, circa 1852.

They wasted little time. On December 3, 1849, Alice Jane gave
birth to their first child, Martha Eleanora, one day before President
Zachary Taylor angered Southerners by proposing the admission of
California and New Mexico as states without territorial status first.[32]
Like the compromise that took shape in Congress over the next few
months, little Martha was frail and brought only a brief period of joy
to her parents. On June 12, 1850, she died and was buried at the small
cemetery in Griffin.[33] The grieving couple was surrounded by the
extended families of Hollidays and McKeys. John Stiles Holliday,
Henry's younger brother, was a prominent Fayetteville citizen, medical doctor, and businessman, with a growing family of his own. Alice
Jane's parents were also nearby. Childhood death was a fact of life in
those days; five of Henry's brothers and sisters had died before the age
of ten. So the young couple coped and planned to try again.

The infant Compromise of 1850 was in trouble, too, by August
14, 1851, when a second child, a son, was born to Henry and Alice
Jane. The boy was likely delivered by John, who came down from
Fayetteville for the occasion. They named him John Henry Holliday,
after his uncle and father, and he became the center of their world.
The Holliday family was both large and close, so John Henry's birth
was a major event in the life of the whole family. As the eldest son of
the eldest son, young John Henry was destined to play a large role in

family life. As he was the primary heir, the guardianship of the family's good name would one day fall into his charge. The Hollidays celebrated and made plans for the future in light of this new birth.[34]

One family source—and curiously only one—recalled that John Henry was born with a cleft palate.[35] Mary Cowperwaithe Fulton Holliday, the wife of John Henry's cousin Robert Alexander Holliday (and a person who never met John Henry herself), reportedly wrote that the "most distressed" John Stiles Holliday consulted with his colleague and cousin by marriage, the renowned Dr. Crawford W. Long, who assisted him in the delicate surgery closing John Henry's cleft palate, using ether as an anesthesia.[36] If true, this was an extraordinary event that should have made news throughout the country, not only for Long, who was involved in a public controversy about the use of ether at the time, but also for Holliday, who would have won accolades for the successful delicate surgery.

In 1842, Long had removed a small cystic tumor from the neck of a patient using ether, but he published no paper on his discovery. In 1846, Dr. John Collins Warren of Massachusetts General Hospital experimented with ether, and in November of that year, Henry J. Bigelow published an article in the *Boston Medical and Surgical Journal* announcing to the world the successful use of ether as an anesthesia. The reputations of Warren and Bigelow gave the procedure credibility, and they were heralded as the discoverers of ether's anesthetic powers.[37]

Once the Bigelow article had been published, Long tried, after the fact, to assert his own claim as the discoverer of ether's use as an anesthesia. Long blamed his failure to act earlier on a "very laborious country practice," and, once his discovery became public in Jackson County where he lived at the time, his practice fell off, he suffered some community ostracism, and one local elder told him that "if he should have a mistake and kill someone with ether, there was not a doubt but that he would be lynched." But by 1851 he was involved in a very public controversy with Warren and Bigelow on the subject. His use of ether at an early date would eventually be verified and recognized, but because he did not publish a report of his discovery, the medical community did not, as the leading medical historian William H. Welch said, "assign to him any influence upon the historical development of our knowledge of surgical anesthesia or any share in its introduction to the world at large."[38] Regardless, in 1851 he was still

Dr. John Stiles Holliday, brother of Henry
B. Holliday, who delivered John Henry
Holliday and played a role in his nephew's
life.

very much involved in an effort to assert his claim, and success in an operation as complex as cleft palate surgery on an infant would have been a noteworthy accomplishment in any case.

Long was living in Atlanta in 1851 and, at least theoretically, would have been available for such a procedure, although no contemporary source has yet been found to confirm it. This seems a little odd, because Long had learned the hard way the importance of reporting medical breakthroughs. Cleft palate surgery on an infant using ether was a formidable challenge, requiring better than average skill and luck as well as specialized tools. The surviving papers of Long, which detail many of his operations—most less significant than the complicated procedures of cleft palate surgery—contain no hint of such an operation, even though he was publicizing his discoveries, documenting examples of their use, and emphasizing their importance during the very time when the operation would have occurred.[39]

A successful cleft palate surgery on a small child was certainly newsworthy—and under anesthesia, extraordinary and groundbreaking. Several innovations were introduced between 1844, when Sir William Fergusson first outlined operative procedures for cleft palate surgery "founded on anatomical and physiological data," and 1877, when Francis Mason published his work "On Harelip and Cleft Palate," but notably the first successful cleft palate surgery under anesthesia was not reported until a physician named Buzzard announced his use of chloroform in 1868.[40] If Holliday and Long did perform such an operation on John Henry, it was a major event, and, in light of his previous battles to gain recognition for his work, Long's failure to publish reports of it was inexplicable.

Cleft palate surgeries were performed as early as possible because of the complications of feeding infants caused by the condition and because of possible speech impediments occasioned by waiting until after a child began to speak before operating. The latter consideration argued for surgery before the second birthday, but surgery within the first several months was discouraged because of the shock to the infant's system, the belief that small children did not "bear the loss of blood well," and the simple fact that early efforts often failed to close the cleft satisfactorily.[41] Given the complexity of the surgery, the specialized knowledge and tools required, and the complications of using anesthesia on an infant at that point in time, such a procedure would have been virtually impossible outside of a hospital or without receiving public notice.

If such a surgery was performed on John Henry, it would have certainly happened in 1851 or early in 1852 at the latest, because Long moved to Athens, Georgia, in 1852. If John Henry was born with a cleft palate, it was never obvious in the photographs of him, even as a baby (the earliest of which was almost certainly taken before any surgery could have occurred). Of course, a posterior cleft would not have affected the lip or the upper jaw and would not have created a facial deformity. According to Mary Holliday, the cleft "extended to, but not through, his lip."

No convincing evidence exists to support the claim of a cleft palate. Still, the possibility of such a surgery must be considered because of the potential impact on both his physical and social development. If he did suffer from such an impediment, it doubtlessly affected him in two ways: first, by tying him closer to his mother and delaying the "dropping of the slips"—the point, usually about age four, when boys began to wear pants—and, second, by causing him to be, in the words of Mary Holliday, "somewhat self-conscious" and "withdrawn." This would help to explain the child's distance from his father and a perception of Doc as a "mama's boy."[42] Unfortunately, the weight of evidence does not provide any real support for the claim.

John Henry was baptized on March 21, 1852, at the Griffin Presbyterian Church.[43] By then, Spalding County had been created, and

Henry Holliday had become the first clerk of the superior court.[44] As he prepared to take office in December 1851, a state convention convened at Milledgeville to consider Georgia's course in light of the Compromise of 1850. On December 10, the attendees agreed to abide by the compromise but warned against further encroachments against slavery.[45] The following year saw the compromise jeopardized, and although Franklin Pierce was elected president supporting it, the Free-Soil Party and the controversy surrounding Harriet Beecher Stowe's best-selling *Uncle Tom's Cabin* guaranteed that the issue had not been resolved. Men clung to the hope that it could be amicably settled but feared it would not be. And in it all, Southern solidarity was growing with a widespread perception that the South's way of life was under siege.

As the linchpin of Southern society, slavery involved much more than morality or even economics. In the South—indeed, in the country at large—the issue was not so much the effect of slavery on blacks but its effect on whites.[46] What was at stake was the very balance of white society, the shattering of all the social conundrums of Southern life, and the anticipated reordering of the Southern way of life from top to bottom along the lines of the hated Yankee model. If Southerners rationalized the evils of slavery, they did so by making the contest one of honor, principle, and will. To the forefront rushed all the personal pride, individualism, and community solidarity that transcended class and welded together a fervent belief that the coming conflict was above all self-defense.[47]

Henry's stance on the issues can only be assumed based on his rising position in the community. Though he was not a planter, he did own slaves, and the perceived threat to Southern institutions jeopardized his upward mobility. Moreover, he shared popular views about Southern rights and Yankee meddling. Ever the individualist anxious to improve his lot and that of his family, Henry doubtless measured his future in terms of Southern unity. There was honor at stake, a way of life, and the images of Henry that have passed down the corridors of family remembrance are reminiscent of a contemporary portrait of the Mississippian Sargent Prentiss:

> Instant in resentment, and bitter in his animosities, yet magnanimous to forgive when reparation had been made . . . [t]here was no littleness about him. Even toward an avowed enemy he was open and manly, and bore himself with a sort of antique courtesy and knightly

hostility, in which self-respect mingled with respect for his foe, except when contempt was mixed with hatred, and then no words can convey any sense of the intensity of his scorn.[48]

The future that Henry sought for himself and his family was linked to the social order that had spawned him. Honor was separate neither from responsibility nor from safety for family and society. And the very solidarity of viewpoint that he shared with his neighbors and kinsmen gave to him and to them a sense of confidence and power, so that there was no loss of optimism about the future, only a fierce, resolute determination to ensure that it would not be disrupted. So then, Henry set his eyes on the tasks at hand, the practical matters of business and family, and he was unwilling to sacrifice the present with fears about the future.

Alice Jane's mother died on January 26, 1853, beginning an eventful year that would involve other changes.[49] In October 1853, Henry sold his house on Tinsley Street and bought a new home and land northwest of Griffin near the railroad tracks.[50] Little John Henry was not yet two years old when Francisco, his name anglicized to Francisco E'Dalgo, moved out to start his own family. He married Martha Freeman in Butts County on June 12, 1854, and settled down there.[51] And even though Henry and Alice Jane had no more children after the birth of John Henry, the house was soon full again. On November 9, 1856, William Land McKey, Alice Jane's father, also died, and Henry became the guardian of his wife's minor siblings, Thomas Sylvester, Melissa Ella, Eunice Helena, and Margaret Ann, as well as guardian of their inheritance and his wife's.[52]

Tom McKey, who was fourteen when his father died, became the older "brother" whom John Henry idolized as he grew. John Henry had already dropped the slips before Tom moved in. He turned six with "bleeding Kansas" in the news. For him, though, the education of a gentleman had begun already, both in the manners of the wellborn taught by his mother and in the stern demands of Southern manhood imposed by his father. Southern boys of all classes were given a surprising amount of freedom as children so as not to limit their aggressiveness or to feminize them with a strict discipline that would break their spirits.[53]

At an early age they learned independence, took to the fields and woods, and began their tutelage in hunting, the handling of firearms, and horseback riding. They were also taught deference to their elders and learned the "Sir" and "Ma'am" required of them in speaking to adults whether highborn or low. Courtesy, spirit, and firmness were all part of the curriculum of individualism that Southern sons learned, but care was taken not to undermine their self-confidence or pride.

So John Henry grew. Nurtured by his extended family, he learned a way not so different from the aristocratic ideal that his mother wanted to teach him. "The result," as Cash wrote of Southerners in general, "was a kindly courtesy, a level-eyed pride, an easy quietness, a barely perceptible flourish of bearing, which for all its obvious angularity and fundamental plainness, was one of the finest things the Old South produced."[54] From his father came a sense of personal honor and discipline; from his mother came a proper sense of manners and the principles of faith. Cousins, uncles, aunts, and neighbors filled out the life of a child growing.

In 1857, John Henry's uncle, Robert Kennedy Holliday, moved to Jonesboro with his family so that most of the Hollidays and McKeys were now within the triangle of Griffin, Fayetteville, and Jonesboro, close enough for support and frequent visits. Robert's wife, Mary Anne Fitzgerald, was a devout Roman Catholic. His daughters, Martha Anne (called "Mattie" by the family), Lucy Rebecca, Mary Theresa, and Roberta Rosalie, added yet another dimension to John Henry's experience. Mary Anne Holliday's uncle, Philip Fitzgerald, and his wife, Eleanor, were also part of the family circle.[55] Then in 1859 Henry agreed to assume the guardianship of a young orphan named Elisha Prichard, who moved in with the family.[56]

The family prospered. Land holdings mounted. Martha Holliday, the sister of Henry and John Stiles, married James Franklin Johnson, a planter, lawyer, and state senator, which extended the family's influence.[57] Close at hand, the future looked bright. Not even the Panic of 1857 dampened optimism. Indeed, Southerners saw its mild impact on them as evidence of the superiority of their system.[58] Griffin grew—its population approaching three thousand by the end of the decade, making it the largest city between Atlanta and Macon—and offered amenities and opportunities found in few Georgia towns, including three colleges and a public library.[59] Despite growth and prosperity for Griffin, however, the boiling clouds and rolling thunder of politics were increasingly difficult to ignore.

The election of 1856 had come and gone. The Democrat James Buchanan gave Georgians little reason for optimism. They found hope

Robert Kennedy Holliday, brother of Henry Holliday and father of Martha Anne "Mattie" Holliday, with whom John Henry had a close relationship.

in the *Dred Scott* decision, but were soon disillusioned by open defiance of its precepts. They were more disturbed by the growing strength of the new Republican Party in the congressional elections in 1858. They saw the Fugitive Slave Law declared unconstitutional in *Ableman v. Booth* and recoiled at news of John Brown's raid on Harpers Ferry, Virginia, in October 1859.

Senator Robert Toombs, known as Georgia's "Son of Thunder" and considered a moderate in Congress by most observers, became convinced that further compromise was impossible, the Georgia legislature passed resolutions condemning John Brown's "aggressions," and Joseph E. Brown, Georgia's fiery governor, set up factories for the production of weapons and gunpowder and ordered the Georgia militia to make preparations for the "inevitable conflict" to come. There were still Georgia voices, like that of Alexander H. Stephens, who urged caution and restraint, but the martial spirit was gaining momentum in Georgia as it was in other Southern states.[60]

The crazy-quilt election of 1860 found Georgia in turmoil. The Democratic Party had divided into Northern and Southern factions, meeting in Baltimore, Maryland, and Richmond, Virginia, respectively, and a splinter group calling itself the Constitutional Union Party added more confusion. The nomination of Abraham Lincoln by the Republicans did not factor into Georgia's election, but still the vote was so close among the other three candidates that the legislature had to decide where Georgia's electoral votes would go. Lincoln was elected president without Georgia's votes so that the exercise was perfunctory at best, so much so that Governor Brown urged the legislature not to bother. Then on December 20, 1860, South Carolina formally repealed its ratification of the U.S. Constitution and seceded from the Union. In Griffin, Fayetteville, and Jonesboro, the Hollidays, McKeys, Johnsons, and Fitzgeralds were caught up in the anger against the North and the debate over what Georgia should do.[61]

In the end, despite the eloquence of men like Stephens, Benjamin H. Hill, and Hershel V. Johnson, who urged moderation and caution, a referendum was held, and the people voted 50,000 to 37,000 to follow South Carolina's example and defend Georgia's honor in the only manner left to it. On January 19, 1861, Georgia declared itself an independent state.[62] It was not immediately apparent what course Georgia would take, but in February Georgians played prominent roles in the convention that convened in Montgomery, Alabama, to draft a constitution for the Confederate States of America. On March 16, Georgia formally adopted the new constitution and became a state in the new Confederacy.[63]

John Henry Holliday's world was about to change forever.

THE WORLD TURNED
UPSIDE DOWN

Defend yourselves, the enemy is at your door!

—Senator Robert Toombs, January 20, 1860

Georgians celebrated. Across the length and breadth of the state, men and women saw secession as liberation from an oppressive central government. They might not have understood all the complexities of sectional politics or even stood united on the issue of slavery, but they responded to the mantra of Southern rights with undeniable fervor. They were confident, too, that the South would have no trouble defending its new independence. When war became certain after Fort Sumter, former senator Robert Toombs, now secretary of state for the Confederacy, told a cheering assembly of recruits at Milledgeville, Georgia's capital, that they would be home within six months and that any good Southern boy could whip six pasty-faced Yankee clerks. "Why," he proclaimed, "we could lick the Yankees with cornstalks!"[1]

That was the sense of the times for Georgians. Theirs was a fight to protect home and honor, and they had no doubts that they were equal to the task. What they lacked in training and understanding of what was to come was covered up with a brash confidence and fierce loyalty as old as the battles of Sterling and Bannockburn. There was no thought that they could be beaten. So they came to Georgia's colors—planters, dandies, clerks, middling farmers, and crackers, young men and old—ready to defend their state's honor and their liberty.

Griffin shared the excitement. The mobilization and the pomp and circumstance that went with it could not have done anything except stir the imagination of an impressionable ten-year-old boy like John Henry Holliday, watching as he surely did the troops moving in and out of town by road and by rail, crowding the train station, and creating an air of excitement on city streets. Camp Wilder became a training center for Georgia soldiers at Griffin, and the need was great enough that Henry Holliday sold 136 acres of his 147-acre farm for the establishment of another training facility.[2] Joseph E. Brown, Georgia's governor, wrote to Alexander H. Stephens, Georgia's former moderate congressman and the new vice president of the Confederacy, that two regiments had gone into training "at Camp Stephens, near Griffin, which I had called in honor of yourself."[3] The war fever had come to John Henry's doorstep.

He saw his hero, Uncle Thomas Sylvester McKey, who was now twenty-one, don the uniform of the Fifth Georgia Volunteers. There were the comings and goings of other Holliday and McKey relatives—his uncles, Robert Kennedy Holliday, John Stiles Holliday, James Taylor McKey, and William Harrison McKey—cousins, and Francisco E'Dalgo besides—as one by one they enlisted to support the cause. They all looked fine in their fresh new uniforms of Confederate gray surrounded by the womenfolk and children as they prepared to leave for the war. Even his cousin George Holliday, only five years his senior, was at the Georgia Military Institute in Marietta preparing for the day he would be a soldier, too. There were tears and good-byes, and then, one after the other, they were gone.[4]

Henry was the last to go. He bought 278 acres south of his property and made provisions for his family as best he could. Finally, on September 2, 1861, Henry Holliday was commissioned a major in the Twenty-seventh Georgia Infantry, and on October 31 he left as well, bound for Virginia with his regiment as a quartermaster officer, arriving in time for the first battle of Manassas.[5] Alice Jane was left to manage family affairs like other Southern women, and the slaves were still there to produce the necessary crops to sustain John Henry and her sisters.[6]

The excitement soon faded into the anxious anticipation of news about the war, and John Henry found himself alone in a house full of women at precisely the age at which Southern boys began their apprenticeship as men. By then he would, if he was typical, have acquired the masculine skills so critical to male identity in Southern society. He surely knew the rudiments of hunting, fishing, wrestling, dexterity with firearms, and horsemanship. Now was the time to hone the basics into expertise. The absence of male role models was doubtlessly compensated in some measure by the martial air that permeated Griffin. So he likely took to the woods not only to hunt and explore but also to imagine himself in battle along with his kith and kin, holding back the Yankee hordes. Doubtless, too, he watched at the fringes of Camp Stephens as recruits trained or stole away to listen to the gossip about the war around the depot and on the streets of the town.

Of the menfolk, only John Stiles Holliday remained close to home. As a medical officer for Company E (the Fayette Dragoons), Second Georgia Cavalry, which was part of Georgia's home guard, he was close enough to watch over the various relatives to some degree. There were, periodically, family gatherings at which John Henry could play with his cousin Robert, but the visits were less frequent. For the most part, he lived in a strangely feminine world in the midst of that most masculine of human enterprises: war.[7]

Southern women, especially those of Alice Jane's class, were controlled and proper and bore their sacrifices stoically, even proudly. The genteel tradition marked them with manners, abstinence, and social restraint. Their honor was linked to marital loyalty and social purity, but they also shared a pride in their menfolk and a surprisingly militant patriotism. Southern women experienced the loneliness of protracted absences by their husbands without complaint, but they had expectations for the development of their sons as men.[8] For young boys like John Henry, the missing fathers were a special burden, and women often overcompensated, either by spoiling their sons or by giving them too much freedom.

John Henry grew close to and protective of his mother, and she strove to make him a gentleman. It's worth mentioning again that in Southern society, there was a certain tolerance of childish aggression among boys to avoid feminizing them or stifling their independent spirit. Alice Jane doubtless did the best she could, but she and her sisters pampered and spoiled the boy. Perhaps it was then, in the absence of Henry's stern demands, that young John Henry first began to show a certain rebelliousness and resentment of his father. To make matters worse, John Henry's mother fell ill. She was confined to bed more and more, apparently the victim of chronic pulmonary tuberculosis, although that is by no means certain.

Tuberculosis was known as consumption or phthisis in the mid-nineteenth century. It was the leading cause of death at the time, accounting for 20 percent of all deaths in the United States. Doctors considered consumption to be noncontagious and believed that it ran in families. Curiously, too, treatment varied according to the gender of the victim of the disease. Women were encouraged to remain within the home and pursue domestic responsibilities as much as possible. They retained their responsibilities for their children and did their best to maintain a cheerful and calm demeanor. They followed a simple diet, but the only regimen prescribed for women in most cases was to continue traditional female roles.

As the disease worsened, the burden fell on female relatives and friends to assume the responsibilities of the household. Yet despite what one contemporary called "the hideous physical symptoms" of consumption, it was a disease that inspired more admiration than revulsion. It was seen as "the most spiritual, the most ennobling, a purger of base qualities and a distiller of lofty ones."[9] These general practices and images blend well with the anecdotal recollections of Alice Jane Holliday, who was seen as a particularly pious and gentle soul who bore her illness with a memorable forbearance. In practical terms, however, Alice Jane's sisters had to grow up fast, and young John Henry's responsibilities increased as well. He was now "the man of the house" in more than just name.

News trickled home in occasional letters from his father, his uncles, Francisco, and other relatives and neighbors. His uncle William H. McKey, serving with the Thirteenth Georgia Volunteers of General John B. Gordon's division in Virginia, was wounded at Malvern Hill and given furlough to recuperate before returning to action. He was back with his unit in time to be elected captain in September 1862.[10] Henry was with the Twenty-seventh Georgia through the Peninsular campaign and spent his spring and early summer at places like Williamsburg, Seven Pines, Mechanicsville, Cold Harbor, White Oak Swamp, and Malvern Hill, where the Twenty-seventh left more than a third of its 1,151 men as casualties. Besides the reports of battles and lists of dead filtering back, the letters of relatives were not encouraging. William continued to be so troubled by his wounds that his recov-

William Harrison McKey, brother of Alice
Jane McKey Holliday, who served with the
Thirteenth Georgia Volunteers in General
John Brown Gordon's division in Virginia.
He survived the war and moved to south
Georgia, where he developed the Banner
Plantation on the Georgia-Florida line
where John Henry visited as a teenager.

ery seemed doubtful, and he was again absent from duty until March
1863. Henry did not fare well, either. Like many on both sides, he suffered so severely from "chronic diarrhea and general disability" that he
resigned his commission in July 1862, and on August 24, 1862, he was
discharged.[11]

Major Holliday came home to a different situation from the one he
had left. The war had already taken a heavy toll on commerce. Goods
were scarce, crops were thin, and food was in short supply. His wife,
Alice Jane, was virtually bedridden. He scarcely had time to recuperate
or to adjust to his wife's worsening condition before his own father,
Robert, the patriarch of the Hollidays, died in Fayetteville in November. As the eldest son, Henry made arrangements for his father's
funeral and oversaw the settling of his father's estate, dividing it
among his brothers and sisters.[12] As he shouldered these responsibilities, he also faced another harsh reality.

With the Union victory at Gettysburg and the fall of Vicksburg in
July 1863, the momentum of the war shifted dramatically. General William S. Rosecrans, who was commanding Union operations in Tennessee, finally began to take the offensive, and by September 9 he had
maneuvered the Confederate forces under General Braxton Bragg out
of Chattanooga. Bragg's incompetence was so great that General Robert E. Lee took the unprecedented step of sending eleven thousand

badly needed troops from Virginia under the command of General James Longstreet to reinforce the lethargic Bragg. On September 19–20, 1863, the armies met at Chickamauga in northern Georgia just south of the Tennessee line.[13]

Longstreet's forces broke through, drove two Union corps off the field, and sent a significant portion of Rosecrans's forces in full retreat toward Chattanooga, while General George Thomas, the "Rock of Chickamauga," stood firm on the Union right, preventing a total disaster. With the Union army virtually besieged in Chattanooga and the Confederates holding the high ground of Missionary Ridge and Lookout Mountain overlooking the city, Bragg seemed to have secured the Confederate position. President Jefferson Davis left Bragg in command over the protests of his officers, however, and a series of bad decisions afterward dangerously divided the Confederate forces.[14]

General Ulysses S. Grant was now commanding the army of the West, and he and General Thomas unified the federal armies before Chattanooga. On November 23, following spirited resistance by Confederates who were greatly outnumbered, General Joseph Hooker took Lookout Mountain. Bragg's forces held Missionary Ridge, but two days later Union troops, in a brash display that panicked Southern troops, took the field. It was, in the words of one Southern official, an "incalculable disaster."[15] The doorway to Georgia was now open.

Confederate forces consolidated at Dalton, Georgia, not far from the Chickamauga battlefield, now commanded by General Joseph E. Johnston, who had been manhandled by Grant and William Tecumseh Sherman in the West because of his predilection for defensive tactics. Now he faced a Union force in Tennessee more than twice the size of his own army, which reinforced his conservative tendencies. Johnston dug in, waiting for General Sherman to make the first move. The mood was somber. One Georgian wrote that "gloom and unspoken despondency hang like a pall everywhere."[16]

It was then that Major, as Henry Holliday was now almost universally called, concluded that he needed to get his invalid wife and his son and young sisters-in-law out of harm's way to a safer place. He recognized that because of the railroads Atlanta would be the Union's primary target in Georgia. He began to sell property in Spalding County to prepare for the move. Between August 1863 and April 1864 Henry raised $23,700 in Confederate currency from the sale of real estate in Griffin and in Spalding County. He also decided to move his family to the little town of Valdosta in southern Georgia. How he decided on Valdosta as a refuge is not clear from the record, except that contemporary papers referred to it as a "safe retreat."[17]

Valdosta was about as far away from the war as his family could get in Georgia, near the end of the rail line deep in the piney woods and wiregrass of an area still largely undeveloped in 1863. When Major first saw it, Valdosta was a dismal place. The town had been founded in 1859 with high expectations, when the Atlantic & Gulf Railroad missed Troupville by several miles, and several of the prominent citizens of that place decided to move their businesses to the railroad tracks. Believing it unlucky to transfer the name, but not wanting to insult former governor George M. Troup, for whom Troupville was named, they named the new settlement after the former governor's plantation, Val d'Aosta.[18]

Valdosta was "just cropping up out from the woods when the war began," as the *South Georgia Times* explained it a few years later, but "the impetus which the railroad gave was suddenly checked by war, and buildings, half finished were left to rot."[19] The Union blockade and two bad crop years threatened to finish off the town. By the time Major first saw the place, both the Methodist and the Baptist churches had blown down, and the town seemed anything but prosperous. Growth had stopped, and what was there seemed to be falling apart. The only thing the town had to recommend it was that it was distant from the war.

In fact, though, the gathering refugees made the place even less attractive. The local population made room for the newcomers as best it could. Most crowded into the only hotel in town, "a long, rambling building, two stories high," on Central Avenue, with narrow hallways and a dark interior. The "furriners" gathered at the courthouse to talk about land and more permanent lodging. Some of the locals expressed their concern about the invasion of newcomers. "I would like to know what so many of you 'furriners' is a'coming here fur," one of them asked a slaveowner looking for land to buy. "You is gwine to hem us in and ruint our ranges."[20] To outsiders, that did not seem likely, and Major must have seen something there, because on February 9, 1864, he purchased 2,450 acres from the estate of James D. Shanks on Cat Creek northeast of the town for $31,500.[21]

Henry may have had second thoughts almost at once, because that month troops from Charleston and Savannah were ordered into Florida to stop reported Union advances west from Jacksonville toward Pensacola. The Thirty-second Georgia Volunteers traveled by train to Valdosta and camped briefly south of the railroad before marching into Florida. On February 20, 1864, the Confederates stopped the Yankee incursion in a bloody fight at Olustee (or Ocean Pond) near Lake City, Florida, which was just south of the Georgia line. It was as close to Valdosta as the war ever came. Union forces at Jacksonville never ventured west again, and Major Holliday was reassured that he had made a wise choice.[22]

Major returned to Griffin, settled his affairs, closed his house, gathered his family and slaves, and took what personal belongings he could when he boarded the train south with other refugees. It was a hard trip to Macon on the Macon & Western Railroad, then east to Savannah on the Central of Georgia. From Savannah, the family moved briefly on the Savannah, Albany & Gulf Railroad, before taking the Atlantic & Gulf into Valdosta. In due course, however, the Hollidays, their McKey wards, and their slaves arrived at what must have seemed a foreign land. Their new neighbors sought as much news as they could get from the refugees, and, for all their misgivings about the newcomers, did their best to make them welcome.

In April 1864 young John Henry found himself in a place completely unlike the red-clay country of his childhood. It must have seemed like a wilderness to him. The pine and oak forests stretched over the rolling countryside for miles with little besides wiregrass under the canopy of trees. The absence of undergrowth gave an openness to the terrain that was compelling in its parklike beauty and yet conveyed a great sense of emptiness. Farther south, lime sinks, lakes, and cypress swamps gave a different look to the land. Rivers and creeks were also abundant.

The population was a mixed group. Many of the locals were free grazers running livestock over the wiregrass as their forebears had done, but there were farmers as well, some of them slaveholders. A few of the local slaveholders owned large farms on sandy loam that was ideal for Sea Island cotton, and they held substantial numbers of slaves. The dirt was black and rich, and newcomers, like Henry Holliday, recognized at once the potential for agriculture. Many of the refugees, like Henry, also brought slaves with them. Those slaves who came from coastal Georgia, with their "geechie" accent that the locals could not understand, troubled whites, and they organized patrols to "keep them under control."[23]

As Henry's family settled in, legitimate news filtered south slowly, mixed liberally with all manner of rumor, little of it good. Alice Jane received a letter from her brother William, who had returned to duty, describing the battle of Spotsylvania Courthouse in May 1864. But his health was still bad, and Captain McKey was honorably discharged on June 17, 1864. William remained in Virginia, however, trying to get back into the fighting. Tom McKey was in north Georgia with Joe Johnston maneuvering against Sherman's forces. On May 10, 1864, the cadet battalion at the Georgia Military Institute was pressed into service, and by May 14 it saw action near Resaca at the very heart of Johnston's efforts to stall Sherman's advance. George Holliday, though almost eighteen, had received his baptism of fire and gave his relatives one more person to worry about.[24]

Sherman was increasingly the primary concern. "Nearly the whole Population is moving off," one Georgian wrote, "taking their negroes south."[25] Robert Kennedy Holliday, serving as an assistant brigade quartermaster with the Seventh Georgia Regiment, had come home to Jonesboro on furlough in February 1864, and before he returned to his unit, he had taken his daughters, Mattie and Lucy, to Savannah, where he enrolled them at St. Vincent's Academy, removing them as much as he could from harm's way.[26]

Johnston's cautious strategy allowed Sherman to advance deeper and deeper into Georgia and siphon off Confederate confidence. On June 27, the two armies clashed at Kennesaw Mountain. Sherman was repulsed, and Confederate morale was rejuvenated temporarily. On July 20, while Sherman and John Bell Hood, the Texas commander who replaced Johnston, probed each other's lines inconclusively, Howell Cobb wrote to his wife from Macon that the "crisis of Atlanta is evidently at hand." He added, "At present every effort to cut off all railroad communication with the place are succeeding pretty well, as the Macon & Western road is the only one now running, and I am just informed that the train that left here this morning has stopped in Griffin in consequence of the telegraphic lines being cut between there and Atlanta."[27]

On August 30, 1864, Hood's troops were badly mauled at Jonesboro, and the following day Sherman hit the rebels hard again. Hood evacuated Atlanta on September 1, destroying everything of military value in the process, and on September 2 Sherman wired Washington, "Atlanta is ours, and fairly won."[28] Far away, Major Holliday and his family had no idea that the war had come so close to their kin at Jonesboro or that George was part of the evacuating forces, but each day brought more news.

Robert Holliday's wife, Mary Anne, called "Mollie" by her husband, was caught in the battle of Jonesboro. In its aftermath, she saw to the burial of Father Emerson Bliemel and Colonel William Grace in her own backyard. Father Bliemel had been killed while giving last rites to Colonel Grace, and Mary Anne saw that they were properly interred before moving her family to her uncle Philip Fitzgerald's farm. She returned home before Union troops set up a temporary headquarters at the Fitzgerald place and destroyed everything in sight. At Jonesboro, she found her house destroyed and the property occupied. She decided then to flee south with her children.[29]

On September 15, 1864, Henry Holliday, who was in Macon at the time, wrote to his brother Robert at Petersburg, Virginia, that he had just received word that Mary Anne and the children had fled Jonesboro and were safe at Gordon, below Macon. Henry also wrote to Mary Anne that he would be back in the area within a week and that he wanted to take her home with him. "Mollie," Robert wrote to his wife on September 24, "you don't know how glad I was to hear that you had left Jonesboro, for I was perfectly miserable thinking how you and our little children could live inside of the yankee lines or even where our own army are [sic], for there is not as much difference in them as there ought to be, but when I heard you had got away I was happy Indeed."[30]

Mary Anne and her children had spent two weeks in a boxcar on the Macon & Western Railroad en route to Gordon. After two more weeks there, she moved on to Savannah and eventually to Valdosta. Apparently, Major was unable to return as planned, but one day early in October, while he was tying his horse to a hitching post near the train station at Valdosta, he looked up to see his sister-in-law and her children standing on the platform. Mattie Holliday would later recall, "He did not know of her coming. She had no means of communication, but God in whom she trusted, arranged for her here as in every other circumstance of that eventful journey." Mary Anne and the children enjoyed the reunion, and Henry "gave them a house on his farm and provided for them."[31]

After the fall of Atlanta, General Hood moved north, hoping to cut Sherman off from his source of supply by striking the rail lines. Eventually, Sherman was able to force Hood's army northwest into Alabama, but he complained that holding "Hood, Forrest, and Wheeler, and the whole batch of devils" at bay would be costly and produce no result. Instead, he proposed a march to the sea. "I can make the march," he assured Grant, "and make Georgia howl."[32] On November 15, 1864, Sherman burned Atlanta and began "marchin' through Georgia." His columns moved swiftly with only Georgia militia and 3,500 cavalry under "Fighting" Joe Wheeler in his way.

Governor Brown wisely decided not to take a stand at the state capitol in Milledgeville, and on November 19 a force consisting of prisoners paroled from the state penitentiary, factory and penitentiary guards, one artillery battery, two militia companies, and the cadet battalion from the Georgia Military Institute, including young George, withdrew from the city by rail toward Gordon. The cadets would continue to be a part of the force attempting to slow the Union advance, but by early December Sherman was approaching Savannah.

Mattie and Lucy escaped from the city during the general evacuation not knowing that Cousin George was part of the force covering the withdrawal. They joined the rest of the family on Major's farm in time for Christmas.[33] It almost seemed a blessing, shortly afterward, when Sherman's forces destroyed the Atlantic & Gulf Railroad tracks near Savannah and further isolated Valdosta. Then Sherman turned north into South Carolina, and southern Georgia was seemingly forgotten.

John Henry was nineteen months younger than his sixteen-year-old cousin Mattie when she and her sister arrived in Valdosta, but he grew closer to her in the months that followed. He was discovering the mysteries of puberty, and Mattie was charming in the tradition of Southern womanhood. She was a bewitching distraction during a desperate time in which he needed some relief from its realities. Although Georgia seemed to have been abandoned by federal troops, Valdosta was feeling the aftermath of Sherman's destruction. John Henry's mother was virtually an invalid, and his father, by his nature, was distant and understandably preoccupied with providing for a house full of relatives. Work was also a part of John Henry's life; there were no slackers in Major's household. Mattie made things bearable.

Practical man that he was, Henry could see that the Union would prevail, and he was already trying to make sure that his family would survive the trauma. With the devaluation of Confederate currency, security seemed to lay in the land. He paid $3,150 in Confederate money for an additional 980 acres from the Shanks estate on January 24, 1865.[34] Beyond that, all he could do was wait for the fortunes of war to be played out.

Southern Georgians did not immediately hear of General Lee's surrender at Appomattox and the end of the war in April 1865. In May, the last of Georgia's troops surrendered to General James H. Wilson, and gradually the soldiers began to return home. Tom McKey had been hospitalized at Macon during the late summer of 1864 in time to miss the fall of Atlanta. When he recovered, he was made ward master over ten wards in the hospital. At year's end, he was once more a patient. Fearing that Sherman might move against Macon, the hospital had been moved southwest, first to Smithville and then to Cuthbert, where Tom was again working as ward master when the war ended.[35] One story claimed that John Henry armed himself, took an extra horse, and went looking for Tom.[36] With the countryside full of desperate men, it was a bold move for a youth not yet fifteen, but, according to the story, he found his uncle on the road and led him to Cat Creek.

Although ordered to retire in June 1864, William H. McKey had managed to stay with the army in Virginia. He was paroled at Gordonville, Virginia, after the surrender and began his journey back to his family. James McKey had served as a field surgeon throughout the war, but he also came home safely. Francisco E'Dalgo was with the Army of Tennessee when it surrendered on April 16, 1865, at Greensboro, North Carolina. It was the same for the Hollidays. John Stiles Holliday, having served throughout the war as a surgeon in Georgia's military hospitals, was never distant from his family or Fayetteville except during the bloody summer and fall of 1864. He was now with his family again. His son, George, a battle-hardened veteran despite his youth, came home as well. When Robert Kennedy Holliday showed up at Henry's place to rejoin Mary Anne and his children, after being released from a Union prisoner-of-war camp, he clearly was a broken man, but he was alive.[37]

Thomas Sylvester McKey, John
Henry Holliday's favorite uncle, who
lived in the Holliday household after
his own parents died. He became
John Henry's boyhood hero.

As tough and uncertain as times were, the Hollidays and the Mc-
Keys had reason to rejoice. All came home. Eventually, Robert took
his family back to Jonesboro to begin the rebuilding process, even
though everything he owned had been destroyed. Other members of
the Holliday family also returned to their homes in the area of John
Henry's childhood. But Major Holliday had found a permanent home
in Valdosta. The McKeys were reunited at Valdosta and settled there
as well. Young Tom was now a man full-grown after four years of war.
William and James were there as well, happy to be with the rest of their
family once again. For the moment, the Hollidays and the McKeys enjoyed the time together, glad the war was over. They gave little thought
to the hard times ahead.

For a while, Valdosta was spared the humiliation of occupation, and
the people did their best to get on with their lives. When Sherman
drove into South Carolina early in 1865, he left General J. G. Foster
in command at Savannah. Foster supervised a difficult occupation, although he faced little military threat. His was, in many ways, the first
Reconstruction experiment in Georgia. After the final surrender of
Georgia troops, federal troops were stationed in Milledgeville, Atlanta,
and Augusta. Governor Brown was arrested, sent to Washington, D.C.,
and held for nine days before being paroled. No civil authority existed
in Georgia, except for whatever local government had survived.
Through all of this, Georgia existed in what one historian called
"a position of suspended political animation" that left places like Valdosta pretty much on their own.[38]

That state of affairs did not last long, however. In the summer of 1865, General Q. A. Gillmore began to distribute forces along communication and transportation routes. A detachment of soldiers moved into the Lowndes County courthouse in Valdosta. On September 27, 1865, Captain C. C. Richardson arrived in Troupville as an agent for the recently organized Bureau of Refugees, Freedmen, and Abandoned Lands to protect the interests of the former slaves and provide them with services. The 103rd Regiment of U.S. Colored Infantry was headquartered at Thomasville, and units were distributed in towns like Quitman, Doctortown, Homerville, and Valdosta. Company G of the 103rd replaced the white troops in Valdosta and set up their more substantial encampment between Patterson and Toombs streets.[39]

Friction was not long in coming. Richardson was conscientious in his efforts to deal with the needs of the freedmen and set about trying to provide jobs, education, and food. Local whites cooperated reasonably well, considering the food situation and the need for labor, but there were problems arising from white attitudes, the shortage of cash for wages, and the belief among some freedmen that emancipation meant that they no longer had to work. Whites were somewhat more recalcitrant when freedmen were put in positions of authority. They objected to the appointment of a black postmaster and armed black policemen.

Black soldiers caused the most concern. The troops encouraged former slaves to bring charges against their former masters. They intimidated whites on the streets. They arrested people on flimsy charges. One farmer was strung up by his thumbs in a stock car and left there for hours. Townspeople also resented the white officers' attention to local girls. To make matters worse, Captain Andrew W. Leonard, a twenty-one-year-old commander, was frequently out of town searching for deserters, and Lieutenant Alberto Marochetti, a former hospital steward, who commanded during Leonard's absences, had little experience and was not respected by locals. Command control was loose at best, and one officer, probably Marochetti, was detested by the townspeople as "the black Dutchman."[40] Trouble was on the way.

In January 1866, a young freedman complained that a nineteen-year-old ex-Confederate soldier named Richard Force had choked him. Force was a newcomer to Valdosta, but he was a veteran who had gone to war at the age of fourteen and was wounded at Gettysburg. He was arrested and confined in a small building near Griffin's store that was used as a headquarters by the troops. When one of the young women of the town attempted to see him, she was ordered to move on at bayonet point. After a few tense days, Force escaped through the back door and returned home, where he saddled his horse, Rex, and rode away. Later, the young people of the town threw a party at Force's home. He made the mistake of slipping back into town for the occasion. While the party was in full swing, soldiers arrived, and, following an argument in the front yard, Force was shot. He received prompt treatment, but despite the efforts of his doctors, Force never recovered. He died five months later, on May 15, 1866, of blood poisoning.[41]

Dick Force became a hero to Valdosta's young people, a symbol of resistance to Yankee oppression, and there were threats of retaliation. Several older men, however, including Henry Holliday, worked publicly and behind the scenes to keep the situation in hand. When Force died, there were further rumors of a violent response, but by then the troops had already left, and again, prominent locals spoke out strongly and managed to calm matters. But Force had left an impression on the youthful and the hotheaded that would not soon disappear in the face of Yankee occupation.

Among those influenced by Force was John Henry Holliday. Tucked away on Cat Creek, John Henry did not have the daily contact with black soldiers and the new order that some townsmen did, but he shared the resentment of his father and neighbors, particularly their contempt for the black soldiers as emblems of their distress. John Henry hated the occupation the way his neighbors did, but he was restless in those days for other reasons, too. Tom McKey, his favorite uncle, and Tom's brothers, Will and James, had purchased the Banner Plantation in Hamilton County, Florida, and moved away.[42] His mother's illness was worse. His father was distant. There was little to temper the growing resentment and rebelliousness in this young man.

There was some progress for the town, though. On March 13, 1866, rail service was restored when the first train arrived from Savannah since Sherman's forces cut the line in 1864. The town's population turned out to welcome it. "Those folks hadn't been so happy since the war broke out," remembered one old-timer.[43] Thannie Smith Wisenbaker remembered, "New improvements were being seen in all parts of town. Lawyers and doctors hung out their signs. The stores were opening and new goods were on display."[44] A new mill was built and with it more and more cabins for the mill workers. In spite of the galling bitterness of Reconstruction, change was coming.

Change was also seen in educational opportunity. Since moving to Valdosta, John Henry had attended school. A Professor Newton, a stern disciplinarian, had conducted classes from sunup to sundown in the courthouse through 1863. In 1864, a Professor Mathis arrived and began holding classes at the renovated Valdosta Institute. Those years had been tough because of the scarcity of paper and textbooks, but things took a turn for the better when Samuel McWhir Varnedoe settled in Valdosta in November 1865. Varnedoe would become something of a local legend. He was himself a model of discipline, learning, and industry. He eschewed the switch for disciplinary purposes and instilled a pride in his students that fostered achievement. The students admired him, and he rewarded them with devoted attention to their needs. He also gave them ample opportunity to show off their newly acquired learning to parents and neighbors. There were outings, too, and, in the coeducational environment, opportunities to improve social skills.[45]

John Henry fit in well. Already well mannered and charming as the result of his mother's instruction and the experience of a large, well-educated family, he learned quickly both in the classroom and in the social arena. He was popular with the girls at dances and was considered a strong-minded, even cocky, young man by his neighbors. He was not quite fifteen when Dick Force was shot, and that event marked a momentous year for him. On May 30, 1866, scarcely two weeks after Force died, Henry Holliday accepted an appointment as an agent for the Freedman's Bureau. The appointment did not sit well with his neighbors, least of all with his rebellious son. Major, ever the independent spirit, soon found himself denounced regularly as a "worthless scalawag."[46] It was an added burden John Henry found hard to bear.

Then, on September 16, 1866, Alice Jane McKey died. Reverend N. B. Ousley, the local Methodist minister, paid this glowing tribute to her:

> She was confined to her bed for a number of years, and was indeed a greater sufferer. She bore her afflictions with Christian fortitude. It has never fallen to my lot to know a more cheerful Christian. It was a

great pleasure to visit her to see the triumph of religion over the ills of life. She was deeply solicitous about the welfare of all she loved. She fully committed them into the hands of a merciful God with the full awareness that God would hear and answer her prayers, and that her instructions and Christian example would still speak. She was deeply anxious about the faith of her only child. She had her faith written so her boy might know what his mother believed. She was for a time a member of the Presbyterian Church and never subscribing in heart to their article on election she determined to change her Church relation as she was not willing to die and leave on record for her boy, that she subscribed to said faith. She therefore joined the M. E. Church whose doctrines she heartily accepted. I visited her a few days before her death; she was calm, cheerful, joyful. She said to me that there was not a dimming veil between her and her God. She thus passed away from the Church militant to the Church triumphant, leaving her friends to mourn not as those who have no hope, knowing their loved one is not dead but sleepeth.[47]

The tribute not only honored Alice Jane; it was also a classic statement of the best in Southern womanhood. The effects of her absence were quickly felt. Alice Jane had been the major restraining force on John Henry. She had taught him and perhaps pampered him to the point of vanity on his part. What is certain is that he took her death hard. The community acknowledged her piety and gentility in glowing acknowledgments of her life, but John Henry struggled with the loss. By custom, the period of mourning was one year. Husbands and sons wore black for nine months and gray for three more. During that time, mourners severely limited their social activities. Anything less was considered to be seriously disrespectful of the deceased.

The town was stunned, then, when a mere three months after his wife was laid to rest in Sunset Hill Cemetery, Major married his neighbor's daughter, twenty-three-year-old Rachel Martin. The marriage was performed by Reverend Ousley, the same Reverend Ousley who had spoken so glowingly about Alice Jane only weeks earlier. He might have overlooked the affront to tradition, but the town did not. There had been no time for a courtship, which raised questions about when the relationship between Henry and Rachel began and suggested a greater impropriety.[48]

More important than town gossip, though, was the impact of Henry's action on the family. John Henry was angry over the disrespect his

Rachel Martin Holliday, Henry Holliday's second
wife and John Henry's stepmother.

father had paid to his mother's memory, and he resented his new stepmother, who was only a few years older than he. To make matters even
worse, Major left his farm at Cat Creek and moved with his family
into a house on Savannah Avenue owned by his new in-laws. The
townspeople soon moved on to new scandals, but the relationship
between John Henry and his father was cooled forever. Living in town
with constant reminders of what had happened, John Henry was an
angry young man.

The removal of Alice Jane's influence and the resentment against
Major soon materialized in John Henry's conduct. Bertram Wyatt-
Brown observed that the socialization of Southern boys included
expected experimentation with "fighting, gambling, swearing, drinking, and wenching . . . all activities that tested the school boy's honor
among his peers." At school one day, John Henry got into an argument with a classmate over some matter that was not recorded. The
way Tom McKey recalled the incident years later, it could have had
tragic results:

> John's opponent in the quarrel challenged him to a duel with pistols.
> Willingly, John accepted the challenge. The two youths met with
> their seconds on the edge of town and two pistols were set out before
> them. When he was offered his choice of the pistols, John replied
> that he had his own pistol and that it was well loaded with balls.
>
> His opponent and the seconds were very much disconcerted over
> this statement by young Holliday. It was supposed to have been a
> "mock" duel [that is, the pistols were only loaded with powder charges

John Henry Holliday's home in Valdosta at 405 East Savannah Street, originally owned by Rachel Martin Holliday's father, where Henry Holliday and his son moved after Henry's marriage to Rachel. John Henry would live here with his father and stepmother until he left for dental school.

that would not inflict a wound] and here was Holliday with a loaded pistol meaning business! They urged him to use one of the powder-loaded pistols but to no avail. He had his own gun and that was the one he was going to use in this affair.

Seeing that they could not persuade Holliday to use one of the harmless guns, the seconds and his opponent had to explain to him that the duel was a kind of joke. But John was satisfied that "the joke wasn't on him." There was no duel, and an amicable settlement was made between the two young men.[49]

An earlier Georgia writer seems to confirm the incident with these remarks, "As a boy and a play-fellow, John was aggressive and nervy, but upon the whole generous. One who was at school with him for several years can recall but one scrap that he had with another boy."[50] Though a single incident, this episode was enough to affirm something of John Henry's spirit, and it may be assumed that he did not miss the pleasures of cards, drinking, horsemanship, swearing, womanizing, and the other tests of manhood of adolescent boys of his time and place, perhaps exaggerated by resentment toward his father that could not be expressed directly.

Alice Jane's brothers and sisters were also upset by Henry's disrespect for their sister. One of the McKey girls had already married, and the rest moved to the Banner Plantation with their brothers. The brothers openly questioned whether Major had been faithful to their sister, given the circumstances of his quick marriage to his closest neighbor's young daughter. Not long after the December 18, 1866, wedding, the rift became public when Tom McKey filed a lawsuit against his brother-in-law to recover his sister's property, which otherwise would have gone to Major as the widowed husband. One of the pieces of property in question was the Iron Front Building in downtown Griffin, Georgia. Playing the role of Solomon, the Lowndes County judge eventually divided the building into two parts, awarding half to the McKeys and half to Henry Holliday as guardian for John Henry. The building was split by a partition running down the center. The judge's wisdom settled the legal issues, but healing family divisions took longer.[51]

John Henry's relationship with his father was further damaged by Major's role as the Freedman's Bureau agent. Thannie Wisenbaker recalled, "The Freedman's Bureau was an institution established in the courthouse and became the headquarters for carpet baggers. The Southern men were tried here and all kinds of lawlessness was heaped upon a peaceful people."[52] Henry was associated in the public mind with Yankee excesses, and his neighbors denounced him as "a deceitful scalawag," a "wicked spy," an "ignorant ass," and a "moral leper" while he served.[53] In fact, his term seemed unexceptional, except to the extent he tried to do his job well. He acted on behalf of a number of freedmen as he was charged without any hint of misconduct or unfairness. Henry did not resign, but on May 2, 1867, he was relieved of his duties.[54]

Overall, resistance to Reconstruction, black codes enacted by Southern states to control former slaves, and the failure of all the Southern states except Tennessee to ratify the Fourteenth Amendment caused Congress, now controlled by Radical Republicans, to move into a second phase of Reconstruction. The South was divided into military districts, and military commanders took charge of the Reconstruction process. General John Pope, commanding the Third Military District, arrived in Georgia on April 1, 1867, to assume command. One of the first actions under the new system was the reorganization of the Freedman's Bureau.

Because so many of the civilian agents were former Confederates who were unable to take the test oath, they were relieved, and districts were consolidated to include more than one county. After Major was removed, Lowndes was combined with other counties under the jurisdiction of the agent at Quitman. Major was replaced by Alvin B. Clark, who used a more aggressive style that caused many of Henry's neighbors to rethink their earlier criticism of him. In retrospect, his management did not seem so bad.[55]

Georgians now watched as their constitutional forms were rewritten. The state constitutional convention convened on December 9, 1867, and continued into March 1868. Georgia's conservative whites were able to limit the changes, and while black voting rights were guaranteed, white suffrage was not limited as it was in some other states. The new district commander, General George F. Meade, ordered an election for April 20, 1868, to ratify the constitution and choose officials under it. What followed was a bitter campaign in which white Georgians worked very hard to keep the state from falling into the hands of carpetbaggers, scalawags, and blacks.[56]

The political rancor was felt in Valdosta as deeply as anywhere in the state. J. W. Clift (called "booby" by the press) was a Republican candidate for the U.S. Congress. He arrived in Valdosta to make a campaign speech on April 4, 1868. Clift disregarded local ordinances and made no effort to get permission to hold a rally, but a meeting was called at the courthouse nonetheless. A substantial crowd gathered for the event, composed largely of freedmen, though including local dignitaries and curious whites. During Clift's speech in front of the courthouse, an explosion interrupted the occasion. No one was injured, but the crowd was scattered. An investigation by local authorities revealed that a group of young men had placed "a modicum of powder" in a keg under the building. The evidence suggested that the incident was more a prank than a serious threat, designed to break up the meeting with no real damage to anyone while putting a scare into Clift and the freedmen. The *South Georgia Times* argued, "It is idle to suppose there was any intention on the part of the boys, if they did it, to blow up their friends and relations."[57]

Community leaders promptly denounced what had happened, and a committee of five was chosen to draft a statement condemning the incident. One of the members of the committee was Henry Holliday. The committee moved quickly, pointing out that Clift had scheduled the rally "without giving to the civil authorities the notice required by military orders—so as to enable said authorities to have a police in readiness to preserve order." The committee's report deplored the actions of those who had set off the explosion and expressed "our condemnation and disapproval of said riotous conduct." The resolutions applauded local authorities for arresting the lawbreakers, but they also called on Mayor M. J. Griffin to replace the city's colored policemen with white officers.[58]

Federal officers took a dimmer view of what had happened. The new Freedman's Bureau agent at Quitman quickly reported to military headquarters at Thomasville that a riot had occurred and that local authorities were "powerless" to do anything about it. On April 6, Corporal John Murray and two soldiers were sent to Valdosta. By then, A. H. Darnell, Iverson Griffin, John Calhoun, Ben Smith, and John Rambo, all sons of locally prominent citizens, had been arrested and released on bond. That did not satisfy the army. On the night of April 13, the three soldiers descended on the homes of the five young men, rousted them from their beds, and started them for Savannah as prisoners in chains before morning.[59]

Local citizens were enraged. T. B. Griffin was sent to Savannah to look out for the "boys," and Mayor Griffin demanded to know by what authority they had been taken. He was advised that they had been arrested on General Meade's order "and will be held for trial by Military Commission."[60] In May, well after the state election, the prisoners were released on $10,000 bond each, raised by the sympathetic citizens of Savannah. The boys received a heroes' welcome when they returned to Valdosta. On the docket for the May term of the Lowndes County Superior Court, the five men originally arrested, five more whites, and thirteen blacks (including one named Henry Holliday) were charged with rioting. Nothing ever came of any of the charges, local or federal, and the case was eventually disposed of in 1873.[61]

In a possibly related episode, the *South Georgia Times* publicly chided the male students at the Valdosta Institute for their recent bad behavior. Local tradition always had it that not all the participants in the plot were arrested or publicly identified because they were so young. John Henry Holliday was said to have been one of them. It certainly would not have been out of character for him to have participated. He was angry and rebellious enough. While no contemporary

Professor Varnedoe's Valdosta Institute, where John Henry Holliday attended school as a boy.

evidence connecting him to the incident survived (beyond reminis-cences), the furor coincided with John Henry's sudden departure from Valdosta for an extended stay with Robert Kennedy Holliday's family in Jonesboro.[62]

John Henry's "summer of discontent" under the same roof with his cousin Mattie, now eighteen and more tempting than ever, formed the basis for what some members of the family saw as a budding romance between them. Her father was struggling to salvage some-thing out of the war's losses. He had taken a position as baggage mas-ter on the Macon & Western Railroad, and it is likely that John Henry worked around the station as well. Doubtless, too, he had opportunity to visit with his other Holliday relatives in the area, including Cousin Robert and the rest of Uncle John's family.[63] How long he stayed or what transpired unfortunately escaped documentation, but in due course, he returned to Valdosta.

That summer of 1868 Georgia was readmitted to the Union and federal troops withdrew. But the friction of Reconstruction was not entirely over. The adjustment to civil and political rights for blacks was galling for most whites, and there were episodes like the riot at

Camilla, Georgia, in September, which left nine freedmen dead and close to thirty wounded. The following year, 1869, would be memorable in Georgia for its political chaos, which was so extreme that in response to Governor Rufus Bullock's request, Congress, on December 22, 1869, sent the army back into Georgia.[64]

Throughout all of this, John Henry's life was more concerned with mathematics, history, literature, science, composition, Latin, and the rest of Varnedoe's rigorous curriculum, as he worked to complete his education. He took a job in 1869 working at the station for the Atlantic & Gulf Railroad in Valdosta. In April of that year, William and Tom McKey bought some land near Troupville, which, happily for John Henry, meant Uncle Tom was spending a little more time with him.[65] By then, another fateful connection had arrived in Valdosta.

Dr. Lucian F. Frink was a Floridian and ex-Confederate soldier who had served with an artillery unit during the war. He had surrendered with Confederate forces in Alabama in 1865. While awaiting parole, Frink made friends with a Union soldier, and the two of them agreed to attend the dental college in Philadelphia once the war was over. He entered the Pennsylvania College of Dental Surgery in 1867 as planned, and on completion of his training moved to Valdosta in 1868. How and when he and young John Henry met escaped the record, but the decision to attend dental school and where was made in Dr. Frink's office. Frink was only five years older than John Henry and probably knew him on a social level as well as a professional one.[66]

In late October 1869, John Henry and his father and stepmother may have traveled to Atlanta, where John Stiles Holliday had moved after the war, to attend the wedding of George Holliday to Mary Elizabeth Wright. Aside from the family reunion and a chance to see the recovering young city of Atlanta, the trip would have given John Henry an opportunity to talk with his uncle about his plans. Apparently, Dr. Holliday encouraged him, because when John Henry returned to Valdosta he began making plans for admission to dental school the next fall.[67] In September 1870, John Henry Holliday, with Dr. Frink's endorsement as preceptor, arrived in Philadelphia to begin his education as a dentist.

The Pennsylvania College of Dental Surgery was one of the best dental schools in the country. Housed in an imposing building at the corner of Twelfth and Filbert streets, it was the outgrowth of the Philadelphia College of Dental Surgery, originally chartered in 1850, which

Pennsylvania College of Dental
Surgery, where John Henry
Holliday studied dentistry.

had opened its doors in 1852. The Pennsylvania College of Dental Surgery was chartered in 1856, after a dispute between the trustees and the faculty of the Philadelphia college led to the mass resignation of the faculty and the creation of the new institution. The college had an average enrollment of fifty to sixty students. Students faced a rigorous curriculum in chemistry, mechanical dentistry, metallurgy, dental pathology and therapeutics, dental histology, operative dentistry, physiology, anatomy and microscopic anatomy, and surgery, as well as clinical instruction in operative and mechanical dentistry.[68]

John Henry began his studies on October 3, 1870. He attended daily lectures and demonstrations morning and afternoon and began immediately to participate in clinical procedures under the direction of demonstrators. He had ample opportunity for the application of his studies. The largest in the world, the facilities were devoted to dental education, and the urban population brought a steady supply of patients to the clinics.[69]

Young Holliday faced a rigorous schedule six days a week, but he also found time for a somewhat broader education as well. Philadelphia was unlike any place he had ever known. The experience had to be both intimidating and exhilarating. For the first time in his life, he was outside the South and away from the control of parents and community, with no constraints except his school's demands for respectability and discretion. Still, he found time for jaunts into the mysteries of urban life, and he doubtlessly learned more than the principles of dentistry during his time in Philadelphia. For one thing, he got to know Yankees apart from the issues that had held his attention since he was old enough to remember. For another, he came to appreciate some of the social amenities of the urban environment. Philadelphia had its share of saloons, gambling dens, and brothels, and it would not be extravagant to think that the cocky young Georgian tasted some of the city's worldly pleasures or even made jaunts to New York City.

He was not in Philadelphia to play, however, and discretion demanded that he be careful. He was apparently a gifted student. For five months, he attended classes, demonstrations, and laboratories in both academic knowledge and rigorous practical training. By the time the term ended, John Henry had become adept at both. The college held a spring session devoted to practical dentistry, but in March 1871 he returned to Valdosta, where he spent the next eight months working with Dr. Frink.[70] The town was continuing its postwar recovery, and young Holliday had plenty of opportunities to practice his skills.

In September 1871, John Henry returned to Philadelphia with much valuable experience that equipped him for his second-year tasks of developing a thesis, demonstrating his mastery of operative dentistry, and preparing artificial dentures. His thesis, "Diseases of the Teeth," and each of the other requirements were met in due course, and he was scheduled to graduate on March 1, 1872. There was one problem, however. Qualification for graduation required that "[t]he candidate must be twenty-one years of age."[71] He was still more than five months shy of turning twenty-one (a requirement for licensing dentists in several states, including Georgia). His name appeared on the graduation announcement, but he would not receive his credentials until August. John Henry would have to work as an assistant to someone else in the interim or find some other use for his time.

Times were changing. Reconstruction in Georgia officially ended on January 12, 1872.[72] Tom McKey and William H. McKey bought more land at the confluence of the Little and Withlacoochee rivers in February.[73] John Henry could have gone home and worked with Dr. Frink and enjoyed the company of his relatives, but, by then, he knew his future did not lie in Valdosta. He had time on his hands before he

John Henry Holliday, D.D.S. This photograph
was taken at Philadelphia at the time of John
Henry's graduation and passed down through
the family from Mattie Holliday, Doc's first
cousin and lifelong correspondent, to Carolyn
Manley.

could open his own practice, so he decided to gain experience and see
a little of the country. One of his classmates, A. Jameson Fuches Jr.,
who wrote his thesis on the same topic that John Henry did, was
returning to his home state of Missouri to practice in St. Louis.
Fuches opened an office on Fourth Street and young Holliday joined
him there.[74]

St. Louis was a bustling, hardy, and bawdy place, full of progress
and the negative payoff of progress. John Henry tasted the excitement
of this place caught between modernization and the frontier. He
gained experience in his chosen profession, and he was attracted to
things more personal as well.

Near Fuches's office was a theater and saloon. One of the employees there was a young woman named Kate Fisher, but that was not her
real name. She was born Mary Katharine Harony in Pest, Hungary, on
November 7, 1850, the first of seven children. Her parents immigrated to the United States in about 1860 and settled in Davenport,
Iowa, with what amounted to a colony of Hungarians.[75] Kate's father
purchased property there in 1863, but by 1866, both he and his wife
had died, leaving the care of the minor Harony children under the
guardianship of the children's brother-in-law, Gustavus Susemihl.
Guardianship soon passed to the family attorney, Otto Smith, however, who reported in October 1867 that Mary Katharine could not be
advised of the mortgage of the family's property "because she went, as
it is said to parts unknown."[76]

"Kate Fisher." This is believed to be a photograph
of Mary Katharine Harony, who lived under the
name of Kate Fisher in St. Louis, where she met
John Henry Holliday. The photograph was given
by Wyatt Earp to Hiram Sutterfield in Colorado.

Kate had run away. One story says that she stowed away on a river-
boat and assumed the name of the boat's captain, a man named Fisher.
Her choice of the name "Fisher" might also have come from one of
the leading actresses of the day, Kate Fisher, whose performances as
Mazeppa, in which she rode across the stage on horseback wearing
only pink tights, scandalized and tantalized audiences across the country.[77] Kate claimed to have entered a convent school in St. Louis, but,
like many runaway girls in that period, she appears to have entered a
somewhat different "school." A "Kate Fischer" was listed in the 1870
census living with eight other women. Seven, including Kate, were
listed as "whores."[78] By 1872, she was working at the saloon near Dr.
Fuches's new office.

She later claimed that she met John Henry in the spring of 1870,
but Kate had trouble remembering dates late in life, and other internal
evidence in her writings suggests that she meant 1872.[79] Apparently,
they had an affair or perhaps a "professional" relationship. In later
years, concerned about the negative image of her in published sources
and determined to salvage her reputation, she even claimed they were
married, but though her account was slanted, even deceptive, it contained details that suggest that she did meet and have a relationship
with John Henry that spring and summer. She would remember that

John Henry Holliday's stay in St. Louis was a brief adventure, and she would also recall that he returned to Georgia to claim an inheritance. In fact, during July he did return to Georgia to claim his inheritance from his mother and to begin his practice. Kate would not forget Dr. Holliday, and, as it turned out, John Henry would not forget her either.[80]

John Henry moved in with John Stiles Holliday that summer. Dr. Holliday had moved to Atlanta after the war and gone into the grocery business with R. W. Tidwell, another Fayetteville transplant. They had been quite successful, to the point that Dr. Holliday gave up the regular practice of medicine. Holliday's son, Robert Alexander, called "Hub" by family members, was working with him as well. John Stiles Holliday was highly regarded in the new Atlanta, and John Henry moved into not only a large and comfortable household but social and professional credibility as well.[81]

Following his return to Georgia, John Henry was introduced to Dr. Arthur C. Ford. Ford was one of the most prominent dentists in the state. He also had a colorful history. He was an Englishman who came to Georgia by way of South Africa. He fought in the Confederate army, was wounded at Sharpsburg, and established himself as a dentist in Atlanta after the war as the partner of Dr. Albert Hape. Ford gained an enviable reputation. He was a charter member of the Southern Dental Association, formed in 1869, and was active in the Georgia State Dental Society.[82] He may have met John Henry through Dr. Samuel Hape, the brother of Ford's partner and owner of the Southern Dental Depot, who was living at the home of John Stiles Holliday. Albert Hape had terminated his partnership with Ford and was moving his practice to Thomson, Georgia. On July 26, 1872, the following notice appeared in the *Atlanta Constitution*:

CARD

I HEREBY inform my patients that I leave to attend the Sessions of the Southern Dental Association in Richmond, Virginia this evening, and will be absent until about the middle of August, during which time Dr. Jno. H. Holliday will fill my place in my office.

Arthur C. Ford, D.D.S.
Office 26, Whitehall Street.[83]

Dr. Arthur C. Ford, the distinguished Georgia
dentist and Confederate veteran with whom
John Henry first practiced in Atlanta in 1872.

It was a grand opportunity. Ford's prominence ensured the right
connections and the best chances for success in the new city. Young
Dr. Holliday turned twenty-one the same day that Dr. Ford returned
to Atlanta, and less than a month later Major signed over the property
he had held in guardianship for John Henry to his son.[84] John Henry's
future seemed bright. In November, he visited Griffin and registered
his deed for the Iron Front Building. He had come of age, and for the
occasion his uncle gave him a Model 1851 Navy Colt revolver like
those he had given to his own three sons.[85] John Henry had reason to
be proud. Never the aristocrat, he was now fairly a Southern gentleman, well bred, educated, and prepared for the successful professional
life he trained for as part of the New South.

GONE TO TEXAS

When he became nearly of age, he studied dentistry and afterwards located in Atlanta. But he had a roving and reckless turn of mind, and like a great many of our southern boys of similar nature he soon sought his fortune out West.

—*Valdosta Times*, June 24, 1882

How quickly things turned. The relationship with Dr. Arthur C. Ford did not last. Ford was not a well man, and on January 4, 1873, he announced that "[O]n account of impaired health, from too close application to my profession, and having determined in consequence to visit Florida for a short period to recuperate, I have this day associated with Dr. J. [?] Cooley, a gentleman of skill and experience, and one in whom my friends and patients may place implicit confidence, who will attend to my practice during my absence." Ford would return to Georgia within a few weeks and be elected president of the Georgia State Dental Society in 1873, but his health would continue to deteriorate. He was consumptive.[1]

John Henry Holliday had obviously moved on, although why is not known. He may also have moved out of John Stiles Holliday's home, because on December 21, 1872, he was registered at the National Hotel in Atlanta.[2] Christmas would be gloomy. On December 31, 1872, the *Griffin News* announced, "Mr. Robert Holliday, who has so long and efficiently occupied the position of baggage master on the Macon & Western Railroad, died at Jonesboro on Christmas night."[3] Mattie Holliday's father had finally succumbed to his disabilities, actually on

Christmas Eve, and the Holliday clan gathered to pay their last respects over a somber Christmas. Mattie later recalled, "Everything gone but one house in Jonesboro, a large helpless family, health wrecked, it is no wonder this jovial, kindhearted man was heartbroken. Seven years struggle with poverty, he died December 24, 1872, after being received into the Catholic Church. He was buried in the Catholic plot in Fayetteville."[4]

John Henry attended the funeral with the rest of the family to comfort Mattie, her sisters, and James Robert Holliday, their brother, called Jim Bob by the family. The Hollidays were close, and Mattie was special to John Henry. Yet beyond the personal and family effects of Robert's passing, his death seemed to mark the beginning of a troubling and confusing time for young Dr. Holliday. On January 13, 1873, Francisco E'Dalgo died of consumption on his farm near Jenkinsburg, leaving behind a young family of his own.[5] Perhaps this loss and a desire to help explained in part why John Henry sold his half of the Iron Front Building in Griffin to N. G. Phillips the very next day, January 14, for $1,800, a surprisingly large sum at the time.[6]

John Henry tried to get past the troubles. He may have tried to make a go of it in Griffin after leaving his association with Ford. It was a booming town with a variety of things to recommend it. Griffin boasted fifteen practicing attorneys, a dozen physicians, fifty stores, twelve barrooms, nine churches, and a variety of other establishments. "Griffin is now the healthiest place in Georgia," the *Griffin News* boasted. "[N]ot all the fruit and watermelons brought to town can get a serious case of sickness for the doctors." The same issue noted that Griffin was "the best policed city in the state."[7]

With three colleges, a major rail station, and only one dentist, R. A. McDonald, the opportunities seemed promising. Even though the local press described McDonald as "one of the cleverest and most successful 'tooth carpenters' in the country," local tradition says that John Henry took a corner office upstairs in the McKey half of the Iron Front Building and began a practice there. The corner office still bears evidence of a dental practice, not McDonald's, which was elsewhere in town.[8]

There might even have been other interests for young Holliday; as the *News* observed, "Think of it, that in the little city of Griffin, gambling holes are as common as pig tracks in the snow."[9] The paper sought "to legalize and tax" them, but John Henry's interest may well

Francisco E'Dalgo, the Mexican orphan taken in by Henry Holliday and reared in his home, who went on to serve honorably in the Confederate army. He died of tuberculosis shortly after John Henry Holliday returned from dental school.

have been less public minded. Here, he could indulge his card playing vice away from Uncle John's view. Besides that, the town boasted the Central College for Young Women, with courting opportunities aplenty for a young professional man.

Of course, Atlanta still had its attractions as well. There, he had renewed his acquaintance with Lee Smith, the "celebrated mixologist" at the Maison de Ville. At twenty-eight years old, Smith was also from Griffin and had known John Henry's parents. But he had led a fast life since leaving home. He launched his career as a bartender in Atlanta at the end of the war and had spent a couple of years in New Orleans mixing drinks at the St. Charles Hotel before returning to Atlanta to open his own saloon. He was affiliated with several establishments before joining the Maison de Ville in August 1872.[10] Smith was a genuine hustler involved in a variety of investments designed to elevate him above the role of bartender.

In April 1872, while operating the Turf Exchange Saloon, Lee Smith was arrested for "Keeping a Gaming Table." Specifically, he was running a faro bank. Faro was a popular game at the time, described by one authority on nineteenth-century gambling as "the backbone of the professional gambler's repertoire and the prime vehicle for the seduction of moneyed innocents."[11] It was a simple game with relatively close odds; *Hoyle's Rules of Games* claimed that odds in favor of the house were no more than 3 percent in an honest game. Faro was played on a cloth layout with images of cards in the deck, and players bet on individual cards or combinations against the house.[12]

Cards were drawn from a box by the house dealer, with the first card drawn winning for players and the second card for the bank. If a dealer turned two cards of the same denomination, the money was split between the house and the player. All bets paid even money except for splits and the last four cards. Faro's popularity was based on its simplicity, but the opportunities for dishonest play were considerable. The cultural impact of the game was significant, contributing expressions such as "from soda to hock," "bucking the tiger," and "both ends against the middle" to the language.[13] In the post–Civil War period, it was still one of the most popular card games, and John Henry Holliday, who would spend a considerable part of his life as a faro dealer, may well have acquired or honed his skills in the game at Smith's tables in Atlanta rather than later after he went west.

Smith was found not guilty of the gambling charge on May 27, 1872, before young Dr. Holliday returned from St. Louis, and he accepted the position at the Maison de Ville not long afterward. Later in the year he was arrested for "Assault with Intent to Murder" but was acquitted on November 12, 1872.[14] Despite his troubles, Smith made an effort to qualify himself as a bona fide "respectable" entrepreneur as well. By March 1873, he was dealing in specie payments at No. 16 Marietta Street as an investment capitalist. That did not keep him from refurbishing and opening the Girl of the Period Saloon on Marietta Street in August 1873 or continuing to dabble in the saloon trade over the next few years. By 1875, when he opened the Big Bonanza Saloon, he was well on his way to financial success.[15]

Smith's friendship with young Holliday suggests that John Henry was already drawn to the world of saloons and gambling before he left Georgia, which should not be surprising. "Sowing wild oats" was expected of young men of his time and place, especially when they had a rebellious streak, as John Henry certainly did. Whatever John Henry's precise activities and their implications, he nevertheless seemed to be focusing on his future, and conversations with Cousin Robert "Hub" Holliday led to Robert's decision to follow John Henry's lead and attend the Pennsylvania College of Dental Surgery in the fall of 1873. John Henry would be Robert's preceptor, and the two of them anticipated a long and respectable partnership once Hub graduated.[16]

His decision to act as Hub's preceptor indicated John Henry's intentions to stay in Georgia. Robert would enter school in October 1873, and he would go on to a distinguished career as a dentist in Georgia.[17]

Robert Alexander Holliday, Doc Holliday's first cousin. John Henry was his announced preceptor for dental school and his anticipated partner. He went on to become a very successful dentist and businessman.

Unfortunately, the planned collaboration was derailed, and by the time Robert graduated, John Henry was gone. Something dramatic had happened to destroy their plans. *What* happened is more difficult to define. Even the anecdotal evidence is maddeningly unsatisfying. Yet something happened that caused John Henry's life to unravel and sent him west to Texas. The details remain shrouded in mystery.

For the record, the earliest published explanation from the *Valdosta Times* in 1882 was that he had "a roving and reckless turn of mind, and like a great many of our southern boys of similar nature he soon sought his fortune out West."[18] The most common explanation is that John Henry learned that he had contracted tuberculosis and decided to go west for his health. No doubt this news would have stunned him. He had watched his mother die, he had buried Francisco, and he knew of Arthur C. Ford's condition. Furthermore, he grasped the ominous prognosis of the disease, he knew its symptoms, and he understood the prescriptions for diet and exercise. Diagnosis might explain anger, disorientation, or denial. As an explanation of his decision to move west, however, such a diagnosis is not sufficient.

In the first place, consumption was an insidious killer. The very term presented an image of a body wasting away, of being "consumed," in frightening and disturbing ways. Diagnosis was itself chilling, and yet at its outset the disease left its victim with the desperate hope that it was not consumption at all. Even though the symptoms were dramatic enough, accurate diagnosis was difficult. The dry cough, the sore throat, the chest pains, the elevated pulse rate, and the difficult breathing were also symptoms of other, less serious or more treatable ailments. In John Henry's time, diagnosis was not based on identification of the tubercle bacillus through medical testing. The microscope and even the stethoscope played little role. Diagnosis amounted to a suspicion, albeit a calculated one in the hands of an experienced physician. The presumption was that any symptoms not corrected with purgatives and emetics most likely meant consumption, but the hallmark of the first phase was uncertainty.

The first response, then, was often disbelief or a stubborn refusal to believe, especially for one who, like John Henry, had seen the horrible reality of the disease. The suspected victim of consumption faced life without the expectation of seeing it unfold while clinging to the cruel hope that his malady was not consumption at all. Treatment was little more than a bland diet, active exercise, and "removal to, and residence in a mild, genial, uniform, and salubrious climate." The patient was admonished to choose an ennobling lifestyle, consoled by the notion that the disease "would purify him and edify his friends." A "perverted sentimentalism" toward the disease that extended into the last third of the nineteenth century became the incubator of both faith and cynicism.[19]

The Hollidays were a close family, and sending one of them away for his health argued against their nature. It was more natural for them to come together in support. This was an important consideration since, at the time, in the treatment of consumption there were as many advocates of a "Southern cure" as of a "Western cure." Ponce de Leon Springs in Atlanta was famous for its curative powers. Indian Springs, just a few miles from Griffin, was known as "the Saratoga of the South," which might explain why John Henry chose to move back to Griffin, if he did, as local tradition there insists. In discussing the pros and cons of what it called the western fever, the *Griffin News* made the argument this way: "There is no country on earth equal to our own Middle Georgia, and nine men out of ten who leave it will find themselves woefully mistaken. Our advice is, remain where you are."[20]

Other options were available. One "JLM" of Hamilton County, Florida, wrote the *News* with this advice: "I desire to call the attention of your people who have a desire to emigrate to the advantages of Florida over the West." He added, "Within a mile of me, is a spring that

excels Saratoga or the celebrated Virginia White Sulphur Springs."[21]
Hamilton County, Florida, was the home of John Henry's McKey relatives, and it is tempting to think that the "L" in the signature of the
News article was a misprint for a "T" (a handwritten capital "T" and
capital "L" are remarkably similar in the florid styles of the 1870s),
raising the possibility that its author was Dr. James Taylor McKey,
John Henry's own uncle and a man with a connection to Griffin that
would explain why a person from Hamilton County would write a letter to the Griffin newspaper. At the very least, the Hamilton County
springs provided another option for John Henry close to his own family, including his father at Valdosta. Dr. Ford would eventually move
to Palatka, Florida, to find treatment for his own consumption. He
died there in 1882.[22]

Perhaps the most compelling argument against an abrupt change
in John Henry's plans because of a diagnosis of consumption was the
chronic nature of the disease. The average life expectancy after diagnosis in 1872 was fifteen to twenty-five years. Commonly, people diagnosed with consumption married, raised families, and built businesses
before succumbing to the ravages of the disease. Indeed, consumption
was almost romanticized. It was thought to be more prevalent in more
sedentary and "bookish" careers such as teaching, the law, the ministry, and even medicine. Consumption might produce a melancholy
fatalism, but it could also inspire "spasms of creative eagerness." Until
the last third of the nineteenth century it was seen as "the muse of
literature."[23]

By the time John Henry was diagnosed, the sentimentalism was
fading, but functioning with the disease, supported by proper diet and
exercise, gave consumptives an almost heroic edge. Climate did matter, and the Western cure was growing in popularity by 1872, but if
John Henry had chosen to move west for his health, Dallas, Texas,
where he eventually did go, was an unlikely choice. Its general climate
was little different from Georgia's—the town had been quarantined
because of yellow fever until weeks before John Henry's arrival there—
and it was not "on the way" to anywhere, because it was the end of the
rail line.[24]

It would not have made sense, then, for John Henry, with bright
prospects for the future, including a planned partnership with his
cousin Robert, to suddenly move west simply because of a diagnosis of

consumption. Even if John Henry's consumption was diagnosed before he left Georgia (which is possible, even probable), the sudden nature of his departure had to be attributed to something else, something personal and shattering that triggered a quick response.

Another possibility sometimes cited as the reason for John Henry's abrupt departure was his feelings for Mattie Holliday. Although the relationship was usually discounted by members of the Holliday family, who insisted that it was a friendship rather than a romance, the family did acknowledge that the two had a special bond. Family recollections also may have been skewed by John Henry's later unsavory reputation as a Western gambler and gunfighter and by Mattie's special place in family lore as the saintly, self-sacrificing nun who inspired the character Melanie in Margaret Mitchell's *Gone with the Wind*. The family almost certainly sought to prevent her reputation from being tainted by his.[25]

Nevertheless, there is a strong circumstantial pattern suggesting an intimate (though not necessarily sexual) relationship between the two of them. She corresponded with him regularly through all those long years in the West. She kept his letters for the rest of her life. His drinking and general moral decline (by traditional standards) were consistent with frustrated love. She never married and eventually became a nun after her cousin became notorious as "Doc Holliday." John Henry's sharp decline in health after she took her vows would also be consistent with lost hope. If a romantic relationship did exist between them, a happy consummation was highly unlikely under the best of circumstances.

The marriage of first cousins was not uncommon in the nineteenth century. Some families even encouraged it as a means of controlling family property. In fact, other first cousins in the Holliday family had married in the past. What made the difference in the case of John Henry and Mattie was that Mattie was Catholic. Not even John Henry's conversion to Catholicism would have made a difference, because canon law forbade the marriage of first cousins.[26] Still, that fact surely was known to both of them before 1873. Did John Henry hope to convert her? Did something else happen that precipitated a crisis? Undeniably, a strong bond existed between them. There are even reports that Mattie's parents disapproved. Definitive answers to the mystery of their relationship were lost. Mattie destroyed some

Martha Anne "Mattie" Holliday, John Henry Holliday's first cousin, with whom he enjoyed a special relationship throughout his life. The exact nature of the relationship is still debated, but she went on to become a nun and the inspiration for the character Melanie Hamilton in Margaret Mitchell's novel *Gone with the Wind*.

of the letters herself before her death, and after her death, a family member chose to burn the rest of the correspondence that Mattie had kept through all her years as a teacher and nun.[27]

Even if they were romantically involved, however, their involvement would require some crisis to explain John Henry's sudden and abrupt decision to go west. Again, consumption would not have been sufficient. There are two distinct claims within different families that John Henry fathered an illegitimate child who was put up for adoption when it was born. In such situations, one common solution among well-to-do families was to "put away" the woman until the child was born, then turn the child over to an adoption group and bring the woman back with some explanation for her absence that protected her and the family's reputation.[28]

Within the families, though, such an event would have created tensions that could well have explained John Henry's decision to move away, and it would have provided an explanation for Mattie's decision to enter a religious order. Such a situation seems highly improbable, however. Within the John Stiles Holliday family there was also a report that John Henry was interested in Sallie Tidwell, the daughter of John's partner in the grocery business.[29] So far, no evidence confirms this attachment, nor would proof of the involvement explain John Henry's move west any more than his connection with Mattie would without a crisis.

Whatever the reason, in the spring or summer of 1873, John Henry Holliday said good-bye to John Stiles Holliday and the rest of the Atlanta Hollidays. They went with him to the train station, and his uncle gave him a diamond stickpin as a going-away gift.[30] According to the version favored by some family members, John Henry left Atlanta bound for Dallas, Texas, by train through Chattanooga, Memphis, New Orleans, and Houston. Through the auspices of John Stiles Holliday, so the story goes, he was to convalesce in Texas until Robert graduated from dental school, during which time he would work in partnership with Dr. John A. Seegar, a former Georgian and an acquaintance of the Holliday family.[31]

More likely, though, John Henry, instead of taking the train north and west, would have taken the train south, back home to Valdosta. If he was indeed planning to go west according to a prearranged plan, this would have been only logical. He would have wanted to say good-bye to his McKey relatives as well as to the Hollidays. His ties to the McKeys were as strong as or stronger than his ties to the Hollidays. If he had already learned that he had consumption, he might well have concluded to test the curative powers of Hamilton County waters near the care of Dr. James McKey, his mother's brother, in a rural environment that would provide opportunities for a more vigorous lifestyle.

The tensions between himself and his father, who had been elected mayor of Valdosta on January 20, 1872, do not appear to have healed, but such a visit gave him a chance to visit with Dr. Lucian F. Frink and some of his old friends.[32] Most important, though, he and his uncle Thomas Sylvester McKey were close. He would have sought advice and comfort from him. For a while, it must have seemed a release as well as a relief to be able to roam over his uncle's lands between the Little and Withlacoochee rivers near the Lowndes County–Brooks County line even as he had explored his father's land on Cat Creek a decade earlier, especially if he left Atlanta under the cloud of some kind of social scandal.

Tom's property on the Withlacoochee was the place where the earliest accounts say that an event happened that forced John Henry to go west. Bat Masterson, who had ample opportunity through the years to hear Holliday discuss his youth, later explained that "the indiscriminate killing of some negroes" was the cause of John Henry's abrupt departure for the West. According to him, young whites and blacks shared a swimming hole on the river until the whites decided that they would no longer share. He wrote, "The negro boys were informed that in the future they would have to go further down the stream to do their swimming, which they promptly refused to do and told the whites that if they didn't like existing conditions, that they themselves would have to hunt up a new swimming hole."[33]

This "defiant attitude" caused the whites to "instantly go on the warpath." Masterson said, "One beautiful Sunday afternoon, while an unusually large number of negroes were in swimming at the point of dispute, Holliday appeared on the river bank with a double-barreled shotgun in his hands, and, pointing it in the direction of the swimmers, ordered them from the river." The blacks "stampeded for the opposite shore," and "Holliday waited until he got a bunch of them together, and then turned loose with both barrels, killing two outright, and wounding several others." Masterson said that Holliday later justified what he did by saying that "the 'niggers' had to be disciplined," but that his family thought it best that he leave for a while, whereupon he went to Dallas.[34]

Other accounts of the mayhem survived. One provided by a Mr. Moore, who worked in Valdosta in 1881, was somewhat simpler:

> There was a swimming pool on the Withlacoochee River near Valdoster [sic] and Doc. and the white boys used to think it was theirs. One day, they came down and some nigger boys were swiming [sic] in it. Doc. had a pistol and some say he shot promiscuously and accidentally killed one of the colored boys. Others say he deliberately shot at and killed three. That I do not know. But it was for this reason he is supposed to have left home.[35]

Curiously, too, the tradition of a fatal encounter at Blue Springs on the Withlacoochee near Troupville between John Henry and young blacks survived among members of the family of Major Holliday's second wife, the Martins, who had little reason to remember Rachel's stepson fondly. According to the version passed down in the Martin family, "there were some words and Doc allegedly killed one of the Black youths with a gun."[36]

In the early 1930s, when Stuart N. Lake's *Wyatt Earp: Frontier Marshal* revived interest in Doc Holliday, the stories of the Withlacoochee shooting were resurrected. What is interesting is that the

John Henry Holliday, Atlanta, Georgia, 1872. This photograph has good provenance within the family but is questioned by some authorities.

family did not deny that such an episode occurred, although it was reported as less bloody. Mrs. Clyde McKey White, the youngest of Tom's children, remembered it this way: "Papa told me Doc shot over their heads. They rode up on the Negroes in swimming in a part of the Withlacoochee River that Doc and his friends had cleared out to be used as their swimming hole. The presence of the Negroes . . . enraged Doc, and he drew his pistol—shooting over their heads to scare them off. Papa said, 'Shot over their heads.' "[37] This recollection squares well with the story that Tom himself told as reported by the *Valdosta Times* in 1931:

> Accompanied by Mr. T. S. McKey, now one of Valdosta's oldest citizens, John one day rode out to a point northwest of the city which was noted throughout this section for its fine "washhole." Arriving there, they discovered that several negroes had been throwing mud into the water and stirring it up so that it was unfit to swim in.
>
> Holliday began scolding the negroes and one of them made threatening remarks back to him. John immediately got his buggy whip

and proceeded to punish this hard-boiled negro. The negro fled and returned in a few minutes with a shot gun. He shot once and sprinkled Holliday with small bird shots. Holliday promptly got his pistol and pursued the fleeing negroes. When the negro who had shot at him saw that the youth meant business, he took to his heels and could not be caught.[38]

It would not be surprising if the family sanitized the shooting for public consumption, but the larger problem is that no account of such an incident has survived in the records of the time. That is not entirely surprising. First, the Valdosta papers for 1873 are incomplete, and the criminal records for that period in Lowndes County were lost. Moreover, white violence against blacks frequently went unreported in the press during those days. Nevertheless, the shooting would have been serious business in a place still recovering from Reconstruction. The detail in Masterson's account, combined with his knowledge that John Henry went to Dallas and the supporting accounts from family sources, is compelling if not definitive.

If John Henry did leave Georgia on the run, he would have slipped into Hamilton County, Florida, long enough to say good-bye to his McKey relatives and gather what he needed for the journey, and then caught the train into Tallahassee and traveled west to Pensacola. From there, he might have continued west into Mobile, New Orleans, and on into Texas. Or, more likely, he boarded a steamer at Pensacola bound for Galveston. One story from a family source, which supports the idea that John Henry left by this more southerly route, claims that John Henry fled from Tom's McKey's home, taking with him a knife Tom had made from a meat cleaver and carried with him through the Civil War. The knife, which Tom called the "Hell Bitch," was heavy, long bladed, and double edged in the manner of a Bowie knife. Doc left behind the sheath, which remained with family members.[39]

The historical sources, both reliable and unreliable, are exasperating because of all the possible motives for secrecy and whitewashing, both at the time the events occurred and in the treatment of those events by the family over time, and because the public records are incomplete. Perhaps the truth was some combination of all these issues. Perhaps John Henry learned he had tuberculosis, pressed Mattie for an answer only to be turned down, returned to Valdosta, and was forced west by the shooting incident. This much is clear: something traumatic and devastating enough to interrupt his plans drove him west that summer of 1873. Coughing spasms, a broken heart, a shotgun blast, or a combination of all three cut him off forever from his past and threw him into an unknown future.

John Henry Holliday headed west in 1873 accompanied by many ghosts and embittered by the destruction of his dreams. Everything and everyone he loved lay behind him, and what he found in Texas hardly gave him hope. Some doctors claimed that whiskey helped consumption, and perhaps it was then that he began to drink more heavily to find relief, with the added excuse of needing to forget. Or perhaps he headed west determined to follow "the path of rectitude" that his mother had taught him, as he himself later claimed.

Galveston was a city with a history back to the days of Jean Lafitte. As the major port of entry on the Gulf of Mexico, it was the gateway to Texas. It was also a city on the move with a large business community and real claims to progress. It boasted an opera house, just a couple of years old when John Henry arrived, and a cotton exchange had been established the year before. But John Henry was just passing through. He caught the Houston & Texas Central one jump ahead of a yellow fever epidemic that closed Galveston.[40] He passed through piney woods, post oaks, and cotton country that must have reminded him of the Georgia he left behind him. He traveled through Houston toward Dallas but almost certainly stopped off at Brenham to see his uncle, Jonathan Level McKey, who had left Georgia in 1858 before the war. Uncle Jonathan had prospered in the area, but the war and Reconstruction had taken their toll, and most of his wealth was gone by the time John Henry arrived. Apparently, he did not stay long once he realized his uncle's plight, and after an appropriate time for catching his uncle up on news of his brothers and sisters back in Georgia and Florida, he moved on to Dallas.[41]

Dallas was scarcely the answer to prayers. It was the end of the line for the railroad and a rude and rough settlement only then transforming into a town of substance, but it had a look and feel that John Henry Holliday would come to know well. Dallas was a boomtown with muddy streets and fresh construction everywhere. The railroad had arrived on July 16, 1872, and in the year that followed, the town grew from a quiet Trinity River farm town of twelve hundred to a burgeoning trade center of more than seven thousand. It was a major source of supply for points west. It was still struggling to find its niche, but the railroad itself held promise enough that the business community grew.[42]

Dallas had problems, however. That spring, before John Henry arrived, it had been closed for four weeks because of a quarantine brought on by yellow fever. Construction added to the noise and confusion, and hogs were allowed to roam free on the streets as a unique measure for cleaning the streets of cattle waste. Beyond the business district, on Main Street past the train depot more than forty saloons and gambling halls stretched out to the Trinity and played host to a substantial floating population including gamblers, saloonkeepers, prostitutes, and various frontier parasites. Cattle and buffalo hides would eventually boost the local economy, but first, in September, the Panic of 1873 further dampened the prosperity of Dallas and left the future in doubt. Instead of a temporary end-of-track town, Dallas became the end of the line for the Texas and Pacific Railroad for the foreseeable future. Population growth stalled, and the town settled in.[43]

It was not mere chance that took young Holliday to Dallas. He knew people there. H. P. Morris, whose daughter, Miriam, had attended the Valdosta Institute with John Henry, had moved to Dallas in 1872 with his family.[44] More important, John Henry knew a prominent dentist in Dallas named John A. Seegar, also a recent emigrant from Georgia. John A. Seegar was the son of John Seegar, who had operated a "respectable house of entertainment for travellers" on the post road that extended from Greenville, South Carolina, through Atlanta to Mobile, not far from the hotel owned by John Henry's grandfather in the two decades before the war.[45]

John A. Seegar had lived in Fayetteville for a time, served in the Confederate army, and after the war attended the Pennsylvania College of Dental Surgery. In 1867, he migrated to Texas and settled in Dallas with his family. He became prominent in local affairs and established a successful practice. In 1869, Seegar advertised for a partner in the *Philadelphia Dental Office and Laboratory*. He wrote, "Will take a young man who has just graduated."[46] Of course, that was three years before John Henry's graduation, but in the same issue of the *Dental Times* that carried Holliday's commencement program, Seegar published a paper titled "Galvanic Action from Amalgam Fillings."[47] Because of family and school connections, then, Seegar was John Henry's best chance. They struck a deal, and, by the summer of 1873, they were partners in a dental practice.

For a time, the partnership seemed to prosper. John Henry's talents were considerable. In October, Holliday and Seegar swept the prizes at the state fair for the best set of teeth in gold, the best set of teeth in vulcanized rubber, and the best display of artificial teeth and dental ware.[48] Holliday later claimed that he also joined the Methodist Church in Dallas and even became a member of a temperance society as part of his effort to achieve respectability.[49] Both would have pleased Seegar—who was a strait-laced man of firm Baptist persuasion—and his family back home.

But on March 2, 1874, the Dallas paper announced that "upon mutual consent" the firm of Seegar and Holliday had dissolved. The item also indicated that Holliday's office was now located above the Dallas County Bank at the corner of Main and Lamar. Further indication that the partnership had ended on less than a happy basis was the announcement that John Henry would be responsible for bills against the firm of Seegar and Holliday. The cause of the breach was never explained, but the likely cause was soon a matter of public record. Young Dr. Holliday, in the parlance of the times, had "slipped from the path of rectitude."[50]

John Henry was drawn more and more into the city's nightlife. He may well have found release from his problems in Fort Worth, a few miles west, where a Dallas professional could drink and gamble with less notice. But over time his drinking increased, and he was soon a regular at Dallas's saloons and gambling halls. Faro, monte, five-card draw, and all the games he had learned growing up in the Deep South now had an allure they had not had before. If he was consumptive, which seems probable, the drinking was easily explained. The liquor helped him to cope with his pain (mental as well as physical), and the gambling not only contributed to his prosperity but also provided a diversion from the ghosts of his past.

He was apparently an apt student. In April 1874, he was arrested for operating a keno game, and on May 12 he was indicted for gambling. On May 22, he appeared in court for the charge.[51] He apparently made an effort to keep his day business, though. On June 1, he paid his property and poll taxes.[52] Curiously, Dr. Seegar's office was destroyed by fire on June 21, but by then Holliday had left Dallas for Denison.

John Henry Holliday, Dallas, 1873. This photograph was discovered by the late Vincent Mercaldo. The original was in an oval frame, and on the back of the photo, in pencil, was inscribed "John Henry Holliday—Dallas—1873."

Denison, another end-of-track town just south of the Red River, was a wide-open town suited to John Henry's newfound avocation. This town had a rougher edge than Dallas, though, because it was on the fringe of the Indian Territory in a spot that had been the home of desperadoes and ne'er-do-wells for years. Denison was organized on September 20, 1872, and the Kansas & Texas Railroad ran its first train through on Christmas Day. The town anticipated becoming a major shipping point for cattle, and before long it even had a refrigerated slaughterhouse capable of processing three hundred cattle a day. The Katy Railroad anticipated shipping beef back east in refrigerator cars. The first year of operation was a good one, which meant jobs in Denison and a substantial floating population of cowboys during the cattle season, one of the attractions for Doc.[53]

Jesse Leigh Hall, who was known as "Red," but who preferred to be called "Lee," was the deputy sheriff in charge of law enforcement. A former schoolteacher at Sherman and the county seat of Grayson County until he became Sherman's town marshal, he was tough and courageous. In 1873, he had been after an outlaw who challenged him to a duel. Hall accepted and shot his man dead out of the saddle, although he was wounded himself. Hall was determined to keep the lid on Denison. Aside from demanding regular cleanups on the part of businessmen, he kept the saloons, gambling houses, and bordellos a block off Main on Skiddy for easier control and better appearances. At the same time, Hall was congenial to the sporting class. He generally ignored the state law forbidding gambling and the sale of spiritous liquors in the same establishments and let gaming flourish so long as there was no trouble.[54]

Holliday kept a low profile in Denison. Dr. R. H. Lampkin, "a very agreeable gentleman," had opened an office in June 1873, and the *Denison Daily News* announced that "[h]e is the only practicing Dentist in the city."[55] By August 1873, Dr. J. Crane had added his services as an option for the citizenry. When John Henry arrived, dental services seemed well met, and he apparently spent more time on Skiddy than on Main. With Red Hall on hand, the gambling halls ran smoothly. John Henry remained there through the fall, learning the culture as well as the games, although he apparently made trips back to Dallas from time to time on the Houston & Texas Central. But when the American and Texas Refrigerator Car Company became another victim of the Panic of 1873, and its packing plant in Denison closed, the negative impact on the economy was felt on both Skiddy and Main.[56]

In the meantime, things had improved a bit in Dallas. Oddly enough, the peculiar combination of the panic and the new technology that made it easier to process buffalo hides spawned a new industry overnight, and Dallas was positioned to take advantage of it. Before long, Dallas was a center for shipping and processing hides from the slaughter of the great southern herd on the plains of western Texas.

On New Year's Eve, John Henry took another significant step in his transformation from Southern professional to Western sport. The *Dallas Weekly Herald* provided the details: "Dr. Holliday and Mr. Austin, a saloon keeper, relieved the monotony of the noise of firecrackers by taking a couple of shots at each other yesterday afternoon. The cheerful note of the peaceful six shooter is heard once more among us. Both shooters were arrested."[57]

Charles W. Austin, called "Champagne Charlie" by the patrons of the St. Charles Saloon, was a Texan and former cowhand who earlier had been a clerk at J. W. Thomas's Butcher Shop in the City Market. The transformation to successful saloonman was noteworthy, for he was soon classified as a "rollicking fellow" with exceptional skills as a bartender. His "rollicking" sometimes got him into trouble, however. The previous year he had been arrested on a charge of assault with intent to commit murder after an attack on the ex-marshal of Dallas, Major G. W. Campbell. He had been acquitted in that matter, and by August 1874 a local paper declared of him, "It is admitted by all that Charlie beats the world mixing drinks, and from our own experience, unqualifiedly assert that Charlie 'understands his gait.'"[58]

The details of the New Year's Eve shooting were not recorded, but while both shooters were arrested, Austin was not held. He clearly had a bigger reputation and more friends in Dallas. On January 18, John Henry was charged with assault with intent to murder, but a week later, on January 25, he was tried and acquitted.[59] It had not been much of an affair, but he was building a reputation as a man who would not back down. John Henry was back and forth between Dallas and Denison that spring. On April 13, he was responsible enough to show up in court for the old keno charge in Dallas. He was fined $10.[60] The books in Dallas were now clear, and he began to think of his future. The inhospitable clime of Dallas and poor prospects in Denison and Fort Worth moved him west in May 1875; he left behind unclaimed mail at Denison.[61]

So far, Doc, as he was now called, had known only the fringe of the frontier. He had met frontier types, and he had heard stories aplenty of life beyond the reach of the railroad, where cowboys, desperadoes, the army, and occasional flare-ups of Indian resistance gave life a hard edge, rough and unfinished. But he had also been told that in the little towns that had grown up near military posts, men who were willing to take chances had the opportunity to make money on the gambling circuit. That winter, one of the more promising spots seemed to be Fort Griffin Flat, a sprawling little village that stood just below Fort Griffin, one of the army's outposts in a cluster of forts on the central plains of Texas.

The buffalo slaughter made the Flat a rendezvous for hunters and a shipping point for hides, and the Dodge City Trail ran past Fort Griffin, bringing great cattle herds and cowboys with them into town for one last party before the dry and monotonous drive toward Doan's Station and on into Dodge City, Kansas. It was a promising combination—soldiers, hunters, and cowboys—bound to attract gamblers, saloonmen, and whores. Doc Holliday, with his respectable reputation wasted in Dallas saloons and gambling houses, took the stage west along the military roads. He may have paused briefly at Jacksboro, near Fort Richardson, but if he did, he did not tarry long, pushing on past Fort Belknap, and then southwest to Fort Griffin and the Flat.[62]

Fort Griffin had done its part in the defense of central Texas from 1867 to 1874, when the Red River War finally broke the back of Comanche and Kiowa resistance. The fort stood on a plateau overlooking the Clear Fork of the Brazos River, kept mostly for mop-up operations and as a force for order in the area. The post was crude but neat and, when Doc reached it, was home to troops from the Tenth Cavalry and the Eleventh Infantry. The Flat curled around the base of the plateau, with a single street, Griffin Avenue, stretching toward the river. One old-timer described the town this way: "Fort Griffin, when I arrived there, was the toughest place I'd ever seen. I believe there were eight or ten saloons there then, and, in addition, there were several dance halls. The Bee Hive Saloon and Dance Hall was the main one. Lewd women infested these places, and all of them had their little huts or shanties, which sprawled along the bank of the Clear Fork of the Brazos River."[63]

In 1874, the Flat had been so lawless that the military had seized control and driven out most of the undesirables, and Rufus Choate, the assistant surgeon at Fort Griffin, reported that "the low whiskey shops and gambling-halls of the flat were weeded out."[64] That same year Shackleford County was created, and, before the year ended, the "Town of Fort Griffin" had gained legal status. On October 12, 1874, Fort Griffin had even become the temporary county seat. That favored position lasted for less than a month, though, because on November 8, Albany (ironically named after the southwestern Georgia town of Albany less than a hundred miles from Valdosta by another postwar Georgia migrant to Texas, William R. Cruger) became the county seat.[65]

By the time Doc arrived, the town was coming back to life. He found a room, most likely at the Planter's Hotel, advertised as the "best" and "only" hotel in town. Outside, Griffin Avenue was alive with sounds and smells. By day, as one old-timer declared, "Fort Griffin was more disgusting, after first glance, than alluringly picturesque."[66] Another added, "Old Griffin had its night life; everything went but murder, arson, and burglary."[67] Don H. Biggers later described his first impression of the town:

At that time the town and the post were in the full bloom of military glory and commercial prosperity, unrestrained recklessness and military discipline. The cosmopolitan population of the place was within itself a theme of no mean consequence. There were buffalo-hunters, bullwhackers, soldiers, cowpunchers, Indians, gamblers, toughs, refined business men and fallen women mingling in one common herd on the streets and in the business houses. The picture of the town that day was one never to be forgotten. There must have been 300 or 400 cowboys in town, many of them belonging with trail herds. In front of every store or place of business there was a long hitching rack, and these hitching racks were lined with horses. Several big hide and meat trains had come in from the range, and dozens of big ox teams were standing about the streets and camped along the creek. Thousands of buffalo hides were stacked here and there and thousands more were loaded on wagons ready to depart for Fort Worth. Everybody had plenty of money, and half a dozen big stores, eight or ten saloons and two or three dance halls and varieties were doing business at full capacity. From more than a dozen places music was being ground out on pianos, fiddles, banjos and guitary, and the whole town was a Babel of boisterous talk, whoops, curses, laughter, songs and miserable music.[68]

Doc slipped into the town's rhythms easily enough, although he doubtlessly watched with some amazement a town "where men drank, gambled, quarreled and fought, indifferently dumped hundreds of dollars over the bar and killed each other over a quarter suspiciously taken in a poker game or because of some trivial, perhaps wholly imaginary insult, [and] daily supplied mule and ox train loads of merchandise to the wants of man."[69] Holliday had met sports, peace officers, and a few toughs in Dallas and Denison, but at Fort Griffin he encountered a rougher and more desperate class at the bars and gambling tables. At the Bee Hive Saloon and John Shaughnessy's place, John Henry found all the action he needed.

One of the characters he met at the Bee Hive was the notorious Hurricane Bill Martin. The amazing thing was that he was free so close to a military post. Martin had gained notoriety in Kansas as a horse thief and was considered by many to be one of the primary causes of the Red River War of 1874 because of his horse-stealing raids on the herds of the Southern Cheyennes. He was, as a contemporary put it, "as slick a rascal as ever escaped justice," which was demonstrated when he took a job as a scout for the army in 1875 while still a fugitive.

He more or less had his way in Fort Griffin, except for the time that the vigilance committee forced him to marry his paramour and full-time whore, Hurricane Minnie. The arrangement did not seem to hamper the activities of either of the partners.[70]

Doc was on hand when Hurricane Bill and a buffalo hunter named Mike O'Brien got into a quarrel. When both men realized they were unarmed, each ran to get their guns. O'Brien, armed with a buffalo gun, moved into the middle of Griffin Avenue and opened fire on Bill's shack, blasting holes into the walls while Bill crouched inside attempting to return the fire. O'Brien fired until he ran out of ammunition, then returned to the Bee Hive for another drink. Bill was left to contemplate his newly ventilated shanty. When they sobered up, both men forgot the quarrel and turned their attention to other matters. Hurricane Bill was a regular at the poker and faro tables, and it was there that he and Doc got to know each other.[71]

Watching, learning, and taking his winnings at the tables, Holliday created no disturbances at Fort Griffin. Unfortunately, in June, not long after he arrived, the legal authorities decided to flex their muscles. The first session of the Shackleford County District Court convened with Judge J. P. Osterhout presiding. Thirty-seven cases were heard in five days, during which a dozen men were found guilty of gambling and illegally selling liquor. Most of the fines were $10 to $15, but several of the men had more than one fine to pay. Among the defendants was "Dock Holliday," who was arrested for playing "at a game of cards at a house used for retailing spiritous liquor," along with Hurricane Bill, Mike Lynch, and Curly, a protégé of Hurricane Bill's. Doc would later claim that some of the outlaws in Tombstone were "part of the old Fort Griffin gang," which raises the possibility that the Fort Griffin Curly was Curly Bill Brocius.[72]

Of the defendants, though, Doc and Mike Lynch decided to leave Fort Griffin rather than pay the fine. On June 30, 1875, an *alias capias* was issued for Doc's arrest and forwarded to the sheriff of Tom Green County at San Angelo.[73] Doc probably took the stage west along the military road to Fort Concho, but he does not appear to have lingered long there. His movements over the rest of 1875 escaped documentation. He recalled later that he spent part of 1875 in Denver, and this has been the most commonly accepted view, placing him on the military roads west to El Paso, then turning north through New Mexico into Colorado. According to this scenario, Doc dealt cards for John A. Babb in Denver through the rest of 1875, then joined "a fresh invoice of Denver gamblers" who arrived in Cheyenne, Wyoming, on February 5, 1876.[74]

John Charles Thompson claimed that Doc was there as well, writing in his history of Cheyenne:

> Run out of Texas because of his lethal propensities, this platinum blond desperado tried Colorado, extinguished several gunmen there, came to Cheyenne and did right well at gambling. The reputation of this dour misanthrope with death gnawing on his lungs caused him to be unchallenged here. Jeff Carr, the town marshal, regarded him dourly, but courageous though the big officer was, he didn't choose to take on a killer of Holliday's ruthless character.[75]

Previous biographers have differed on whether Doc joined the Black Hills gold rush and moved to Deadwood. One view claimed that he remained in Deadwood until the spring of 1877, when he returned to Cheyenne and Denver en route back to Texas, while another returned Doc to Denver with Colorado statehood in August 1876, where he remained until early 1877 gambling under the name "Tom McKey."[76] These are not the only possibilities.

Kate Elder claimed that she and Doc were together at Cantonment Sweetwater, later Mobeetie, Texas, during the winter of 1875–1876, and said that they were both on hand when Bat Masterson killed Corporal Melvin King on the night of January 24, 1876. Kate doubtlessly was there, but Doc's presence seems likely an artifice of Kate's to cover up her real reason for being in Sweetwater. She was one of the girls in Tom Sherman's dance hall, having moved from Dodge along the wagon road when the Sweetwater camp was established. Bat Masterson never mentioned Doc's presence at Sweetwater and always claimed that he met Doc in Dodge City, more than two years after King's death.[77]

Kate did leave a partial trail. After John Henry returned to Atlanta in 1872, Kate apparently fell in with Silas Melvin. She claimed he was a dentist, that they later moved to Atlanta, and that her husband and child both died there of yellow fever. She also claimed that she renewed her acquaintance with Doc and married him in Valdosta on March 25, 1876, before moving west in 1877. Of course, the dates do not fit. Melvin was, in fact, an attendant at the County Insane Asylum in St. Louis and had married Mary Virginia Bust on October 10, 1871. Most likely, Kate had an affair with Melvin, but other relationships escaped notice.[78] At some point, she gave up the name "Kate Fisher" and started using "Kate Elder." She was fined for prostitution using that name in the summer of 1874 in Wichita, Kansas. Bessie Earp, the wife of James Earp, and Sallie Earp, who may well have been Sarah Haspel, the consort of Wyatt Earp from Peoria, Illinois, were also arrested at that time.[79]

Curiously, Wyatt Earp always called Kate "Kate Fisher," which suggests that he may have met her before she changed her name. Perhaps she became Kate Elder in Wichita. The first marshal of Wichita was Ike S. Elder, and he was still around in 1874. Bessie and Sallie established their house in January 1874, and Kate may have worked for them. In that case, Kate would have met not only her employers but James and Wyatt as well. That would explain Kate's bitter distaste for the Earps, especially for Wyatt later on. In 1875, however, Kate left Wichita for Dodge City, where she went to work for Tom Sherman at his dance hall. Sherman then took some of his girls to Sweetwater when that camp sprang up in the fall of 1875.[80]

John Henry almost certainly headed southwest to Fort Concho in June 1875, which generated the *alias capias* to Tom Green County, but he could have trailed south rather than west from there, toward more civilized environs like San Antonio or Austin, perhaps moving on to Laredo or even looping back north to Fort Worth or Dallas. He could have easily wintered in familiar haunts in Dallas or Denison, or on new grounds like San Antonio or Austin, without notice. He was not well known and, after all, had little to worry about over a gambling fine. He was far from a seasoned frontiersman, and his health was fragile, both of which mitigated against him getting too far away from established roads. Early in 1876, however, he was on the move again, and he may well have gained enough confidence to return to Fort Griffin. Shackleford County authorities did issue a second *capias* for Doc on the old charge at the May term of court, which provides circumstantial evidence that he had returned to the area. But by then something had happened that already had caused Doc to run.

Bat Masterson, whose account of Doc's life, while flawed, is reliable in broad form, claimed that Doc killed a black soldier at Jacksboro.[81] No such event was reported in either the papers or the records of the time, but an incident did occur at Fort Griffin that might well have been the shooting Masterson recalled. On the night of March 3, 1876, Private Jacob Smith, who was "absent without authority" from Fort Griffin in the Flat, was shot and killed by an unknown party.[82] Perhaps it was a coincidence, but John Henry Holliday was soon on the run, using the alias Tom McKey, not something likely precipitated by a $10 fine for gambling.

Masterson said that after the soldier was killed, Doc "lost no time in getting out of town, and seated on the hurricane deck of a Texas cayuse, was well on his way to safety by the time the news of the homicide reached the fort."[83] Masterson claimed that Doc struck out for Denver across the Texas Panhandle, no-man's-land, and New Mexico. But again, Doc was not an experienced plainsman, and even taking the stage roads west was a grueling journey. More likely, he would have headed east, caught the train at Dallas, and traveled north through Denison and on into the Indian Territory. At Vinita, in the Cherokee Nation, he would have changed trains and traveled into Missouri, perhaps going as far as St. Louis, where he hoped to find his old friend, Dr. A. Jameson Fuches Jr. If that was his intent, he was disappointed, because Fuches had moved across the river into Illinois, where he pursued a very successful career as a dentist and a physician.[84]

Doc may well have encountered his old friend Kate Elder there. St. Louis was a big gambling town in those days, which attracted a lot of the sporting circle that spring. After returning to Dodge from Sweetwater, she may have found her way east to a "warmer nest" in her old stomping grounds at St. Louis. At least, she was not further associated with Dodge. As previously noted, she would later claim that she married Doc on May 25, 1876. No proof of such a union survived in the rather complete St. Louis marriage records, and Kate's recollections were far from trustworthy, but the timing was appropriate for a reunion of some sort.[85]

The big news that spring was the Black Hills gold rush, and Doc soon would have left Kate and St. Louis, catching the train to Kansas City and taking the spur from there to the Union Pacific. He may well have headed west to Cheyenne, though later than generally supposed, and, before the spring was over, arrived in Deadwood. After a brief stay, he caught the stage back to Cheyenne. On June 26, 1876, the day after General George Armstrong Custer's fall at Little Big Horn, a man named J. H. Holliday was one of the victims of a stage robbery, losing his cash and a fine, engraved gold watch. Apparently, this Holliday was a St. Louis businessman, but the timing would have fit Doc's movements.[86]

Americans were celebrating the nation's centennial, and Doc almost certainly arrived in Denver just after the grand July 4 celebration and just in time to hear the news of Custer's disaster. Denver was a booming city, with broad streets and prosperous neighborhoods, but it still had a frontier edge. There was a large sporting district that was populated with some of the West's most successful gamblers. Apparently, Doc took a job dealing cards for Charley Foster at Babb's Variety House and found a room over Long John's Saloon on Blake Street nearby. He settled in, using the alias T. S. McKey, after his favorite uncle, indicating that he was still on the run.[87]

Members of the Holliday family later claimed that that summer Pinkerton agents called on the John Stiles Holliday household asking for photographs of John Henry and that one of the girls quickly removed his picture from the family album and hid it under her dress before handing the album to the agents.[88] If this incident did occur, the reason was never revealed. Jacob Smith's murder was not likely the reason. Apparently, the army did not have a clue as to who had killed Smith, nor did it usually put up much of a fuss over a black trooper killed while absent from duty without leave.

Denver had its share of fights and crime, and at the time of Doc Holliday's death in 1887, one of the newspaper obituaries mentioned an 1876 fight between Doc and another gambler named Bud Ryan in which Doc slashed Ryan with a knife. According to the report, Doc "was a quiet, modest man, with a smile that was child-like and bland." The reporter added, "[B]ut one night he electrified the town by nearly cutting off the head of Budd Ryan, a well-known Denver gambler."[89] Bat Masterson would also repeat the story in 1907, noting that Ryan was still living in Denver, though scarred by the encounter. A Bud Ryan was in fact living at 1653 Arapahoe in Denver in 1890.[90]

If Doc did carve up Ryan with the "Hell Bitch"—and it is noteworthy that the Denver reporter knew that he went by the alias Tom Mackey—the incident escaped direct notice in the surviving papers.

On November 28, 1876, however, the *Rocky Mountain News* did report an incident at 19 Holladay Street, referred to simply as "Saturday night's affair," as if everyone was familiar with the details. Two days later, the *News* reported that Judge O. A. Whittemore had "settled the Holladay street affair by charging the accused $30 and costs." Interestingly, the very next day the *News* reported letters for "T. S. McKey" in its list of undelivered letters at the post office.[91]

Doc headed east. He could not know that the gambling charges against him in Fort Griffin had been dismissed in November, but he apparently felt confident that he was not being pursued on more serious charges. He may have stopped in Laclede, Kansas, long enough to visit his aunt Rebecca Annaliza Holliday McCoin, who was living there with her family, but by January 1877 he was back in Dallas using his own name. There were two gunfights in Dallas within a matter of days after he returned, including one at a saloon on Jefferson Street, which indicated that the town was still lively. He settled into the bars and gambling halls, and on January 8 he was arrested on three counts of gambling.[92]

Holliday's movements after his arrest are unclear. What is clear is that he was a different man than the one who had arrived in Dallas a few years earlier. The aspiring dentist had given way to the seasoned and hardened professional gambler. John C. Jacobs, who met him later that year at Fort Griffin, remembered him as follows:

> This fellow Holliday was a consumptive and a hard drinker, but neither liquor nor the bugs seemed to faze him. He could at times be the most genteel, affable chap you ever saw, and at other times he was sour and surly, and would just as soon cut your throat with a villainous looking knife he always carried, or shoot you with a .41-calibre double-barreled derringer he always kept in his vest pocket.[93]

Doc may have wintered in Dallas despite its inhospitable treatment of gamblers. He may have returned to Denison or traveled to Eagle Pass, especially since the Dallas papers were praising Maverick County and claiming that "there is no more healthy country."[94] He may have visited Fort Worth, San Antonio, or other points south and west of Dallas. Newspapers of the time frequently reported (or complained) of the sports in town, but they rarely named them, unless they were famous, which Doc decidedly was not. On May 8, 1877, the January cases were transferred to the court of the justice of the peace.[95] By June, the papers were reporting the growth of the new town of Breckenridge in Stephens County, Texas, and Doc joined other sporting men in a migration there.

On July 4, Holliday had an altercation with another gambler named Henry Kahn, a relative of Dallas's prominent clothiers. Reviving a Southern tradition, Doc severely caned Kahn. The police intervened and hauled both men into court, where they were fined. Later that same day, the two met again, and Kahn shot Holliday, seriously wounding him.[96] The cause of the dispute escaped documentation, but Kahn was himself probably on the run. He was indicted in Shackleford County in August for forgery, and thereafter slid through the fingers of Texas justice. On July 7, the *Dallas Daily Herald* reported, "Our reporter was told in Fort Worth yesterday that a young man named Doc Holliday, well known in this city, was shot and killed at Breckenridge last Wednesday by a young man named Kahn."[97] Of course, reports of Doc's demise were premature.

Apparently, Doc's family was notified, and George Henry Holliday was sent by them to tend Doc during his recovery and perhaps to persuade him to return home. George arrived on July 21 and looked after his cousin briefly before being convinced that John Henry was able to take care of himself and had no intention of returning home.[98] Doc's recovery was marked by another arrest for gambling in Dallas in September, and this time he decided to move on.[99]

His destination was Fort Griffin. Fort Griffin had become a different place since his last visit. The town was booming. It was a major stop for Texas cattle headed north, with as many as 150,000 head covering the plains around the town the previous spring. In July, John Golden had been killed by officers of the law, and Hurricane Bill, once a cock-of-the-walk in Fort Griffin, escaped jail and departed for parts unknown. John Larn was the new law in Griffin as the Shackleford County sheriff. He was a man of questionable character himself, and he would eventually run afoul of the still active vigilance committee.[100]

Perhaps the most notable addition to Fort Griffin society in Doc Holliday's absence was "Lottie Deno." Actually named Charlotte Tompkins, Lottie arrived in the spring of 1877 and immediately became a local celebrity. She was a mysterious, well-mannered, and attractive woman who was both a whore and immune to the rough and rowdy climate of the saloons and gambling halls. She quickly obtained an interest in the Gus, a saloon and boarding house. Despite her business success and her reputation as "the poker queen"—she was successful in poker games and at the faro table—Griffin's respectable element denied her the social acceptance of other saloon owners. This was, after all, the Victorian era, and not even her beauty and manners could overcome the public perception of her as a fallen woman.

Lottie may have followed a former Georgian named Frank Thurmond, who was also a San Antonio gambler on the run, to Griffin. Using the alias Mike Fogarty, he was employed periodically as a bartender at the Bee Hive, although he also ran cattle at times or worked as a shotgun guard on stagecoaches. Lottie was also involved with a gambler named Johnny Golden, but Golden had been killed by Marshal Bill Gilson and Deputy Sheriff Jim Draper in July before Doc returned to town in September. After Golden's death, Lottie became increasingly reclusive, but she did emerge to support herself at the gambling tables.[101]

Doc checked into the Occidental Hotel, owned by Hank Smith and run by his wife, Elizabeth, known locally as "Aunt Hank." Doc opened an account at Smith's bar on September 14. Within a week he amassed a liquor bill of $120, while spending just over $20 for room and meals.[102] Whether he relocated after that week or moved on to other towns is not clear, but he did have notable experiences while there. For one thing, he appears to have met his former acquaintance Kate Elder and struck up a relationship with her that would last for a time. One of the apocryphal stories about Doc in Griffin was provided by John Jacobs:

> In your recent letter you asked if faro was a popular game at old Fort Griffin. It certainly was popular; every gambling house there had a faro bank. I remember well one instance where a lot of money changed hands, and Lottie Deno coming about three thousand dollars ahead, winning it all from Doc Holliday at the Bee Hive. It seems that Holliday had won over three thousand dollars and the layout from Mike Forgarty [*sic*], who operated the gambling resort, when Lottie Deno, who was lookout for Fogarty, proposed to Holliday that she be given a chance to recoup Fogarty's losses. Holliday agreed to this, and the game was resumed with a fifty dollar limit. The game did not last very long, for Lottie Deno copped every bet, and left Doc Holliday completely strapped for the time being at least, for he was not one who let poor luck get him down and keep him there.

He got into a poker game the next night and won $500 and a dia-
mond ring from an army officer stationed at the fort.[103]

Another story claimed that Kate grew jealous of Lottie, and one
night Kate accused her of trying to steal her man. Supposedly, Lottie
sprang to her feet, shouting, "Why you low-down slinkin' slut! If I
should step in soft cow manure, I would not even clean my boot on
that bastard. I'll show you a thing or two!" Both Lottie and Kate drew
weapons, and bloodshed was avoided by Doc Holliday stepping
between them and defusing the episode—or at least that is the way the
story was told.[104]

Such tales notwithstanding, Fort Griffin quieted down quickly in
late September with the end of the cattle season and the evaporation
of the floating population, and the press was soon reporting, "A Fort
Griffin letter says all is quiet and there is less business now than in the
summer."[105] Doc was gone by then, and when he left, Kate was with
him. She later recalled that she and Doc traveled through south and
southwest Texas, stopping "at every place where there was money to
be made at his profession." They stopped briefly at Laredo, then
moved up the river to Eagle Pass. "While there," Kate recalled, "Doc
went across the Rio Grande to Piedras Negras, a Mexican army post,
and called on the commanding officer to inform he [sic] that he was a
dentist. The commandante told Doc he would arrange quarters for him
to practice in, and asked him to report next morning at 10 A.M. We
remained at Eagle Pass for more than three months, and Doc went
across the river every morning."[106]

While in Eagle Pass, Doc and Kate stayed at the National Hotel
and gambled at the saloon of Blue Vivian, who had moved into the
area early with his brother, Charlie. "Old Blue" passed stories down
through the family about Doc's days there.[107] In December, the situation at Eagle Pass grew tense when the Mexican authorities refused to
turn over to American authorities a man accused of murdering a blind
man on the Texas side of the river. That may well have been the reason that Doc decided to move on, although Kate said that when they
left Eagle Pass, the Mexican "commanding officer would not accept
anything in the way of rent for the office Doc had occupied."[108]

From Eagle Pass, Kate recalled that she and Doc moved to San
Antonio, where they remained for "a few weeks" before moving on "to

Bracketville [*sic*] across the river from Fort Clark, and then to Jacksborough where we remained two months. The next town we hit was Griffen [*sic*], Texas."[109] Kate may have confused this itinerary (for example, she placed it in the fall and winter of 1875–1876), because in her recollections she frequently telescoped events and confused time lines, but the movements in question were consistent with the gamblers' circuit at the time and fit, circumstantially, with other sources and anecdotal material.

Sam Baldwin, who was a buffalo hunter in Texas in the 1870s and later a mining man in New Mexico, knew Doc at Fort Griffin in "the early spring of 1878." He became acquainted with him because his partner, Bob Fambro, and Doc "were from the same neighborhood in Georgia." Baldwin provided one of the few descriptions of Doc during the Texas period: "He was a tall, slim fellow; was a dentist by trade and had a Southern drawl. His hair was almost red and he was blue-eyed. Didn't have a mustache."

Baldwin said that early that spring "a bunch of race horse gamblers" arrived in Fort Griffin anxious "for anything that might come up." Things were dull, so they decided to have a foot race (a surprisingly popular sport in the 1870s and 1880s). A local named Sam Diedrich, a one-armed freighter, fancied himself a racer, so the gamblers brought in a character called Sugar Foot. Diedrich "didn't have a chance with Sugar Foot," but the gamblers bet heavily on Diedrich against their own man. Even Sugar Foot quietly placed bets on Diedrich.

On the day of the race, the crowd gathered on the flat below the military post about a hundred yards from the army's haystacks. Quite a crowd gathered, and the race was about to start when Doc Holliday drove up in a wagon. Baldwin recalled:

> It was about a hundred and twenty yard race. And he stepped over and said, "Boys, what kind of race is this? I have got a lot of money to bet on this!" They said, "It is up and going." He said, "My idea is . . . Sugar Foot could win this race." And said, "Sugar Foot, you know you could." Sugar Foot said, "I don't know."
>
> Doc steps to his wagon, picks up a double barrel shotgun, he was quick speaking anyway, had kind of a whining voice, and said, "Boys, you can't get out of this race. You are going to run it."
>
> He said, "You know that Sugar Foot can beat Diedrich and can win it. There are sixteen buckshot in each barrel and I am going to

empty it into Sugar Foot if he don't win it!" And they called the race, and that fellow fairly flew. By golly, he did fly! Doc walked over and said, "I knowed he could beat him."

Baldwin's recollections concerning other matters are generally reliable, and his account affirms Doc's presence in Fort Griffin in the spring of 1878 as the legend always insisted. In fact, Wyatt Earp claimed that he first met Doc there in the winter of 1877–1878. Earp did have an altercation in a Fort Worth saloon in January 1878, and before the month was out, the Dodge City, Kansas, papers were reporting him at Fort Clark, so he could have met Holliday at Fort Griffin on his way to Fort Clark, as he claimed, although Kate's chronology makes it possible that they met at Fort Clark. Earp may well have remained at Fort Griffin nearly a month before moving on to Clark. However, at some point in time, at one place or the other, he and Doc met, and they talked at length about Dodge City. Doc asked questions and seemed genuinely interested in what Earp had to say.[110]

Earp was the source of the story of another encounter between Doc that became one of the mainstays in the Holliday legend. He said Doc and Kate had departed Fort Griffin because of an argument over cards while he was en route back to Griffin from Clark:

> Doc Holliday was spending the evening in a poker game which was his custom wheneer faro bank did not present superior claims on his attention. On his right sat Ed Bailey, who needs no description because he is soon to drop out of this narrative. The trouble began, as it was related to me afterward, by Ed Bailey monkeying with the deadwood, or what people who live in cities called discards. Doc Holliday admonished him once or twice to "play poker"—which is your seasoned gambler's method of cautioning a friend to stop cheating—but the misguided Bailey persisted in his furtive attentions to the deadwood. Finally, having detected him again, Holliday pulled down a pot without showing his hand which he had a perfect right to do. Thereupon Bailey started to throw his gun around on Holliday, as might have been expected. But before he could pull the trigger, Doc Holliday jerked a knife out of his breast-pocket and with one sideways sweep had caught Bailey just below the brisket.[111]

According to Earp, Doc was locked up in a hotel room while a crowd clamored for his blood. He said that Kate heard about the incident, saw the predicament Doc was in, and set fire to a shed behind the hotel, and when she hollered "Fire," everyone rushed out to fight the flames, leaving the marshal and the constables with the prisoner. Kate then marched into the room, pointed a revolver at the marshal, tossed a pistol to Doc, and, with a laugh, said, "Come on, Doc." Earp said that Doc "didn't need any second invitation" and that the two of them hid in the willows along the creek until a friend brought two horses and clothes for both of them, after which "they got away safely and rode the four hundred miles to Dodge City, where they were installed in great style when I got back home."[112]

No record concerning such an incident at Fort Griffin has been found, although some claim that a large file on Holliday disappeared from the county records at Albany and that a case against Kate for arson was made. Kate later denied that such an incident ever occurred. Reacting to the story as related in Stuart N. Lake's *Wyatt Earp: Frontier Marshal*, she denied that Doc ever killed "a man named Bailey over a poker game, nor was he arrested and locked up in a hotel room." She told Anton Mazzanovich that she "got a hearty laugh" out of the story of her alleged rescue of Doc. She said, "Just think of it. . . . A woman weighing only one hundred and sixteen pounds, standing off a deputy, ordering him to throw up his hands, disarming him, rescuing her lover and hustling him to the waiting ponies. It reads fine, but there is not a word of truth in that fairy story."[113]

Still, Earp, who told the story more than once, did not claim to be an eyewitness to the Bailey stabbing and sometimes confused names, places, and details in his recollections, so that it is possible that the incident in question happened somewhere else in Texas. For example, Brackett, the town near Fort Clark, had a murderous reputation. A report written about the time that Doc and Earp were there proclaimed that

Brackett is a fast place. There are seven dry goods stores, twelve or more retail whiskey shops, 1080 regular thoroughbred monte-dealers. . . . [W]hy sir, it is nothing to hear from fifty to one hundred shots fired here every night, and to hear the next morning of two or three men and as many women being shot or robbed or thrown into Los Moras Spring to feed the fish and flar [*sic*] the water. Six men broke jail last night, and seven are still there.[114]

Given Holliday's peregrinations and Earp's known movements, the Bailey episode could have happened somewhere other than Fort Griffin at some place like Brackett or San Angela, whose records are scarce or nonexistent and whose townships had no newspapers. Much that happened in those camps off the beaten path escaped attention. At any rate, that spring Doc and Kate headed north to Sweetwater and, from there, took the wagon road to Dodge City. Wyatt Earp returned to Dodge in May, and he later said that Doc had already arrived and had settled in by the time he got back. This time, Doc Holliday had left Texas for good.[115]

COW TOWNS AND PUEBLOS

It was easily seen that he was not a healthy man for he not only looked the part, but he incessantly coughed it as well.

—Bat Masterson, *Human Life Magazine* (1907)

John Henry Holliday never looked back. He was through with Texas. He wrote to Mattie Holliday back in Georgia that he had "enjoyed about as much of this [Texas] as [I] could stand."[1] Doc had heard about the Kansas cattle towns often enough, told all scary the way that drunk drovers told everything at poker tables and faro banks, but there was enough truth in their bragging and yarn telling to intrigue a man like Doc. He might have talked about Kansas—and especially Dodge City—with Charles Rath, the former Dodge City entrepreneur who now had a base of operations in Fort Griffin, or with Henry M. Beverley, the Texas agent of Wright, Beverley & Company, which had taken over Rath's business in Dodge.[2] Doubtless, too, he had talked about Dodge with Wyatt Earp, and the bottom line was that there was money to be made there.

Dodge City was seven years old that May 1878, and by the look of it, it was quite a different place from the little end-of-track buffalo camp it had started out as. Now it was "the queen of the cow towns," the "beautiful, bibulous Babylon of the plains." It had a reputation for wildness and violence, although, truthfully, the rowdy cow town Dodge could not hold a candle to the hellhole Dodge had been when buffalo hides guaranteed most of the capital for the city's entrepreneurs.[3] The cowboys could still have their fun with the blessing of the town fathers, but there were limits. Dodge City's police force had gained a reputation for toughness and keeping things under control.

Only weeks before Doc arrived, Edward J. Masterson, the town marshal, had been murdered in the line of duty.[4] Charles E. Bassett, a veteran officer and past sheriff whom one old-timer described as "a pretty good man, too, better than his associates," was appointed to replace him. Ed's brother, Bat Masterson, was the sheriff of Ford County and was making a reputation for himself as the bane of horse thieves.[5] On May 12, the *Dodge City Times* reported Wyatt Earp's return from Texas and predicted that he would be rehired. Three days after that, the *Ford County Globe* confirmed the prediction: "Wyatt Earp, one of the most efficient officers Dodge ever had has just returned from Fort Worth, Texas. He was immediately appointed Asst. Marshal by our City dads, much to their credit." In fact, the *Times* seemed pleased with the entire police force, noting:

> Dodge City is practically under an efficient guard. The city fathers have wisely provided for the honor, safety and character of the city by the appointment of an excellent police force. We believe no better men for the position can be found anywhere. The city's guardians are named as follows:
>
> Marshal—C. E. Bassett
> Assistant Marshal—Wyatt Earp
> Policemen—John Brown and Charles Trask[6]

Later in the summer, Charles Trask was replaced by Jim Masterson, and Dodge was ready for the cowboy invasion.

Doc arrived as the town was preening itself for the cattle season. The *Dodge City Times* told the story:

> This "cattle village" and far-famed "wicked city" is decked out in gorgeous attire in preparation for the long horn. Like the sweet harbinger of spring, the boot black came, he of white and he of black. Next the bar "with his lather and shave." Too, with all that go to make up the busy throng of life's faithful fever, come the Mary Magdaleens [*sic*], "selling their souls to whoever'll buy." There is "high, low, jack and the game," all adding to the great expectation so important an event brings about.

Front Street, Dodge City, Kansas, as it looked in 1878 when Doc Holliday arrived from Texas.

The merchants and the "hardware" dealer has filled his store and renovated his "palace." There are goods in profusion in warehouse and on shelves; the best markets were sought, and goods are in store and to arrive. Necessarily, there is great ado, for soon the vast plains will be covered with the long horn—and the "wicked city" is the source from which the great army of herder and drover is fed.

The season promises to be a remarkable one. The drive is reported to be large, and the first herd will probably reach this point within a couple of weeks. There has been no undue preparation, and the earlier season has stimulated activity to the greatest measure of expectation.[7]

With sixteen saloons, ranging from upscale operations such as the Long Branch and the Alamo to southside dives, Dodge seemed primed for profit for a man like Doc Holliday. "Everybody is supposed and expected to visit these places," an observer noted, "and 'everybody' does. Some of these places are fitted up with a view to the comfort of the patrons, especially the 'Long Branch,' where sweet music is dispensed nightly by a band, consisting of eight pieces led by Mr. Beeson, the gentlemanly proprietor of the establishment."[8]

Doc watched as the herds arrived, sprawling south of the tracks in surprising numbers. At the stock pens, buyers plied their trade at a feverish pace. By June 9, 110,000 cattle had arrived, with 40,000 ready for shipment. While owners and foremen closed deals, drovers hit Front Street, gawking through the store windows and pondering how to spend their fresh pokes. On the south side, saloonmen, gamblers, and whores were ready to help them make their decisions. On May 20, the *Ford County Globe* reported "[n]umerous cowboys under the influence in town."[9] This was why Doc had come.

Dodge City was opportunity knocking. There was high-toned play at places like the Long Branch and the Alamo, and the town did not have a practicing dentist. Day or night, there was money to be made. Doc rented a room at the Dodge House and was soon immersed in his new world. He wired his old colleague in Dallas, John A. Seegar, and had him ship the dental chair he had left behind in Texas. When the chair arrived in June, Doc posted the following notice in the *Dodge City Times*:

DENTISTRY

John H. Holliday, Dentist, very respectfully offers his professional services to the citizens of Dodge City and surrounding county during the summer. Office at Room No. 24 Dodge House. Where satisfaction is not given, money will be refunded.[10]

Holliday apparently behaved himself in Dodge City, because his name did not show up either in the press or in the police court records. What survived are anecdotes that have an apocryphal feel about them. Perhaps the most interesting story is the one told by Robert M. Wright, a prominent Dodge City pioneer businessman and political leader; it is particularly compelling because Wright mentioned Wyatt Earp only briefly in his *Dodge City: The Cowboy Capital*, and then misspelled his last name as "Erb." Wright's account, if true, would almost have to have happened shortly after Doc's arrival in town, and in light of his later association with a man called Turkey Creek Jack Johnson, the story is all the more intriguing because of reference to a male companion known only as "Creek." Wright claimed to have first made their acquaintance when

two gentlemen, elegantly dressed and groomed, made their appearance at the Long Branch Saloon. One could see at a glance that they were educated and refined, and both men had lovely manners and

Dodge House, where Doc roomed and practiced dentistry. Inset: Doc Holliday's advertisement from the *Dodge City Times*, June 8, 1878.

PHOTOGRAPHED FROM DODGE CITY TIMES, ISSUE OF JUNE 8, 1878

DENTISTRY.

J. H. Holliday, Dentist, very respect-fully offers his professional services to the citizens of Dodge City and surrounding country during the summer. Office at room No. 24, Dodge House. Where sat-isfaction is not given money will be re_funded.

exceedingly great persuasive powers. They were quiet and unassum-ing, both were liberal spenders as well as drinkers, but they were never under the influence of liquor. It was only a short time until they had captivated a lot of friends, and I among the number.[11]

Wright claimed that as their "friendship ripened," he learned that they were not "elegant gentlemen" but "big crooks and gold brick men." He said that they confided to him the details of the shakedown of a banker in Leadville during the first year of the Leadville boom. Doc and Creek allegedly convinced the banker that they were the last members of a gang that had stolen gold bullion bars in stage robberies between the Black Hills and Cheyenne and offered to sell the banker the gold bricks for $20,000. After they convinced the banker that the bricks were real, he gave them $20,000, but insisted that one of them go with him to Chicago as surety while he arranged for transporta-tion of the gold. Creek was the designated hostage. En route, how-ever, a man claiming to be an officer of the law arrested both the banker and Creek. While in custody, Creek suggested that the banker attempt to buy off the marshal. The marshal, following a proper show of righteous indignation, did offer to let the banker go for a payment of $15,000. "It is needless to say that the United States Marshal was no one else but Doc Holliday," said Wright. Later, they returned to Dodge for a time before heading south in style: "They were sports every inch of them, if they were crooks and both dead shots with the six-shooter."[12]

Another tale, collected by Dr. Frank Dunn, the first dental historian to become interested in Holliday, recalled a time when Doc arrived in the Alhambra Saloon appearing more the derelict than the dandy. Amused by him, a group of cowboys invited him to have a drink. When he refused, one of the cowboys poured him a tumbler full of whiskey, pointed a pistol at him, and insisted that he drink it. Doc made awful faces as he downed the liquor, and the cowboys laughed, insisting that he have yet another. Filling a third, Doc downed it, and as he drained the fourth, the cowboys realized that it was they who had been had.[13]

A third anecdote was told by Charles Lowther, who claimed that when he was a child he had arrived in Dodge City with his minister father, only to be denied lodging at Dodge House. When his father protested, the hotel clerk explained that he was afraid to give him a room because Doc Holliday, "a gambler and general all around bad-man," was on a bender and might want the room. Later, the Lowthers were told more about Doc: "Nobody crossed him, lest they get him started shooting. In Dodge City he held dominion. It was because the night clerk had sought to favor him by holding several rooms vacant for Doc Holliday that we had to occupy the parlor from about three o'clock till breakfast time."[14]

These stories, all of which seem unlikely, did foster an enigmatic view of Holliday's character. In them, he was a charmer, a con man, a drunk, and a hellion. They do not fit easily into the chronology of Doc's sojourn in Dodge City, but they were consistent with the image of his complex personality. He made an impression on Dodge City's folklore if not its historical record. In fact, the images were symptomatic of the moodiness and moral ambiguity that had come to mark John Henry Holliday's life. Cynical, bitter, and morose, especially when drinking, he still had the capacity to play the gentleman and amuse others with his humor, which made him seem both dangerous and charming and explained the contradictory perceptions of him.

Bat Masterson, who first met Doc in Dodge, provided perhaps the most familiar portrait of Doc in his 1907 *Human Life* series: "He was slim of build and sallow of complexion, standing almost five feet ten inches, and weighing no more than 130 pounds. His eyes were of a pale blue and his mustache was thin and of a sandy hue."[15]

Although later in life he claimed never to have liked Doc, Masterson provided a more complex view of him in his description of Doc's Dodge City days, noting that "[d]uring his year's stay in Dodge at that time, he did not have a quarrel with anyone, and, although regarded as a sort of grouch, he was not disliked by those with whom he had become acquainted." While in Dodge, "he showed no disposition to quarrel or shoot," Bat said. Doc's behavior convinced many that "much of the trouble he had had been forced on him," but Bat believed "that it was pretty much all of his own seeking." What he did confirm, though, was that Doc moved with ease in Dodge and was accepted by the fraternity there.[16]

Dodge City had an easygoing, tolerant feel to it. Things were quiet for a time, with the *Times* bragging in late June about the light court docket.[17] Of course, there were incidents, and the papers did complain about "gaslight robberies," nighttime muggings of citizens and visitors, and one critic suggested "that the police officers be compelled to patrol the streets of the city during the night, instead of hanging around the dance halls as much as they are in the habit of doing."[18] The *Ford County Globe* opined that "[i]f less protection was given to the pimp, the bawdy house loafer and the robber, and more protection given to visitors and others engaged in legitimate business, it would be much better for the community."[19] And this only days after the *Globe* had said, "Wyatt Earp is doing his duty as Ass't Marshal in a very creditable manner.—Adding new laurels to his splendid record every day."[20]

Tensions would mount in July and force changes. Early on the morning of July 13, a "low skulking vagabond" called "Limping Tom," who was being teased and harassed by saloon patrons at the Long Branch, became "terribly incensed at the bickerings of the party, suddenly sprang to the bar where H. T. McCarty was standing, and grasped McCarty's pistol from the latter's side, flourishing it for half a moment, and then fired one shot, which took effect in the right groin [of McCarty] severing the femoral artery." McCarty, a recently appointed deputy U.S. marshal, was not involved in the harassment.

Wyatt Earp (seated) and Bat Masterson, 1876. Earp was assistant city marshal and Masterson was sheriff when Doc arrived in Dodge City in 1878.

Limping Tom, a Texan whose name was Thomas O'Herron (alias Thomas Roach) and who was the camp cook for the Shiner brothers outfit, was shot by one of the bystanders. McCarty died within the hour. Limping Tom survived and would later be sentenced to twelve years and three months for his crime.[21]

The killing of another lawman so soon after the murder of Ed Masterson sobered Dodge and caused the police force to tighten controls on the drovers and to be less tolerant of cowboy high jinks. The day following the shooting of McCarty, Wyatt Earp intervened in an altercation between C. C. Pepperd, a prominent and troublesome rancher from Comanche County, southwest of Dodge, and the prostitute Anna Slater. Robert M. Wright later wrote, "Pepperd was one whom the officers disliked to see come to Dodge. Invariably rows began then, and he was in all of them." Doc Holliday may even have known him, for he reportedly had killed a man at Fort Griffin.[22]

In this instance, Pepperd pleaded guilty and was fined. His arrest stayed out of the papers, but it seems to have raised tensions in the town still further, especially against Wyatt Earp. Thereafter, Dodge's police force saw a flurry of activity; they arrested drovers, whores, and gamblers as if to gain a tighter grip on the town. The drovers, resentful of the clampdown, tested the limits. On July 25, Earp arrested

Charles Reid for "unlawfully discharging a pistol." The same day, James Masterson arrested K. M. May for a similar offense.[23]

Matters came to a head at three o'clock on the morning of July 26 when a small party of drovers from the crew of Tobe Driskill, most likely including George Hoy, Joe Day, Harrison French, and Charles French, charged by Ben Springer's recently opened Comique Theater and fired into the building as they rode. Inside the Comique, all was confusion. Eddie Foy, who was performing at the time, recalled the scene:

> Everybody dropped to the floor at once, according to custom. Bat Masterson was just in the act of dealing in a game of Spanish monte with Doc Holliday, and I was impressed by the instantaneous manner in which they flattened out like pancakes on the floor. I had thought I was pretty agile myself, but those fellows had me beaten by seconds at that trick. The firing kept up until it seemed to me that the assailants had put hundreds of shots through the building. They shot through the wall as well as windows, for a big .45 bullet would penetrate those plank walls as if they had been little more than paper.
>
> The firing had been going on for a minute or so when we heard a volley from another quarter—this time out on Main Street. Some of the city police and deputy sheriffs were attacking the gunfighters in flank.[24]

Wyatt Earp was standing outside, leaning against an awning post when the shooting began, and he immediately began to fire after the cowboys, as did James Masterson and several citizens who joined the fray. Near the bridge, George Hoy fell from his horse, wounded in the arm. Hoy was a likable young man, although a fugitive from Texas for cattle theft. "The marvelous part of the whole affair," Foy remembered, "was that aside from a few harmless scratches and some perforated clothing, nobody in the dancehall was hurt." Hoy was not so lucky. He died on August 21 of complications from his wound, attended to the end by his companions, Day and the French boys.[25] No charges were ever filed against any of the cowboys involved.

By the time of the Hoy shooting, Doc and Wyatt Earp had become friends. Doc also deepened his sense of belonging with the gambling and saloon crowd. William H. Harris, Chalkney Beeson, Bat Masterson, and their associates accepted him in a way he had never known in Dallas, Fort Griffin, Denver, or any of the other places he

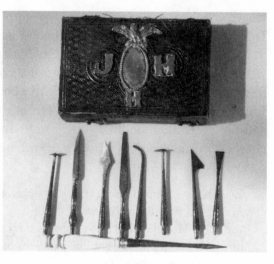

John Henry Holliday's pocket dental kit. The medallion at center bears the inscription "A Pocket Dental Office, J. H. Holliday, 24, D. H., Dodge."

had traveled. He had found a congenial place, and he apparently had decided to stay. He made for himself what he called "[a] Pocket Dental Office," a kit of basic dental tools, inscribed "J. H. Holliday, 24, D. H., Dodge," fitted into a gold-worked ambrotype case. The case indicated Doc's gold-working skills, but the inscription also suggested an intent to settle down.[26]

His association with Earp was also about to become closer. Earp would later state the reason succinctly: "I am a friend of Doc Holliday because when I was city marshal of Dodge City, Kansas, he came to my rescue and saved my life when I was surrounded by desperadoes." In a more dramatic statement ghostwritten for him, Earp said that Doc "saw a man draw on me behind my back. 'Look out, Wyatt!' he shouted, but while the words were coming out his mouth he had jerked his pistol out of his pocket and shot the other fellow before the latter could fire."[27]

Unfortunately, the local papers did not record Holliday's intervention. Stuart N. Lake, the author of the somewhat fanciful biography *Wyatt Earp: Frontier Marshal*, placed the episode in September 1878. He also claimed that the incident in question involved the ranchers Tobe Driskill and Ed Morrison. According to Lake, Earp met the Driskill-Morrison crew on Front Street near the Long Branch. They were closing around Earp when Holliday stepped out of the Long Branch and, with a string of expletives, ordered the cowboys to throw up their hands. "There were times . . . when Doc Holliday swore beautifully," Lake quoted Earp as saying. According to this version, Doc's intervention gave Earp time to draw his own guns. Still, one of the cowboys made a play, and Doc shouted a warning to Wyatt while simultaneously shooting the drover in the shoulder.[28]

There is another version that is more directly attributable to Wyatt Earp that states:

> It happened that Doc Holliday was seated at a monte table and glancing through the window he appraised the situation in an instant. Turning to Frank Loving, the dealer, he said, "Have you a six-shooter?" He handed his gun over to Holliday who sprang without hesitation through the doorway into the sidewalk, and throwing both guns down on the crowd, said, "throw up your hands!" This rather startled them and averted their attention. In an instant I had drawn my gun, and the arrest of the crowd followed. They were confined in jail over night and fined and released the following day. It was because of this episode that I became the friend of Doc Holliday ever after. This event happened at about 7 o'clock in the evening late in August 1876 [sic].[29]

The newspapers of the period never mentioned either Earp or Holliday specifically in connection with such an incident, but at least two episodes could be the incident in question, given the local papers' habit of speaking of "officers" without identifying them. The first came in late August and fits well with Earp's recollection that the incident took place in August:

> Another shooting affair occurred on the "south side" Saturday night. It appears that one of the cow boys, becoming intoxicated and quarrelsome, undertook to take possession of the bar in the Comique. To this the barkeeper objected and a row ensued. Our policemen interfered and had some difficulty in handling their man. Several cattle men then engaged in the broil and in the excitement some of them were bruised on the head with six shooters. Several shots were accidentally fired which created general confusion among the crowd of persons present. We are glad to chronicle the fact that none were seriously hurt and nobody shot. We however cannot help but regret the too ready use of pistols in all rows of such character and would like to see a greater spirit of harmony exist between our officers and cattle men so that snarling cayotes [sic] and killers could make their own fights without interesting or draging [sic] good men into them.[30]

The second incident occurred on the evening of September 19, 1878, and it fits with Earp's insistence that the incident involved Tobe Driskill and Ed Morrison. On September 14, the *Times* issued a special edition announcing that the Northern Cheyennes had fled their reservation in the Indian Territory in a desperate attempt to return to their traditional home in Montana. Over the next several days, rumors spread rapidly that the Indians were killing cattle and drovers and raiding homesteads. The Cheyennes were especially interested in horses, and on the morning of September 16 they ran off fifty-five head from the camp of the Driskill brothers. The following day the Driskill brothers, Doc, Tony Day, and close to twenty other cowboys joined Captain William C. Hemphill's company of cavalry in pursuit of the Cheyennes. After a sharp engagement on Wednesday, September 18, the cowboys showed up in Dodge, and the following morning Hemphill arrived with his company.[31] Later that same day, September 19, before the cavalry and the cowboys took the field again, two incidents occurred:

> There was a scrimmage Thursday night between the officers and the party that were going on the Indian hunt. Several shots were fired. One man carries a bandaged head and a soldier was severely wounded in the leg. A disgraceful row occurred in the afternoon in which it was said that the officers failed to appear. These occurrences are the subject of much comment on the conduct of the officers.[32]

The timing and circumstances of the Thursday night "scrimmage" fits with Earp's recollections. First, Earp said that the incident occurred at the time of the Dull Knife raid (as the Indian outbreak was called in Kansas). Second, most of the men involved were from the crew of Tobe and Bud Driskill, men with a grudge against Dodge City's police over the Hoy shooting. Third, though the account differs from Lake's version, one man was in fact wounded in the fracas.[33]

In any event, the distraction of the Indian scare caused some breakdown in law enforcement. On September 24, the *Globe* observed that "[n]o less than half a dozen shooting scrapes occurred in our city during the past week. We are glad to state, however, that no one was seriously hurt. The last one occurred night before last. There seems to be more danger in being shot in the city than there is danger of being scalped by the Red Man on the plains."[34]

Just when Doc and Kate Elder left Dodge for points west is far from clear, although Kate suggested that it was late November or early December. The decision to move was based on several things. First, on August 6, 1878, the town council had passed ordinances outlawing gambling and prostitution. In fact, the true purpose of the ordinances was to regulate gambling and prostitution through fines, not to eliminate either, while giving authorities the ability to get rid of undesirables. Nevertheless, it did increase the costs of gambling even for the favored ones.[35] More practically, gambling opportunities declined once the cattle season was over.

Second, Doc would later claim that he left because he was falsely accused of burglary. On December 11, 1878, an attempt was made to burglarize Jacob Collar's store, although no connection to Doc is implied in news accounts. A different story claimed that in Dodge, Doc had made the acquaintance of Charles Wright, who ran crooked faro games, commonly called "brace games," in Chicago and had a shady reputation in Dodge. Wright, a Canadian-born gambler and saloonman, was related to the Dodge City businessman and town father Robert M. Wright. When money went missing from Wright & Beverley's store, Charles Wright was suspected, but he accused Doc of taking the money. Robert believed Charles's story and blamed Doc. Doc could not buck a man as important as Robert Wright, so he left town rather than face further trouble. This incident was said to have increased tensions between Robert Wright and Wyatt Earp, who resented the accusations against his friend.[36]

The most critical reason for Doc's move, however, was his health. Kate later claimed that she and Doc left Dodge for Las Vegas, New Mexico, to take advantage of the famous Montezuma Hot Springs near the town that was already becoming a mecca for consumptives. Clearly, Kansas had not been kind to Doc. Bat Masterson recalled that "[i]t was easily seen that he was not a healthy man for he not only looked the part, but he incessantly coughed it as well." None of the Texas recollections of him—and they are sparse—made any real point of his poor health.

Masterson's comments and Kate's recollections suggest that Doc was moving into the "second phase" of consumption in the inhospitable climate of Kansas. His voice began to develop a deep hoarseness as the result of throat ulcers that would periodically make it difficult for him to speak above a whisper or to eat. His cough became more severe, constant, and debilitating, producing a thick dark mucus of greenish hue with yellow streaks and laced with pus. The cough was attended by "hectic fever" that rose and fell with an accelerating pulse rate. The fever contributed to a ruddy complexion that seemed deceptively healthy yet alternated with a "deathlike paleness." Even so, most doctors were reluctant to confirm the diagnosis of consumption because the same symptoms might appear with problems like bronchitis. Even in the second phase, the symptoms could become more severe and then subside.

At the least, though, the hollow rattle of Doc's cough and the frequent pallor of his face suggested that his condition was worsening as the fall snows began to blanket Dodge City. He and Kate took the train as far as Trinidad, Colorado, where Doc's health worsened to the point that they were forced to lay over for ten days. They were on hand when the first train departed Trinidad and took them along the winding track over the pass to end-of-track in New Mexico. The railroad was still a long way from Las Vegas, however, and with snow in the mountains during a particularly bitter December, Doc and Kate had to seriously consider their next move.[37]

According to Bat Masterson, within a week from the time Doc reached Trinidad, "he shot and seriously wounded a young sport by the name of Kid Colton [Earp called him Kid Dalton], over a very trivial matter." Masterson claimed that it was this incident that forced Doc to move on again.[38] The shooting did not make it into the record, if it occurred at all, but something convinced the pair to challenge heavy snow and bitter cold rather than winter in Trinidad. Kate recalled that Doc's health was so bad that once they reached end-of-track they "had to hire an outfit to take us to Las Vegas, New Mexico. We traveled with a big freight outfit." George Lail, a teamster who was hauling supplies to the Santa Fe's end-of-track, confirmed that he transported Doc, whom he remembered as being in bad shape, and his "woman friend," who spoke with "a German accent," into Las Vegas that December.[39]

Doc settled in at Montezuma Hot Springs in Gallinas Canyon, a few miles northwest of the town's plaza. An army hospital had been built there during the Mexican War. It was later abandoned, and Dr. Oscar H. Woodworth reportedly established the first private spa there in 1864. Next, W. Scott Moore took over and renovated the abandoned hospital as the Old Adobe House. When Doc arrived, he most likely stayed there with several other consumptives drawn from across the country to take treatments in the sulfurous waters. When not resting in the steaming pools, he practiced dentistry at the Adobe House. Once his tuberculosis seemed under control again and weather permitted, Doc and Kate moved into quarters on the plaza in Las Vegas. Las Vegas was the destination of the Atchison, Topeka & Santa Fe Railroad, but in the winter of 1878–1879 it was still some distance and months away. Las Vegas was a stable and well-established community. Doc and Kate wintered there in what was perhaps the quietest environment they had known in years.[40]

Later, he opened an office near the plaza in a building that also housed a tubercular young jeweler named William Leonard, who would play a significant role in Doc's life. Both of them were young, both were consumptives, and both specialized in gold work, albeit for different purposes. They had, however, a respect for each other's skills. Leonard already had something of a reputation as an unsavory character and a gunhand. In September 1878, he had shot a man named Jose Mares in front of Ilfeld's store and was "pounded" severely by Mares's friends. But Doc was used to such company. They had much in common and were soon friends. In March 1879, a local grand jury returned indictments against Leonard in the Mares case, but Leonard skipped town rather than face the charges.[41]

The climate and springs revived John Henry physically, and he was soon plying his trade as a gambler in Las Vegas saloons. Unfortunately, the territorial legislature passed a law against gambling that winter, and on March 8, 1879, about the time that Leonard took off, Doc was fined $25 because he "did keep a gaming table called monte." He may have used this as an excuse to leave, because he left before paying the fine, and papers were issued ordering the collection of the fine by August.[42] He headed north toward the end-of-track for the railroad being built into New Mexico, where he caught the train to Dodge City without Kate. He may have been included in this notice from the *Ford County Globe* of March 23: "A fresh invoice of gamblers arrived last Monday. Foy and Thompson are back in the Comique."[43] Once back in Dodge, Doc assisted Bat Masterson in the organization of a group of fighters for the Atchison, Topeka & Santa Fe Railroad.

The problem was that the discovery of silver at Leadville set off a rivalry between the Santa Fe and the Rio Grande because the only feasible route to Leadville was through the Royal Gorge. The Royal Gorge was an awesome work of nature with thousand-foot walls. It simply was not big enough for two sets of tracks, and each railroad company was determined to have the gorge for itself. The Rio Grande had already leased its road to the Santa Fe for a period of thirty years, but General W. J. Palmer, the president of the Rio Grande, took the Santa Fe to court, claiming that it had violated the lease. He also sent armed men to keep the Santa Fe out of the gorge.[44]

At that point, the Santa Fe went to Dodge City for help. As Robert M. Wright later wrote, "It was only natural for them to do so, for where in the whole universe were there to be found fitter men for a desperate encounter of this kind. Dodge City bred such bold, reckless men, and it was their pride and delight to be called upon to do such work."[45] In Dodge, Holliday continued his efforts as a recruiter, attempting to enlist Eddie Foy, the entertainer, in the effort. Foy recalled (though with a somewhat strained Georgia accent for Doc):

> "But listen, Mr. Holliday," said I. "I'm no fighter. I wouldn't be any help to the gang. I couldn't hit a man if I shot at him."
>
> "Oh that's all right," he replied easily. "The Santy Fee won't know the difference. You kin use a shot-gun if you want to. Dodge wants a good showin' in this business. You'll help swell the crowd, and you'll get your pay anyhow."
>
> But I declined to join the expedition, much to Doc's disappointment.[46]

On March 25, the *Globe* announced the nature of the expedition:

> Last Thursday evening, Sheriff Masterson received a telegram from officers of the Atchison, Topeka and Santa Fe road at Canon City, asking if he would bring a posse of men to assist in defending the workmen on that road from the attacks of the Denver and Rio Grande men, who were again endeavoring to capture the long contested pass through the canyon. Masterson and Deputy Duffey immediately opened a recruiting office, and before the train arrived Friday morning had enrolled a company of thirty-three men. They all boarded the morning train, armed to the teeth, Sheriff Masterson in command and started for the scene of the hostilities.[47]

Offered three dollars a day, board, and a little excitement, the Dodge City recruits included the Texas gambler and gunfighter Ben Thompson, Deputy Sheriff Joshua J. Webb, Kinch Riley, Dave Rudabaugh, and a number of others. At Canon City, Colorado, the Santa Fe army found the mouth of the gorge held by nearly fifty men under the leadership of J. R. DeRemer, a tough-minded Rio Grande engineer. The situation was very tense, but, to his credit, Bat Masterson kept control of the situation, realizing that the Rio Grande fighters held the high ground and hoping that the courts would resolve the issue. On April 21, the courts did hold that the Rio Grande held prior claim to the gorge, but the matter of the lease still had to be resolved. So, for a time, Bat and company returned to Dodge, and Doc returned to New Mexico.[48]

Holliday did not immediately return to Las Vegas, however. Instead, he settled in the little railroad town of Otero, north of Las Vegas. Otero was a monument to the tenacity of its namesake, Don Miguel Antonio Otero, already an entrepreneur par excellence in New Mexico. He now watched as the Santa Fe moved into New Mexico over Raton Pass and down toward Las Vegas. The first railroad town and station was named Otero in his honor. The town had a boomtown flavor, and Doc settled into a dental practice with a partner named Fagaly.[49] He may even have purchased property there, for as late as 1891 a parcel of land, with past due taxes outstanding, was recorded as the property of "John Holiday."[50] Later, Dr. T. O. Washington, a physician, "purchased a half interest in the room occupied by Holliday & Fagaly." Perhaps the biggest surprise for Doc, though, was the town marshal. Even the editors of the *Otero Daily Optic* could scarcely hide their disbelief:

An individual taller than the majority of men, wearing a large revolver strapped in sight, and more than ordinary determined expression of countenance, is apparent, always, day and night, prominent upon our streets. A history of his life would not be adopted for Sunday school reading—"it fills a want long felt" in the heart of a train boy. His experience has been something of an Illiad. He was well known in Kansas, Texas, and all over the frontier. His name is Hurricane Bill. As marshal of Otero he is unquestionably doing a good work. It is claimed that this is the most orderly city, and from the start has been, that this road has found west of Atchison. Hurricane

Bill having brought an experience with the Vigilance Committee of the Lone Star, and the Indians in the vicinity of Pawnee Rock, to this territory, has contributed not a little to this quiet. His reputation is at stake; he is interested in keeping order, and is equally as active in keeping the peace as he ever was successful in breaking it.[51]

That must have brought a smile to John Henry's lips, but it gave a certain familiarity to the games of chance at Henry & Robinson's Saloon. The *Otero Optic* reported that Doc, Hurricane Bill Martin, and eight others were on hand there when "a splendid violin was raffled off" at five dollars a chance. Samuel Burr "was the lucky individual [to win], he throwing higher dice than any of the others."[52] Eventually, Hurricane Bill would be fired for "drunkenness and incompetency." Dr. Washington proved to be a mistake, too. His quick temper eventually led him to stab a man to death. He moved to Raton afterward, where he made advances to a female patient. Her fiancé threatened Washington, after which he was put in jail at Otero, but a mob followed and hanged him on the town water tank.[53]

By then Doc had left Otero in the service of the Santa Fe railroad once again. He may even have been retained by the Santa Fe, because he apparently did some recruiting for the railroad in Cimarron and other points en route back to Dodge.[54] Fearful of the outcome of court action, W. B. Strong, the vice president and general manager of the Santa Fe, had decided to make a show of force to prevent the Rio Grande from seizing the road before countermeasures could be taken legally. The result was described by the *Denver Rocky Mountain News*:

> Three extra trains came in from the south and east yesterday with the following men: Paddy Welsh and forty-five of Dick Wooten's deputy sheriffs from Trinidad; Bat Masterson, sheriff from Dodge City, Kansas with sixty-five men; Charles Hickey, sheriff of Bent County, with eighteen men. An extra went to Colorado Springs last night with a lot of bad men from Dodge City. Bat Masterson goes to Canon City this afternoon to regulate Hadden and DeRemer. Does the governor care to hear of this?

It was a short jaunt, as it turned out, and less heroic than some hoped and expected. Bat Masterson concentrated his force, including Holliday, at the roundhouse and rail station at Pueblo, the pivotal spot in the railroad system, but once General William J. Palmer figured out that the Santa Fe planned to hold its positions until the court's decision could be appealed, he decided to move quickly. At six o'clock in the morning on June 11, the Rio Grande forces moved against all the Santa Fe positions. Two men were killed and more wounded at Cuchara, and sharp fighting occurred at Colorado Springs, but the Dodge City force held its ground at Pueblo.[55]

Pat Desmond, Pueblo's town marshal and a deputy sheriff as well, was a tough Irishman with long experience on the frontier who had seen more than his share of group violence, having been a participant in the Bear River riot of 1867 alongside "Bear River" Tom Smith, who later made a name for himself as a peace officer in Abilene, Kansas.[56] Now, Desmond and J. A. McMurtrie, Palmer's chief engineer, decided to move against Masterson's men. It was a bold decision. Masterson had more men, and they were holed up inside the roundhouse with a cannon pointed up the street. Armed with bayoneted rifles, Desmond's force charged the telegraph office at the depot, overwhelmed the defenders, and forced them out the back windows. One Santa Fe fighter, Harry Jenkins, was shot in the back there, and Josh Webb had a tooth knocked out in the melee. After taking the telegraph office and cutting Bat off from any communication with his superiors, the Rio Grande force laid seige to the roundhouse.

R. F. Weitbrec, the senior Rio Grande official on the scene, then called for a meeting with Masterson and pointed out that the roundhouse defenders were the last holdouts of the Santa Fe fighters, that he had a legal writ to take control, and that it was foolish to risk further loss of life. Bat agreed, and his men were soon en route back to Dodge. "Sheriff Masterson and party of fifty men returned from Pueblo on Thursday morning," the *Times* reported. "He had been placed in charge of the railroad property there but surrendered his authority upon writs served by U.S. officers. The Denver & Rio Grand [*sic*] has possession. And 'our boys' didn't smell and burn powder. Their voice is for peace."[57]

Not everyone was happy about the outcome, but the Royal Gorge War was over. A few days later, locals assuaged their disappointment with the news that "[t]he boys and girls across the dead line had a high old time. . . . They sang and danced, and fought and bit, and cut and had a good time generally, making music for the entire settlement."[58] The *Times* also reported that Josh Webb was sporting a new gold tooth in the place of the one he had lost at Pueblo, doubtless the work of the Santa Fe force's personal dentist, John Henry Holliday. In fact, neither Webb nor Doc lingered long in Dodge. Webb went to Pueblo and, shortly, to a position on Pat Desmond's police force. Doc headed back to New Mexico. They would soon meet again.

Doc was always comfortable with the Dodge City crowd and appeared to win their respect, if not their friendship. Young George D. Bolds remarked in his recollections that men like "Earp and Holliday were not the friendly type." Bolds met Doc that summer of 1879, describing him as a "slim man with ash blond hair and the mark of tuberculosis on his gaunt face," but he said Doc "barely nodded" when introduced. Bolds described the longest conversation he ever had with Doc, "'How old are you kid?' he asked in a hoarse voice. When I told him, he said, 'I'm just ten years older.'"[59] Still, he knew that Doc was a man who could be counted on in a fight, and Kate later claimed that Bat Masterson showed his appreciation by giving Doc a nickel-plated revolver before he left Dodge.[60]

Holliday did not reopen his dental practice in Otero, although John Myers Myers, his first biographer, claimed that before he left, he "was arrested on charges of killing an unnamed, and probably unknown gunman, albeit under circumstances that led the court to exonerate him on the broad Western grounds of 'self-defense.'"[61] If so, the incident did not make it into the Colfax County records. Considering that there was only one surviving issue of the *Otero Daily Optic* and few town records, the episode could have evaded documentation, but it was more likely a latter-day addition to the Doc Holliday legend.

That spring, Otero was almost literally boxed up with the terminal and shipped via the Santa Fe to be reassembled at Las Vegas. Said the *Optic*, "Otero so busy and bustling six months ago, is now passing into peaceful obscurity—saloons all gone."[62] The Santa Fe had advanced to Las Vegas by then, and Doc followed. "We came over Raton summit from Colorado into New Mexico, on the switchback, the tunnel not being then completed, and the last hundred miles of the journey was made in platform cars, with a caboose built on one of them for the ladies," an old-timer recalled. "There was a mixed crowd of passengers, of old-timers, tourists, Spanish-American families with pretty daughters demurely expectant of the grand baile [*sic*] which was to conclude the opening day, with a sprinkling of gamblers and other professionals going south to be on hand at the start of the new terminal on the road."[63]

East Las Vegas, which was located on the flats east of town where the tracks ran, was taking shape as a true end-of-track town in contrast to the ancient pueblo of West Las Vegas. The end-of-track settlement had the usual supply of entrepreneurs and frontier vagabonds. Even Russell A. Kistler, the editor of the *Otero Daily Optic,* soon relocated in what came to be called New Town, and he opened the *Las Vegas Daily Optic.* On July 4, 1879, both Old Town and New Town celebrated in style, with speeches, grand balls, and dance hall fandangos. By then, tents and makeshift buildings were already dispensing liquor, whores, and opportunities for gambling. The celebration was a high old time that seemed to forecast the future, at least for a while.[64]

Doc saw opportunity in New Town, as did others, and he entered into partnership with another recent arrival, Jordan L. Webb, a twenty-one-year-old transplant from Iowa, to open a saloon on Center Street. Webb was probably the younger brother of Doc's Dodge City crony, Josh Webb, which would explain the partnership. In any event, it did not take Holliday long to get into trouble there.

Las Vegas had more than its share of gamblers, con men, whores, thugs, and vagrants, all the usual flotsam that followed boom camps. Among them was a former army scout from the Fifth Cavalry named Mike Gordon, who had a weakness for women. Gordon was quite a traveler. He may have been in Wichita in the early 1870s, where a "Gordon" was the boyfriend of Ida May. He was in Dodge City in 1875. He got into more trouble at Fort Elliott in the Texas Panhandle in 1878 over a woman. In Las Vegas, though he was still in his late twenties, Gordon already sported a disfigured face as the result of a brawl in which his opponent had bitten off his nose. He was also a mean drunk.[65]

On the night of July 19, Gordon was drunk and apparently had been for several days. Several "places of amusement" opened that night. "His mistress was at a hall on Center Street [actually Holliday and Webb's saloon]," the *Las Vegas Gazette* reported. "Gordon tried to persuade her to accompany him to another hall on Railroad St. When she refused to go, he flew into a drunken rage and swore that he would kill someone or be killed himself before morning." The *Gazette* provided the rest of the story:

Gordon was standing in the street to the right of the hall after some of his threats and drew a revolver and fired, the bullet passing through the pants leg of a Mexican and struck in the floor in line with the bartender who was standing at the rear of the bar.

Other shots were fired immediately but it is difficult to tell how or by whom.

It is said that Gordon fired a second shot. Every person there says three shots were fired, while several maintain that five in all were fired.

Gordon at once ceased firing and disappeared. An hour or two later a Mr. Kennedy went into his tent some thirty or forty yards away, to go to bed and hearing groans investigated and found Gordon laying on the ground outside. The news soon spread and his woman arriving on the ground had him taken to her room east of the Court house, where he died at 6 o'clock Sunday morning. In the afternoon the Coroner held an inquest and the jury returned a verdict of excusable homicide.[66]

The paper reported that the bullet had struck Gordon in the right breast just below the collarbone and exited below the shoulder blade. The *Gazette* added that although a crowd witnessed the shooting, no one seemed to know who fired the fatal shot for fear of being called to testify.

John Henry Holliday's name was not mentioned at the time, quite probably for the reason stated by the *Gazette*, although town records for July 1879, which would include criminal charges, seem to have disappeared, making it impossible to state with certainty that they did not mention Holliday. Nor was he mentioned in the account provided by the *Las Cruces Thirty-Four*: "Mike Gordon got drunk in a dance hall in Vegas and began a 'bluff' by drawing a 'pair of sixes' and firing promiscuously around the room. Some unknown person 'called his hand,' and Gordon was 'froze out.' He was buried at the expense of the county next day. Vegas is a bad town to 'bluff.' " Two years later, however, an article by Russell Kistler, the editor of the *Optic* (who was crusading for reform in Las Vegas at the time), cited troubles involving Doc at Tombstone and described him as "the identical individual who killed poor, inoffensive Mike Gordon."[67] Still later, in another *Optic* account after Doc and the Earps left Tombstone, Kistler noted that Doc "will be remembered as having killed Mike Gordon in this place at an early day in the history of the town."[68]

In 1886, Bat Masterson gave another account of what happened that night, noting that Doc "had some trouble with Mike Gordon, a tough gambler," at his saloon, after which Gordon left. "About an hour afterward, though, Gordon came back and fired a shot from the side-walk into the saloon." Bat described what happened next: "The bullet whizzed a couple of inches from Holliday's head and went crashing through a window at the rear of the room. 'Doc' drew his gun and rushed to the front door and saw Gordon standing on the sidewalk with a revolver in his hand. Gordon raised his revolver to fire a second time, but before he could pull the trigger, 'Doc' had shot him dead."[69]

The reason Holliday was not identified at the time may well have been that the coroner was Hyman G. Neill, known as "Hoodoo Brown," who was the boss of New Town, a justice of the peace, and the leader of what was known locally as the Dodge City Gang. The group included the town marshal Joe Carson, Mysterious Dave Mather, Dave Rudabaugh, Frank Cady, John "Bull Shit Jack" Pierce, William P. "Slap Jack Bill" Nicholson, and others. Hoodoo Brown supposedly came from a respected family in St. Louis but had plied his trade as a gambler and con man for a number of years before arriving in Las Vegas with the railroad. He was described as "a tall thin man, has light hair, small mustache, and a rakish look which is a terrible giveaway, and one would at once set him down as a desperate charac-ter, and a man to beware of." Rightly or wrongly, Doc was accused of being part of the Dodge City Gang, and, in fact, Jordan Webb, his partner, was a known associate of Hoodoo Brown's. The *Optic* later claimed that Doc had "crept through one of the many legal loop-holes that characterized Hoodoo Brown's judicial dispensation." It was a plausible explanation of what happened. County authorities never fol-lowed up on the matter.[70]

Masterson also claimed that the day after Gordon was killed, "a Mexican gambler who had been a friend of Gordon swore out a com-plaint against all the saloons and gambling houses in town. Among others, Doc was indicted. Afterwards, Doc, Jim Pearson and two of their friends met the Mexican in front of a saloon. A fight was of course the inevitable result. During the row, the Mexican was killed and Doc had to leave Las Vegas."[71] Masterson was wrong both with the timing and with the result, but there were odd coincidences over the next few weeks that make it impossible to dismiss his commentary out of hand.

On July 15, four days before the Gordon shooting, Jim Pearson and his two brothers (the two "friends" of whom Masterson wrote) assaulted a Mexican gambler named Epifanio Baca in a dispute arising out of a card game, not out of the Gordon killing, which had not yet occurred.[72] John Henry was not involved as far as the record shows. He was concerned with other, more mundane matters. On July 30, ten days after Gordon died, Holliday purchased an additional parcel of land adjacent to his saloon. He once again seemed to be making an effort to settle down, rather than move on. On August 1, however, he was called as a witness, along with Charles Hennessey and James Dunnigan, in a gambling case against Hoodoo Brown, and later the same night Doc was arrested for gambling himself, for which he posted a $200 bond.[73]

Then, on the night of August 5, 1879, John McPherson, a former marshal of Old Town Las Vegas, was mortally wounded "at the dance-hall kept by Pierson [sic]" in New Town. During the fight, McPherson also shot Charles Karth, a henchman of Hoodoo Brown's commonly called Charley Slick, Slick Charley, or Slicky. Slick was apparently the instigator, and the papers would later suggest that Hoodoo Brown was behind the incident. Initially, McPherson's assailant was identified only as a "little policeman," who admitted pursuing McPherson from the dance hall into the "exchange saloon" with the intent of killing him. Gossip was rampant that the policeman was allowed by Brown, in his capacity as justice of the peace, to escape. On August 9, however, McPherson signed a deathbed statement identifying Jim Pearson as the man who shot him. That same day, the chief justice of New Mexico's Supreme Court brought local law enforcement officers before him and insisted that they strictly enforce local ordinances against carrying deadly weapons. "Every difficulty that occurs in town grows out of a violation of this law," he told them.[74]

The San Miguel County grand jury was in session at the time, and its members listened to the judge if the police did not. On August 12, indictments were brought against the Pearson brothers on charges arising out of the Baca incident, and the next day, August 13, Jim Pearson was charged with murdering McPherson and for carrying a deadly weapon. Curiously, Doc Holliday was also indicted on August 13 for carrying deadly weapons on the night of August 5, the same evening that McPherson was shot. No connection was ever shown or implied publicly between Doc and the Pearson brothers' crime spree until Masterson's later account linking Doc with Jim Pearson and "their two friends," but the combination of evidence with Masterson's account creates a strong circumstantial case of a relationship of some sort between Doc and the Pearsons.[75]

Pearson was "not found," but Doc did not leave town. He did, however, begin to rethink his position in Las Vegas. Shortly after his indictment, he surrendered his saloon to Thomas L. Preston, his liquor wholesaler and possible mortgage holder, apparently in settlement of accounts, and, on August 18, Preston sold one-half interest in the saloon to Samuel N. Lacy. On September 1, Preston and Lacy leased the property for $75 a month to B. O. Bertholf, who also ran the Globe Theater, a few doors east of the saloon. John Henry and Jordan Webb appear to have continued gambling in the saloon, but ownership had passed on to others.[76]

During that summer, Holliday may have played cards with Jesse James and Billy the Kid, as they both were reportedly in town between July 26 and 29, even having dinner together with other locals at the new Las Vegas Hotel at Montezuma Hot Springs.[77] That year, Easterners had bought the property and had constructed a new three-story hotel on the grounds, along with a new bathhouse that made the facility even more attractive. Doc still took treatments there, and the arrival of the railroad meant a new accessibility to the curative waters. It was characteristic of the town for the notorious and the respectable to coexist, but that was about to change because of the flagrant excesses of Hoodoo Brown.

Later in August, two stagecoaches were robbed near town, and again locals suspected that the Dodge City Gang running East Las Vegas was responsible. On August 24, 1879, after the first robbery, the *Gazette* deplored the fact that "the town is evidently filling up with a good many of those bad characters who usually congregate in new and growing railroad towns." In a long editorial, the paper deplored the "burglars and highwaymen" who had settled into the community: "The robbery of the coach and mail so near town and the tracing of the culprits directly back to town shows that we have some bold, bad men in the community who will not scruple to commit any crime for money." On August 30, the second robbery occurred between Las Vegas and Tecolote, with similar suspicions about the perpetrators.[78]

The situation was serious enough that express companies, apparently not trusting local authorities, sent their own operatives into the area. Josh Webb, Doc's old associate and comrade in arms from Dodge City, signed in at the Mackley House on Railroad Avenue in New Town in September, apparently as an undercover man for the Adams Express Company. Later in the month, the *Ford County Globe* reported that "Webb is engaged in some very mysterious business up there," and gave him credit for "quietly capturing two or three mail robbers out in New Mexico."[79] Perhaps his undercover operations explained why he fell in with the Dodge City Gang initially, since Hoodoo Brown and his cronies were primary suspects in the robberies. His effectiveness in blending in with the gang would eventually prove costly, however.

In early September, the *Globe* announced that "Mr. Wyatt Earp, who has been on our police force for several months, resigned his position last week and took his departure for Las Vegas, New Mexico."[80] After an appropriate farewell party, Earp headed west with a young woman named Mattie Blaylock, his brother Jim, and Jim's family. Curiously, Earp later claimed that Doc Holliday left Las Vegas and returned to Dodge City looking for him but arrived three days after he left Dodge for Las Vegas. He said that Doc caught up with him at Trail City near the Colorado line (at the time it was still known as Sargent) and traveled with the Earp party back to Las Vegas, arriving there before September 23, when a Las Vegas correspondent wrote the *Globe* that "Dodge City is well represented here, N. F. Kelly, Henry Sherer, Dr. Milligan [Holliday?], J. J. Webb, Wyatt Earp, and many others are here, not excepting 'Crazy Horse' [Thompson] with his cap and ball death dealer."[81]

If Doc did leave town in time to reach Dodge just after Wyatt left, he missed another important event in Las Vegas. On September 11, Jordan Webb, his former partner, was arrested while dealing keno in the saloon they formerly owned. He was charged with complicity in the August 30 stage holdup. Webb was transferred to Santa Fe for trial. He would face three trials and would not be acquitted until February 1881, long after Doc Holliday had settled in Tombstone. More likely, Doc did not leave Las Vegas and was on hand when Earp arrived. Kate later claimed that Holliday encountered Earp on the Plaza in Old Town and accompanied him to his camp on the edge of town for a reunion.[82]

Doc's old friend from Atlanta, Lee Smith, also checked into the Mackley House late in September for a surprise reunion with John

Henry.[83] Whether the meeting was by chance or was planned was never clear from the surviving record, but the visit hints that the two were at least haphazard correspondents. Smith's investments had paid off, and he was expanding his interests into Western mining, which may have been prompted by Doc's letters. His investments would eventually take him to Denver. The visit gave Doc the opportunity to catch up on what was happening back home in Georgia. Briefly, John Henry was able to escape the world of Hoodoo Brown.

Earp stayed in Las Vegas for nearly a month, long enough to be remembered later as one of the "hoodoo fellows." Oddly, a Dodge City paper would later report that he was also working "as a special messenger by Wells, Fargo & Co., on a division of the railroad in New Mexico" when he left Dodge. On October 14, 1879, masked men robbed a train near Las Vegas, and Charles E. Bassett, Chalk Beeson, and Harry Gryden showed up from Dodge to investigate the robbery for the Adams Express Company.[84] It almost appeared that there were two Dodge City gangs in the area for a while. If Earp was involved somehow with the express companies, it was a temporary assignment passed on to others. Robberies in New Mexico were not his primary concern.

Earp had learned of the silver strike in southeastern Arizona from his brother, Virgil, who was living at Prescott, the territorial capital of Arizona. Wyatt planned to give up law enforcement and open his own stagecoach operation out of the new boom camp of Tombstone in partnership with his brothers. He painted a glowing picture of opportunities there and encouraged Holliday to join him. With his partner in jail and suspicions doubtlessly directed at him, the environment in Las Vegas was dangerous enough to give Doc concerns, and when the Earps pulled out of Las Vegas bound for Prescott, Doc and Kate left with them, much to Kate's chagrin.[85]

In October 1879, W. G. Ward, the carpenter who had built the Holliday Saloon, filed a claim against Doc for an outstanding balance of $137.50 still owed him out of the $372 contract for the construction of the Holliday Saloon. Included in the record was a copy of Ward's contract, which recorded $45 received from Doc on July 20, leading some researchers to conclude erroneously that the construction of the saloon was not begun until July 20. Clearly, the contract was for "work done on house or building" before that date. In any event, he still owed Ward a balance on the saloon construction, and when Doc left town, Ward filed the claim.[86]

Curiously, the legal documentation provided by the contract supported Kate's later claim that she and Doc were married: "J. H. Holliday being first by me informed of the contents of this instrument did confess upon separate examination independent and apart of his said wife that he executed the same voluntary and with[out] the compulsion or illicit influence of her [sic] said wife." Something seemed to be implied by this phraseology that was never made clear in the record, so that its main significance is the support it provided for Kate's claims of marriage.[87]

Of course, by the time Ward's claim was filed, Doc was in Prescott, a town that proved to be interesting to both John Henry and Kate. They moved into a hotel, while the Earp party looked for Virgil. But when the Earp clan pulled out for Tombstone in mid-November, Doc and Kate stayed behind. Perhaps Doc was discouraged by reports like this one from the *Prescott Miner*:

> We are told that travel of late has been brisk to Tombstone, but during the past few days it has taken a backward move, where one goes in, four are leaving. It is true that they have a few good mines there, but nothing to justify the great immigration that has gone on there during the last three months. It is asserted authoritatively that not more than one out of every four living at Tombstone are employed. It is enough to kill any new town.[88]

By March, however, the *Miner* was describing Tombstone as "that new and flourishing city."[89]

Prescott was a nice change with attractions that boom camps did not have, including a level of stability and a more settled and cosmopolitan society that must have appealed to something deep and almost forgotten in John Henry Holliday. Curiously, though, Doc made no effort to establish a dental office there; indeed, after Las Vegas he apparently never practiced his profession again. He was a professional gambler now, and he found his place on Whiskey Row, Prescott's gambling district. Doc passed the winter there.

Kate, in her recollections, said that "a short time later" Doc received a letter from Wyatt Earp urging him to come to Tombstone. She and Doc quarreled over the letter, and she told him that she would not go to Tombstone: "If you are going to tie yourself to the Earp Brothers, go to it. I am going to Globe." She said that Doc replied, "All right. I will be in Globe in a few days too. I don't think I will like it in Tombstone anyway." They traveled as far as Gillette together, she claimed, and then parted company, Doc going to Tombstone and Kate to Globe. She added, "I didn't hear from Doc for some time." Since Kate never mentioned Doc's return to Las Vegas and noted a long separation, Doc appears to have changed his plan and decided to settle his affairs in Las Vegas before testing the waters at Tombstone.[90]

That winter, Hoodoo Brown and his cronies finally went too far. In fact, the situation there may have contributed most to John Henry's decision to make a permanent move to Arizona. At any rate, events had taken a turn for the worse in Doc's absence. As the *Dodge City Times* reported, "shooting scrapes" were all too frequent in Las Vegas, and New Town seemed out of control. On January 22, 1880, Marshal Joe Carson was killed in a gunfight with four men at Close and Patterson's Saloon. Dave Mather killed one of them outright and wounded the others. Two managed to escape but were caught later by a posse that included Dave Rudabaugh and Josh Webb. The killers had been housed in the local jail only hours when a mob stormed the jail and dragged them to the windmill at the center of the plaza in Old Town to hang them there. Before the two killers could be hanged, however, the mob opened fire on them and riddled them with bullets.[91]

Afterward, Mysterious Dave Mather was named marshal, and Webb was appointed policeman. Neither appointment really pleased the better class of citizens because of the two men's suspected complicity in the Dodge City Gang's activities. Their reputation was not helped when three days after Carson was killed, Mather shot and killed a railroad man named Joseph Castello. He was promptly exonerated of any wrongdoing by a coroner's jury with Hoodoo Brown presiding.[92]

Things finally came to a head on March 2, 1880, when two men were killed in unrelated incidents. One killing occurred that evening when James Allen, a waiter at the St. Nicholas Hotel and an associate of Hoodoo Brown's, shot and killed the traveling salesman James A. Morehead, who was well thought of by the local business community. The fight began over a remark by Morehead about the food at the St. Nicholas. Morehead, who was the bigger of the two men, was besting

Allen, when Allen pulled a gun and ordered Morehead to his knees. When Morehead tried to grab the pistol instead, Allen shot him.[93]

The other episode, which occurred earlier on March 2, near four o'clock in the morning, had a more dramatic effect. It involved Doc's friend Josh Webb. In the Goodlet and Robinson Saloon, Webb ordered a man named Michael Kelliher to surrender his pistol in compliance with the local ordinance. Kelliher refused, and, in the melee, Webb shot and killed him. Webb was then arrested by his friends Dave Mather and Dave Rudabaugh, of all people. It seemed an open-and-shut case of self-defense, and a coroner's jury quickly ruled the shooting a "justifiable and absolutely necessary" act.[94]

The town was finally fed up with Hoodoo Brown's shenanigans, however, and since the coroner's jury consisted of members of the Dodge City Gang, the county's grand jury reviewed the case, concluded that it was premeditated murder, and indicted Webb for murder. Hoodoo Brown and John "Dutchy" Schunderberger, Hoodoo Brown's right-hand man, were named as accessories. Significantly, immediately after arresting Webb, Mysterious Dave Mather resigned his post as marshal and left town by train bound for Dodge City. He cited "the inadequacy of pay" as his reason, but he may well have recognized the handwriting on the wall. With Mather gone and Webb in jail, New Town was "without a police force," and the *Optic* opined that "some action should be taken at once."[95]

Local authorities wasted little time. On March 4, the *Optic* reported, "The boys are skipping out. The Grand Jury is in session, you know." And on March 5, the *Gazette* announced, "Justice of the Peace, H. G. Neill, commonly known as Hoodoo Brown, quietly stepped aboard yesterday morning's east bound train and left for parts unknown. A boy known by the name of Dutchy went with him."[96] That left Webb to face the music alone. On March 10, he was convicted of murder and, two days later, sentenced to hang. News of Webb's conviction created a storm in Dodge City and set in motion efforts to help him. Michael Sutton, the county attorney, left immediately for Las Vegas to aid in an appeal of the verdict.[97]

Dodge City residents could not believe that Webb was guilty of murder, and they may well have been right. Webb may have been set up by Hoodoo Brown and Dutchy, motivated both by their greed and by their desire to get "payback" for Webb's undercover activities. Webb insisted that he was told by Hoodoo Brown's associates that Kelliher was planning to kill him and that he believed he had to kill Kelliher or be killed by him. Moreover, Hoodoo Brown misrepresented the amount of money Kelliher had on his person and kept the larger portion for himself. Even the local press seemed to think murder was out of character for Webb, but the verdict was guilty nonetheless. In April, there was an inept attempt by Jack Allen and Dave Rudabaugh to free Webb. After that, he languished in jail while the appeals process unfolded. The courts affirmed his conviction, but Governor Lew Wallace commuted his sentence to life in prison, citing "extenuating circumstances." Eventually, Webb escaped with Dave Rudabaugh (who had been jailed on charges relating to the earlier robberies), only to die two years later of smallpox.[98]

Curiously, especially in light of the crackdown on criminal activity, the same day that Webb was sentenced to hang, John Henry Holliday appeared in the San Miguel County District Court, where the old charge against him for gambling was dismissed and refunds ordered. Because of the heavy calendar, the charge for carrying a deadly weapon was continued, but it, too, would eventually be dismissed and his bail of $300 refunded in August 1880. This was orchestrated by Sydney A. Hubble, the acting district attorney and longtime New Mexico officeholder who had no part in Hoodoo Brown's misdeeds.[99]

Apparently, given the events happening at the time, Doc had escaped being linked with Hoodoo Brown and the Dodge City Gang, in spite of his friendship with Josh Webb and his former partnership with Jordan Webb. Doc remained in Las Vegas for a time, and in mid-April paid off his outstanding debt to the carpenter Ward. During this period, Doc became acquainted with Miguel Antonio "Gillie" Otero Jr., the son of the prominent New Mexico entrepreneur who was a mover and shaker in the Santa Fe railroad organization. Gillie supervised many of his father's operations, including his mercantile business in Dodge City. He saw Doc often and "found him to be a very likeable fellow."[100]

Doc and Kate remained separated through the summer, and Gillie's recollections offer an interesting observation on Doc's love life. He wrote that Doc had told him that March when he was in Las Vegas that he had originally gone west because he had been "jilted" by a young woman back home. That event "became the turning point in his life."[101] Gillie's comment was made long before information about John Henry and Mattie Holliday ever came to light or anyone publicly suggested that his feelings for Mattie might have been a factor in Doc's decision to go west. Perhaps the memories were crowding in, especially since Kate was not there, and the youthful Gillie became his confidant. Despite inaccuracies of detail, Doc must have shared something.

How long Doc remained in Las Vegas escaped the record, but he apparently was involved in another shooting incident before he left. Gillie recalled that Doc had had "some serious difficulty" with a man named "Charlie White" in Dodge City. While in town, Doc learned that White was working as a bartender in an Old Town saloon. After having dinner in New Town, Doc went to the saloon on the Plaza. Gillie described what happened:

> Doc entered the saloon with a cocked revolver in his hand and began hostilities at once, without previously making his presence known. White was in the act of serving some thirsty customers, but recognizing his old enemy from Dodge City, he ducked behind the bar just in time, while the customers ducked to the floor. White quickly emerged with a six-shooter, and [a] duel began in dead earnest, many shots being exchanged at short distance without effect.
>
> The meeting was so sudden that both participants were evidently somewhat off their accustomed good marksmanship, but finally White dropped to the floor. At first it was thought that the shot had killed him, and Holliday feeling that he had fulfilled his mission in Las Vegas, departed for the New Town, to mingle with his old friends of Dodge City. A doctor was called at once for White, and it was found that while the bullet only grazed the skin, it had been so near the spine as to stun him temporarily. He was up and around in a couple of hours as good as ever.[102]

Gillie reported that no arrests were made: "It was simply allowed to pass, as no one was interested in either Holliday or White, and the peace officers in Las Vegas were much too busy looking after their own games." Gillie claimed that White left Las Vegas on the next train heading east.

Actually, White was Charles Wright, not Charlie White, the selfsame Charles Wright who had caused Doc trouble in Dodge. He apparently followed the railroad to Las Vegas and was still working as a "saloonkeeper" when the census taker arrived that year. Wright's Place, a keno parlor and club advertised as "A quiet place for gentlemen to congregate," was still operating in June.[103] Wright did leave Las Vegas that summer, though, moving to several locations before eventually landing in Fort Worth, Texas. There, in December 1890, he ran afoul of another former Dodge City resident, Luke Short. From a hiding place he shotgunned Short, but he bungled the job and left town to avoid facing the consequences against a recovered Luke Short.[104]

Doc left Las Vegas after settling his affairs and most likely returned to Prescott, although there are tales that he visited Albuquerque. The Santa Fe tracks reached Albuquerque on April 10, and shortly thereafter the Palace Saloon was opened, owned by "Holliday and Sanguinette." William S. Sanguinette was a thirty-three-year-old clerk, described as "one of the most popular and influential citizens of New Mexico's metropolis." The Palace Saloon did not last long, but Sanguinette continued a career as an Albuquerque bartender into the twentieth century, and Doc, if he was indeed Sanguinette's partner, moved on.[105]

Holliday did return to Prescott, Arizona, in time for the census taker in June, and moved into a boardinghouse on Montezuma Street without Kate. On the census record, he was listed as "single." John Henry's bachelor summer was an interesting departure from his recent past. Back in Prescott, he shared quarters with Richard E. Elliott, a miner and temperance advocate, and John J. Gosper, the secretary of Arizona Territory.[106] He gambled, of course, but he also had opportunity to debate temperance issues and to hear Gosper talk politics and complain about the absences of Arizona's governor, John Charles Frémont, which made him the acting governor. John Henry was associating with potentially influential people. He may even have met other men who would play roles in his future: John P. Clum, an ex–Indian agent and newspaperman, Thomas J. Fitch, one of the territory's leading attorneys, and John H. Behan, a politician and office seeker, all of whom were in Prescott that summer.

And, like all of them, he was listening to tales of Tombstone.

THE PRICE OF A REPUTATION

And the Behan side whenever they got a chance to hurt me over Holli-
day's shoulders they would do it. They would make a lot of talk about Doc
Holliday.

—Wyatt Earp (1926) during the Lotta Crabtree case

Prescott did not hold John Henry Holliday's attention for long. It was a busy town, with its own kind of excitement as the capital of Arizona Territory. It even had a raw edge unlike the political centers of most other states and territories. Its sporting community was still active and profitable. Yet Doc was only one gambler in a town full of gamblers, even if he was rooming with the acting governor of the territory. It was not the anonymity that Doc minded. The truth of things was that he needed the reckless excitement and less careful clientele of the boom camps, and ultimately, he could not resist the reports of Tombstone. Late that summer of 1880, he left Prescott, most likely in August, then paused at Tucson before moving on to Tombstone in September.

Doubtless, he was attracted to the San Augustin Festival that ran from August 27 to September 16 in Tucson. Gamblers from all over the region poured in to the "Old Pueblo," including faces Doc certainly recognized, such as John Shaughnessy, his old friend from Fort Griffin. John H. Behan, the erstwhile lawman and politician from Prescott, was in town and, like Holliday, en route to Tombstone.[1]

The gambling competition was fierce, and Doc may well have seen either Virgil Earp or Wyatt or both, since they were in town during the festival at least briefly. Perhaps it was then that he finally decided to accept Wyatt's invitation, catching the train to Benson and making the rest of the journey on Kinnear & Company's stageline to Tombstone. He may even have ridden on the same coach with John Behan and his son, Albert, who arrived on September 14. He must have been there by then, because on September 17, 1879, the day after the San Augustin Festival closed in Tucson, John Henry Holliday registered to vote in Tombstone.[2]

If the crowded, dirty, uncomfortable ride to Tombstone did not discourage Holliday, first impressions of the town itself could hardly have given him much reason for optimism, except that Doc had long since learned what to expect of new camps in his path. It was true, as Clara Brown, a recent arrival, reported, that Tombstone was still "an embryo city of canvas, frame, and adobe, scattered over a slope." She accurately added, however, that "[t]he only attractive places visible are the liquor and gambling houses, which are everywhere present and are carpeted and comfortably furnished." On the whole, she thought Tombstone was still "one of the dirtiest places in the world." The town sprawled over the flats and boasted dirty streets that were "simply disgraceful, lined from one end to the other with refuse of all kinds, from waste paper to rotten fruit."[3]

Of course, "the liquor and gambling houses" were Holliday's primary interest anyway, but he soon sensed that Tombstone, Arizona, was more than a typical boom camp. The clapboard shanties and tents were giving way to a growing community with a sophistication rare in mining camps. Once Doc settled in at the Cosmopolitan Hotel, Brown's, or one of a few other rooming places, he quickly realized that this was not Fort Griffin or even Las Vegas. Something was afoot here already that those places never had, and he knew, at once, that he wanted to be part of it.

Though it still had the look and feel of a newly born mining camp, Tombstone boasted a more urbane and stable business community than most boomtowns. There were not only plush saloons but also fine hotels, a public library at J. Goldtree & Company's cigar store, complete with a carpeted and well-decorated reading room, and a school under construction. There were also Masons, a brass band, a miner's union, a miner's hospital, the Home Dramatic Association, the Tombstone Social Club, a fire department, two daily newspapers, and a variety of other social and political clubs. Waterworks, large-scale mining operations, investment companies, freighting operations, and an assortment of professional offices and mercantile stores testified to the diversity of the community. Not long after Holliday settled in, the *San Francisco Exchange* predicted that Tombstone was "destined within a year or two to be as important a place as Leadville or Virginia City."[4]

Yet Tombstone was still a town "with the bark on." Besides the miners and freighters regularly employed, Tombstone had a large floating population of young, rootless ne'er-do-wells. Unemployed miners, drifters, cowboys in from surrounding ranges, tin-horn gamblers, and adventurers crowded its streets. It was also a culturally diverse population that included Hispanics, Chinese, Irish, and other immigrants. It was a volatile mix, with real potential for trouble. In the beginning the absence of law enforcement was notable, and the prospects of wealth attracted many who plainly intended to make their fortunes thieving, pilfering, and conning. In that respect, at least, Tombstone was no different from other boom camps.[5]

Fred White, the thirty-two-year-old town marshal, had his hands full. Fights, shootings, and killings gave the town, what George W. Parsons called "a hard reputation." Not even the passage of Ordinance No. 9, forbidding the carrying of weapons in town, solved the problems. Still, Clara Brown noted early in July 1880, "The camp is considered a remarkably quiet one—only one murder since my arrival." But on August 3, she modified her appraisal, noting, "The boasted quietude of the camp has been disturbed of late, and fears are entertained that the end is not yet. Two murders have been committed within the last ten days, both the result of drinking and gambling. When saloons are thronged all night with excited and armed men, bloodshed must needs ensue occasionally."[6]

It was a hard truth, and local authorities were taking steps to tighten controls. On July 27, Wyatt Earp was appointed deputy sheriff of Pima County. The *Tombstone Epitaph* called the appointment "an eminently proper one" and announced to the local population that "Wyatt has filled various positions in which bravery and determination were requisites, and in every instance proved himself the right man in the right place."[7] By the time Holliday arrived, Earp had established a credible record as an effective officer that convinced most Tombstoners that the *Epitaph* was right.

Wyatt and his brothers had come to Tombstone hoping to move up the social ladder by way of economic success in more respectable pursuits. They had planned to establish a stageline but found two operations already in place. Wyatt sold his equipment to Kinnear & Company when he saw that door closed. Virgil had taken a post as a deputy U.S. marshal en route to Tombstone, and Wyatt had become a shotgun guard for Wells, Fargo & Company, as they slipped back into economic pursuits more suited to their experience and social position.[8]

Nevertheless, they continued to look for openings for economic success and social progress. They invested in mining properties and tried to broaden their base at least. By the spring of 1880, reports had reached Dodge City of their success:

> We understand that our fellow townsman Mr. Harry Finaty is contemplating a trip to the Tombstone district of Arizona to look after his interest in a mine which was recently sold by his partner Mr. Wyatt Earp for thirty thousand dollars. The mine is called the "Cooper Lode" and is not worked at present owing to the quantity of foul air that has accumulated in the shaft.[9]

The Earps continued to dabble in mining properties, but the Dodge City report was far more optimistic than their real success, which forced them, again, to fall back on their experiences as lawmen and gamblers.

In July 1880, at the request of the army, Virgil Earp, as a deputy U.S. marshal, joined the pursuit of six stolen army mules with a detachment of soldiers under Lieutenant Joseph H. Hurst. This would be the first encounter between the Earps and men who would come to play fateful roles in their lives, including Frank and Tom McLaury, Pony Deal, Sherman McMaster, and A. T. Hasbrough.[10] The episode soured the taste of both the Earps and the McLaurys for one another. By the time Doc Holliday reached Tombstone, Virgil and Wyatt were both officers of the law, and Morgan had taken Wyatt's place as a shotgun guard for Wells, Fargo.

Saloons, gambling halls, and brothels flourished—and openly—but the saloonkeepers, gamblers, and whores who made most boomtowns primarily purveyors of vice for the exploitation of workers were balanced by businessmen and entrepreneurs who were able to quickly

Virgil Earp, Wyatt Earp, and Morgan Earp, the "fighting Earps," who were friends of Doc Holliday in Tombstone and whom Doc supported whenever the need arose.

establish Tombstone as a solid business community. For those arriving from more conventionally Victorian communities, there was certainly shock at the coexistence of saloons, gambling halls, and whorehouses with the more respectable business community. It was not that such establishments did not exist in other places, but that Tombstone had not yet swept its vice into a corner. The town had grown fast, and it was too fresh to have installed the moral niceties demanded by Victorianism, even to the extent of having a separate redlight district or saloon row. That would come later. Moreover, some of Tombstone's gambling fraternity and saloonmen played prominent roles in local economic and political decisions.[11]

By the timing of Holliday's arrival in Tombstone, he may have been recruited rather than enticed by Wyatt's general invitation, which, after all, he had resisted for more than a year. Doc moved to Tombstone at the onset of a conflict between rival gambling factions, later identified as the Easterners and the Slopers. Both terms were somewhat misleading. Easterners referred generally to gamblers who came from east of the Pacific Slope, while Slopers were mostly California based. Still, the Easterners included some West Coast gamblers, and the Slopers counted Texans and Montanans in their numbers. It was never clear how organized the gamblers' war was, but it was real enough.[12]

At the center of the conflict was the Oriental Saloon on the northwest corner of Fifth and Allen streets. Opening in July 1880, the Oriental was lauded as "the most elegantly furnished saloon this side of the favored city at the Golden Gate." Actually owned by Jim Vizina and Benjamin Cook, the bar and restaurant were leased to Milton E. Joyce, a former blacksmith who dabbled in mining in California and Nevada before settling in Tombstone, and Joyce's young protégé, William Crownover Parker, a well-heeled youth from a prominent San Francisco family, while the gambling concession was run by a consortium of gamblers headed by Lou Rickabaugh of San Francisco. Richard Clark, a well-known sporting man with years of experience in Colorado, Kansas, and California, and William H. Harris, Chalkney Beeson's old partner at the Long Branch Saloon in Dodge City, completed the partnership. The Oriental was a lavish, profitable operation, which created considerable envy among other saloonkeepers and sporting men.[13]

Within the gambling community, however, some other establishments had ties to Rickabaugh and his associates. James Earp was working at Vogan & Flynn's. Earp, in turn, had connections to Robert J. Winders and Oregin C. "Charlie" Smith, who controlled the gambling concession at Danner & Owen's Saloon. The Alhambra, another upscale saloon, owned by Thomas H. Corrigan and operated by John Meagher and Joseph Leonard Mellgren, was the saloon where Doc settled in as a faro dealer. Together with the Oriental group, these men represented what might have been called the gambling establishment in Tombstone.[14] Naturally, there were others who envied what seemed to them to be the control exercised by these men.

By August 1880, a group of them were bent on disrupting the gambling arrangements in Tombstone. Apparently, they were led by John E. Tyler, a veteran gambler who hailed from Jackson County, Missouri, and who had gained experience in Kansas and California. At least he was the most visible of the Slopers. He was also a troublemaker who had killed a man in California before coming to Tombstone. Tyler took a job as a dealer working for Smith and Winders soon after his arrival, but he was more often associated with men like Elliot Larkin Ferguson (known in Tombstone as Pete Spence or Peter Spencer), Thomas J. Duncan, Andrew Ames, and Andy McCauley, a shift miner who apparently ran with a faster crowd when not working in the mines.[15]

Perhaps it was coincidental that Doc Holliday arrived in Tombstone soon after the disruptive behavior of Tyler and company began.

Perhaps Bill Harris spotted him in Tucson and invited him to Tombstone. At any rate, Holliday hit town just as the trouble between the gamblers heated up. On September 23, 1880, only days after Doc's arrival, Tyler and Tony Kraker, another gambler with ties to the Easterners, got into a fracas at Vogan & Flynn's Saloon, and weapons were drawn. Before things got out of hand, "friends interfered and further hostilities were prevented."[16] Less than three weeks later, Doc would have his turn with Tyler.

On Sunday evening, October 10, Holliday got into an argument with Tyler near the Oriental "which boded a shooting scrape." Marshal White or Officer James Bennett disarmed both men to defuse the situation and deposited their pistols behind the bar at the Oriental. Later, both men returned to the Oriental, where the argument was renewed. Milt Joyce asked Tyler to leave the saloon, "as he didn't want trouble." Tyler left, but when Joyce "remonstrated with Holliday," Doc, who was apparently intoxicated, got into an argument with Joyce, during which Joyce "bodily fired" Doc out of the saloon. Doc was no physical match for the burly former blacksmith, who easily threw him into the street. Uncowed, Doc returned and demanded the return of his pistol from behind the bar. Joyce refused to give it to him.

Infuriated and humiliated, Holliday left again, found another pistol, and returned. He approached Joyce, who was coming out from behind the bar, "and with a remark that wouldn't look well in print, turned loose with a self-cocker." Joyce pulled his own pistol and charged Doc, perhaps firing at him once, before using it to knock Doc to the floor with a blow to his head. As they struggled, Marshal White and Officer Bennett arrived and separated them. In the melee, several shots were fired. Joyce was wounded in the hand, and William Parker was shot in the big toe of his left foot. Gus Williams, a bartender, also had fired a shot, which hit no one. Doc was bleeding badly from the blow to his head, and observers thought at the time that he "was severely, if not fatally, hurt." He was lifted into a chair, and Joyce was escorted out of the saloon. When it was clear that Holliday was not critically injured, he was arrested.[17]

The following day, Fred White secured a warrant against Holliday sworn out by Joyce on a charge of "assault with a deadly weapon with intent to kill," before Justice of the Peace James Reilly. The next day

Milton E. Joyce, saloonkeeper and member of the Cochise County Board of Supervisors, who became Doc Holliday's bitter foe after an incident in the Oriental Saloon in which Holliday shot Joyce and Joyce severely beat Holliday.

Doc pleaded guilty to assault and battery even though no witnesses appeared against him in Reilly's court. He was fined $20 plus $11.25 in court costs.[18] Doc got off light, but the episode generated animosity between him and Joyce.

Joyce's physical wound healed slowly. At one point he feared he might lose his hand, but eventually he fully recovered. He did not forget Doc Holliday, however, and the incident seemed to sour his relationship with the men who ran the Oriental's gambling concession, driving him into the Slopers' camp, and, critically, predisposing him against the Earps in the months that followed. The witnesses called to testify in Holliday's hearing had included not only Joyce but also John Behan and West Fuller. Like Joyce, they failed to appear, and both of them would figure prominently in the troubles to come. John Tyler, who must have taken some pleasure in the trouble he had caused, continued to deal for Smith and Winders for a time, and the owners of the gambling concession at the Oriental, concerned about the situation, hired Luke Short to protect their interest. The fall passed with tension in the air, but October ended with a sensational affair that drew attention away from the gamblers' war.[19]

Shortly after midnight on the morning of October 28, a group of revelers were gathered at the Alhambra Saloon. Four cowboys from the San Simon Valley, Curly Bill Brocius, Frank Patterson, Edward

Collins, and Dick Lloyd, had been discussing a cattle deal with the stockman Jerome E. "Jerry" Ackerson. Business ceased being an issue as the liquor flowed. The cowboys fell in with three part-time miners and hangers-on with the cowboy crowd: James Johnson, a resident of Charleston; Andy McCauley, an associate of Pete Spence and Johnny Tyler; and Andrew Ames. Together, this band of celebrants spilled out of the saloon into the street. Near Sixth, some of them began to fire their pistols in the air. At that point, Patterson apparently tried to quiet the situation, and two of the group, McCauley and Johnson, ran to the south side of Allen Street to get away from the fuss. As they ran, they heard Curly Bill shout, "This won't do," as he followed them behind a cabin off Sixth halfway to Toughnut Street.[20]

At the first sound of gunfire, Marshal Fred White headed for the scene. Deputy Sheriff Wyatt Earp left his card game at the Bank Exchange Saloon and sprinted toward the sound of the guns as well. Near the scene he encountered his brother, Morgan, and Fred Dodge, borrowed a pistol from Dodge, and continued on. He spotted Marshal White just as White approached Brocius demanding that he surrender his pistol. Curly Bill was pulling his pistol out of its holster when Wyatt threw his arms around him from behind. At that point, White shouted, "Now, you Goddamn son-of-a-bitch, give up that pistol!" As he jerked the pistol from the cowboy's hand, it discharged, sending a bullet into the marshal's groin and tearing into his intestines. Wyatt Earp buffaloed Brocius and, with the help of his brothers Virgil and Morgan, arrested most of the others in the party. Once the prisoners were deposited in the jail, Wyatt left Morgan and Dodge standing guard, and with Virgil, Turkey Creek Jack Johnson, and Doc Holliday he sought the others, not sure if there would be more trouble. Dodge recalled that "we passed through the night without another killing. And in the morning everything was quiet and orderly, as all things were that Wyatt Earp had anything to do with."[21]

The following day, Ames, Collins, Johnson, and Lloyd were fined $10 each on weapons charges, and Patterson was released without charges for his effort in trying to quiet the revelers. McCauley had not been arrested, and Ackerson, after presenting his credentials as a cattle dealer, had posted a cash bond the night of the shooting. Sentiment was building against Brocius as White's condition deteriorated, so much so that Judge Michael Gray ordered the case transferred to the county seat at Tucson. Wyatt Earp took charge of the transfer. With Virgil, Morgan, George "Shotgun" Collins, and a few others, including Holliday, he took Brocius to Tucson.[22]

On the day of the shooting, Virgil Earp had been appointed assistant city marshal at a salary of $100. Two days later, Fred White died, and Virgil became marshal temporarily until elections could be held. On October 31, White was followed by a large cortege representing "all classes and conditions of society, from the millionaire to the mudsill" to his final resting place.[23] Ironically, as White was laid to rest, word reached Tombstone that Jerry Ackerson, the cattle buyer who had been one of the revelers that night, had been found murdered and robbed of $100 thirty miles away on the Southern Pacific line at Groton Springs.[24] Brocius, whose reputation was not well known in Tombstone at the time, was eventually discharged in December, based largely on White's deathbed statement that the shooting had been accidental, which was supported by the testimonies of Wyatt Earp and Jacob Gruber, a gunsmith who testified that Brocius's pistol was defective, allowing it to fire at half-cock. Others testified that Brocius had tried to quiet the revelers before the encounter with White occurred.[25]

Doc would later claim that Curly Bill had been part of the Fort Griffin crowd and had an unsavory reputation even then, and during the course of his trip to Tucson in the custody of Wyatt Earp, Bill had admitted to being a fugitive from Texas. None of that was relevant at the time, though, and Curly Bill was set free to play a greater role in the unfolding Tombstone story. Within a matter of weeks, his antics once again would have him in the news, but for the moment, Curly Bill was a free man and of no concern to Doc Holliday.

The White killing led to a temporary increase in law enforcement in Tombstone. A public outcry about the "epidemic of shootings" was matched by demands in the press that local gun ordinances be strengthened. The town council appointed a new group of policemen and scheduled a special election for marshal on November 12, with Virgil Earp, James Flynn, and Ben Sippy as candidates. Interestingly, the council also appointed Buckskin Frank Leslie as a special deputy authorized to keep the peace and make arrests in the Oriental Saloon.[26] And perhaps unnoticed at the time was that the relatively unknown John Henry Holliday was playing a backup role whenever the Earp brothers needed men they could depend on in a fight. In fact, in light of subsequent events, his new role appeared short lived at best. Politics took care of that.

In the general election that was held on November 2, 1880, the race for sheriff of Pima County was closely watched. Charlie Shibell, the incumbent and a Democrat, had a spotless record, but his Republican opponent, Robert H. "Bob" Paul, had an imposing career as a law enforcement officer and Wells, Fargo detective. At first, Shibell appeared to be reelected by a slim margin of 42 votes, but when the results from Precinct No. 27, the San Simon district, showed 103 votes for Shibell and only 1 for Paul, the Republicans cried foul. Balloting had taken place at the home of Joe Hill, a Texan with a questionable reputation whose real name was Joseph Greaves Olney, and poll officials included Isaac Clanton and John Ringo, other men with less than sterling reputations, even though their appointments had been revoked days earlier.[27]

Paul challenged the outcome, but his suit was not scheduled to be heard until January 1881. In the meantime, Shibell was sworn in for a second term. On November 9, 1880, Wyatt Earp resigned his post as deputy sheriff because, as he put it, he did not think it proper to work on Paul's behalf in the election dispute while serving under Shibel. The *Tombstone Nugget* lamented his departure, stating, "Wyatt Earp's resignation as deputy sheriff was noted by his many friends with regret. During the time he has held the office he has been active and prompt in the discharge of all duties and every citizen had the consciousness that his life and property were as well protected as they could be by any single officer."[28]

There were suggestions, however, that he had resigned under pressure from Shibell because of his perceived disloyalty to the man who had hired him in the first place. A local observer noted that the Earps' "ingratitude to one who had always been their friend has been marked by his many friends in Tombstone, and retribution has already reached one."[29] Virgil was the victim of retribution referred to by the correspondent. On November 12, Ben Sippy defeated him in the special election for city marshal of Tombstone by a vote of 311 to 259, after James Flynn dropped out of the race to go into business with T. E. Fitzpatrick at the Cosmopolitan Saloon. Virgil resigned as assistant marshal shortly thereafter.[30]

These developments left the Earps without official credentials except for Virgil's role as deputy U.S. marshal and Wyatt's continued work with Wells, Fargo. Wyatt also began to work on Paul's behalf in the election dispute. Their election problems prompted the Earps to sell some of their properties. After selling land lots in Tombstone for $6,000 earlier in the year, Wyatt and Andrew Neff, who was a partner in some of his investments, sold the Comstock mine for $3,000 and an option on the Grasshopper claim next to it; while both were undervalued, they eventually became profitable to Alfred H. Emmanuel, who developed them.[31]

Perhaps the sales underscored the lack of experience of the Earps and their partners, but the quick sales did not end their speculations. A few days after Wyatt resigned as deputy sheriff, Doc witnessed the survey of the Mountain Maid mine by Wyatt and Bob Winders. The Earps and their partners still owned mines called the Long Branch, the Dodge, and the Mattie Blaylock, and they were dabbling in other projects with several partners, including Albert Steinfeld and C. G. Bilicke.[32]

John H. Behan replaced Wyatt as Shibell's deputy sheriff in Tombstone. The appointment was scarcely a surprise, and it was welcomed by Democratic observers throughout the territory. At the time, his appointment seemed tenuous and wholly dependent on the outcome of the Pima County sheriff's suit. Behan was well connected, however, and he almost certainly took the position with full knowledge of the movement afoot in Prescott to create new Arizona counties. He understood, if Wyatt had not, that holding the position of deputy sheriff of Pima County would be an asset if Tombstone became part of a new county. And with his connections in Prescott and his political skill, Behan had the inside track for appointment as sheriff if a new county were created.

Behan had to have been impressed with Earp's record as Pima County deputy, and, knowing that Earp would likely seek the sheriff's appointment himself, should it become available, Behan approached him with a proposition. He proposed that if Wyatt did not apply for the position of sheriff, he would appoint Wyatt as undersheriff. Wyatt would be the chief law enforcement officer, while Behan concentrated on tax collection and politics. The arrangement had unmistakable appeal to Wyatt because it was similar to the role he had played as assistant marshal to Larry Deger and Charles E. Bassett back in Dodge City.[33]

Because of his friendship with Wyatt Earp—and perhaps unwittingly—Doc Holliday was being drawn into local politics. Oddly, he registered to vote before the Earps did. He was already partnered with the Earps and R. J. Winders in mining claims, and as events unfolded that fall, his sense of loyalty would involve him in other enterprises as well. He was out of town for a time in November, perhaps gambling in Tucson or Prescott or visiting Kate in Globe.

But he was back in Tombstone in December. On the evening of December 6, 1880, Shotgun Collins, another former resident of Dodge and one of those who had helped Wyatt Earp on the morning of Fred White's fatal shooting, exchanged pistol fire with a man named Scott, which resulted in no injuries but cost both of them $10 for discharging firearms in public. By December 10, George Parsons was complaining that shooting was a nightly affair and musing that it was "[s]trange no one is killed." Cowboys openly defied the gun ordinances and hurrahed the town on a regular basis. Doc, though, stayed clear of gunplay.[34]

On January 4, 1881, John P. Clum, the editor of the *Tombstone Epitaph* and a former Indian agent, was elected mayor after a campaign that focused on title to town lots. Clum would prove to be an important ally to the Earps in the months that followed. Ben Sippy defeated his challenger, Howard Lee, in the marshal's race. The new year also brought the big news that Curly Bill had been acquitted for the killing of Fred White, and it was soon apparent that he had not learned much from the experience. On January 9, 1881, he "celebrated" at Charleston by shooting up the town and disrupting a church service and making the preacher dance at gunpoint. The next day he hit Tombstone, "captured the Alhambra Saloon," and hurrahed the town. No one tried to stop him; it would be the beginning of a lively year.[35] On January 14, Doc was again pressed into service by Wyatt. On that day, Michael O'Rourke, commonly called "Johnny-behind-the-Deuce," shot and killed Richard Schneider, a local mining man, during a card game at Charleston.

Because of Schneider's prominence, a crowd gathered, and George McKelvey, the local constable, fearing a mob, started for Tombstone in a buggy with O'Rourke. En route, he met Virgil Earp out exercising one of Wyatt's horses. Virgil took O'Rourke up behind him and raced to Tombstone ahead of McKelvey and the Charleston crowd. He stopped at the Wells, Fargo office, where Wyatt happened to be. Although neither he nor Virgil held any official position, Wyatt took a shotgun and moved the prisoner to Vogan's Bowling Alley, while Virgil rushed off to find Marshal Sippy. Gathering a cadre of men including Morgan, Doc, Fred Dodge, West Fuller, and a few others as guards, Wyatt sent Warren home to saddle horses for the group. By the time the mob arrived, the situation was under control. Sippy and Virgil had joined the group, and Wyatt led them through the crowd that had gathered—both curiosity seekers and the mob that had trailed Virgil from Charleston—announcing that they were taking the prisoner to Tucson. Once joined by Deputy Behan, the entourage moved out, and O'Rourke was saved.[36]

The mood in Tombstone was grim, prompting Parsons to declare on January 21, "Town unsafe—some decisive steps should be taken." In the aftermath of the Johnny-behind-the-Deuce affair, a citizens' vigilance committee was established and matters settled down.

Tombstone was deceptively calm as February began, and Doc, who was also speculating in mining properties, joined a new partnership that focused on the important matter of water rights. Opportunity seemed to lie in the Huachuca Mountains west of the San Pedro River; at least claims in the area appeared to be worth the gamble. Besides Doc and Wyatt Earp, the unlikely business partnership included Dick Clark and Jim Leavy. Clark was the "boss gambler" of Tombstone and a partner in the Oriental's gambling operation. He was also a man well known throughout the mountain West and "regarded as a professional man of high rank." Jim Leavy, a gambler and gun handler, called "the top-notcher of them all except Wild Bill," had respect as a deliberate and honest man, whether handling cards, money, or revolvers. Known far and wide as the man who had killed Charles Harrison in Cheyenne, Leavy was by far the best known of the quartet of investors who set out from Tombstone to stake water claims.[37]

On February 2, 1881, the four men staked out their first claim in Hayes and Turner's Canyon (later renamed Garden Canyon), calling it the Wyatt Earp Water Right. The following day, they staked out the Clark Water Right in Mormon Canyon (later called Miller Canyon), and the Holliday Water Right about a mile and a half from the mouth of Ramsey Canyon. At each of the claims, the partners left a "board of location" nailed to a tree. They did not choose a fourth claim to bear Leavy's name, but each of the staked locations was to be owned jointly by all four partners. Their work done, they headed back to Tombstone. En route, however, they encountered Sherman McMaster, a former Texas Ranger, a suspected horse thief, and a hanger-on with the San Simon crowd, who told them that a horse that had been stolen from Wyatt was at Charleston in the possession of eighteen-year-old Billy Clanton. Earp decided to go to Charleston to reclaim his property at once, and Doc—and possibly Leavy—went along. Clark returned to Tombstone to file the claims.[38]

Wyatt and Doc found the horse as reported, and Wyatt immediately wired his brother Jim in Tombstone to secure the appropriate papers to recover his property. When young Clanton learned of Earp's presence, he attempted to remove the horse, but Earp would not let him do it. When Warren Earp arrived with the documents, young Clanton surrendered the horse without trouble but asked Earp sarcastically if he "had any more horses to lose." Earp assured him that he would watch over his stock more carefully in the future and "give him no chance to steal them."[39]

While Doc and Wyatt were in Charleston, Behan, Leslie Blackburn, and Lawrence Geary rode in from Tombstone looking for Ike Clanton to serve him a subpoena ordering him to appear in court in the sheriff's election fraud case. Earp and Behan exchanged pleasantries, but Behan later claimed that when he met Ike Clanton afterward in Tucson, Clanton informed him that he had come near to getting "into a hell of a fuss." Clanton claimed that Wyatt Earp had told him about the subpoena and that Behan was coming to his ranch with a posse of nine men to arrest him. "Then he told me that he had armed his crowd and was not going to stand for it," Behan later maintained.[40]

Based on this unconfirmed exchange, Behan concluded—or later claimed that he concluded—that Earp had gone to Charleston to warn Clanton so that he would hide out and not testify in the fraud case. As Clanton was Shibell's key witness, his failure to appear would doom Shibell's case and make Bob Paul sheriff of Pima County. Earp would admit later that he had promised to testify favorably at Curly Bill Brocius's trial for the murder of Fred White if Brocius convinced his cowboy friends to admit the San Simon election fraud.[41] Apparently, Wyatt Earp had a political agenda as well.

On February 2, 1881, while Doc and his partners were claiming water rights, Tombstone became the county seat of the newly created Cochise County, and, as expected, on February 10, John Behan was appointed sheriff. At that point, Wyatt was still confident that Behan would appoint him undersheriff. On February 21, Tombstone was granted a city charter, and the city council abolished the office of town marshal and created a police department with Ben Sippy as the chief of police. These activities suggested that the town was growing up, and, appropriately, most of February passed without gunplay.[42]

Even the gamblers' war seemed to have managed a cease-fire, although posturing and maneuvering continued. Leslie was still watching the bar and restaurant at the Oriental, and Luke Short was acting as lookout in the gambling room. Then, on February 8, 1881, Bat Masterson left Dodge City for a reunion with his Dodge City buddies at Tombstone, where he expected "to remain next summer."[43] On February 24, the *Dodge City Times* reported that Harris had written to Chalk Beeson, his old partner, that Masterson had arrived in Tombstone. Masterson's reputation appeared to further stabilize the situation at the Oriental—but not for long.

Soon after Masterson's arrival, the Slopers imported their own new gun hand. Charles S. Storms was a well-known gambler and gunman in both Colorado and the Black Hills country. His family lived in California, but he came to Tombstone from El Paso, Texas. A contemporary paper said of him, "He was what the men of the West call 'gritty,' and had been in a number of shooting affairs where he showed plenty of nerve. He had great confidence in his ability to cope with any antagonist."[44] Upon arrival in Tombstone, he wasted little time.

On February 25, he got into a game at the Oriental. Rickabaugh was dealing; Storms—with too much liquor and fight on the brain—attempted to pick a quarrel. Luke Short, who was in the lookout chair, intervened, and Storms turned his wrath on Short. The situation was at flash point, but before they could draw their pistols, Bat Masterson, who knew Storms from Colorado and considered him a friend, stepped in and hustled Charlie off to his room at the San Jose House. Bat was still working to calm Short down outside the Oriental when Storms reappeared about noon.

Storms approached Short, demanding to know, "Are you as good a man as you were this morning?"

"Every bit as good," Short calmly replied as he pulled his pistol.

Short shot Storms through the heart and once more before he hit the ground. According to George Parsons, Storms "was game to the last and by a desperate effort steadying revolver with both hands fired—four shots I believe." Said the *Santa Fe New Mexican*, "self-reliance finally brought him to his grave."[45]

The games at the Oriental "went on as if nothing had happened," but two days later, on February 27, another incident took place that was apparently related. The *Phoenix Herald* described what happened: "A slight fracus occured [*sic*] in Tombstone, Sunday night last, owing to some misunderstanding between one Lyons (better known as Dublin) who was a partner with the late C. S. Storms in the gambling business, and Wyatt Earp. Dublin was ordered to leave town, which he did." That same week, "Mr. Louis Rickabaugh, who has been running a faro game in Tombstone, in an altercation with a person whose name is not stated, hit his antagonist on the head with a pistol."[46]

Then on March 1, still less than a week after Charlie Storms died, "a man named Al McAllister shot a one armed man named Kelly in Tombstone in self defense" at the Oriental. Alfred McAllister was a Galeyville butcher with a hard reputation. One-armed Kelly was a gambler known on the circuit, as described by a correspondent called "Cactus" in this commentary from the *Las Vegas Optic*: "One-armed Kelly, who was outlawed from Leadville six months ago and came to Vegas, shot the window out of Burton's restaurant, was run in for three months, went to Tombstone, where it has been reported that he was handed down for the worms of that consecrated soil."[47]

The Kelly incident proved to be too much. Milt Joyce closed the gaming room. "Oriental a regular slaughter house now," wrote George Parsons.[48] Just how long the Oriental remained closed is unclear from the record, but Short and Masterson had established a presence at the Oriental that changed the equation between the Easterners and the Slopers, and while they could hardly be praised for maintaining order, the gamblers' war did subside after a bloody last week in February. Johnny Tyler remained in Tombstone, but he stayed clear of the Oriental.

The most serious ill effect of the troubles appeared to be resentment on the part of Milt Joyce toward the Rickabaugh group, which he apparently blamed for the troubles. He already identified them with Holliday, even though Doc did not work at the Oriental. Over time this friction would deepen. Of course, Doc Holliday was only peripherally involved in most of these events, but his unfortunate encounter with Joyce would have effects far beyond the gamblers' war—and sooner than he could have expected.

Doc had settled in. He kept a low profile for a time, dabbled in mining properties and water rights, ran a regular faro bank at the Alhambra, and tried to restore his relationship with Kate Elder. Kate said later that she had opened a hotel in Globe and that she made two or three trips to Tombstone to try to patch up her relationship with Doc. The first of these trips was in late February or early March. Not much changed between them, however, and they were soon arguing again. On March 10, Doc was arrested. The *Daily Epitaph* told the story:

> A "man about town" named "John Doc," last night, while under the influence of too much family disturber, grew noisy and disorderly, and officers Ramsey and Kirkpatrick proceeded forthwith to take him in. While that transaction was in progress, the inevitable "gun" made it's appearance, and in the melee was somehow discharged, the shot fortunately striking no one. The shootist was taken before Judge Wallace, and when that official got through with "Doc," the latter was $25 poorer.[49]

From the flavor of the article and the reference to "too much family disturber," the cause of Doc's arrest was probably the renewed quarreling with Kate. And, from the tone of Kate's memoirs, the source of the argument was almost certainly Doc's relationship with the Earps and her desire to get him to leave Tombstone with her. She did not succeed, and at that point, at least, Doc made some effort to distance himself from her temporarily by seeking the company of friends.

John Henry was a man not likely to forget friendships even when they did not serve him well. One such "friend" was William Leonard, the jeweler he had known in Las Vegas. Leonard had arrived in Tombstone in time for the 1880 census, and at that time was living with Frank C. Marsh, a local jeweler. Time had not been kind to the consumptive Leonard. He was frail, weighed scarcely 120 pounds, and was addicted to morphine. To make matters worse, he soon fell in with a rough crowd. Wyatt Earp explained the circumstances of Doc and

Leonard's relationship to the writer Walter Noble Burns many years later:

> Holiday [sic] was a friend of Lenard's [sic], having known him in Las Vegas New Mexico where Lenard was established in the jewelry business. And was considered at that time a respectable citizen. And from Las Vegas he came to Tombstone and with Harry Head, Jim Crane, also Bill [Luther] King and himself all went batching in a house two miles north from town which was known as the Wells. And all three remained there for several months. Holiday would make them a visit now and then knowing Lenard so well, which many people knew how friendly they were.[50]

Perhaps their association was based more on their shared battle with consumption than on anything else. Whatever the case, the relationship would prove costly to Doc. Leonard and his companions all had hard reputations and ran with the Cow-Boys. Rumor had it that Leonard's skills as a jeweler were put to use melting down gold and fencing stolen jewelry. Doc had lived on the edge for so long that he would have paid little attention to such matters. They were of no direct concern to him in March 1881, but things were about to change.

On March 15, 1881, Doc rented a horse at Dunbar's stable and left Tombstone. He later claimed that he went to Charleston to join in a high-stakes poker game he had heard about, but he found that the game had broken up by the time he arrived. During his trip back to Tombstone, he came across Old Man Fuller, who was driving a water wagon, and rode with him back to Tombstone, where he stabled his horse, had dinner, and went to work operating his faro bank at the Alhambra. Wyatt Earp told the story somewhat differently to Burns, though with the same ending:

> Holiday [sic] went to the livery stable on that day, hired a saddle horse which he did quite often to visit Lenard [sic] at the Wells. The horse came from Dunbar's stable, and not Tribletts [sic], as Triblett did not have any stable in Tombstone. Holiday remained there until 4 P.M. Old Man Fuller was hauling water into Tombstone at that time and leaving the Wells with a load of water Holiday tied his horse behind the wagon and rode into town with Fuller. And which many people knew. After Holiday ate his dinner, he went to playing

faro. And he was still playing when the word came to Tombstone from Bob Paul to me that there had been a hold up.[51]

The two stories were not incompatible. After leaving Charleston, Doc might well have stopped at Leonard's place en route back to Tombstone, afterward joining Old Man Fuller at the Wells and riding with him into town. Earp would also insist that Doc was playing faro against Wyatt at the time of the crime, adding "that Holliday hocked his big watch chain for $40 to get faro money that evening."[52] All of this would be important later.

The regular run of the Kinnear & Company's stagecoach from Tombstone to Benson departed as usual that evening for Benson with Eli "Bud" Philpott driving and Bob Paul riding shotgun for Wells, Fargo. The stage stopped at Watervale, two miles out of Tombstone, and picked up two additional passengers. The stage was loaded, so one of them, a young man named Peter Roerig, had to ride up top. Afterward, the coach proceeded toward Benson. At about ten o'clock under a bright moon, the stage horses slowed to a walk as they passed through a wash and mounted an incline near Drew's Station beyond Contention. Close to the top, a man stepped onto the road from the east and shouted, "Hold!"

"By God, I hold for nobody!" Paul thundered as he lowered his shotgun to fire. By then more men were on both sides of the road. Paul fired, wounding one of the would-be robbers, as the group opened fire on the stage. Philpott was hit at the first fire and toppled dead from the seat into the traces, carrying the reins with him as the horses bolted into a run. The stage careered past Drew's Station pell-mell for nearly a mile as Paul tried to gain control of the team. He managed to slide into Philpott's seat and apply the brake, gradually slowing the horses to a walk. He then dropped to the ground and recovered the reins. Once he had the stage stopped, he discovered that Roerig was badly wounded. Paul drove as rapidly as possible to Benson. There, he telegraphed Tombstone, learned that Roerig was fatally wounded, and started at once back to the scene of the attempted robbery.[53]

When the stage passed Drew's Station out of control, the men there rushed outside in time to see the would-be robbers riding away at a dead run and Philpott's lifeless body on the road. As soon as word reached Tombstone, Marshall Williams, the Wells, Fargo agent,

Sheriff John Behan, Virgil Earp (as deputy U.S. marshal), and his brothers, Wyatt and Morgan, started for the scene. Others offered their services, but Behan declined them all and requested only the Earps. Bat Masterson, who was one of the passengers on the stage, according to Paul, had manhunting experience and joined the posse at Wyatt Earp's insistence. At the scene, the posse found fifteen shell casings, three wigs, and a beard of rope yarn. The bandits tried to cover their trail, but the pursuers were dogged. The evidence indicated that there were four robbers, and spots of blood suggested that Paul's shotgun blasts had taken a toll.[54]

The posse pursued the outlaws for nearly three days before approaching the ranch of Len Redfield, who was known to be sympathetic to the Cow-Boys. There, Wyatt spotted a man milking a cow while armed with two revolvers, a gunbelt, and a rifle. He and Morgan quickly arrested him. Wyatt then insisted that Sheriff Behan not allow the prisoner, who turned out to be Luther King, to talk with either Len Redfield or his brother, Hank. While Earp conferred with Paul, however, King talked freely with the Redfields, and one of them quickly saddled up and rode off, presumably to warn King's associates. Under interrogation, though, King confessed to holding the horses for the robbers at Drew's Station. At that juncture, the posse decided that Behan and Williams would return to Tombstone with the prisoner, while the rest would pursue the other fugitives.[55]

The posse was close behind the fugitives. They found a campfire nearby, but the fugitives had apparently acquired fresh mounts from the Redfields and had struck east once they were warned of the posse's approach. Paul, the Earp brothers, and Masterson continued the hunt for six more days before their horses were so worn out that Paul's mount died and Wyatt and Masterson were forced to walk back to Tombstone from a distance of eighteen miles. On March 21, Virgil wired Sheriff Behan from Tres Alamos to bring fresh horses. He also telegraphed U.S. Marshal Crawley P. Dake at Tucson: "I left the night the stage was stopped with two of my brothers and Bill [sic] Masterson. Have not lost a foot print. Have caught one. Will follow as long as I can find a track."[56]

Behan left Tombstone on the afternoon of March 20 with Marshall Williams, Buckskin Frank Leslie (who had a reputation as a tracker), William M. Breakenridge, and Ed Gorman, which meant that the horses Virgil had requested arrived after they left town. Behan's group rejoined Virgil at Helm's Ranch on the south side of the Dragoons on March 24. By then, Wyatt and Bat had returned to Tombstone.[57]

Tombstone was already full of rumors about the outlaws. On March 20, George Parsons had noted in his diary, "Marshall Williams in from hunting stage robbers. Told me at ball that they would have them and who they are. Know one of them—Leonard—very well by sight and have had business with him. Know him to be a hard case."[58] Others doubtless knew as well. On March 23, the night Wyatt returned from the hunt, he wasted no time. Though it was late, he sent for Doc Holliday. Kate recalled what happened:

> One night after we had retired, Warren Earp came after Doc and said that Wyatt wanted to see him at his house. He was gone one hour and a half. I could see that he was very much put out about something. He kept saying "the damned fool. I did not think that of him." Then he said, "I have to get up early in the morning, but I will think about it." This was after the stage holdup. He did not get up until 9:00 A.M., when we went to breakfast. "Well, I don't know what I am going to stack up against today. I am getting tired of it all."[59]

The reasons for Doc's concerns were about to become public. The next day, March 24, the *Tucson Star* reported the source of his worries, with these revelations about the fugitives:

> The names of the three who are traveling are Bill Leonard, Jim Crane, and Harry Hickey [*sic*]. The fourth is at Tombstone and is well known and has been shadowed ever since his return. This party is suspected for the reasons, that on the afternoon of the attack he engaged a horse at about 4 o'clock, stating he might be gone seven or eight days [or] he might return that night. He left about 4 o'clock, armed with a Henry rifle and a six-shooter, he started toward Charleston, and about a mile below Tombstone cut across to Contention, and when next seen it was between 10 and 11 o'clock, riding into the livery stable at Tombstone, his horse fagged out. He at once called for another horse, which he hitched in the streets. Statements attributed to him, if true, look very bad indeed, and which, if proven, are most conclusive as to his guilt either as a principal actor or an accessory before the fact.[60]

In light of what was said and happened later, the "fourth" alluded to in the *Star* was most likely Doc Holliday, although that was not apparent at the time and might have fit other residents of Tombstone. Bill Leonard was the "damned fool" whom Kate had heard Doc talking about. And he understood the import of Leonard's involvement for him. That was why Wyatt had called him to his house so late at night. Later accounts, rumors, and accusations complicated perceptions of just what the rumor mill was saying at the time, but Doc clearly knew that his friendship with Leonard would cause problems for him. Kate did not linger in Tombstone. She returned to Globe, and based on her later actions and recollections, she apparently believed the worst. And so did others.

Billy Breakenridge would later report a rumor that when the stage stopped at Watervale late on the afternoon of March 15, "Doc Holladay [sic] who was there on horse back brought out a drink of whiskey and wanted Paul to take it but Bob refused telling him he never drank while on duty." Breakenridge believed the whiskey to be drugged and Paul lucky he did not take it, though on what basis he would have arrived at such a conclusion other than prejudice against Holliday is far from clear. Afterward, Breakenridge said that Doc "got on his horse and road [sic] off and the stage proceeded on its way to Benson."[61]

Rumors about Doc disturbed Wyatt. Representing Virgil as a federal posseman, and perhaps acting as a Wells, Fargo operative in Tombstone (with Marshall Williams again out of town), Wyatt did as much investigating of the case as he could until James B. Hume, the company's chief detective, arrived to act for the company. Reward posters were printed over Bob Paul's name as "Special Officer of W. F. & Co," dated March 23, 1881, offering rewards amounting to $3,600 for Leonard, Head, and Crane. No reference was made to a fourth fugitive, and certainly not to Doc.[62]

Hume was convinced that Luther King was the key to successful prosecution of the case. Marshall Williams also told the reporter of the *Tombstone Daily Gossip* that King had "made a full confession to him [Williams] and Sheriff Behan showing how the matter had been planned, and where the robbers were to bivouac after its commission."[63] If King did make a full confession, he did not name Holliday, because if he had, Behan surely would have arrested Doc as soon as he reached Tombstone. Clearly, neither Hume nor Williams remotely implied a Holliday involvement, even though rumors reported as many as nine men involved in the planning and execution of the robbery. They, at least, were sure of King's story that the robbery attempt and murders were the spawn of a four-man operation. King was in the care of the new undersheriff, Harry M. Woods, who was also the editor of the *Tombstone Nugget*, while Behan was on the chase. Then on the evening of March 28, the unthinkable happened. Luther King escaped by simply walking out the back door of the jail to a waiting horse.

The *Tombstone Evening Gossip* explained what happened:

> At about 7:30 last evening Harry Jones entered the Sheriff's office to draw up a bill of sale for King, he being desirous of selling his horse to Mr. Dunbar, and while so engaged King stepped out of the back door taking Deputy Campbell's pistol as he went. Jones having occasion to ask King some questions in regard to certain marks on the horse turned to speak to him, and discovered that King had gone. The officers immediately rushed to the back door but he had vanished. Search was unavailing, and they had to acknowledge that King had escaped. Where he has gone or which way to look for him nobody knows.[64]

What made the episode particularly egregious was that Jim Hume had that very afternoon "warned the officers who had King in charge to guard him very closely, as there would be an attempt made in the evening to release him from custody, and that it was very little encouragement for men to leave their business and go out into the mountains after these men, and after capturing them have them let loose."[65] Virgil Earp elaborated, "Hume got Wyatt to go with him to the Sheriff's office to notify them, and they asked as a favor of the Under Sheriff to put King in irons. He promised to do so, and fifteen minutes afterward King escaped, going on a horse that was tied back of the Sheriff's office."[66]

Undersheriff Woods quickly concocted a most remarkable and brazen newspaper item for the *Nugget* that doubtless left knowledgeable people speechless and men like Wyatt Earp and Jim Hume livid. He claimed that Leonard had been gone only seconds when he was missed, but he could not be found, adding, "It was a well planned job by outsiders to get him away. While there might at the time have been more watchfulness on the part of those in charge of him, still through the days and nights since his arrest a guard has been kept over him, and a single unguarded moment, but not without the aid of accomplices on the outside."[67]

The *Nugget's* explanation stank to high heaven, along with Woods's negligence, and contempt rained on those who had let it happen. George Parsons noted with indignation, "King, the stage robber, escaped tonight early from H. Woods who had been previously notified of an attempt at release to be made. Some of our officials should be hanged. They're a bad lot."[68] The *Tucson Citizen* expressed its disdain in plain terms: "The escape was the result of an inexcusable and culpable negligence on the part of the officer in charge as he had been notified of the intended escape of King."[69] The *Epitaph* joined in, adding, "King did use the boys at the Sheriff's office rather rough, that's a fact. He never said a word about going—never whispered 'tra-la-la.'"[70] Jim Hume sadly wrote to his fiancé, "Tombstone has a population of six thousand—five thousand of them are bad—one thousand of them known outlaws. I don't want much of Tombstone."[71]

Disgust and barbed humor aside, people were angered because of the seriousness of the crime involved. The *Epitaph* underscored the significance of what had just happened: "The escape of King is very important, not only in connection with the late murder near Contention, but with the extensive stock stealing now being perpetrated in Southern Arizona. He is possessed of valuable information, and it is thought under proper treatment he might have been induced to 'give the business away.'"[72]

The *Epitaph* predicted that King would "make good his escape." A week later, the *Tucson Star* reported a rumor that the Cow-Boys had hanged King in the Huachucas, explaining that "believing that King had 'given them away' to the officers," the Cow-Boys had "resolved on punishing him, and with that purpose in view assisted him to escape."[73] If so, his friends were convinced that he already had given the business away. The *Star's* story was never verified, but Luther King had vanished.

By then, the pursuit of the other principals, Leonard, Head, and Crane, had been abandoned. Clara Brown explained why succinctly: "The party in search of the stage robbers returned to Tombstone after an unsuccessful quest of over two weeks, enduring considerable hardship and wearing out their horses before giving up the chase. They were four days and a half without food and thirty-six hours without water."[74] The local press praised the efforts of the possemen, but there were plenty of reasons to be disappointed. "Their intention was good, but their luck was bad," explained the *Prescott Miner*.[75]

King's escape reshuffled the deck in Cochise County. It left unanswered questions and room for rumors to flourish. It marked the real beginning of friction between Wyatt Earp and John Behan. Earp saw in the appointment of Harry Woods as undersheriff a betrayal by Behan, who had promised him the post. He had learned of Woods's appointment only after his return to Tombstone, and the escape of King added suspicions to resentment. To make matters worse, Behan refused to pay Virgil and Morgan for their part in the pursuit of the outlaws.

Virgil later described what happened:

> Behan brought in a bill against the county for $796.84. We supposed it was to pay expenses for the whole party, but he rendered it as a private account. I went before the Board of Supervisors and they said Behan must vouch for us. This he refused to do, saying he had not deputized us. Everybody but myself and my brothers were paid, and we did not get a cent until Wells Fargo found it out and paid us for our time. From that time our troubles commenced.[76]

Behan had played his hand, and now anything he could use to justify his decision not to make Wyatt undersheriff would benefit him. Furthermore, Milt Joyce was no longer just Behan's friend; he was also a member of the Cochise County Board of Supervisors, nursing a grudge against Doc Holliday and supporting Behan's decisions. Joyce may well have been one of those most closely involved in promoting the rumors about Doc's involvement in the Drew's Station attack. He had both motive and means, as the next few weeks amply demonstrated. The rumors did persist, and there were those in town willing to feed them, either because of their distaste for Holliday himself or because the gossip hurt the Earps. Wyatt was not a politician, and he was more or less blindsided by this combination of events.

If Wyatt Earp was the real target of the rumors and had the most to lose politically, the man left most vulnerable by these developments was Doc Holliday. At the very least, Doc had a bull's-eye painted on his chest, and everybody in Tombstone knew it. He was not a popular man to begin with. His relationship with Leonard was well known, and many people—even some close to the Earps—were prepared to believe the worst. And Doc had a nasty way of giving people additional reasons to dislike him. As Wyatt Earp later wrote, "He was his own worst enemy."[77]

As if to prove the point, on April 13, 1881, Doc found himself again in Justice A. O. Wallace's court facing charges of "threats against life." Apparently, the incident arose from accusations linking him to the Benson robbery attempt and Philpott's murder. One story that made the rounds later was that Doc had threatened anyone who accused him of complicity in the robbery attempt, declaring, "If I had pulled that job, I'd have got the $80,000. . . . Whoever shot Philpot was a rank amateur. If he had downed a horse, he'd have got the bullion." The most reliable account claimed that the arrest came after yet another altercation between Doc and Milt Joyce. In this version, Joyce saw Holliday come into the Oriental and remarked, "Well, here comes the stage robber." Doc, in turn, explained to Joyce what he intended to do to him, but before trouble could happen, Sheriff Behan arrested both men. Joyce then swore out the warrant for "threats against life" that took Holliday back to Wallace's court on April 13.[78]

Earlier in April, Bat Masterson had received an urgent message from his brother in Dodge City, and on April 16 he climbed down from the eastbound Santa Fe passenger train at Dodge and into a gunfight, known afterward as the battle of the Plaza. Bat's return was not welcome under the circumstances, and he did not linger in Dodge, but he did not return to Tombstone. In May, the charges against Luke Short for the killing of Charlie Storms were dismissed, and Short soon departed Tombstone as well. William H. Harris followed Masterson and Short, and he was soon back in business with Chalk Beeson at the Long Branch Saloon in Dodge City. Rickabaugh and Clark were left without a partner or a protector, and it was probably at this time, rather than earlier, as most accounts have assumed, that the partners offered a one-quarter interest in the Oriental game room to Wyatt Earp, much to the chagrin of Milt Joyce.[79]

Johnny Tyler was still in town at that point, for the *Tucson Citizen* reported him involved in the highest-stakes game in the history of the camp with Dick Clark, John Marshall Nichols (known locally as "Napa Nick" or "Judge Nichols," a faro dealer at the Crystal Palace), and a man named Billy Frees.[80]

Doc still could not free himself from the past or his nemesis, Milt Joyce. On May 30, the *Epitaph* announced, "Doc Holliday has been indicted by the Grand Jury on account of participation in a shooting affray some time since. He was released on bonds."[81] The charges did not derive from the Benson stage robbery attempt, but from his fight with Milt Joyce the previous fall. Though the case had been dismissed in Justice Wallace's court, Joyce had pressed the matter with his friend Sheriff Behan, and with his clout as a county supervisor, he was able to get the indictment.

Curiously, the charge against Holliday was listed simply as "Indictment for Felony." The original warrant was sworn out under the case title *Territory of Arizona v. Doc Holliday*. When he first appeared before Judge William H. Stilwell on June 2, he was asked if Doc Holliday was his true name. He replied that his name was "J. H. Holliday," and the judge ordered that the indictment be amended. On June 3, Doc's attorney, A. G. P. George, asked the court to dismiss the case "on the ground that it was found by a Grand Jury illegally impaneled." The motion was denied. In an unrelated case, the firm of Goodrich and Goodrich also unsuccessfully protested against "irregularities in empaneling the Grand Jury" without better success with Judge Stilwell. On June 4, George asked for a "demurrer to the indictment and a change of venue," but Stilwell scheduled the trial for June 6. On June 7, the case was continued until October 6, 1881.[82]

Strangely, Joyce's grudge, the gamblers' feud, and the unresolved issue of the robbery attempt and murders near Drew's Station now melded together in a most unusual way. First, Wyatt Earp had apparently spent considerable time and energy simmering over Behan's betrayal, and at some point he made the decision to challenge Behan for the office of sheriff in the next election. He also still had a burr under his saddle about the escape of King and the failure to catch Leonard, Head, and Crane, which he saw as a viable issue to use against Behan. If he could find the fugitives and bring them in, he could solve the crime, greatly enhance his chances of winning the election, and stop the persistent rumors about Holliday's involvement.

Early in June, Earp approached Ike Clanton, the Cow-Boy leader, with a proposal. As Wyatt explained it later:

> I had an ambition to be Sheriff of this County at the next election, and I thought it would be a great help to me with the people and businessmen if I could capture the men who killed Philpot. There were rewards offered of about $1,200 each for the capture of the

robbers. Altogether there was about $3,600 offered for their capture. I thought this sum might tempt Ike Clanton and Frank McLaury to give away Leonard, Head, and Crane, so I went to Ike Clanton, Frank McLaury, and Joe Hill when they came to town. I had an interview with them in the back yard of the Oriental Saloon. I told them what I wanted. I told them I wanted the glory of capturing Leonard, Head, and Crane and if I could do it, it would help me make the race for Sheriff at the next election. I told them if they would put me on the track of Leonard, Head, and Crane, and tell me where those men were hid, I would give them all the reward and would never let anyone know where I got the information.[83]

Earp was shrewd enough to know that men like the Clantons and the McLaurys, who were engaged mostly in rustling and fencing Mexican cattle, had no particular use for stage robbers and murderers. In fact, such men drew attention to operations that otherwise were largely ignored and even tolerated for economic reasons. Before making a bargain, though, Clanton had concerns. He told Wyatt that the trio would make a fight, so he had to know if the reward would be paid dead or alive. Earp promised he would find out. Without revealing anything about his negotiations with Clanton, Wyatt had Marshall Williams wire Wells, Fargo headquarters, and on June 7, Williams received the following response: "San Francisco, June 7, 1881. Received at [blank] June 7, 1881, 4 o'clock P.M., To Marshall Williams. Yes we will pay rewards for them dead or alive. L. F. Rowell."[84]

Though almost obsessive about secrecy in his negotiations with Wyatt, Clanton also approached Virgil Earp about the deal. Virgil, who apparently was not aware of Wyatt's negotiations and not particularly happy about them once he found out, asked Clanton why he did not just capture or kill the trio himself. "Jesus Christ!" Clanton responded. "I would not last longer than a snowball in hell if I did that. . . . The rest of the gang would think we killed them for the reward and they would kill us."[85]

In all, Wyatt had four or five conversations with Clanton, McLaury, and Hill, trying to reassure them of his commitment to absolute secrecy. Wyatt added one more thing for emphasis, "I told Ike Clanton in one of those conversations that there were some parties here in town that were trying to give Doc Holliday the worst of it by their talk, that there was some suspicion that he knew something about the

Joseph Isaac "Ike" Clanton's deal with Wyatt Earp to betray the Benson stage robbers created secrets that would eventually lead to trouble between the Clantons and their friends, on the one hand, and the Earps and Doc Holliday, on the other.

attempted robbery and killing of Bud Philpot, and if I could catch Leonard, Head, and Crane, I could prove to the citizens that he knew nothing about it."[86]

Eventually, Clanton's fears seemed sufficiently allayed that Joe Hill left Tombstone to put the plan into motion. He returned ten days later and announced that he had arrived too late; Leonard and Head had been killed the day before he arrived. On June 10, Leonard and Head were shot by Ike and Bill Haslett near the New Mexico line after the Hasletts had been warned that Leonard and Head had threatened to kill them on sight to gain control of their ranch. Leonard still had "two big holes in his belly" from the robbery attempt and begged to be put out of his misery after the confrontation with the Hasletts. Both Leonard and Head soon died. A short time later, Crane and fifteen to twenty Cow-Boys caught the Hasletts and an immigrant named Sigmund Biertzhoff in a saloon and riddled them with bullets.[87]

The deaths of Leonard and Head short-circuited Wyatt Earp's plan and deprived Ike and his friends of any possibility of rewards. What was left was a potentially deadly secret between them, and the summary vengeance by the Cow-Boys against the Hasletts gave Ike Clanton legitimate reason to fear what would happen if the secret ever came out. Finally, the deaths of Leonard and Head reduced the chances of being able to exonerate Doc of the suspicions against him. Virgil's concerns turned out to be justified and potentially troublesome for him as well.

The town fathers were not entirely happy with Marshal Ben Sippy, so when he asked for a two-week leave of absence on June 6, it was granted. Virgil became acting city marshal in his place. He immediately impressed locals with his attention to duty and his even-handedness. On June 9, Ike Clanton got into a quarrel with Denny McCann (also known as Daniel Burns), a gambler known to be friends with the Earps, in a saloon on Allen Street. McCann slapped Clanton, after which both men left to get their guns. They met again outside the Wells, Fargo office prepared for gunplay, when Virgil and Constable Hugh Haggerty "stepped between them and spoiled a good item," as the *Epitaph* put it.[88]

While Wyatt Earp's plot with Ike Clanton was unraveling, on June 19 the press reported, "There was a little triangular matinee between a couple of gamblers and another party Sunday morning, which had one time threatened a good sized item, but it fortunately ended without bloodshed." It was a discreet but tantalizing notice, especially since Virgil Earp arrested Wyatt and hauled him into Recorder's Court before Judge Wallace and charged him "with disturbing the peace and fighting in violation of an ordinance." Wallace fined him $20 and discharged him.[89]

The details of the "little triangular matinee" escaped direct documentation, but circumstances suggest that this may have been the occasion of Johnny Tyler's final attempt to cause trouble at the Oriental. Rickabaugh had just opened his new club rooms above the saloon on June 11. Milt Joyce was arrested on that very day by officer James Coyle for "fighting" and paid court costs in Wallace's court. Wyatt would say later that Tyler was "sent to hoorah [the] place," but he never said by whom, and no reliable account of what followed has been located. Earp's biographer Stuart N. Lake claimed that Tyler brought "a dozen followers" to disrupt play at the Oriental. According to him, Tyler braced Rickabaugh at his own faro table. That was bold enough in itself, for Rickabaugh had a reputation as a fighter. Still, according to the story, Tyler laid his money on the queen and coolly told the big man that if he did not win his bet, he would blow away the chips. Unperturbed, Rickabaugh drew the card from the box. It was not a queen.

Before Tyler could make good his threat, he was dragged from his seat as Wyatt Earp seized his earlobe between his thumb and index finger. Tyler had not been aware of Earp's presence, and when he realized who had him, he protested that he did not know that Earp had an interest in the Oriental. According to Lake, Wyatt assured him that he did and told him to tell his friends that it was the "fighting interest," after which he propelled Tyler out of the saloon into Allen Street. Holliday was on hand that evening to keep Tyler's friends from stepping in. He covered them with his six-gun and greatly enjoyed Wyatt's humiliating dispatch of his foe with appropriate commentary.[90]

If this, or some less melodramatic incident involving Tyler, was indeed the affair for which Earp was arrested in June, the expulsion of Tyler was rendered anticlimactic when, on June 22, the Oriental burned to the ground in a disastrous fire that leveled several blocks of downtown Tombstone. Joyce desperately tried to rescue $1,200 from his safe, but he was driven out by the flames. Afterward, he decided to get out of the saloon business and transferred his interest in the Oriental to Rickabaugh and his partners. It was weeks, though, before the Oriental was able to reopen under new management. By then, the gamblers' war was effectively over, and Johnny Tyler was in Leadville, Colorado.[91]

Milt Joyce now turned his attention primarily to politics as chairman of the Cochise County Board of Supervisors. At the time, Cochise County law allowed county officials to keep a percentage of local taxes for themselves. Though not uncommon, this practice was not popular. "Much dissatisfaction is manifested at the high rate of taxation decreed by the County Supervisors—$2.83 on $100—and at their course in allowing the Sheriff 10 per cent for collecting it, a percentage whose exorbitance is without a precedent," wrote Clara Brown. With Harry Woods as undersheriff as well as editor of the *Nugget*, it was no surprise that the *Nugget* supported the county government. Nor was it surprising that the Republican *Epitaph*, edited by Mayor John P. Clum, attacked Joyce as the leader of the "Ten-percent Ring," while suggesting that Behan was so preoccupied with collecting taxes that law enforcement was practically an afterthought.[92]

In the meantime, Virgil Earp was continuing to prove himself to be a capable officer. During the fire that destroyed downtown Tombstone, Virgil won praise for using his police force to support the fire-fighting effort and afterward mobilizing a large special police force to protect property, prevent looting, and displace lot jumpers who had squatted on choice lots in the burned-out district. His prompt and firm action was approved by businessmen and the leaders of the Citizens Safety Committee. It was no surprise then, that on June 28, when it was clear that Sippy was not coming back, Virgil was appointed marshal permanently. On July 4, 1881, he was officially sworn in.[93]

Joyce's political clout was about to strike closer to the Earps and Holliday than tax use, however. Kate came back to Tombstone for another visit in June and lost little time catching up on local gossip. Arguments with Doc followed, with all the old issues rehashed once again, and Kate began to drink heavily. In this vulnerable state, she encountered John Behan, and possibly Milt Joyce, who sympathized with her and baited her until she signed an affidavit accusing Doc of complicity in the attempted stage robbery and murders of Bud Philpott and Peter Roerig.[94]

On July 5, 1881, Sheriff Behan arrested Doc Holliday. Charges were brought against him both for attempting to rob the U.S. mail and for the murder of Bud Philpott. Holliday was taken before Justice Wells Spicer and released on a bond of $5,000 guaranteed by Wyatt and Doc's employers, John Meagher and J. L. Melgren. A hearing was set for nine o'clock on the morning of July 9.[95] Later on the afternoon of July 5, Virgil Earp arrested Kate for being drunk and disorderly. Apparently, her binge was not over, and Virgil kept her in jail overnight. The next morning she was fined $12.50 and released. The *Nugget* observed, "Miss Kate Elder sought surcease of sorrow in the flowing bowl. She succeeded so well that when she woke up she found herself on the Chief's register with two 'Ds' appended to it. She paid her matriculation fee of $12.50 and departed."[96]

Her education was not yet completed. Sober, but still angry, she directed her ire at someone (the record is silent on whom, although several were properly in her sights) with sufficient fervor that she was arrested again, this time for "threats against life." In Judge Andrew J. Felter's court, she was pronounced guilty, but she promptly hired Wells Spicer and appealed her case to the commissioner of the first judicial district, T. J. Drum, who granted her a writ of habeas corpus and discharged her. Said the *Nugget*, "Such is the result of a warrant sworn out by an enraged and intoxicated woman."[97]

Kate always claimed (and it seems logical) that during her quadrille with Tombstone's judiciary, the Earps pressured her to change her story. In fact, Kate's version of affairs had a more deeply sinister hue that revealed even decades later an almost pathological hatred of the Earps. Her affidavit of accusations against Doc was not the result of intoxication, she said, but of her desire to get Doc away from the Earps. She blamed what happened on them and explained the situation this way:

> I became desperate and in a vain hope of breaking up their association with Doc, whom I loved, I swore out a warrant charging him with the murder of Philpott and Roegrig [sic] and he was arrested by Sheriff Behan. But Wyatt Earp and others of his gang of legalized outlaws furnished $5,000 bail to get him out. It took all of the persecution of the Earps and other law officers aligned with them to make me quit. In doing it I had known I was taking a desperate chance, and I was not astonished when I lost out.[98]

Kate never explained how accusing Doc of robbery and murder was going to help him. Nevertheless, she claimed that Behan took her to Spicer and that he interrogated her at length about the complicity of the Earps in the robbery attempt and grew impatient with her when she did not provide specific details. She also claimed that Virgil locked her in a room at the Cosmopolitan Hotel and pressured her to recant her story. "Of course," she said, "I am not positive about the hold-ups. . . . But although I have no positive knowledge of the Earps and Doc having held up those stages between Hereford, Charleston, and Bisbee, I do know that they went often at night to those places. And now and then Doc dropped significant remarks that had me worried."[99]

In yet another version of her story, Kate was more specific. "All I know is how Doc acted that afternoon before the stage was held up," she wrote to Anton Mazzanovich. She explained that Doc came to their room and quickly changed clothes. When she asked why he was in such a hurry, he said he had business and would not be able to take her to supper. Later, Warren Earp came to her door with a note from Doc, asking her to send his rifle to him by Warren. Warren told her he did not know why Doc needed the rifle. She said, "Doc did not come home until late that night. He did not bring his rifle back. It was four or five days after the holdup that he brought the rifle back. I thought that after the holdup things looked very suspicious about the Earps and Doc. Something tells me that Doc was in with Wyatt, Virgil, and Morgan in that affair."[100]

According to Kate, the most substantial evidence she had of wrong-doing came from Mattie Earp, Wyatt's second wife, several years later when she told Kate that the Earp women believed their husbands were involved in illegal activities. Kate also alleged that Wyatt had once shown her masks made of rope similar to those found at the scene of the crime. She would claim that after she was released, Napa Nick invited her to take a buggy ride with him. She declined, she said, and was told later by Mattie that the gambler had been hired by the Earps to kill her.[101]

In yet another account, however, Kate did not even mention her role in Doc's arrest. She recalled being in Tombstone at the time of the robbery attempt, with no reference to the events of July. She even appeared surprised at the allegations:

> Now, after all these years I see it in print that it was the Earps and Doc Holliday [who attempted to rob the stage and killed Philpott and Roerig] and that Doc Holliday was the one that killed Bud Philpot [*sic*]. Although Doc did not come to his room until late that night that does not mean that the Earps and Holliday were in that hold-up. There were plenty of people in Tombstone who knew where the Earps and Holliday were that night. There was no arrest made. Nothing was done about it. There could not be.[102]

The great difficulty with these statements is that they are all recollections written by a woman anxious to protect her own reputation. They consist primarily of speculations and suspicions and are short on facts. Unfortunately, her sworn affidavit accusing Doc of complicity in the affair has not been found, so the question of exactly what she said at the time remains unanswered.

Nevertheless, the case was handed to Lyttleton Price for prosecution. Price investigated the charges, and at ten o'clock on the morning of July 9 Doc appeared before Justice Spicer:

> The District Attorney, addressing the court, said that he had examined all of the witnesses summoned for the prosecution and from their statements he was satisfied that there was not the slightest evidence to show the guilt of the defendant; that the statements of the witnesses did not even amount to a suspicion of the guilt of the defendant, and he was therefore asking that the complaint be withdrawn and the case be dismissed.

Spicer dismissed the case, and "thus ended what, at one time, was supposed to be an important case."[103]

Doc's innocence could hardly have been stated more emphatically. And yet, the *Nugget*'s assessment of the outcome was not completely accurate. Doc was free of legal jeopardy but not of suspicion. If anything, suspicions had increased among those looking for reasons to be suspicious. Doc's friendship with the fragile, flawed, addicted, consumptive Bill Leonard first aroused suspicions, but Kate's charges spawned a whole new set of speculations that extended beyond Doc to the Earps themselves.

Some were already raising questions about the Wells, Fargo agent Marshall Williams's ties to the stage robbers; he may have been the person referred to in the earlier report that "it is certain that several men around Tombstone, among them one who was a participant in the preliminary pursuit, are under surveillance." And in the minds of others predisposed to believe the worst anyway, the possibility of a conspiracy involving the Earps now seemed plausible, or at least politically useful. Once the public accusation had been made against Holliday, however implausible it was, a few nurtured and exploited the notion of the Earps' involvement. As Wyatt recalled years later, "I was Holliday's friend and they tried to injure me every way they could."[104]

Unfortunately, Holliday never made a public statement on the issue or left a clear presentation of his version of what happened. Even some of the Earps' friends who did not care for Doc had lingering questions. For the moment, though, the feelings were largely unspoken or at most whispered. Still, Virgil knew what Wyatt would not admit: Doc Holliday had become a liability to the Earps. Ironically, the whole affair revolved around loyalty: Doc's loyalty to Bill Leonard and Wyatt's loyalty to Doc. The truth of what happened may have escaped the recovery of history, but no credible evidence ever linked Doc Holliday to the attempted robbery.

Wyatt Earp made perhaps the most telling observation when he told Walter Noble Burns that "Doc was not in on the Benson stage hold up." Wyatt emphasized that Holliday "never did such a thing as holdups in his life."[105] Wyatt understood Doc's character. Doc lived on the edge. He was guilty of many things. He was quick-tempered when he drank and had a penchant for getting himself into trouble. He did not always choose his friends well, but nothing in his life before or after the Benson stage robbery attempt indicated that he was the type of man who would participate in the kind of affair that happened on the Benson road.

Still, Doc may well have known more than he said. Frederick Bechdolt would later write, after speaking with Earp, "He does not try to exonerate Holliday from knowledge of the robbery, although he makes a show of claiming Holliday was entirely innocent of knowledge."[106] If, as Wyatt believed, Doc visited Leonard that day in March, Doc may have learned of his friend's intent. Perhaps that was why he made a point of riding back to Tombstone in the company of Old Man Fuller or why he offered Bob Paul a drink of whiskey at Watervale—to make sure that he had an alibi. He kept quiet out of loyalty to one friend and created troubles for another, better one. However, riding with Old Man Fuller and offering Bob Paul a drink of whiskey could as easily be explained by his Southern breeding (which emphasized both conviviality and congeniality) and need not imply either an attempt to build an alibi or something more sinister as suggested by Breakenridge.

Kate's account of Doc being called out late at night and returning to sit on the bed saying, "The damned fool. I did not think that of him," almost certainly applied to Leonard. After all, the names of the suspects in the case were not publicly announced until after Wyatt Earp returned to Tombstone from the chase, and Doc's alleged comment, "Well, I don't know what I am going to stack up against today. I am getting tired of it all," was appropriate to his realization that his friendship with Leonard would raise questions and make him a suspect.

Now, in July 1881, a thicket of rumor and suspicion encircled the Earps on Doc's account, and Wyatt found himself with his own potentially explosive secret growing out of the scheme with men he could not trust and who could be depended on to do whatever it took to save their own hides. For the moment, though, the troubles were largely hidden from view. No public accusations were made against the Earps, and, in fact, they continued to enjoy the confidence and support of Tombstone's citizenry, especially the business elite. Stuart Lake said that Doc offered to leave town, but that Wyatt told him all that he asked was that Doc send "that woman" away. Both are plausible. After his recent experiences, Doc did not need much encouragement concerning Kate. She was soon on her way back to Globe.[107] Ike Clanton and his friends could not be sent away, however, and they were the greater threat.

FRIENDS AND ENEMIES

[H]ere is a man who, once a friend, is always a friend; once an enemy, is always an enemy.

—*Gunnison Daily News–Democrat*, June 18, 1882

At midsummer of 1881, John Henry Holliday found himself with an unenviable notoriety in Tombstone. Although he had been legally cleared of charges relating to the Benson stage robbery attempt and the murders of Bud Philpott and Peter Roerig, suspicions remained. For many people, including some of Wyatt Earp's friends and supporters, Doc represented what was wrong with Tombstone. "Yes. 'Doc [Holliday] was a tough citizen and a bad egg,' and I was fully aware of the situation between Doc and Wyatt," Fred Dodge would recall later. "Doc never played square with anyone in that country."[1] Dodge would always believe that Doc was involved in the stage robbery attempt at Drew's Station, whatever the district attorney and judge had said, and he was not alone. Wyatt Earp, though, stood by his friend.

Doc was experiencing something he had not known before. He had had his troubles in the past, but he had been, at most, a peripheral figure in the public life of other towns. Now, when the dapper, well-dressed young man walked down Fremont or Allen Street or took his chair at the faro bank in the Alhambra, people looked at him with a combination of fear and deference. For the first time, too, he had an avowed enemy—a nemesis—in the person of Milton E. Joyce. With all of this came a grudging respect for a dangerous adversary. Though generally quiet and restrained, he could be quick-tempered and vocal, especially when drinking. Though usually unassuming, he had a sense of honor that at times smacked more of inferiority complex than principle. Whatever it was, when it was violated, he was not afraid to seek redress of grievances at the point of a gun.

He was healthier and stronger than he had been in years. No doubt, he was visiting Dr. Glendy King's hot springs, and the general climate of southern Arizona benefitted him, as he had hoped, even with his long hours in smoky saloons and gambling halls. He was reported to have regained some of his sense of humor, and, although it seems unlikely, the story was told that "if any stranger entered Tombstone wearing a post hat he would follow him round the street ringing a dinner bell."[2] He was robust enough to ride with the Earps and from time to time joined posses and other expeditions. He was associated in the public mind with the Earps, but, in truth, he was never Wyatt Earp's lackey as legend would later portray him. Had he been, he would have caused Earp less trouble. The most troubling thing was that Doc remained under bond on the charges brought against him by Joyce awaiting disposition by the courts.

Not everyone in Tombstone saw him as a bad man. In 1881, young Billy Hattich, along with his mother and two sisters, moved to Tombstone to join his father, Bartholomew Hattich, who owned a tailor's shop at 528 Allen Street. Doc, always the dapper dresser, was a customer. Doc took an interest in young Billy and used him to run errands for him. Doc paid the boy fifty cents to a dollar for carrying notes to other people. Billy liked Doc. Hattich said that Doc was friendly, generous, soft-spoken, and a favorite among the town's kids because he always carried candy in his pocket.[3]

In spite of everything, John Henry was still his own man, still living by a code that dictated his responses, though modified by the less genteel environment of his Western life. Even his outbursts confirmed that he was his father's son, jealous of his reputation and quick to brace anyone who impugned it. It was more than his record as a gunfighter that caused men to respect and fear him. They knew that he would not hesitate at flash point, which made him a dangerous adversary and a dependable ally. For much of the summer of 1881, though, he had little role to play in the unfolding drama of Cochise County beyond that of professional gambler and local character. His movements from mid-July until October were not recorded with any dependability, but he was reportedly out of town through much of that time. Most likely, he simply tried to escape the heat, perhaps following the gamblers' circuit as far away as Prescott to find more congenial climes or journeying to Globe to see Kate as she later insisted he did. Later on, however, some would claim darker explanations of his movements. And all of those started with the men known as Cow-Boys.

Doc had known men like them since his days in Texas. They were not merely cattle drovers, or cowboys, in the ordinary usage of the terms, although they shared characteristics with them. The favored press usage, "Cow-Boys," suggested more than profession; it designated a harder, restless, free-wheeling, lawless lot. Most of them arrived on the heels of the silver boom, many already on the run from other parts of the West and drawn to both the boom phenomenon and the relative isolation that southern Arizona afforded. They were what Virgil Earp called "saddlers," men with no homes save their saddles, no loyalties except to themselves and one another.[4] A Galeyville hotel owner, who came to know many of the Cow-Boys, provided an insightful portrait of them:

> They are wild, reckless men from all over the world. They do not claim a home, a business or close affiliation with civilization. Some are miners from Colorado and the Black Hills, others are escaped criminals and refugees from all parts of the world. Some are mere reckless adventurers who have followed the line of new railroads since the first rail was laid from the Missouri River or in the Sacramento Valley. They do not work, and they are never without money. They live in a style that you city folks would despise no doubt, but still they are never actually without food, a good horse, arms, ammunition and blankets. They are not all brave, and often sneak away from danger, but in my twenty years' intercourse with them I never knew one of them to whine and squeal when he knew he had to die.[5]

John Henry could admire that attitude and see in those hard men reminders of the free grazers of his native Georgia. Some of them even had a kind of honor that a man like Doc could appreciate. In the beginning, the Cow-Boys were of little concern to John Henry, except when they sat across the table from him at faro, monte, or poker. Virgil explained why:

> As soon as they are in funds they ride into town, drink, gamble, and fight. They spread their money as free as water in the saloons,

John Henry Holliday, in a photograph believed to
have been taken at Tombstone. This photograph was
first published by Bat Masterson in his *Human Life*
series, "Famous Gunfighters of the Western Frontier."
It was also identified as Doc by both Kate Harony and
Josephine Earp. Still, despite this strong provenance
by people who knew him, some recent studies have
questioned whether it is he.

dancehouses, and faro banks, and this is one reason they have so
many friends in town. All that large class of degraded characters who
gather the crumbs of such carouses stand ready to assist them out
of any trouble or into any paying rascality. The saloons and gambling houses into whose treasuries most of the money is ultimately
turned receive them cordially and must be called warm friends of the
cowboys.[6]

For a man like Doc, then, there was no inherent animosity. The
Cow-Boys helped pay his bills and provide the standard of living he
sought. And he was not one to judge the source of the coin and green-
backs that filled his coffers. Doc even claimed to have known some of
them in Texas before coming to Arizona. As Tombstone grew and more
of the Cow-Boys frequented the town, however, they were increasingly
the subject of news reports and editorial commentary. Both in terms of
local incidents and as a larger territorial problem, they concerned public officials, community and territorial leaders, and the law enforcement agencies from top to bottom.[7] Of themselves, such matters
might have been little more than curiosities to Doc, but for the Earps,
as law enforcement officers and agents for the express and mining
companies, the behavior of the Cow-Boys was another matter. It was
this simple connection that drew John Henry into the controversy.

The Cow-Boy problem evolved over time, although it had already
attracted attention before Tombstone and its satellite towns sprang up

in southeastern Arizona. Along the border with Mexico from El Paso to Yuma, smuggling and international theft had been a problem for years, and, in fact, the practice of stealing Mexican cattle for sale in the United States to fulfill government beef contracts and swell the herds of Southwestern ranchers was tolerated, even encouraged. It was a clandestine practice, largely out of the public eye so long as the border regions were thinly populated. The development of mining towns like Tombstone changed that, first, by increasing demand for beef, and, second, by inevitably making the illegal activities more visible. The problem developed "on account of the tide of miners flooding in, thus creating demand for Mexican goods," as Special Agent R. M. Moore of the U.S. Customs Service put it. The increased volume of illegal cattle and other smuggled goods also swelled the volume of Mexican protests in official circles as well as the raw numbers and boldness of the Cow-Boys. By the end of 1879, the border problem was increasingly the subject of both diplomatic discourse and editorial commentary in the territory's newspapers.[8]

Some of the Cow-Boys had arrived relatively early and owned ranches in the area. Newman Haynes "Old Man" Clanton and his sons, Phineas (called Fin), Ike, and Billy, moved into southern Arizona in the mid-1870s. Locating near Fort Bowie, they enjoyed a mixed reputation almost from the beginning, as both reputable settlers and as parasites looking to profit from government contracts. Old Man Clanton counted Henry Hooker, the Sierra Bonita rancher, and John P. Clum, then still the Indian agent at San Carlos, as friends. Of the Clantons, Ike was the most troublesome, because he was quick-tempered and boastful. He was prone to run with a rowdy crowd, but Old Man Clanton generally kept him in check. In 1877, the Clantons settled at Lewis Springs below Charleston and constructed a fortlike adobe atop a hill. When the Tombstone boom occurred, Ike even ran a restaurant in town for a time. But they were mainly stockmen. Curiously, though, the Clantons did not have a registered brand in Pima or, later, Cochise counties.[9]

Robert Findley "Frank" McLaury and Thomas Clark McLaury came to Arizona from Iowa by way of Texas. They appear to have been in Arizona as early as 1877, although there was a report that they worked for John Chisum in New Mexico for a time. They were clearly in southeastern Arizona in 1878 and employed on Walter Vail's Empire

Ranch. By the time silver was found at Goose Flats, and before Tombstone boomed, the McLaury brothers had laid claim to a stretch of
prime grazing land west of Tombstone between the Babacomari and the
San Pedro rivers. Later, they sold these lands to John Slaughter and settled at Soldier's Hole in the Sulphur Springs Valley east of Tombstone.[10]

In the beginning, at least, both the Clantons and the McLaurys
were regarded as respectable ranchers by some of the area's citizens.
William M. Breakenridge, no friend of the Earps, would state flatly in
his memoir that "the Clantons looked after the rustlers' interests on
the San Pedro," while "the McLaurys looked after the stock brought
up through Mexico through Agua Prieta, where Douglass now stands,
into the Sulphur Spring[s] Valley."[11] And John H. Behan, Cochise
County's sheriff who would be charged with collusion with them, said,
"The Clanton brothers and McLowrys [sic] were a tough lot of rustlers,
who were the main perpetrators of that rascality rife in that region."[12]

Other men, like Joe Hill and Frank Patterson, ran small operations. Together, these men controlled lands in the San Pedro near
Tombstone, the Sulphur Springs Valley, Rustler's Park in the Dragoon
Mountains, and east to Galeyville and the Animas Valley in New Mexico, and south into Mexico. With government contracts to be gar-
nered and big ranchers like Walter Vail and Henry Hooker in the
market for cattle, slipping into Mexico was easy enough. Buyers in the
settlements asked few questions, and stealing Mexican cattle enjoyed a
semirespectable position in the economy of the region.

Special Agent Moore explained that "[a]s matters now are, Cattle
men drive large droves of cattle from Mexico on to their ranches and
report what number they please at the Customs House in Tucson, and
from what I can learn I am of the opinion that not over 25% of the
duties have heretofore been collected upon cattle."[13] The process was
simple enough, according to a friend of the Cow-Boys: "Whenever a
man wants a herd of cattle and contacts any of the leading spirits
among them that he wants a bunch of stock, and a price is agreed
upon, the cattle are forthcoming."[14]

Most of the ranchers in the area ventured south less and less as the
freebooters moved in. These more desperate types were often fugitives from other territories and states and sometimes added stolen cattle from New Mexico and as far away as Texas to their stock. Robert
Martin and his gang, numbering more than a hundred, arrived early.

By the time of Martin's demise in December 1880, the numbers had swelled, creating the appearance of organized gangs, when in fact most were independent operators, loosely linked by a common cause. "The 'cowboys' have no chief, nor do they run in gangs as is generally supposed," explained a local. "No sir, the 'cowboys' don't band together in droves but come and go about their own personal business whenever they desire to go."[15]

The prototype of this sort was John Ringo. Born in Iowa, Ringo had traveled with his family to California as a child, witnessing along the way the accidental self-inflicted fatal shooting of his father. Already troubled as a young man, Ringo went to Texas, where he acquired a reputation as a desperate man and a man killer before he moved on to Arizona in 1879. There, he shot a man named Louis Hancock in the neck for refusing to take a drink with him. In July 1880, he, Ike Clanton, and several others were involved in another violent spree at Safford. He was a morose, brooding man and a heavy drinker. He appears to have been well read and well mannered, which helped to spawn the story that he was well educated. Even in his own time, he was romanticized by some who knew him, but he was still feared as a dangerous loner.[16]

Ringo and Curly Bill Brocius were perceived as Cow-Boy leaders, probably based on their frequent escapades in the mining camps, but together with men like Pony Deal, Zwing Hunt, Hank Swilling, Johnny Barnes, Milt Hicks, Bill Hicks, "Rattlesnake Bill" Johnson, Florentino Cruz, Jake Gauze, Jim Hughes, Charlie Snow, Alex Arnett, Bud Snow, Charlie Green, Tall Bell, Charlie Thomas, Jim Crane, Luther King, Harry Head, and dozens—perhaps scores—more, they formed a loose league of rustlers and thieves that was often perceived to be an organized gang. Their links to the McLaurys, the Clantons, Joe Hill, Frank Patterson, and other ranchers did not go unnoticed, which first roused suspicions that the ranchers were part of the Cow-Boy scourge, as well.

Richard Rule, a capable journalist employed for a time by the *Tombstone Nugget*, would summarize the situation neatly:

> There is no doubt that most of the cattle sold in the vicinity of Tombstone—more in the vicinity than in the town itself—during the past two years have been stolen. It is a current saying that all a man needs there is a band of fifty cattle to draw to, and he can come out

with as many as he wants. It is necessary, though, that he have a small band to start with. A good many of the cowboys have ranches and live in the guise of simple cattle farmers. Those who make a business of stealing horses and cattle [a]re wild reckless fellows, but in their business with the men of Tombstone have a pretty good reputation. They pay their bills, and with the balance of their money are very liberal, and that of course brings them many friends of one class.[17]

For a time, then, the Cow-Boys enjoyed a kind of immunity from the law as authorities "looked the other way" and businessmen in the camps operated as witting and unwitting partners. Not everyone was so tolerant, however. As early as January 1879, protests were being registered with Governor John Charles Frémont at Prescott about Cow-Boy depredations, and by April 1880 U.S. Customs Agent Moore was reporting that over the previous two years "not less than 8000 or 9000 head of beef cattle that paid no duties" had been driven up the San Simon Valley out of Sonora. Moore noted in particular Walter Vail's "crooked transactions," which consisted primarily of purchasing illegal cattle.[18]

Not all cattlemen were pleased with the situation. T. W. Ayles complained that "[h]onest dealers in stock must either have protection or join the band of robbers and their accessories, the purchasers and hiders."[19] And following the disturbance near Safford involving Ike Clanton, Joe Hill, and John Ringo, the mill supervisor Jerome B. Collins said of the Cow-Boys, "It will be God's blessing for this valley to get rid of them."[20] That would be easier said than done, and, over time, the Cow-Boys would prove problematic even to their associates among the ranchers, who acted as the primary middlemen between the rustlers and the government contractors, mining camp butchers, and other purchasers of beef. Not only were the Cow-Boys less choosy about whose cattle they stole but also, as the towns grew, they saw opportunity in other forms of criminal activity, including horse thievery and hold-ups.

On May 21, 1880, a stagecoach bound west from Shakespeare, New Mexico, was accosted on the downgrade through Granite Pass nine miles east of San Simon Station. Four men, two on each side of the road, ordered the driver to halt and immediately opened fire. The driver, John Henry, was shot twice in the leg, and Antonio Chaves, who was beside him, was killed. At first fire, the horses broke into a dead run, and Henry managed to reach San Simon Station. It would not be the last such incident in the region.[21]

In August 1880, under the headline THE RUSTLERS, the *Tombstone Epitaph* offered the following report: "Through George Fitzpatrick, recently from New Mexico, we learn of the existence of a gang of cattle and horse thieves, organized near the Arizona line under the above title. The band is comprised principally of young Americans. Several instances have occurred in which they have dismounted parties and taken their horses. So far as heard from, they have not engaged in anything but theft."[22] The Cow-Boys eventually became so brazen that they stopped a freighter using oxen to pull his wagons, stole them, and drove them to San Carlos, where they sold them as beef cattle, "When the contractor remonstrated with the cowboys as they were plundering his train, they told him he must be a d——d fool to team with oxen in Arizona. He ought to use mules."[23]

The extension of criminal activities to stage robbery and horse theft on American soil changed things. For men like Hooker and Vail and even for Old Man Clanton and the McLaurys, the crime associated with the new Cow-Boys was problematic because investigation of these activities drew attention to the practices that had been tolerated in the past and tarred the ranchers with the same brush as hold-up men and horse thieves. Indeed, by the spring of 1881 the U.S. Customs Service was actively investigating, although Agent Moore declared, "It is evident that we have not reached the bottom of all the crooked cattle transactions."[24] Yet, except for the bigger operators like Hooker, ranchers were more or less forced to coexist with the outlaw newcomers because of their own vulnerability to the depredations of the Cow-Boys. The dilemma was illustrated by the episode that first drew the Earps into contact with the Cow-Boys.

It happened before Doc ever reached Tombstone. In July 1880, Lieutenant J. H. Hurst led a squad of four soldiers west from Camp Rucker in search of stolen army mules. At Tombstone, Hurst approached Virgil Earp, a deputy U.S. marshal, and requested his assistance. Virgil, Wyatt, Morgan, and Marshall Williams, the Wells, Fargo agent, joined Hurst's expedition. The McLaurys, Billy Clanton, and Pony Deal were suspects in the case. On July 25, when Hurst's command and Virgil's posse reached the Babacomari ranch of the McLaurys, they caught men red-handedly changing brands on the army mules.

Frank Patterson, who seemed to be in charge, negotiated an arrangement to return the mules if no arrests were made. Hurst agreed and waited for the return of the mules at Charleston.

The mules were not returned as promised, and Patterson, the McLaurys, and Billy Clanton reportedly rode into Charleston and taunted Hurst for his gullibility. In response, the infuriated Hurst posted notices naming Pony Deal, A. T. Hansbrough, and Mac De-Masters (most likely Sherman McMaster, a former Texas Ranger, who had fallen in with the Cow-Boys) as the thieves and also naming the McLaurys and Patterson as accomplices. Frank McLaury reacted angrily, posting a paid notice in the *Tombstone Nugget* denying complicity in any theft and claiming that he had actually tried to find the mules for Hurst. He defended his reputation for honesty and accused Hurst of being the real thief.[25]

McLaury then confronted Virgil Earp and told him in no uncertain terms that if he ever came after them again, he would have to fight. Virgil told McLaury that if warrants were put in his hands, he would have to serve them.[26] Later, Wyatt was named deputy sheriff of Pima County, but apart from occasional actions required by their positions, such as the arrest of Curly Bill and associates on the night Fred White was fatally shot, the Earps had no open conflict with the Cow-Boys or those who dealt with them. Curly Bill, John Ringo, William Claiborne, Pony Deal, and others drew attention for their high jinks at Charleston, Contention, Galeyville, and Shakespeare, with the quarrels, pranks, and gunplay that bemused as well as caused concern, but after White's death, the Cow-Boys generally stayed clear of Tombstone.

In February 1881, the *Tucson Citizen* reported a series of raids that had occurred along the U.S.-Mexican border between October 5, 1880, and January 30, 1881, concluding that

> [t]hese facts show a deplorable state of affairs near the border, where the settlers are completely at the mercy of marauding parties of cowboys destitute of any protection from either the United States or Mexican government. They are liable to lose all their stock at any time, and in fact they consider their present condition as far less secure than in former days when the Indians controlled that part of the county. If the condition of matters continues long, many settlers will be compelled to abandon their homes and seek safety for their lives in the larger settlements.[27]

The *Citizen* demanded strong action, "else citizens may be forced to combine and offer a bounty for cowboy scalps as the people of New Mexico do for those of Indians." The *Citizen's* competitor, the *Tucson Star*, agreed that "the question of how the cow-boys are to be dealt with is assuming greater importance every day" and recommended a striking force of two companies of cavalry to patrol the border.[28] Governor Frémont saw the merit of the plan and requested the creation of a state militia to break up the rustlers and to preserve peace along the border. He later explained, "In view of the increasing lawlessness of the frontier and of the representations made to our Government by Mexico, I asked the Legislature at its last sitting for 700 men to enforce the laws. A bill was introduced for this purpose but passed only one house and left me unprovided with any means to maintain order on our boundaries."[29] The attitude of the territorial legislators toward the plan was best explained by L. Wollenberg, who said that "the raids of the cowboys [are] less detrimental to the territory than would be the proposed raid on our treasury."[30] In the absence of governmental action, the situation on the border worsened.

One Arizona mining man later explained the difficulty of trying to deal with the Cow-Boys:

> The cowboys would be suppressed in short order if they did not have so many friends among people who claim to be respectable and who cannot be reached by the law. Don't think that this friendship is the result of any maudlin sympathy for the cowboys. Not at all. It is business. Tombstone is in Cachise [*sic*] County and in Cachise county are not less than 200 cowboys, mostly cattle thieves. Their headquarters are on the Barbocomari [*sic*] creek and the San Pedro river, where they rendezvous with the stolen cattle which they supply to Tombstone butchers. The cowboys have an alliance with most of the butchers and are also on friendly terms with two or three leading business houses. The butchers like to purchase beef at low rates, and ask no questions, and it is cheaper for some business men to pay the cowboys a tribute than to fight them. This is the situation now because a lot of officials in Cachise county are in with the cattle thieves.[31]

The Cow-Boys were taken more seriously after the attempt to rob the Benson stage at Drew's Station. The *Star* continued its crusade for action on the border. The Cow-Boy problem was underscored again on

May 13, 1881, when Juan Vasquez, a Mexican rancher, and his vaqueros caught up to Cow-Boys who had stolen between four and five hundred cattle from him and had killed four men, including George Turner and Alfred McAllister, the Galeyville butcher, who had shot One-Armed Kelly near the Oriental. Vasquez was also killed in what came to be called the Fronteras massacre.[32]

With rumors rampant of a planned raid to "clean out" Fronteras, these highly visible activities not only increased demands for a solution to the Cow-Boy problem at all levels of government on both sides of the border but also reminded ranchers of the potential costs of being associated with the Cow-Boys. This reality, apart from the hope of financial reward, probably was what tempted Ike Clanton, Frank McLaury, and Joe Hill to consider helping Wyatt Earp when he approached Clanton in June 1881 about William Leonard, Henry Head, and Jim Crane. There was no real love lost between the Clantons and the McLaurys, on the one hand, and the Benson stage robbers, on the other. Still, the Clantons and the McLaurys were in bed with the Cow-Boys, and there was danger in crossing their associates, as Cow-Boy revenge against the Haslett brothers for the killings of Leonard and Head proved. The Clantons and the McLaurys clearly saw the deal struck with Wyatt Earp as a genuine threat to their own safety after that episode.

Doc Holliday had little reason to pay attention to any of it. Except as it may have been the subject of conversation, until the deaths of Leonard and Head and the revenge against the Hasletts, the Cow-Boy problem was at best a curious subject for barroom banter. Even Wyatt's deal with Ike Clanton was kept from Doc because it involved a betrayal of Doc's friend, Bill Leonard, if for no other reason. Wyatt could not be sure how John Henry would react. So, Doc concentrated on his own legal troubles and changes that were taking place in Tombstone.

Unwittingly, though, Doc may have contributed to his future difficulties by stepping into a personal conflict with Sheriff John Behan. In the spring and summer of 1881, Behan was involved in an affair with Josephine Sarah "Sadie" Marcus. Marcus was a free-spirited young actress from San Francisco who had moved in with Behan. Later in the summer of 1881, she would meet Wyatt Earp on the streets of Tombstone and ignite the sparks that would eventually lead to a lifelong relationship. In the spring and early summer, however, she was still "Johnny's woman." Doc would later claim that Behan became "a deadly enemy of mine" because of her. He explained that Behan started a quarrel at his faro bank one night and that he refused to allow the sheriff to play anymore. "We were enemies after that." Doc explained why: "[I]n the quarrel I told him in the presence of a crowd that he was gambling with money which I had given his woman. This story got out and caused him trouble."[33] Such an incident certainly would have created animosity between them, and if Behan's "woman" was indeed Sadie Marcus, Doc may well have known her before Wyatt did.

Virgil Earp's appointment as the chief of police proved to be a good one. As acting chief, during the month of June he and his deputies made forty-eight arrests and collected fines amounting to $323; he also won praise for his handling of the aftermath of the town's disastrous fire. With an eight-man police force, sixty arrests were made in July, and $384 worth of fines were levied. In August, Virgil reported things quiet and suggested that the police force be reduced to two officers besides himself. Virgil worked days and James Flynn and A. G. Bronk had nights. Virgil had put the lid on Tombstone.[34]

Doc was hardly visible after Justice Wells Spicer threw out the charges against him in the death of Bud Philpott and the attempted stage robbery. In July, he was party to a suit filed by Marcus Smith on behalf of the Last Decision mine against the Intervenor Mining Company. The suit commenced on August 6, 1881, but Doc was not directly involved.[35] In fact, Doc was out of town for at least a part of August, most likely somewhere on the gambling circuit or in Globe with Kate.

Doc had become a close friend of Morgan Earp's and probably spent some time in Benson, where Morgan gambled and hung out so much that some mistakenly associated him with Big Ed Byrnes and the "top and bottom" crowd that controlled the place. Doc was certainly savvy enough to appreciate the humor when Sheriff Behan appointed Morgan a special deputy at the request of Deputy Sheriff Charley McComas to help control some of the more notorious citizens of Benson. Morgan proved valuable though, when he arrested J. J. "Off Wheeler" Harlan, a refugee from Las Vegas, who started a quarrel with an Indian that led to gunplay.[36]

While Doc was conspicuous only by his absence, the Cow-Boy scourge was increasingly the subject of press attention as the bandits

grew bolder and Mexican protests stronger. The reason was underscored by George Holt, the foreman of the Grant County, New Mexico, grand jury, at the end of July:

> There seems to be a very bad state of affairs existing in the southern
> part of this country near the border of Old Mexico. It almost seems
> that a law abidindg [sic] citizen can hardly live there with any safety
> to himself or property. There seems to be a band of men living in
> that section of the county who live by robbing and stealing, and defy
> the authority. We ask that our Sheriff and law abiding citizens use
> every effort to suppress this lawlessness, and if it cannot be done oth-
> erwise, to call on higher and more powerful authority to assist in so
> doing, as such a state of affairs seriously effects the prosperity of our
> county.[37]

On July 26, a running fight occurred between Cow-Boys and
Mexican vaqueros over a herd of cattle on the plains near Guadalupe
Pass in New Mexico that resulted in the rout of the Mexicans.[38] On
July 27, at Cajon de Sarampion, Cow-Boys attacked a party of sixteen
Mexicans moving into the United States, killing four, although initially as many as nine were thought to have been killed.[39] On August
11, Cow-Boys attacked Ochoaville, killed a horse, wounded a Mexican, and took what they could.[40] Also during August, the papers reported an effort to steal cattle near Charleston and an attempt to steal
gold and silver from three Mexican soldiers. The editor John P. Clum
went so far as to say that without effective law enforcement "the people are justified in taking the law into their own hands and ridding
themselves of the dangerous characters who make murder and robbery
their business."[41]

This flurry of seemingly uncontrolled criminal activity aroused
more than editorial ire and official correspondence. On the morning
of August 13, 1881, the Mexicans took a measure of revenge when
they attacked a party of men encamped in Guadalupe Canyon near the
Mexican border with a herd of Mexican cattle purchased from rustlers.[42] The leaders of the Americans were William Lang, a recent
arrival in the region, who, along with his father, had purchased lands
from John Slaughter and John W. Roberts, and Old Man Clanton.
With them were Dixie Lee Gray, the son of Judge Mike Gray, Jim
Crane, the last of the Benson stage robbers, Billy Byers, Harry Earnshaw, and Charles Snow.[43]

The attack commenced about dawn, when Snow rode out of the camp to investigate a disturbance of the herd. Lang believed a bear was threatening the cattle. Snow rode directly into the concealed Mexicans, who were waiting for first light to attack. They killed Snow with the first volley, then opened fire on the camp. Clanton, Gray, Lang, and Crane were also killed. Byers was seriously wounded, but survived by stripping off his clothes and playing dead to make the Mexicans believe that he already had been killed and stripped by others in their party. Earnshaw hid in the brush. Hours later, he stumbled onto the ranch of John Plesant Gray with the news that Mexican soldiers had attacked them and killed his companions.[44]

The Guadalupe Canyon affair stunned the citizens of southeastern Arizona. Rumors flashed across the area of planned retaliatory raids against Fronteras by as many as four hundred Cow-Boys, one organized by the fathers of Gray and Lang, and another put together by the Clantons. The threat seemed real enough that federal troops were ordered "to intercept all armed parties raiding into Mexico with hostile intent and disarm them, or if found returning, to aid the civil authorities to arrest them."[45] The *Tombstone Nugget* went so far as to suggest that war with Mexico would be fully justified.[46] A few days after the killings, Buckskin Frank Leslie came across the bodies of three Mexicans at Blackwater near Guadalupe Canyon, and the *Nugget* suggested "that the work of retribution has already commenced."[47] As events unfolded, however, the Gray-Lang group turned out to be a burial party, and the Clanton group never materialized.

Other observers saw things differently. Clara Brown reported that "the Mexicans were not the first to inaugurate the present unhappy state of affairs along the border. They have suffered greatly from the depredations of those outlaws who, under the guise of 'cowboys' infest this country and pursue the evil tenor of their ways with no attempt at interference on the part of those whose duty it is to suppress crime."[48] George W. Parsons observed, "This killing business by the Mexicans, in my mind, was perfectly justifiable as it was in retaliation for killing of several of them and their robbery by cowboys recently."[49] The *San Francisco Daily Report* expressed the view that the Cow-Boys posed a greater problem than the Apaches and urged that "the cowboy element [be] wiped out hip and thigh by any rightful means."[50] And General Adolpho Dominguez, the adjutant to General Jose Otero in Sonora, made clear the Mexican government's intent to take "active steps to protect our citizens and repel raiders."[51]

The Guadalupe Canyon affair changed the balance in the region. The Cow-Boy problem could no longer be ignored. Federal and local authorities had to respond. The incident helped to finally unseat John Charles Frémont, Arizona's governor in absentia, even though, ironically, Frémont had been one of the first to demand action against the Cow-Boys. It was also at this point that John Clum took dead aim at John Behan and Harry M. Woods, declaring that "[t]here is altogether too much good feeling between the Sheriff's office and the outlaws infesting this county."[52]

U.S. Marshal Crawley P. Dake and his one-armed chief deputy, J. W. Evans, already understood the importance of addressing the border situation. On August 11, two days before the Guadalupe Canyon affair, Evans advised Dake that the Mexican government had expressed "great dissatisfaction at the seeming neglect of our Gov't and threaten to take vengeance on all Americans in Sonora."[53] Scarcely a month later, Deputy Sheriff William Bell reported that "a few days ago he had occasion to cross the line and go into Sonora, and says that no one is allowed in that state without a pass from the governor or military commander."[54] The border situation had reached a dangerous state.

The killings also fed the rumor mill to the point of hysteria. Early in September, the *New Southwest and Grant County Herald* reported a second massacre south of George W. Lang's ranch near the site of the Guadalupe Canyon killings, listing the deaths of five men, including John Gray, Billy Clanton, and Charlie Snow (whom the paper erroneously reported had "escaped from the other killing"). The paper reported that "both these massacres were perpetrated by parties of Mexican regular troops, who were identified by their uniforms."[55] By the end of September, the U.S. Customs officer at Arivaca reported "roving bands of 'Cow Boys' have been seen in the vicinity several times in the last week or ten days" and expressed concern about a raid on the town.[56] Both reports proved to be false, but they underscored the state of the public mind.

The presence of Jim Crane at Guadalupe Canyon also excited controversy, linking Old Man Clanton and the others to the known stage robbers. "Am glad they killed him," Parsons opined about Crane. "As for the others—if not guilty of cattle stealing, they had no business to be found in such company."[57] John Plesant Gray would later claim that Crane had joined the party the night before the attack with the intent of accompanying it to Tombstone, where he planned to surrender to the sheriff, "as we had talked him into doing."[58] Later, Milt Joyce would try to link the Earps to the Guadalupe Canyon affair, but both surviving eyewitnesses, Billy Byers and Harry Earnshaw, insisted that the attackers were Mexicans.[59] Nevertheless, the affair did bring the Cow-Boy problem directly to the doorsteps of the Earps and John Henry.

Jim Crane was the last link to solving the Benson stage robbery. Crane was the one man who could exonerate Doc beyond all doubt. His death made it impossible for Doc to satisfy those predisposed to believe the worst about him, and it gave Joyce and others the basis for linking Doc and the Earps not only to the Guadalupe Canyon killings but also to stage robberies in the area, by claiming that the primary purpose of the attack was to kill Crane. In this way, the enemies of the Earps created the appearance of impropriety, really for the first time since the Earps had arrived in Tombstone. This was doubtless in response to Clum's revival of charges against the sheriff's office for the escape of Luther King.[60]

John Clum might be able to editorialize that Crane was "a fugitive from justice and an outlaw, and the six bullets that struck him were certainly well expended," but his death also heightened Ike Clanton's apprehensions about the secret between himself and the Earps at precisely the point in time where his father's restraining hand was removed in the same bloody encounter at Guadalupe Canyon.[61] Old Man Clanton had always managed to maintain some sense of propriety and respectability and had even gotten along reasonably well with the Earps. Now Ike's insecurity, bravado, and temper had no effective check.

As a deputy U.S. marshal, Virgil Earp now faced increased pressure to act against the Cow-Boys, and the businessmen of Tombstone who were feeling the economic pressure created by the Cow-Boy situation explained their concerns to the Earps, who were the most likely to act. Practically, though, J. W. Evans was the deputy U.S. marshal who had taken charge of operations against the Cow-Boys, and, for the moment, Virgil still concentrated on his duties as the marshal of Tombstone with such efficiency that the *Epitaph* quipped, "Cowboys don't seem to visit our city very much. Don't they like the climate? We feel slighted."[62]

The high profile of the Cow-Boy problem did require that Virgil cooperate with Sheriff Behan in both his role as the chief of police and his role as the deputy U.S. marshal at precisely the moment the strain between the Earps and Behan was approaching the breaking point, especially in light of Clum's renewed criticism of the sheriff's office. On September 9, with word that Pony Deal had been arrested by Bob Paul for robbing the Globe stage in February, Virgil and Behan attempted to arrest Sherman McMaster, but McMaster managed to escape, with Virgil firing after him. Behan gave chase but soon lost the trail.[63] It was later reported that McMaster and John Ringo stole two horses at the Contention mine. Ringo, who had also been in Tombstone, was wanted for robbing a poker game at Galeyville. McMaster's escape produced more criticism of Paul, Earp, and Behan. When the acting governor, John J. Gosper, visited Tombstone in September to personally investigate the Cow-Boy problem, he found Behan and Earp criticizing each other for failure to cooperate "in capturing and bringing to justice these outlaws." He reprimanded both and demanded strong action at once.[64]

By September, the situation was having a detrimental effect on business. Even the *Tombstone Nugget* reported that "the Mexicans are very aprensive [*sic*] of the cowboys and are afraid to come to Arizona," noting that a party of twenty came to Tombstone with Deputy Sheriff William Bell, "trusting that in his official capacity they would find ample protection." The *Nugget* also reported other effects of the Cow-Boy problem:

> The playful pastimes of the festive cowboys in stealing cattle and shooting the owners as a mark of affection is having its effect on the lumber market. It is almost impossible to procure any kind of lumber at this time for immediate use in the mines or for building purposes. Several orders for lumber have been telegraphed to San Francisco as men owing teams suitable for hauling lumber positively refuse to take any more chances outside of the city limits so long as the present state of insecurity for stock exists. The scarcity of hemp and rope factories is a serious drawback to all new and unsettled countries.[65]

The apprehension of business was not about conditions in Tombstone, but about the interruption of commerce created by the apparent lawlessness around Tombstone that not only posed the direct threat of stolen horses, shortages of timber, machinery, and other commodities necessary to business operations but also threatened to have a potentially more disastrous impact on investments in the area. Both in Arizona and California the demand for action was shrill, almost hysterical. One resident declared that the Cow-Boys "now virtually control this section of the country." They had been "emboldened by repeated success," he said and lamented, "There have been but few arrests made, and, so far as I know, no convictions of this class of outlaws."[66] Many citizens plainly perceived a crisis of monumental proportions. Moreover, the situation suggested an organized operation, not merely random thievery and violence.

Some began to suggest the use of vigilance committees of "honest men banded together to rid the country of murderers and robbers." The *Epitaph* took the suggestion to heart in a strongly worded summation of the situation:

> "Committees of Safety" are not always safe defenders of the law, and should only be organized as a last resort; however, Cochise county has very nearly reached that point. As it is now the cattle men are afraid to say anything. As one stated to the writer the other day, "I can only live among them by keeping my mouth, eyes and ears constantly closed. I tell them if they want any of my stock to help themselves, only I would prefer they would not take the cows and heifers." Whether it is through fear or not, it is a well known fact that the principal apathy is exhibited by the stock men themselves. Some of the principal ones never lose a head of stock, which leads one to believe they are not entirely guiltless themselves. The only remedy we can suggest is organization, and never rest until the last thieving desperado is killed or driven out of the country. Desperate diseases require heroic treatment.[67]

These feelings intensified after the robbery of the Bisbee stage on the night of September 8, 1881. Robbers, at least two in number, perhaps more, stopped the stage three miles south of Hereford and took $2,500 from the treasure box, $600 from the passengers, and a gold watch. Two posses, one consisting of Harry Woods, David Neagle, and Billy Breakenridge of the sheriff's office, and another led by Virgil Earp as a deputy U.S. marshal, consisting of Wyatt Earp, Morgan Earp, Marshall Williams, and Fred Dodge, went after the robbers.

Three days later, the Earp posse brought in two suspects: Deputy Sheriff Frank Stilwell and Pete Spence. They were released on bail. Charges were dropped against Spence because of a lack of evidence. Stilwell, who was held on the basis of a boot print at the robbery scene and his habit of using the word "sugar" to describe money, was also released for insufficient evidence early in October.[68]

The Earps were convinced Stilwell and Spence were the guilty parties, however, and the incident heightened tensions between them and the Cow-Boy crowd. Both the *Epitaph* and the *Nugget* reported that "a number of cowboys" had threatened the lives of the Earps because of the arrests of Stilwell and Spence.[69] A few days after the arrest, Frank McLaury, perhaps recalling the strongly worded *Epitaph* recipe for dealing with outlaws and its criticism of ranchers as accomplices of the outlaws, stopped Virgil Earp and demanded to know if he was raising a vigilance committee to go after him and his brother, the "Clantons, Hicks, Ringo and all us cowboys." Virgil denied any such intent, but McLaury said, "Now . . . I'll tell you, it makes no difference what I do, I never will surrender my arms to you. . . . I'd rather die fighting than be strangled."[70]

McLaury also accosted Morgan Earp in front of the Alhambra in the presence of John Ringo, Ike Clanton, and the Hicks brothers. He told Morgan that he would never forgive Spence for allowing himself to be arrested by the Earps, then added, "If you ever come after me, you will never take me." Morgan responded that if circumstances required it, he would arrest him. McLaury then responded, "I have threatened you boys' lives and a few days later I had taken it back, but since this arrest, it now goes." Wyatt Earp later reported that at least nine or ten men told him of threats against his life and the lives of his brothers by Ike Clanton, the McLaury brothers, John Ringo, and Joe Hill.[71]

Stilwell and Spence had strong ties to the Cow-Boys. Both men had faced criminal charges before in two separate cases of murder. They also hung out in the Cow-Boy haunts at Charleston, where they had ample opportunity to meet and become involved with the cattle thieves and other ne'er-do-wells causing trouble in the area. Stilwell owned several businesses in Charleston, including a saloon, a livery stable, and a lumberyard, and could have been quite useful in the fencing of stolen horses. In fact, in October 1880 Spence had been charged with stealing mules. Still, why McLaury chose the September arrests of Stillwell and Spence to defy the Earps openly was puzzling, because until that moment nothing approaching a feud existed between the Earps and the Cow-Boys.

Some good news did make the papers, although it was almost lost in the flurry of reports of Cow-Boy outrages. On August 23, "The 'top and bottom' gang of confidence men, who have so long infested Benson to the discomfiture and pecuniary loss of many Eastern tourists was ... broken up, and the members driven from the town."[72] The occasion of this event was a quarrel between Big Ed Byrnes and Martin Mahain, two of the leaders. A shooting incident resulted in which Deputy McComas was shot in the thigh. Outraged citizens finally had enough. They attacked the headquarters of the gang and piled all the furniture into the street and burned it, after which they "notified the party that if they did not leave town on the next train there would be some hanging done." Byrnes was arrested and incarcerated at Tombstone. The rest of the gang caught the westbound train on August 24.[73]

If problems were not bad enough, early in October a breakout was reported from the San Carlos Indian Reservation. In the wake of this report, there was a flurry of livestock thefts including horses, mules, and cattle. By then, reports of Indian hostilities were viewed skeptically by some:

> The cow-boys in Southeastern Arizona are having a pretty good time now; they can rob and murder and put the blame on the Indians. A border community always keeps a few "straggling hostiles" on hand for this purpose. After a party of ruffians has murdered a teamster or a rancher it comes into towns and reports the sight of Indian stragglers in that neighborhood; armed citizens go out and don't find any Indians, but they find the body of a man "massacred by the red devils," go back to town, hold a meeting, and pass resolutions that they ought to have the reservations right away, and that "every Indian in the country should be exterminated."[74]

Whether Apaches were responsible for the raids or white thieves simply took advantage of the situation was never really determined in this instance, but a party of volunteers from Tombstone, led by John Behan, with Virgil Earp as second in command, rode into the Sulphur Springs Valley to investigate reports of Indian raids. The expedition camped at the Soldier's Hole ranch of Frank and Tom McLaury, who had reported fourteen horses stolen. There, the Cow-Boy war seemed temporarily suspended as Virgil Earp and Curly Bill Brocius, described by George Parsons as "Arizona's most famous outlaw at the present time," greeted one another. They "shook each other warmly by the hand and hobnobbed together some time."[75] Wyatt Earp did not join in the pleasantries, however, and shortly Bill and two companions rode off. It was the most memorable moment of the whole enterprise, because the expedition proved a waste of time, and the volunteers returned to Tombstone with little to show for their efforts.

On October 8, the Benson stage was robbed north of Contention. Five days later, both the *Nugget* and the *Epitaph* reported that Wyatt and Virgil Earp had arrested Frank Stilwell and Pete Spence for the robbery.[76] In fact, the Earps had arrested them on federal charges, claiming new evidence in the Bisbee stage robbery. Virgil, acting in his capacity as deputy U.S. marshal, took the pair to Tucson on October 13, where they were scheduled to appear before T. L. Stiles, the U.S. commissioner, on October 20.[77] Virgil returned to Tombstone on October 14 and had a busy few days as marshal handling minor infractions. On October 18, he, Marshall Williams, and Sheriff Behan left for Tucson to attend the Stilwell-Spence hearing. Ike Clanton, William Allen, and Ham Light—all friends of Stilwell and Spence—also traveled to Tucson to be on hand for the hearing. In Virgil's absence, Wyatt served as acting marshal.[78]

Doc Holliday was not a party to any of these happenings—intrigues, arrests, and expeditions. He was, after all, a gambler, and he was, for most of the time, where he was expected to be: at faro banks or poker tables, seeking his fortune apart from politics and criminal intrigues. He likely attended the San Augustin Festival in Tucson, which opened on August 28 and continued into September, and it may well be that he shared that experience with Kate, who always claimed that Doc attempted a reconciliation with her when her boardinghouse burned at Globe that summer.[79] He certainly knew the opportunities for gain at the festival, and he may well have been one of those described by the *Tucson Citizen*, which noted in August that "as the Feast approaches, all sharpers of all kinds gather into the city" and warned that "thieves, burglars, pick-pockets, and cut throats will be here in large numbers."[80] Of course, not all gamblers fit these disparaging descriptions, and Doc, remembering the previous year, surely tried his hand there.

On September 29, the *Tucson Star* reported, "Over two hundred people have left Tucson to attend the feast at Magdalena [in Mexico] on the 4th proximo, it being the regular annual feast of San Francisco. This includes a number of the sporting fraternity."[81] Doc was back in Tombstone only briefly at the end of September, and he left again on October 1, just before the feast opened in Magdalena. That he had been out of town in September was confirmed by the unclaimed letter for "John Hallady" listed in the *Epitaph* on October 1, the same day he left town again.[82] Doc did not appear to have been on hand when Lou Rickabaugh reopened the refurbished Oriental Saloon on October 11, and the *Daily Epitaph* listed a letter for Kate in its issue of October 15, suggesting that she and Doc were still out of town. Kate also claimed that at midmonth, "Doc asked if I would like to go to see the Fiesta." She continued, "I said, 'I don't mind going.' We left that evening for Tucson. We were there about four days."[83]

Her memory after so many years was confused. There was no fiesta in Tucson in October, but she placed Doc in Tucson at the right time. Doc and Kate probably attended the fiesta at Magdalena (the fiesta she remembered), coming back through Tombstone at midmonth before going on to Tucson. The *Epitaph* noted a quarrel in which an unnamed gambler beat his woman and then left town on October 18, but there is no reason to believe this was Doc and Kate.[84] His alleged abuse of Kate, so oft written about in recent years, was not documented at the time or reported by her in her memoirs. Kate's "four days" would put Doc in Tucson on October 19, which meant he was apparently "bucking the tiger" in Tucson about the time that Virgil returned to attend the Spence and Stilwell hearing. In fact, Kate claimed that Doc lost her last $75 in the Congress Hall Saloon during this trip to Tucson.[85]

Virgil and Sheriff Behan returned to Tombstone on October 21. The next day, charges against Spence were dismissed, and Stilwell was bound over for trial. On his return to Tombstone, Virgil resumed his duties as marshal and appointed Wyatt "'a special,' to keep the peace with the power to make arrests."[86] While Virgil was out of town, something dramatic had happened. One night while drinking and before going to Tucson, Marshall Williams had told Ike Clanton that he knew about his deal with Wyatt to betray Leonard, Head, and Crane. Enraged, Clanton found Wyatt and accused him of breaking his word by telling Williams their secret. Wyatt denied it and told Ike that Williams was just guessing. When Ike returned from Tucson, he accused Wyatt of telling Doc Holliday about the deal as well. Wyatt told Ike he would prove that Doc knew nothing when Doc returned to town. Ike then swore that Doc himself had told him that he knew about their deal, whereupon Wyatt said he would ask Doc about it when he came back.[87]

On October 21, Wyatt sent Morgan to Tucson to get Holliday to hurry back to Tombstone. Kate recalled what happened:

> One evening at the Fiesta, Doc was bucking at faro. I was standing behind him, when Morgan Earp came and tapped Doc on the shoulder and said, "Doc, we want you in Tombstone tomorrow. Better come up this evening." Doc said, "all right." He cashed in his chips. Morgan Earp did not want Doc to take me back with them, although he did not say anything. Doc said to me, "You had better stay here. I will come after you tomorrow or in a day or two." I said, "No, I am going back with you." Then he said, "We are going back on a freight train." I said, "If you can go on a freight, so can I." Then he said, "We are going to Benson on a freight. Then we have to ride on an open buckboard." I said, "If you can ride on an open buckboard, so can I." They saw that there was no way of getting rid of me, so the three of us went back to Tombstone.[88]

The trio of Doc, Kate, and Morgan reached Tombstone on the evening of October 22. Doc settled Kate into his room at C. S. Fly's and went with Morgan to find Wyatt, but by then Ike Clanton had left town for his ranch on the San Pedro River above Charleston. Nevertheless, Wyatt explained the situation to Doc. Doc denied knowledge of any deal or having discussed it with Ike, and he told Wyatt that he would speak with Clanton when he could.

That same evening, Deputy Sheriff Breakenridge arrested Milt Hicks for possession of stolen cattle. Two days later, while the jailor Billy Soule was out of the office, Hicks, Charlie "Yank" Thompson, and Jim Sharp surprised Charles Mason, the assistant jailor, when he unlocked the cell to serve the prisoners dinner. After a brief struggle, they locked Mason in the cell and fled. Mason was able to raise the alarm, and soon Sheriff Behan, Breakenridge, and the three Earp brothers gave chase without finding the prisoners.[89]

Behan and Virgil Earp, along with Deputies Breakenridge and David Neagle, searched further without success. Behan then ordered Breakenridge and Neagle to continue the pursuit. This would prove to be important because it took two more deputies out of Tombstone while Undersheriff Harry Woods was in El Paso, Texas, to take into custody suspected horse thieves who had been arrested in El Paso del Norte, Mexico, on October 18. He arrived in El Paso on October 23, started extradition proceedings, and did not take possession of the prisoners until October 26, 1881. This meant that Behan's force was seriously reduced at what turned out to be a critical moment.[90]

During this period, Doc had returned to his faro bank at the Alhambra. Ike Clanton had not tarried long at his ranch, but soon left on unspecified business for three days in the Sulphur Springs Valley. On October 25, he was en route home in a light spring wagon when he encountered his younger brother, Billy, and the McLaurys, Frank and Tom. They rode together as far as Jack Chandler's Milk Ranch, nine miles east of town, near the foot of the Dragoons, where they had breakfast together. They agreed to meet again in Tombstone in a day or two, after which Tom decided to ride with Ike into town to handle some business matters. Between ten and eleven o'clock on the morning of October 25, Ike and Tom arrived in Tombstone and put up their horses and wagon at the West End Corral, where they also checked in their weapons. They then split up to take care of business matters. At the time, Tom and Frank apparently were planning to leave Cochise County to attend their sister's wedding back in Iowa, and they had to settle some affairs before going. Ike was mostly involved in tasting the wares of the town's numerous saloons.[91]

That evening, Doc Holliday spotted Ike in the lunchroom of the Alhambra Saloon and approached him as he had promised Wyatt he would. "I understand that you say the Earp brothers have given you away to me, and that you have been talking about me?" he said bluntly. Doc told Ike that Earp had told him nothing and that Ike should stop talking about him. Doc was doubtless less than polite, but Ike was drunk, so drunk that he would later report the conversation as having taken place in three different saloons![92] He likely was so drunk that he would not remember the conversation clearly, but he was surly in response, repeating the accusations and advising Doc in plain terms that he did not believe him.

Doc, in turn, called Ike a liar for telling Wyatt that he had told Ike anything about things of which he had no knowledge. Doubtless, too, now that he knew that Clanton had planned to sell out Leonard, Head, and Crane, he expressed contempt for Clanton and his mercenary character. Holliday lost his temper and told Clanton it was time for him to pull out his gun and go to work. "Doc's vocabulary of profanity and obscene language was monumental and he worked it proficiently in talking to Ike," Fred Dodge remembered.[93] Ike Clanton later testified:

> While sitting down at the table, Doc Holliday came in and commenced cursing me and said I was, "A son-of-a-bitch of a cowboy," and told me to get my gun out and get to work. I told him I had no gun. He said I was a damned liar and had threatened the Earps. I told him I had not, to bring whoever said so to me and I would convince him that I had not. He told me again to pull out my gun and if there was any grit in me, to go to fighting. All the time he was talking, he had his hand in his bosom and I supposed on his pistol.[94]

A serious row was in the making. At the time, Wyatt Earp was seated at the lunch counter eating, and Morgan Earp was standing at the Alhambra bar talking with the bartender. Wyatt testified, "I called him over to where I was sitting, knowing that he was an officer and told him that Holliday and Clanton were quarreling in the lunch room and for him to go in and stop it."[95] Morgan climbed over the lunchroom bar and took Doc by the arm and led him out of the saloon, with Ike following close behind. Ike claimed that Doc said as he left, "You son-of-a-bitch, if you ain't heeled, go and heel yourself," and testified, for good measure, that Morgan had added, "Yes, you son-of-a-bitch, you can have all the fight you want now."[96] The exchange continued in the street and was still going on when Wyatt walked outside.

The disturbance was loud enough that Virgil Earp, who was next door at the Occidental Saloon, heard it and came out to investigate. He told Doc and Ike in plain terms that if they did not stop quarreling, he would arrest them both. With that threat, the argument broke up, Wyatt led Doc away, and Ike crossed the street to the Grand Hotel. Virgil returned to the Occidental, and Morgan went home. After calming Doc down, Wyatt went to the Eagle Brewery Saloon to check on one of his games, and Doc went to the Oriental. A short time later, Ike Clanton caught up to Wyatt at the Eagle Brewery.[97] According to Wyatt, he was now armed. Wyatt recalled, "He told me when Holiday [*sic*] approached him in the Alhambra that he wasn't fixed just right. He said that in the morning he would have man-for-man, that this fighting talk had been going on for a long time, and he guessed it was about time to fetch it to a close. I told him I would not fight no one if I could get away from it because there was no money in it. He walked off and left me saying, 'I will be ready for you in the morning.'"[98]

Ike still did not let matters go. He followed Earp to the Oriental, where he told him, "You must not think I won't be after you all in the morning." He threatened Doc again, whereupon Wyatt told him that "Holliday did not want to fight, but only to satisfy him that this talk had not been made." After closing his game at the Oriental, Wyatt met Doc on the street between the Oriental and the Alhambra and walked with him down Allen Street until they separated to go to their lodgings.[99] After leaving Wyatt, Ike went to the Occidental Saloon, where, curiously, he joined an all-night poker game with Tom McLaury, John Behan, Virgil Earp (of all people), and a fourth unidentified man. Ike lost some money, but continued to drink. He also became irritated because Virgil kept a pistol in his lap as he played. The sun was already coming up when the game ended. Virgil explained what happened next:

> On the morning of the 26th, somewhere about six or seven o'clock, I started to go home, and Ike Clanton stopped me and wanted to know if I would carry a message from him to Doc Holliday. I ask [*sic*] him what it was. He said, "The damned son of a bitch has got to fight." I said, "Ike, I am an officer and I don't want to hear you talking that way at all. I am going down home now, to go to bed. I don't want you to raise any disturbance while I am in bed."[100]

Virgil turned to walk away, but Clanton persisted in his demand. "You won't carry the message?"

"No, of course I won't," Virgil replied.

"You may have to fight before you know it."

"I made no reply to him and went home and went to bed," Virgil testified later.[101]

Ike Clanton did not follow suit.

THE FREMONT STREET FIASCO

Damon did no more for Pythias than Holliday did for Wyatt Earp.

—Bat Masterson, *Human Life Magazine* (1907)

Near eight o'clock on the morning of October 26, 1881, Ike Clanton picked up the pistol and rifle he had left at the West End Corral, "expecting to meet Doc Holliday on the street," as he later claimed. In fact, he began to roam the streets looking for Doc or for any of the Earps, as he made clear to anyone who would listen. Only a few minutes after leaving the West End Corral, he ran into Ned Boyle, a bartender at the Oriental. "He said that as soon as the Earps and Doc Holliday showed themselves on the street, the ball would open, and that they would have to fight," Boyle recalled later. Boyle saw that Ike had retrieved his weapons and hurried off to Wyatt Earp's house to warn him. Wyatt listened, then went back to sleep.[1]

In the meantime, Ike had moved on to Julius A. Kelly's ornate Wine House, where Kelly overheard him talking to the bartender Joe Stump about the previous night's difficulties. Kelly asked him what the trouble was, and Clanton told him that the Earps and Holliday had insulted him the night before when he was not armed, but that he was armed now "and that they would have to fight on sight." Kelly warned him against further talk, because he believed the Earps would fight if pushed.[2] Ike continued his tour of the saloons, leaving a flood of rumors in his wake. Eventually, there were enough of them that Officer A. G. Bronk woke up Virgil and told him there was liable to be "hell." Virgil thanked him, then rolled over and went back to sleep.[3]

The Earps simply did not take Ike Clanton seriously. He was a blowhard and a braggart, and they fully expected that he would eventually crash, and that on awakening with a hangover the fight talk would wilt. However, Ike was still going at noon when he told R. F. Hafford that the Earps and Holliday would have to fight. Hafford also warned him that he had better go home.[4] Instead, he found his way to Fly's boarding house looking for Doc, who was still asleep. Mollie Fly found Kate in the rear gallery of the photographic studio behind the boardinghouse looking at pictures and told her that Clanton, fully armed, was asking about Doc. Kate went back to Doc's room and woke him up to tell him. Doc sat up on the side of the bed and responded, "If God lets me live long enough to get my clothes on, he shall see me."[5]

At about the same time, Virgil finally got up and started downtown. He was scarcely out of the house when Daniel Lynch, a young housepainter, caught up to him and said, "Look out for Clanton, he's on the prowl and allows to kill you on sight." Next, Virgil met his brothers Morgan and James, who asked if he had seen Clanton, explaining, "He has got a Winchester rifle and six-shooter on, and threatens to kill us on sight."[6] These warnings would not be the last threats reported to Virgil, but they were sufficient to give a new seriousness to the situation. In the meantime, Wyatt walked into the Oriental to be told by Harry Jones, an attorney, that Clanton was looking for "you boys." Wyatt wearily and nonchalantly said, "I will go down and find him and see what he wants."[7]

On his way out of the saloon, Wyatt ran into Virgil and Morgan. They told each other what they had heard, then split up to look for Ike, with Wyatt walking down Allen Street and Morgan and Virgil proceeding up Fremont. In the meantime, Mayor John P. Clum passed Ike on the corner of Fourth and Fremont. "Hello Ike. Any new war?" he asked innocently. A few steps farther on, Clum met Charles Shibell, who was in town from Tucson, and struck up a conversation with him. As they spoke, they saw Virgil and Morgan turn onto Fourth Street, both armed.

"What does that mean?" Shibell asked.

"Looks like real trouble," Clum answered.[8]

They watched as the two Earps approached Ike, who had moved into an alleyway off Fourth. He was watching Wyatt, who was coming down Fourth from the opposite direction off Allen. Virgil recalled what happened next:

> I found Ike Clanton on Fourth Street between Fremont and Allen with a Winchester rifle in his hand and a six-shooter stuck down in his breeches. I walked up and grabbed the rifle in my left hand. He let loose and started to draw his six-shooter. I hit him over the head with mine and knocked him to his knees and took his six-shooter from him. I ask [sic] him if he was hunting for me. He said he was, and if he had seen me a second sooner he would have killed me. I arrested Ike for carrying firearms, I believe was the charge, inside the city limits.[9]

Virgil still was not taking Ike seriously enough. Instead of putting him in jail to sleep off his drunkenness or charging him with some more serious offense, he hauled him off to Judge A. O. Wallace's court on a simple weapons charge, expecting that a fine and the headache received in the buffaloing would get Ike's attention sufficiently to sober him up. He miscalculated. Wallace was not at the courtroom, and Virgil went to look for him, leaving Clanton in the charge of Morgan. At that point, Wyatt came in, followed by Rezin J. Campbell, a deputy sheriff and clerk of the Cochise County Board of Supervisors. A crowd of curiosity seekers soon packed the little courtroom; they were not disappointed. Wyatt sat down near Morgan, who still held Clanton's rifle and pistol.

Clanton's defiance had not withered. He was soon in a heated exchange with Morgan. "You fellows haven't given me any show at all today," he thundered. "You've treated me like a dog." Clanton strutted. "Fight is my racket, and all I want is four feet of ground." Then, turning on Morgan, he said, "If you fellows had been a second later, I would have furnished a coroner's inquest for the town." He threatened, "I will get even with all of you for this. If I had a six-shooter now, I would make a fight with all of you."[10]

Morgan reacted by angrily offering Ike his revolver, saying, "Here, take this; you can have all the show you want right now." At that point the crowd scattered. One eyewitness said, "You should have seen that crowd light out just then. In less than half a minute everybody was about a block away. I ran with the crowd, but as no shooting was heard, in a short time we all went back again, when we found out that Ike had refused to take the gun. But I tell you, pard, that was the worst scared crowd I ever saw."[11] Actually, Ike did jump up, but before he could grab the pistol, Deputy Sheriff Campbell pushed him into a chair. Wyatt had heard and seen enough. He yelled at Clanton, "You have threatened my life two or three times and I have the best evidence to prove it and I want this thing stopped." Then he thundered, "You cattle thieving son of a bitch, and you know that I know you are a cattle thieving son of a bitch, you've threatened my life enough and you've got to fight." He then turned and left the courtroom in a rage.[12]

As he walked out, Wyatt almost collided with Tom McLaury, who was rushing to see what kind of mess Ike had gotten himself into. Earp snapped at McLaury, and McLaury fired back, "If you want to fight, I will fight you anywhere."

"Are you heeled? Right here, right now!" Earp quickly replied. In the same instant, Wyatt slapped him, jerked his own pistol, and knocked Tom to the ground with it. He stormed away muttering, "I could kill the son of a bitch," while McLaury struggled to regain his feet and fumbled to find his silver hatband, which had been knocked off when Earp struck him. Tom had had enough. Still groggy, he made his way to the Capitol Saloon and deposited his pistol behind the bar.[13]

Wyatt claimed later, "I was tired of being threatened by Ike Clanton and his gang and believed from their movements that they intended to assassinate me the first chance they had, and I thought that if I had to fight for my life with them I had better make them face me in an open fight."[14] That was postfight rationalization. At the moment, the usually calm Wyatt Earp had lost control in a fit of anger. Still steaming, Wyatt walked to Hafford's corner at Allen and Fourth streets, bought himself a cigar, and stood there puffing away to regain his composure after a rare display of emotion.

In the meantime, Virgil had returned to the courtroom with Justice Wallace, and the courtroom settled down to business. Wallace fined Ike $25 and court costs for carrying weapons. Afterward, Virgil asked Ike where he wanted to pick up his weapons. The still defiant Clanton said sharply, "Anywhere I can get them, for you hit me over the head with your six-shooter." Virgil told him he could pick them up at the Grand Hotel.[15]

At that point, the Earps were sure they had taken care of things.

Shortly after noon, Frank McLaury and Billy Clanton arrived in town from Antelope Springs, in company with J. R. Frink, a cattle dealer

Tom and Frank McLaury. Both brothers were killed in the
street fight with the Earps and Doc Holliday on October 26,
1881, Tom shotgunned by Doc and Frank killed after
exchanging words with Doc during the fight.

known locally as "Major," to meet their brothers. Frink was arranging
to provide a herd of six hundred cattle to supply beef for the Union
Meat & Poultry Market, and he was working with the McLaurys on
the deal. They reined up in front of the Grand Hotel without any
knowledge of what had happened so far. They met Doc Holliday as
they started toward the hotel; he pleasantly stuck out his hand to Billy
Clanton and asked, "How are you?" Despite later efforts to give the
gesture some sinister meaning, it was likely nothing more than common Southern courtesy.[16]

Doc walked on to find breakfast, and the new arrivals were moving
toward the hotel when a local named William Allen, who had connections with some of the Cow-Boys, joined them and asked if they knew
what was going on. At the Grand Hotel bar, he quickly filled them in
as Frank ordered drinks. Frank asked why Wyatt had hit Tom. When
Allen said he did not know, Frank grew somber and said, "We won't
drink." Outside, he and Billy unhitched their horses and as they led
them away, McLaury said to Allen, "I will get the boys out of town."[17]

As they headed off in the general direction of the O.K. Corral,
they encountered William Claiborne, the youngster who was making a
reputation for himself as the "second Billy the Kid" because of his
Cow-Boy high jinks. He was even then awaiting the disposition of a
case in which he had killed a man in Charleston. Claiborne told them

that he had taken Ike to Dr. Charles Gillingham's office to have his head wound treated. Together, they walked to find Ike, with Billy Clanton saying, "I want to get him to go out home." They found Ike shortly, and he promised Billy he would leave "directly." In fact, Ike claimed that he saw the stableman from the West End Corral at that point and asked him to hitch up his team for him. Then they all walked together to Spangenberg's Gun Shop behind Brown's Hotel.[18] On another day, it would have gone unnoticed, but in a situation already taut with rumors and suspicion, the visit to a gun shop seemed deliberately provocative.

Moments later, a group of miners stopped Virgil and asked, "Ain't you liable to have some trouble?" Then one of them told the marshal, "I seen two more of them just rode in. Ike walked up to them and was telling them about your hitting him over the head with a six-shooter. One Cowboy said, 'Now is our time to make a fight.'" At that point, Virgil concluded that the situation was more serious than he had believed. He walked to the Wells, Fargo office and borrowed a ten-gauge shotgun. By then, there were small knots of men gathering on the streets to talk about the situation.[19]

From his vantage point at Hafford's corner, Wyatt watched as the Clanton crowd passed by on Fourth Street and disappeared into the gun shop. Having regained his composure, he decided to investigate. As he approached the gun shop, Frank's horse stepped onto the sidewalk and stuck its head into Spangenberg's. This violated a city ordinance, so Wyatt grasped the bridle to move the horse off the sidewalk. This movement brought Billy Clanton to the door with his hand on his gun butt. Frank followed and took his horse from Wyatt by the bridle. Earp told him he had to get the horse off the sidewalk and gave him chapter and verse on the law. Frank coolly backed his mount into the street, then, without a word, went back into the shop. Wyatt said that afterward, "I saw them in the gun-shop changing cartridges into their belts." In fact, George Spangenberg refused to sell Ike Clanton a pistol because he "had been in trouble."[20]

Virgil was still at the Wells, Fargo office when Bob Hatch rushed in and said, "For God's sake get down there to the gun shop, for they are all down there and Wyatt is all alone. They are liable to kill him before you get there!" Virgil ran to the scene, arriving just as Frank reentered the shop. He watched, too, as Billy Clanton filled his belt with cartridges. Wyatt and Virgil then walked back to Hafford's corner.

They watched the Cow-Boys pass by and eventually turn in to the Dexter Corral.[21] Tom McLaury, after having his head treated, stopped off at Everhardy's Eagle Market to take care of some business before catching up to the others at Dexter's Corral. As he came out of Everhardy's, "his pants protruded as if there was a revolver," and J. B. W. Gardiner observed that he was sorry to see that Tom was now armed.[22]

By then, Tombstone was full of buzz about what was happening, and any sense of reality was quickly slipping away. Citizens and groups were approaching the Earps with all sorts of ominous warnings about what the Clantons and McLaurys had said. Rumor had it that Ike had been seen in the telegraph office, which created the fear that he had wired for backup, and, indeed, the Earps believed—in error—that Ike had telegraphed Frank and Billy that morning. Meanwhile, Frank and Billy, who had not seen Ike's performance before they arrived in town, now believed that the Earps were out to get them. The recipe for tragedy was almost complete.

About the only person in Tombstone who did not seem to know what was going on at that point was Sheriff John H. Behan. He ambled into Barron's Barber Shop for his daily shave and was soon enveloped by gossip about the situation. Back on the street, Behan ran into Charles Shibell, who had witnessed Virgil surprise Ike earlier, and the two of them went off together to find the marshal. Along the way, they were stopped by R. F. Coleman, who told them that the Clantons and the McLaurys were up to no good. They had crossed over Allen into the O.K. Corral, he said, and he told the sheriff, "You should go and disarm that bunch!"

Coleman got to Virgil before Behan and Shibell did and repeated his report of Cow-Boy mischief. When the sheriff caught up to Virgil in a crowd of bystanders at Hafford's corner, the marshal was clearly frustrated. When Behan asked Virgil what was going on, Virgil snapped, "Some sons-of-bitches have been looking for a fight and now they can have it!"

"You had better disarm them. It is your duty as an officer," Behan replied.

"I will not. I will give them their chance to make a fight."[23]

Sensing Virgil's agitated state, Behan eased the marshal into Hafford's Saloon with an invitation to take a drink. Virgil must have realized how ill advised his public outburst had been, and he joined Behan and Shibell at the bar. Virgil declined a drink, but as the bartender brought the sheriff his drink, William B. Murray, a local stockbroker and a leader of the Citizens Safety Committee, pulled the marshal aside and told him, "I know you are going to have trouble and we have plenty of men and arms to assist you."[24]

Calmer now, Virgil told him, "As long as they stay in a corral, the O.K. Corral, I will not go down to disarm them. If they come out on the street I will take their arms and arrest them."

"You can count on me if there is any danger," Murray assured him as he left.

Behan questioned Virgil about what "that son-of a bitch Strangler" wanted, but Virgil brushed the question aside and asked Behan to help him arrest the Cow-Boys. Behan refused but offered his own plan: "Don't undertake to disarm that bunch, or they will kill you. They were just down at my corral [the Dexter] having a gun talk against you and threatening your life. I will go down to where they are. They won't hurt me. And I will get them to lay off their arms."[25]

Virgil agreed. Anything seemed worth a try to avoid a fight. Behan hurried off. As Virgil walked out of the saloon, H. F. Sills, a Santa Fe railroad engineer on furlough and a stranger in town, stopped him and told him that he had seen the Cow-Boys at the O.K. Corral and that he had overheard them threatening Virgil's life and the lives of his brothers.[26] Most likely this was more of Ike's liquor talk, but each new report made the situation seem more and more ominous. And when Morgan and Doc joined Virgil and Wyatt, West Fuller, the young gambler, decided he should warn his friend, Billy Clanton. He headed for the O.K. Corral, but along the way he was sidetracked when he met Mattie Webb, a young madam, and stopped to talk with her.[27]

After his late breakfast, Doc had walked to the Alhambra Saloon to check on business. Morgan caught up to him there, filled him in on the situation, and walked with Doc to Hafford's corner.[28] Doc was dressed like a dandy in a gray suit and a pastel shirt with a stiff collar and tie. He wore a slouch hat and a long, gray overcoat and carried a silver-headed cane. As Doc approached Wyatt and Virgil, he asked what the situation was. Exactly what was said between them was not recorded at the time, but Wyatt and others later recalled an exchange that went something like this:

"Where are you going?" said Doc.

"We're going to make a fight," replied Wyatt.

"Well, you're not going to leave me out, are you?"

"This is none of your affair."

"That is a hell of a thing for you to say to me!"

"It's going to be a tough one."

"Tough ones are the kind I like."[29]

Wyatt may well have protested, as this dialogue suggests, but Virgil settled the matter when he handed Doc the Wells, Fargo shotgun, telling him to hide it under his overcoat. "I did not want to create any excitement going down the street with a shotgun in my hand," he explained.[30] Doc took the shotgun and handed Virgil his cane. Virgil's decision to involve Doc would prove costly.

Close to twenty minutes had passed since Behan left to find the Cow-Boys when John L. Fonck, formerly a captain on the Los Angeles police force and another leader of the vigilantes, offered the help of ten men. Virgil told him much the same thing that he had told Murray, that as long as the Cow-Boys were getting their horses to leave town, he would do nothing, but that if they came onto the streets, he would have to arrest them. Fonck responded, "Why, they are all down on Fremont Street now."[31]

Fonck was right. What he did not know was that Virgil concluded that the Cow-Boys had had ample time to leave if that was their intent. Their number had already grown from two to five, and he clearly worried that more might be on the way. He had turned down the best offers of help. He did not trust Behan. His regular officers were asleep. And the town's affairs had been disrupted long enough by the threat of armed men on the streets. It was time. His credibility as chief of police was on the line. Further delay would almost certainly produce criticism for allowing the situation to go on for so long. "Come along," the marshal said to his brothers and Doc.

Morgan spoke up at that point, "They have horses. Had we not better get some horses ourselves, so that if they make a running fight we can catch them?"

"No. If they try to make a running fight we can kill their horses and then capture them," Wyatt offered. And the four of them started toward Fremont Street. As they walked, Doc whistled quietly and nodded to the people he passed.[32]

If the Clantons and the McLaurys did intend to leave town rather than put up a fight, they waited too long. First, the McLaurys had business with James Kehoe at the Union Market, which they stopped to attend to. That was where Sheriff Behan caught up to them. The Clantons and Claiborne had turned down Fremont Street toward the West End Corral and stopped on the eighteen-foot vacant lot between Fly's Photograph Gallery and boardinghouse and a small house owned by William Harwood to get out of the cold wind until the McLaurys caught up. The coincidence of being so close to Doc's living quarters would not be missed by the Earps.

At the Union Market, Behan told Frank McLaury he wanted him to give up his arms. Frank replied, "Johnny, as long as the people of Tombstone act so, I will not give up my arms."[33] Behan then threatened to arrest him if he did not, and Frank reconsidered. He would go with the sheriff willingly, he said. They then proceeded down the street to catch up to the rest of the party for the same message to be delivered. At the vacant lot, Behan surveyed the scene and asked how many there were. "Four," he was told, as Claiborne insisted he was not one of the group. Because he was awaiting grand jury action in the Hickey shooting at Charleston, Claiborne had a reputation that caused concern, but he told Behan that he had deposited his weapons at Kellogg's Saloon the day before.[34]

According to Behan's testimony, both Ike Clanton and Tom McLaury said they were unarmed, and he checked Ike to be sure. Tom McLaury pulled back the lapels of his coat to show that he was unarmed, but Behan confessed that he "might have had a pistol and I not know it."[35] Frank and Billy were both plainly armed, and Frank flatly refused to give up his weapon. He insisted that he did not want a fight, but he said he would not surrender his arms. Ike Clanton later testified, "Then Frank McLowry [sic] said he had business in town that he would like to attend to, but he would not lay aside his arms and attend to his business unless the Earps were disarmed."[36] Behan was in a tough spot. Frank was obstinate, and Behan knew that his demand to disarm sworn peace officers was unreasonable.

These negotiations delayed the Cow-Boys just long enough for the Earps and Doc Holliday to turn off Fourth Street onto Fremont. Someone yelled, "Here they come!"

Behan looked up and saw the marshal's party walking briskly toward them along the sidewalk. He said to the Clanton group, "I won't have no fighting, you must give me your firearms or leave town immediately."[37]

"You need not be afraid, Johnny, we are not going to have any trouble," came the reply. Sheriff Behan accepted that statement, but he left the Cow-Boys still armed when he hurried off to stop the marshal's party. The townspeople were fully alerted to what was happening, and several were trailing the Earps to see what would occur next. As the Earps passed the Union Market, Martha J. King, a customer annoyed by the distraction of the employees from business that afternoon, looked out in time to see the wind blow Doc's coat back to reveal the shotgun underneath. She testified later that she overheard one of the men say, "Let them have it," as they passed, and heard Doc reply, "Alright." Placing the worst construction on what she saw and heard, she hurried to the back of the store in fright.[38]

Outside, Sheriff Behan reached the Earp party as it passed the market. With his hands outstretched, he urged, "Hold up boys! Don't go down there or there will be trouble."

"Johnny, I am going down to disarm them," Virgil grimly responded.

"I have been down there to disarm them," Behan replied. The Earps and Doc Holliday pushed on by him. Clearly, they interpreted what Behan had said to mean that he had already disarmed them. Virgil relaxed. He tucked his pistol into his pants on his left hip and shifted Doc's cane to his gun hand. Wyatt relaxed also, slipping his own revolver into his overcoat pocket. Behan did not return to the vacant lot with the Earps to complete his mission of preventing a fight. The problem was that the Cow-Boys had not been disarmed. As Sheriff Behan himself put it, "I doubt whether they considered themselves under arrest or not, after I turned to meet the other parties."[39] Ike Clanton later testified that he did not consider himself under arrest since he was leaving town, and Frank McLaury had made his position clear on the matter as well.

As the Earps approached Fly's, the Cow-Boys stepped back into the vacant lot away from the street. Doc moved out into the street apart from the rest of the Earp party. He understood that his role was that of backup, so he positioned himself to prevent escape from the vacant lot. When Virgil turned in to the lot, he found Ike Clanton standing in the middle of the lot between the buildings. Along the side of the Harwood House stood the McLaury brothers and Billy Clanton. Two horses, Frank's and Billy's, both of which had Winchester rifles in the saddle boots plainly in view, stood with the Cow-Boys.

Apparently, Billy Clanton had walked away from the McLaurys to speak with Claiborne and handed the reins of his horse to Tom McLaury. As the Earps approached, young Clanton stepped back against the wall alongside the McLaury brothers. He was nervous, but he was wearing a gunbelt and a holstered revolver. Frank also had a pistol in plain view. The Earps were caught off guard by the sight of armed men and by the presence of Billy Claiborne and West Fuller, who had finally reached the scene too late to warn his friends. At that point, Wyatt may well have muttered a shocked, "Son-of-a-bitch!" under his breath, accounting for later prosecution claims that Wyatt used the expression in a threatening way.[40]

Doc watched as Virgil moved into the lot toward Ike, with Wyatt following behind and Morgan lingering on the sidewalk. He himself stayed in the street but moved closer to the center of the lot. Virgil stepped up and raised his right hand—with Doc's cane still in it—over his head. "Throw up your hands, boys. I intend to disarm you!"

"We will!" Frank McLaury said as he stepped forward and grabbed the revolver on his hip. The inexperienced Billy Clanton also reached for his gun, and Tom McLaury grabbed his coat lapels and threw them back in a movement much like the motion of reaching for a weapon under one's coat. With Frank and Billy going for their pistols and none of the others obeying Virgil's order, Wyatt Earp took no chances and pulled his own revolver. With these movements, Doc lifted the shotgun into view from underneath his coat, pulling back the hammers of the sawed-off ten-gauge with an ominous click-click.[41]

Virgil was losing control. "Hold! I don't mean that," he shouted, as he stood exposed with Doc's cane in his gun hand high above his head.

The first shot came from Wyatt Earp's revolver, and it tore into Frank McLaury's belly left of the navel, while Billy Clanton fired wide of Wyatt. There was a pause as Virgil tried to shift the cane to his other hand and awkwardly fumbled for the pistol out of place on his hip, and the Cow-Boys stood frozen as Frank stumbled from the impact of Wyatt's shot and Doc moved a step closer to Tom McLaury, who was moving behind one of the horses. Ike broke the indecision, charging up to Wyatt, grabbing him, and wrestling with him for a moment before Wyatt shoved him away and said, "The fight's commenced. Go to fighting or get away!" Clanton "broke and ran." He stumbled through the door of Fly's and into another vacant lot, then through Kellogg's Saloon and into Toughnut Street before he stopped. In the flurry of gunfire, both Ike Clanton and Billy Claiborne would later claim that the Earps shot at them, and the Earps believed that someone fired at them from just east of Fly's. In all probability, in both cases, they were simply shots that went wild in the confusion.[42]

The mortally wounded Frank McLaury and young Billy Clanton put up a fight, both firing rapidly. Virgil went down with a bullet in his calf, most likely fired by Frank. Another bullet tore across the back of Morgan Earp, chipping a vertebra as it did so and causing him to shout as he fell, "I am hit!" As he scrambled to get to his feet again, he stumbled over a mound of dirt beside a ditch dug for new water pipes.

Once the fight began, Doc, as containment man, closed in on Tom McLaury, who had taken refuge behind one of the horses. He was reaching across the mount either to fire a pistol or to get the Winchester in the saddle boot. The horse was plunging in the chaos, and when for a split second Tom's body was exposed, Doc squeezed the triggers on the shotgun. Tom staggered away with twelve buckshot in his right arm and side and crumpled by the telegraph pole at the corner of Third and Fremont while the horse ran off down Fremont Street. Doc threw the empty shotgun to the ground and drew his nickel-plated revolver.

By then, Billy Clanton had been hit twice, once in the chest and once in the wrist. Falling back against the wall of the Harwood House and sliding to the ground, Clanton gamely shifted his pistol to the other hand. He continued to fire with his pistol propped on his knee.

Frank McLaury, still holding on to the reins of his horse, now began to move into the street, trying to use the horse as a shield. He fired once at Morgan before his horse broke loose and ran away. Frank squatted in the street from exhaustion, but as Doc followed him, he regained his feet, and, lifting his pistol, said to Doc, "I've got you now."

"Blaze away!" Doc said calmly. "You're a daisy if you have."

They fired together. Doc's shot struck Frank in the chest at the same instant that Morgan shot him in the side of the head. McLaury's shot tore into Doc's coat and grazed his hip. "I'm shot right through," Holliday yelled. Frank went down hard, but when he seemed to still be moving, Doc ran toward him shouting, "The son-of-a-bitch has shot me, and I mean to kill him."[43]

By then the fight was over, except for young Clanton gamely trying to reload his pistol as Bob Hatch and C. S. Fly, two of the witnesses, approached him. "Give me some cartridges," Billy demanded. Without a word, Fly took the pistol from his hand.

The fight was over, but the confusion was not. The witnesses who had scrambled for cover when the shooting began now came out of hiding and milled about with other citizens crowding onto the scene. The two McLaurys and Billy Clanton were carried into the house on the corner of Third and Fremont, just beyond the Harwood House. Young Clanton said that he had been murdered and told people to go away and let him die. Frank was already dead, and Tom died without ever speaking. The confusion on the vacant lot was such that there was certainly no securing the scene, which meant that pieces of evidence could have been picked up by gawkers. The Earps were convinced that Tom fired the shot that wounded Morgan, and Wyatt would claim that Old Man Fuller later told him that West Fuller had picked up Tom's pistol in the postfight confusion.[44] Much of the town did not know what had just happened, and some panicky citizens thought that either the Cow-Boys or Indians were attacking the town. Within minutes the Vizina mill whistles brought dozens of armed men into the streets, as the vigilantes turned out for action.

Wyatt, the only one of the marshal's party not hit, was busily seeing to his brothers, when Sheriff Behan reappeared. "I have to arrest you, Wyatt," Behan said.

"I won't be arrested," Wyatt said. "You deceived me Johnny, you told me they were not armed. I won't be arrested. I am here to answer for what I've done. I am not going to leave town."

There was a tense moment before Sylvester Comstock, a local attorney and leader of Tombstone's Democratic Party, interceded. "There is no hurry in arresting this man," he said. "He done just right in killing them, and the people will uphold them."

"You bet we did right," Wyatt added. "We had to do it. And you threw us off, Johnny. You told us they were disarmed."

Behan let the matter go for the moment. Later, when Ike was located, he was taken into custody by the sheriff's office. Fin Clanton came in from the ranch and, after seeing Billy's body, put himself in Behan's custody as well, with ten extra deputies hired to protect him and Ike. In response to a rumor "that a mob would attempt to take Ike Clanton from the jail and lynch him and to prevent any such unlawful proceedings a strong guard of deputtes [*sic*] was placed around that building and will be so continued until all danger is past."[45]

Doc did not linger at the scene once the fight was clearly over. He retired to his room at Fly's. Kate recalled:

> After the fight, Doc came in, and sat on the side of the bed and cried and said, "Oh this is just awful—awful." I asked, "Are you hurt?" He said, "No, I am not." He pulled up his shirt. There was just a pale red streak about two inches long across his hip where the bullet had grazed him. Then he went out to see what had become of the two Earps that were wounded; they were afraid to leave them for fear that the cow rustlers would take them in the night.[46]

That evening, John Behan called on the Earps at Virgil's home. He found the two injured Earp brothers there, along with James Earp and three of the Earp wives. Winfield Scott Williams (a lawyer about to take office as an assistant district attorney) and another unidentified man, described by Williams as a "red-faced man, about 5 feet 8 inches high, dressed in a ordinary suit of clothes," were also present.[47] The mood between the marshal and the sheriff was tense. Virgil was clearly angry because he believed that Behan had misled him about the Cow-Boys. Behan's admission that he had tried to disarm the Cow-Boys, but that he had not done so when the Earps came down Fremont Street, did not help. Virgil and Williams would both contend that Behan told Virgil that he had heard the marshal tell the Cow-Boys to throw up their hands and that he had seen Frank McLaury pull his pistol and begin firing. Both Virgil and Behan claimed to be friends, but when Behan left, both still had hard feelings.[48]

Wyatt came in after Behan left. He and Doc had been together trying to get a sense of what to expect next. There were fears of a Cow-Boy raid. These concerns were overblown, but Wyatt did warn his brothers that they would all most likely be charged. After Wyatt left, Morgan told Virgil's wife, Allie, "If they come, Al, you'll know they got Wyatt. Take this six-shooter and kill me and Virge before they get us." Allie and Louisa, Morgan's wife, stacked mattresses in front of the windows, and Allie sat up all night with a pistol in her lap. "I would have used it, too," she recalled, "if they had come to kill Virge and Morg."[49]

Nothing happened that evening. In fact, initially, the public reaction was surprisingly favorable to Marshal Earp, his brothers, and Doc Holliday. As expected, Clum's *Epitaph* strongly justified what had happened:

The feeling among the best class of our citizens is that the Marshal was entirely justified in his efforts to disarm these men, and that being fired upon they had to defend themselves, which they did most bravely. So long as our peace officers make an effort to preserve the peace and put down highway robbery—which the Earp brothers have done, having engaged in the pursuit and capture, where captures have been made, of every gang of stage robbers in the county—they will have the support of all good citizens. If the present lesson is not sufficient to teach the cowboy element that they cannot come into the streets of Tombstone in broad daylight, armed with six-shooters and Henry rifles to hunt down their victims, then the citizens will most assuredly take such steps to preserve the peace as will be forever a bar to further raids.[50]

The *Nugget*'s account confirmed the view that when Virgil called on the Clantons and McLaurys to throw up their hands, "Frank McLowry [*sic*] made a motion to draw his revolver, when Wyatt Earp pulled his and shot him" to precipitate the tragedy. The *Nugget* did note that the McLaurys "did not bear a reputation of being of a quarrelsome disposition, but were known as fighting men, and have generally conducted themselves in a quiet and orderly manner when in Tombstone." This surprisingly balanced view indicated that Richard Rule wrote the account, because Harry M. Woods was still in El Paso.[51]

News of the street fight spread quickly. The *San Francisco Daily Report* was laconic: "A dispatch from Tombstone describes the killing of three desperadoes by the City Marshal and his assistants and then says 'The town is quiet and the authorities are fully able to maintain order.' Considering the summary disposal of the desperadoes the remarks about the quietness of the town and the power of the authorities are somewhat superfluous."[52]

The *San Francisco Exchange* celebrated, "The people of Tombstone have reason to congratulate themselves that they have not only courageous Marshals but Marshals who are dead shots. That performance yesterday, wherein three cowboys were left dead on the field and one lodged in jail, is among the happiest events Tombstone has witnessed, and especially so as it was attended with so little injury to the law vindicators."[53]

The first real clue that the shootout would not pass without controversy came when the bodies of the McLaurys and Billy Clanton were

propped up in their ornate caskets under a sign that read: MURDERED
IN THE STREETS OF TOMBSTONE.[54] Many were stunned by the size of
the crowd that gathered for the funeral. The procession, led by a brass
band, two hearses, Ike and Fin Clanton in a wagon, three hundred
people on foot, twenty-two carriages and buggies, a stagecoach, and
an entourage of men on horseback, was the largest in Tombstone's history. Curiosity seekers lined the sidewalks, and the whole affair was
made all the more sobering because it occurred the day after the fight
before many in the outlying areas had time to find out about the fight
or make the trip to Tombstone.[55]

Clara Brown rightly noted, "The divided state of society in Tombstone is illustrated by this funeral." She was skeptical that the reasons
were based on right or wrong, however, noting:

> While there are many people of the highest order sojourning here,
> whose business is honorable and whose voices are always heard on
> the side of law and order, there yet remains a large element of unscru-
> pulous personages, some outwardly regardless of restraining influ-
> ences, and others (more than one would suspect) secretly in sympathy
> with the "cowboys," acting in collusion with them. Even the officers
> of the law have not escaped the stigma of shielding these outlaws,
> some of them being believed to have accepted bribes to insure that
> silence. One must not judge the whole by a part, but it is undeniable
> that Cochise county started out upon its career hampered by a set of
> officials which might be improved; and doubtless will be at the next
> election.[56]

Still, even with that strongly held view, she was certain that the
community was divided on whether the killings had been justified, and
she concurred with George W. Parsons, who observed grimly, "It has
been a bad scare and the worst is not yet over some think."[57] They
were right. On October 28, at ten o'clock in the morning, a coroner's
inquest convened. John Behan took the stand, and a different view of
the fight unfolded as he testified:

> When they [the Earps and Doc] got to the party of cowboys, they
> drew their guns and said, "You sons-of-bitches, you have been look-
> ing for a fight and you can have it." Someone of the party, I think
> Marshal Earp, said, "Throw up your hands! We are going to disarm
> you!" Instantaneously with that, the fighting commenced. They fought
> around there, and there was from 25 to 30 shots fired.

All the time before the shots were fired, I was talking to all parties, saying, "Put up your guns!", not to shoot. I heard Billy Clanton say, "Don't shoot me! I don't want to fight," or something to that effect. . . .

Tom McLowry [sic] said, "I have got nothing," and threw his coat back to show that he was not armed. This was instantly with the shooting, almost at the same time. The order to throw up their hands and this remark and the shooting were almost simultaneous.[58]

By the time the coroner's jury had finished hearing testimony, Ike Clanton and Billy Claiborne had sworn that the Cow-Boys had thrown up their hands when commanded to do so, except for Tom McLaury, who threw open his coat to show he was unarmed. Other witnesses testified, but Behan, Clanton, and Claiborne presented the view that the Earps provoked the fight and then opened fire on the unresisting Cow-Boys. They also shifted the firing of the first two shots from Wyatt Earp and Billy Clanton, as reported by both Tombstone newspapers, to Doc Holliday and Morgan Earp.[59]

The coroner's jury avoided placing blame, stating simply that the Cow-Boys had died "from the effects of gunshot wounds by Virgil Earp, Morgan Earp, Wyatt Earp, and one Holliday—commonly called 'Doc' Holliday." The *Nugget* noted with deep sarcasm that the verdict reassured them: "We might have thought they had been struck with lightning or stung to death by hornets."[60] Regardless, no one in Tombstone missed the point that the Cow-Boys and Sheriff Behan were building a case for murder. More important, the failure of the coroner's jury to declare the Earps' action justifiable opened the door for criminal charges against them. George Parsons understood the implication: "Looks bad for them all thus far."[61]

On October 29, warrants were issued for the arrest of Virgil, Wyatt, Morgan, and Doc, on the strength of a complaint by Ike Clanton sworn out before Justice of the Peace Wells Spicer. Spicer denied bail, but because of the seriousness of Virgil's and Morgan's wounds, only Wyatt and Doc were taken into custody. Once defense attorneys submitted affidavits of fact, Spicer granted bail, but at the stunning (for the time) amount of $10,000 each. O. C. "Charlie" Smith, James Earp, Lou Rickabaugh, John Marshall Nichols, Fred Dodge, Robert J. Winders, W. H. Savage, Charles R. Brown, A. C. Bilicke, and Thomas J. Fitch were bondsmen for Wyatt Earp, raising a total of $27,000, and

Smith, Dodge, Winders, James and Wyatt Earp, Savage, Dan O'Toole, and William J. Hutchinson were bondsmen for Doc Holliday, raising $14,500 more. Interestingly, the largest individual sum for Doc's bond was $7,000, furnished by Wyatt.[62] The money pledged was far more than the amount required and indicated strong support for the Earps and Doc Holliday.

The day the arrests were made, Mayor Clum called a special session of the town council with the following result: "Mayor Clum stated that [the] meeting was called to consider grave charges against Chief of Police Earp and it was ordered that pending investigation of said charges Chief Earp be temporarily suspended and James Flynn act as Chief during such suspension."[63] The following day, Virgil Earp blundered by requesting a company of cavalry from Fort Huachuca to protect the town from Cow-Boy retaliation. General Orlando Willcox put a company at readiness and wired Acting Governor John J. Gosper, but the primary effect was to win ridicule for Virgil.[64] By then, Harry Woods had returned from El Paso and had taken charge of the *Nugget*'s editorial campaign against the Earps. He belittled Virgil's request and took a very different approach to what had happened on Fremont Street. He provided a heartrending account of the fate of the McLaurys and Billy Clanton:

> With great holes pierced through their bodies by the leaden messengers of death, their sole anxiety seemed to be to return shot for shot, and only when the spark of life ceased to burn did they relinquish their hold on the death dealing revolver, and they sank to earth while the smoke from their weapons ascended as from a funeral pyre. Before death claimed them for his own they saw Morgan Earp fall only to raise up and renew the murderous fire, and the chances for each man's life engaged was a thousand to one against him. Who says it does not require courage to stand and listen to the music of half a dozen sixshooters singing a dead march in unison every time the hammers come down? But these men died, as they would probably have chosen to die had they had their choice.[65]

"To read such stuff as this," scoffed the *San Francisco Daily Report*, "is enough to make the healthiest feel sick." The *Nugget*, the *Report* declared, "indulges in the customary gush over the 'sand' and 'grit' the well-served desperadoes exhibited." The San Francisco editor's disgust then overflowed: "To such papers as the *Nugget* are due the troubles from which the Territory has suffered or is suffering. They are always toadying to the criminal element and standing in with the rings. If we are to gush over the courage of murderers and desperadoes when they resist arrest, why not eulogize the skill of burglars, the boldness of garroters, and the enterprise of incendiaries."[66]

For the business-minded editors of California, the issue seemed simple enough: the law was primarily about maintaining order to produce an environment conducive to commerce and social stability. In Arizona, however, things were considerably more complex. What was right was not just about what was good for business. In Tombstone especially, even many of those who deplored the Cow-Boy problem in broad terms could hardly help asking whether such a bloody affair on the city streets had been necessary. For most Tombstone residents, the Cow-Boys were faceless beyond the few notables like Curly Bill Brocius and John Ringo, whose exploits made the papers. In street discourse, the question for many was not the "character of the parties killed," but the motives of Marshal Earp and his deputies.

The views expressed by Arizonans were not more pristine, however. Politics was already spilling over into what should have been a simple issue of law enforcement. The Democrats could not fail to see the potential value of the Earps' troubles for them at both the territorial and county levels. Surely, the case benefitted Behan, who expected Wyatt to run against him in the next election for sheriff. Undersheriff Woods was now in the perfect position to promote Behan's cause at Wyatt Earp's expense. Criminal conduct on the part of the Earps also had the potential to benefit the opponents of John Clum within the city. Moreover, economic connections with the Clantons and the McLaurys and a certain class resentment of the power structure in Tombstone caused some to question Marshal Earp's decision. Ironically, even some of those who had no love for the Cow-Boys but for whom appearances mattered worried that the street fight would be bad for business. Those like Clum—and other public officials all the way to Prescott—as well as the Earps and their allies saw the Fremont Street fight as an opportunity to reinforce the urgency of dealing with the Cow-Boy problem, but they found its usefulness diluted by the sensational nature of what had happened.

At three o'clock in the afternoon on Monday, October 31, Justice Spicer convened a hearing to determine whether sufficient evidence

existed for the grand jury to consider bringing the Earp brothers and
Doc Holliday to trial on charges of murder. The hearing opened behind closed doors by defense request in accordance with territorial law.
The coroner H. M. Matthews provided the only testimony of the day
with details of the wounds received by the deceased and served to prove
that keeping the proceedings secret would be impossible when the
Nugget printed Matthews's testimony on November 1.[67] By the time
William G. Allen took the stand as the lead witness that morning, the
chances of keeping the testimony secret had already evaporated.

The hearing would quickly become something much more than a
perfunctory review of evidence to determine probable cause. Indeed, it
became something more than an investigation into a shooting. District Attorney Lyttleton Price faced a genuine challenge in prosecuting the case. Friends of the Cow-Boys doubted his zeal, and friends of
the Earps were upset that he pursued the case at all. His Republican
credentials and the earlier efforts of Cochise County Democrats to
deny him the post combined to make his handling of the case controversial from the beginning and explained why other attorneys joined
him to help secure the indictment he was charged to seek, including
the able Ben Goodrich, who had defended Cow-Boys in the past, and
the well-respected Marcus Aurelius Smith, who was excused from testifying before the coroner's inquest apparently because he had been
retained by Ike Clanton.[68]

The Earps and their friends did not take the situation lightly. They
retained former Nevada congressman Thomas J. Fitch to lead the defense team. He was clearly the most distinguished attorney on either
side of the case, experienced, colorful, and, at forty-three, already heralded as "the silver-tongued orator of the Pacific." The firm of Howard
& Street represented the Earps, and T. J. Drum, the court commissioner who had granted Kate Elder's writ of habeas corpus when Virgil
incarcerated her for "threats against life" back in July, was hired to defend Doc. Clearly though, Fitch would manage the case and, despite
possible conflicts of interest among the defendants, he would ensure
that they presented a united front in the courtroom. That proved to
be critical, because by the time the hearing convened, the prosecution's strategy seemed clear and Doc Holliday was at its center.[69]

The Earp brothers, particularly Virgil and Wyatt, had credible records that made it difficult to pin charges of murder on them, but a
notorious gambler with a questionable record and outstanding charges

against him for another violent crime was a different matter, especially in light of his public confrontation with Ike Clanton the night before the fight. At the very least, Virgil could be criticized for poor judgment in calling on Holliday to help arrest the Clantons and the McLaurys, particularly if the case could be made that he was the "loose cannon" who precipitated the fight. If the prosecution could add to that basic premise a convincing argument that the Earps lost control and made the confrontation personal, they would be in deep trouble.

Once Ike Clanton pressed charges, Doc—and everyone else—knew that he and his reputation would be central issues in the case. An anonymous letter from Tombstone, dated November 1 and published in the *Tucson Star*, laid the prosecution's strategy out clearly: "Admit the worst that can be said of these boys [the Clantons and McLaurys] as proven facts, and they stand in Angel robes of innocence as compared with the cut-throat who shot Tom McLowry [*sic*] with buckshot while he was protesting that he was unarmed."[70]

When the testimony began, the prosecution stressed its premise that Doc Holliday and Morgan Earp opened fire while the Cow-Boys were trying to surrender. Billy Allen and John Behan portrayed the Earps as angry and out of control, although they did not explain why. By placing the blame on Doc and Morgan and initially suggesting a case of negligence against Virgil Earp, the prosecution seemed to be following the best route to a conviction on some charge, since neither witness gave any strong evidence of premeditation on the part of the Earps. Prosecution strategy changed when William R. McLaury, the brother of Frank and Tom, arrived in Tombstone from Fort Worth, Texas, on the evening of November 3, before Behan had completed his testimony.

Will McLaury was himself a lawyer, and he was quickly unhappy with the prosecution's style and approach. After sitting through the end of Fitch's cross-examination and Price's redirect of Behan and the testimony of Martha J. King, who testified that one of the Earps had said "let them have it" as they passed the Union Market, McLaury approached Price about having Doc and Wyatt remanded to jail. King's testimony appeared to give evidence of premeditation, and he was incensed that Price and the other attorneys for the prosecution would not support him in the matter. McLaury saw their reason as fear, writing that none of the attorneys would seek to have bail revoked, "and would not permit me to do so and said they did not want

William R. McLaury, brother of Tom and
Frank McLaury, was a lawyer from Fort
Worth, Texas, who arrived in Tombstone after
his brothers' deaths determined to convict the
Earps and Doc Holliday of murder. He played
a significant role in the strategy of the
prosecution in the hearing before Wells Spicer
and threatened more severe action after the
charges were dismissed.

to get me killed and to prevent me from making this motion refused
to support me if I made it."[71] McLaury was determined, however.

On November 7, West Fuller took the stand to support the prosecution's case that the Clantons and the McLaurys attempted to surrender.
The court adjourned for lunch, and when the proceedings reconvened
at one o'clock, McLaury surprised the defendants and their lawyers by
moving "that the defendants be remanded to the custody of the Sheriff without bail." After some haggling, Justice Spicer ruled that when
"the proof became evident and the presumption great" that the defendants were guilty, then the court was "bound" to remand the defendants
to custody. Fitch demanded that they be allowed to make application
for bail, but for the moment, Doc and Wyatt were again in the custody of Sheriff Behan. Spicer's decision was important because it could
be interpreted as an indicator that the prosecution's case was making
points with him.[72]

On cross-examination, Fitch caught Fuller in some confusion on
several points and asked him specifically who fired first, eliciting the
response "Morgan Earp and Doc Holliday." Then he finished off his
questions with the following exchange:

Q. What are your feelings toward the defendant, Holliday?
A. We have always been friendly.

Q. Are you so now?
A. Yes sir.

Q. Did you not on the 5th day of November, 1881, about 5 o'clock
in the afternoon in front of the Oriental saloon, in Tombstone,
say to, or in the presence of Wyatt Earp, that you knew nothing
in your testimony that would hurt the Earps, but that you
intended to cinch Holliday, or words to that effect?

A. I told Wyatt Earp I thought Holliday was the cause of the fight.
I don't think I used the words that I would cinch Holliday. I will
not be positive.[73]

That night, Doc and Wyatt were returned to jail. A "strong guard"
was placed around the jail, although there was some dispute about
who they were. Some claimed that Harry Woods placed the guards
there at Behan's instructions, but acting governor Gosper said that the
vigilantes were there to prevent harm from coming to the defendants.
Heavily armed guards remained in place around the jail throughout
Doc and Wyatt's incarceration. In some respects, that night marked
the low point in the proceedings for the defendants. In the meantime,
McLaury was exultant. By his account, he spent the evening shaking
hands with supporters.[74]

When Billy Claiborne took the stand the following morning, he
summarized the prosecution's case:

When they got to the corner of Fly's building they had their six-
shooters in their hands, and Marshal Earp says, "You sons of bitches,
you have been looking for a fight and you can have it." Marshal Earp
says, "Throw up your hands;" Billy Clanton threw up his hands, Ike
Clanton threw up his, Frank McLowry threw up his and the shooting commenced. At this time, Tom McLowry was standing holding
open his coat by each side with his hands on the lappels [sic] and said,
"I have nothing," or "I am disarmed;" the shooting commenced in an
instant right then by Doc Holliday and Morg Earp; the shots fired
by Earp and Holliday were so close together that I could hardly distin-
guish them; I saw them shoot; Doc Holliday shot at Tom McLowry,
and Morg Earp shot at Billy Clanton; when Doc Holliday fired Tom
McLowry staggered backwards; Billy Clanton fell up against the corner
of the house and laid himself down on the ground; Frank McLowry
had hold of a horse about the corner at a post; Ike Clanton when I
saw him was dodging and trying to get away; well, there were about
six or eight shots fired by the Earp party in rapid succession; Billy
Clanton was lying on the ground and drew his six-shooter, rested
across his arm and commenced firing; Frank, at that time, was out in

the middle of the street with his six-shooter; I did not see Frank pull his pistol; I saw it in his hand. Frank did not have a six-shooter in his hand until after six or eight shots had been fired by the Earp party.[75]

Claiborne also insisted that Doc Holliday had a nickel-plated pistol in his hands when the Earp party arrived on the scene and that he fired his first shot from that pistol.

On the surface, Billy Allen, Sheriff Behan, West Fuller, and Billy Claiborne had provided a cohesive prosecution case that was plausible enough to raise doubts and cause some to rethink their position on the case. The *Tucson Star* said, "It is to be hoped that every means within the power of man will be used to reach the bottom of the whole affair, and if the Marshal's posse were doing their duty, let them not only be set free but commended. But if under color of authority, they wreaked their vengeance on these victims, as set forth, then let the law claim its due, no matter what the consequences."[76] Even the *San Francisco Examiner* observed, "Public feeling which at first was for the Earps and Holliday, seems to have taken a turn, and now nearly all the people of Tombstone condemn the murderers."[77] Will McLaury exulted, "I think I can hang them."[78]

Doc Holliday took an active role in the hearing. He was reported taking notes and consulting with attorneys during the sessions. Incarceration could not have been helpful to his consumption, and while he was in jail another personal problem developed. John Ringo checked into the Grand Hotel on the same day that Doc and Wyatt were remanded to jail. He played no role in the Spicer hearing, but he did provide comfort for Kate Elder, who was stuck in Tombstone (by her own account) because of a lack of funds. Loyalty did not seem to be an issue with her, as she herself explained:

> I kept close to my room at Mrs. Fly's during the Earp-Holliday trial.
> . . . Ringo had come to town and visited me at Fly's twice. The second time he advised me to return to Globe, but I told him I did not have enough money to do so as Doc had lost all my money, about $75.00, playing faro while we were at the Tucson Fiesta. He said the Clantons were watching for Doc to come to the room and intended to get him there.
>   "If you haven't enough money to go," he said, "here is fifty dollars." So I left that evening.[79]

Other witnesses followed, but when Ike Clanton took the stand on November 9, Fitch and the defense saw an opportunity to draw attention back to the causes of the street fight, through a review of both the events of the night of October 25 and the morning of October 26, and the arrangement between Wyatt and Ike that lay at the root of the matter. As expected, on direct examination Ike confirmed the scenario set forth by Allen, Behan, Fuller, and Claiborne. He, too, claimed that Doc and Morgan fired first. He also portrayed himself as a victim of the Earps' malice and cast himself in a somewhat more gallant role in the fight itself than even his friends had portrayed.[80] He claimed that he struggled with Wyatt Earp to keep him from firing at his brother and that he left the scene under fire himself. When he had finished his direct examination, Spicer postponed cross-examination "to accommodate one of the counsel for the defense." With that, other witnesses appeared for the prosecution.[81]

On November 12, Fitch began his cross-examination of Ike Clanton. He eased into his questions, reviewing the events between his confrontation with Doc on the evening of October 25 and the street fight, seeking to establish the pattern of Clanton's threats. He also tried to question him about an earlier conversation between Clanton, Frank McLaury, and William Daley about threats against the Earps, but Spicer did not allow it. Fitch then asked if Clanton had not said within the past two months that "'They,' meaning the Earps, 'are in our way any way, and will have to be got out,' or words of similar import?" The prosecution objected, and the defense did not press the question.

Next, Fitch subtly introduced the question of Ike's agreement to sell out the Benson stage robbers by presenting him with a copy of the Wells, Fargo telegram to Marshall Williams agreeing to pay rewards for William Leonard, Harry Head, and Jim Crane, dead or alive. Clanton denied ever having seen it. After establishing that Clanton knew the three outlaws, Fitch asked him whether Wyatt Earp had approached him, Frank McLaury, and Joe Hill in an effort to get them to help him to capture Leonard, Head, and Crane. This was potentially explosive material. Clanton dodged this by claiming that Earp said that he "would either have to kill them or else leave the country." He claimed that Wyatt confessed to him that he and Morgan "had piped off to Wm. Leonard and Doc Holliday the money that was going off on the stage . . . and he was afraid some of them would be caught and would squeal on him."

Fitch pressed Clanton on the matter, and he continued to deny any kind of deal with Wyatt Earp while insisting that Earp wanted to kill the outlaws to protect himself. He further denied that he had accused Wyatt of "giving him away" to Marshall Williams and Doc Holliday. On redirect, the prosecution tried to return the focus to the events of October 26, but on recross, the defense quickly slipped back to the arrangement between Wyatt and Clanton. Clanton claimed that Doc had confessed to him that he was involved in the Benson stage robbery and stated that Doc, Morgan, and Bill Leonard had all separately admitted to him that Doc had killed Bud Philpott. Under Fitch's questioning he went further, insisting that Wyatt, Virgil, and Morgan had all admitted to him at various times that they were involved in "piping off" Wells, Fargo money and hoped to kill Leonard, Head, and Crane to prevent them from revealing the Earps' illegal activities. Ike claimed that he feared for his life and used these alleged conversations to provide the motive for a premeditated attack on him, his brother, and the McLaurys at the vacant lot off Fremont Street.[82]

Why all the Earps and Doc Holliday would confess to Ike Clanton was not clear, and Fitch went after him relentlessly, belittling his claims and effectively punching holes in his testimony, and concluded by asking, "Did anybody else beside Doc Holliday, Wyatt Earp, Virgil Earp, Morgan Earp, or any one of them confess to you that they were confederates in stopping the stage and murdering Bud Philpot [sic]?" The prosecution objected. The defense asked, "Did not James Earp, a brother of Virgil, Morgan, and Wyatt, also confess to you that he was [a] murderer and stage robber?" The defense objected again, but the point was made. Believing Ike Clanton required believing that Doc Holliday and the three Earp brothers had all confided damning, incriminating information about themselves to Ike Clanton. The skillful cross-examination had laid important groundwork for the Earp-Holliday defense, which would focus on Wyatt's deal with Ike as a causal factor in the street fight. At the same time, Ike had succeeded in raising questions in the public mind about the Earps and their troublesome friend, Doc Holliday, that were unlikely to go away whatever the outcome of the hearing.

Wyatt Earp took the stand on November 16, prepared to read a written statement in his own defense. After some haggling, Justice

Spicer ruled that reading the statement was acceptable under Arizona statute.[83] Wyatt reviewed the history of his relationship with the Clantons and the McLaurys, beginning with the incident of the stolen mules at the McLaury ranch. He then reconstructed the details of his arrangement with Ike Clanton, Frank McLaury, and Joe Hill concerning the Benson stage robbers. He said that later Clanton and McLaury claimed that he had given them away to Marshall Williams and Doc Holliday, "and when they came to town they shunned me, Morgan, Virgil, and Doc Holliday, and we began to hear of their threats against us." Wyatt took particular care to acknowledge the nature of his relationship with Doc, stating, "I am a friend of Doc Holliday because when I was City Marshal of Dodge City, Kansas, he came to my rescue and saved my life when I was surrounded by desperadoes."

Wyatt carefully recounted incidents in which the Clantons and the McLaurys made intimidating remarks to the Earps, and he listed the names of people who warned the Earps about additional threats—Farmer Daley, Ed Byrnes, Old Man Winter, Charlie Smith, and others. All of this was critical to his recounting of the events of October 25 and 26, because it provided the context of those events. It was in this frame of reference that he said:

> I believe I would have been legally and morally justifiable in shooting any of them on sight, but I did not do so, nor attempt to do so; I sought no advantage when I went, as Deputy Marshal, to help to disarm and arrest them; I went as a part of my duty and under the direction of my brothers, the marshals; I did not intend to fight unless it became necessary in self-defense or in the rightful performance of official duty; when Billy Clanton and Frank McLowry drew their pistols, I knew it was a fight for life and I drew and fired in defense of my own life and the lives of my brothers and Doc Holliday.[84]

It was an effective opening of the defense case, despite the criticism of Wyatt's use of a written statement. The defense team built on the history of Cow-Boy threats that Wyatt provided and emphasized Ike Clanton's provocations in the hours before the street fight. This approach enabled the fight to be cast as a justifiable police action against men who chose to resist arrest. Wyatt's admission that he fired the first shot in response to Frank McLaury's move for his gun called into question the prosecution's premise that Doc opened the fight with a shot from his nickel-plated pistol, and the witnesses who followed hammered away at the prosecution's case by documenting Cow-Boy threats and Wyatt's version of the way the fight opened.[85]

Virgil Earp's testimony affirmed the defense's case, and the prosecution had little impact on cross-examination. The most stunning testimony came after Virgil stepped down, when H. F. Sills, the Santa Fe Railroad engineer on leave who had warned the Earps about Cow-Boy threats the day of the fight, took the stand and essentially affirmed the defense case through the eyes of a nonpartisan stranger. Sills's testimony was powerful in its impact, opening the way for the defense to detail the threats against the Earps that had come earlier on the day of the fight and virtually demolishing the idea that the Cow-Boys had thrown up their hands at Virgil's command.[86] After Sills's testimony, the defense moved that Doc and Wyatt be released on bail. Spicer agreed in the sum of $20,000 each, and two prominent mining men, E. B. Gage and J. M. Vizina, immediately pledged the funds.[87] The case had definitely taken a turn in favor of the defense.

Doc Holliday was not called to testify. He likely would have been a good witness. As containment man for the Earps in the fight, he was in the best position of any of the Earp party to see what happened in the fight, and he certainly was involved in the preparation of the defense's case. He was bright and savvy enough to have handled himself well on the stand; he could have even submitted a written statement as Wyatt had. The defense never explained why Doc was not called. Practically, he would have added little to what Wyatt and Virgil had said, but he would have provided the prosecution opportunity to exploit his unsavory reputation and raise questions about his previous brushes with the law in Tombstone. Since the prosecution's case focused on Doc's role in precipitating the fight, the defense wisely chose not to put him on the stand. The risks outweighed the advantages.

One of the most important moments of the hearing occurred when Winfield Scott Williams, the assistant district attorney who had been present during the conversation between Sheriff Behan and Virgil Earp at Virgil's home following the fight, affirmed Virgil's version of the conversation and directly contradicted Behan's. He even said that Behan had agreed that Virgil had called on the Cow-Boys to throw up their hands and that Frank McLaury had drawn his pistol in response.[88]

Fitch brought more witnesses to the provocations of the Cow-Boys, then had one more surprise. On November 27, Addie Borland, a dressmaker who lived across the street from Fly's, took the stand. Her account was succinct:

> I saw five men opposite my house, on the afternoon of October 26, leaning against the small house west of Fly's, and one of them holding a horse; the man with the horse was standing outside. I supposed these five to be cow-boys. I saw four men coming down the street toward them. A man in a long coat walked up to the man with the horse and put a pistol to his stomach, and then the man with the coat stepped back about three feet. I was sitting in my house at the window when I saw this. Then shooting commenced in a very few seconds after this. I don't know which party fired first; it was impossible to tell. I was looking at both parties, but no one in particular. I did not know the man with the long coat at the time of the shooting. [Witness points out Doc Holliday as the man with the long coat on.]
>
> Q. Did you notice what kind of a weapon he had in his hand?
> A. It was a very large pistol, a dark bronze.
>
> Q. Was it a nickel-plated pistol?
> A. It was not a nickel-plated pistol.
>
> Q. Did you see, at the time of the approach of the party on Fremont Street any of the cow-boys throw up their hands?
> A. I did not.

Borland said that after the first flurry of gunfire, she got up and went into her back room. Curiously, the prosecution did not cross-examine her. Borland's testimony was not entirely a blessing for the defense, but it established two critical points: first, that Doc Holliday was not holding a nickel-plated pistol at the beginning of the fight, and, second, that the Cow-Boys did not raise their hands. One of the most curious events of the hearing occurred during the lunch break when Justice Spicer called on Borland to ask her further questions and took it upon himself to recall her to the stand that afternoon. The prosecution objected, but Spicer did not rule against himself. She reiterated that she did not see anyone raise his hands. Perhaps her most powerful statement came during the prosecution's further cross-examination granted by Spicer:

> Q. Didn't you say this morning that you did not see who fired the first shot?
> A. I did say so.

Q. Did you say this morning there were two shots fired close together?

A. I did not.

Q. Did you say there were any shots fired at all?

A. I did.

Q. Did you say this morning that when the first two or four shots were fired you were excited and confused, and got up from the window and went into the back room?

A. I did not say how many shots were fired, for I did not know when I went into the back room.

Q. What conversation did you have with Judge Spicer, if any, with reference to your testimony to be given here since you signed your testimony this morning?

A. He asked me one or two questions in regard to seeing the difficulty, and if I saw any men hold up their hands, and if they had thrown up their hands whether I would have seen it, *and I told him I thought I would have seen it* [emphasis added].

Q. Did not you testify this morning that those men did not throw up there [*sic*] hands that you saw?

A. Yes, sir, I did.[89]

Borland's testimony was potentially a mixed blessing for the defense. Her statement that Doc had approached one of the Cow-Boys, shoved a large bronze pistol into his stomach, and stepped back could be seen as a provocative act not mentioned by any other witness, but the prosecution did not pursue it, apparently because it countered their own theory of what happened. It proved important to the defense, however, because it challenged two of the primary points of the prosecution, and, as in the case of Sills, was from a nonpartisan witness.

The defense then finished by calling J. H. Lucas, the same J. H. Lucas who had earlier denied the writ of habeas corpus to Wyatt and Doc. He testified that Billy Clanton did not go down in the first fire and confirmed that two shots were fired, followed by a brief pause before the shooting became general.[90] Perhaps most important, he represented the "better class" of Tombstone's citizenry supporting the Earps. The prosecution finished with a whimper, on rebuttal providing only brief testimony by Ernest Storm, a butcher, that Tom McLaury did not get a weapon in his shop on the afternoon of the fight.[91] With that, the case was submitted to Judge Spicer without argument by either party on the morning of November 29.

Justice of the Peace Wells Spicer heard the testimony against the Earps and Doc Holliday in the preliminary hearing and released them.

At two o'clock on the afternoon of November 30, 1881, Justice Spicer rendered his decision. It was a long, carefully constructed opinion. From the beginning, the prosecution had to see the way the decision would go because Justice Spicer chose to emphasize Ike Clanton's belligerent behavior on the day of the street fight. He did note that "[i]n view of these controversies between Wyatt Earp and Ike Clanton and Thomas McLaury, and in further view of this quarrel the night before between Isaac Clanton and J. H. Holliday, I am of the opinion that the defendant, Virgil Earp, as chief of police, subsequently calling upon Wyatt Earp, and J. H. Holliday to assist him in arresting and disarming the Clantons and McLowrys—committed an injudicious and censurable act."

If those comments gave the prosecution any hope, Spicer quickly squelched it by adding:

[A]lthough in this he acted incautiously and without due circumspection, yet when we consider the conditions of affairs incident to a frontier country; the lawlessness and disregard for human life; the existence of a law-defying element in [our] midst; the fear and feeling of insecurity that has existed; the supposed prevalence of bad, desperate and reckless men who have been a terror to the country and kept away capital and enterprise; and consider the many threats that have been made against the Earps, I can attach no criminality to his unwise act. In fact, as the result plainly proves, he needed the assistance and support of staunch and true friends, upon whose courage, coolness and fidelity he could depend, in case of an emergency.

Spicer said that he was convinced that Virgil "honestly believed" that the Clantons and the McLaurys intended to do them harm or at least to resist arrest and that his belief was "reasonable" in light of the threats made that day. What was missing, Spicer said, was any evidence of "felonious intent" on the part of the Earps. He brushed aside the notion that Tom McLaury was unarmed, saying that "if Tom McLowry was one of a party who were thus armed and were making felonious resistance to an arrest, and in the melee that followed was shot, the fact of his being unarmed, if it be a fact, could not of itself incriminate the defendants, if they were not otherwise incriminated."

Spicer concluded that Frank McLaury and Billy Clanton did in fact resist when called on to surrender. He dismissed the claim that the fight was an effort to "assassinate" Ike Clanton to cover up their confessions to him and emphasized Sheriff Behan's testimony that the Cow-Boys had "demurred" from surrendering their arms to him. He dismissed as "a proposition both monstrous and startling" McLaury's demand that the "Chief of Police and his assistants should be disarmed." There was no "criminal haste" on the part of the Earps nor "felonious intent then and there to kill and murder the deceased." Rather, Spicer said, "[t]hey saw at once the dire necessity of giving the first shots, to save themselves from certain death!"

Accordingly, he reasoned, "I cannot resist the conclusion that the defendants were fully justified in committing these homicides—that it was a necessary act, done in the discharge of an official duty." Spicer said that he did not believe the evidence would warrant "a conviction of the defendants by trial jury of any offense whatever." He pointed out that the grand jury was then in session and could choose to indict, but he concluded his duties by ordering Wyatt Earp and John Holliday released.[92]

Spicer's decision was legally sound, but it was not greeted with universal approval. The *Tombstone Nugget* immediately questioned Spicer's motives and used innuendo rather than reason to disagree: "The remarkable document which appears in another column purports to be the reasons which actuated the judge in his final actions. But the suspicion of reasons of more substantial nature are openly expressed upon the streets, and in the eyes of many the justice does not stand like Caesar's wife, 'Not only virtuous but above suspicion.'"[93] The *Nugget's* allegations were not only unsubstantiated but also irresponsible, although they clearly reflected the street verdict of many of Tombstone's citizens. Clara Brown captured the moment with her report that "[t]here being two strong parties in the camp, of course this verdict is satisfactory to but one of them. The other accepts it with a very bad grace and a smoldering fire exists, which is liable to burst forth at some unexpected moment."[94]

The controversy, then, was not about Spicer's legal conclusions (for all the rhetoric) but about the predisposed opinions of the factions that the street fight had brought into the open. In point of fact, Spicer's opinion was almost inevitable, based on the evidence presented and the rigorous standard to which he was held. Territorial law required him to determine the likelihood of conviction, not to determine whether sufficient evidence existed to justify a trial. The defense made a strong case that the Earp party had acted consistent with correct police procedures. Even the question of whether Tom McLaury was armed was rendered irrelevant by the resistance of his companions. Virgil's only legally damaging mistake was involving Doc Holliday.

Yet, the prosecution ultimately misplayed that ace. If "blame" could be placed for the failure of the prosecution, it lay in the prosecution's own overzealous strategy, with its emphasis on premeditation (insisted on by Will McLaury, with support from Ike Clanton). The unbelievable scenario Ike presented in court, combined with the more reasonable case presented by the defense, undermined what initially appeared to be a strong case for the prosecution. Even in the court record itself, Spicer's shift of opinion was obvious—belying any notion of prejudice one way or the other—and it followed Clanton's self-destruction and the introduction of nonpartisan witnesses by the defense who supported the more plausible testimony of Wyatt and Virgil Earp.

At that moment, however, legal analysis was not the standard. The same angry emotion that characterized Will McLaury's letters to his family combined with politics to cause at least some of the population to believe the worst about Spicer as well as about the Earps and Doc Holliday. Something peculiar had happened in the hearing that swung opinion against the Earps, and Doc was at the center of it. Before the hearing, the Earps had reputations as effective law enforcement officers. Even the *Nugget* had commended them without any hint of wrongdoing on their part. So, too, the *Tucson Star* had made Cow-Boy depredations a point of editorial emphasis. The Earps might have been perceived as cold, no-nonsense, and clannish, but they stood clearly for law and order in the public mind.

Stripped of all the rationalizations, postfight justifications, and prevarications, the most famous gunfight in the history of the Old West was a bloody miscalculation that neither side really wanted but that both sides believed the other side wanted. The Spicer hearing provided no evidence that the Clantons and the McLaurys came to Tombstone for the purpose of goading the Earps into a fight. In fact, the Cow-Boys most likely were about to leave town before Behan delayed their departure. Still, Ike's threats did produce a situation that Virgil Earp, as chief of police, could not ignore. Neither was there any evidence that the Earps went to the vacant lot on Fremont Street to gun down the Cow-Boys. They simply had no motive for doing something so damaging to their own interests.

The Fremont Street fiasco was a testament to the costs of braggadocio, miscommunication, and rumor. Although Virgil and his brothers felt fully justified and were supported in that view by Judge Spicer, the Cow-Boys saw themselves as victims, and the townsfolk both oversimplified and complicated what had happened until what really happened on the vacant lot off Fremont Street on October 26, 1881, scarcely mattered at all. Instead, the bloody miscalculations of that afternoon were filtered through preconceptions of what or who was right or wrong, based on personal, economic, and political animosities, and those prejudices shaped the next phase of the Cow-Boy war and finally made the Earps and Doc Holliday central players in it.

Doc's participation in the fight also did more than anything to cause a shift in public opinion toward the Earps after the shootings. The prosecution's attempt to place the blame on him for firing the first shot, although discredited in court, was believed by many. Doc's public confrontation with Ike Clanton the night before, his feud with Milt Joyce, and Kate's accusations about the murders of Bud Philpott and Peter Roerig and the attempted holdup of the Benson stage gave him a bad reputation even among many of the Earps' friends. Believing the worst about him in the fight provided the easiest explanation for what happened.

The one blemish on the Earps in Tombstone before the street fight was their association with Doc Holliday. And initially that seemed to be the focus of the prosecution in the Spicer hearing. It was the view summarized by Ridgely Tilden, a freelance journalist who worked for the *Nugget* for a time, in the *San Francisco Examiner* after the decision. He said, "Doc Holliday is responsible for all the killing, etc, in connection with what is known as the Earp-Clanton imbroglio in Arizona. He kicked up the fight, and Wyatt Earp and his brothers 'stood in' with him, on the score of gratitude. Everyone in Tombstone conversant with the circumstances deprecates the killing of the McLaurys and Clanton." What people could not find was justification for the deaths on October 26, and Doc's unsavory reputation seemed to provide the logical explanation. That is why John P. Clum, a staunch friend and supporter of the Earps, would write later in his life, "I have always believed that if he [Holliday] had not been in that street battle on Dec. [Oct.] 26, 1881, the affair would have been relieved of much of its bitterness."[95]

Of course, that conclusion made the Earps guilty of bad judgment, anger, and personal animosity, not premeditated murder. It did not make them the murderers Will McLaury saw in his grief. The hearing gave Ike Clanton a forum for accusing the Earps of being involved in stage robberies, "piping off" Wells, Fargo shipments, and planning murders to hide their misdeeds. These allegations were wild and unsupported and would have been dismantled in a full-blown trial, but they provided fodder for those who opposed the Earps and tarnished their reputations among the citizenry. Will McLaury bought Ike's story, with all its embellishments, because it fit his perceptions of the defendants. He wrote his brother-in-law:

> The cause of the murder was this [:] sometimes ago *Holliday* one of the murderers attempted to rob the express of Wells Fargo & Co. and in so doing shot and killed a stage driver and a passenger and the other parties engaged in the murder with him. . . . [T]he Earp brothers were interested in the attempt at the Exp—robbery and young Clanton who was killed, a boy 18 years old knew the facts about the attempted robbery and had told his brother J. I. Clanton and Thos and Robt and they had got up facts intending to prossecute [*sic*] him (Holliday) and the Earp Bros. and Holliday had information of it. It is now known that two other men who knew of the murder in the attempted robbery have since then been killed in Mexico, the report was by "Greasers" but at the time they were killed Holliday was out of town "said to be visiting in Georgia" there will be an indictment agst Holliday and I think two of the Earps and one *Williams* for the murders in the attempted robbery [emphasis in original].[96]

Things did not happen the way McLaury hoped, but his response to Ike's story was an interesting precursor to the public response to Ike's testimony. Ike did not succeed in getting his adversaries convicted of murder, but he did raise questions about their character and conduct while providing an alternative view of his "arrangement" with Wyatt Earp that took him off the hook with his Cow-Boy associates. Doc and the Earps won their freedom in Spicer's court, as they should have, but, ironically, Ike Clanton, the braggart most responsible for the Fremont Street tragedy, succeeded in planting doubts about the Earps in the public mind that doomed their future in Tombstone.

VENGEANCE

The Earps and a desperado named Doc Holliday are running things with a high hand at Tombstone, Arizona.

—*Albuquerque Morning Journal*, January 31, 1882

After Judge Wells Spicer's decision was rendered, someone in Tombstone wrote a letter to John Henry Holliday's father, Henry Holliday, in Valdosta, Georgia, about what had transpired. According to the *Valdosta Times*:

> He received a letter signed by a large number of citizens of Tombstone entirely exonerating John from the charge of willful murder. He also received a copy of the Tombstone *Epitaph* in which a long decision, delivered by the local Judge in the committment [*sic*] trial, was published, exonerating and discharging Holliday and the Earps. We have read it, and from the summary of evidence given there is no other conclusion to arrive at than that Holliday, with the Earps, was acting in self-defense, while performing the duties of the positions they held.[1]

Things were not so plain in Tombstone, however. On December 1, George W. Parsons noted in his diary, "Earps released today or yesterday. Grand jury may indict but I doubt it. Fights in both saloons opp[osite] and underneath last night. Quite a circus about one a.m."[2] Doc may have been involved in one of the episodes, because on December 3, 1881, the *Nugget* reported that he had been arrested for firing a pistol.[3] The details of the incident escaped the record, but given the temper of the time, it could have been an inconsequential moment, resulting from celebration of his renewed freedom, or it could have been the result of an altercation over some remark about the outcome of the hearing. After that trouble, though, John Henry became less public.

William R. McLaury was still in town, hoping for a grand jury miracle, but the *Nugget* was not optimistic, noting that "from the confessed and known bias of a number of its members, it is not probable that an indictment will be found."[4] On December 16, the grand jury confirmed the *Nugget's* prophecy and shattered McLaury's hopes of a legal solution to his bitterness and anger. He lingered in Tombstone, working to settle his brothers' affairs and nursing his rage. Rumors were rampant of Cow-Boy retaliation. Will McLaury had warned back in November that "in the event they escape by any trick or otherwise then if you read the papers there will be more 'Press dispatches.'"[5] Later, after his sister cautioned him "to leave it to God" to punish the killers of Tom and Frank, he had responded:

> Now when these men are dead by one means or another and there [*sic*] friends who aided them are dead all of which may occur soon then I will go home perhaps. . . .
>
> I think their only hope is in escape and should they escape from Jail their bones will bleach on the mountains. . . .
>
> I am trying to punish these men through the courts of the country first if that fails—then we *may* submit.[6]

It was not just talk. Mrs. J. C. Collier, a visitor in Tombstone who had witnessed the street fight herself, wrote an account of her experiences in Arizona for the *Kansas City Star.* She reported one threatened raid on the Oriental Saloon:

> The night before we left, the cowboys had organized a raid on the saloon. Fifteen or twenty cowboys heavily armed were in the saloon. Just on the edge of the town were thirty more and others scattered around the town ready to jump in the fight at the signal. A fire broke out and so rustled them that they gave it up for a time. You see we became intimately acquainted with a gentleman who boarded at the same hotel we did and was in sympathy with the cowboys, and acquainted with all their plans. He told us about this raid being in contemplation and said that this was the second time they had been prepared to make a raid, and were thwarted by a fire breaking out and calling all the people out on the streets. He said, "You're going away, and I don't mind telling you this."[7]

In fact, on the night of December 9, a fire did break out at the Grand Lodging House on Toughnut Street where R. F. Coleman lived with his son. Crowds of people swarmed into the street, and some of them worked together with the Rescue Hook & Ladder Company to prevent another disaster like the fire of June 22. That night, James Flynn, the town marshal who had replaced Virgil, ordered all the saloons closed at eleven o'clock, which could well have helped to quell any Cow-Boy plans.[8]

Acting governor John J. Gosper had mixed emotions about the situation in Cochise County. His visit to Tombstone in November had reinforced his belief that the Cow-Boys had to be suppressed, but he also believed that some "officers of the law are often themselves in league with the 'Cow-Boy' element to obtain illegal gains." He also deplored the political situation, particularly the "strife" arising from the rivalry of John H. Behan and Wyatt Earp for the position of sheriff of Cochise County. He was distressed by the partisanship of the local newspapers and the interplay of county and city patronage. He condemned the practice of citizens handling stolen property and profiting from the theft of the Cow-Boys, which meant that a large portion of the population sympathized with them.

He advocated to U.S. Marshal Crawley P. Dake the appointment of "a man of well known *courage* and *character* of cool sound judgment, which your good judgment can secure, who with a suitable posse of men, can first *fully comprehend* the true nature of the situation, and then with proper discretion and courage, go forward with a firm and steady hand bring as rapidly as possible the *leading* spirits of this lawless class to a severe and speedy punishment." He also suggested the removal of Sheriff Behan by the appropriate authorities and advocated that Dake employ "[d]eputies to the end that men possessing the confidence of the public" be appointed.[9]

Dake, however, used Spicer's decision as a vindication of the Earps and chose to pursue Gosper's goals using them as the agents of choice. On December 3, he wrote to S. F. Phillips, the acting attorney general:

> The Earps have rid Tombstone and neighborhood of the presence of this outlaw element.—They killed several Cow boys in Tombstone recently—and the Sheriff's faction had my deputies arrested—and after a protracted trial my deputies were vindicated and publicly complimented for their bravery in driving this outlaw element from this part of our Territory. The magistrate discharged my deputies on

the grounds that when they killed Clanton and the McLowry's, they were in the legitimate discharge of their duties as my officer.

Hereafter my deputies will not be interfered with in hunting down Stage Robbers, Mail Robbers, Train Robbers, Cattle thieves and all that class of murdering *banditti* of the border.

I am proud to report that I have some of the best and bravest men in my employ in this hazardous business—men who are trusty and tried, and who strike fear into the hearts of these outlaws.[10]

With this overly optimistic endorsement, Dake promised that the war on the Cow-Boys had just begun, and he gave the Earps his firm support as the men who could carry out the mission. If he conveyed these feelings directly to Virgil, and it is probable that he did, he may well have given the Earps renewed confidence, especially when combined with the support of prominent Tombstone citizens—a renewed confidence that may well have affected their behavior in the weeks that followed. If Dake thought that the troubles were over, however, he was badly mistaken, and the Earps knew it. They expected the worst, but they also prepared themselves, confident that they would be supported in what they did.

In any event, enough tension existed in Tombstone that John Henry and the Earps stayed together for protection with their supporters to the point that some who had previously supported them now saw them as bullies. They armed themselves and headquartered at the Oriental. The Cow-Boys reportedly had a room in the Grand Hotel overlooking the street where the Earps and Holliday could be watched in their movements. More ominously, prominent Earp supporters as well as Justice Spicer, Mayor John P. Clum, the Earps, and Holliday received threatening letters. Clum went so far as to telegraph acting governor Gosper, asking that he provide weapons for the Citizens Safety Committee, and on December 9, Gosper urged the repeal of the Posse Comitatus Act so that the military could be used to suppress the Cow-Boys.[11]

On the night of December 14, Clum left Tombstone on the Sandy Bob stage for Benson, planning to visit his brother in Tucson before traveling east. En route, the stage was accosted by holdup men who fired on the stage. Whistling Dick Wright, the driver of a bullion wagon following the stage, was wounded in the leg, but both the stage and the wagon managed to get to safety before one of the horses fell dead from a wound received in the flight. Clum, who was convinced the incident was an assassination attempt, left the stage and walked seven miles before securing a horse and riding on into Benson.[12]

The *Nugget* belittled Clum as a coward, and the *Epitaph* chastised the *Nugget* for making light of an incident that placed lives in jeopardy and resulted in at least one injury.[13] Clum later claimed that "it was whispered that the Death List had been prepared with most spectacular and dramatic ceremonials enacted at midnight within the recesses of a deep canyon, during which the names of the elect had been written in blood drawn from the veins of a murderer." Such melodrama did not work well with the community, and he even added, "We did not believe all we heard. Nevertheless, we realized that the situation was extremely serious."[14]

On the morning of December 15, Virgil Earp encountered Milton E. Joyce in the Oriental. Joyce could not resist remarking about the attempted stage holdup of the previous evening that "he had been expecting something of the sort ever since they [the Earps and Holliday] had been liberated from jail."[15] Virgil instantly slapped Joyce across the face, and several of Virgil's friends sprang forward to his side. Joyce wisely let the moment pass, saying as he reached the door, "Your favorite method is to shoot a man in the back, but if you murder me you will be compelled to shoot me in the front."[16] Said the *Nugget*, "[H]is coolness and good judgment saved Tombstone from disgrace of another bloody tragedy, all who are cognizant of the peculiar characteristics of the Earp party will readily admit."[17]

The following day, Joyce returned to the Oriental, found the Earps in the gambling area, and, "with a six-shooter in each hand, asked them if they wanted to fight as bad as they did the night before." William M. Breakenridge recalled, "Sheriff Behan followed Joice [*sic*] into the saloon and coming up behind him grasped him around the waist, turned with his back toward the Earps and carried Joice out of doors, and arrested him for carrying weapons. He was fined fifteen dollars for carrying the guns. Up to this time Joice and Behan were close friends, but from this time out Joice was very bitter toward him."[18] The *Epitaph* reported, "It is understood that a little unpleasantness occurred in the Oriental Saloon yesterday, which under any circumstances is seriously to be regretted. Under the present state of public excitement it becomes all good citizens to avoid provocation for all disturbance."[19]

Also on December 15, the *Nugget* reported that the Citizens Safety Committee had suggested that Sheriff Behan and others unfriendly to the Earps should leave town, but the threats by friends of the Cow-Boys were more plentiful.[20] On December 18, the *Epitaph* published a letter from "A Miner" warning Wells Spicer that he was "liable to get a hole through your coat at any moment." Spicer responded with a long letter in which he curiously absolved the Clanton brothers from responsibility. He did defend himself from the charge that he acted in a partisan way in writing his decision:

> It is but just to myself that I should here assert that neither directly or indirectly was I ever approached in the interest of the defendants, by them or for them. Not so the prosecution—in the interest of that side even my friends have been interviewed with the hope of influencing me with money, and hence all this talk by them and those who echo their slanders about corruption. And here too, I wish to publicly proclaim every one who says that I was in any manner improperly influenced is a base and willful liar.[21]

Spicer defied the "Miner" to come after him and expressed his contempt for the "low-bred, arrant cowards" who made anonymous threats.

Two days later, the other side was heard, in a letter to the *Nugget* written by James A. Reilly, the former justice of the peace who had had troubles with Wyatt Earp the previous year. After denouncing threats against Milt Joyce, Buckskin Frank Leslie, and others who had condemned the Fremont Street killings, Reilly declared, "I am convinced that seven out of ten of the stage robberies committed in Arizona for the last fifteen years have been put up and engineered by the trusted agents of the post office, of Wells Fargo & Co.'s agents, and agents of the stage companies."[22] By innuendo, then, he had cast aspersions on John Clum (as postmaster), Marshall Williams, and the Earps.

He chastised the Citizens Safety Committee as a dangerous and misguided organization. "Is it, or is it not true," he demanded, "that the Earps and Holliday, while undergoing examination, threatened that when they got out they would make those men who called the killing of the McLaurys a murder, 'take it back' and that since they got out they have gone around town armed, abusing and picking quarrels with men of that opinion and have threatened many persons, telling them they had better leave?" Doc and the Earps were not "good men," Reilly proclaimed, "for if good men are unfortunate enough to be compelled to kill, they regret it; they are sorrowful, modest, and ask only to be allowed to live down the prejudice excited against them by good conduct and submission to the laws. They do not by threats, assaults and braggadocio, attempt to bulldoze a whole community into giving countenance to their acts."[23]

Reilly's missive prompted a response in the *Epitaph* from Ned Boyle, the bartender from the Oriental who had testified for the defense at the Spicer hearing. He began by accusing Reilly of having himself been involved in a stage robbery while he lived at Yuma. He also reminded readers of Reilly's less than exemplary history in Tombstone, including his record as a lot jumper. With reference to the Earps, he wrote, "I shall speak only of one of them, Wyatt Earp; he is one of the partners in the firm I am working for, and a more liberal and kind-hearted man I have never met." Boyle denounced Reilly as a "lying mountebank" and challenged him to respond.[24]

And so the charges and countercharges went. "Tombstone seems to be in a nice condition of disorder," the *San Francisco Daily Exchange* declared.[25] What was lost in the process was the contrast between the orderly state of affairs in Tombstone before October 26, while Virgil was marshal, and the chaos that reigned in December. The political ramifications were hardly missed by anyone. Virgil's wounds were far greater than the gunshot wound that caused him to limp, and while Wyatt still hoped to challenge Behan for sheriff in 1882, the politically astute already knew that something dramatic would have to happen to give him a fighting chance.

Oddly, the Earps made no public effort to defend themselves. They made no public statements, and while they kept many of their warmest and most respectable supporters close by, they appeared confused and dazed. They seemed unwilling to believe that public opinion had turned against them. They assumed they were right, and they could not believe that people would fail to see it. Always politically naive, Wyatt was surprisingly off balance, even bewildered, by the public reaction. Virgil might have been more politically aware, but he kept a studied silence as if waiting and watching to see what would come. Clara Brown summed up their situation: "If the Earps were not men of great courage, they would hardly dare remain in Tombstone."[26]

City elections were scheduled for January 3. Clum had decided not to run for reelection, and Virgil could not afford to risk total repudiation. On December 13, a petition signed by 170 men, including several of the friends of the Earps, called on Lewis W. Blinn, a lumberman, to run for mayor, and four days later he agreed. James Flynn announced his bid for chief of police. On December 24, a group calling itself the People's Independent Ticket nominated John Carr for mayor and David Neagle, Behan's feisty enforcer, for chief of police. Interestingly, the situation broke both Republican and Democratic solidarity. Locally, at least, the Earps had friends and enemies in both parties. A nasty campaign, with the Earps' reputation at the center of it, followed, as the *Nugget* and *Epitaph* harangued local citizens.[27]

On December 21, the Bird Cage Theater opened. A few nights later, Deputy Breakenridge was walking along the street opposite the theater hugging the walls against the rain when "I ran up against a gun-barrel which was placed against my breast. Looking up, I saw it was Frank Stilwell." Breakenridge remembered:

> I asked him what he was trying to do, and he said that a certain party had boasted that he was going to get him that night, and that he would not do it if he saw him first. I told him that it was too late for him to kill any one that night, that he was in enough trouble already, and to put up his gun and go home. He did as I told him, and went down the side street, and I turned back wondering whom he was after, but about the middle of the block I met Doc Holliday, who roomed a short distance up the street, on his way home. It flashed through my mind that I had inadvertently saved Holliday's life that night.[28]

If Stilwell was gunning for Doc, it was a forecast of things to come. The Cow-Boys stood watch in their room in the Grand Hotel facing the Cosmopolitan Hotel. They kept the shutters closed, except for a single slat that had been removed to enable them to watch the Earps' rooms. Early in December, one of them was at the window with a Winchester, waiting to shoot Lou Rickabaugh, who was walking down the street. Another Cow-Boy arrived and stopped his friend by reasoning that Rickabaugh had done nothing more than "spend his money for his friends, the Earps," something he could not be faulted for.[29] Later, a clerk at the Grand, Jack Altman, warned the Earps that Curly Bill Brocius, John Ringo, Pony Deal, Ike Clanton, and others fre-

quented the room, watching their movements and waiting for opportunities to shoot them.[30]

The Christmas season, then, was hardly a time of good cheer or
peace on earth in Tombstone that December. It was hard to be grateful for the freedom won with things so bitter for John Henry and,
especially, for his friends the Earps. He, at least, had lost no post, nor
any hope of one; they stood to lose everything they had built in
Tombstone, not the least of which was their reputation as responsible
men and capable peace officers. And already they saw some of those
who had called them friends turning away as they passed by or criticizing them for what was done and denying them support in their crisis.

John Henry stood by them because, in truth, his future as well as
his past was linked to theirs. The rancor was bitter for them all as the
Earp wives set the Christmas table. There was no pride in the moment,
but no shame either. What was done was what had to be done, and not
to good men. And the worst of it was that the cause of it all—Ike
Clanton—walked free and slandered the names of better men to take
his revenge and cover his own record of treachery and betrayal.

It could be argued that Doc alone profited from what happened, if
"profit" is the proper word. Doc achieved something in the street
fight, but it was not something he sought or even wanted. If the reputations of the Earps were sullied in the street fight, the reputation of
Doc Holliday grew as a man to be feared—and respected—for his courage if not for his character. Men gave him room after that. But what
he gained was as much a burden as a boon, a burden that intruded on
the private man that Doc really was. Notoriety was not something he
reveled in, but it had its use in making men think twice about bracing
him. Most important, though, Doc had found a cause, a reason that
gave his life a sense of purpose it had not had for a very long time. He
was fighting for something that mattered. Life now had meaning.

In the rhetorical battles of the *Epitaph* and the *Nugget*, Doc was
unseen for the most part. There was little to be gained from celebrating or denigrating him. The Earps were the point of controversy, and,
in truth, both newspapers missed the mark. The *Epitaph*, with its excesses, hardly served the Earps well, and the *Nugget* had to ignore
much to make the case they tried so desperately to make. Ironically, as
the *Nugget*—and the *Tucson Star*—reversed field to minimize the Cow-
Boy threat, men in the areas frequented by the Cow-Boys finally began
to grow tired of their antics. While the Spicer hearing plodded on

through the month of November, Curly Bill was in jail in Lordsburg, New Mexico. On November 9, 1881, citizens of Shakespeare lynched Sandy King and William "Russian Bill" Tettenborn.[31]

While Tombstone residents hurled barbs at one another over the Earps, federal and territorial officials kept their focus on the Cow-Boy problem. Following Mayor Clum's request for guns to arm the Citizens Safety Committee, Dake forwarded the message to President Chester A. Arthur with the admonition, "Give us the use of the military and we will give you peace on the border."[32] President Arthur did ask Congress to rescind or alter the Posse Comitatus Act to allow the use of the army in pursuit of outlaws whose acts threatened to disrupt relations with other countries, but Congress did not respond at first.[33]

However, that was all far away from Tombstone on the night of December 28, 1881, when Virgil Earp left the Oriental Saloon to return to his rooms at the Cosmopolitan Hotel. From the darkness of a construction site on the southeast corner of Fifth Street came the roar of shotguns. Virgil was knocked to the ground by the force of the blasts. George Parsons noted in his diary, "Doc G[oodfellow] had just left and I tho't couldn't have crossed the street—when four shots were fired in quick succession from very heavily charged guns, making a terrible noise and I tho't were fired under my window under which I quickly dropped, keeping the dobe wall between me and the outside until the fusillade was over."[34]

Virgil regained his feet and walked back to the Oriental, where he told Wyatt he had been shot. Wyatt hastened him back to his rooms and sent for Drs. H. M. Matthews and George Goodfellow. Parsons initially thought that Dr. Goodfellow had been shot, "knowing how pronounced he was on the Earp-cowboy question." Parsons criticized the police, whom he described as "cowardly, apathetic guardians of the peace," for their failure to pursue the shooters. By the time he reached Virgil's room at the Cosmopolitan, the hotel and its halls were filled with armed men.[35]

Virgil's left arm was shattered. Other shots had torn into his thigh and struck his kidney, liver, and spinal column. More shots had crashed through the window of the Eagle Brewery Saloon and passed over the heads of the patrons. Nineteen shots were counted in the outside wall and awning posts. The doctors wanted to remove Virgil's arm, but he was adamant against that procedure, so they removed five and one-half inches of humerus bone from the arm. He told his wife, Allie, "Never mind, I've got one arm to hug you with."[36] George Parsons said, "Patient doing well. It is surmised that Ike Clanton, Curly Bill, and McLaury did the shooting. Bad state of affairs here. Something will have to be done."[37]

In fact, Curly Bill's whereabouts were unknown (assuming he had been released from the Lordsburg jail), and Will McLaury had gone home to Fort Worth. Virgil later said he saw Frank Stilwell entering the construction site as he left the Oriental, and Ike Clanton's hat was found at the rear of the building. With Virgil wounded and perhaps dying, Wyatt telegraphed Marshal Dake:

> Virgil was shot by concealed assassins last night. His wounds are fatal. Telegraph me appointment with power to appoint deputies. Local authorities are doing nothing. The lives of other citizens are threatened.
>
> WYATT EARP[38]

Dake immediately telegraphed the appointment to Wyatt, "instructing him to spare no pains or expense in discovering the perpetrators of the deed."[39] Accordingly, Wyatt deputized a group of men including Doc, Morgan, Warren, Sherman McMaster, Texas Jack Vermillion, Turkey Creek Jack Johnson, Dan G. Tipton, O. C. "Charlie" Smith, and perhaps a few others.[40] It was a hard group, but Wyatt wanted a tough crowd experienced in gunplay, and these men were. Doc must have smiled at the thought of being a duly appointed federal lawman. Now, his cause had legitimacy too.

The attack on Virgil was serious. The *Epitaph* offered its opinion without restraint, seeing in what happened more validation of its stance on the Cow-Boy question:

> This further proves that there is a band of assassins in our midst, who, having threatened the lives of Judge Spicer, Mayor Clum, Mr. Williams, the Earp brothers and Holliday, have attempted on two occasions to carry their threats into execution, first upon Mayor Clum and second upon Virgil Earp. The question naturally arises, Who will be the next subject? And a further question, How long will our people stand this sort of thing? It is no fault of these damned assassins that several persons were not killed in their dastardly attempt to murder a United States officer last night; for there were many people in the Eagle brewery, over the heads of whom the passing shots flew

on their course. A few inches lower and there would have been corpses prostrated upon the floor in place of frightened people wondering what had happened to cause the bombardment.[41]

The *San Francisco Stock Exchange* said that people should stop justifying the Cow-Boys as "a benefit to the town" for economic reasons, saying flatly, "it is time for respectable citizens to take the law in their own hands, if the officers are powerless to enforce the laws. . . . [T]his seems to be one of the cases in which a Vigilance Committee and a few hangings would be justifiable."[42] The *Nugget*, however, kept up its campaign against the Earps, with James Reilly now claiming that Bud Philpott's death was "the result of a well-concocted scheme" to kill Bob Paul and to gain control of Tombstone's criminal life. Reilly not only accused the Earps of stage robbery and murder but also of malfeasance in office.[43] Oddly, then, the attempt to assassinate Virgil did nothing to bring Tombstone to its senses, but, on the contrary, divided the town even more.

In that environment, city elections were held on January 3. The *Epitaph* warned that a vote for Carr as mayor and Neagle as chief of police would ensure that the "ten-percent-ring" would control the city as well as the county. The *Nugget* proclaimed, "Doc Holliday and the Earps are solid for Blinn and Flynn. So is the Daily Strangler." The *Nugget* argued that if Blinn and Flynn were elected, Flynn would resign and Blinn would reappoint Virgil Earp as chief of police: "The election will to-day decide whether Tombstone is to be dominated for another year by the Earps and their strikers. Every vote against the People's Independent Ticket is a vote in favor of the Earps. Miners, business men, and all others having the welfare of our city at heart should remember this."[44] Its arguments apparently won the day, because Carr beat Blinn by 830 votes to 298, and Neagle defeated Flynn by a vote of 590 to 434, with Leslie Blackburn polling 103. Reilly, at least, was defeated by A. O. Wallace for city recorder.[45] The *Nugget* crowed and the *Epitaph* acquiesced, but the troubles were not over.

Carr did make a strong effort. He beefed up the enforcement of Ordinance No. 9 and revoked a number of concealed weapon permits. His administration dropped the 10 percent surcharge on taxes to shatter that projection, and Marshal Neagle at least commanded the respect of the Earps and their supporters. The Earps no longer had a clear political presence, but they did continue to have a political base with the same "law and order" types who comprised the Citizens Safety Committee and some of the most prominent movers and shakers in the business community. The support was not as visible as before, but it was still there.

On January 6, and again on January 8, stage robberies reminded the residents of Cochise County that a city election in Tombstone had not cured all their problems. The W. W. Hubbard & Company coach for Bisbee was attacked on January 6. Even though Charley Bartholomew, a Wells, Fargo guard, fought the attackers, a horse was killed and the robbers took $6,500. Two days later, the Sandy Bob stage from Benson was hit between Contention and Tombstone. The robbers got little more than small change from the passengers (missing $1,500 that was hidden), but they humiliated James B. Hume, the Wells, Fargo chief of detectives, by stealing his two prized revolvers. Hume continued to Tombstone, where he met with Wyatt Earp, whose ties to Wells, Fargo were still strong. He now had fresh reason to support the Earps and to be critical of Sheriff John Behan.[46]

In fact, Wells, Fargo was so infuriated by the latest robberies that it temporarily closed its Bisbee run, giving rise to rumors that Tombstone would soon be closed as a Wells, Fargo destination as well. The rumor was not true, but the threat itself was enough to concern the business interests in southeastern Arizona, which gave Wells, Fargo influence and leverage in law enforcement, and that reality alone extended the life of the Earps in Cochise County. Wells, Fargo officials never believed the tales about the Earps' involvement in stage robberies that surfaced after the Spicer hearing, and, on the contrary, saw them as the best hope for ending the crime spree.

The cause of the Earps with Wells, Fargo was boosted when Marshal Dake traveled to San Francisco. There,

[h]e called upon Mr. John J. Valentine, and represented that in the matter of the disturbance at Tombstone in Cochise Co., Arizona. A. T., that he, Dake, was powerless to do good as U. S. Marshal for want of funds, and if the Company would advance him $3,000, he would use in quieting the disturbance and return the amount as soon as the vouchers could be approved at Washington and the money could be gotten in return—upon which representation by Dake, Mr. Valentine advanced $3,000, taking Dake's receipt for the sum.[47]

John Peters Ringo, the Cow-Boy
leader who challenged Wyatt Earp to
a fight on the street in January 1882,
and was in turn challenged by Doc
Holliday. The police intervened, but
the incident would be used to imply a
rivalry between Ringo and Holliday.

This support would be welcome. The Earps were feeling financial
pressure as a result of recent events and, not surprisingly, began to
look for funds. The *Nugget* soon reported that "Wyatt Earp has sold
his interest in the Oriental Saloon to Ricabaugh [*sic*] and Clark," and
two days later the *Epitaph* reported that Lou Rickabaugh and Richard
Clark had sold out to Milt Joyce.[48] On the evening of January 10,
Joyce took over the operation of the Oriental with the best wishes of
both of the town's newspapers. It would be only the first move in the
gradual draining away of the Earps' assets in Tombstone.

The relative peace did not last, however. On January 17, George
Parsons wrote in his diary:

> Much blood in the air this afternoon. Ringo and Doc Holliday came
> nearly having it with pistols and Ben Maynard and Rickabaugh later
> tried to kick each others [*sic*] lungs out. Bad time expected with the
> Cow-boy leader and D. H. I passed both not knowing blood was up.
> One with hand in breast pocket and the other probably ready. Earps
> just beyond. Crowded Street and looked like another battle. Police
> vigilant for once and both disarmed.[49]

The venue was Allen Street near the Grand and Cosmopolitan
hotels in front of the Occidental Saloon. For a few seconds, a fight
between the two most feared men in Tombstone, John Ringo and Doc
Holliday, seemed certain. Everyone who was there remembered it as a
tense moment almost certain to erupt in gunplay, but contemporary
accounts were cryptic at best, especially about the preliminaries. Over
time, a web of recollections developed that reflected the interests and

prejudices of the various factions. The tale that emerged from that morass of accounts was pure melodrama, with Ringo offering to fight a handkerchief duel with Holliday, who was all too willing to oblige him, declaring in one version, "I'm your huckleberry. That's just my game," before the authorities stepped in to prevent another gunfight on Allen Street.[50]

Some accounts, especially those partial to the Cow-Boys, had Ringo publicly berating the Earp crowd and challenging Wyatt to settle things one on one. Billy Breakenridge claimed that Ringo approached Wyatt Earp and said to him, "Wyatt, let's end this row. It has gone on long enough. Let Holliday and me get out here in the middle of the street and shoot it out. If you get me, the cowboys will go home and consider the feud ended. If I am the winner, you agree to do the same and it will be all over." Ringo then turned on his heel and started for the middle of the street, but, said Breakenridge, "This arrangement . . . was not acceptable to the Earp party, and they all went into the saloon." Other old-timers would dismiss the entire Earp crowd as cowards for walking away and portrayed Wyatt cringing with fear at the very thought.

Still other versions portrayed Wyatt as coolly and wisely refusing to fight in order to defuse the situation, but, as Wyatt turned away, Doc stepped forward to accept Ringo's challenge. In Wyatt's own accounts of the affair, he claimed that Ringo's challenge was made directly to Holliday, who responded by preparing to fight. He claimed that Chief of Police James Flynn grabbed Ringo by the arm at that point and that men in the crowd shouted, "Turn him loose!" Wyatt said he then stepped through the crowd, took Doc by the arm, and led him away. Billy Breakenridge even claimed that the crowd broke up after the Earps went into Hatch's Billiard Parlor and that he later arrested Ringo himself.[51]

Doubtless, Tombstone narrowly avoided another shootout. George Parsons recalled that as he passed through the crowd, he heard Holliday tell Ringo, "All I want of you is ten paces out in the street." But the credit for preventing further trouble went to Chief of Police Flynn, who had not yet turned his duties over to newly elected David Neagle. It was his moment in the Tombstone story. The *Nugget* recounted:

> A difficulty occurred yesterday afternoon in front of the Occidental
> Saloon, Allen street, between John Ringo and Doc Holliday, that very

nearly terminated in bloodshed. The parties had been on bad terms for some time past, and meeting yesterday morning words were exchanged and both parties stepped back, placing their hands on their weapons with the intention of drawing and using them. Fortunately Chief of Police Flynn was at hand and placed both parties under arrest. They were taken to Judge Wallace's court and fined $32 each for carrying deadly weapons. Some little feeling was evinced by the occurrence, which fortunately died out before anything serious occurred. The streets were crowded at the time, and had the shooting commenced it is probable that more than one life would have paid the penalty and another serious tragedy been enacted in our streets.[52]

Actually, Flynn arrested Wyatt Earp as well as Ringo and Doc for carrying concealed weapons, which suggests he was involved somehow, but Wyatt was released because he was a federal officer with the right to carry a pistol. The other two were fined and released.[53]

Lou Rickabaugh's encounter with the Cow-Boy partisan Ben Maynard was also clearly related to ongoing troubles. Rickabaugh was himself a feisty partisan with a quick temper who had been involved in more than one scrape in Tombstone. On November 15, during the Spicer hearing, he got into an argument with C. D. Dill during a faro game. Dill struck him on the head with a six-shooter, which discharged. Chief Flynn arrested both men, and Judge Wallace fined Dill $20 for carrying concealed weapons and Rickabaugh $15 for "using profane and indecent language." Rickabaugh's fight with Maynard on January 17 let everyone know where he stood. Maynard, for his part, had not seen the last of the Earps.[54]

Ringo's arrest on January 17 was sufficient to remind Judge William H. Stilwell that Ringo had not been tried for the Galeyville robbery, and the judge decided that, given his behavior, the bond in his case was insufficient. On Friday, January 20, Ringo was taken into custody and lodged in the county jail, where he remained over the weekend.[55] During the same day, Dake deposited the $3,000 he received from Wells, Fargo in the Hudson & Company Bank, minus $15, for use "to arrest all parties committing crimes against the United States." The following day, John Thacker of Wells, Fargo went with Wyatt to the bank to authorize his use of the account.[56]

The Earps and their friends were quietly making plans to track down the men who had shot his brother. With his new authority as a deputy U.S. marshal, Wyatt sought and received warrants through Judge Stilwell, and Mayor Carr issued a proclamation calling on the citizens of Tombstone not to interfere with his efforts.[57] Some people were surprised at Carr's stance on the matter, and the *Nugget* placed the proclamation with other legal notices rather than give it prominence. It also editorialized that "a large majority of our citizens believe that the recent killing in our streets was a murder in reality, but done under the cover of a city marshal's authority. To again place such power, in a slightly different form, in the hands of the perpetrators of the former act, is an outrage upon the public that could only be committed by a stupid or vicious magistrate."[58]

Judge Stilwell was neither stupid nor vicious. He was one of a growing number of citizens who were put off by the failure of Behan's office to deal with recent criminal activity in Cochise County. The warrants were issued to duly constituted officers of the law. On January 23, Wyatt left Tombstone with a party of men including Morgan and Warren Earp, Doc Holliday, Texas Jack Vermillion, Sherman McMaster, Creek Johnson, and two others. Wyatt carried warrants in his pocket for Ike and Fin Clanton and Pony Deal, but his destination was not announced.[59]

Ringo was still incarcerated when the Earp posse left Tombstone, so he called for his attorney, Briggs Goodrich, to expedite his bail. Goodrich advised Sheriff Behan that bail would be granted shortly, and Behan released Ringo before the judge had officially acted. Ringo immediately left town to warn his friends of Earp's posse. James Earp, seeing Ringo leave, filed an affidavit calling Ringo "an escaped prisoner" who left "the custody of the Sheriff of said county without the approval of any bond." He charged, further, that Ringo's purpose was "to intercept Wyatt S. Earp, a Marshal entrusted with the execution of warrants for the arrest of divers persons charged with violations of the laws of the territory and duly issued for the arrest of said persons and deponent believes that the purpose of said Ringo is to obstruct the execution of said warrants."[60]

At that juncture, a second posse was formed under John H. Jackson for the specific purpose of rearresting Ringo; they departed on January 24 at four o'clock in the morning. Ringo reached Charleston in plenty of time to raise the alarm about the Earp posse, but when Jackson's party arrived, he agreed to return to Tombstone with the posse. His attorney arrived after that, however, and, following a conversation with his client, told Jackson that Ringo would surrender to the authorities in Tombstone. Ringo then rode back to Tombstone and was again lodged in the county jail.[61]

The following day a party of more than thirty riders from Tombstone led by Charley Bartholomew, the Wells, Fargo guard, joined the Earp group that had been reconnoitering the backcountry, and together they descended on Charleston. En route they met Ben Maynard and forced him to return to Charleston with them to help locate the Clantons. By then, because of Ringo's warning, the Clantons had left town. The Earps controlled Charleston overnight and the following day returned to Tombstone with nothing accomplished, except having created more ill will toward themselves.[62] That day, Sheriff Behan received the following telegram:

> CHARLESTON, A. T., January 26.—TO J. H. BEHAN, Sheriff of Cochise County—DEAR SIR: Doc Holliday, the Earps and about forty or fifty more of the filth of Tombstone are here armed with Winchester rifles and revolvers, and patrolling our streets, as we believe, for no good purpose. Last night and to-day they have been stopping good, peaceable citizens on all the roads leading to our town, nearly paralyzing the business of our place. We know of no authority under which they are acting. Some of them, we have reason to believe, are thieves, robbers, and murderers. Please come here and take them where they belong.
>
> CHARLESTONIAN[63]

On January 30, Ike and Fin Clanton surrendered to a posse led by Bartholomew and were taken to Tombstone, where they were surprised to find that they had not been arrested for armed robbery as they supposed but for "assault with intent to commit murder, the specific offense being the waylaying and shooting of Virgil Earp some weeks ago."[64] After some dilatory moves to delay any action, the Clantons reversed their tactics and boldly decided to face the charges at once.

The trial was held on February 2. The evidence was circumstantial—Ike Clanton's hat found on the construction site and Sherman McMaster's testimony that he was at Charleston the night of the shooting and heard Ike say after he learned that Virgil had not been killed that he "would have to go back and do the job over." Against this was the testimony of seven men—including George McKelvey, the constable, and J. B. Ayers, the saloonman who also apparently worked undercover for Wells, Fargo—that the Clantons had been in Charleston the night of the shooting and could not have participated in the attempt on Virgil's life. They were acquitted.[65] Wyatt always claimed that Judge Stilwell told him afterward, "Wyatt, you'll never clean up this crowd this way; next time you'd better leave your prisoners out in the brush where alibis don't count."[66]

On the same day that the Clantons were arrested, Sylvester Comstock filed charges of perjury against John Behan, though the case was quickly dismissed. Sherman McMaster was also arrested by David Neagle at Wyatt Earp's camp at Pick 'Em Up near Tombstone. He was quickly released on bail. Accused of malfeasance in office and distrusted by court officials, Sheriff Behan also found himself under seige. The legal and law enforcement situation in Cochise County was chaotic at best. Parsons noted in his diary on February 4, "People suspicious on roads. Every stranger I met mounted was cause for me to remove gauntlet so I could handle pistol freely."[67]

Some had had enough. On February 3, Marshall Williams quietly left Tombstone with a lady of the evening. Later, Wells, Fargo determined that he left behind irregularities in his books.[68] Also on February 3, Richard Rule replaced Harry M. Woods as editor of the *Nugget*. Afterward, the paper, though hardly pro-Earp, was more responsible in its views, and Sheriff Behan no longer had immunity from criticism.[69] On February 6, Frederick A. Tritle, an Arizona mining man and partner of William B. Murray, one of the leaders of Tombstone's Citizens Safety Committee, was named governor of Arizona Territory. On February 7, Lou Rickabaugh left Tombstone for San Francisco on an extended visit.[70]

By then something remarkable had happened. The continued criticism of the Earps finally had an effect. On February 2, the *Epitaph* and the *Nugget* published a letter of resignation signed by Wyatt and Virgil, which said in part:

> [W]e realize that notwithstanding our best efforts and judgment in
> everything which we have been required to perform, there has arisen
> so much harsh criticism in relation to our operations, and such a per-
> sistent effort having been made to misrepresent and misinterpret our
> acts, we are led to the conclusion that, in order to convince the public

that it is our sincere purpose to promote the public welfare, independent of any personal emolument or advantages to ourselves, it is our
duty to place our resignations as deputy United States marshals in
your hands.[71]

Shortly thereafter, Marshal Dake arrived in Tombstone, and after a
meeting with local citizens, he appointed John H. Jackson as his deputy
in Cochise County, but, curiously and significantly, he did not accept
the Earps' resignation. He, at least, had no problem with their style.[72]

Wyatt apparently was making some effort to change public perception of him and his motives. At the same time he resigned as a
deputy U.S. marshal, Wyatt sent a message to Ike Clanton asking for a
meeting to reconcile their differences and end the animosity between
them. Clanton refused. The *Nugget* reported that "Mr. Clanton emphatically declined to hold any communication whatever with Earp."[73]
Instead, on February 9 the Clantons boldly swore out warrants in
Contention City for Virgil, Wyatt, and Morgan Earp and Doc Holliday for the murders of Billy Clanton and Tom and Frank McLaury.
Behan took all except Virgil into custody, and once again, Doc, Wyatt,
and Morgan appeared in court to account for their conduct in the Fremont Street fight. Ike wrote to Billy Byers, "I have got the Earps all in
Jail, and am not going to unhitch. I have got them on the hip and am
going to throw them good."[74]

Thomas J. Fitch was out of town, so the Earps hired William Herring as their attorney. He filed for a writ of habeas corpus before T. J.
Drum. Drum declined to hear the matter because he had served as
Doc Holliday's attorney during the Spicer hearing, and Judge J. H.
Lucas refused to act. On February 14, a substantial party of twelve
armed riders accompanied Doc, the Earps, and their attorney to Contention. There, after Herring opened with the statement, "Your
honor, we come here for law, but we will fight—if we have to," Justice
of the Peace J. B. Smith wisely ordered the hearing moved to Tombstone.[75] Still, people were worried. Parsons wrote:

> Earps were taken to Contention to be tried for killing of Clanton.
> Quite a posse went out. Many of Earp's friends armed to the teeth.
> They came back later in the day, the good people below beseeching
> them to leave and try case here. A bad time is expected again in town
> at any time. Earps on one side of the street with their friends and Ike
> Clanton and John Ringo with theirs on the other side—watching
> each other. Blood will surely come. Hope no innocents will be killed.[76]

On February 15, the case was postponed again, but this time Judge Lucas granted Doc and the Earps a writ of habeas corpus, declaring, "Whether Petititioners are guilty or not, it is apparent to any reasonable being, that an examination at this time would serve no good purpose. Unless new evidence or circumstances occur subsequent to the first examination, it would only duplicate the first hearing."[77] Lucas's order would be the last legal action in the case; the legal process was finally over. Trouble was not over, however, a fact that was underscored that day when Ben Maynard and Dan Tipton came close to getting into a fight. The police intervened, and they were fined $30 each for carrying concealed weapons.[78]

Free again, Wyatt prepared to take the trail, and on February 17, he and Morgan, Doc, Sherman McMaster, Creek Johnson, Charlie Smith, Texas Jack, and perhaps one or two others rode out. The *Nugget* noted, "It is supposed they are acting in the capacity of U.S. Deputy Marshals, their resignations not having been accepted or their appointment revoked by U.S. Marshal Dake, as was generally supposed some time ago."[79] Outside of town the posse split up, ostensibly looking for Pony Deal, Al Tiebot, and Charles Haws, who were wanted for the January 6 robbery of the Bisbee stage. As it turned out, all three were in jail in Cisco, Texas, but the Earp posse did not return to Tombstone until February 24.[80]

Doc Holliday's life had changed dramatically in the weeks since Virgil was shot. He had exchanged the smoke-filled saloons and gambling halls for the trail. At the very least, his participation in the posses suggested that his health was better than it had been. It had to have been to follow the life of a posseman as opposed to that of a gambler. After the Earp posse returned to Tombstone, Doc returned to the gambling tables temporarily, and by March 10, Clara Brown wrote, "There being a lull in cowboy criminality (which we hope is something more than temporary) and the Indians apparently having left the Dragoons, Tombstone people have been obliged to look to other causes for excitement."[81] One was a smallpox scare, and there were fires. But hopes that the Earp-Clanton troubles were over were about to be shattered.

On the evening of March 17, Wyatt saw activities that concerned him. The following day, he met Briggs Goodrich, one of the attorneys favored by the Cow-Boys, on the street and stopped him for information and advice. "I think they were after us last night," Wyatt said. "Do you know anything about it?"

"No," Goodrich replied.

"Do you think we're in any danger?" Wyatt persisted.

Goodrich responded plainly that they "were liable to get it in the neck at any time."

Earp said, "I don't notice anybody in particular in town now—any of the crowd."

"I think I see some strangers here that I think are after you," Goodrich replied, adding, "By the way, John Ringo wanted me to tell you that if any fight came up between you all, that he wanted you to understand that he would have nothing to do with it; that he was going to look out for himself, and anybody else could do the same."[82]

That evening, a play opened at Scheifflin Hall, billed as "2 Hours of Incessant Laughter." *Stolen Kisses*, staged by William Horace Lingard and Company, seemed a safe outing, and, despite warnings from Wyatt, Morgan Earp, Doc Holliday, and Dan Tipton attended. At the theater, Goodrich warned them, "You fellows will catch it tonight if you don't look out."[83] After the play, Doc went to his rooms, but Morgan and Tipton walked down Fourth Street intending to go to Campbell & Hatch's Saloon and Billiard Parlor, which had become the Earps' headquarters since the sale of the Oriental.

At the corner of Allen Street, they met Allie Earp, Virgil's wife, out to buy candy for her husband. Morgan inquired about Virgil, then said wistfully, "Wish he'd get better. I'd like to get away from here. Tonight."[84] Morgan escorted Allie back to the Cosmopolitan, then proceeded to Campbell & Hatch's. At the door, he and Tipton met Bob Hatch, and Morgan challenged Hatch to a game of pool.

Inside, Hatch and Morgan found a pool table near the back door, and the pair was soon involved in a game. Tipton took a chair next to the table. Wyatt and Sherman McMaster were sitting nearby. Hatch and Morgan finished the first game and started another. Hatch leaned over the table with his back to the rear door while Morgan stood watching him line up his shot. Suddenly, there were two gunshots, and Morgan fell hard to the floor. Wyatt, Sherman, and Tipton quickly pulled him out of the line of fire, while Hatch ran through the card room and into the backyard looking for the shooters. By then the assassins had fled. Back inside, Morgan was dying. The bullet had struck him in the back to the left of his spinal column, passed through the left kidney and the liver, traveled through his body, and emerged on the right side near the gallbladder. The bullet then struck George

A. B. Berry, a mining man who was warming himself by a stove near the front. A second bullet had hit the wall above Wyatt Earp's head, proving that he too had been a target of the assassins.

Dr. William Miller ran to the scene after hearing the gunfire, and Drs. Goodfellow and Matthews soon followed. After an initial examination, Morgan was moved to the card room and laid on a lounge. When they lifted him to his feet to move him, he said, "Don't. I can't stand it." Once he was laid on the lounge, he said to Hatch, "I have played my last game of pool." With his brothers and friends around him, including Virgil, who had come to be with him from his sickbed, and Doc, who was awakened, Morgan passed his last minutes. Finally, he said, "It won't be long. Are my legs stretched out straight, and my boots off?" Those around him assured him that they were. Then he whispered to Wyatt, "Do you know who did it?"

"Yes," Wyatt said grimly. "And I will get them."

"That's all I ask," Morgan whispered, "but don't let them get you, brother."[85]

That night the equation in the Tombstone troubles changed. The story that Doc went on a rampage, kicking in doors looking for the men he held responsible, appears to have been a fanciful, latter-day addition to the story, but, at the very least, he and Wyatt came to an unspoken agreement.[86] Something had to be done. So far none of the Cow-Boys had been convicted of any criminal activity. Virgil was maimed for life, and Morgan was dead. Wyatt had never been a violent man—the street fight had been the exception in his life. But now, what Judge Stilwell had told him finally rang in his ears: "Leave your prisoners out in the brush where alibis don't count." It was a solution that a man reared on the antebellum Southern code of honor like Doc could appreciate, with the law seemingly impotent, and it likely took no more than a glance at Wyatt to confirm the next step. Others knew what to expect as well. Parsons wrote, "Murderers got away of course, but it was and is quite evident who committed the deed. The man was Stilwell in all probability. For two cowardly, sneaking attempts at murder, this and the shots at Virgil E when I came nearly getting a dose, rank at the head. Morg lived about forty minutes after being shot and died without a murmur. Bad times ahead now."[87]

The next day was a Sunday, Wyatt's thirty-fourth birthday, and he and a group of friends escorted Morgan's body to Contention to be placed on the train. James Earp accompanied his brother's remains home to his parents and to Morgan's wife in Colton, California. Back in Tombstone, Wyatt made plans to send Virgil and his wife home to California as well. The wives of James and Wyatt were also settling their affairs. Wyatt had work to do, and he wanted no distractions. On Monday, Doc rode with Wyatt, Warren, Sherman McMaster, and Creek Johnson to escort Virgil and Allie to Benson. Hearing that Frank Stilwell had traveled toward Tucson ahead of them and that Stilwell, Clanton, and two other Cow-Boys were watching every train with the intention of killing Virgil, Wyatt decided to see his brother through to Tucson and make sure that he departed for California safely.[88]

Doc Holliday was the first man off the train at Tucson. Carrying two shotguns, he greeted Deputy U.S. Marshal J. W. Evans on the platform and stored the guns in the railroad station. Then, the Earp entourage walked to Porter's Hotel facing the tracks for dinner. Afterward, Wyatt and Virgil both stopped to speak to Evans before Wyatt escorted Virgil and Allie back to the train. Doc asked one of his companions, probably Sherman McMaster, to recover the shotguns from the station. Inside the train, a passenger told Virgil that men were lying on a flatcar near the engine. Wyatt saw them, too. He recognized one as Frank Stilwell; he believed the other to be Ike Clanton. He slipped into the space between the tracks and moved toward them. When they saw him, they both ran, and Wyatt chased after them. Stilwell's companion disappeared in the darkness, but Wyatt was intent on catching Stilwell. "I ran straight for Stilwell. It was he who killed my brother." Eventually, Stilwell froze in his tracks. Wyatt would later recall, "What a coward he was. He couldn't shoot when I came near him. He stood there helpless and trembling for his life. As I rushed upon him he put out his hands and clutched at my shotgun. I let go both barrels, and he stumbled down dead and mangled at my feet."[89]

Doc, Warren, Sherman, and Creek caught up to Wyatt about then, and a volley of gunfire followed, riddling the body of the fallen Stilwell. Wyatt looked for Stilwell's companion or companions (he believed Clanton and Hank Swilling were both there), but when he could not find them, he moved alongside Virgil's train car as the train began to move out, holding up a single finger and saying, "One for Morg."[90] Stilwell's body was not found until morning. By then, Wyatt and his companions had walked to Papago Station, where they flagged down a freight headed to Benson. Late in the afternoon of March 21, they reached Tombstone. Even before their arrival, however, they had been declared fugitives.

Stilwell's body was proof enough that Wyatt had never intended to arrest him. George Hand, who saw Stilwell, called him "the worst shot up man I ever saw."[91] A shotgun blast had torn into his abdomen and shredded his liver. A second load of buckshot shattered his leg. A rifle slug had struck him under one armpit and traveled through both lungs to the other side. There were also gunshot wounds in his upper left arm and his right thigh. His left hand was burned, which confirmed that he had grabbed at the shotgun when Wyatt caught up to him.[92] Oddly, Wyatt Earp later claimed that "Doc and I were the only ones in Tucson at the time Frank Stillwell was killed. Others remained in Benson."[93]

The citizens of Tucson were outraged at such a cold-blooded killing in the Old Pueblo. The *Star* pointed out that Stilwell had been in town to appear in court to face stage robbery charges, and interviewed Ike Clanton. Clanton, who was in Tucson for Jerry Barton's murder trial, claimed that he was near the depot with Stilwell to meet a witness from Charleston, which gave both men reasons for being in Tucson other than to make another attack on the Earps. Clanton said that when he saw the Earp entourage, he left at once and Stilwell "walked down the tracks between the cars and hotel."

The *Star* did not hold back in its condemnation of the Earps, although the source of its "facts" was a puzzle then, as now:

> In regard to the Earp party, no doubt but what they have some warm friends who are good citizens. And undoubtedly it is this fact which has given them so long suffrage in Tombstone. If one-twentieth part of what is said of their record is true, they are certainly no desirable acquisition to any community. They are a roving band; their path is strewn with blood. Strange as it may seem, wherever they halt in a settlement stage robberies follow and human life ceases to be sacred. Their late escapades at Tombstone are only their records repeated in other frontier towns, and, if we judge the honest sense of justice and peace abiding disposition of our citizens, they will never dare another such foul murder as was committed last Monday night. If they must take human life they must seek other localities than our city. It will not be tolerated.[94]

Notably, the same papers that announced the death of Stilwell also reported that Jerry Barton had been acquitted, giving further substantiation to the claim of Earp partisans that the courts had never convicted any one of the Cow-Boy crowd.

While a coroner's jury in Tucson found the Earps responsible for a brutal killing in the case of Frank Stilwell, another coroner's jury in Tombstone was determining, indirectly, that no blow had been struck amiss at Tucson. No one in Tombstone had ever seriously doubted Stilwell's part in Morgan Earp's death, and on the very day that Wyatt and his companions returned to Tombstone, Maria Duarte Spence, the wife of Pete Spence, gave damning testimony concerning the plot to kill Morgan and Stilwell's critical part in it.

Maria Spence identified Morgan Earp's killers as Frank Stilwell, Pete Spence, a man she identified as "Freis" who was actually Frederick Bode, and two Indians, one of whom she identified simply as "Charley." The "Indians" were identified later as Florentino Cruz and Hank Swilling. She testified, "Four days ago, while mother and myself were standing at Spence's house, talking with Spence & the Indian who came home with him [Charley], Morgan Earp passed by, when Spence nudged the Indian and said, 'That's him, that's him.' The Indian then started down the street, & got ahead of him to get a good look at him."

On the night of the shooting, she said, she and her mother heard the shots. A few minutes later, Stilwell and Charley came into her home and a short time later Spence, Bode, and the other Indian followed, all very excited. She testified that the following morning Spence told her that "if I said a word about something I knew about he would kill me; that he was going to Sonora and would leave my body behind him." She concluded, "Spence didn't tell me so, but I know he killed Morgan Earp." Based on the evidence, the coroner's jury concluded that Morgan had been murdered "at the hands of Pete Spence, Frank Stilwell, a party by the name of Freis, and two Indian half-breeds, one whose name is Charlie and name of the other was not ascertained."[95]

For one final twist, Briggs Goodrich testified that Stilwell had told him that "there were some boys in town who would toe the mark, and the worst of it was the Earps would think he was in it, as they did not like him." Goodrich said, "I told him I would tell the same for him as I did for John Ringo, and he said no, that he would rather die than let them know that he cared a damn what they thought."[96]

Parsons succinctly offered his appraisal of what had happened: "A quick vengeance and a bad character sent to hell where he will be the chief attraction until a few more accompany him."[97] He was not alone in his verdict. A Tombstone correspondent wrote, "On receipt of the news of the killing of Stilwell, many people said the right man had been killed. He was seen on the night of the killing of Morgan Earp, and the next day was in Tucson, having ridden there that night."[98] Even Cow-Boy partisans would affirm that Stilwell traveled to Tucson on a fast horse after Morgan's murder.

So when the Earp party entered Tombstone on the afternoon of March 21, the stage for high drama had been set. The Earps rested and gathered their belongings at the Cosmopolitan. That afternoon, the local telegraph office received a telegram from Tucson for Sheriff Behan advising him that the Earps were wanted for the murder of Stilwell. The office manager, who was a friend of Wyatt's, showed him the telegram first, and agreed to delay giving it to Behan until the Earps were ready to leave town.[99] Near eight o'clock, Behan got the telegram and proceeded to the Cosmopolitan to arrest them. William M. Breakenridge would later claim that Behan told him and David Neagle to get their shotguns because he had to arrest the Earps. "We had not gone a block on our way to get our weapons when they came out of the hotel," he recalled. "Behan met them on the sidewalk as they were getting on their horses and tried to arrest them alone."[100]

As the Earp party passed through the Cosmopolitan's office, they encountered Behan at the door. "As Wyatt advanced to the front and approached Behan, the sheriff said to him, 'Wyatt, I want to see you.' Wyatt replied, 'You can't see me; you have seen me once too often,' or words to that effect. He passed out into the street and turned around and said, 'I will see Paul,' and then the party passed on down the street." Wyatt later claimed that as they passed Heyman Solomon's bank, the banker stopped him and asked if he needed anything. "Yes," Wyatt replied. "Doc Holliday has no gun." Solomon went into the bank and returned with his own Winchester, which he gave to Wyatt along with his best wishes.[101]

Wyatt's posse, joined by Charlie Smith and Dan Tipton, saddled their horses at P. W. Smith's Corral at the corner of Third Street and rode out of town. They set up camp at nearby Watervale and slept that first night within easy reach of Sheriff Behan. "Behan claims they resisted arrest," reported Clara Brown, "but the bystanders claim this was all that passed, and that nothing was said about an arrest. He also asserts that every one of the party drew their guns on him, which is denied by the spectators. All were heavily armed, but no motion was made."[102]

George Parsons expressed his disgust with Behan, "The Earp party returned this afternoon and Behan tried to arrest them tonight upon a telegram. They refused arrest and retired from town, first though waiting for Behan and Neagle to do what they threatened. Bad muss this. Sheriff is awake now that one of his friends is killed. Couldn't do anything before. Things are very rotten in that office. Fine reputation we're getting abroad."[103] The following morning, Behan left Tombstone with six men. At Contention, they met Sheriff Bob Paul from Tucson. Paul then proceeded to Tombstone, and the papers reported, "The whereabouts of the Earps is unknown."[104]

That was about to change. The Earp party rode straight for Pete Spence's wood camp off the Chiricahua Road below South Pass in the Dragoons. They approached Simon Acosta, a wood cutter, and Theodore Judah, a teamster, inquiring about Spence. They were told he had returned to Tombstone that morning to appear in court for an assault charge. The party started back toward Tombstone, then turned off the road. The workers watched as the Earps pursued Florentino Cruz, who was "running and jumping from side to side." There was a flurry of gunfire, and the workers watched as the Earp party rode leisurely away. They found Cruz lying face down under a tree. He had been shot four times; two of the shots were fatal.[105]

Wyatt always claimed that before he was shot, Cruz named Curly Bill Brocius, John Ringo, Hank Swilling, Frank Stilwell, and himself as parties to Morgan Earp's death. He did not mention Pete Spence, and Wyatt would believe afterward that Spence was not involved. Cruz reportedly told Wyatt he was paid $25 to hold the horses. "That twenty-five dollar business just about burned me up," Wyatt said.[106] He claimed to have given Cruz a chance to draw against him, although the evidence of Cruz's body argues against such a mano a mano duel. This was blood vengeance, not a fast-draw contest.

News reached Tombstone quickly, and Pete Spence surrendered to Behan. On the same day, Deputy Sheriff Frank Hereford arrested Frederick Bode, and Deputy Sheriff William Bell brought in Hank Swilling. The rats were scurrying for cover, and Parsons applauded, "More

killing by the Earp party. Hope they will keep it up."[107] Not everyone
agreed, of course. J. S. Browder, a mine owner, wrote, "I very much
question whether law abiding people [should] sanction the kind of justice which is administered from the muzzle of guns in the hands of
Doc Holliday and the Earp party."[108] Across the Southwest, even some
of the Earps' former supporters agreed. Wyatt left no doubt that
vengeance was his motive.

Clara Brown reminded her readers "that it was not the Earps who
first disturbed this quiet, and that their criminal actions since have
been from the determination to avenge the murder of a dearly loved
brother. I do not present this as sufficient excuse for their conduct, or
approve any act contrary to law; but there are certainly extenuating
circumstances to be taken into consideration."[109]

Ironically, Wyatt's vendetta served to undermine rather than vindi-
cate John Behan's reputation as sheriff. He had been surprisingly
impotent as a lawman since the street fight, so much so that even the
Nugget eventually took him to task. He opened himself to further criticism when he assembled a posse of twenty-five, including a dozen
Charleston-based Cow-Boys that numbered Curly Bill, John Ringo,
and Fin Clanton among them. Breakenridge explained that "he took
those men knowing that the Earp party would resist arrest, and, on
account of the feud between them, he believed the cowboys would
stay and fight."[110]

That dubious logic prompted Bob Paul to refuse to join Behan's
posse. Paul explained that Behan "persists in cloaking the most notorious outlaws and murderers in Arizona with the authority of the law. I
will have nothing to do with such a gang." Even the *Tucson Star* approved of his decision, stating, "He refused to pursue the parties, as he
felt that they could not be taken with the posse raised, inasmuch as
they are most all hostile to the Earps and a meeting simply meant
bloodshed, which he believed ought to and could be avoided, and yet
get the parties into custody. All things considered, we do not see how
Sheriff Paul could have done otherwise."[111]

Brown wrote that Paul had explained that "he was assured, by
friends of the Earps, that the men would, in a few days, either give
themselves into his hands, or leave the country."[112] Parsons added his
own perspective on Paul's conduct: "He is a true—brave man himself
and will not join the murderous posse here. If the truth were known

he would be glad to see the Earp party get away with all of these murderous outfits. . . . Behan will get it yet."[113]

Behan did arrest Charlie Smith and Dan Tipton, who had returned
to Tombstone. Because they had left the Cosmopolitan with the Earps,
they were held for "resisting officers and conspiracy." A Tombstone
correspondent of the *Tucson Citizen* advised Tucson readers that "[t]he
charge cannot be sustained as Sheriff Behan made no attempt to arrest
any one and made no mention to any of the Earp party that he wanted
to arrest them."[114] The Earps' allies quickly came to the aid of Smith
and Tipton. William Herring arranged bail. Robert J. Winders, Bob
Hatch, James Earp's son-in-law Thaddeus S. Harris of the Tombstone
Foundry, and Frank Walker, the superintendent of the Sycamore Springs
Water Company, acted as sureties. And, on March 25, Judge Andrew
J. Felter released them because "at the time of Behan's attempt to
arrest the Earp party he had no legal process."[115] Smith left at once to
rejoin the Earp party; Tipton remained in town.

Behan's Cow-Boy posse, which appears to have divided into two
separate groups, was back in the field, and before the end of the day
on the twenty-fifth, word reached Tombstone that Curly Bill had been
killed in a fight with the Earps. George Parsons provided an overview:

> A very disagreeable day, indeed. Tip and Smith discharged this a. m.
> Rumors of a battle and four of the Earp party killed received this
> a. m. Discredited. I got strictly private news though later that "Curly
> Bill" has been killed at last—by the Earp party and none of the latter
> hurt. Sheriff Behan has turned all of the cow-boys loose against the
> Earps and with this lawless element is trying to do the worst. I am
> heartily glad at this repulse and hope the killing is not stopped with
> the cut-throat named. Feeling is growing here against the ring, Sher-
> iff, etc., and it would not surprise me to know of a necktie party
> some fine morning. Things seem to be coming to this pass. "Then
> let it come the time is ripe and rotten ripe for change."[116]

The death of Curly Bill was the result of an unexpected collision
between Earp's party and the Charleston posse of Cow-Boys. George
Hand spotted the Cow-Boys and described them in his diary: "They
are well mounted, well armed, and seem intent on biz. They are in
search of the Earp party who took breakfast two miles above here this
morning."[117] In the meantime, Wyatt Earp was running out of funds.

Daniel G. "Big Tip" Tipton, an Earp partisan who left Arizona with the Earps and Doc Holliday in 1882. He traveled with Doc from Albuquerque to Colorado. Later he was a customs officer in El Paso, Texas. He was eventually prosecuted for illegal activities as a customs agent; the photo was taken at the Ohio State Penitentiary in 1897.

He met Charlie Smith near Tombstone and sent him to ask E. B. Gage for a $1,000 loan. Smith was instructed to deliver the funds at Iron Springs in the Whetstone Mountains the following day. Smith was taken into custody by Marshal Neagle, and Tony Kraker and Whistling Dick Wright were picked to deliver the money to Warren Earp at Iron Springs.[118]

The following day, March 24, Wyatt, Doc, Sherman, Texas Jack, and Creek were approaching Iron Springs unaware that Curly Bill and his Cow-Boy posse were camped there. As Wyatt and his companions neared the springs, the Cow-Boys opened fire on them. In the first blast of gunfire, Texas Jack Vermillion's horse went down, pinning Jack to the ground, while the rest of the party, including Doc, scattered in retreat. Only Earp held his ground. He dismounted, threw his reins around his arm, and unlimbered his shotgun. With his horse plunging about nearly out of control, Wyatt recognized Curly Bill blasting away at him. Some accounts claim that McMaster and Doc yelled, "Curly Bill!" at first fire. Wyatt, who had not realized that "[e]very mother's son, including my old pal Doc Holliday, one of the bravest men I ever knew, had turned tail in the first volley and gone scampering into the distance as fast as their horses could run," returned the fire. Curly went down with a yell, his chest torn open by buckshot.[119]

Earp had loosened his gunbelt to be more comfortable during the ride. When he realized how exposed he was, he found that the belt had slipped down his legs, so that when he attempted to remount, he could not swing into the saddle. As he tried to pull the gunbelt up with one hand, bullets tore off the saddle horn, hit one of his boot heels, and shredded his coattails. Finally remounted, he stopped long enough to help Texas Jack get free and then rode for cover.[120]

Doc met Wyatt and, expecting him to be wounded, prepared to help him from the saddle. "You must be shot all to pieces," Doc said. Everyone, including Wyatt, thought he had been shot, and they were amazed to find that he had not been hit. Doc then suggested that they make a charge on the Cow-Boys, but Wyatt said, "If you fellows are hungry for a fight you can go on and get your fill."[121] With that, the Earp group fell back. Doc later provided his own account:

> The facts are these: We were out one day after a party of outlaws, and about 3 o'clock on a warm day after a long and dry ride from the San Pedro river, we approached a spring which was situated in a hollow. As we did so
>
> EIGHT RUSTLERS ROSE UP
>
> From behind the bank and poured from thirty-five to forty shots into us. Our escape was miraculous. The shots cut our clothes and saddles and killed one horse, but did not hit us. I think we would have been all killed if God Almighty wasn't on our side. Wyatt Earpp [sic] turned loose with a shot-gun and killed Curley [sic] Bill. The eight men in the gang which attacked us were all outlaws, for each of whom a big reward has been offered.[122]

So the Earp party withdrew. Later, Kraker and Wright rode into Iron Springs expecting to find Warren Earp. Instead, they found themselves looking down the barrels of Cow-Boy guns. Kraker caught them off guard by yelling, "What are you doing here, you lop-eared Missourian?" Whistling Dick quickly concocted a story about looking for lost mules, and he and Kraker ended up eating a meal with the Cow-Boys and listening to an account of Wyatt Earp's one-man charge against them. Afterward, they returned to Tombstone without delivering the money and gave a *Nugget* reporter an account of the gunfight.[123]

The shootout at Iron Springs happened. The various accounts agreed on the main particulars to an amazing degree. The only real point of dispute was the outcome: Did Wyatt Earp kill Curly Bill Brocius? Wyatt and his companions believed he did. That is certain. Wyatt, Doc, and Warren all gave separate accounts that agreed on that, and Johnny Barnes, who was wounded in the same fight, confirmed it to Fred Dodge. However, the Earps did not retrieve the body, which left room for doubt. And the Cow-Boys and some of the area newspapers chose to question whether Brocius was even there.[124]

One plausible story told by old-timers was that Bill was seriously wounded and was carried by wagon to Frank Patterson's ranch, where he died and was buried. This would explain one discrepancy between the first accounts: the Earps claimed eight or nine Cow-Boys present, while Kraker and Whistling Dick found four men at Iron Springs. This would also explain why the Cow-Boys did not tell Kraker and Wright of his death. Wyatt Earp later claimed that he told John Thacker of Wells, Fargo of Brocius's demise and that Thacker had a man dig up and identify the body.[125]

No body was produced for the public to see, however, leaving the debate over Curly Bill's death to become a staple Wild West controversy, beginning with the *Nugget* saying that "the notorious and wily William is, beyond a question of doubt alive in New Mexico," and the *Epitaph* responding, "Suffice it to say that Curly Bill is as dead as two loads of buckshot can make him."[126] Across the West, others took up the debate. The *San Francisco Exchange* used sarcasm to note how he would be missed, but concluded, "This makes the fourth the Earp party has scored to the cowboys' one. We are beginning to doubt the courage and invincibility of that much-talked-of class and are willing to give long odds on the murderous superiority of the Earps."[127]

What the Curly Bill debate did do was to draw attention back to the Cow-Boy question and the real source of lawlessness in southeastern Arizona. Bill's name had become synonymous with the rustlers, while Stilwell and Cruz did not have that association outside of Cochise County. Killing Curly Bill in an open gunfight somehow made Wyatt Earp seem less a rogue lawman on a path of personal vengeance, and gave his supporters more of an argument in justification of their course. On March 24, proceedings were to begin against Pete Spence in the murder of Morgan Earp before Justice A. O. Wallace, but the dilatory actions over the next few days gave little reason for optimism, and by April 4 all the remaining conspirators named by the coroner's jury had walked, confirming the Earps' fears and providing for some citizens validation of his course.[128]

On the night of March 25, the murder of Martin R. Peel at the Tombstone Milling and Mining Company, near Charleston, by Cow-Boys made the case of the law-and-order crowd even stronger, especially after Peel's father, Judge Bryant L. Peel, sent this public letter to the *Epitaph*:

> *To the People of Tombstone:* Perhaps I am not in a condition to express a clear, deliberate opinion, but I would say to the good citizens of Cochise county there is one of three things you have to do. There is a class of cut-throats among you and you can never convict them in court. You must combine and protect yourselves and wipe them out, or you must give up the country to them, or you will be murdered one at a time, as my son has been.—B. L. Peel.[129]

Such a public endorsement of vigilantism by a judge had its impact, and Parsons summed it up, "Now that it has come to killing of upright, respectable, thoroughly law abiding citizens—all are aroused and the question is now, who is the next."[130] Even earlier, a Tombstone correspondent of the *Tucson Citizen* reported, "Feeling is rapidly changing to sympathy for the Earps since the Coroner's jury rendered a verdict in the case of the killing of Morgan Earp."[131] On March 27, when Governor Frederick A. Tritle arrived in Tombstone, he saw at once that dramatic measures had to be taken. Tritle was the former partner of William B. Murray, a leader of the Citizens Safety Committee, and he stayed at the home of Milton Clapp (another prominent vigilante, who was handling money for Earp's posse) while he was in Tombstone.

After consulting with these and other Tombstone leaders, Tritle organized a posse to go after the Cow-Boys. Significantly, he did not put this group under Behan's control, but under the command of Deputy U.S. Marshal John H. Jackson with directions to restore order. In fact, Behan's failures were cited as justification for the creation of the group. Tritle urged local citizens to set up an emergency fund to pay special deputies. He then wired President Arthur, pinning the troubles on "the utter failure of the civil authority and the anarchy prevailing; the international trouble likely to grow out of this cattle thieving along the border, the fact that business is paralyzed and the fairest valleys in the territory are kept from occupation by the presence of the cowboys."[132]

Behan took considerable heat for his seeming indifference to Peel's death, and he was still in the field in his ineffective pursuit of the Earps when E. M. Harley, the chief deputy in charge in Behan's absence, dispatched Billy Breakenridge to Chandler's Milk Ranch to capture Zwing Hunt and "Curly Bill's Kid," Billy Grounds, who were believed to be Peel's killers. On the morning of March 29, a gunfight ensued in which Hunt and Grounds were wounded (Grounds mortally) and Deputy Sheriff John A. Gillespie was killed.[133] With two more of the well-known Cow-Boys taken for their criminal activities, the focus was shifting back to their depredations rather than the Earps. "Calky times very," Parsons recorded on March 30. "14 murders and assassinations in ten days. More than one a day. A hanging bee anticipated tonight—But not carried out. Cowboy raid on town expected tonight. . . . A regular epidemic of murder is upon us. What and when the end will be—God only knows."[134]

THE OUT TRAIL

The claim I make is that some few of us pioneers are entitled to credit for what we have done. We have been the fore-runners of government. . . . If it hadn't been for me and a few like me there never would have been any government in some of these towns.

—Doc Holliday, *New York Sun*, 1886

In March 1882, John Henry Holliday was a more robust and tougher man than he had been when he first arrived in Tombstone in September 1880. It was more than notoriety and a healthier climate that explained the difference. Doc had changed. For the first time in a long time—perhaps since before he left Georgia—he had a sense of purpose that extended beyond survival or self-indulgence. He did not see himself as a killer or even as a vigilante. Rather, he saw himself as an instrument of justice and an agent of progress. Perhaps it was a rationalization, but if it was, it was validated by important men and forces all the way from Tombstone to Washington, D.C. He had a new perspective that would have surprised his relatives back in Georgia—a Republican, business-oriented perspective in tune with the spirit of the Gilded Age.[1]

Doc and the rest of the vendetta posse shared the role of federal marshals, Pinkerton agents, "company men," and other enforcers of the new industrial establishment, and, like them, Doc may have been viewed by his patrons as a necessary evil. Even so, he had a part in the search for order that gave his life a fresh meaning. He was more than a mercenary, as he had been in the Royal Gorge War; this time he had

258

a stake in what happened that was consistent with the lingering code of honor and a half-forgotten sense of right and wrong that even his father would have understood. In the saddle for a cause—and with friends and comrades around him—he had finally stepped beyond the preoccupation with self that had characterized his life since he left Georgia for the West. His link to the Earps, beginning with the street fight and especially after Morgan's murder, went far beyond loyalty to a friend. He had a sense of belonging he had not known since those long-ago family gatherings. John Henry's life had a new meaning in his own mind, quite apart from the measure of Doc Holliday by other men. What they made of him was another matter, not bound by the truth of things. Already, he stood on the edge of legend.

Legends grow, and rarely by design. Like the wisteria in Doc's native Georgia, they spread, encircle, constrict, and hide the damage they do to the truth in a cascade of tales that, like foliage and flowers, cause people to forget everything else. But, like the wisteria, they have an unmistakable beauty that makes them nearly irresistible until they become a part of the landscape of history. That spring of 1882, Doc Holliday was swept along by events, caught up in something larger than himself, something larger than a settling of accounts with a friend's enemies. The newspapers and politicians would not let it be that, nor, for that matter, would Wyatt Earp and his compatriots, who saw what they did as justice gained the only way it could be under the circumstances: at gunpoint.

Doc saw the changes in his friend, too. Nothing in Wyatt Earp's life, before the vendetta or after it, ever hinted that he was homicidal by nature. The vendetta was the great anomaly in a life as devoid of vigilantism as it was of murder. The man who had protected Curly Bill Brocius and Johnny-behind-the-Deuce took the law into his own hands because he believed the law had failed. He believed that the legal system was so corrupt and impotent that he had no other way to keep his promise to his brother but to go after Morgan's killers himself. He was smart enough, however, to listen to advice and to know there would be consequences, and he kept counsel with men of position and respectability who—privately, at least—encouraged and applauded his trail of retribution as useful to their sense of the future.

On Saturday, March 25, 1882, the same day that news reached Tombstone of the killing of Curly Bill, the Earp party returned to the

edge of Tombstone for a meeting with supporters and apparently ren-
dezvoused with O. C. "Charlie" Smith and Warren Earp. They may
have also met with John Thacker of Wells, Fargo. Unfortunately, Tony
Kraker and Whistling Dick Wright had not returned, so they did not
recover the $1,000 sent by E. P. Gage.[2] Instead, they struck north.
They ate along the way with a group of miners in the Winchester district and had dinner at Summit Station on the Southern Pacific line
through the Dragoon Mountains, where they apparently boarded a
train looking for someone, most likely a courier with the money they
expected.[3] Then they proceeded to the ranch of Hugh and Jim Percy.
Although sympathetic to the Earps, the Percys feared the Cow-Boys,
so they reluctantly fed the group and asked them to leave before
morning. Apparently, they were not the only guests at the ranch: the
Dos Cabezas Gold Note reported, "Barney Riggs informs us that on
Tuesday night the Earp party stopped at Perseley's [*sic*] ranch for supper. A promising young deputy sheriff, whose initials are Frank Hereford sought safety in a corn crib near the house. He and Riggs were in
the house which the party approached."[4]

About three o'clock in the morning of March 27, the Earp posse
left the Percy ranch, moving toward the Sierra Bonita ranch of Henry
C. Hooker, where Wyatt hoped to reoutfit and wait for the Gage loan.
Somehow, Wyatt had sent a message to Tombstone, because the *Nugget*
reported that "D. G. Tipton, well-known as one of their friends, was
called out of bed about 4 o'clock and left on the 5 o'clock stage, and
arrived at Willcox on the morning train. He immediately obtained a
horse and started at a rapid pace to overtake the party, evidently knowing their destination."[5]

In the meantime, Earp's group had arrived at Hooker's ranch. The
cattleman welcomed them, and when told about the death of Curly
Bill, Hooker reportedly said, "Good work, Wyatt! Keep it up, and
when you have finished I'll get you pardoned."[6] Although Hooker told
them to make themselves at home, Wyatt told him that what he really
needed was fresh horses and that he was willing to pay for them.
Hooker fed the little band and allowed Wyatt and his friends to pick
fresh mounts but refused to take any money for them. Late on the
afternoon of March 27, John Behan's posse was spotted in the distance. Hooker encouraged Earp to make his stand at the ranch, but
Wyatt decided to move to a hill about three miles from the ranch headquarters in the direction of the Galiuro Mountains called Reilly Hill.[7]

Sheriff Behan and his posse arrived at the Sierra Bonita on the morning of March 28 and faced a very different reception. When Behan explained his purpose and asked Hooker if he knew where the Earps were, the rancher told the sheriff that he did not know where they were and that he would not tell him if he did know. At that point, Behan said to Hooker, "You must be upholding murderers and outlaws then."

"No sir, I am not," Hooker replied. "I know the Earps and I know you and they have always treated me like gentlemen; damn such laws and damn you, and damn your posse; they are a set of horse thieves and outlaws."

At that, one of the "honest farmers," as the *Epitaph* derisively called them, spoke up and said, "Damn the son of a b——h, he knows where they are and let us make him tell."

A moment later, Billy Whelan, Hooker's foreman, stepped up and pointed a Winchester at the Cow-Boy. "You can't come here into a gentleman's yard and call him a son of a b——h! now you skin it back! [S]kin it back! If you are looking for a fight and come here and talk that way you can get it before you find the Earps; you can get it right here."

Hooker remained cool and in control, but seeing Fin Clanton, John Ringo, and the other Cow-Boys in the sheriff's posse, he told Behan again, bluntly, "These are a pretty set of fellows you have with you; a set of horse thieves and cut-throats."

At that point both Behan and Harry M. Woods responded, "They are not our associates; they are only here on this occasion with us."

"Well, if they are not your associates I will set an extra table for you and set them by themselves," Hooker replied.[8]

After eating, Behan approached Whelan and offered him a diamond stickpin if he would not tell what had happened there. Then he told Hooker, "If I can catch the Earps, it will help me in the next election."[9] With that, he and his posse rode away, but not in the direction of the Earps on the bluff. William Breakenridge would later claim that Behan did not go after them because "the Earps were fortified in a stone house up in the mountains."[10] Instead, Behan rode to Fort Grant, where he offered Colonel James Biddle $500 for the services of Indian scouts. During the discussions, he made the mistake of telling Biddle that he had been to Hooker's and that Hooker had told him he did not know where the Earps were and that he would not tell him if he did. At that Biddle abruptly ended the negotiations, saying, "Hooker said that did he? Well, if he did, you can't get any scouts here."[11]

Behan returned to Hooker's the next day. This time the rancher told him he would not need scouts to find the Earps and pointed out the hill where they were camped. Behan told Hooker that he was going back to Tombstone instead, because his expenses were pretty high—$13,000 for ten days of riding. Hooker told him what he thought about his expenses in no uncertain terms, and Behan left. Hooker always expressed the view that Behan was willing to ride anywhere in Arizona except where the Earps were.[12]

After Behan left, the Earp party returned to the ranch and stayed for several days. Reportedly, Hooker offered Wyatt Earp the $1,000 reward offered by the Arizona Cattlegrowers Association for Curly Bill, but Earp turned it down, saying that he would not take any reward for keeping his promise to Morgan. While Earp, Doc, and the others rested at Hooker's place, Dan Tipton arrived with the $1,000 from Gage and stayed to be a part of the group. Before they left, Lew Cooley, a former stage driver, also rode into Hooker's with another $1,000 from Wells, Fargo & Company, for Wyatt Earp.[13]

All things considered, it was a remarkable moment. While Earp and his riders were enjoying the hospitality of one of Arizona's most prominent ranchers, he received money from one of Tombstone's leading mining men and from Wells, Fargo. Such a dramatic demonstration of the establishment's support of Earp and his mission was striking. James B. Hume, in an interview with the *National Police Gazette*, would deplore the fact that "the inhabitants fear and harbor" the Cow-Boys "rather than incur their wrath." He also accused "the sheriff of the county of being in with the cowboys."[14] More dramatically, on March 23, in a remarkably detailed review of events in Tombstone, Wells, Fargo had taken the astonishing step of publicly defending Wyatt Earp and endorsing his actions.

Doc Holliday was even mentioned as part of the company's defense of Earp and his record at Tombstone, and although the officials scarcely gave a ringing endorsement of Doc and his character, they did take care to defend him from charges that he was involved in the Benson stage robbery:

> Doc Holliday, although a man of dissipated habits and a gambler, has
> never been a thief and was never in any way connected with the

attempted stage robbery when Philpot [*sic*], the stage driver, was killed. For three-quarters of an hour after the stage passed the Wells, two and a half miles from Tombstone, he was seen at the latter place, so drunk that he was helped upon his horse, and the robbery occurred thirteen miles from Tombstone, so that it was utterly impossible for him to be there. Neither did he form a part of agent Williams' and detective Paul's posse afterward. The statement that he was present on the occasion of that robbery was put forth by the cowboys and their friends to throw further discredit upon the Earp brothers and their friends.[15]

Wyatt had conveyed his intent to Bob Paul earlier when he sent word to him that he would either surrender to him or leave the country. Paul was now back in Tucson, content to let events follow their course. By the end of March, it was clear that Wyatt had decided to leave the country, but it was also clear that he was consulting with powerful forces with respect to his plans and the expectation of a full pardon. Wyatt's posse rested at Hooker's briefly, then prepared for a final sweep in search of Cow-Boys. A member of the posse—likely Doc, although others in the posse had the skill—wrote a letter to the editor of the *Tombstone Epitaph*:

In Camp, April 4, 1882

Editor Epitaph:—In reply to the article in the Nugget of March 31, relating to the Earp party and some of the citizens of Graham and Cochise counties, I would like to give you the facts in this case during our trip to Cochise and Graham counties. Leaving Tombstone Saturday evening March 25, we went into camp six miles north of town. Next morning we were overtaken by three prospectors on the road from Tombstone to Winchester district, who asked us to partake of a frugal meal, which we ate with relish, after which we traveled in company with them on the main road to Summit station where we had dinner and awaited the arrival of the passenger train from the west expecting a friendly messenger.

From here we continued our journey on the wagon road to Henderson's ranch where we had refreshments for ourselves and horses. Here we were informed that a gentlemanly deputy sheriff of Cochise county, Mr. Frank Hereford (for whom we have the greatest respect as a gentleman and officer) was at the ranch at the time of our arrival and departure, and have since learned the reason for not presenting himself, was fears for his safety, which we assure him were groundless.

Leaving this ranch we went into camp on good grass one mile north. At seven next morning we saddled and went north to Mr. H. C. Hooker's ranch in Graham county, where we met Mr. Hooker, and asked for refreshments for ourselves and stock, which he kindly granted us with the same hospitality that was tendered us by the ranchers of Cochise county.

As regards to Mr. Hooker outfitting us with supplies and fresh horses, as mentioned in the Nugget, it is false and without foundation as we are riding the same horses we left Tombstone on, with the exception of Texas Jack's horse, which was killed in the fight with Curly Bill and posse, which we replaced by hiring a horse on the San Pedro river. In relation to the reward offered by the Stock Association, which the Nugget claims Mr. Hooker paid to Wyatt Earp for the killing of Curly Bill, it is also false, as no reward has been asked for or tendered.

Leaving Hooker's ranch on the evening of that day, we journeyed north to within five miles of Eureka Springs. There we camped with a freighter and was cheerfully furnished the best his camp afforded. Next morning, not being in a hurry to break camp, our stay was long enough to notice the movements of Sheriff Behan and his posse of honest ranchers, with whom, had they possessed the trailing ability of the average Arizona ranchman, we might have had trouble, which we are not seeking. Neither are we avoiding these honest ranchers as we thoroughly understand their designs.

At Cottonwood we remained overnight, and here picked up the trail of the lost Charlie Ross, "and a hot one." We are confident that our trailing abilities will soon enable us to turn over to the "gentlemen" the fruits of our efforts, so they may not again return to Tombstone empty-handed. Yours respectfully,

One of Them[16]

The Earp posse did not immediately leave the area, choosing instead to scout the watering holes of the area with the hope of encountering other Cow-Boys. For more than a week they sought their quarry, but the Cow-Boys had scattered. The Earps returned to Tombstone for one last consultation with members of the Citizens Safety Committee before making a final sweep of the area on their way out of Arizona. Thacker was there, and Judge William Herring advised them to leave the territory while legal options were explored.[17]

By then, Jack Stilwell, the brother of Frank Stilwell and a famous and respected character noted throughout the West as a scout and

Indian fighter—the hero of the Beecher's Island fight—had arrived in Tombstone and was searching for the Earps with a new posse that included Ike Clanton, John Ringo, and close to thirty others, mostly Cow-Boys. There was some safety in numbers, after all. Stilwell apparently sensed the kind of men he was riding with, though, for he soon gave up the chase, perhaps realizing, at last, what his brother had become. Afterward, several of the Cow-Boys headed south to Mexico for safety.[18]

Through all of this, the papers were filled with rumors and inflammatory rhetoric, but most people were simply sick of the whole affair and ready for it to be over. The *Star* did not slow its attack on the Earps, but it did admit that there was a greater problem: "The officials of Cochise County, with all of the available strength they can muster, seem to avail nothing in putting down the blood-thirsty class infesting that county. Ex-City and United States officials have taken to the hills as so many Apaches. A lot of loose, marauding thieves are scouring the country killing good industrious citizens for plunder. The officials are out in every direction but nothing is accomplished."[19] And the *San Diego Union* declared, "We cannot escape the conclusion that the people of Cochise County are incapable or unfit for self-government."[20]

The Earps had stepped over the line, and the simple fact that they were "Deputy United States Marshals sworn to protect and sustain the laws of the country" overshadowed everything else. What most saw was simply a "spirit of revenge"; the cause was immaterial. What mattered was the impact of the daily reports on public opinion. The *Los Angeles Express* blamed the Earps for circumstances that had existed long before the vendetta ride began:

> The Earp vendetta, with its train of bloodshed, is more damaging to the Territory than would be a protracted Apache war. It has brought people to believe that there is no security whatever for life there, and that the law is utterly impotent as against the desperadoes who ride around the country killing whomsoever they please. It is not a pleasant or inviting picture to a contemplating settler in Arizona, nor will it tend to make capitalists feel safe in investing in mining enterprises in that Territory. Money will not go freely into any country where the laws are set at defiance and life is at the mercy of every ruffian who delights to pull the trigger. The impunity with which the Earp gang has carried out its programme is anything but reassuring to persons who have put their money in Arizona property. It is but a step from this kind of outlawry that destroys human life to that other

kind that has no appreciation of the ownership of property, and men of means who have been entertaining propositions to invest in Arizona enterprises will refuse to risk their substance in a Territory where there is no protection outside of the strong arm.[21]

The *Los Angeles Herald*, with more awareness of the complexity of the situation in Cochise County, added its view that "[t]he law should be supreme in Arizona as elsewhere. Every man who is going about with arms in his hands, whether he belongs to the Earps or the cowboys, should be made to lay them down, and to submit his case to the arbitrament of a jury of his peers, even if it should require the whole power of the Federal government and the whole force of the people of Arizona!"[22]

These sentiments doubtlessly pricked the sensibilities of even the warmest allies of the Earps. The businessmen of Tombstone may have approved of Wyatt's vendetta, even applauded or conspired to support it, but they were businessmen. They needed the lifeblood of investment, and the vendetta had stirred up such a firestorm that they worried about its economic and political consequences. The message conveyed to Wyatt on his last visit to Tombstone by the vigilantes was likely very simple: "We appreciate what you've done, but it is time to end it all. When things cool down, and we have a chance to show the good you've done, you can come back."

The Earp party stopped at Camp Grant on their way out of the territory. Wyatt asked for a notary public. He met with Henry Morgan, who reported that Earp signed some properties over to his sister and then mailed the documents. Afterward, Wyatt and the others met with Colonel Biddle, who told them, "Wyatt, I'm going to have to hold you here. They're looking for you and there are warrants out for your arrest. We're going to have to hold you. But come in and have something to eat first." Wyatt and the others sat down to eat, expecting to be arrested, but then Colonel Biddle suddenly excused himself. When they finished their meal and walked outside, they found fresh horses waiting for them by the gate.[23] Wyatt, Doc, and the rest rode away, bound for New Mexico.

The departure of Wyatt Earp and his men from Arizona was part of a plan. Behind them, the next phase of the plan was already in motion. Despite the anti-Earp tone of the press, a combination of forces was at work to see that Wyatt Earp and his companions would not be brought to trial in Arizona or otherwise be called to account for what they had done. A conspiracy of sorts was afoot, involving prominent Tombstone businessmen, Arizona's U.S. marshal, the governors of Arizona and New Mexico, officials of Wells, Fargo & Company, and even the Southern Pacific and Santa Fe railroad companies.

Personally following up the company's interest in the Cochise County troubles, John J. Valentine, the general superintendent of Wells, Fargo, arrived in Arizona in April and is believed to have consulted with James Hume and John Thacker about the situation. These consultations produced the $1,000 that Lew Cooley carried to Wyatt Earp at Hooker's ranch. Cooley, a former Wells, Fargo employee, became a go-between for Earp and the company. On April 14, Cooley reported to Valentine in his railroad car at Benson. At Willcox, after leaving Valentine, Cooley was arrested by Sheriff Behan for "aiding and abetting the Earps." He was held only briefly, and Valentine proceeded east into New Mexico by rail following the Earp party.[24]

Wyatt, Doc, Warren, Sherman McMaster, Turkey Creek Jack Johnson, Texas Jack Vermillion, Dan Tipton, and Charlie Smith reached Silver City, New Mexico, on April 15, as described by the *New Southwest and Grant County Herald*:

> Last Saturday evening at about 10 o'clock the Earp boys' party and Doc Holliday arrived in Silver City. They went at once to the Exchange hotel to find the stage agent to make arrangements to leave the next morning on the Deming coach. They slept in some private house up town and took breakfast next morning at the Broadway restaurant, and as they had not registered at any hotel it was not known they were in town until after their departure. The party came on horseback, and put up at the Elephant corral. They were all well mounted and armed to the teeth. One of the men, when asked his name, answered John Smith, and another Bill Snooks. This excited the suspicion of Mr. White, proprietor of the corral, and the next morning when they offered to sell him their horses, he refused to buy them, fearing to get himself in trouble. They offered six of their horses for $300, but as the horses were worth much more than that, this offer was also looked up as unfavorable to them. They finally sold the six horses to Mr. [Levi] Miller, who is about to start a livery stable here. This done they spoke to Mr. White about hiring a team

to take them to Fort Cummings, but he advised them to go by stage which they decided to do. The saddles and two horses they failed to sell were left here with Charley Bagsby.[25]

The network of support was already at work. On the afternoon of April 15, O. R. Smythe, the local stageline manager, had received a telegram from Wells, Fargo requesting a special coach to Deming for the Earp party on April 16. Wyatt went directly to the agent when he arrived. One unverified source later claimed that most of the Earp party slept that evening in the basement jail of the Grant County Courthouse as the guests of Sheriff Howard Whitehill, while Wyatt stayed at the sheriff's home. The "private house up town" could have been the home of D. P. Neff, a relative of Earp's mining partner from Tombstone, A. S. Neff.[26]

Charlie Smith said his good-byes to the rest of the vendetta posse at Silver City and returned to Arizona. Wyatt, Doc, and the others rode the stage as far as Deming and then boarded a train for Albuquerque. By then, Superintendent Valentine was already in Albuquerque, and, in fact, he dispatched Agent Frank Stevens to Deming on the morning of April 16 to replace the agent there who had been injured in an accident at Rincon but who was in a position to be a messenger to Wyatt Earp, since the Earp party changed trains at Rincon that same day.[27] After one more brief stop at Socorro, the Earp posse completed the trip to Albuquerque.

Curiously, the destination of the Earps was well known before they arrived. On March 28, before the Earp party left Arizona, the *Albuquerque Morning Journal* reported, "Last night, at a late hour, a *Journal* reporter learned that the famous Earp boys were headed for Albuquerque, and that they were on the Atlantic express which arrives in this city this morning at 6:18. . . . It is not likely they will remain in this city if they stay at all, because they are too shrewd to stay in this locality." Perhaps a plan was already in motion after the powder house meeting in Tombstone on March 25.

When the Earp posse did reach Albuquerque on the Atlantic & Pacific train on April 16, Wyatt found Frank McLain (also known variously as McLean, McLane, and McClain), an acquaintance from Dodge City, waiting for him at the station. McLain took the Earp party under his wing in Albuquerque, later giving Earp $2,000, which suggests that McLain was acting as an agent for forces in collusion with Wyatt, most likely the Atchison, Topeka, & Santa Fe Railroad, which had always had strong ties with the old Dodge City crowd. In John H. Flood Jr.'s manuscript written with Earp's collaboration in the 1920s, the author cryptically noted, "At Albuquerque, Earp visited a friend." Doubtless, this was McLain.[28]

The Earp party remained in Albuquerque for close to two weeks and managed to keep a surprisingly low profile that was possible only with help. During that time, Wyatt conferred with Valentine and possibly C. C. Wheeler, the general manager of the Atchison, Topeka, & Santa Fe Railroad, who was also in town. He may have been involved in the discussions of these men with Governor Lionel A. Sheldon about the Earps remaining in New Mexico at least for a time. Sheldon shared concerns about the Cow-Boy problem and had asked the territorial legislature for assistance in January 1882. In fact, Major Albert Jennings Fountain was even then in the field with the First Battalion of Volunteer Cavalry of the New Mexico Territorial Militia searching for Cow-Boys in Soccoro, Grant, and Sierra counties.[29]

Also most likely drawn into the discussions was Don Miguel Antonio Otero. Otero was a leading Democrat in New Mexico, with strong connections in Washington, but he was also a banker and railroad man, with interests in both the Southern Pacific and the Santa Fe. As vice president of the Santa Fe, he had overseen the building of the road into New Mexico, and he was eventually responsible for the connection with the Southern Pacific at Deming. He also knew of both Wyatt Earp and Doc Holliday through his mercantile operations in New Mexico and Kansas and had knowledge of both men through the firsthand accounts of his son Miguel A. "Gillie" Otero Jr., who had befriended Doc in Las Vegas in 1880.[30]

Interestingly, Otero had arrived in Albuquerque early in April for a brief period while Governor Sheldon was in town, before returning to Las Vegas for festivities at the dedication of Montezuma's Castle at the hot springs near Las Vegas. Shortly thereafter, both Otero and his son departed for Denver, where the elder was "taken in" by a con man named Charles "Doc" Baggs at about the same time the Earps arrived in Albuquerque.[31] Still, Otero may well have been the person who made the accommodations for Wyatt, Doc, and company with the local establishment before the Denver trip. After securing Baggs's arrest,

Gillie apparently returned to Las Vegas and proceeded to Albuquerque, where he acted as a go-between for the Earps.

In 2001, the historian Chuck Hornung discovered a letter apparently written by Gillie Otero in 1940, which, while still controversial, appears to throw new light on the Earp party's Albuquerque sojourn. In it, Gillie recalled that "[f]ather sent me to see to the comfort of the Earp posse because his railroad supported the boys." Specifically, he said that "Blonger and Armijo kept watch over the boys." Sam Blonger was the marshal of New Town. He was out of town during most of the Earps' time in Albuquerque—in Denver, interestingly enough—but his brother and chief deputy, Lou Blonger, was acting as marshal in his stead. Perfecto Armijo was sheriff of Bernalillo County. He had appointed Blonger marshal, subject to the approval of the New Albuquerque Board of Trade.[32]

Another of Don Miguel Otero's friends and associates in Albuquerque was Henry N. Jaffa, a prominent Jewish merchant with operations in Trinidad, Colorado, and Las Vegas, New Mexico, as well as in Albuquerque. Jaffa competed with the Otero family in the mercantile business, but he was also their political ally. He likely was also familiar with Wyatt Earp and Doc Holliday because of their Trinidad and Las Vegas connections. He was exactly the kind of man the elder Otero would have called on for help.

While in Albuquerque, Gillie said, "Earp stayed at Jaffa's home and the other boys were around town." The weather was very cold that spring, and Otero recalled that "Jaffa gave Earp an overcoat from his store, Earp's had been ruined in a fight with the Cow-boys. I remember that cold wind even today. I do not remember that the boys had much money." He also claimed to have driven Jaffa and Earp to the river to see the work being done on the new bridge, noting that "Earp remarked how it reminded him of the big bridge at Wichita."[33]

Eventually, Wells, Fargo "arranged safety in Colorado," and the Santa Fe provided passage from Albuquerque to Trinidad. Before that happened, however, Doc and Wyatt quarreled, and Doc left ahead of the rest of the posse in company with Dan Tipton. According to the *Albuquerque Evening Review*, Doc "became intoxicated and indiscreet in his remarks, which offended Wyatt and caused the party to break up."[34] Doc later downplayed the incident, saying, "We had a little misunderstanding, but it didn't amount to much."³⁵ Still, over time, the incident did precipitate speculation.

Kate Elder would claim years later that the split had to do with a steel vest allegedly worn by Wyatt Earp, which prompted Doc to say, "You should take the same chances I take. I'm out."³⁶ How Kate knew that, she did not explain, nor did she clarify why the falling out would take place after they were well out of harm's way.

The "steel shirt" story first appeared in print in William Breakenridge's *Helldorado*. According to him, two Cow-Boys named Pink Truly and Alex Arnold claimed to have been at Iron Springs when the Earp party approached and that they, not Curly Bill, fired on the Earp party. They said that one of their shots struck Wyatt, and that he was saved by a steel vest. Other old-timer accounts, including Kate's, appear to have derived from Breakenridge's story.³⁷ Wyatt Earp was infuriated when the story appeared in *Helldorado*, insisting, "I never wore a steel vest, and I never had such a thing in my possession[,] another one of his dam [*sic*] lies."³⁸ Perhaps more to the point, such contraptions, although available, were hardly practical by 1882, and as an explanation for the dispute between Wyatt and Doc, it never had credibility.

Gillie Otero provided a completely different explanation in his 1940 letter:

> Earp and Holliday had a falling out at Fat Charlie's one night. They were eating when Holliday said something about Earp being a Jew boy. Something like Wyatt are you becoming a damn Jew boy. Earp became angry and left. Charlie said that Holliday knew he had said it wrong, he never saw them together again. Jaffa told me later that Earp's woman was a Jewess; Earp did mu——[illegible, apparently a misspelling of *mezuzah*] when entering his house.³⁹

What makes Otero's comment even more interesting, if his letter is authentic, is that in 1940 when he wrote it, Wyatt's early connection to Sadie was not well known. Even Allie Earp, Virgil's wife, did not remember her being in Tombstone. In March 1882, following Morgan Earp's murder, Wyatt's wife, Mattie, had gone to Colton, California, with other members of the Earp family, but by then Earp was clearly interested in, if not involved in an affair with, Sadie Marcus. That would explain his interest in Jewish custom. Holliday's remark, if indeed he did make it, was more likely based on Wyatt's staying in better quarters and spending extended periods of time with Jaffa than on some deep-seated anti-Semitism. Doc may also have disapproved of Sadie, either because of her earlier connection to John Behan or because he disapproved of Wyatt's disloyalty to Mattie. Most likely, the comment was an unguarded remark fueled by too much alcohol, but it was exactly the sort of indiscretion that would best explain Wyatt's reaction and the subsequent split between him and Doc.[40]

The split was serious enough that news of it spread rather quickly. Within a short time the *Tombstone Epitaph* reported, "It is pretty well understood that a row has taken place in the Earp camp."[41] About the first of May, Doc left Albuquerque ahead of the others in company with Dan Tipton, but the circumstances were not clear. Doc may have left angry, and Tipton decided to join him. Wyatt may have feared that Doc would cause trouble for the negotiations under way, so he sent him on to Trinidad with Tipton, either to make preparations for the posse there or simply to get him out of town to where he could do less harm.

The Albuquerque hiatus of Wyatt, Doc, and friends, far from bringing an end to the debate over the Cow-Boy war, merely exacerbated it. Speculation and diatribe reached new levels in waves of justification and condemnation that pushed the names of Wyatt Earp and Doc Holliday beyond "the news" and into the realm of legend. It was then, in late April and May 1882, with Earp and Holliday out of public view, that the vendetta began to transcend the narrow confines of history.

Even before the Earp posse left Arizona, the reputation of the Earps was undergoing a reconstruction. In an article portraying Frank Stilwell as an honest citizen, the *Tucson Star* acknowledged that the Earp brothers had "some warm friends who are good citizens," but added, "If one-twentieth part of what is said of their record is true, they are certainly no desirable acquisition to any community. They are a roving band; their path is strewn with blood. Strange as it may seem, wherever they halt in a settlement stage robberies follow and human life ceases to be sacred. Their late escapades at Tombstone are only their records repeated in other frontier towns."[42]

Such a gratuitous misrepresentation of the record transformed the Earps into the cause of Cochise County lawlessness and minimized the Cow-Boy problem that had been the subject of public outrage and editorial commentary for more than two years. Even the ambush attack on Virgil and the murder of Morgan were lost in the coverage or rationalized as the fruit of their own misconduct. The reversal of roles for the Earps in the press did not pass unchallenged. On April 24, a Tombstone correspondent replied to a strongly worded editorial of the *Los Angeles Express* blaming the Earps for the troubles:

> Things are in an anomalous condition in Cochise County. The Earps are hunting assassins and robbers, and the Sheriff, with a set of Cow-boys and cut-throats, are hunting the Earps [on the] *suspicion that they had a* hand in the killing of a stage robber in Tucson. Said stage robber was supposed to have assassinated Morgan Earp. But there is no proof that the Earps killed the robber. However, the friends of the robbers have made complaint against the Earps, and sent a warrant to our Sheriff. Our Sheriff is so anxious to avenge the death of the stage robber that he seems to have forgotten all other duties. The day after M. R. Peel, son of our esteemed townsman, Judge Peel, was assassinated, the Sheriff, with eighteen or twenty deputies, left in search of the Earps, leaving the warm and bloody corpse of poor young Peel at Tombstone, and from that day to this if he, or any of the Cowboy deputies, have ever done one thing towards detecting the murderers, no one in Cochise County has heard of it. Judge Peel declares that the Sheriff has never spoken to him, or noticed him, since the death of his son. All of the good people are shocked at such conduct. The Governor has equipped thirty men and put them under a United States Marshal. They and the people are doing all they can to detect the assassins. Since the Earps left the county there have been five or six cold-blooded murders and robberies, and if our Sheriff or his gang have ever noticed or made the least effort to arrest one of the fiends no one knows it.
>
> It is now said that the Earps have left the country, and we expect to have a series of crimes soon, as the Earps were the only men here that these fellows were afraid of. The citizens are thinking of petitioning the Governor to recall the Earps and put thirty men under their control.[43]

Responding to further criticism of Doc and the Earps in the *Las Vegas Optic*, the same correspondent challenged the charges and added, "Another petition is being quietly circulated requesting the governor to recall the Earps, as the citizens claim they were the only ones who dared cope with the cattle thieves and stage robbers. I find the feeling is universal among the law and order party, that the Earp party are the only ones that can restore order and security of life and property."[44]

As far as the Arizona press was concerned, only the *Epitaph* and the *Tucson Citizen* actively reminded readers of the history that had led to the vendetta, and that changed in April, after the Earps left Cochise County, when John P. Clum and Charles D. Reppy sold the *Epitaph*. The *Epitaph* had been the great defender of the Earps, and, more important—because the *Epitaph* had controlled the Associated Press wire service—it had been largely responsible for the positive view of the Earps nationally. The new editor, Sam Purdy, a friend and former partner of James A. Reilly, an old enemy of Wyatt Earp, came to Tombstone from Yuma, where he had published the *Yuma Free Press*.[45]

Purdy's arrival on May 1 marked a dramatic shift in the *Epitaph*'s editorial position. Indeed, Purdy was the primary architect of the anti-Earp view of the Earps as stage robbers, thugs, and murderers who victimized the Cow-Boys, and he promoted the lie that there had been no Cow-Boy problem. Purdy was a newcomer to Tombstone; as such, his viewpoint had to come from Reilly and the other enemies of Wyatt Earp. Purdy now gave editorial sanction to the lies that Ike Clanton had first told on the witness stand at the Judge Wells Spicer hearing.

This left the *Tucson Citizen* as the single strong editorial voice in Arizona to remind other journals of the history of Cow-Boy depredations in their own back files, while Democratic papers used the Earps to attack the Republicans, suggesting that "[t]he rope that hangs the Earps will strangle the Republican party." Even before Purdy arrived in Tombstone, the Democratic press intimated that the Republican Party supported the Earps. Lyttleton Price, the Republican district attorney in Tombstone, had been under fire from the *Tombstone Nugget* from the beginning of his tenure in 1880. As early as November 8, 1880, the *Nugget* complained in a criminal case that "[a]s is usual in Price's prosecutions, the defendant was discharged." During the Spicer hearing, Will McLaury expressed the view that Price's prosecution of the Earps and Doc Holliday was less than enthusiastic. On April 1, 1882, in one of the last blows against local authorities before Richard Rule replaced Harry Woods as editor, the *Nugget* attacked Price directly for his handling of cases involving the Earp party, especially Milt Joyce's case against Doc: "Probably the District Attorney of Cochise county will arise and explain to the people why so many 'straw' bonds have been accepted and the criminals allowed to escape. Maybe he will explain why an indictment against Doc Holliday has not been placed on the criminal calendar, and while on this subject, why did he not present it at the last term of court when requested to do so by a ledsing [leading] prosecuting witness?"[46]

Significantly, under the editorship of Richard Rule, the *Nugget*, though no friend of the Earps, became more moderate in its tone and steered clear of the political excesses of the *Tucson Star* and the propaganda of the *Epitaph*. The *Tombstone Commercial Advertiser* took a somewhat different and practical view of the Earps: "It seems that at this time the people and city have lost their old staunch champions, and perhaps it is just as well that it be so, and better, that both city and people look out for themselves and fight their own battles."[47] Some of the Earps' old allies, at least, thought that good advice.

The Earp posse had already left Tombstone when William Tecumseh Sherman, the general of the U.S. Army, arrived on April 7, 1882. He stayed long enough to talk with some of the locals on both sides of the controversy (although that was not his mission), and he advised the U.S. attorney general that the "Civil Authorities have not sufficient force to make arrests to hold prisoners for trial or punish when convicted." He supported the Gosper-Tritle plan, which called for federal funds to create "a suitable posse to aid the sheriff & marshal" or a revision of the Posse Comitatus Act to allow federal troops to be used.[48]

Sherman's opinions contributed to President Chester A. Arthur's decision to follow the advice of Governor Frederick A. Tritle and to issue his "Proclamation Respecting Disturbances in Arizona" on May 3, 1882, which authorized the use of troops to enforce the laws and ordered the "insurgents" to disperse. The proclamation declared that it had "become impracticable to enforce, by ordinary course of judicial proceeding, the laws of the United States."[49] The reaction to the proclamation was swift and strong.

Sam Purdy and the *Epitaph* set the tone by announcing that indignation meetings were planned to protest the proclamation and declaring, "Cochise County is as peaceful a state as any other section of the country. There is no outlawry, no outrages, no resistance offered to the exception of the law."[50] In reprinting the article, the *San Diego Union* interjected at this point, "Let us wait a minute and get our breath."[51] The *Epitaph* went on to declare that "Tombstone is as peaceful a city as there is in the Union, having a perfect police system and efficient officers. Public opinion is unanimous in calling the President's action an outrage." The *Union* proclaimed, "for absolute, steel-plated cheek, the foregoing dispatch has never been equalled," adding, "It is, however, surpassed by the one that follows."

The *Union* then published a long editorial from the *Tucson Star* that deplored the proclamation and blamed federal authorities for any difficulty there: "There has been no time when the law could not have been executed in Arizona with the assistance of Federal officials, and criminals at any time could have been brought to punishment with their help. There has been no terrorism, and no difficulty in the administration of justice, save that inaugurated by them." The *Star* went on to assert, "The origin of this scandalous condition is simply this: A band of Deputy United States Marshals engaged in the most wanton and criminal practices under the color of their official authority. They murdered innocent people, and when the Sheriff of the county in which these crimes were committed sought to arrest them, they interposed their official position and resisted the execution of the law. These are the facts."[52]

These editorials aroused other reactions to their bald-faced effrontery. "The cattle thieves and stage robbers of Arizona are in a state of virtuous indignation. The proclamation of the President has seriously wounded their feelings," declared the *Union* in response. It then expressed this firm opinion:

> Now it is perfectly useless to enter into any serious argument with people who gravely utter such expressions as we have quoted, in the face of the actual occurrences in southeastern Arizona in the last six months. The very fact that gamblers, murderers, stage robbers, and cattle thieves of that section are strong enough to be represented in the local administration of affairs, and to obtain the sustenance of a portion of the press, tells its own story, and needs no comment.[53]

The *San Francisco Exchange* dripped sarcasm in its review of Cow-Boy outrages: "It is pleasant to hear that these pastimes no longer exist in Cochise county, but we believe they do all the same."[54] The *Tucson*

Citizen observed, "To read the Tombstone papers one would imagine that the great enemies of the prosperity of the country were not the robbers and murderers but those who punish and denounce the crimes." In subsequent issues, the *Citizen* quoted at length from the back files of the *Star* and other papers to expose the hypocrisy of their stance. "Their news columns give the lie to such editorial utterances," the *Citizen* declared. "It is a notorious fact that lawlessness prevails and it is equally well known that a reign of terror exists in the city of Tombstone that makes it next to impossible to correct the existing disorder of things by the ordinary means of civil justice."[55]

The *Citizen* went on to point out Sam Purdy's reaction in the *Yuma Free Press* about Tritle's visit to Tombstone and his proposals: "He has come to the conclusion that law and order must prevail at any cost, and is taking sensible and energetic steps in the direction of such a consumation." There, Purdy had deplored "THE EXISTING LAWLESSNESS IN COCHISE COUNTY." The president's proclamation was not "an infringement upon the rights of individuals and local governments," the *Citizen* proclaimed. Rather, "we are inclined to the opinion that the quiet which these papers now declare to exist is due to the establishing of some authority which will not be deterred from enforcing the law either through fear or favor."[56]

On the evening of May 10, the promised indignation meeting was held at Tombstone with Marcus Aurelius Smith, a Republican from Tombstone, and Judge Robinson, a Democrat from Tucson, as the primary speakers, prompting the *San Diego Union* to ask, "Are murder, robbery, and gambling so firmly intrenched in the Tombstone section that their endorsement is non-partisan?" Actually, the meeting was disappointing to its sponsors, so much so that the *Tombstone Nugget* could not resist belittling it for "falling flat as a cold potato," and the *Phoenix Arizona Gazette* called it a "complete farce." And when Charleston announced an indignation meeting, the *Citizen* had its say:

> If any place in the Territory is entitled to indignate, Charlestown [*sic*] is that place. It is there that the Cowboys have broken whiskey glasses just as they were raised to the lips of terror-stricken citizens, broken the tops of beer bottles and snuffed out candles with their revolvers. It is in Charleston that clergymen have been compelled to dance and sing in the midst of religious services to gratify the humor of Curley Bill et al. It is here that merchants have been compelled to

open their safes and turn over their ready cash to the festive Cow-
boys. It is here that the Clantons and McLowreys [*sic*] tied up and
disarmed a peace officer for attempting to arrest one of them for disturbing the peace. It is here that M. B. Peel and a half dozen others
have been murdered in cold blood within the past five months. We
would suggest that they embrace these facts in the preamble to the
resolutions they will be called upon to pass. It will establish their
knowledge of the characteristics of the festive cowboy and strengthen
their statement that no lawlessness exists.[57]

One of those who directly challenged Sam Purdy's portrayal of
peace in Cochise County was Deputy U.S. Marshal John H. Jackson,
just back from twenty days and four hundred miles through the countryside with his rangers. He pointed out that two years earlier there
were ranches, livestock, and development. Then he wrote, "Yes, Mr.
Epitaph, there is peace; and the reason is evident—there is nothing
more to steal. The rancheros were literally broken up by the thieves,
and had to abandon their homes and corrals and move into town to
save their own lives, because their lives were threatened if they
reported on the thieves. Is it to secure the favor of the vandals who
committed these outrages that the Epitaph is advertising to the world
that we have so much peace and quiet in Cochise county?"[58]

The *Nugget* endorsed Jackson's letter by saying that it was "written
by a gentleman of integrity and unquestioned veracity, a resident of
over three years' duration, and who knows whereof he writes." Purdy
retaliated by blaming the deserted ranches on federal Indian policy,
not on the depredations of Cow-Boys, and belittling Jackson for
spending twenty days in the field and finding "nothing but grass and
timber—not even a cowboy or an Earp." He accused Jackson of being
politically motivated and set off another controversy in Cochise
County. That was another story, however.[59]

Not all those who criticized the proclamation followed the *Star-
Epitaph* line. Some simply thought it was the wrong solution. Judge
Bryant L. Peel of Tombstone, a staunch Democrat who was still bitter
over the murder of his son, addressed the issue directly:

> I have read these editorials until I am disgusted. I know the object of
> such articles. It is to cover the deficiencies of a set of county officials
> in Cochise County. The most outrageous crimes had been commit-
> ted by the wholesale and not an arrest made nor an attempt made to

arrest. Farmers at their homes, engineers in their offices, teamsters on the road and miners in their camp, had been murdered in cold blood, and our county officials took no pains to ferret out the perpetrators of these crimes. These things caused the best citizens of Tombstone to appeal to the Governor for relief. I was one of that number. The Governor had two classes of advisers when he came here. One advised him to call out 100 militia and head them and take this class of outlaws, as a class, and shoot them wherever found, which I think is the only way to deal with fiends. A more conservative class advised him to call on the general Government for aid. He took the advice of the latter and asked the president for $150,000 and permission to remove inefficient officers. The President asked Congress for permission to use the military to aid the civil authorities—a thing that nobody asked for, nor no one wanted. But that was not the fault of Governor Tritle, nor shall he be blamed for it. All that Governor Tritle said is true, and we stand ready to prove it to the world.[60]

Criticism from the *Virginia City (Nevada) Enterprise* prompted Tritle to write to the editor there, pointing out that he had requested help because the territory could not provide needed funds and that all the criticism was from the Democratic press. "The Republican press has no indignation meetings," he wrote. "Those were held only where cowboys abound." Like Peel, the *Enterprise* thought the president's use of martial law was unnecessary (calling it "ridiculous"), but it added, "Those acquainted with the character of the depredations committed by the cowboys understood very well that all that was required to bring the desperadoes under subjection was the exhibition by a few determined officers of a bold front toward them. The Earp brothers nearly succeeded in bringing them to terms, and had they been backed by the sentiment of the community in which they operated, their success would have been complete."[61]

In the mind of moderate editors, including the newly balanced *Tombstone Nugget* (which never played down the levels of violence that prompted the proclamation) or the Republican press, Tritle was not to blame for the president's overreaction. By May 16, Tritle was claiming that the proclamation was serving its purpose. Even the threat of a federal military presence had had a salutary effect. The press was still debating whether the cause was the governor's action or the fact that the Earps were gone, but there were at least fewer claims that southeastern Arizona had been peaceful before the vendetta ride. Now, the questions were overtly political, which meant, simply, determining who had been to blame. What happened was giving way to what best served the parties. That political controversy would be around for a while.

The one thing missing from most of this public debate was the Earp posse. Nothing was clear about its movements during late April and early May. The same *Epitaph* article that reported the "row" in the Earp camp also reported Dan Tipton killed en route to Colorado with Holliday. He was allegedly thrown from a train. Texas Jack was also reported killed riding on a train near Las Vegas. According to this account, Jack defended the Earps as "brave, honest men and true patriots, in fact that they were anything that was not bad." He also attacked the Cow-Boys as "a pack of murdering thieves, villains and stage robbers." When someone expressed a contrary view, the story alleged that Jack left the car, and a few minutes later the conductor returned to say that he had jumped from the train traveling sixty miles an hour. Both of these tales apparently derived from the *Las Vegas Optic* report that "an unknown man was murdered on a freight train between this place and Otero and the remains [were] thrown off the cars."[62]

To cap off all of this, another source reported that Sherman McMaster had been killed and Wyatt Earp seriously, if not fatally, wounded. When it finally got around to describing the Earp stay in Albuquerque, the *Review* reported:

> Notwithstanding the fact that the newspapers did not speak of their arrival here, it became known in Arizona, and Tombstone supplied a party of man-hunters, who, it appears from Arizona papers received this morning at last found their prey. The Epitaph gives an account of the killing of Wyatt Earp near Hooker's, Arizona, last Monday, by a party which ambushed and attacked him while the Citizen indorses the news, adding the statement that Tipton was killed last week while with Doc Holliday. No particulars are published of the killings as both papers received their information through private sources. Wyatt met his death while returning from a visit to his wounded brother, at Colton, California, who had but the week before assured a citizen of Tombstone that all of them would, as soon as he was well, return to Arizona and stand trial on the charges preferred against them.[63]

Clearly, the rumor mill was in high gear. In another story, Virgil Earp supposedly told the press that he had received a letter from "his brothers in Illinois." The wire service reported, "The boys say they left the country for fear of killing some good men."[64] The rumors provided some cover for the Earp posse as they prepared to leave Albuquerque, in pursuit of an arrangement to provide an unofficial sanctuary in Colorado. The elder Otero was a friend and business associate of Frederick W. Pitkin, the Colorado governor. Pitkin was a pragmatist, but he apparently saw no problem with the Earps taking refuge in the state so long as there was no push for their extradition, which seemed unlikely, given Governor Tritle's predisposition to favor the Earps.

On May 13, well after the Earp posse had left New Mexico, the *Albuquerque Review* got around to publishing its account of their sojourn in Albuquerque, which supported the belief that powerful forces were working on behalf of the Earps:

> On the morning after their arrival [in Albuquerque], and before more than one or two knew of their presence, Wyatt Earp called at the Review and Journal offices, and had an interview with the reporters of both papers. He stated that they had come to Albuquerque to escape persecution while awaiting the result of an effort by Governor Tritle to secure their pardon from the president; that they were being sought for by their foes; and that they would not give themselves up to the Arizona officers without resistance. In view of these facts, Earp requested of both papers that their temporary sojourn in Albuquerque remain unnoticed until they could be assured that the knowledge of their whereabouts would not bring a party of cow-boy avengers down on them. To back his assertions regarding Governor Tritle's feeling toward them, Earp presented The Review several convincing documents, and his request was accordingly granted by this paper, as it was by the Journal.[65]

The *Review* indicated that about fifty people knew of their presence in Albuquerque. The *Journal* denied that the "Earp desperadoes" called at its offices, but the *Review* offered a contrary view of their character, noting, "The party, while in Albuquerque, deported themselves very sensibly, performing no acts of rowdyism, and in this way gained not a few friends for their side of the fight."[66]

Doc Holliday would have enjoyed the newspaper dialogue in Arizona had he been able to follow it, but at the very least, he realized that he had become involved in something much larger than revenge for the death of a murdered friend and brother. It was never simply that, and through the early months of 1882, he witnessed the whole process becoming more complicated, involving corporations and government officials as well as his new friends. Doc found himself on the side of the consolidating power of the new industrial order. With six dead Cow-Boys, possibly more never recovered in the brush (as rumor always claimed), and many scattered into Mexico, New Mexico, and other points, the vendetta ride could fairly be called a success.[67] There would be political costs, mainly for Wyatt Earp himself, but he knew—and so did his supporters—that he and his riders had given the business development of Arizona a bloody shove toward the stability and order his supporters sought.

The vendetta touched ancient issues about law and justice that resonated with people far beyond Tombstone and Arizona. There was something primal in what became known as the Earp-Clanton feud. Violence is most likely to occur where the authority structure is insufficient, where the authority structure is undermined by inefficiency, corruption, or lack of public support, and where the authority structure itself feels threatened. All three factors played a role in the troubled region of southeastern Arizona. The Cow-Boy troubles originally derived from an insufficient law enforcement presence. Over time, inefficiency, corruption, and a general distrust of both Sheriff Behan and Marshal Earp led to a lack of public support for the legal systems of Tombstone and Cochise County. The authority structure itself—the new order represented by mining, shipping, and banking interests—saw its interests threatened, and it was willing to support a heavy hand to set things right.

The new industrial order was redefining class relations in ways that challenged traditional assumptions and justified violence in defense of the community. The same arguments that played out in Arizona over what Doc and the Earps were doing were part of the debate not only over events like the Lincoln County War and the Johnson County War but also over events like the Great Strike of 1877, the suppression of the Molly Maguires, the Homestead Strike, and the Haymarket Riot, with one side condemning the violence and the other justifying it as necessary for the establishment of order. The managerial philosophy adopted by most business leaders during the Gilded Age encouraged the quick suppression of perceived threats to the new order, while more traditional thinkers worried about the possible abuse of law presented by the resort to force too quickly, which made the cure worse than the disease.[68]

Few Arizonans doubted that there was trouble in southeastern Arizona; the question was whether the Earps were part of the cause or the cure. Many Arizonans deplored the Earps' vendetta as ruthless vigilantism of the worst sort for which there was no justification. They believed the Earps posed a serious threat to the rule of law. Many others, including most of the business elite in the territory, pointed to the failure of the law to deal with the Cow-Boy scourge as justification for what the Earps did. What is the relationship of law and justice? At what point, if ever, can men justify going outside the law to achieve justice? This debate was not confined to Arizona in 1882, or in other times before or since.

Violence attended growth, and the right or wrong of it depended on whether it was perceived as a necessary agent of change or a needless usurpation of law. The *Citizen* offered one view: "The only way to make the country safe and secure for immigration and capital is to wipe out the lawless element by any means possible."[69] The *Star* offered another: "The question is law or no law; which shall prevail? The people say the former must."[70] And while that debate went on, Wyatt Earp, Doc Holliday, and the rest were simply pawns in the larger game. They had served their purpose, and now they withdrew as heroes or villains (depending on the point of view) to await the vindication they had already been promised.

A HOLLIDAY IN DENVER

Doc Holliday, I have you now!

— Perry Mallon, *Denver Tribune*, May 16, 1882

Trinidad was southern Colorado's door to New Mexico through Raton Pass. In 1882, it boasted a population of sixty-five hundred. Its businessmen, ranchers, and miners were ambitious, calling their town "the Pittsburg of the West," but like many such places in the West, the real mother lode for some was found in the gambling halls and saloons rather than in the mine shafts. On April 17, 1882, about the time that Wyatt Earp's posse reached Albuquerque, Bat Masterson became the marshal of Trinidad. Only a day before, the former Dodge City policeman John Allen mortally wounded Cockeyed Frank Loving, John Henry Holliday's old buddy from Dodge, who had also "killed his man," as the expression went. Masterson calmed things down and soon won the praise of the town fathers and a skeptical press.[1] He had just begun to settle in when Doc and Dan G. Tipton arrived from Albuquerque amid the press speculations that Tipton had been killed.[2] Bat doubtless got his first real accounts of the past weeks from them, but shortly thereafter the rest of Wyatt Earp's posse slipped off the train at El Moro just outside of Trinidad for a brief reunion before disbanding.

It was the end of the vendetta trail. Wyatt, Warren, Doc, Texas Jack Vermillion, Turkey Creek Jack Johnson, Tipton, and Sherman McMaster said their good-byes, and by May 3 most of them had departed.[3] Wyatt enjoyed his reunion with Bat, recounting the bitter months just past, and Doc found congenial company in smoky, more familiar climes

284

free of trail dust and Cow-Boy posses. The town had more than a dozen gambling halls and saloons and a number of familiar faces from his earlier days at Trinidad in 1878 and from Dodge City, Las Vegas, and other points in his past, which made the experience something of a reunion for him as well.

Doc and Wyatt parted company there. Perhaps the strain on their friendship from the incident at Albuquerque was still fresh; perhaps Doc had already made his plans to visit the silver mining camps in the Wood River country in northern Colorado. More likely, the deal struck at Albuquerque simply meant that Wyatt did not need him anymore, and they parted company at Trinidad on good terms. Wyatt, Warren, and Tipton left about May 4, bound for Gunnison in the mountains, but not before the *Trinidad News* reported, "Messrs. Wyatt and Warren Earp are still with us. Their brothers went south Wednesday morning. Again the *News* takes great pleasure in saying they are all 'way up' boys—gentlemen of the first water."[4]

Bat probably accompanied the Earps as far as Pueblo to attend the prize fight scheduled there on May 5 between the pugilists Thomas B. Walling and Bryan Campbell.[5] Despite reports that both fighters were "in good trim," the match turned into a debacle when the only man the principals could agree on as referee refused to take the job. A riot seemed imminent until some promoter cooked up an impromptu dog fight that lasted until one of the dogs' backers "threw up his tail for lack of a sponge."[6]

The affair was the occasion for an editorial on the brutality of prize fighting, and to add to the sporting men's woes, "the police made a raid upon all classes of gambling and houses of prostitution in South Pueblo" that night and "pulled all the inmates, between forty and fifty all told." Said the *Pueblo Chieftain*, "It is very evident that the South Pueblo authorities mean to root out the evil which has been let alone so long, and in this the best class of citizens back them up. Nearly all parties arrested put up for their appearances this morning."[7]

In this righteous atmosphere, Bat said good-bye to Wyatt and returned to Trinidad and his duties. The Earps stayed in Pueblo a day or two longer, minding their manners, before catching the train to Gunnison with Tipton.

Doc lingered in Trinidad a few days longer than the others, gambling and renewing acquaintances with companions from his past.

William B. "Bat" Masterson, marshal of Trinidad
in 1882. He took an active role in the effort to
prevent Doc Holliday from being extradited back
to Arizona.

Relying on the arrangements made at Albuquerque, he gave little
thought to danger arising from the vengeance trail he had recently
traveled, although he knew that warrants had been sworn out for him
in the Frank Stilwell and Florentino Cruz killings.

On May 8, 1882, in Tombstone, the old case against him in the
matter of his fight with Milt Joyce was called before Judge William H.
Stilwell, and when Doc did not appear, Stilwell declared his bond forfeited and closed the books on that matter.[8]

About May 10, John Henry moved on to Pueblo. He continued his
gambling in South Pueblo, where things were back to normal after the
short-lived crackdown on the sins of the flesh. There, too, he introduced himself to local authorities and spent considerable time with
Pat Desmond, a constable, former Pueblo chief of police, and acquaintance of Doc's from the days of the Royal Gorge affair.[9] He behaved
himself and made sure that everyone knew that he had been acting as a
peace officer during the vendetta ride. As in Trinidad, "He made no
effort to conceal his identity, and when questioned as to his doings in
Arizona, said he had nothing to fear from that quarter, as he had
received full pardon from the governor for his bloody work, in consideration of the effective services he had rendered to the authorities."[10]

Doc would have had no reason to notice the brief item in the
Chieftain of May 11, which noted simply, "Perry Mallen [*sic*], Esq., of
Ogden, Utah, is in the city on his return from Los Angeles, California,
and autographed at the Lindell," but it was a name he would soon be

unable to forget. On the night of May 12, a "small man, with reddish face and bearing, with small ferrety eyes, and not an inviting cast of features" approached him in Tom Kemp's variety theater. The man introduced himself as Perry Mallon and thanked Doc for once saving his life in Santa Fe. Doc replied that he must be mistaken because he had never been in Santa Fe, but the little stranger persisted with his story and warned Doc that he had seen "Josh" Stilwell, the brother of Frank Stilwell, on the train and that Stilwell was gunning for him. Mallon then curiously threatened to kill Doc if he said anything and capped off the encounter by taking down his clothes to show Doc what he claimed were scars from gunshot wounds. Doc laughed, shrugged Mallon off as an eccentric of some sort, and promptly forgot the incident.[11]

On Sunday, March 14, in company with Texas George Robinson and Sam Osgood, two gambler friends, Doc departed Pueblo for Denver. The *Chieftain* announced why: "The races began in Denver yesterday and there was quite an emigration of sporting men from this point, who hope to see some of the proceeds of the pool box."[12] On the train Doc and his friends ran into Bat Masterson, who was also on his way to the races. Arriving in Denver on May 15, Doc checked into the Windsor Hotel and, as he had done in Trinidad and Pueblo, announced his presence to the authorities. He spent the day at the fairgrounds, in company with Masterson and his gambler friends, but he also talked with David J. Cook, the head of the Rocky Mountain Detective Agency, and Chief James Lomery of the Denver police department, among others. He certainly did not act the part of a fugitive, and, in fact, was not even armed.[13]

That evening he planned to meet John N. Vimont, the superintendent of the Big Pittsburg mine in Leadville, at the Windsor Hotel. Vimont was a friend from Tombstone, a mining speculator who had pulled out in 1881 before the troubles started and had gone to work for Horace A. W. Tabor, the father of the Leadville boom, lieutenant governor of Colorado, and brother of Maxie Tabor, whom Doc had met during the Royal Gorge War. Vimont had apparently agreed to loan Doc money for his planned trip to the Wood River country. Why he was willing to finance Doc was a question never answered, but he and Tabor may have expected Doc to investigate investment opportunities in the north.[14] At any rate, Doc never kept the appointment.

Instead, near nine o'clock in the evening, as Holliday walked along Fifteenth Street toward the Windsor, a small, strange-looking man

Perry Mallon, the confidence man whose melodramatic arrest of Doc Holliday and tale of a seven-year manhunt in pursuit of Doc led Denver authorities to hold Doc until Arizona authorities could process extradition papers to have him returned to face charges.

stepped up to him, pointed two revolvers at him, and shouted dramatically, "Throw up your hands. Doc Holliday, I have you now!" as two deputy sheriffs, Charles T. Linton and Barney Cutler, took Doc into custody and hustled him off to the sheriff's office a short distance away. Only after arriving at the sheriff's office did Doc recognize the man who had accosted him as Perry Mallon, the eccentric he had encountered in Pueblo.[15]

The scene in the sheriff's office was chaos multiplied. Even there Mallon continued to nervously point his revolvers at Holliday, causing Doc to remark, "Oh you can drop that. Nobody is trying to get away from you. I have no weapons."

This set off a heated verbal exchange between the two. Mallon dramatically declared, "No, you won't get away from me again. You killed my partner, you blood-thirsty coward, and I would have taken you at Pueblo if the men I had with me had stood with me."

Disgusted, Doc made it clear that he did not intend to be abused and appealed to a growing number of men gathering in the room that he be allowed to make a statement.

The officers were visibly nervous about the crowd, and Deputy Linton impatiently reminded Doc, "This is not a court or jury."

Doc persisted, demanding to know "[i]f it is customary in this country to deny a citizen the right of speech? Is it right? Is it justice?" The melodrama continued as Doc told the onlookers he could expose Mallon as a fraud, and Mallon flourished his pistols again. "I can show you his reason for bringing me here," Doc exclaimed. "I can show—"[16]

At that point, Linton cut him off, but Mallon rambled on about Doc having killed his partner, until Holliday was hustled into a hack and taken to the county jail. As the officers started out the door with their prisoner, a *Tribune* reporter asked Doc if he could come along. Doc responded, "Come on; you are just the man I want to see."[17] The news of the arrest had spread quickly because the *Tribune* reporter was only one of several reporters there, along with a number of citizens including what the *Tribune* described as "rough looking characters" from out of town whom no one seemed to know. Once he arrived at the jail, Doc grew more reticent, declaring that he wanted to speak with Bat Masterson and an attorney before he said any more. Not until Doc was pushed into a cell did the reporter hear someone call him "Doc" and realize who the prisoner was and why the sheriff's department was so officiously nervous.[18]

Bat Masterson must have caught wind of what was happening early on. Doc had hardly been lodged at the jail before Bat and Frank A. Naylor, a prominent Denver attorney, moved to secure a writ of habeas corpus. En route to see the judge, they encountered the *Tribune* reporter. Bat told him "that Holliday was a responsible man, a Deputy United States Marshal, and for a time Deputy Marshal of Tombstone, and that the cowboys only wanted to assassinate him as they had Virg and Morgan Earp."[19]

Bat also told the *Denver Republican*'s reporter, "I tell you that all this talk is wrong about Holliday. I know him well. He is a dentist and a good one. He was with me in Dodge City where he was known to be an enemy of the lawless element."[20] By 3:30 A.M., Bat and Naylor delivered papers signed by Judge Victor A. Elliott to the sheriff's office ordering Sheriff Michael Spangler to have Doc in court later that very morning. Clearly, Bat was prepared for action and already acting as manager of the situation on Doc's behalf.

Denver residents awoke to a flurry of reports about the "celebrated" prisoner and Perry Mallon's "manhunt." Over breakfast and throughout the day, Doc Holliday was the main topic of conversation. At the outset, most of Denver's papers took Mallon's story at face value, and it was a dramatic one at that. Mallon claimed to be the sheriff of Los Angeles County, California, and said that the story had begun seven years earlier when Doc Holliday murdered his partner, Harry White, in St. George, Utah. Mallon laid it on thick. At his hands, Doc became "one of the most noted desperadoes in the West." The *Denver Republican* declared:

> In comparison, Billy the Kid, or any other of the many Western des-
> peradoes who have recently met their fate, fade into insignificance.
> The murders commited by him are counted by the scores, and his
> other crimes are legion. For years he has roamed the West, gaining
> his living by gambling, robbery and murder. In the Southwest his
> name is a terror. In fact, he is no other a personage than the leader of
> the murderous gang of cowboys who have been lately operating in
> the vicinity of Tombstone, Arizona, and the head of the lawless ele-
> ment of Tucson, Arizona.[21]

Mallon gravely showed reporters a missing little finger on his left hand that he attributed to Doc's marksmanship, adding, "And six other bullets from his pistol have perforated my body." He claimed that Doc had callously killed his partner as the result of a quarrel over cards. "A more cold-blooded murder never came to my knowledge," Mallon intoned. "Poor Harry never moved; bullet after bullet was shot into his body, and Holladay [*sic*] had so many friends at his elbow that any resistance on my part would have been useless." Mallon said that he resolved at that point that he would track Holliday down, which led to a manhunt that took him on a trail through Arizona, California, Kansas, the Indian Territory, and eventually to Tombstone.

He made Doc the Cow-Boy leader, turned Frank Stilwell into a martyr, accused Doc of killing a railroad conductor named Clantry, and capped it all off with this revelation: "Six week[s] ago, while a man known as Curly Bill, and myself were searching for him in the moun-tains, we suddenly came upon him, and during the encounter, in which over 100 shots were fired, 'Curly Bill' was killed at my side from a shot fired by Holladay [*sic*]."

After murdering six men at Tucson, Mallon went on, Doc left Ari-zona headed for Fort Dodge or the Indian Territory. He followed, he said, noting the outcome:

> I stopped at Trinidad, and there gained my first clue. I went to
> Pueblo, and one night saw the object of my search in a box at the
> Comique theatre. Not wishing to show myself, I went out to get an
> officer, and when I returned he had gone. I thought he had recog-
> nized me, and left in consequence. I remained there for several days,
> but could not find my man again. Three days ago, I came to Denver.

I was taking my chances. Yesterday I saw him on the street and you know of the capture.[22]

It was a wild yarn, but many Denver citizens, including the sheriff's department, appeared to take it at face value, although Deputy Sheriff Linton was put off by Mallon's style. The *Denver Rocky Mountain News* proclaimed Mallon a hero and gave him credit for a bit of verbal wizardry, so bizarre that it almost had to be deliberate, when it informed its readers that Mallon "has been on the track of Doc since the desperate fight he had with the gang by the sheriff's force of Tucson, Arizona, six weeks ago in which Sheriff Stilwell was killed in an attempt of the gang to murder Charley, a brother of Deputy Sheriff Clintry, murdered by one of the Earps in a billiard parlor at Tombstone a few weeks ago."[23]

"Sheriff Mallon deserves great credit for the persistence with which he followed up the man," the *News* intoned. The *Republican* initially added its voice to the view that Doc's crimes were "legion," his murders were "counted by the score," and that Mallon was a brave officer.[24] For the moment, Mallon basked in the glory of having brought down the West's most notorious outlaw. His ruse, with all of its calculated fantasies, could not withstand scrutiny for long—but then, it did not have to prove true to hold Doc until the processes for extradition in Arizona could be put into motion. It was a bold charade.

Not everyone was conned. The *Tribune* quickly judged that Mallon's story was "a very sensational one, and, in fact, too highly colored throughout to bear the impress of truth." The *Tribune* noted that "Mallan [sic] had a little silver-mounted revolver such as a cow boy would disdain to carry. The manner in which he handled his pistol showed that he was afraid it would go off every moment, and that he was more frightened than Holliday was evident. It looked like the affectation of a tyro to hold a pistol on a defenseless and unarmed man as Mallan did in the Sheriff's office." The *Tribune* said that "Holliday does not think Mallan was ever a cowboy or in the habit of handling a pistol."[25]

By contrast, the paper pointed out that "Holliday has not been in hiding nor has he disguised his name or features." John Henry did not overplay his hand with claims or accusations. His story was understated and reasonable. The *Daily Times* reported:

Holladay [sic] claims with considerable show of reason that the only fault committed by the gang was a vigorous effort to enforce law and order and bring the cowboys to justice. This claim is sustained by the fact that the *Epitaph* was a firm adherent of Earp and his followers until the proprietors were compelled by threats and attempted assassinations to sell out the paper, and also by the position taken by the federal authorities, which under orders from Washington have taken measures to suppress the lawlessness inspired by the doings of the cowboys. It is possible that one part was as bad as the other, but the facts developed and the history of the trouble known to the readers of the daily papers through the associated press dispatches point to a different conclusion. . . . Mr. Holladay's story . . . is plausible, and is certainly told with an air of candor and straightforwardness that carried conviction. It will not be surprising if it turns out that the matter grows out of the Arizona troubles, and that Mallen's [*sic*] story was made up to give him an excuse for making the arrest and for giving him tone as a seven-years' avenger of a friend's death.[26]

To the *Rocky Mountain News*, Doc recounted the rivalry between Wyatt Earp and John H. Behan for the sheriff's position in Cochise County, including Behan's failure to appoint Earp undersheriff as promised. The *News* reported that "Earp is said to have become an active partisan of the United States Marshal in his efforts to suppress lawlessness, while Behan took the side of the cowboys." The Cow-Boys then determined to drive Earp and his friends out of the territory, while the respectable element of Tombstone supported the Earps and Holliday. Eventually, the Earps decided to leave the country with the sheriff and a posse of Cow-Boys chasing them.[27]

Doc's appearance and demeanor were also inconsistent with Mallon's portrait of him as a cold-blooded killer. One by one, Colorado's newspapers drew surprisingly consistent word portraits of Doc. "When Mr. Holladay came out of his cell," the *Times* said on May 16, "the reporter was surprised to find, instead of the typical western ruffian, a delicate, gentlemanly man, apparently not weighing more than one hundred and thirty pounds, perhaps thirty-five years of age, with a prematurely gray head, and a heavy sandy mustache."[28] The *Pueblo Chieftain* described him similarly: "'Doc' Halliday [*sic*] is a man of light weight, rather tall, smoothly shaven, and is always well dressed. Streaks of gray can be seen in his hair which grows from a head a phrenologist would delight in examining. His eyes are blue, large, sharp and piercing. He is not over thirty five years of age, and is straight as an arrow."[29] The *Tribune* portrayed him as a thin, spare man with a blonde moustache and a piercing eye, which glanced covertly and suspiciously from under the brim of a black slouch hat. . . . The stranger's hair was lightly streaked with gray, his clothes were custom made and such as are worn in civilized communities, and altogether there was nothing to denote that he was the desperate, blood thirsty and notorious murderer, stage robber and villain which he was soon afterward represented to be.[30]

Moreover, those who came forward to speak on Doc's behalf added respectability as well as credibility to Doc's version of things. Even the *Rocky Mountain News*, which tended to support Mallon, noted that "Holladay [*sic*] is well known by General D. J. Cook and others of the Rocky Mountain detectives, and has also many other acquaintances in Denver, who put a good deal of faith in his story. Some of his friends say that Holladay's arrest is merely a ruse to get him down to Arizona in order to give the cowboys a chance to murder him."[31] Not only did Doc have the support of Bat Masterson, Dave Cook, Pat Desmond, Chief Lomery, and others in the law enforcement community, but respectable citizens like George Tritch and George Reppy, the brother of Charles D. Reppy of Tombstone, spoke out on his behalf as well.[32] Reppy produced a letter from his brother that supported Doc's version of things, and Tritch, who had recently returned to Denver from southern Arizona, told the *Times* staff that he believed "that the story told by Holladay [*sic*] is correct," explaining:

> During his visit to Tombstone he conversed with a large number of the most substantial and influential citizens, all of whom told him the story precisely as told by the prisoner. This is an important corroboration of the situation from Holladay's standpoint, and affords a strong support for his opinion that if he is taken back to Arizona, it will be, not for the purpose of bringing him to trial for an alleged crime but in order to get him back for the purpose of giving the cowboys an opportunity of murdering him.[33]

On May 17, the *Pueblo Chieftain* provided information that Mallon had conned "considerable money" from "several Akron [Ohio] gentlemen" and added, "Those who know him here say he holds no official position whatever, which goes far to strengthen the belief that he is simply after the blood-money which may be given to him by the cowboys of Arizona for the capture of Holliday."[34] That view was virtually confirmed by the report in the *Republican*, almost lost in the melo-drama, that

> As soon as the arrest was made, Officer Mallen telegraphed to the Sheriff at Tombstone and late last night received the following reply:
>
> Tombstone A. T., May 15.
>
> Perry Mallen.
>
> Five hundred dollars delivered to me at Denver. Answer when arrested.
>
> J. H. Behan, Sheriff.

Said the *Republican* without realizing the implication of its report, "The total amount of rewards on his head will reach probably $5,000. It is a big capture, and will be hailed with delight by the citizens of Arizona and the Southwest."[35]

Unfortunately for Doc, none of this was enough to free him. The sheriff's department remained firm: "The Sheriff's officers incline toward the opinion that Mallen's story is the correct one, and that Holladay is the outlaw he is represented to be. They do not attempt to reconcile the opinion, however, with the fact that he was a deputy United States marshal, contenting themselves with the belief that one party was as bad as the other, which may be the fact without weakening the statement made by Mr. Holladay."[36]

Doc's hearing was not held on May 16 as planned. Judge Elliott postponed it until the eighteenth. Masterson knew that delay worked against Doc, so he concocted another scheme to spring Doc. Under Colorado's extradition law, priority was given to charges against an individual arising within the state. With this in mind (and perhaps brought to mind by Doc's lawyer), Bat contacted Marshal Henry Jameson of Pueblo, and the very next day Jameson left for Denver with a warrant for Doc's arrest on a larceny count in Pueblo that charged "Holladay [*sic*] with being an operator in a confidence game . . . by which a 'sucker' was relieved of $150."[37]

On the afternoon of May 18, Jameson, who was quickly labeled as "a friend of Holladay," marched into Sheriff Spangler's office and presented his warrant. Spangler told him that his warrant could not be considered until after the habeas corpus hearing that afternoon. Near five o'clock, Doc was transferred to the sheriff's office in the county

building expecting to appear before Judge Elliott, but the judge postponed the hearing again because of illness. A crowd of people, many
of them sporting men, had gathered and were witnesses to a bold
move on Jameson's part. According to the Denver papers, the Pueblo
marshal stepped up to Doc, read the warrant to him, and told him,
"You are my prisoner; I want you to go with me."

Jameson's boldness caught the sheriff's deputies off guard for a
moment, but Sheriff Spangler quickly regained control, seizing the
Pueblo marshal "by the arm and sending him through the door in the
most one-two-three-bounce 'em style," with the command, "Here,
you get out of here and d——d quick, too." Spangler then turned on
the bystanders, "I don't want any money acting . . . and all of you men
who have no business here will get out in quick order."[38] Jameson
denied that he had trouble with Spangler. He said he had words with
Mallon, but that he was on "the best of terms" with Spangler and his
men. Spangler, though, expressed the view that "the arrest by the
Pueblo parties is a put-up job to secure Holladay's [*sic*] release." The
sheriff was suspicious enough of the whole situation, however, to say
that he would not surrender Doc to Arizona officers without "the
proper authority."[39]

Whatever the truth of Jameson's encounter (and Spangler seemed
to have the best of it), Doc was returned to the county jail, and the
Tribune reported that the sheriff had "good reason to fight all efforts
to release Holladay. He has received stacks of telegrams from the California and Arizona officers to hold Holladay at all hazard, and by fair
means or foul. This he now intends to do."[40] Already, the story was
shifting to Mallon's true purpose, which could not be hidden by his
tale of a seven-year manhunt. Ironically, a report that Sheriff Behan
was en route to Denver with a requisition from the governor of Arizona to Governor Frederick W. Pitkin of Colorado led the *Republican*
to assert that it settled Mallon's standing. "He has been attacked here
by certain newspapers as the enemy of law and order and a cowboy
representative; all of which insults he has born [*sic*] in silence," the
paper declared. "He has been relieved of this odious notoriety by the
dispatch."[41]

Yet, the truth was that Mallon was already becoming a curious footnote in the larger story. The *Pueblo Chieftain* noted that "[t]he Denver
reporters have nearly all arrived at the conclusion that Mallen [*sic*], the

man who did the arresting, is an imposter and a deadbeat." The Pueblo paper also announced that Mallon would probably be arrested if he returned to Pueblo for "obtaining money on false pretenses."[42]

There was no shortage of opinions about the right and wrong of things. One unidentified "gentleman, recently from Arizona," told the *Rocky Mountain News* that the Arizona war was simply a struggle between "bunco-steerers" and Cow-Boys. He claimed that the "better class of citizens" preferred the bunco men to the Cow-Boys because of the rowdiness of the latter. The bunco-steerers were, in general, "a peaceable, quiet class of people who outside of the bad habits of lying and stealing, would make quite respectable Sunday-school super-intendents." They had treated the cowboys treacherously, however, and the Earps and Doc Holliday were associated with the bunco men. He even claimed that Virgil Earp was shot—killed, he erroneously reported—because of a con game. This explained why Denver's confidence men generally supported Doc, said the *News*, but it did not "explain the fact that there are many men in Denver, thoroughly respectable and having no possible connection with 'crooks,' who believe the doctor thoroughly."[43]

Despite the journalistic war in Colorado, the real battle had shifted to Arizona. Sam Purdy's *Epitaph* announced that Holliday's arrest was due entirely to the "exertion" of Sheriff Behan. Purdy claimed that Behan had spared no effort in trying to locate the Earps and that when he learned that the Earps were headed for Colorado he had contacted Sheriff Spangler. Spangler had then advised Behan that he had Holliday in custody, and Behan, who apparently believed that the Earps were in custody as well as Holliday, advised Spangler to hold them securely until he could get the necessary papers and make the trip to Denver. Later, Spangler reportedly sent the following dispatches:

> Denver—Habeas corpus served. Can hold them three days. Can you get here in time with papers and reward? Answer quick, specifying crime, so we can hold them. M. Spangler, Sheriff.

> Denver—Have arrested Doc. Holliday. The Earpps [*sic*] are here. As soon as you come will take them. Answer. Sheriff.

Behan responded that he would start at once, and then he applied to Governor Frederick A. Tritle for the proper extradition papers. He then received the following telegram from Tritle:

J. H. Behan, Sheriff:

Cannot issue requisition until indictment and warrant are presented to me. Am ready to issue requisition at once. District Attorney absent at Benson. Have not at present the proper papers. When it is issued, the requisition must go to Prescott for the territorial seal. F. A. Tritle

Behan immediately wrote to the governor underscoring the importance of the case and urging him to act quickly. Later in the day, he received another dispatch from the governor:

John H. Behan, Sheriff:

Mr. Horton acting for District Attorney, asks for the requisition in the name of Sheriff Paul. F. A. Tritle

This was followed by another telegram from the assistant district attorney of Pima County, which brought surprising news:

John H. Behan:

Farley not here. Paul has made application for a requisition, and will leave tomorrow morning for Denver.

W. B. Horton.[44]

Behan was stunned, and Purdy was convinced that "Governor Tritle is conniving with Sheriff Paul." The *Epitaph* declared,

The friendship of Paul for the Earps is notorious, and it is a well known fact that he has made no effort to effect their capture. On the other hand, Sheriff Behan left no stone unturned to effect their capture. He has offered large rewards and went to much personal expense to bring the outlaws within range of justice. The opinion is advanced by a great many that the action of the Governor has not been fair to Behan, and that he has favored Paul for political or individual reasons.[45]

The matter was not quite that simple. Papers could be issued only if there was an arrest warrant, and the only warrant was the one issued by the Pima County grand jury's indictment of the Earp posse in the death of Frank Stilwell. Tritle claimed that if Behan had submitted papers for a requisition first, he would have had no choice but to grant them. However, after the governor's telegram to Behan, W. B. Horton, acting on behalf of Hugh Farley, the Pima County district attorney, urged that the requisition be granted to Paul. Horton's request was supported by two Pima County supervisors, based on the argument that "as the expenses of the arrest and delivery of the prisoners would devolve upon this county [Pima], it was right that a resident officer of this county should have the work to do."[46]

District Attorney Farley explained, "Now for the Governor under such circumstances, to have gone around the Sheriff of this county and appointed some one else to have brought the Earps here, would to say the least, have been an unusual and unfounded deviation." The supervisors also pointed out that Behan had already presented a bill for more than $2,000 against Pima County for his Cow-Boy posse's expenses. The *Star* openly questioned why Behan had not requested a requisition on a Cochise County warrant, and Farley openly speculated that it was to put the costs on Pima County. Tritle agreed with the Pima County arguments.[47]

Even so, the *Epitaph*'s charges were doubtlessly true that Tritle favored Paul over Behan, because Tritle had no confidence in Behan and may well have delayed long enough to allow the Pima County intervention. More important, Tritle was content just to see the Earps gone. Had it not been for the seemingly serendipitous arrest of Doc by Mallon, Pima County likely would not have pressed extradition. Tritle had no plans for extradition proceedings until Mallon forced the situation, and Pima County authorities moved quickly to block Behan in an after-the-fact gesture. Once set in motion, Paul and Pima County acted in good faith, but few outside Cochise County were anxious to see the return of any of the Earp party.

Paul started for Denver without the requisition in hand but with assurances that the papers would follow by express. The *Republican* erroneously reported that Behan was en route to Denver, based on a statement by Mallon, who claimed to have received a telegram from Tombstone.[48] He may well have received such a telegram, but if Behan did send it, he was stopped dead in his tracks by the governor.

Tritle's seeming to give preferential treatment of Paul over Behan set off an angry exchange between the *Epitaph*, on the one hand, and the *Star* and the *Citizen*, on the other, giving the Tucson papers common cause for the first time in months. The *Citizen* went so far as to claim that Behan had "notoriously failed" to arrest criminals in Cochise

County and had allowed the escape of a half-dozen prisoners. The *Epitaph* retorted that Paul was known to be a friend of the Earps and had in fact conspired in their escape from Arizona. The *Star,* so recently in common cause with the *Epitaph,* reacted strongly to the implication, declaring that "[t]he impression shared by many that Sheriff Paul will not bring the Earps to Tucson but will permit them to escape in transit, the *Star* considers an injurious suspicion which is not justified by the high reputation of the officer."[49]

In the meantime, Sid Byers, the marshal at Gunnison, Colorado, had telegraphed Marshal David Neagle at Tombstone and Sheriff Paul at Tucson and asked if those officers wished him to arrest the Earps. The *Epitaph,* which believed that the Earps were under arrest in Denver, denounced Byers as "a fraud and a delusion."[50] Spangler had left the impression that the Earps were also in custody with the broad statements "Have your men in jail" and "The Earps are here." Spangler denied having ever said that he had the Earps under arrest, and the feeling was widespread in Colorado that "the arrest of the Earp boys, the Arizona outlaws, is not desired for some reason or another. It is believed that it would not be a difficult thing to get them if they were wanted." All of this demonstrated, as the *Denver Times* put it, that the "whole affair is badly mixed."[51]

Bob Paul arrived in Denver on May 19 and ratcheted up the drama at once. In company with Deputy Sheriff Barney Cutler, Paul met Mallon at the Windsor Hotel. After about fifteen minutes, the trio was joined by Bat Masterson. Reporters deduced that Mallon was concerned that he was being pushed out of the picture, which led to a discussion of Mallon's claim that he had been trailing Doc for seven years for the murder of his partner. Masterson stood him down by stating that Doc had never been to Utah, and "Mallon finally acknowledged that he might have been mistaken."

Paul initially tried not to take a public stance, but the *Times* immediately said that he "confirms the truth of Holliday's story."[52] The *Tribune* agreed. "He is reticent and does not desire to commit himself in the affair," the paper declared, "but the simple fact as to where his sentiments and personal opinions lay cannot be concealed."[53] Paul would not be able to maintain a low profile. His career and character would be explored at length. The *Republican* reviewed his heroics at the attempted holdup near Drew's Station in March 1881, without any mention that some had accused Holliday of having a part in that episode. His career with Wells, Fargo, his reputation on the Pacific Slope, and his record as sheriff of Pima County won kudos aplenty. Bat Masterson concluded, "That's the kind of a man . . . who will take Holladay back and you [can] bet they will have to kill him before they kill his prisoner."[54]

On Monday, May 22, the *Denver Rocky Mountain News* carried an extended interview with Paul, which was yet curious in its ambiguous slant, given Paul's known sympathies. The paper observed that Paul was "reticent" to talk about the affair, but he did comment about Doc in the following exchange:

"Mr. Paul, have you known 'Doc' Holliday for a considerable length of time?"

"Yes; I believe about three years."

"Was he a member of what is called the Earpp [*sic*] gang, which created so much excitement in Tucson by their desperate encounters with the cowboys?"

"He was, and in fact was one of the leaders. The so-called Earpp gang, or faction if you please, was composed entirely of gamblers who preyed upon the cowboys, and at the same time in order to keep up a show of having a legitimate calling, was organized into a sort of vigilance committee, and some of them, including Holliday, had United States Marshal's commissions."

"Was Holliday regarded as a desperate character?"

"Not by any means. He was always decently peaceable, though his powers when engaged in following his ostensible calling, furthering the ends of justice, made him a terror to the criminal classes of Arizona."

There followed a review of the quarrels between the Earps and the Cow-Boys, somewhat garbled in that it implied that Morgan Earp had been killed and Virgil "fatally wounded" in a fight with the Cow-Boys that led to the killing of Stilwell in Tucson. The interview then continued:

"What is the sentiment of the people of Arizona in regard to the crime and its alleged perpetrators?"

"That, sir is a difficult thing to answer. The feeling is, however, very strong, especially among the more respectable citizens who have been terrorized for years by the cowboys and the Earpp gang and justice will no doubt be meted out to Holliday and his partners."[55]

The *News*'s slant created a strong impression that contrasted sharply with Paul's view as presented in the other papers. The *Tribune* had reported Paul as saying that "[t]he fight was a factional and political one. The cowboys, who represented the worst element of Arizona, were Democrats to a man. Holladay and the Earps represented the Republican element of Tombstone and the best class of citizens."[56] The *Daily Times* went further:

> Sheriff Paul was selected instead of Sheriff Behan, of Cochise county, because of the fact that under him the prisoner was reasonably certain of being protected from the designs of the cowboys or "rustlers," while with Sheriff Behan his life would not be worth a hawble. Sheriff Paul confirms the truth of Holladay's story in regard to the affair. Holladay was formerly a deputy under Paul, and while acting in that capacity was engaged in the effort to suppress the depredations of the cowboys, which have made life a burden in that part of the territory. It is more than probable that Holladay will have a fair trial. Under Sheriff Paul he is likely to reach the jail in safety, and will doubtless take a change of venue from Cochise county, as in the disturbed condition of affairs there it will be almost impossible to secure a fair jury.[57]

On the same day that the Paul interview was printed, the *Denver Republican* published the first real interview with Doc Holliday. Doc finally got to speak for himself, and it was a masterful performance. The *Republican*'s reporter noted that Holliday's appearance was "as different as could be from the generally conceived idea of a killer," and described him as follows:

> Holladay is a slender man, not more than five feet six inches tall and would weigh perhaps 150 pounds. His face is thin and his hair sprinkled heavily with gray. His features are well formed and there is nothing remarkable in them save a well defined look of determination from his eyes, which the veriest amateur in physiognomy could hardly mistake. His hands are small and soft like a woman's, but the work they have done is anything but womanly. The slender forefinger which has dealt the cards has dealt death to many a rustler with equal skill and quickness, and the slender wrist has proved its
>
> MUSCLES OF STEEL
>
> In many a deadly encounter, when a quick motion of a six shooter meant everything. Holladay was dressed neatly in black, with a colored

linen shirt. The first thing noticeable about him in opening the conversation was his soft voice and modest manners.

Doc was then allowed to tell his story, which was understated for the most part, but included a few misstatements that had to have been calculated:

The men known as cowboys are not really cowboys, in the early days the real cowboys, who were wild and reckless gained a great deal of notoriety. After they passed out their places were taken by a gang of murderers, stage robbers, and thieves, who were refugees from justice from the Eastern States. The proper name for them is Rustlers. They ran the country down there and so terrorized the country that no man dared say anything against them. Trouble first arose with them by the killing of Marshal White by Curly Bill. Marshal White fell into my arms when he was shot and I arrested Curly Bill. The trouble since then is familiar to all."

"Do you apprehend trouble when you are taken back?" asked the visitor.

Holladay paused for a minute and gazed earnestly out of the window of Jailor Lamberts room

INTO THE RAIN,

Outside and then said slowly, "If I am taken back to Arizona, that is the last of Holladay." After a pause he explained this by saying, "We hunted the rustlers, and they all hate us. John Behan, Sheriff of Cochise County, is one of the gang, and a deadly enemy of mine, who would give any money to have me killed. It is almost certain that he instigated the assassination of Morgan Earpp [*sic*]. Should he get me in his power my life would not be worth much."

"But Sheriff Paul, of Tucson, will take you to that place will he not."

"Yes and there lies my only chance for safety. I would never go to Tombstone alone. I'd make an attempt to escape right outside this jail and get killed by a decent man. I would rather do that than be hung by those robbers there."

"Cannot Paul protect you?"

"I AM AFRAID NOT.

He is a good man, but I am afraid he cannot protect me. The jail is a little tumble down affair, which a few men can push over, and a few cans of oil thrown upon it would cause it to burn up in a flash, and either burn a prisoner to death or drive him out to be shot down. That will be my fate."

"Haven't you friends there who would rally to your assistance?"

"Yes, the respectable element will stand by me, but they are all intimidated and unorganized. They will never do anything until some respectable citizen is shot down, when the people will rise and clean them out, as they did at Fort Griffin, where twenty-four men were hung on one tree when I was there. The Tombstone Rustlers are part of this Fort Griffin gang."[58]

And so the interview went. When asked about the killing of Frank Stilwell for which he was charged, Doc said simply, "I know that Stillwell [sic] was a stage robber, and one of Morgan Earpp's assassins, and that he was killed near Tucson, but I do not know that I am in any way responsible for his death." He accused Behan of instigating Morgan's murder because he was affiliated with the Cow-Boys and because he had quarreled with Morgan on several occasions and hated him. He recounted his personal disagreements with Behan and claimed that the proof that Behan was involved with the outlaws was that he had "five Rustlers under him as deputies," including John Ringo (doubtless a reference to the Cow-Boy posse).

Doc then recounted his initial meeting with Perry Mallon and described him as a "crank," adding, "One thing which Mallon tells gives him away bad. He said in your paper that he was standing alongside Curly Bill when the latter was killed." He then recounted "the facts":

We were out one day after a party of outlaws, and about 3 o'clock on a warm day after a long and dry ride from the San Pedro river, we approached a spring which was situated in a hollow. As we did so

EIGHT RUSTLERS ROSE UP

From behind the bank and poured from thirty-five to forty shots into us. Our escape was miraculous. The shots cut our clothes and saddles and killed one horse, but did not hit us. I think we would have been all killed if God Almighty wasn't on our side. Wyatt Earpp turned loose with a shot-gun and killed Curley Bill. The eight men in the gang which attacked us were all outlaws, for each of whom a big reward has been offered. . . . If Mallon was alongside of Curley Bill when he was killed, he was with one of the worst gangs of murderers and robbers in the country.

Doc then told the interviewer that the Earps were in Gunnison and that his quarrel with Wyatt was "a little misunderstanding, but it didn't amount to much." When asked if the Earps would help him, he replied, "Yes, all they could; but they are wanted themselves, and of course couldn't go back with me without putting themselves in danger, without doing me any good." He concluded by belittling Mallon's claim that he had killed his partner in Utah, pointing out that at the time he was supposed to have murdered the man in Utah he was in Denver "dealing for Charley Foster, in Babbitt's house, where Ed. Chase is now located."[59]

It was a tour de force performance on the very same day that the *News* declared that Doc's hope was "vanishing into thin air."[60] Holliday's habeas corpus hearing, scheduled for that Monday, was postponed yet again, but at ten o'clock on the morning of May 23, Doc appeared in court before Judge Elliot, who examined the papers by which Doc had been held after Mallon's dramatic arrest and announced that there was no evidence to hold him and ordered the prisoner discharged. One paper said "a faint smile crept over" Doc's face, but Deputy Sheriff Linton stepped forward with a warrant authorizing the arrest of John Henry in the murder of Frank Stilwell. Doc was remanded to the jail to await the requisition from Arizona Territory, and Doc's lawyers, from the firms of Decker & Yonley and Deweese & Naylor, immediately filed for another writ of habeas corpus. The hearing on that motion was scheduled for Friday, May 26, based on news that Sheriff Paul had received a telegram that the Arizona requisition had been sent and should arrive at any time.[61]

These developments pushed Perry Mallon completely out of the picture, but on the day that the charges growing out of his arrest of Doc were thrown out, Mallon wrote a letter that did throw fresh light on how he had become involved in the case. He claimed that he had visited Tombstone, and while there Sheriff Behan had offered $500 to anyone who would arrest Doc. He said that he offered to do it, "whereupon he gave me undoubted authority. The County Commissioner also offered a reward of $1000, who also clothed me with proper authority." He said that when he arrived in Denver, he told Sheriff Spangler and explained the situation, and that Spangler had given him permission to proceed. When Doc arrived in Denver, then, Mallon telegraphed Behan, who replied, "Arrest him immediately."[62]

Mallon's "card" offered a plausible explanation for what had happened except for two things. First, if Mallon did make arrangements in Tombstone, as he claimed, why would Behan have singled out Doc rather than the Earp party in general? If Behan did do such a thing, it would appear to confirm Doc's statement that Behan had a special grudge against him, and it would also suggest that the county commissioner in question was Milton E. Joyce, Doc's nemesis, the only commissioner with a reason to single Doc out. Second, if the plan was concocted in Tombstone, how would Behan and Mallon have known that Doc Holliday would be in Denver, separate from the rest of the vendetta posse? A more likely scenario is that Mallon saw Doc in Pueblo and telegraphed Behan, making the arrangements by telegram. Once he had confirmation of the promised rewards from Cochise County, he followed Doc to Denver, contacted Sheriff Spangler as he said, telegraphed Behan again, and then made the arrest.

The papers from Arizona did arrive on Thursday, May 25, which produced an unexpected result. The newspapers expected the habeas corpus to be decided first, but the extradition proceedings before Governor Pitkin took precedence over the habeas corpus hearing, and "[o]wing to the absence from the city of Governor Pitkin, the hearing of the case was postponed to Monday." The *Republican* expected Doc to be returned and acquitted in the murder of Frank Stilwell, but it believed he would face a tougher time if sent to Cochise County for trial in the murder of Florentino Cruz. The editor wrote, "As Sheriff Paul is an open friend of the Earps, who as officers, assisted him in suppressing lawlessness, Holladay will be protected at all hazards. In Tucson he is safe, and there will be no call for him to go to Tombstone, as his lawyers can swear that his life is not safe there, and secure a trial in Pima County in the same judicial district."[63]

Curiously, the papers reported that the debate over the case had fallen largely silent. "Mallon is still in the city, but is keeping quiet, while Holliday's friends *have entirely disappeared* [italics added]."[64] It was also reported that Bat Masterson had left the city and that there was a rumor circulating "that he is organizing a party to guard the train upon which Holladay will be taken back."[65] This was likely true, because the *Las Vegas Optic* had already announced that "Bat Masterson, the new marshal of Trinidad, went south today, presumably on business connected with the arrest of his friend 'Doc' Holliday."[66] And precautions were warranted, because the *Albuquerque Review* had said that "[t]he cow-boys have all left Tombstone, and it is thought that they have gone out in order to intercept Sheriff Paul as he returns from Denver with Doc Holliday, and assassinate his prisoner. They have threatened that Holliday will never again enter Tombstone alive."[67]

On March 26, the *Rocky Mountain News* made its final case for the return of Holliday—who the paper reported was "completely broken up by the arrival of the requisition"—to Arizona. The *News* doubted that Judge Elliott would surrender Holliday without assurances that he could be protected from mob violence. This, the paper alleged, was viewed by Paul "as a piece of impertinence," and Paul's conduct was "an excellent refutation of the statement that the arrest is simply for the purpose of getting Holliday into the hands of the cowboys." The *News* took another strong slap at those working to help Doc: "Desperate efforts are being made by Holliday's friends to prevent his removal, not the least disreputable of which is the circulation of a story intended to prejudice the authorities here against Arizona authorities. This is that Holliday and the Earpps were Republicans, and acted under the United States Marshal, while the local authorities were Democrats, and that the troubles arose from this fact."[68]

The *News* concluded that there was no real reason "to defeat the ends of justice" by not honoring the requisition. With that flourish, the public debate was largely over. The newspapers had taken their stands, but the behind-the-scenes activities on Doc's behalf went on. From the beginning, Doc's public advocates were numerous, including Bat Masterson, Dave Cook, and Chief Lomery, all affiliated with law enforcement; George Tritch, a prominent hardware merchant; George Reppy, Charles Reppy's brother; and more. The *Denver Tribune*, which initially went along with the portrayal of Holliday as a dangerous criminal, soon became his champion. And was John J. Valentine's presence in Denver the week before the case was settled a coincidence?[69]

That Doc was represented by attorneys of the caliber of W. S. Deckard, Frank Naylor, and Colonel John T. Deweese did not fail to impress the observant, although it might have also raised questions about where a frontier gambler, on the run for more than a month, found the resources to hire them. Masterson had Naylor working on Doc's behalf within an hour of his arrest, and a Pueblo paper curiously noted that "[s]everal United States officers, as well as the marshal of Trinidad, are making strenuous efforts to secure his liberty," raising the instant question of which federal officials were involved and why.[70]

Governor Pitkin was in a difficult spot. In all probability, given their mutual connections, he and Governor Tritle of Arizona had already arranged sanctuary for the Earps in Colorado, which would account for the string of newspaper reports that the Earps already had been "pardoned" by Tritle before they arrived in Colorado. Mallon was the fly in a carefully prepared ointment. The arrest of Doc Holliday in such a sensational, public way forced both governors to consider the political implications of pushing forward with the private deal. That was the reason so much energy had to be expended on Doc's behalf. The Earps' friends could take no chances.

Lieutenant Governor H. A. W. Tabor might have been expected to be a spokesperson for Holliday, given his association with Doc's friend, John Vimont, and other associates of Doc and the Earps, but he kept a low profile, most likely because he and Governor Pitkin were involved in a political squabble at the time.[71] It is also likely that U.S. Marshal Crawley P. Dake was applying pressure on his counterpart in Colorado, which would account for the "United States officers" whom the *Chieftain* mentioned. Just how much Wyatt Earp knew about what was going on from his haven in Gunnison was never clear, but almost certainly the management of Doc's situation was out of his hands.

In the meantime, Paul's delay in returning to Arizona and reports that only Holliday was actually in custody produced anger even in papers, like the *Tucson Star*, that had argued for his right to act over Behan's. "But this concession is based on the presumption that Paul had the intention and the courage to perform his duty," the *Star* fumed. "His return with only Holliday in custody will be simply an outrage upon public decency."[72]

Governor Pitkin returned to Denver on Sunday, March 29, to find a cauldron waiting for him. George Tritch called on him that afternoon and advised him "that from his knowledge of the cowboys and their hatred of Holladay [sic], he was confident that the latter would be killed by them were he taken back there." Tritch also made a statement to the *Daily Times* to the same effect. Bat Masterson returned to Denver on Sunday as well and, having no direct access to the governor, visited the offices of the *Denver Tribune*, where he pleaded Doc's case to E. D. Cowen, the paper's capitol correspondent. He insisted, as well, that Doc would be murdered if he were returned to Arizona. Late that evening, Cowen called on the governor and presented the case against granting extradition. Cowen later claimed that his presentation persuaded the governor to order a public hearing.[73]

Still another advocate on Doc's behalf was Lee Smith, his friend from Georgia. Smith was living in Denver at the time, speculating in mining properties. He, too, called on the governor and made the case that "[i]t was certain death to Holliday to go back to Tombstone."[74] However, the critical voice may have been that of his friend and business partner George W. Crummy. Crummy was a saloonkeeper, but he also had mining investments in Custer and Hinsdale counties, southwest of Denver in the San Juan district, along with Pitkin. Wyatt Earp later claimed that Crummy was also his friend, and when he received word from Bat Masterson that "it would be necessary to use the last resort as the papers were flawless," he spoke to Crummy, who left at once for Denver. Wyatt recalled:

> As he stepped into the Governor's office, the governor was glancing over the requisition papers trying to find a flaw.
> "Governor, can you drive a four in hand?" inquired Crumy [sic].
> The Governor replied that he could.
> "Well then drive a four in hand through that," said Crumy, pointing at the papers, and the papers were returned to Arizona.[75]

Whether Crummy's influence with the governor was the deciding factor or not, it certainly was consistent with other pleas on Holliday's behalf and may have swung the balance, although, as it turned out, the papers were not "flawless" as Earp later said. Clearly, though, Crummy was one of the key players, as he would later prove.

On May 30, Governor Pitkin made his decision. Assistant Arapahoe County District Attorney I. E. Barnum, Deputy Sheriff Linton, and Sheriff Paul attended to present the case for extradition. Barnum presented the state's case, arguing that John Henry Holliday "should be delivered to the Arizona authorities as they were demanding him on a clearly-worded indictment, for a capital crime, and with a direct requisition from the Governor of the Territory." He argued that as a matter of equity, the case against Holliday in Arizona was of greater significance than the larceny case against him in Colorado and should take precedence. Holliday's lawyers argued, by contrast, that a person arrested for a crime in one state should be held to answer for that crime before being turned over to another jurisdiction. They argued further that the indictment from Arizona was faulty.[76]

When Deputy Sheriff Linton pointed out to Barnum that the warrant against Doc in Pueblo was dated a day *after* Doc had been arrested in Denver, Barnum made that point to the governor, who replied, "You forget Mr. Barnum, that he is not to be tried on the warrant, but on the complaint."[77]

With that, Governor Pitkin announced that he would not grant extradition. First, he claimed that the Arizona papers were not in order. An act of Congress required that the governor of the state or territory making demand for a fugitive should certify the authenticity of the indictment attached. In this case, Governor Tritle had not authenticated the indictment, and the certificate of the clerk of court was defective. He asserted his belief that the indictment "would not hold up in any court of record in the country." Since the papers did not conform to the requirements of an act of Congress, he could not hold the prisoner if a writ of habeas corpus had been applied for. Furthermore, Pitkin ruled, a warrant was in the hands of officers for the arrest of Holliday for the crime of larceny in the state of Colorado, so that even if the Arizona papers had been in order, Holliday was first subject to trial in Colorado. Accordingly, Pitkin refused to grant extradition.[78]

With that, Holliday was carried before Judge Elliott, where Barnum stated that he had no reason for holding Holliday on the charge in question, and Undersheriff Farmer, who was called on to answer by what right he held Holliday, declared that he had no proof of crimes in Arizona nor papers under which he could be held. With that, the writ of habeas corpus was granted, and Elliott ordered Doc discharged. Before he could be processed, however, an arrest warrant for the crime of larceny at Pueblo was presented, and he was remanded to custody yet again.[79]

On the morning of May 31, Doc Holliday, in the custody of Deputy Sheriff Linton and accompanied by Bat Masterson and Bob Paul, took the train to Pueblo, where that same afternoon he was taken before Judge McBride on the charge of having swindled Charles White out of $400. Holliday waived examination and was bound over to the July term of court. Bail was furnished in the amount of $300, and Doc was released from custody for the first time since Mallon's dramatic arrest in Denver. Bob Paul attended the proceeding at Pueblo, and the following day he made preparations for his return to Tucson, arriving home on the evening of June 2.[80]

On the day after Pitkin's decision, the *Rocky Mountain News* claimed that Sheriff Paul "gave Governor Pitkin a piece of his mind yesterday in strong but temperate language." That would have been characteristic of Paul, because he believed the governor's decision would set a bad precedent. Paul spoke with a reporter for the *Tucson Star* on the evening of his return and gave a more detailed and revealing view of the whole affair. He explained that he had, indeed, had an appointment with the governor before the governor made his decision. Pitkin had advised him of the Pueblo charge. Paul said that Pitkin "also said that he had been informed by prominent citizens of Denver that if Holliday was placed in my custody he would be murdered by cowboys before reaching Tucson." Paul advised the governor that he already had men placed at Deming, Willcox, and Bowie to advise him of potential trouble, and even proposed to take Holliday back to Denver by way of San Francisco to throw off any Cow-Boys who might have murder on their minds. Pitkin refused to honor the writ, however, because Governor Tritle had not signed it.[81]

Paul also provided other new insights into what had happened. He said that when he arrived in Denver, he received a telegram from Gunnison advising him that the Earps were there (with Wyatt ill) and that they could be arrested at any time. Paul purchased a ticket to Gunnison but "was influenced to remain in Denver and look out for Holliday." He telegraphed the sheriff at Gunnison for more information and was told that Wyatt and Warren had left town in a wagon but could be caught if he had papers. "I hadn't the requisition papers and hence could do nothing," Paul said.[82]

Interestingly, he claimed that Holliday had told him that he intended to return to Tucson to face the charges against him when court opened. He then provided Holliday's statement about the Stilwell killing:

> He does not deny or acknowledge the killing of Stilwell. He however states that when his party were at the depot in this city some of them were standing on the rear platform of the train. Two men approached. One he was sure was Stilwell, and the other it was presumed was Ike Clanton. The latter leveled their guns at the Earp party, when he and his friends dodged into the cars, procured guns and jumping from the train started down the track after the other two. At this point Holliday stopped the story and would not say what occurred afterwards.[83]

Bob Paul had acquitted himself well, winning the unanimous praise of the Colorado press, even the *Rocky Mountain News*, which had pointed out his friendship with the Earps. That was no mean accomplishment, but the Arizona papers could not resist a parting shot or two. The *Tombstone Epitaph* quipped, "Sheriff Paul's trip to Denver, although intended for a Holliday, proved to be anything but an enjoyable one."[84] The *Star* called him "a remarkable man," then added, "He resembles the distinguished soldier who never fought a battle nor won a victory." In yet another piece, the *Star* got closer to its real complaint: "Sheriff Paul's return to Arizona without the prisoner he ostensibly went to secure really creates no surprise. It was not expected he would bring them. It was not believed that those who commissioned him to do so intended that he should discharge his duty. The Republican officials could not afford to have the Earps or any of their crowd returned for trial; and of course the papers were defective. It was the easiest way out of the difficulty."[85]

The *Star* struck closer to the truth than perhaps even it realized, although probably not for the overtly political reasons that it imagined. The Earp vendetta was not simply a mission to avenge the murder of Morgan, nor was it about party politics. The forces that came together to support the Earps—corporations like Wells, Fargo and the Santa Fe Railroad, government agencies from U.S. Marshal Dake's office to cabinet-level departments in Washington, business leaders from three states, and two, possibly three, governors—made the Earp posse quite literally a force for order when the legal establishment appeared to have failed. What happened was consistent with appeals to violence in other milieus of American history, and especially in the age of incorporation of which it was a part. This was not simply about Cow-Boys and gamblers, cattle rustling and stage robbery; it was about mining and industry and the search for order—issues that were easily lost in simple and simplistic views of the misnamed Earp-Clanton feud. The Earps and Doc Holliday were at best tools of larger forces at work.

The Earps initially did not realize how things had changed. On June 4, less than a week after Doc was discharged, Wyatt Earp broke his silence. Asked about the future, he told a reporter:

My lawyers will have a petition for a pardon drawn up. Everybody in Tombstone knows that we did nothing but our duty. Anyway I'd do it over again under like circumstances, and all the best people there will sign the petition. Governor Pitkin knows the facts pretty well and will sign it too. We look for a pardon in a few weeks, and when it comes I'll go back; but if no pardon is made I'll go back in the fall anyway and stand trial. I'd go now, but I know we would have no show. They'd shoot us in the back, as they did my brother.

Asked if he anticipated trouble if he went back, Wyatt replied, "I don't know. . . . I suppose so. I'm going to run for sheriff this fall. Behan knows he can't get it again, and that's what makes him so hot towards me. I hear the gang is breaking up and a good many are going to other parts of the country."[86] In California, Virgil Earp also said that Wyatt would return to Tucson in the fall, arguing that they did not want to languish in jail through the summer, but asserting that "when the court sits again they will give themselves up, and, with fair play, will be acquitted."[87]

Both Doc and Wyatt promised at one time or another to return to southern Arizona to face the charges against them, and they most likely meant it. They did not return, because the men who had sponsored them and appreciated what they had done also believed that they had served their purpose and that for them to return would generate political problems too great to master. They had restored order—and the case could be made that they had broken up the Cow-Boy combination—but their return could itself be a fresh threat to order. Republicans could continue to defend the Earps, as papers like the *Tucson Citizen* did, and still be glad the Earp brothers and Doc Holliday were gone.

Politics triumphed in the end. Pitkin's decision may well have been a foregone conclusion. Tritle's failure to sign the documents may well have been deliberate to provide Pitkin with an easy way to dispose of the case (for both of them). The *Star* could declare that "[t]he Republican party in Arizona has taken shelter under the Earpumbrella," and then confess that in the matter of the Earps, it had "only treated the political aspect of the Earp difficulty and has not sought to prejudge their personal responsibility for individual crimes."[88] Virgil Earp lamented the political turn of the controversy: "I am sorry to see the thing taken into politics as a personal measure, because the true aspect of the trouble will be lost and new enmities are likely to be created."[89] But that was the way of things in Arizona, and history would soon be rewritten to fit a simpler scheme, with the Earps' voice largely missing.

Doc Holliday and Wyatt Earp were now linked forever, and yet, in an ironic way, because of the Denver episode, Doc was, at least briefly, the better known of the two to the public at large. Because of Perry Mallon, Doc was approaching the edge of legend. The wild tale Mallon told of his pursuit of Doc over seven years and his characterization of Doc as a bloodthirsty villain of the worst sort put the spotlight on him, although it was, as the *Tribune* put it, "a cock and bull story," full "of absurdities and monstrosities."[90] At least two of the Denver papers initially bought Mallon's tale at face value. The *Tribune* was more careful and soon raised questions about the tale. Mallon miscalculated, though. He was an experienced confidence man, with a reputation larger than he himself imagined. He had been recognized by several men from Akron, Ohio, as a confidence man from their home state, but Mallon did not expect that the publicity he gained in the Holliday case would itself expose him. Not long after Denver became enthralled with the Mallon-Holliday melodrama, an elderly gentleman named A. H. Rublee living in Denver, who had been conned two years earlier in Omaha, Nebraska, in a deal involving a threshing machine purportedly invented by Mallon, recognized him and brought the earlier scam to the attention of the *Tribune*, which reported it.

Mallon boldly challenged the *Tribune* to produce proof, which it was able to do, since Rublee lived in Denver and still had the papers drawn up for the "deal" by which Rublee was cheated out of $50, along with copies of other documents relating to his efforts to reclaim the money. Eventually, Rublee confronted Mallon at the sheriff's office. Mallon offered him $50, but Rublee turned the matter over to Frank Naylor, who was also Doc's lawyer, to secure $100 as provided in the contract. On May 24, the *Daily Times* announced, "Perry Mallen [*sic*], who arrested 'Doc' Holladay, has been made to pay W. H. Ruble [*sic*], of Omaha, $100, which the latter alleges Mallen swindled him out of by the sale of a patent threshing machine."[91]

Once it was clear that Mallon was not going to claim the rewards promised to him by the Cochise County authorities, he decided to leave town. Before doing so, however, he borrowed two revolvers from a man named Kent and a third from another named Greenstreet, then borrowed $310 from Julius Schweighardt, one of the owners of the Great Western Hotel. He also borrowed another $130 from Charles Morgan, a friend of Schweighardt's. Mallon had letters of introduction to Schweighardt from Los Angeles businessmen who may have been the object of a swindle from the beginning. At any rate, he told Schwei-ghardt that he was en route to Kansas City to arrest a criminal and claim a reward of $1,500, and Mallon offered him a part of the reward in exchange for the loan. Schweighardt accompanied him to Kansas City, where they registered at the St. James Hotel and called on the chief of police. Then Mallon told Schweighardt that he was going to Wyandotte to make the arrest. After several days, Schweighardt realized he had been conned and returned to Denver, where he reported what had happened to the police. When Morgan learned that he had been conned, he boarded a train for Albuquerque pursuing a report that Mallon had gone to New Mexico.[92]

Mallon, a career thief and con man, was gone. He was born in Akron, Ohio, in 1855, and from the time he was admitted to the Lancaster Reformatory in Akron for "incorrigibility and vicious conduct," he was an intelligent but troubled and troublesome person. He eventually made his way west to Nevada. He later turned up in Ogden, Utah, where in 1880 he abandoned a young wife and infant daughter. In January 1882, his wife divorced him for "unkind, harsh and cruel" behavior and "a roving disposition." She had not seen him in more than a year, and the divorce was granted only two months before his encounter with Doc Holliday.[93] Mallon was a small-time confidence man who was able to move at ease between his native Akron, Ohio, and the West Coast because he was also an employee of the Central Pacific Railroad for at least part of his career. Colorado would be glad he was gone.

Mallon left a trail, though. On May 29, the *Cincinnati Enquirer* published a sensational story about Doc that would have embarrassed Ned Buntline, the dime novelist. Datelined Denver and signed "Winston," its beginning was enough to raise the most gullible eyebrow: "Now that Jesse James body lies slumbering in the grave, and the excitement of his death considerably subsided, one would naturally suppose that any incident, however sensational, would cause but a slight ripple of excitement in comparison. This is not true, however, for here in Denver, in a crowded thoroughfare at night, was made one of the most important captures the world ever saw, and one that will cause a fervent 'Thank God' to arise from the lips of all in this Southwestern country."

The story went downhill from there. He was called "Doc," so the story went, because of a "peculiar dexterity" he had in the care of gunshot wounds. He was described as "a tall, dark looking man of about forty years of age, with a form herculean in its activity and strength." One could not look at him, "Winston" intoned, without feeling "that he is enjoying the society of a human tiger, only more fierce and relentless than that animal." Doc started his outlaw career in Missouri because of his "socialistic ideas concerning the ownership of various cattle in that section[, which] caused a slight misunderstanding with the presumed owner." Doc fled Missouri with a posse after him and landed in St. George, Utah, where he murdered George White, the "bosom friend" of Perry Mallon. Doc fired shot after shot into "poor White," but Mallon could do nothing because Holliday was secure among his friends.

When Doc moved on to Fort Yuma and a lucrative career as a cattle rustler, Mallon took up his trail as part of a sheriff's posse. Pursuing Doc's gang into the Calico Range, the sheriff's posse was defeated, with Holliday killing three men and severely wounding Mallon. Mallon did not give up, however, and pursued him through southern California, and from there to Fort Dodge, Kansas, where Doc murdered a judge. From there Holliday led the heroic Mallon into the Indian Territory, where he headed a gang of "thieves and cut-throats" until he followed the mining fever to Tucson, Arizona, in 1877, where he became the leader of "the murderous gang of cow-boys which has since proved the great terror of that country." It was there that "he became a devil incarnate, and truly his horned godfather had no cause to feel ashamed of his namesake." Shot six times by Holliday over the years, Mallon persisted and eventually caught him in Denver.

Winston then claimed an interview with Mallon in Denver, who treated him with "true border civility":

"Who is this Doc Holladay?"

"Well, that's hard to say," said Mallen [sic] thoughtfully, "unless perhaps, that he is the greatest scoundrel that ever went unhung."

"Precisely what they said of Jesse James. Which was the greatest villain of the two?"

"Why Doc Holladay [sic] of course. . . . He has not one germ of true manhood; he is vain as vanity itself, and his heart is as a stone. No cry of anguish or suffering deterred him from his purpose, and like a savage wild he gloried in his deeds of blood!"

"How many lives has he taken?"

"That is a hard question to answer, but they approach close to fifty."[94]

And so it went. The *Denver Republican* published this preposterous tale in full, with appropriate commentary, declaring that "[f]or a genuine romance of crime with detectives, bloody avengers, bulldogs, and dark lanterns thrown in, the country has never produced anything half as good as the Doc Holladay case." Referencing the *Enquirer*'s piece, its editors added, "These facts round off the hideous tale with a burst of laughter and turns what was nearly a tragedy into a roaring farce." The *Republican* summarized the case well: "The villain of the first act becomes the hero of the second, and the avenger and detective in one, the man who has devoted his life to his dead comrade, and has been shot so often that he has trouble in retaining his food, proves to be a petty swindler."[95]

A copy of the *Cincinnati Enquirer* also reached Pueblo containing the "column of twaddle devoted to this case," and the *Chieftain* observed, "The article in question has caused much amusement among Holladay's [*sic*] friends."[96] That same bunch must have also enjoyed the *Denver Republican*'s note that Doc was "resting quietly at Pueblo in the bosom of his constituency; a hard lot, to be sure, but not half as bad as Mallen [*sic*]."[97] On June 6, Mallon was reported to have been arrested in Pittsburg, Pennsylvania, where he was expected to be held until a requisition from Colorado could be forwarded to Pennsylvania.[98]

Doc rested a few days at Pueblo, but after about ten days, he left for a reunion with Wyatt and Warren in Gunnison. He was quickly recognized on the streets of that mountain town, "dressed in a dark close fitting suit of black, and wore the latest style of round top hat. His hair was seen to be quite gray, his moustache sandy, and his eyes a piercing dark blue." The reporter appreciated his "strong free and friendly grip of a hand, which said very plainly, 'here is a man who, once a friend, is always a friend; once an enemy, is always an enemy.'" Doc, "half jokingly and half in seriousness, told the reporter, 'I'm not traveling about the country in search of notoriety, and I think you newspaper fellows have already had a fair hack at me.'"

Doc gave a congenial, free, and open interview that revealed more about himself than he had ever told in any public forum, including details of his background, education, and travels. It was an interesting, if not entirely candid discourse that provided clues to his past and personality. Doc was asked about Mallon, and he said that Mallon left when he realized that Doc would be released. Asked if he would appear at Mallon's trial, he responded, "No, that is not my way of doing. I avoid trouble. My father taught me when young to attend to my own business and let other people do the same. I shall let him alone if he does me." He expressed the view that Mallon would be sent to prison "for a few years" because "the fraternity will spend a thousand dollars if necessary to send him there."[99]

Mallon did not remain in custody in Pennsylvania, however. By the end of June, he was in Vienna, Michigan, where he represented himself as an heir to a fortune and married a young woman. He then announced that he had to leave to go to his mother's deathbed in the West. He and his new wife showed up next in Toledo, Ohio, where he "cheekily entertained the police with great stories of himself and of what he was going to accomplish as a detective." He represented himself as a U.S. marshal from California. The next day, he beat his new wife, threatened to kill her if she did not sign over to him property she owned, and found himself arrested after a disturbance at the Union Depot.

Mallon pled guilty to being a suspicious person and creating a disturbance on July 30, 1882. He was fined $65. He did not have the money, so he served four months in jail at hard labor, while the father of his bride tried to have him charged with assault and battery. His exploits in Toledo won him mention in the *National Police Gazette*, along with a portrait. While he was incarcerated, authorities in Indiana contacted the police in Toledo and requested his photograph concerning a case arising from Mallon's marriage to a woman in that state.[100]

Doc remained in Gunnison for the rest of June. The rift with Wyatt seemed resolved, and the men enjoyed the time together. Judd Riley, who was on the police force at Gunnison, later recalled:

> The bunch was well heeled and went armed. Earp was a fine looking man, tall with a drooping mustache that curled at the ends. He was quiet in manner and never created a bit of trouble here, in fact, he told us boys on the police force we could call on him if we needed help at any time. He was a dead shot, I guess, always wore two guns high up under his arms, but he never used them here. Doc Holliday was the only one of the gang that seemed to drink much, and the minute he got hilarious, the others promptly took him in charge and he just disappeared.[101]

Doc was still in Gunnison on July 1, but he soon parted company with the Earps to make his court date in Pueblo. The *Salida Mail* recorded on July 8 that "'Doc. Holliday,' late of Arizona is in town with Osgood and Robinson. They will remain several days. The Arizona authorities tried to get Holliday [*sic*] back to that territory on a charge of murder but Governor Pitkin refused to honor the requisition."[102]

On July 11, the grand jury indicted Doc on a charge of larceny, whereupon the judge issued a capias for Doc and advised the sheriff that he could admit Doc to bail in the amount of $500. At that point the district attorney "and the said defendant in his own proper person as well as his counsel, W. G. Hollings, Esq., also came and being ready to plead to the indictment said defendant says that he is not guilty in manner and form as charged in said indictment, and puts himself upon the county, and the said people, by their said attorney, say they do the like."[103] On July 18, the case was continued, and, on the very same day, the *Leadville Daily Herald* announced that "Doc Holliday is visiting Leadville."

A LIVING–AND DYING–LEGEND

This is funny.

— Doc Holliday, November 8, 1887,
Walter Noble Burns, *Tombstone*

The Tombstone experience was the defining moment of John Henry Holliday's life. Everything before it was prologue; everything after, postscript. It was at Tombstone that Doc found a purpose greater than himself. Loyalty to a friend was part of it, and the part most remembered at that, but loyalty, though a character trait he embodied, was not the greater part of it. He saw what he did at the street fight and afterward as a duty, and he never once described what happened as anything less than service to the community. Doubtlessly, such sentiment curled the lips of many who knew him into cynical smiles, as the notion would for many who studied his life later. But honor mattered to him at a level few realized. He needed to be doing more than simply dying. He had lived for so long without hope or purpose that when he took a stand with the Earps against the Cow-Boys, he came to believe that he was doing something right and good. Perhaps it was a delusion, but there was little doubt that he believed it. And when the vendetta was over, he found his sense of purpose atrophying as surely as his lungs.

Yet his Denver ordeal made him something more than a gambler, or even a gunfighter. In a way that was much less satisfying personally, the publicity surrounding the extradition effort finally made Doc Holliday a "legend in his own time." Before that he had enjoyed something of a reputation on the gamblers' circuit as a "well-known sport." The O.K. Corral fight and subsequent events raised his stock as a "bad man to tangle with." He was notorious in Arizona by the spring of 1882, but the publicity he received during the extradition proceedings did more than spread his notoriety to Colorado, it ensured that his name would spread across the country. For the first time in his life, the mere mention of his name created an image in men's minds, and the sight of him caused men to stare and whisper. Stories of all kinds—good and bad—proliferated. They were not satisfying to him in the way the experiences in Arizona had been, but they helped him rationalize, justify, and conclude that he had been right, after all.

Back home in Georgia, Lee Smith was cornered by reporters suddenly interested in these tales of a native son. The reporter for the *Atlanta Constitution* found Smith at the Markham House on one of his visits home. Smith painted a dramatic portrait of the quiet "Georgia boy" who became "a terror to evil doers" in Arizona. His description of the street fight, which he described as "one of the most remarkable pieces of fighting that I have ever heard of," quickly parted company with the facts, pitting Doc Holliday (armed with "a double barreled, breach-loading shotgun") and the "four Earps" against the "McLowry crowd," consisting of six men. Smith went on:

> I don't know exactly how the fight first arose, but I know that the marshal and his deputies demanded a surrender which was answered by a volley. The fire was returned, and almost before you could think the McLowrys [sic] were wiped out. Doc Holliday shot four times and killed four men. He never missed a single shot. All the six were killed, four of them died instantaneously and two subsequent to the affray. The McLowry party was absolutely wiped out, and strange to say, not a man of the marshal's party was hurt.

Smith then described the retaliation of the Cow-Boys that led to an attempted assassination of Virgil and the assassination of Morgan Earp. He declined to blame Doc for the killing of Frank Stilwell, saying only that Stilwell was a deputy sheriff who "was known to have been one of the men who assassinated the Earps." He recounted the fight at Iron Springs and the melee in which Curly Bill Brocius was killed. He would say only, "It was supposed that Wyatt Earp killed Curly Bill." He went on then to describe the arrest of Doc by Perry

Mallon and the peril Doc faced as a result. Finally, the reporter asked, "Does Holliday ever speak of coming back to Georgia?"

"He would be back here today were it not for the fear that he would be turned over to the authorities of Arizona and Tombstone."[1]

The story was appealing if not accurate. Smith also spoke with the *Atlanta Post-Appeal*, where he tried to provide a more personal touch. "Well, I guess I do know 'Dock' Holliday," he told the reporter:

> I know the whole Holliday family, father, mother and son, and a finer family never grew up on Georgia soil and "Dock" Holliday is one of the best boys that ever lived, if he is left alone, but you mustn't impose on him or you will smell powder burning. I've a letter in my pocket now from "Dock" that I expect to answer to-day, and only a few days since gave Dr. J. H. [sic] Holliday, an uncle of "Dock" a paper containing an article about his nephew.

Smith then recounted Doc's career in even more detail than he had for the *Constitution*, with the same errors of fact. If anything, he was consistent. He claimed that Wyatt, "Dock," and "Johnson" were escorting Morgan (confused with Virgil) through Tucson when Stilwell was killed. "The fact that Holliday was known to be in the vicinity when the crime was committed, together with the fact that Stilwell was killed with a shot gun was circumstantial evidence enough to convince Stilwell's friends that Holliday killed him," Smith advised, concluding that Holliday "will be credited with the killing of every man in that section so long as he lives there, who dies from being shot down with a shot gun."[2]

Later in July, Sam Purdy's *Epitaph* published a response to the *Denver Republican*'s interview with "the now notorious Doc Holliday," which had finally made its way to Tombstone. "If the statement before us is a specimen of Doc's veracity," Purdy intoned, "there is no questioning the strength and power of his imagination." Purdy then reviewed several "lies" from the interview, including the statement that Doc was an "honest, peaceful citizen while in Arizona and contributed more than any other one towards preventing stage robberies and outrages of all kinds." Purdy also objected to the suggestion that when John H. Behan was nominated for sheriff, the Cow-Boys "packed the convention" and with "a flourish of revolvers and bowie knives forced his nomination." The editor was especially peeved by the statement that the Cow-Boys had forced with a "revolver argument" change in the editorial policies of the *Epitaph* to make it a "cowboy organ" and that they forced the departure of Charles D. Reppy, the former editor, from the country.

The *Epitaph* took special exception to claims that it was the tool of the Cow-Boys or that Reppy had been intimidated in any way by Cow-Boy threats. The paper published a curious report that contradicted the accounts provided to the Denver papers by Reppy's brother, who had defended Doc using letters from his brother, Charles:

> An *EPITAPH* reporter met Mr. Reppy after reading the interview and inquired if he had seen it. An affirmative answer, accompanied by a laugh, was given, supplemented by the statement that Holliday was the most thoroughly equipped liar, and smoothest scoundrel in the United States. The reporter then inquired if Mr. Reppy was not a friend of the Earps and Holliday, and was immediately answered in the negative. He said that he was never on intimate terms with any member of the gang, and believed that the greatest blessing ever bestowed on Arizona was their departure from beyond its borders. Reppy said his attention was called to the interview while in Colorado, but it was too absurd, and too thoroughly pregnant with glaring falsehoods, about the people of Arizona, to take serious notice of.[3]

And so the legend took shape, with point and counterpoint built loosely on what had happened in Arizona and the notoriety Doc gained as a result of his arrest in Denver. For the moment, he enjoyed more attention than Wyatt Earp or anyone else in the Tombstone story. Almost instantaneously, he went from a relative unknown in the communities where he lived to a hero or an archvillain, with both views written in purple prose devoted to melodrama rather than to what actually happened. The tales that he had a frontierwide reputation before Tombstone that writers and chroniclers produced about him in 1882 and afterward were actually after-the-fact representations designed to build his celebrity status in Denver. They implied pre-Tombstone notoriety, but the stories exaggerated his earlier adventures to make him bigger than life. What they really demonstrated was the impact of those tense days in May 1882 on the reputation of Doc Holliday. And, at a personal level, he found it hard to decide whether the hullabaloo was a blessing or a curse.

On June 14, 1882, the *Rocky Mountain News*, which had opposed Doc throughout the Denver episode and became Governor Frederick W. Pitkin's chief critic in the aftermath, noted:

A gentleman recently from Pueblo stated to a *NEWS* reporter yesterday that the notorious "Doc" Holliday is still in that city, awaiting
the action of the grand jury, on the charge of larceny which has been
preferred against him. Holliday is enjoying a splendid time, his
numerous friends in Pueblo giving him all that he could desire. He
feels perfectly safe against any and all proceedings that may be begun
against him in the neighboring territory of Arizona, being protected
by Colorado state authorities.[4]

The *News* carried the hint of sarcasm in that report, but it did
demonstrate that Doc's life was no longer his own. The Tombstone
legend was already swallowing him up, or perhaps his troubles were
feeding it. However defined, Doc had become the symbol of the Cow-
Boy war, which had captivated readers in the Southwest and Pacific
Slope for months and which had made its way into the eastern press
and even into the *Congressional Record.* That would change, of course,
but the peculiar circumstances of his incarceration made him the focus
of the debate for the moment. Oddly, with Wyatt Earp safe in Gunnison, Doc Holliday became the leader of the "Earp gang" in the public
mind.[5]

On July 14, 1882, two days after Doc's court appearance in Pueblo,
John Ringo's body was found in Morse's Canyon in the Chiricahua
Mountains east of Tombstone with a single gunshot wound to the
head. Apparently brought down by his own melancholy despondence,
he was one of the few real victims of his .45 Colt revolver. The coroner's jury proclaimed that the cause of death was "unknown," and
more than a decade would pass before anyone would claim that his
death was anything other than a suicide. With time, however, Ringo
also became a mythical figure in the Tombstone saga, not unlike Doc
in the portrayal of him as an educated loner, honorable, morose, a veritable Don Quixote, lost in mysterious self-absorbed tortures of the
mind. Arguably, in Arizona at least, where he had already been proclaimed "the King of the Cowboys," in life, Ringo was more notorious
than Doc Holliday. Over time, the mystery of his death would tanta-
lize old-timers and future generations of writers tempted by what-if's
and might-have-been's, but in 1882, his was an Arizona story.[6]

Perhaps inevitably, Ringo and Holliday would become each other's
bête noire in the evolving legend of Tombstone, the mavericks on
each side of the Earp-Clanton feud, different, yet much alike in their
brooding, dark ways. This theme had no firm basis in the reality of

what happened. It was based largely on the January 1882 confrontation on the streets of Tombstone that was cut short by prompt police work by a man whose name is all but forgotten, and perhaps later on the reported rivalry between the two of them over Kate Elder. The claim would eventually be made that Doc was part of a band of men who slipped back into Arizona and killed Ringo to fulfill Wyatt's promise to Morgan. Some even suggested that he was perhaps the man who fired the fatal shot.[7] But it was a fantasy, born of a need to make Ringo's death more dramatic, more meaningful, and more satisfying in the Tombstone saga. As two lost souls, each reminding the other of his own failed life, Doc and Ringo presented a temptation too great for latter-day mythmakers to resist.

That would be a twentieth-century addition of the ought-to-have-happened variety. The simple fact was that in July 1882 Doc Holliday could not have been a party to Ringo's death, because his presence in Pueblo was clearly documented and because the risks were simply too great for him—or Wyatt Earp for that matter—to undertake such an unlikely expedition. At the time, Doc was concentrating on more mundane and practical matters as he prepared to head north to Leadville or perhaps on to the Wood River country as he had originally planned. It would be hard to say when he learned of Ringo's passing, if he ever did. That summer Holliday was the man dealing with the attention, although it is doubtful that he either realized it or wanted it.[8]

What Doc needed most was money, not fame.

Leadville was quite literally "a field of dreams." From the time placer miners found gold in California Gulch in 1860, hope flooded the area as high as the ten-thousand-foot peaks. The real boom began in 1877 when the silver carbonate beds were discovered, and by 1880 Leadville was the "queen of the silver camps," boasting a population of forty thousand people and a monthly mining payroll of $800,000. More than a few millionaires walked the town's busy streets as fair game for the sporting crowd, who soon found the hunting good. At its heyday, Leadville boasted 120 saloons, 118 gambling halls, 110 beer gardens, and 35 brothels, besides churches, schools, department stores, a plethora of other businesses, and 3 newspapers.[9]

Doc certainly knew of Leadville long before he arrived, because its riches had generated the Royal Gorge War between the Santa Fe and the Denver & Rio Grande railroads, in which he had played a part, and because he had known more than a few men who had sought their fortunes there. The town's boom had already peaked when Doc first arrived. Growth had stalled. The silver mining operations were experiencing trouble, but there were still plenty of opportunities to be had. Along Harrison Avenue at upscale establishments like the Texas House, the Board of Trade, the Monarch Saloon, Hyman's Saloon, and more, Doc saw opportunity aplenty. Besides, he knew people there. He knew the superintendent of the Big Pittsburg mine, John N. Vimont, the acquaintance from Tombstone he had been going to meet when he was arrested in Denver.[10] There were also acquaintances from the gamblers' circuit. And horse races were scheduled to start the week after he arrived, which surely provided opportunities to make a little money. For all those reasons Leadville made perfect sense to John Henry.

However, Leadville, Colorado, was the last place Doc Holliday needed to be that summer of 1882. Its climate was deadly for a man suffering from consumption; even the promotional literature for the region said so. "Persons troubled with weak lungs or heart disease should give the new camp a wide berth," advised the *Tourist's Guide to Leadville and the Carbonate Fields*. "The rare atmosphere accelerates the action of both these organs and unless they are in perfect condition, serious results may follow."[11] He probably gave the subject little thought. He was in the best shape he had been in years. He had ridden the vendetta trail without complaint, and he was in good enough condition when he arrived in Colorado that not a single Denver paper mentioned that he had a lung condition during his incarceration. All of that would change in Leadville.

He would not have known that Robert Koch, a German doctor and a pioneer of research into infectious diseases, had identified the tubercle bacillus and had announced in a presentation to the Physiological Society of Berlin just weeks earlier, on March 24, 1882, that all forms of consumption were the product of the bacillus. Other work, particularly a study of cholera in Egypt, prevented him from pursuing his findings for a time, and, as a consequence, the importance of his discovery was not immediately realized or spread.[12] For victims of the disease like John Henry, the delay in the spread of knowledge oddly had benefits.

Some researchers, in both Europe and the United States, explored the implications of the new understanding, which transformed consumption into tuberculosis. The knowledge that tuberculosis was a contagious disease would create a "phthisio-phobia" in the late 1890s and early 1900s. For the time being, people like Doc Holliday were spared the discrimination that the next generation of victims would face, while missing some of the changes in understanding the disease and how best to treat it that might have given them greater hope.[13]

In the beginning, things went well for Doc. His reputation helped, although he did not make a point of it. He settled in with a lifestyle that was anything but flamboyant. He checked into a hotel and arranged to receive mail at the local Western Union office located at 106 East Second Street. He quickly found work as a faro dealer at Cyrus Allen's Monarch Saloon at 320 Harrison Street, and with a little luck playing poker at the Board of Trade and the Texas House, Doc eventually took better quarters at 210 West Third. At first, Cy Allen was pleased with the attention his new dealer attracted; Doc Holliday was good for business.[14]

During that time, John Henry became acquainted with some of the high rollers, such as John G. Morgan, who owned the Board of Trade, Elmon G. Hall, who ran Marble Hall, Ben Loeb, the owner of a variety theater, Mannie Hyman, the owner of Hyman's Saloon, Colonel Sam Houston, and more.[15] Doc made a favorable impression as a fair dealer and a model citizen. He stayed out of trouble and did well. His good behavior doubtless was influenced by his ongoing legal problems in Colorado and the possibility that the Territory of Arizona would make yet another attempt to bring him back to Tucson or Tombstone for trial. He simply could not afford to risk trouble that would wear out his welcome in Colorado. His good behavior pleased men like Cy Allen, who could boast the services of the famous Doc Holliday without having to worry about trouble.

However, trouble was lurking nearby. The one thing that might have given Holliday pause as he settled in was the discovery that old enemies were already well entrenched at Leadville. The most notable of them was John E. Tyler, the same John Tyler who had crossed John Henry in Tombstone. Tyler had moved to Leadville after his humiliating exit from Tombstone and had ridden the Leadville boom with relative success. The old Sloper had not changed his ways, however. He had bounced around for a while and was suffering from a streak of bad luck when Elmon G. Hall, a well-known saloonman formerly associated with the Texas House, hired him to run his gambling operation when he opened Marble Hall at 210 Harrison Avenue about the first of May 1882. Hall said later that he was looking "for some honest man to manipulate his cards and to handle his cash" when Tyler applied for a job. According to press accounts, Hall had known Tyler for twenty years and hired him. Hall even advanced Tyler money to pay off his debts at the time.

Hall soon became suspicious when his faro table, perhaps the most patronized operation in his place, consistently lost money. Eventually, one of Hall's friends confided to him that he believed Tyler was dishonest and stealing from him. On Sunday night, May 28, Tyler was in the lookout chair beside the faro table, and, when he took a break, Hall counted the money in the drawer—$50. When Tyler returned, Hall stood nearby, ostensibly in conversation but actually watching Tyler. He saw Tyler take a $10 bill from the cash drawer. At that point, Hall approached Tyler and asked him how much money was in the drawer. The suddenly uncomfortable Tyler uneasily answered $50. Hall then demanded that Tyler count the drawer. After stammering and stalling, Tyler could produce only $40, at which point Hall accused him of stealing and fired him on the spot. Hall publicly said that he had no idea how much money Tyler had stolen from him but expressed the opinion that "he has been stealing ever since he first went to work."[16]

Given Hall's prominence in the sporting community and the very public exposure of Tyler's larceny, that Tyler was not prosecuted or run out of town was surprising. However, Tyler soon found work in another house before Doc arrived a couple of weeks later and even had established something of a following among the gamblers. One of them was Thomas J. Duncan, who had been an associate of Tyler's in Tombstone. He arrived in Leadville sometime in 1881 and soon proved himself to be an unsavory character. He also managed to ingratiate himself with some of the high rollers on Harrison Avenue, which afforded him opportunities for improving his lot. In the beginning, Tyler and Duncan made no public display of their dislike of Holliday, and it seemed for a time that they would let the old troubles stay quiet if not forgotten.[17]

Doc also had friends and acquaintances in Leadville, perhaps one of more recent association than anyone in Leadville imagined. At the time, the press had generally reported that Wyatt Earp's posse scattered after arriving in Colorado, with only Dan G. Tipton lingering in Colorado, but Turkey Creek Jack Johnson was likely in Leadville during the summer and fall of 1882. Johnson had turned against his Cow-Boy friends originally in exchange for Earp's promise to help secure a pardon for his brother, Allen Blount, who was imprisoned at Yuma. Blount was pardoned, and Wyatt Earp would later testify that Johnson's name was actually John Blount, who was himself a fugitive in Arizona when he was known as Jack Johnson.

Allen Blount was in Leadville while Doc was there along with J. W. Ritchie. Ritchie was another alias used by Creek Johnson. In fact, in 1885 Wyatt Earp and a man named Ritchie were arrested in Hot Springs, Arkansas. Wyatt would also later say that Blount did in fact go by the name Ritchie. Furthermore, later on, Lee Smith would specifically identify one of the men with the Earps and Doc in Tombstone as J. W. Ritchie. In view of these circumstances, Doc may well have continued his acquaintance with Creek Johnson in Leadville.[18]

Of course, Leadville had more than its share of low lifes. One of them was a character named Harry C. Neil, a hard case described as "a cadaverous looking fellow, with a stringy lock of hair hanging over his forehead in a masher-like way. His face is covered with pots like a cranberry marsh and he looks like a regular dance-hall steerer." Neil bore a striking resemblance to Hyman G. Neill, the old "Hoodoo Brown," although not riding quite so high. They could have been the same person, although reports after Neill left Las Vegas claimed that he was arrested in Nebraska in April 1880 and later killed in Buena Vista, Colorado, in June of the same year. Other reports suggest that he lived in Kansas, Texas, and Colorado before dying in Torreon, Mexico, several years later. If by some chance he did beat the odds, as he had been in the habit of doing throughout his misspent life, he had fallen on hard times by the time he reached Leadville.[19]

Leadville's Neil ran with a "short stumpy fellow" by the name of Edward B. Dempsey, who looked "like a professional leisure man" and "carried the evidence of hard times on him."[20] Neil and Dempsey were sometimes seen in the company of another rounder called Curly Mack. His name was actually Harvey Rustin, a gambler with a mixed reputation.

On April 30, 1882, these three watched as a miner called "General" Ward partied at a joint called the Red Light. He made the mistake of flashing a roll of $1,700 in cash, and when he left the place, Neil, Dempsey, and Curly Mack followed and mugged him. Neil and Dempsey were arrested a short time later, and Curly Mack left town on the run.[21] He would be arrested later in Cheyenne, Wyoming, while working in a dance hall under the alias "Frank Miller." Reportedly, he was planning to move on to the Wood River country as soon as he had a stake, which would indicate that he had not carried off much of General Ward's poke.

The officer who arrested Curly Mack was Marshal T. J. "Jeff" Carr, Cheyenne's justifiably well-known peace officer. Carr notified Leadville authorities and discovered that the Lake County grand jury had returned a true bill against the unsavory trio. He then loaded Curly Mack on the train without further legal amenities and delivered him to Sheriff Pete Becker of Lake County at the Denver railroad station on June 2, 1882, just after Doc Holliday had been released. Curly Mack waived the legal requirements for proper requisition forms and agreed to go with Becker. The *Denver Tribune* reported that Curly Mack "denies all knowledge of the crime with which he is charged, and refuses to give any particulars concerning the affair."[22] Back in Leadville, the charges against Neil, Dempsey, and Curly Mack were eventually dropped, and Doc would have dealings with all three men after he arrived.

By contrast, Doc Holliday stayed clear of trouble. He had a chance to change some things in his life, and he apparently made a good faith effort to do so. Despite his Southern roots, his experiences in Arizona and Colorado had converted him to the Republican Party, and he was an avid student of politics.[23] In 1882, Doc became involved in the political process in a way that also gave him a chance to repay some of those who had helped him. Colorado's Republican Party was divided at the time as the result of a controversy over one of its U.S. Senate seats.

In 1878, Jerome B. Chaffee, one of Colorado's U.S. senators, announced that he would retire from politics for health reasons, and Nathaniel P. Hill declared that he was interested in the vacant seat. Later, Chaffee decided to continue in office. Hill got the appointment, but bad feelings were created within the party. When Governor Frederick W. Pitkin announced that he would not seek reelection to the governorship in 1882, Chaffee backed Norman H. Meldrum (hoping eventually through him to return to the senate), and Hill supported Henry R. Wolcott. At the Republican convention in September, however, Lake County Republicans pushed Ernest L. Campbell, a Leadville attorney, and Chaffee switched horses to support him when it was obvious he had the votes to win. Shortly thereafter, the Democrats nominated J. B. Grant by acclamation.[24]

Hill refused to support Campbell and ordered the editors of the *Denver Republican*, which he owned, not to print anything that could be construed to support the Republican nominee. The *Denver Tribune*, whose city editor was E. D. Cowen, one of Doc's champions in Denver, followed suit. Lake County Republicans supported Campbell, of course, and Doc might have supported him and joined one of the many Campbell clubs that sprang up to help elect Leadville's favorite son. However, the *Republican* and especially the *Tribune* had been the Denver papers that had embraced Doc's cause during the extradition proceedings. With Hill and the two Denver papers fostering an "independent" stance by opposing both the Republican and Democratic candidates for governor, the Lake County Independent Club was organized at Leadville.[25] One of the primary organizers was Dr. John Henry Holliday.

Considering his recent arrival in Colorado, his record of attachment to the Republican Party in recent years, and Campbell's being a Leadville mover and shaker, Doc's involvement with the Lake County Independent Club was almost certainly payback for the support of Hill's paper and Cowen's advocacy of his cause. Loyalty still mattered to him. On October 20, 1882, Doc Holliday presided over the meeting at Turner Hall that adopted a resolution, declaring, "Whereas there are numerous political clubs forming throughout this county, we as members of the Lake County Independent Club do pledge ourselves not to consolidate with the same."[26]

Along with Doc, 123 men signed the resolution including John Morgan, Ben Loeb, Ben Pentland, Frank Lomeister (who would become one of Doc's closest friends in Leadville), Allen Blount, J. W. Ritchie, Harry Neil, Edward Dempsey, and perhaps most peculiar of all, John Tyler. The resolution's impact was questionable, since it took no stance one way or the other. Campbell won the election, oddly taking every county in the state but Lake County. There, Grant beat Campbell by 115 votes, so perhaps Doc's venture into politics made a difference at least locally.[27]

Doc did not have time to celebrate much, because he had to leave Leadville for a court date in Pueblo. On November 22, the Pueblo paper reported that "'Doc' Holliday, who among others has not been to Arizona this fall, is in town attending court." Three days later, "On application of defendant by his attorney H. G. Hollins, Esq., It is ordered that this cause be continued to the next Term of the Court." The next day the *Chieftain* stated that "Doc Holliday, Charles Utt and John Nugent went to Denver last night."[28] He wasted little time getting back to Leadville, and he was on hand for a bit of excitement.

Early on the morning of December 6, 1882, shortly after the Texas House had closed, a lamp exploded, and the prestigious gambling hall burst into flames. The fire department fought the fire for more than two and a half hours before bringing the blaze under control. By 8:30 in the morning, "what was a few hours before the elegantly equipped Texas house, was a mass of charred and blackened ruins, with nothing but the smoking walls left of what was once the finest gambling hall in the west." The firefighters did manage to keep the fire from spreading, and except for water damage to neighboring businesses, Leadville had avoided a major disaster. The *Leadville Evening Chronicle* applauded the work of the fire department, but it also noted, "The firemen acknowledge with thanks the services rendered by Sandy McCusick, Doc Holliday, Thomas Flood, Thomas Ransom, and George Fonda."[29]

That moment seemed a grand testament to Doc's emergence as a good citizen, but three days before Christmas, he apparently was arrested for being drunk and carrying a concealed weapon. The demons from Doc's past were stirring, but he fought them for a time, and the local authorities tried to help, after a fashion.

On Christmas night two drunks got into a fight over remarks one made about the other's wife. Timothy Breen shot Patrick Mooney. Mooney would linger until March 1883, but he eventually died. Breen was exonerated of blame at that time. Two days after Christmas, Matt Wells, also known as Charles Perry, shot John Kerr, a faro dealer at St. Anne's Rest, in a quarrel over a debt. Wells would eventually go to prison at the Colorado State Penitentiary for the offense.[30]

As a result of these incidents, on December 29, both county and city officials announced that they would strictly enforce prohibitions against carrying concealed weapons. The announcement seemed to have a salutary effect, because in January the *Evening Chronicle* reported, "The sporting fraternity in the city is observing the law in reference to carrying concealed weapons very strictly. It is said that there are nearly a hundred revolvers deposited by this class of men in a certain place in the city for safe keeping."[31]

Doc took the ordinance seriously, although he may have been the gambler who made the *National Police Gazette* on March 31, 1883, in a story about "an unpleasant guest" who crashed a party of tourists at a Leadville hotel:

> A cowboy, who by some mysterious process (probably stage robbery) had acquired a boodle, has been touring four or five states of the west getting rid of his money. This tough tourist considered himself one of the party, and in spite of all protests made his way into the ballroom where the festivities were at their height. He displayed murderous weapons in ridiculous profusion and made a thrilling sensation. A little chap, a gambler well known in the town, a mild mannered little fellow with a cold, glittering steel grey eye that we read of often in romances but rarely see in life, took the gigantic ruffian down instanter, however, and in the most humiliating manner. Covering him with his pistol he commanded the ruffian to drop his revolvers, to open his jaws and let slip the bowie he had between his teeth and to unload of his weapons generally. Then he made him take off his hat and back out of the room, bowing and apologizing according to the dictated phrase as he went. Leadville is no place for cowboys on a lark as they are doubtless convinced by this time.

The description of the gambler fit Doc, and it certainly sounded like something he would have done. Sentiment, at least, argues that it was he.

The Pueblo case was still a matter of concern to Doc, and it was finally disposed of in April 1883. Seemingly by design, Doc did not appear. Instead, after being "three times solemnly called in open Court to appear and answer to the indictment presented against him for the crime of larceny," the court declared the bond posted by his sureties, William Brady (possibly from Leadville) and George W. Crummy (the same George Crummy who had pleaded Doc's case with Governor Pitkin), forfeited.[32] And that was the end of that, the deal closed exactly as planned. Everyone knew, anyway, that the charge was phony. The case did introduce a new word in Colorado legal circles— "Hollidaying"—which referred to using fake indictments to prevent the prosecution of an individual on other, more serious criminal charges.[33]

Doc kept a low profile through the spring, but he did leave Leadville for a while, and his name was soon highlighting press dispatches again. His old acquaintance from Dodge and Tombstone, Luke Short, had returned to Dodge City and eventually bought Chalkney Beeson's share of the Long Branch Saloon. His partner, W. H. Harris, also a man with a past in Tombstone, decided to run for mayor in 1883 against Larry Deger, the former Dodge City marshal, who had the backing of ex-Mayor A. B. Webster, who also owned the Alamo Saloon, the primary competition for the Long Branch. Running on a reform platform, Deger won, and, after taking office, the new city council passed new ordinances against vagrancy and prostitution.

The laws, which most saw as a form of taxation consistent with common practice in the cow towns for years, were instead strictly enforced—against the Long Branch and only the Long Branch. Three women were arrested there and none elsewhere. When Short realized this, he headed for the city jail to protest. En route he met L. C. Hartman, the city clerk and special policeman. Hartman, who was no gun player, overreacted to the chance encounter, pulled his pistol, and fired at Short. He missed, and when Short drew his own revolver, Hartman ran. Short's shot missed too, but Hartman stumbled and fell.

Short thought he had killed him and surrendered only after being assured that Hartman was okay and that he faced only a fine. When he gave himself up, however, Short was charged with assault and jailed. The following morning, he was released on $2,000 bond and then immediately rearrested along with L. A. Hyatt, Johnson Gallagher, W. H. Bennett, and Doc Neil, other gamblers and saloonmen. Harris tried to reach Short, but the arrested men were held incommunicado, then marched to the railroad station and told to choose a train east or west.[34]

Luke headed east to Kansas City and wired Bat Masterson in Denver to come at once. This was the beginning of an affair that came to be called the "Dodge City War." It would be fought largely in meetings, letters, and the press, although the rumor mill constantly and ominously promised a shooting war. George Glick, the governor of Kansas, was reluctant initially to take any action in the matter, but by May 12, when he realized that Short had been denied due process, he threatened to send the state militia into Dodge if Sheriff George Hinkle could not protect all citizens and guarantee them their rights. Glick suggested that Short return to Dodge, but Short insisted on an escort. Bat Masterson, who had been at Short's side throughout the fight so far, left to provide one, traveling to Colorado for a rendezvous with Wyatt Earp.[35]

The gathering place for Luke's "escort" was Silverton, Colorado. That spring, Wyatt Earp was operating the club rooms of Silverton's new and luxurious Arlington Saloon and Gambling Hall, owned by George Brower of Denver. Initially, Wyatt denied any involvement in the Dodge City troubles and wrote a letter to the *Denver Republican* stating that he had no intention of becoming involved. Both the *Silverton Democrat* and the *La Plata Miner* affirmed that Earp was "a peaceable and law-abiding citizen of Silverton, and has not been in Dodge City for the last four years." Things were about to change, however. Bat Masterson arrived in Silverton at midmonth, and Doc Holliday most likely arrived about the same time. Local tradition says that Doc checked into the Grand Hotel in May, and Bat Masterson was still receiving mail there as late as June 4, 1883, well after he had returned to Dodge. Obviously, their intent was to recruit Wyatt as a fighter on Luke's behalf.[36]

The press was soon full of stories about gunmen en route to Dodge. Rumors flew hot and heavy through the last two weeks in May. On May 15, the *Kansas City Journal* announced that Bat Masterson's presence in Kansas City meant that he was preparing for his visit to Dodge City: "Masterson precedes by twenty-four hours a few other pleasant gentlemen who are on their way to the tea party at Dodge. One of them is Wyatt Earp, the famous marshal of Dodge, another is Joe Lowe, otherwise known as 'Rowdy Joe,' and still another is 'Shotgun' Collins, but worse than all is another ex-citizen and officer of Dodge, the famous Doc Halliday [*sic*]."

The *Journal* went on to describe each of them, saying of Doc, "Among the desperate men of the West, he is looked upon with the respect born of awe, for he has killed in single combat no less than eight desperadoes. He was the chief character in the Earp war at Tombstone, where the celebrated brothers, aided by Halliday, broke up the terrible rustlers." The gathering of these worthies, the *Journal* observed, "means exactly that these men are going to Dodge City," noting:

> They all have good reason to go back. Masterson says he wants to see his old friends. Short wants to look after his business. Earp and Holliday, who are old deputy sheriffs of Dodge, also intend visiting

friends, so they say, and Collins is coming along to keep the others company. "Rowdy Joe" . . . goes about for pleasure. Altogether it is a very pleasant party. Their entrance into Dodge will mean that a desperate fight will take place.[37]

The *Kansas City Star* provided an even more detailed review, stating that Jonathan Calhoun of Caldwell had arrived and after conferring with Short and Masterson left for Topeka, adding another description of Masterson's "formidable delegation" that included an imposing description of Holliday:

> Next to Masterson Doc. Holliday has probably the most exciting history and is the hardest man in a fight. He also was a United States marshal at Tombstone during the troublesome times and has laid away many a cow boy under the daisies, or more properly speaking, cactus. Absolutely reckless of his life he has unaided cleaned out many a saloon of hard characters and on one occasion when a plot was formed to assassinate him, literally shot his way out of a dozen men. So much for the gentle "Doc," who is a quiet spoken man and formerly a dentist—hence his title.[38]

The following evening, the *Star* narrowed its focus to Masterson, Lowe, and Holliday in the feature "About Some Bad Men." The description of Doc was blood and thunder from first to last, but it is arguably the earliest account to say that Doc went west "because his physician told him he had incipient consumption and would die at home," although the author made the mistake of making "home" the state of Iowa. "He is the last man anybody would ever take for a 'killer,'" the *Star* observed, "slim, stoop shouldered, dressed in black, his sandy hair streaked with gray, his complexion sallow; he looks like a professional man who devoted himself strictly to business, and did too much desk work for his health."[39]

While newspaper readers were fed a steady diet of melodrama, maneuvering of a more serious nature continued. The list of gunfighters prepared to descend on Dodge grew apace. The *Dodge City Times* added a list of men with nothing but sobriquets: Black Jack Bill, Dynamite Sam, Dirty Sock Jack, Cold Chuck Johnny, and more. Governor Glick sent Thomas J. Moonlight, the attorney general, to investigate, and a veritable reunion of Dodge City luminaries took place at Caldwell as Frank McLain, Charles E. Bassett, Neal Brown, and others assembled there.

Finally, on May 31 Wyatt Earp arrived in Dodge on the morning train. According to his recollections, a group including Johnny Millsap, George "Shotgun" Collins, Texas Jack Vermillion, and "Crooked Mouth" Johnny Green came with him. According to Earp, when Mike Sutton, the district attorney, saw them, he said, "My God, Wyatt, who are these people you've got with you?"

Wyatt replied, "Oh, they're just some bushwhackers I've brought over from Colorado to straighten you people out."[40]

On June 2, an anonymous writer advised in a letter to the editor of the *Topeka Commonwealth*:

> Masterson, Wyatt Earp, and all the sports in the country, held a meeting at Silverton and decided to take Dodge City by storm. Short is at Caldwell but will meet the party at Cimarron, 18 miles west of Dodge, perhaps Sunday night or soon after. Horses will be taken at Cimarron and the whole party will rendezvous at Mr. Oliver's, two miles west of Dodge. Doc Holliday and Wyatt Earp are now secretly in Dodge City, watching matters. When the time for action comes a telegram will reach them worded as follows: "Your tools will be there at ———," giving the time agreed upon. The plan is to drive all of Short's enemies out of Dodge at the mouth of the revolvers.

The author insisted that he had the information "from undoubted authority," and this may have been the plan. The *Commonwealth* added, "As if to confirm the report, we learn that Earb [*sic*] and Short were registered at Kinsley on Sunday at the eating house. They probably left Dodge for further consultation with friends and are preparing to carry out the plan outlined above."[41] If there was such a plan, it was never implemented. Wyatt claimed that he laid out terms and refused to compromise until the Deger-Webster faction folded, making an invasion unnecessary. He then left Dodge on June 2 and met Short, Masterson, and William F. Petillion, the court clerk of Ford County who had been drawn into the affair by Governor Glick, at Kinsley, east of Dodge. On Sunday, May 3, he returned to Dodge with Short, still half expecting a fight. It did not happen, and Masterson arrived the next day. Bassett, Brown, McLain, and others also slipped quietly into Dodge. The *Globe* reported simply, "Luke Short returned to the city Sunday afternoon, and we believe he has come to stay."[42]

On the evening of June 4, Sheriff Hinkle telegraphed Governor Glick, telling him that he thought it impossible to prevent a fight, explaining, "An agreement was made allowing Luke Short to return to Dodge City on condition he would send his fighters out of town which he has failed to do. I think a fight immenent [*sic*]." The next day, in a remarkably understated note, the *Ford County Globe* reported, "Wyatt Earp, a former city marshal of Dodge City arrived in the city last Thursday. Wyatt is looking well and glad to get back to his old haunts, where he is well and favorably known." But the paper could not resist adding, in another column, "Wyatt Earp has returned to the city. Wonder if it has any political significance? Eh, Deacon?"[43]

Two days later, the *Kansas City Star* reported, "The much talked of band of noted killers who were to congregate here and accompany Luke Short, the exile, back to Dodge City, Kan., are in part at least, at that place now. Advices from there state that Luke Short, Bat Masterson, Charley Bassett, and Doc Holliday at present hold the fort and that trouble is liable to ensue at any moment."[44] The failure of the Short forces to leave led to a proclamation closing all gambling establishments in the city. The arrival of Attorney General Moonlight from Topeka finally settled things when he organized the Glick Guards, a quasi-military organization that included men from both sides of the controversy. By June 10, most of the fighters had left, and Luke Short himself, his point made, would take leave of Dodge not long afterward. The Dodge City War was over.[45]

Whether or not Doc Holliday was actually one of Wyatt Earp's fighters, the Short faction made excellent use of his reputation. He was given a high profile in the feature articles written about Short's allies, and he was subtly mentioned in several of the more understated news accounts. Neither Bat Masterson nor Wyatt Earp mentioned him in their later reminiscences about the affair, and none of his biographers have given him a role. Yet, he was certainly part of what transpired, even if he never left Colorado. He was mentioned more often than several of those known to have been involved, and the list of hard cases Wyatt named as getting off the train with him were never mentioned at all in the papers. At the very least, people were conscious of the possibility that he was one of the fighters, and it was a tribute to his reputation in 1883 that the very mention of him made a difference.

One additional source suggests that he may have been there. Alice Earp Wells, the daughter of Newton J. Earp, Wyatt's half-brother, recalled years later that Wyatt Earp and Doc Holliday visited their home while her family lived at Garden City, Kansas. She said that one afternoon two riders approached their home. She recognized her uncle, and spoke to him, but he barely acknowledged her and went into the house to speak with her father. The other man stayed outside with her.

Alice did not recognize the man with her Uncle Wyatt, but he smiled and asked her if he could sit with her. She said yes, and the two of them talked for a while about all kinds of things. She was charmed by him because of his interest in her. Eventually, he asked her if she would excuse him for a little while. She said yes and watched him ride away. A short time later, he returned and gave her a rag doll with his compliments and another smile. When her uncle's visit with her father was over, her uncle and the handsome stranger left, and her father told her, as they stood watching them ride away, that the man with Uncle Wyatt who had been so kind to her was "the notorious Doc Holliday."

Alice was infatuated with him because of his kindness to her and the interest he took in her, and years later she would proudly show visitors "the doll Doc Holliday gave me." She always remembered the visitor as Doc Holliday, "a kindly gentleman," in contrast to her uncle's cold demeanor. She kept Holliday's gift until she died. And her story was consistent with the behavior of Doc Holliday remembered by Billy Hattich, who had known him at Tombstone.[46]

Alice gave the date of this visit as 1884, when she was nine years old, but it is difficult to place either Wyatt or Doc in Kansas during 1884. For the record, Newton lived in Garden City from 1880 until 1896, when he moved to Casper, Wyoming, so the visit could have taken place at some other time. In June 1883, after the Dodge City War, the *Garden City Irrigator* reported that "Bat Masterson and Wyatt Earp alighted from the west bound train, Sunday, and had a confab with Marshal [Newton] Earp. They were on their way to the recently discovered silver mines at Silver City, N. M."[47] Perhaps Alice, being so young at the time, confused Masterson and Holliday. Given Bat's personality, that would have been possible, but she always insisted that her father had called him "the notorious Doc Holliday."

Whatever the truth about the Kansas adventure, Doc returned to Leadville by midsummer and passed it quietly enough. Leadville's attractions were compelling, as a correspondent for the *Boston Post* recorded:

Leadville by gaslight is a revelation to one unacquainted to the strange life of these western mining camps. Harrison avenue, the main thoroughfare is brilliantly illuminated from one end to the other, and from the hotel window I can look down upon throngs of people. The street is fairly lined with pedestrians, and handsome turnouts and fast horses make the boulevards lively. What this town must have been in '78 I cannot imagine, it is so full of life now. This mountain town, which seems so dull and prosaic by daylight is certainly a most charming and picturesque spot by gaslight.[48]

One observer was surprised at the gambling halls. "Enough to say," he wrote, "I saw money, the amount I could only conjecture—won and lost without a change of countenance, but in many instances high up in the thousands. Here the most punctilious regard was observed to the usual courtesies; the utmost order was maintained; here was nothing to indicate an unusual state of affairs."[49] Not everyone was so impressed. One English writer was astonished that "[g]ambling halls abound without the least attempt at concealment." He was also repulsed by the saloons, theaters, and "worst haunts still, where vice, and dissipation, and immorality were rampant."[50]

On the morning of September 10, E. D. Cowen, Doc's champion in Denver, who had recently taken a position as city editor of the *Leadville Herald*, "was most brutally beaten and kicked by Alderman C. C. Joy" at the Board of Trade. The altercation occurred when Cowen had claimed that he could name the next street commissioner. Joy bet him that he could not, and when Cowen wrote his choice on a piece of paper and placed it in an envelope, Joy, who wanted him to announce the name out loud, grew angry. The alderman, who had been drinking, struck the editor twice, knocking him to the floor, and then proceeded to beat and stomp "his face with his heavy boots in a horrible manner." The brutal beating caused quite a stir, and the press used the occasion to speak out against crime in general, using the Joy-Cowen episode as an example because Joy had been quickly released on bail while Cowen remained in critical condition.[51]

Doc must have smiled when he read the reaction to the incident in the *Chronicle*: "There is but one remedy. If the agents of the people will not execute the will of the people then it is time the people should interfere. And a frequent interference on the part of the people with the duties of the courts will produce a most salutary effect, not only upon the courts themselves, but also upon the criminals."[52] So the editors of the *Tombstone Epitaph* and the *Tucson Citizen* were not the only ones who felt that way.

The *Denver Tribune* took up the cause as well, announcing that Thomas J. Fitch, of all people, had been hired to assist in the prosecution of Joy and asking, "Is there no rope in Leadville? We can send some if it is necessary and have a committee to escort the rope." Nothing so dramatic ever happened. Joy was suspended from the city council, and when his case came up for trial, he was granted a change of venue to Breckenridge. He went through two trials, with both ending in hung juries. After that, the case was dropped and Joy was reinstated on the city council.[53] For a time, Cowen was out of Leadville, recovering, but he would return to be on hand for other episodes involving the good Doc Holliday.

Early in October, an incident occurred at Hyman's between the policeman William Steadman and George O'Connor, which led later to a fight in which Officer Steadman was severely beaten. Later in the month, Frank Gallagher killed James B. "Tex" Garvin in a gunfight at the boardinghouse where they both lived. Gallagher would later be released on the grounds of self-defense. However, Doc was not interested in such matters.[54]

That October, he received news from home that could not have been wholly unexpected but may well have affected him deeply. Martha Anne Holliday—his dear cousin Mattie—had written to him faithfully through the years, and she must have told him of her intentions to enter a religious order. However, intending to do something and actually doing it were two different things. Family tradition always said that Mattie was an "unreconstructed rebel" who blamed the Yankees for her father's premature death. As a result, she would not enter a Northern convent. She waited for an opening in the South, and on October 1, 1883, she entered the Religious Order of the Sisters of Mercy at Saint Vincent's Convent in Savannah, where she took the religious name Sister Mary Melanie.[55]

Sisters of Mercy—Doc must have pondered the thought and reflected on the Sisters of Charity he had seen on the streets of Leadville working to relieve the suffering of men and women there and maintaining a local hospital. The effect of her decision on John Henry can only be imagined, since the true nature of their relationship remains a mystery, and it may have been merely coincidental that her decision seemed to mark a significant shift in his fortunes and quality of life, but it did.

In November, a dispatch concerning "old-time Tombstoners" made the rounds of regional newspapers, noting among other things that "Doc Holliday is the chief engineer of three faro games in Leadville, and Johnny Tyler is holding his own in the same camp."[56] Other old-time Tombstoners must have chuckled at the thought of Holliday and Tyler coexisting in the same town, but they had so far kept their animosities at bay. That, too, was about to change.

At some point that fall or winter, Cy Allen discharged Doc at the Monarch. Exactly when and why was lost, but it was likely the combination of Doc's drinking and his worsening consumption that caused it. Without a doubt, Doc's social and economic woes deriving from his disease multiplied in Leadville; they were not the result of stigma arising from the disease, but of consumption's debilitating effects on his capacity to work. The stage-two symptoms of his disease were increasingly obvious: he had a persistent cough, an accelerated heart rate, and a deepening hoarseness resulting from the ulcers in his throat. At times, he could scarcely speak above a whisper, and in his weakening condition, he suffered recurring bouts with pneumonia. Still, the symptoms that were most obvious were likely more attributable to the treatment than to the disease itself. Doc's drinking, which was a standard treatment to relieve symptoms, had surely become alcoholism long before he reached Leadville, and, as the symptoms worsened there, he seems to have begun the use of laudanum as well. Nearly all consumptives used some form of opiate to quiet the cough, control diarrhea, and reduce stress. The druggist Jay Miller, at the corner of Harrison and Sixth Street, provided Doc with laudanum at no charge. In time, these addictions affected his ability to deal cards as well as his judgment and self-control.[57]

Still, Doc's dismissal from the Monarch may not have been about either his disease or his dissipation. Cy Allen had struck up a friendship with Tom Duncan, Tyler's old Sloper buddy from Tombstone, who was also pimping for Mollie Price, a madam who operated an upscale whorehouse on West Fifth Street. Clearly, he was not a savory character. In January 1884, Duncan got drunk while circulating saloons on Harrison. A friend of his called on Mollie and asked her to

Hyman's Saloon, where Doc
Holliday was employed for part
of his sojourn in Leadville,
Colorado, with inset of Mannie
Hyman, "the Leadville Sport,"
a prominent gambler and
saloonman in Leadville.

take him home. She found him at Shea & Hillary's Saloon at 423 Harrison. He ignored her efforts to get him to go home with her until she grabbed his hat and started to leave with it. Duncan followed her into the street, where he grabbed her by the hair, dragged her home, and beat her severely. She never pressed charges.[58]

Despite this incident, Duncan had managed to ingratiate himself with many of the sporting crowd. He had been one of the greeters who welcomed John L. Sullivan, the heavyweight boxing champion, when he visited Leadville in December 1883. The others were Mannie Hyman, John Morgan, and Sam Houston, all notable sporting men friendly to Doc.[59] Among those with whom Duncan had won favor were Cy Allen and A. E. Scott, the owners of the Monarch, so that it was probably not by chance that Doc was fired or that Johnny Tyler replaced Doc at the faro tables in the Monarch. Doc's enemies would later claim that he did not take the firing well. They claimed that he exchanged heated words with both Cy Allen and Johnny Tyler. And, based on what Doc himself said later, that could have happened.[60] This incident may have restarted the old controversy in earnest. Without a doubt, Doc believed that the firing was part of a plot of the Slopers against him.

Doc was not yet without resources. He was still welcome at other places on Harrison Avenue. He began to hang out at Mannie Hyman's saloon, two doors down from the Monarch, and he still frequented John Morgan's Board of Trade. He dealt for Hyman for a while, and doubtless would have recovered easily enough had his health not failed. The Leadville winter took a heavy toll. Not only was Doc drinking and combating worsening symptoms of consumption, but that winter his recurring battles with pneumonia increased. Hyman was not a sentimentalist. He expected his dealers to be at their tables, and when they could not be depended on to be there, he replaced them. When Doc did make it to the gambling halls, he was left to find work where he could, mostly "bucking the tiger" against the house or playing poker when he had cash enough for a game. Still, he struggled on. He lost coordination, dexterity, and powers of concentration. The vigor he had shown when he first arrived in Colorado from Arizona was gone. He was dropping weight as well, to the point that men described his condition as "delicate."

It was then, when Doc was fragile, broke, and down on his luck, that Johnny Tyler and his crowd began to prod Doc in every way they could, hoping to provoke an incident or to humiliate him publicly. As a Leadville correspondent of the *Tucson Citizen* would later put it, "The old imbroglio was rankling in their breasts here, and Tyler and his friends did everything they could to prejudice the public against Holliday."[61] Though sick, Doc was still game, but they knew they had him at a disadvantage. He did not want to do anything that might cause him trouble with the authorities, and the frail body and the tremor in his hands made a confrontation seem foolhardy. For the first time in his life, Doc asked for help. On several occasions, he complained to the police that a plot was afoot to kill him and requested them to help him. Johnny Tyler showed his true colors then. Despite everything, he was still unwilling to face Holliday directly and alone.

The trouble simmered through the spring and was public enough that the Slopers' bully tactics won John Henry friends and supporters. The local police were concerned enough that they frequently searched Doc for concealed weapons, almost to the point of harassment. On July 21, 1884, some of Tyler's bunch accosted Holliday in Hyman's Saloon, "and several of them called on him to 'pull his gun.' He said he had none, and as he passed out was called filthy names." The next day, the *Leadville Daily Democrat* reported what had happened:

The well-known Doc Holliday claims to have been the victim of a put-up job to murder him in Hyman's saloon yesterday morning, and the place has been on the verge of a shooting match ever since. At an early hour Holliday and John Tyler, another sporting man, got into an altercation in which the latter used very abusive language. Holliday said he didn't want to have trouble, and Tyler called on him to draw. Friends interfered and there was no blood shed. There were some bad threats made during the day, and trouble is anticipated. Tyler killed a man in Frisco and is regarded as "bad."

Doc Holliday states that the trouble arose over an old grudge in Arizona where Tyler tried to put up a job to kill him, but failed to make it work. Tyler's friends say he wants to fight a duel with Holliday.[62]

The following day, Doc spoke with a reporter for the *Democrat*, most likely E. D. Cowen, who had left the *Herald* and was now working for the *Democrat*. With "tears of rage coming from his eyes," Doc told his friend that they dared to do it because they knew he could not retaliate: "If I should kill some one here . . . no matter if I were acquitted the governor would be sure to turn me over to the Arizona authorities, and I would stand no show for life there at all. I am afraid to defend myself and these cowards kick me because they know I am down. I haven't a cent, have few friends and they will murder me yet before they are done."[63]

The reporter did not doubt that what he said was true. Nor did most other folks. On July 24, the *Carbonate Chronicle* added its opinion about the disturbance at Hyman's: "It looks very much as though a gang of would be bad men had put up a job to wipe Doc Holliday off the face of the earth. There is much to be said in favor of Holliday—he has never since his arrival here made any bad breaks or conducted himself in any other way than a quiet and peaceable manner. The other faction do not bear this sort of reputation."[64]

All of this made something that had happened earlier somewhat baffling—it seemed to be at least a serious lapse of judgment on Doc's part. Doc had pawned most of his belongings when Lady Luck abandoned him, and sometime in late June he borrowed five dollars from William J. Allen, a bartender at the Monarch Saloon.

Billy Allen was a former Leadville police officer who now worked as a special policeman and bartender at Cy Allen's place. Leadville's Billy Allen was not Tombstone's Billy Allen, the man who testified against Doc and the Earps in the Spicer hearing, as has usually been supposed. Tombstone's William A. Allen already was safely settled in Arizona when Leadville's William J. Allen became a policeman in Leadville in 1880. Leadville's Billy was from Freeport, Illinois. He was athletic and had enjoyed a successful career as a foot racer (then a popular sport with the sporting crowd) as a young man, successful enough that he eventually used an alias (Murphy) to be allowed to run in the important races. He apparently had killed a man in Illinois, although Leadville locals did not agree on whether he had been acquitted or had jumped bail in the case.[65]

Allen was a tough man who proved his mettle as a police officer. In June 1880, he stood off a mob of miners to protect a militia colonel during a labor dispute. In July 1880, he was shot in the groin while attempting to arrest Charles E. Bakewell, who had already killed two policemen. In September, he was involved in raids against several brothels that resulted in the arrest of some prominent local politicians. His role in that affair won him powerful enemies. Afterward, he patrolled the Second Ward, which included the infamous State Street and environs, clearly the most dangerous area of Leadville. There, he was shot in the leg while trying to arrest a man on Chestnut Street, and still later, while approaching a burglar in "Cat Alley," a bad place in a bad neighborhood, the burglar shot him in the chest and then stabbed him. He survived all these incidents, "owing to a splendid constitution."[66]

Following the local election in April 1881, he was discharged as a policeman. He worked for a time with the fire department as a fitness trainer but was never given the appointment he wanted as the foreman of a hose company, apparently because of the political enemies he had made. Instead, he was given a job as special policeman, first at the Grand Central Theater and then at the Monarch Saloon, where he also became a bartender. He was considered to be fearless, and he may have worked at the Monarch when Doc was a faro dealer there, although he most likely went to work there after Doc left. His only link to Tombstone was Johnny Tyler, who apparently fed him plenty of information about Doc's alleged bad character.[67]

Because of Allen's connection to the Monarch Saloon—and thus to Tyler and Duncan—why Doc accepted money from him has always been a mystery. However, since Doc may have worked with Allen at the Monarch before the changes, or simply because Doc knew him as

William J. "Billy" Allen, saloonman and former
police officer, who was shot by Doc Holliday at
Hyman's Saloon over a five-dollar debt. Allen
recovered and had a long career as fire chief, peace
officer, and saloonkeeper.

an independent sort of man, Doc probably did not consider him to be
a part of the Sloper clique. If he did already consider Allen one of the
Tyler crowd, which seems unlikely, then the transaction simply
demonstrated Doc's desperation. Given Allen's association with the
Monarch Saloon and the crowd that hung out there and in light of
what happened later, some believed it was part of a setup to either
humiliate Doc or kill him. More likely, Allen was a late convert to the
Tyler camp because his personal disagreement with Doc over the
money made him more responsive to Tyler's vicious prattle.

At any rate, Doc did borrow the money. He said later that he told
Allen he would repay him "in five or six days or a week." He explained
to Allen, "There is a young man owing me money, and when he pays
me I will pay you." Unfortunately, Doc's friend, who was at Sowbelly
Gulch, a camp outside Leadville, gambled away the money and could
not pay Doc, so when the time came for him to repay Allen, he did
not have the five dollars. He insisted to Allen that he intended to pay
as soon as he had the funds. Allen was not happy, but he could not do
anything about it.[68] When Doc continued to make excuses during the
weeks that followed, however, Allen began making very public demands that Doc pay up. Doc did go to Sam Houston, John Morgan's
manager at the Board of Trade, and asked him for a loan. Houston refused to give him the money.[69] At that point, Doc's pride took
over, and he refused to go through the humiliation of being turned
down again.

Allen was persistent and increasingly belligerent. The tension in the air prompted the *Democrat* to question a local police officer about the enforcement of the local ordinance concerning concealed weapons and asked him specifically what he would do if he saw someone carrying guns. "I wouldn't do anything as long as the man is sober and doesn't draw it," the officer replied. "[T]his country's like Texas, a man may go a long time without needing a revolver, but when he does want it, he wants it at once and damned bad. I don't know why he should not have the right to carry it."[70] His bluntness was far from comforting.

After the July incident at Hyman's—if not sooner—Doc believed that Allen was part of the Tyler crowd and that the debt had become a pretext to get him. On August 15, Doc went to the Monarch. Why he did so was never explained, but he clearly never avoided the place. Given his nature, he most likely wanted everyone to know that he was not intimidated by either Allen or Tyler and his cronies. When he was leaving, Allen came out from behind the bar and approached him. Holliday would later testify that he was wearing an apron and had his hand under the apron as if holding a gun. Doc stopped, and Allen told him, "Holliday, I'll give you til Tuesday to pay this money, and if you don't pay it, I'll lick you, you son of a bitch."

Doc replied simply, "My jewelry is in the soak and as soon as I get the money, I'll give it to you."[71]

Allen gave Doc until noon of Tuesday, August 19, to pay up "or else." Doc's physical condition, his obvious hard luck, and the relatively small amount of money involved made Allen's threat seem to Doc's friends to be calculated to provoke a fight rather than to collect a debt. The same day Allen sent for Pat Sweeney, a gambler friend of Doc's, and told him that he had heard that Sweeney had said that if Allen jumped on Doc, Sweeney would jump on him. Sweeney called it a "damned lie" and said Doc could take care of himself, but Allen told him that if Doc did not pay up by noon of the nineteenth, he "would knock him down and kick his damned brains out." Allen also made a point of calling Frank Lomeister, a bartender at Hyman's, Doc's roommate at the time, and arguably Doc's best friend in Leadville, aside that same day and repeating his threat to "start hunting for him" if Doc did not pay up by Tuesday.[72]

Over the next few days several men warned Doc to be on his guard against Allen because they had heard him threaten "to do" or otherwise injure Holliday. Ed Doude and Patrick "Blackie" Lorden both said they had heard such threats. James Ryan told Doc that Allen had said that if Doc did not pay up, he would take his gun away from him and pawn it to satisfy the debt. All these men would later swear that Allen had threatened Doc; why they did not help him with the debt to avoid the trouble was another matter never explained. Most likely they offered—or would have if he had asked—but Doc was too bullheaded to accept it.[73]

On Monday evening, August 18, Officer Charles Robinson approached Doc and told him "that someone had told me to search him for a gun and for him not to carry one, because he was a friend of mine and I didn't want to arrest him." It turned out later that the "someone" was Billy Allen. Nevertheless, Doc took this message to heart. Near six o'clock on the morning of August 19, he retired to his upstairs room at 405 Harrison Avenue in the Star Block, after a night's work, knowing that he did not have the funds to pay the debt.[74]

Doc later testified that he slept until three o'clock in the afternoon, but that never quite fit the extended pattern of testimony. More likely, unable to sleep, Holliday walked to Hyman's shortly after noon. Looking at the clock, he remarked to Mannie Hyman in an offhanded way, "The time's up." Hyman did not understand the import of the remark, and Doc went into the card room. Near three o'clock, Pat Sweeney came into the saloon and called Doc out of the gambling room. He told Doc that Allen was looking for him, and Doc remarked that he was going to have trouble. He then asked Sweeney to go to his room and get his pistol for him, which Sweeney refused to do. Reportedly, Doc then said, "I'll go get the gun," and the two of them left the saloon together. Doc went to his room, and Sweeney returned to Hyman's.

Later, Billy Allen came into Hyman's, walked into the gambling room, looked around, and left. At that point, Sweeney headed to Doc's room. In the meantime, Doc was growing restless and told Lomeister that he did not want to stay cooped up in his room all day and asked Lomeister to find Marshal H. S. Faucett or Captain Edward Bradbury for him because he wanted protection from Allen. Lomeister left to find one of the officers, and Doc decided to return to Hyman's. He met Sweeney in the stairwell. They returned to Doc's room, where Sweeney told him that he had seen Allen in Hyman's looking for someone and that he was armed. Doc asked Sweeney what to do, and

Sweeney said he did not know. Doc then said that he did not think it was right for one man to be able to carry a gun and not another. He then asked Sweeney to find Faucett or Bradbury. Together, they left Doc's room, and Sweeney left to find one of the officers.

En route to Hyman's, Doc ran into Marshal Faucett in front of Sands & Pelton's, and asked him if Allen was in fact a special policeman. Faucett told him that he was, but said he was authorized to carry a gun only in the saloon where he worked. Holliday declared his intention of defending himself, saying, "I'll get a shotgun and shoot him on sight." Faucett told Doc that he would locate Allen and end the matter. The marshal headed for the Monarch to find Allen. He missed him by minutes, but Cy Allen pleaded with the marshal to tell Billy to stay out of trouble when he did find him.[75]

In the meantime, Doc ran into E. D. Cowen. "I wish you would do me a favor," Doc reportedly said to him. "Bill Allen is after me. I want you to come around and see me wing him when the ball comes off. He isn't worth killing."[76] Cowen declined the invitation, but with that announcement of intent Doc proceeded to Hyman's—he later said to wait for Faucett, although he was clearly prepared for other alternatives. There, he explained the situation to Hyman and asked him to look out for an officer "as I would not carry a gun, for I had no money to pay a fine, and I did not want to be murdered."[77] Someone—not likely Doc himself, given his concerns—had taken Doc's pistol to Hyman's and placed it under the bar. While Doc waited, he stood beside the cigar case next to the bar, where he could watch the entrance. His revolver—a Colt revolver, identified variously as a .41 or .44 caliber—was just under the bar near his right arm.

In the meantime, Allen had been looking for Doc. Near five o'clock, he had his boots polished and then went to the Monarch to begin his shift, missing Marshal Faucett by only a few minutes. He was behind the bar when he saw Doc Holliday pass by on his way to Hyman's. He pulled off his apron, put on his coat, and started for the door. Cy asked him where he was going. Billy replied, "I am going to hunt this party."

"For God's sake don't go into Hyman's," Cy Allen responded, "as Holliday is in there."[78]

Moments after Billy Allen left, the marshal returned to the Monarch looking for him. Cy told him that Billy was on his way to Hyman's. Outside Hyman's, Blackie Lorden, an employee, told Captain Bradbury, who happened to be standing there, "If Allen puts his foot inside the door there will be trouble." As Allen approached, Bradbury stopped him and asked him what the problem was. Allen told him that Doc owed him five dollars and would not pay him. Bradbury warned him not to go into Hyman's because there was sure to be trouble, but Allen pushed by the officer, saying that he intended to speak to Doc.

As Allen stepped through the door with his hand in his pocket, Doc reached behind the counter, pulled out the revolver hidden there, leaned over the cigar case, and fired. Allen, who apparently had not seen Doc, turned at the report and tried to run as the bullet crashed into the door facing next to him. When he heard the shot, he wheeled around, stumbled, and fell, catching himself on his outstretched hands. As he scrambled to get up, Doc fired again. The second bullet tore into Allen's right arm halfway between the shoulder and the elbow. Henry Kellerman, who was mixing a drink behind the bar, jumped and grabbed Doc as he tried to squeeze off a third shot. Kellerman already had him subdued when Bradbury sprang through the door shouting, "Doc, I want your gun!"

Doc surrendered his pistol without resistance and said to Bradbury, "Alright, I want you to protect me," as he was led away.[79]

Billy Allen had collapsed into Blackie Lorden's arms, and Cy Allen, who had followed Billy from the Monarch, quickly took charge of him by helping him into a taxi and moving him away to receive medical treatment. The bullet had entered the back of the arm below the shoulder and passed through it, ripping open the artery and cutting the muscles. He was bleeding profusely, but the doctor was able to close the artery and save Allen's life.[80]

Immediately, the question was raised whether Allen was armed. He and other witnesses testified that he was not, but several swore that he had his hand in his pocket and at least two said they saw a gun. His quick exit after the shooting did not allow the police to determine whether he was carrying a pistol or not.[81] The *Democrat's* reporter pressed the issue in his interview with Doc:

"What has Allen got particularly against you?"

"He is the tool of the gang?"

"How do you account for no pistol being found on him?"

Doc seemed surprised at the question, but he brushed it aside quickly: "His friends spirited it away—that's all."[82]

When Allen was asked whether he had a weapon, he replied, "Nothing, not even a pen knife."

Allen also said that the affair was about the five-dollar debt. Doc insisted, on the contrary, "That was just a pretext. It is the old trouble, and Allen was picked out as the man to kill me."[83]

Some locals agreed, and many expected the trouble not to end with the Allen shooting. One man predicted "the biggest free fight Leadville ever saw in one of the gambling houses." "Mark my word," he said, "there is going to be a whole lot of trouble before this thing is over." He suggested that it did not matter whether the fight was over a "private grievance" or not, because Allen was a friend of the Tyler crowd, and they would use it as a pretext for going after Holliday. As for Doc, the informant said he would not cause any fight. "To do him justice, he isn't trying to get up a fight, but is sick, and knows he has a hundred times the worst of it and would be glad if they would let him alone."[84]

Others derided predictions of further violence as "bosh of the worst sort." One observer insisted that Allen would tell his friends to let the matter drop and even predicted that he would not press charges. He added that Allen was "a man of sense and isn't going to precipitate any general trouble when a word or two from him can avoid it." He then made an observation that was true beyond a doubt: "The proprietors of several sporting resorts have become considerable alarmed over the status of affairs and are not anxious to have a shooting match in their houses. The consequence is they are pouring as much oil as possible upon the troubled waters. The police are also putting a damper on hostilities by frequently searching all the parties, and do not propose to permit them to carry weapons."[85]

Captain Bradbury arrested Doc on a charge of "assault with intent to kill" and had him incarcerated in the city jail. In Judge W. W. Old's office on the afternoon of August 20, bail was set at $5,000, and John Morgan, the owner of the Board of Trade, and Colonel Sam Houston, who was now working at the reopened Texas House, signed his bond. On August 22, the *Daily Democrat* reported that "[t]here is some talk of further trouble among the Holliday and Tyler factions, but the police have their eye upon them and will see that they don't do any damage." The report added, "The police are making a quiet raid upon everybody who carries concealed weapons."[86]

Allen was reported "decidedly on the mend," although because of "the excessive internal hemorrhage of the wound" the doctors feared that gangrene might set in. It was an "ugly wound . . . likely to give him trouble in after life." He was confined to his home and expected to suffer a stiff arm for a longer period. "Allen takes the matter philo-sophically," one paper said, "and bears his sufferings like a game man." He would not be able to appear at the legal proceedings about to begin.[87]

The preliminary hearing was scheduled for Monday, August 25, and promised "to attract a good deal of attention." It was an accurate prediction. When court opened on Monday, "an enormous crowd was waiting." District Attorney William Kellogg and C. A. Franklin acted for the prosecution, while attorneys M. L. Rice and Charles L. Fish-back represented Holliday.[88]

The hearing elicited few surprises. Captain Bradbury testified that he advised Allen not to go into Hyman's. He said that he saw Doc through the window after Allen pushed by him and saw Doc fire: "Allen, so far as I could see, made no motion to shoot." However, he also said that he "could not see Allen's right hand, as his left side was toward me." Curiously, he also testified that at the time he did not know that Allen had threatened Holliday.[89] Dr. Frederick D'Avignon described Allen's wound and said he was out of danger. Henry Keller-man, the bartender who subdued Doc, said that Holliday had told him that Allen was going "to do him up" and that he would not be mur-dered. He testified that he turned at the first shot and saw Doc "reach over the counter and fire the second shot." On cross-examination, he told the judge that Holliday said that it was hard to go disarmed when Allen was armed. He also said that Holliday had asked Marshal Faucett to protect him. With that brief accounting, the prosecution rested.[90]

The defense presented a string of witnesses who testified primarily about Allen's threats. Pat Sweeney swore that Allen had told him he would "kick his damn brains out" if Holliday did not pay him and that Allen had a gun in his pocket the first time he came into Hyman's on the day of the shooting. On cross-examination, he said that he had told Holliday of Allen's threats. Kellerman was then recalled and sim-ply said that Allen was "a good deal Heavier than Holliday."[91] Frank Lomeister said that he roomed with Holliday and had told Doc that Allen had a gun and was looking for him. Lomeister reported that Doc had told him he didn't want to be "coped [sic] up" and asked him to find Marshal Faucett or Captain Bradbury and tell him he wanted protection. He said he went to look for those officers, but that Holliday found Faucett first.[92]

William Reynolds swore that Allen had his hands in his pockets when he came into the saloon earlier in the day, though he did not see a pistol. He did say that he had heard that Cy Allen had tried to head trouble off and that when he saw Bradbury, he assumed the trouble had been squelched.[93] Officer Robinson reviewed his conversation with Doc Holliday, and, over the objections of the prosecution, revealed that Billy Allen had warned him that Doc would be armed on the day of the shooting.[94] James Ryan, a gambler at Hyman's, testified concerning Allen's threats the previous week, and Blackie Lorden testified that Cy Allen had tried to prevent Billy Allen from going to Hyman's and that he (Lorden) had told Bradbury that "if Allen puts his foot inside the door there will be trouble." He also said Allen had his hand in his pocket, though he did not actually see a pistol.[95]

At that point, the defense called Mannie Hyman. The laconic Hyman protested that he had not been subpoenaed, but the judge informed him that it did not matter and that since he was in the courtroom he would testify. He protested further, but the judge persisted, so he took the stand. In testimony that enlightened observers more about Hyman's nature than about the case, Hyman said simply that Doc Holliday had worked for him in the past and used his saloon as his headquarters.[96]

Doc then took the stand. He reviewed the history of his trouble with Allen and tried to introduce the earlier troubles with the Tyler crowd, but the judge ruled that topic irrelevant, which may well have prevented the full truth about what happened from ever coming out. He then described his efforts to obtain protection from the police on the day of the shooting. He admitted to shooting Allen, then added, "I knew that I would be a child in his hands if he got hold of me; I weigh 122 pounds; I think Allen weighs 170 pounds. I have had the pneumonia three or four times; I don't think I was able to protect myself against him." Under cross-examination, he told the court, "I had been told he had a gun and was looking for me; when he came in his right hand was in his pocket; he was about three feet inside of the door when I shot; when I shot the first time, he turned and fell; I did not see where his hands were when I shot the second time; I supposed he was going to get there if he could, for I thought he had come there to kill me." He said that he saw the butt of a revolver and added, "Of course I couldn't let him murder me so I fired."[97]

The prosecution called Cy Allen as a rebuttal witness, and he testified flatly, "I took Billy Allen home. He had no pistol. His pistol was behind the bar in the saloon at the time of the shooting." He insisted that he told Faucett to tell Billy Allen not to cause any trouble and that in a later conversation Allen told him that he was not looking for trouble. "He said he would go in, but just to tell Doc. he didn't want any trouble." This was powerful, potentially damaging, and perhaps the most compelling testimony presented against Doc.[98]

With Allen's testimony fresh in the judge's mind, Prosecutor Franklin presented closing arguments for the prosecution. Doc's attorney, Fishback, then delivered on Doc's behalf "one of the finest speeches ever delivered by that eloquent gentleman," followed by Rice, who spoke for half an hour on the right of a man to defend his life. He pointed out that Holliday had stayed in his room to avoid trouble, that he had tried to find a police officer to protect him, and that Billy Allen was a dangerous man. He concluded by saying that a jury could not be found in Lake County that would convict Holliday on the evidence presented. District Attorney Kellogg spoke last, arguing that Doc's act was premeditated, that it was not self-defense, and that the prosecution had a strong case. Judge Old apparently thought that the district attorney was right, because he bound Holliday over for trial in the criminal court and raised his bail from $5,000 to $8,000.[99]

The judge's decision was not popular, but the *Daily Democrat* gave a perceptive analysis of the situation:

> After the decision of the court was made it received some criticism from those illy posted in the law. The judge, when approached by one of these prejudiced individuals, stated the fact, which should be evident to all, that he had nothing to do with anything but the law in that case, whatever his opinion might be as to Holliday's moral guile. The evidence was clear that he had shot Allen, and that it was not in self-defense, for Allen had made no break for him, and until he did so, Holliday was not legally justified in shooting, whatever previous provocation he may have had in the way of insult or even threats, so long as no move was made to execute the latter.
>
> The public sentiment, however, which has nothing to do with the law, is largely in favor of Holliday. His friends were making every effort, up to a late hour last night to secure bondsmen for him, the

trouble not being that there was any lack of those willing to guarantee his appearance when wanted, but the difficulty in finding moneyed men, on short notice, ready to come to the front. Holliday has been, without doubt, an abused individual. The manlier class of the community not only appreciate this, but have little criticism to make as to his action in connection with his trouble with Allen, for whatever the latter's intentions may have been, Holliday had reasons, whether or not they are good in law, for believing that past persecutions were to be concluded by a violent assault.[100]

When the judge increased Doc's bail to $8,000 and remanded him to jail, however, he created problems for Doc of a more serious nature than was immediately realized. On August 27, Doc still did not have bondsmen, and he was still in jail. This raised concern about Doc's health. One reporter observed, "Should Holliday be obliged to remain behind bars up to the day of his trial it would probably go very hard with him, as his constitution is badly broken and he has been really sick for a long time past."[101] The judge soon agreed to reduce the bail to the original figure of $5,000 in consideration of Doc's poor health. However, at that point, for reasons never explained, Sam Houston withdrew as a bondsman, so that the process was delayed further.

On September 2, the *Democrat* reported that "[f]rom the appearance of things, Doc Holliday's case will come up inside of fifteen days, before the criminal court, if he cannot give bond; his friends desire to [illegible] as soon as possible so as to keep him in jail the shortest time. The case will certainly excite a great deal [of] interest when it comes up." The next day the paper announced that "[s]trenuous efforts are still being made to secure Holliday's bond." As late as September 6, the belief was that "[i]t now seems to be a sure thing that Doc Holliday will stay in jail until the day of his trial."[102] By then, however, the bond situation had been worked out. Papers were filed on September 5, naming John Morgan, W. E. Reed, John H. Hillary, and L. H. Carland as sureties in the case.[103] On September 7, the public learned that "Doc Holliday is at liberty again. He was finally released on bond last evening, and was about the streets today, the cynosure of all eyes."[104]

The trial was set for the December term of court. On September 9, the *Democrat* reported, "Doc Holliday expresses the utmost confidence over the result of his case. He is busy looking up testimony."[105] The weeks passed quietly enough as Doc worked with his attorneys on his defense.

In the meantime, Billy Allen was on the road to recovery. He was again on the streets as early as September 1, prompting the observation that he is "one of the most active, agile, and powerful men in the city. To this he doubtless owes his swift convalescence." He told reporters, "That he did not desire to speak of the Holliday case, and had not yet determined what he would do." Many thought he would drop the case, "as he has thus far showed no desire to prosecute." He told the *Chronicle* he was still suffering a lot of pain, and added, "I have no control over the arm whatever, and not a particle of pulse can be felt in it. As far as use is concerned the limb is just as good as dead to me." A short time later, he left town for a while "to recover from the effects of Holliday's shot."[106]

That fall, a report circulated in Arizona that Doc had shot a policeman named Patrick A. Kelly, but it was a confused account of the Allen shooting, and Kelly was still on the force at Leadville unscathed.[107] In fact, he would soon replace Faucett as Leadville's marshal.

On October 26, Doc inadvertently caused a small stir when he appeared at the train station to observe the High Line's inaugural run as a section of the Union Pacific. He caused some consternation and considerable comment among passengers who were on an excursion train to Breckenridge, although the train departed on schedule and Doc was left behind still on his best behavior.[108]

As it turned out, according to the *Chronicle*, when the excursionists boarded the train at Breckenridge for the return trip, they encountered a "crowd of drunken bloods" and a "dangerous gambler" who created some excitement for the travelers. The "bloods" were rowdy and mischievous, but not particularly dangerous; the gambler, who "was drunk and gloried in it, seemed to wish to make himself conspicuous as a desperado." When a political discussion grew somewhat heated, he "chipped in," drew a gun, "variously described as from nine inches to three feet in length, cocked it, and laid it across his arm, ordering everybody to leave the car." Most of the passengers followed his orders at once, but a small boy "who thought he would stay to see it out, had the cocked pistol pressed against his body to accelerate his movements."[109] The unnamed gambler's behavior soon made the passengers forget about the "notorious" Doc Holliday.

After the shooting, Billy Allen had the good sense to dissociate himself from the Slopers, who were out to get Doc. He insisted throughout that he was not part of a conspiracy. In fact, after an initial attempt on the part of the Sloper crowd to stir up trouble against Doc's "element," Johnny Tyler and the rest quietly retreated from view. Allen decided to prosecute Doc, despite efforts of the friends of both men to quietly resolve the matter. It was fair to say that they "did not entertain the most brotherly feeling toward each other."[110]

On December 15, Judge George Goldthwaite convened the criminal court and scheduled Case No. 258, *The People v. John H. Holliday*, for trial on Tuesday, December 23, at ten o'clock in the morning, but on December 18, Doc's counsel requested a continuance. Doc, "clad in a huge camel's hair overcoat," sat near his attorney, showing evidence again of the effects of the high country winter on his health. "The motion was vigorously opposed by District Attorney Kellogg," the *Chronicle* reported, but "the court reserved his decision until Saturday morning. On Saturday, December 20, Judge Goldthwaite granted the motion and set the trial for the spring term in 1885.[111] Doc's roommate was lauded in the press the next day with the statement that "Frank Lomeister sticketh to his friends closer than a brother."[112] The attention of the public was soon absorbed in several ore-stealing cases, and Doc received a brief respite.

Doc's health even improved slightly, along with his luck. He was a guest at the first dance sponsored by the Miner's Union on the night of February 27, 1885. The crowd enjoyed an "elegant" supper, an excellent orchestra, and an evening of dancing. According to the *Chronicle*, "Everything went off harmoniously and all agreed that the ball was a signal success."[113] Also at the end of February, the partnership of A. E. Scott, Cy Allen, and Tom Duncan took over the management of the Opera House Club Rooms at 308 Harrison, which was part of the Tabor Opera House.[114] There were still little things that galled Doc, but he had little time to worry about them. "Every effort was made to compromise the matter before it reached the courts," a Denver paper would report, "but Allen stood firm for the prosecution."[115] Doc's trial was at hand.

The trial itself, which convened on March 21, 1885, was anticlimactic. J. W. Taylor and Scott Ashton had replaced Fishback and Rice as Doc's attorneys, and Kellogg was assisted by A. Danford and W. H. Dunfield for the prosecution. The lawyers haggled over motions for a while, and considerable time was spent before a jury could be empaneled.

Danford opened by declaring that the evidence would show that Holliday had made "frequent threats" to kill Allen, that Allen had not seen Holliday on the day of the shooting until the shooting occurred, and that Allen gave Holliday no cause to fire, entering the saloon "in a quiet and peaceful manner." He read the definition of the crime of assault with the intent to kill and stated that if the jury accepted his propositions, it would be justified in convicting Holliday.

The defense responded that if the evidence proved the prosecution's case, then, of course, the jury should convict, but, he said, the testimony would not sustain such a scenario. Instead, the evidence would show that "on account of a financial transaction," Allen had promised to kill Holliday and walked the streets "carrying a deadly weapon" with the intent of carrying out the threats. Holliday had talked with the authorities about the threats and asked for protection. Furthermore, he told the jury that Holliday had been repeatedly informed by friends that Allen was looking for him and would kill him. As a result, the defense argued, Holliday would be justified in "taking a gun and killing Allen."[116]

Billy Allen was the first witness called, and he gave his first detailed public statement of what happened since the shooting:

> [H]e said that on the 19th of August last he was at his room until about 4 o'clock P. M. when he came down town, and after getting some tickets to go to the theatre, went to the Monarch saloon, where he was tending bar; from the Monarch he went into Hyman's, and had no sooner got inside the saloon than some one began shooting at him; after the first shot he turned to run out the door, and saw Holliday leaning over the show case with a revolver pointed at him; before he got out the door he slipped and fell, and as he rose, with his hands on the floor, a second shot struck him in the right arm below the shoulder, the effect of the wound was to paralyze the arm, and to disable him for a long time; for two weeks he was confined to his bed, and two months elapsed before he could do any work.

Allen swore that "he had no particular object in going to Hyman's at the time and did not know Holliday was in there." Under cross-examination, the defense asked if he had not threatened to kill Holliday, which led to an argument over whether the question was proper, with the prosecution saying that the direct testimony did not lay a basis for this improper cross-examination. The court eventually allowed it, and Allen proceeded to deny systematically virtually all the testimony in the preliminary hearing witness by witness.[117] The tactic of denying the existence of a confrontational situation between him and Holliday basically backfired when the prosecution's own witnesses reasserted many of the points Allen had denied. Marshal Faucett testified that "Holliday seemed to think Allen was hunting for him with a gun. . . . [H]e said that he carried no gun; he had been frequently searched for one, but the boys had never found one upon him."[118]

The defense's case was largely a replay of the preliminary hearing with the addition of other witnesses. Edward Donnell even claimed that after the confrontation between Allen and Holliday earlier at the Monarch, Allen had told him that "he had taken a revolver away from Holliday and one of his friends and pawned it."[119] If this was true, it was virtually an admission that Allen had recovered his five dollars before the shooting. After a number of witnesses appeared, Doc took the stand. He gave his version of the shooting and justified his actions on the basis that he thought his life was in jeopardy. He also recounted some of "the stirring events of his life."[120] Officer Charles Robinson was then recalled to rebut Allen's denial that he had told Robinson to search Holliday for weapons, after which Allen was recalled to rebut Donnell, and court adjourned while the judge gave instructions to the jury.

Taking a somewhat unusual approach, Judge Goldthwaite presented instructions prepared by both the prosecution and the defense as part of his presentation. The key point of the prosecution was that "mere threats alone of personal violence will not Justify the person threatened with taking the life of the person making the threats." The defense emphasized that "it is not necessary in this case for the defendant to prove that William Allen, the prosecuting witness, actually had a deadly weapon at the time of the shooting. It is sufficient if the defendant had reason to believe that he had one: and if the Jury find from the evidence that the defendant so believed at the time he fired at the said Allen you must acquit him." The defense also reminded the jury that the law did not require "that Holliday should avoid Allen." The judge presented the arguments of both sides on points of law and added a few remarks that took no stance as to Doc's guilt or innocence.[121]

The judge then advised the attorneys that they would be limited to one hour for each side to present their arguments and then adjourned until seven o'clock in the evening. The lawyers proceeded with no surprises. When they were through, "The court room was then cleared for the purpose of allowing the jury to deliberate, and after a very short time the verdict of acquittal was rendered." Doc was once again a free man.[122]

The defense had been able to show that even some of the prosecution witnesses were sympathetic to Doc and had built a strong case that even if Allen was unarmed, his threats justified Holliday's shooting him. Doc was acquitted not because his counsel proved that Billy Allen was gunning for him with the intent to kill him, but because the jurors were convinced that Doc *believed* that Allen was on the prod with the intent of doing him bodily harm. Allen may well have been unarmed when he entered Hyman's Saloon that afternoon, but Doc did not know that, and given the web of rumors and reports that had kept Harrison Avenue abuzz for several days before the shooting, Allen's true intent—whatever it was—became irrelevant. John Henry was convinced that he had done everything he could do avoid trouble, but when Billy Allen stepped through that door, he was also convinced that he had to defend himself. And Leadville agreed, with the jury affirming the "no duty to retreat" doctrine, plainly and simply.[123] Moreover, Allen apparently never got his five dollars.

The Billy Allen case dispelled two of the most common interpretations of Doc Holliday's character and personality: that he wanted to die and that he was a mean-spirited, obnoxious drunk whom nobody liked. Of course, it is possible that his view of life changed as death approached, but his conduct throughout his Leadville years revealed a man clinging tenaciously to life. Moreover, he received an astonishing amount of public support in a case in which his opponent was a local man who was respected and liked in the community. There was none of the fatalism that later writers would attribute to him, none of the brash temptations of death with other men that legend makers would celebrate. Nor was there evidence at Leadville that he was a social pariah. In his last pitiable, if not pitiful, gunfight, he aroused more sympathy than disgust, more admiration for his fortitude than disdain for his weakness.

Doc Holliday was not run out of Leadville after the Billy Allen case as some of his biographers have alleged. Sentiment and family tradition do suggest that he may have left Leadville shortly after his acquittal, however. In mid-April, Doc's father traveled to New Orleans to attend a reunion of Mexican War veterans. W. A. "Zan" Griffith, a

William Alexander "Zan" Griffith, a Georgian who visited Doc in the West and escorted Doc's father to New Orleans in 1885 to attend a convention of Mexican War veterans and a reported reunion with Doc. He lived out his life in Valdosta, Georgia, where he told others of his friendship with Doc.

young resident of Valdosta who had visited Doc in the West, accompanied the aging Henry Holliday on the trip, and later recalled that Doc met them in New Orleans. Griffith said that he was present at the meeting of father and son and that they sat up most of the night talking. Major Holliday tried to persuade his son to return to Georgia. Doc would not agree, but they parted on good terms, according to Griffith, having laid to rest some of the issues between them.[124]

Earlier that month, from April 1 to 4, Robert Alexander Holliday, Doc's cousin "Hub," with whom he once had planned to go into practice, attended the Southern Dental Association meeting at New Orleans. He was the recording secretary for the association and the chairman of the publications committee. Some biographers have speculated that Doc visited him, but given the dates of Doc's trial and the association meeting in New Orleans, they could not have met unless Hub stayed in New Orleans until his uncle Henry, Doc's father, arrived. The World Exposition was in New Orleans at the time, and Doc could well have slipped into the city without much notice. Although no firm confirmation has been found that Doc met either his cousin or his father, Griffith's confirmation of family stories makes it likely that Doc did visit his father. The stories have a certain sentimental appeal in any case.[125]

If he did make the trip, Doc was back in Leadville by June, in time for an episode with a touch of irony in light of the Allen case. Doc's old acquaintance, Curly Mack, the ne'er-do-well gambler who had been in Leadville since his earlier brush with the law, owed him fifty dollars. He had apparently owed the debt to Doc for some time when Doc collected it in an unusual way, as the *Aspen Times* reported:

> Some nights ago, Curley [*sic*] was seated at a faro bank with a big stack of "reds" before him. Luck was with him and he made a winning of a hundred and fifty dollars. Holliday was standing behind him deeply interested in the game. Just as Curley was about to "cash in" his creditor stepped to one side so that Curley could see him, and drawing a six-shooter from the waistband of his pants he coolly remarked, "I'd like that fifty to-night Curley." When the player looked up and saw the muzzle of the gun and the cold, hard face of "Doc" with its determined expression he shoved the whole pile of chips over and said, "take them all." "Doc" counted out his fifty dollars and pushed the others back to the winner and walked out, and that settled it.[126]

In October 1885, street gossip revived talk of the old rivalry between Doc's friends and the Tyler-Allen group and predicted the possibility of gunplay. Pat Kelly, who had succeeded Faucett as marshal, kept both groups under close surveillance, and the talk never progressed to action.[127] Johnny Tyler, who remained strangely mute through the whole Holliday-Allen affair, despite his role in stirring things up in the first place, remained in Leadville. His luck appears to have waned too, because he soon dropped from view. He was still in Leadville in 1886, and a John Tyler was working as a porter at the Palace of Fashion as late as 1890. He was reported to have left Leadville for Japan at some point and vanished into obscurity.[128] Frank Lomeister prospered in Leadville. When Mannie Hyman reopened his saloon on April 3, 1886, after renovation "that imparts to the famous old resort a brand new appearance as well as a most airy and attractive one," Lomeister and Henry Kellerman were still operating the bar. Lomeister was still in Leadville at the turn of the twentieth century, when he was serving as town marshal.[129]

Billy Allen remained in Leadville after his encounter with Doc before moving to Garfield County, where he served as a scout during the Ute Indian troubles in 1887. Afterward, he apparently lived in Denver and Pueblo briefly, then moved to Chicago. In 1892, he moved again, this time to Salt Lake City, Utah, to be near his sisters. He even joined one of the land rushes in Oklahoma, but he would eventually settle in Cripple Creek, Colorado. There, in 1896, he became chief of the

Cripple Creek Fire Department. Shortly before his arrival, most of the town had been destroyed by fire. He took charge and quickly put together a fine working department. Later, he became embroiled in a controversy that spoke well of him. When the "old town" of Cripple Creek, where Allen was fire chief, and West Cripple Creek were combined under a single city government, Allen was appointed chief of the new combined fire department, but when the city council passed over his firemen in favor of the West Cripple Creek men, Allen resigned in protest. Later, when the manager of the insurance underwriters for the state of Colorado came to Cripple Creek for an inspection, he said that he "was very sorry, indeed, that any change was made in the Cripple Creek department. I do not wish to reflect on the incumbent, but insurance men always object to a change in any fire department when it is in efficient hands. I have known Billy Allen for a long time, and know him to be a good organizer, a strict disciplinarian and a strong, brave, determined man."[130]

Shortly thereafter, Allen was reinstated and allowed to hire his own men. Allen remained at Cripple Creek for a time after that, but in June 1898 he joined the Klondike gold rush. He later moved from Dawson to Nome, Alaska, and he was appointed fire marshal for Nome by the city council, over several other candidates, and praised for his energy and ability by the *Nome News* on October 9, 1899. A year later, he was appointed deputy U.S. marshal by U.S. Marshal Cornelius R. Vawter, in time to be part of the effort to clean up Nome. As a part of that job, he arrested Doc's old friend, Wyatt Earp, who was running the Dexter Saloon in Nome at the time. He stayed in Alaska for a while, and then moved to Seattle, Washington, where he was deputy sheriff of King County. In 1930, he entered the Old Soldiers' Home in Orting, Washington, where he died on March 21, 1941.[131]

Doc lingered in Leadville through the autumn of 1885, but he did not choose to chance another winter in Leadville and moved back to Denver before year's end. Doc's luck seemed to turn for the better in Denver. At least he did not have to battle pneumonia, and he was able to support himself. Apparently, he headquartered at the Chucovitch Saloon owned by Vaso Chucovitch, an associate of Ed Chase's who was considered to be the kingpin of Denver's underworld, although Doc reportedly "flited [*sic*] from the Arcade, the Argyle, the Missouri gambling place, and other resorts for gamblers and gambling."[132] For a time he enjoyed the opportunities and pleasures of the big city. He also had time to meet ghosts from the past.

One night, Doc met Milton E. Joyce, his old nemesis from Tombstone, on the street. Joyce had prospered after the Cow-Boy war. He had remained active in politics and had established the Magnolia Ranch in January 1883. He could not avoid controversy, however. He was embroiled in an election-day fight with David Neagle in November 1882. In January 1883, he and John O. Dunbar were accused of tampering with county funds as the result of an audit by George W. Parsons. He beat that rap and became leader of the Tombstone Rangers, a militia company formed to invade the San Carlos Reservation and stop Apache raids once and for all. The group caused more trouble than it solved and dealt Joyce's reputation another blow. As a result, he left the management of his ranch in the hands of one of his partners, Buckskin Frank Leslie, and moved to San Francisco, where he opened the Baldwin Billiard Parlor in the Baldwin Hotel with J. M. Vizina (an Earp partisan in the old days) and James W. Orndorff. Later, he and Orndorff opened the Café Royale, which was touted as "the finest saloon and billiard hall on the coast."[133]

In 1885, Joyce was on his way back to San Francisco after a business trip when he encountered Doc Holliday in Denver. At the time of Joyce's death in 1889, Orndorff provided Joyce's account of what happened:

> Joyce was one of the closest-mouthed men I ever knew, . . . and it was pretty hard to get him to talk about the game he had been in.
>
> Just before we went into business together at the Café Royal [sic], after we left the Baldwin, he went East. One night, soon after his return, as we were talking, I spoke about a man from Arizona who said he saw Joyce's fight with Doc Holladay [sic], and I asked if he had met Holladay since they left Arizona.
>
> "Only once," he said, "and then I made a blanked fool of myself."
>
> "I stopped over in Denver," he said, "on my way home. One evening, as I was coming out of a barber-shop, who should I see but Doc Holladay [sic]. He evidently had been waiting for me. As I reached the sidewalk he came along the edge of the crowd and brushed against me.
>
> "Restraining my first impulse, I ignored what I thought was a challenge, and kept on my way. When I got half way to my hotel a thought struck me that maybe he imagined I was afraid of him because I was in a strange city where he had all his friends and satellites

about him. Turning on my heel, I walked back and looked for him till [*sic*] I found him in the saloon where he hung out. I deliberately brushed against him, the same as he had against me.

"I looked at him and he looked at me, but neither of us spoke a word. Some old Arizona men who knew us both were in the place, but they didn't have any remarks just then. I walked around him three times, just to give him a chance if he wanted it, and to remove any idea he might have that I wanted to run away. He didn't look at all scared, but he wasn't looking for any more trouble.

"I have thought of it lots of time since then, and have thought how foolish I was to go back, but the impulse struck me to do it, and I couldn't help it."[134]

Joyce's version of the incident is the only one that survived, but his observation, "He didn't look at all scared, but he wasn't looking for any more trouble," was doubtless the truth of what happened.

A more poignant reunion occurred in a Denver hotel that summer or fall. In May 1885, "Wyatt Earp and wife [of] Texas" moved to Aspen, and, in partnership with H. C. Hughes, opened a saloon there called the Fashion.[135] While in Colorado, the Earps visited Denver from time to time, and on one of their visits they encountered Doc Holliday in the lobby of the Windsor Hotel. Wyatt and Josephine Earp had met H. A. W. and "Baby Doe" Tabor and learned that Thomas J. Fitch was also staying at the hotel. One day the Earps were sitting in the lobby talking with Fitch and his wife when, as Josephine recalled, "an exclamation from my husband caused me to look up." She remembered:

There coming toward us was Doc Holliday, a thinner, more delicate appearing Doc Holliday than I had seen in Tombstone.

I have never seen a man exhibit more pleasure at meeting a mere friend than did Doc. He had heard that Wyatt was in town, he said, and had immediately looked him up.

They sat down at a little distance from us and talked at some length, though Doc's almost continuous coughing made it difficult for him to talk.

Wyatt repeated their conversation to me later.

Doc told Wyatt how ill he had been, scarcely able to be out of bed much of the time.

"When I heard you were in Denver, Wyatt I wanted to see you once more," he said, "For I can't last much longer. You can see that."

Wyatt was touched. He remembered how Doc had once saved

his life. Wyatt was arresting one drunken cowboy, when another was about to shoot him from behind. Doc risked his own life to extricate Wyatt and for this he had always felt grateful. My husband has been criticized even by his friends, for being associated with a man who had such a reputation as Doc Holliday's. But who, with a shred of appreciation, could have done otherwise? Besides my husband always maintained that the greater part of the crimes that were attributed to Doc were but fictions created by the woman with whom he lived at times when she was seeking solace in liquor for the wounds to her pride inflicted during one of their violent disputes. . . .

Wyatt's sense of loyalty and gratitude was such that [if] the whole world had been all against Doc, he should have stood by him out of appreciation for saving his life.

"Isn't it strange," Wyatt remarked to him, "that if it were not for you, I wouldn't be alive today, yet you must go first."

Doc came over and chatted with us for a few minutes then he and Wyatt walked away, Doc on visibly unsteady legs.

My husband was deeply affected by this parting from the man who, like an ailing child, had clung to him as though to derive strength from him.

There were tears in Wyatt's eyes when at last they took leave of each other. Doc threw his arm across his shoulder.

"Good-bye old friend," he said. "It will be a long time before we meet again." He turned, and walked away as fast as his feeble legs would permit.

Only a short time after this we heard that he had died.[136]

Josephine, who described Doc as a "misanthropic Dentist, whose mysterious attraction to Wyatt was more than a liability to the peace officer's reputation than an asset" and who said that "Wyatt's loyalty to the irascible tubercular was one of gratitude not unmixed with pity," never mentioned her own obligation to Doc for his financial help to her when she was with Behan in Tombstone.[137] Her account seemed designed more than anything else to protect Wyatt's reputation from the taint of his association with Doc by rationalizing their friendship.

In February 1886, John Henry received a letter from Georgia announcing the birth of his cousin Hub Holliday's son. Hub's wife, Mary, later recalled that Doc wrote them back, congratulating them and expressing interest in Hub's efforts to establish a dental college. "Yet, it was not perfunctory," she recalled. "Rather, it was quite long. Specifically, I recall his disappointment in the failure of President Cleveland's administration to increase the government's purchasing of silver." Having spent so many years in the silver camps, Doc had taken a strong interest in the silver issue, which would be increasingly important in the 1880s.[138]

Clearly, Doc still had some life in him. He was in Denver through the spring of 1886, living at the Metropolitan Hotel at 1325 Sixteenth Street, when the *Denver Tribune-Republican* began a reform crusade to rid Denver of gambling houses and prostitution.[139] Initially, the results were predictable. Saloon owners, gamblers, and prostitutes were rounded up, arrested, fined, and turned loose to resume business as usual. In May, Doc left town to visit his old haunts in Pueblo and then traveled west to Silverton. He stayed there long enough to generate a feature article for the *New York Sun* that was soon being reprinted everywhere from Tombstone to Valdosta. Most of it was the contrived sensationalism that people had come to expect in stories about Doc Holliday, but he did claim in it "to have been a benefactor to the country." And the article concluded with a statement that reflects the themes that Doc had voiced since he left Arizona in his comments to the press: "The claim I make is that some few of us pioneers are entitled to credit for what we have done. We have been the fore-runners of government. As soon as law and order were established anywhere we never had any trouble. If it hadn't been for me and a few like me there never would have been any government in some of these towns. When I have done any shooting it has always been with this in view."

"The Doc's auditors listened attentively, nodded assent, and gradually slipped away," the reporter for the *Sun* informed its readers. "He has been arrested but once, and nobody here will undertake the job."[140]

Not in Silverton, perhaps, but Doc was on his way back to Denver.

Doc returned to his room at the Metropolitan, but he soon realized that the reform effort was serious. Denver was "growing up" and becoming respectable. Reform-minded city fathers took a much dimmer view of the gambling fraternity than had been the case in former times. The sporting element found itself under siege, and Doc felt the pressure along with the rest, perhaps more so because of his notoriety. Denver's police force was using the vagrancy laws to crack down on gamblers and confidence men. He had not been back in Denver long when, on the night of July 6, a serious fire destroyed the Academy of Music and several other buildings near the Metropolitan Hotel. The hotel itself and several other buildings were damaged by the fire and smoke.[141] The police took advantage of the fact that he was homeless, at least temporarily, to advise him to leave town or run the risk of being arrested as a vagrant, since a gambler was regarded as "a person with no visible means of support."

Doc left, but he returned three weeks later, "in company with a score of other confidence men, thieves, and sure-thing workers [a characterization of all professional gamblers by the reform minded]."[142] The influx of gamblers was probably due to horse races scheduled in July and August. On the evening of August 3, Doc was arrested standing on Sixteenth Street, as were J. S. Smythe, a night watchman, and Kenneth McCoy, a bartender. The trio was arrested for vagrancy by Officer Michael B. Norcott, although the *Tribune-Republican* added a curious twist to the story: "They were locked up in jail and opposite their names on the prison slate were marked with the words 'safe keeping.' When asked why such a charge was preferred the reporter was informed that if a charge of vagrancy was preferred the prisoners must necessarily be arraigned in the Police Court in the morning, where the sentence, in all probability would be a slight fine only."[143]

Actually, the cases were heard the next day, and the cases of Doc and McCoy were continued while Smythe's case was tried. Doc was the only one not regularly employed, so he was again asked to leave town.

The editorial staff of the newly combined *Tribune-Republican* conveniently forgot that both the *Tribune* and the *Republican* had championed Holliday's cause in 1882, in prose that both papers had strongly denied and corrected earlier:

> Doc. Holladay [*sic*] has the reputation of being a "killer." He gained his notoriety as an Arizona rustler in 1881–3. He was a member of the noted Earp Brothers gang, who are reported to have killed a dozen or more men in those bloody days of Arizona's history. Holladay is credited with doing his full share of the killing. The country finally became too "hot" for Holladay and he came to Colorado, where he was joined by Wyatt Earp, the most noted of the Earp Brothers. Within a few months after his arrival here, Holladay was arrested on Sixteenth street by an Arizona officer. The prisoner protested against being taken back to Arizona, saying that he would surely be lynched. After two weeks parleying the Governor refused to sign the extradition warrant, and Holladay was released. He then went to Leadville, and soon engaged in two shooting scrapes, which he got out of by leaving town. . . .

He then came to Denver, and since that time has been living here—that is, when the police did not drive him out of town. His only means of living was gambling in its worst form and confidence work.[144]

Doc was too tired to argue. The police escorted him to the train station, and he caught the train "home" to Leadville. He wintered there in 1886–1887, working again for Mannie Hyman, who seems to have found some sympathy in his makeup at last. But John Henry knew that his time was running out.[145]

In May 1887, he caught the Carson stage for Glenwood Springs in a last desperate attempt to prolong his life. Glenwood Springs was a small but prosperous camp in a quiet valley nestled among the mountains on the western slope. It drew its name from the sulphur springs that the Utes believed had curative powers, and Doc, who had "taken the cure" at springs in New Mexico and Arizona, thought it worthwhile to give these springs a try. He settled into the Hotel Glenwood, a modern facility with electricity and hot and cold running water, and tried his hand at the town's gambling halls.

Marshal J. W. Scott watched him carefully at first, but Doc had not come to cause trouble. He was quiet and would be remembered as a "well dressed, soft-spoken southern gentleman who was politely cordial to the ladies."[146] Doc soon gained employment as a faro dealer and bartender, and during the first four months of his stay in Glenwood Springs, despite his failing health, he managed to support himself. Judd Riley later claimed that Doc helped him guard a coal claim at a mine near Glenwood Springs at the rate of ten dollars a day for a time. Kate Elder would say that he served "as undersheriff of Garfield County under Sheriff Ware," although there was no evidence of this and the sheriff at the time was James Kendall.[147]

The summer passed quickly, and "by his quiet and gentlemanly demeanor during his short stay and the fortitude and patience he displayed . . . [Doc] made many friends."[148] The big excitement came in August when Sheriff Kendall raised a posse to help suppress a reported Ute uprising. Billy Allen, who was living in Garfield County at the time, served as a scout. The "war" was reported over by September 1. By the end of September, Glenwood Springs was dressing up the town in preparation for the arrival of the Denver & Rio Grande Railroad.

The springs Doc had hoped would relieve his symptoms seemed to exacerbate rather than ease his suffering. He knew enough about the difference between consumption and "galloping consumption" to recognize the meaning of the sores that began to appear on his body and other telltale signs that his time was short.

Doc must have realized that he had moved into the terminal stage of consumption. His body was emaciated, his face hollow, and his eyes sunken and staring. His body was wasting away. His shoulders slumped, and he found it increasingly difficult to walk because of the pain in his joints and the swelling in his legs. His pulse accelerated and slowed, accelerated and slowed. Breathing became increasingly difficult, and his cough became the distinctive "graveyard cough" that was hard to mistake. Then came the almost uncontrollable diarrhea, sweats, and coliclike pain. In the most graphic ways, Doc was being consumed by his disease. He may have suffered from the sensation of suffocation as his lungs filled and he struggled to free them from the accumulated matter in them, or he may have experienced profuse hemorrhaging with blood pouring from his nostrils and mouth. And yet, consumption defied timetables. Even in the terrible last stage, the symptoms might suddenly abate, cruelly giving hope in a hopeless situation. And through it all, the mind remained clear.

It was during this period that Doc struck up friendships with both Father Edward T. Downey, a Catholic priest, and Reverend W. S. Rudolph, a Presbyterian minister. It was not unlike Doc to hedge his bets even when it came to eternity, although he may well have surprised them both with his knowledge of theology. Through Mattie, he doubtless had learned much about Catholic beliefs; in fact, he may have known Father Downey at Leadville because his ministries included both places and everything in between.[149] And though his mother's Methodist faith was deeply embedded in his mind, he remembered his father's stern Presbyterian beliefs as well.

The arrival of the Denver & Rio Grande would also bring Dr. W. W. Crook, who had met Doc in Leadville, to Glenwood Springs as a physician and surgeon for the railroad. He later recalled that Doc "was a likeable fellow and not looking for trouble but one could get it from him at any time they wanted it."[150] Each day brought Doc closer to the end, and he lacked both the energy and the inclination for trouble. One old-timer recalled, "He walked the streets with a feeble tread and a downcast look. If he heard a shot, he raised his head with eager attention and glanced this way and that."[151] Another resident of Glenwood Springs would remember that "[t]he man was breaking to pieces."[152]

The Hotel Glenwood, shortly after its opening in October 1886. Doc
lived here for the last few months of his life; he died here on November 8,
1887.

Art Kendrick and George Weirick were bellboys at the Hotel Glenwood, and they would recall later that when they gave him a wakeup call each morning, he always gave them two dollars, one for a bottle of whiskey and the other for a tip. His generosity indicated that he was still making a living for himself.[153] In September, he was still tending bar at a local saloon when he fell victim to another bout with pneumonia that forced him to bed. He never recovered. On October 5, the Denver & Rio Grande finally reached Glenwood Springs, and the town's leaders celebrated with a parade, fireworks, and a banquet in the Hotel Glenwood that lasted late into the night; it was followed by a two-day celebration.[154]

Doc was unable to participate, but after that Dr. Crook was on hand to supervise his care. For thirty-three days after he was forced to bed, he was able to get up only twice. For the next two weeks after that, he was delirious and slipped in and out of a coma. For twenty-four hours before his death, he did not speak, and at ten o'clock on the morning of November 8, 1887, he died. Kendrick said later that he and other locals took turns tending to Doc during those last weeks.[155] Kate, whom Doc had not seen since she slipped out of Tombstone while Doc was in jail during the Spicer hearing in November 1881, would claim that Doc contacted her during his last illness. She wrote, "I went to him and we made up. I nursed him and attended him until he died."[156]

Such a reunion would have been fitting, perhaps, but so far, no contemporary evidence has been found to support it. Instead, the record indicates that Doc died among strangers, without any dramatic last words. The first published report of his death, which appeared in the *Aspen Daily Times*, November 9, 1887, was simple and direct: "Glenwood Springs, Colo., November 8.—Doc Holliday died here this morning at the Hotel Glenwood and was buried this afternoon and was followed to the cemetery by a large number of kindred spirits."

Father Downey was out of town attending to his duties as chaplain for the U.S. Army at Leadville, and the *Glenwood Springs Ute Chief* reported, "Rev. W. S. Rudolph delivered the funeral address, and the remains were consigned to their final resting place in Linwood cemetery, at 4 o'clock on the afternoon of November 8th, in the presence of many friends."[157] Expenses for the funeral were paid from a collection taken up among the gamblers, saloonmen, and other locals who had come to know Doc during those last months. The *Chief* also noted, "He only had one correspondent among his relatives—a cousin, a Sister of Charity [*sic*], in Atlanta, Georgia. She will be notified of his death, and will in turn advise any other relatives he may have living. Should there be an aged father or mother, they will be pleased to learn that kind and sympathetic hands were about their son in his last hours, and that his remains were accorded Christian burial."[158]

The *Denver Evening Times* responded to the news with the simple statement, "Doc Holliday died in Glenwood on the 8th with his boots off."[159] Those would not be the final words on the subject of Doc Holliday, however. The man may have died, but his legend was still very much alive.

THE ANATOMY OF A
WESTERN LEGEND

Doc Holliday is ten feet tall and weighs a ton.

—*Tucson Daily Star*, June 11, 1882

Lorenzo D. Walters, in his book *Tombstone's Yesterday*, preserved a tale about John Henry Holliday traveling to Deadwood, South Dakota, in the summer of 1882, after he left Denver. According to the yarn, Doc observed a bartender harassing a miner who came in for a drink simply because he would not order a second drink. When the harassment turned to threats, and the bartender drew a pistol to force the miner to buy another round, Doc intervened and shot the bartender in the wrist. The shot brought a crowd on the run, and when it turned on Doc, Doc stood with folded arms and dispersed the mob by simply saying, "Gentlemen, I am Doc Holliday of Tombstone."[1]

John Henry would probably have found that story amusing, especially since in it he was the champion of a person being abused, the wounded bartender apologized for his rude behavior, and the whole crowd had a round of drinks afterward just to celebrate a happy ending. That, after all, is the way that stories about bona fide legends ought to end. However, in the earliest stories of Doc Holliday the image was always more ambiguous, more confused, as if the legend makers could not quite make up their minds about who and what he was. Even when Doc was a hero, he was a dark hero, a man with demons who struggled as much against himself as with the forces arrayed against him. And yet, what is most remarkable is how quickly the image of Doc Holliday jelled into a surprisingly consistent image.

Sometimes, of course, the portrayal was simple—and sinister. The nationally circulated article from the *Cincinnati Enquirer* that came hard on the heels of his Denver adventure portrayed Doc as an evil man. Perry Mallon's claim that Doc's "record of shameless murders and robbery during this time throws the deeds of Jesse James, Billy the Kid or any other desperado entirely in the shade" was ludicrous on its face. Of course, this piece of nonsense was the setting for Mallon's moment of glory with Doc's arrest in Denver. The reporter who penned the piece said that he asked Mallon who Doc Holliday was: "'Well, that's hard to say,' said Mallen [*sic*] thoughtfully, 'unless perhaps, that he is the greatest scoundrel that ever went unhung.'" He said Doc was far worse than Jesse James, having a lesser reputation simply because he was so far removed from civilization. He claimed Doc had killed close to fifty men. With Doc's arrest, "there's no doubt that the future welfare and prosperity of Arizona is assured."[2]

But Mallon's attempt to influence the public view of John Henry Holliday failed as miserably as his effort to profit from Doc's arrest. The image of Doc Holliday as a profligate and conscienceless man killer simply did not hold. In a *New York Sun* interview in 1886, that image began to subtly turn:

> A crowd following a rather good looking man around, stopping when he stopped, listening as to an oracle when he had anything to say, and all time gaping at him in open-mouthed wonder, proclaimed the fact than an important personage was in town.
>
> "Who is that duck?" an old miner asked.
>
> "Sh-h-h!" replied a companion: "That's Doc Holiday [*sic*]. He's killed thirty men in his day, and there's no telling when he'll turn himself loose again."

The article presented stories not unlike those in Mallon's piece. One of many unnamed "early settlers" destined to talk about Doc proclaimed:

> I remember one time in Tombstone he killed two men in one night, and the next day he called on the editor of the paper and said that, as he was opposed to sensational literature, he hoped there would be no undue prominence given to the occurrences of the evening before.
>
> When the paper came out in the afternoon it had a three-line item saying that it was understood that two men had been found

dead on the streets, but the reporter had not learned there [*sic*] names. The same issue had a long editorial article on the advantages of Arizona as a health resort.

The "early settler" repeated some stuff straight out of the Mallon presentation and concluded, "He could be tried now in any one of a half dozen States or Territories, and hanged for murder, but there is no disposition to press him, as it is remembered that the country was pretty wild in those days."

Another "witness," in a tale that was lifted almost entirely from the earlier Mallon piece, told the reporter about his run-in with Holliday and his gang near Fort Yuma and how "we ran like cowards."

The *Sun* article did not leave the matter there, knee-deep in gore. It gave Doc a chance to respond, even though the feature writer took some obvious liberties with his comments. He had Doc admit to several killings, but then allowed him to justify what he had done. Doc told the crowd, "When any of you fellows have been hunted from one end of the country to the other, as I have been you'll understand what a bad man's reputation is built on. I've had credit for more killings than I ever dreamt of." He then detailed examples of false charges against him, adding, "If you take the trouble to examine a good many of the crimes that I am charged with, you will find that when I have been charged with murder I have always been a long way off—never near at hand. That looks odd, don't it? But it is just because I didn't do it."[3]

Doc finished by claiming for himself a positive role in the settlement of the Southwest. How much of the monologue was Doc's and how much the reporter's embellishments is hard to judge, but it gave a new kind of balance to Holliday's story that took it beyond pure murder and mayhem.[4] What emerged was the more complex figure that had been suggested, at least, in other writings from the Denver press during the extradition process in 1882. This view, while not always accurate in detail, had always stuck closer to the outlines of Doc's life, and, perhaps more important, it carried with it the tantalizing mystique of the "good bad man" that captured Victorian readers already infatuated with "the passing of the frontier."[5]

This image was furthered in Holliday's obituaries in 1887. The tone of some of those death notices was doubtless the result of the sentimentality characteristic of Victorian obituary writing. It was fashionable not to speak ill of the dead, and obituaries had a way of

Doc Holliday's last photograph. This photograph was taken in 1887 by August W. Dennis, who was in Glenwood Springs for only one year, and an attached note on the back of the photograph was dated not more than twenty years later than the photo itself. It states that the picture was given to Wyatt Earp by Dr. Crook of Glenwood Springs. It was later given to Hiram Sutterfield by Wyatt Earp.

being generous to the worst of scoundrels. Still, although often some-what confused on the facts of his life, they contributed insights and helped to build the image of Doc Holliday that would be remembered. The *Denver Republican* said that "[h]e had the reputation of being a bunco-man, desperado and bad man generally, yet he was a very mild mannered man; was genial and companionable and had many excellent qualities." After mentioning his "bloody encounters," the editorial writer then described him: "He has strong friends in some old-time detective officers and in certain representatives of the sporting element. He was a rather good looking man and his coolness and courage, his affable ways and fund of interesting experiences, won him many admirers. He was a strong friend, a cool and determined enemy and a man of quite strong character."[6]

"Of him it can be said that he represented law and order at all times and places," the *Glenwood Springs Ute Chief* declared in yet another obituary statement.[7] In Valdosta, Georgia, his hometown newspaper said simply, "Dr. John Holliday, than whom no man was better known in the far west for the last ten years is dead. He was raised in Valdosta and was the son of Maj. H. B. Holliday, who has been a prominent citizen and for a number of terms major of our town." It then reprinted the *Republican* obituary.[8] The *Denver Field and*

Farm noted his passing and added, "He always expected to die with his boots on, and his demise at Glenwood Springs must have been a considerable surprise to him."[9] These statements gave a shape to a far more interesting Doc Holliday story than the one-dimensional caricature that Perry Mallon had promoted.

As the century closed, even "blood and thunder" needed more than one killing after another to sell. At the very same moment that reformers were moving the sporting element from its semirespectable status in many communities of the West to the underworld, fascination with the frontier past and its characters was stronger than ever. Self-reliant men-at-arms were welcome as heroes, and they were all the more intriguing when they tested the limits of Victorian morality.[10] Doc Holliday fit this mode, and through the decades on both sides of the new century, Doc Holliday's image became surprisingly consistent regardless of whether he was viewed either as a positive or a negative figure.

"Thus departed one of those characters formerly quite common in the West, but now, like the Indian and the buffalo, becoming rare," observed the *Denver Republican* in an important feature article written a few weeks after his death. "The doctor was as mild mannered as Byron's 'Pirate' and perhaps he was not, after all, such a bad man."[11] This article, which included comments from "police officers and sporting men" who had actually known Doc, for all its sentimentality, might well be regarded as the first real effort to assess his life.

Here was presented a reasonably accurate chronology of his life. The details were not always correct, and these misstatements would add to the legendary image of the "good bad man," but the story did include details that would be of value to later writers trying to reconstruct his life. One was Doc's use of the alias "Tom Mackey" while in Denver in 1876. Another was the insight it provided into the extradition process in 1882. Two of the reporter's informants were the Denver detective Charles T. Linton, who had been the deputy sheriff assigned to the case when Doc was arrested in Denver in 1882, and John T. DeWeese, one of the attorneys who had represented him during the extradition process.

Linton regretted having helped Mallon arrest Doc. He deplored Mallon's "abuse" of Doc and believed "that the crazy-headed actions of the Arizona deputy [Mallon] precipitated the troubles that followed and which resulted in Holliday's never seeing Arizona again, but in making Colorado his personal residence." Mallon's imprudence stood in sharp contrast to Bob Paul's cool and determined manner. "Had he come here first instead of the imprudent Arizona deputy, Mr. Linton believes things might have ended differently," the *Republican* reported. The article also confirmed that Bob Paul had tried to convince Governor Frederick W. Pitkin that he could protect Doc if the requisition was granted, but that in the end, the influence of Doc's friends on the governor was simply too great.

DeWeese, who provided some of the details about the extradition proceedings, was also cited as the source of another memorable quote attributed to Doc: " 'The doctor,' says Colonel Deweese, 'had just as lief kill a man as not. All he looked out for usually was to have the law on his side. I said to him one day: "Doctor, don't your conscience ever trouble you?" "No," he replied, with that peculiar cough of his, "I coughed that up with my lungs long ago." ' "[12]

This article provided useful insights into Doc's life, not so much in detail as in terms of contemporary perceptions of who he was among those who knew him. At the same time, here the life and legend of Doc Holliday began to blend in ways that made separating the two even more difficult. Even the mistakes were more subtle. Misstatements were less exaggerated; they seemed possible, at least. Some of the reporter's informants were closemouthed, like the one who "put forward the usual sporting phrase," that "[h]e's come of good people back East and I won't say nothing agin him." Others attributed a certain style to him:

> "It can be set down as a fact," says a man who knows "Doc" Holliday well, that the doctor has killed at least sixteen men. He usually looked out to have the law on his side and then blazed away at them. The doctor was a peculiar one and was a trifle deceptive in his methods. He would seem to back out and hesitate and act as if afraid, then suddenly he would rush on his antagonist and before the latter knew what was coming he was perhaps laid out stiff with one of the doctor's bullets in his carcass.[13]

The *Denver Republican*'s treatise prompted other items, including a noteworthy account from the *Macon (Georgia) Telegraph* titled "A Gritty Georgian." Recalling that Doc began his career as a dentist on Whitehall Street in Atlanta, "where he was quite popular," the author said that his Atlanta friends remembered that "he was a small man of the blonde type, and weighed about 125 pounds. His manners were free and genial, and his company was much sought after on account of his social qualities." Once he went west, "Holliday was thrown on his own resources, and he soon learned that he would have to take care of himself, and not depend too much on any friends or associates that circumstances might make for him." Here followed a recounting of Doc's fights in Texas, Colorado, New Mexico, and Arizona, culminating in his appointment in Tombstone as a deputy town marshal, Wells, Fargo detective, and special guard "to go with express messengers whenever valuable packages were sent off in the express."[14]

Most of the article was devoted to the street fight and bore the mark of his old friend Lee Smith. The article briefly recounted Doc's troubles in Colorado, and then closed with a comment on the source of the information for the article who had "quite a number of letters from Holliday, written in recent years." The source, doubtless Smith, then added this commentary on Doc:

> He was a warm friend, and would fight as quick for one as he would for himself. He did not have a quarrelsome disposition, but managed to get into more difficulties than almost any man I ever saw. He seemed to be peculiarly unfortunate in this way and invariably when he killed a man or gave him the worst of the fight, it turned out that he was justifiable. When I lived in Colorado it was common talk that he had killed more men than any other one man in the West. I think he got credit for killing a good many more men than he really did kill.[15]

Wyatt Earp himself would further stabilize the legend of Doc Holliday in a series of articles for William Randolph Hearst's *San Francisco Examiner*. Wyatt was affiliated with the Hearst family at the time, and the article was almost certainly ghostwritten. Its florid, melodramatic style could hardly have been produced by Earp; it was most likely Hearst's ace feature writer, Robert Chambers, who put the series together. The newspaper that fathered yellow journalism could hardly be expected to do less than put one of its best on the job, particularly when it took the time to publish an editorial on the importance of the Earp articles.

The August 1896 article "How Wyatt Earp Routed a Gang of Arizona Outlaws" gave considerable space to Doc Holliday. It was the

first time in print that Kate Elder, Doc's companion, was referred to as
"Big Nose Kate." The article stated, "Nor shall a heroine be wanting
for Big Nose Kate was shaped for the part by nature and circum-
stances." There followed an accounting of a key component of the
Holliday legend, if not his life: the story of his knifing of Ed Bailey at
Fort Griffin and his subsequent rescue from the authorities by Kate.
This story led to arguably the most quoted description of Doc Holli-
day and what might be called the standard view of who he was:

> Such, then, was the beginning of my acquaintance with Doc Holli-
> day, the mad, merry scamp with heart of gold and nerves of steel;
> who, in the dark years that followed stood at my elbow in many a
> battle to the death. He was a dentist, but he preferred to be a gam-
> bler. He was a Virginian [sic], but he preferred to be a frontiersman
> and a vagabond. He was a philosopher, but he prefered to be a wag.
> He was long, lean, an ash-blond and the quickest man with a six-
> shooter I ever knew.[16]

Here, and in two other articles in the series for the *Examiner*,
Wyatt laid out his friendship with Doc while describing his own life.
In the process, he fixed the image of Doc as his "faithful sidekick" dur-
ing the Tombstone drama.

It was an appealing image. In December 1898, Doc was reported
en route to Cuba, in company with Bat Masterson and Wyatt Earp, on
the heels of the opening of a saloon in Havana by prizefighter Jim
Corbett. The *Kansas City Journal* decided to set the record straight in
an article that was widely reprinted across the country. After noting
that Doc had died "six years" earlier with "his boots off" in "Colorado Springs," the writer offered this portrait of Doc:

> A braver man, or a more loyal friend never drew a gun on an oppo-
> nent than "Doc" Halliday [sic]. He was a misfit in his environments.
> Although as gentle naturally as a child and with a heart as tender as a
> woman's, he became a "man killer" through necessity, and in a career
> on the frontier of less than ten years he was credited with having sent
> unprepared to their Maker no less than fifteen human souls.
>
> Men who were in Tombstone, Arizona in the palmy days of that
> great chloride camp well remember "Doc" Halliday. He was a thor-
> ough gambler, rather temperate in his habits and was always taste-
> fully dressed. Although young in years his hair was iron-gray and
> marks of care and sorrow heavily lined a face that had at one time
> been handsome. Of his past he rarely spoke, of the present he gave

no thought and the horizon of his future did not reach beyond the small cemetery on the mesa. He had the innate gallantry of the true southerner and would resent an insult to a woman, no matter how degraded, as quickly as he would face a bully with murder in his eye.

A great lover of fair play, he was generally the self-constituted referee of saloon fights which were frequent in the mining camp, and once a fight began it was never permitted to end until a decision was reached.[17]

There followed an admixture of fact and fantasy that did, at least, try to follow the general outlines of his life. The author offered the tale that Doc had practiced dentistry in San Antonio until one of his patients, "a beautiful and imprudent woman," caused talk about the nature of her relationship with Doc: "The inevitable happened. Her husband indulged in threats and hunted for Halliday. When the smoke cleared away the husband lay a corpse in the dusty street. Halliday was arrested, tried and acquitted. Later a friend of his victim took up the quarrel, sought satisfaction and was killed at the first shot. Again Halliday was subjected to a trial and acquitted."

That ended his dental career, and he became a gambler in the mining camps of the West, until at last he came to Tombstone and struck up a friendship with the "kings of the camp," the four Earp brothers. Doc became their ally, and "[a]lthough weak physically and the possessor of a hacking cough of a consumptive Halliday never shirked in the performance of his self-imposed duties. No trail was too difficult for him to follow, no act of bravery he would not smilingly perform. He laughed at death, while courting its embrace." The elements of the legend continued to fall into place.

The article confused Ike Clanton and Tom McLaury with each other, and its account of the street fight centered on Doc:

> The first shot was fired by "Doc" Halliday. His weapon was a cut-off double-barreled shotgun. The first charge entered Tom McLowry's [sic] breast; the second went wild, as Tom staggered around a corner only to fall dead in his tracks. Frank McLowry, as he reached for his Winchester, slung to the saddle of his now frantic horse, was shot in the abdomen, and Billy Clanton received a bullet in his left breast. Shot after shot rang out and in the midst of the smoke "Doc" Halliday, ankle deep in dust of the road, a six-shooter in each hand, could be seen alternately firing at Frank McLowry and Billy Clanton, the latter on the ground, dying as bravely as ever a hero died.

"Now it's my time," Frank McLowry was heard to cry out, "I'll get you now!"

"You'll be a dandy if you do," replied Halliday, with a smile, and taking deliberate aim he planted a bullet in his game adversary's forehead.

McLowry threw up his hands when the bullet struck him and fell over backwards. His finger convulsively pulled the trigger of the weapon he still held, and the last bullet of the terrible fight of October 25, 1881, grazed Wyatt Earp's hand, bringing blood.[18]

The author then gave an accounting of the vendetta, beginning with the shooting of Virgil Earp and continuing in some detail through the fight at "Burleigh springs" where "Curly Bill was killed by either Wyatt Earp or 'Doc' Halliday" before the Earp posse slipped out of Arizona. In another article also prompted by the report that Doc Holliday was en route to Havana, the author concluded, "A great many untruthful stories have been printed about him. But the truth is, 'Doc' Holliday was one of that brave band of men who drove to cover the desperadoes of the West, and helped to civilize that section. It took desperate men, in a certain sense, to administer the drastic medicine. Holliday helped to carve out a future for that country."[19]

This Holliday was hardly innocent, but he was compelling. The image in all these articles was tragic and sympathetic. Of course, during this period Doc was the subject of occasional articles that portrayed him as simply a cold-blooded killer, but the more complicated view of a man who was the victim of circumstances that led him to an errant lifestyle, yet who did the right things when faced with hard choices, was the view that gained acceptance. C. P. Thomas, a Montana old-timer who claimed to have known a number of the old-time gunfighters, underscored one quality in another article, published in 1906: "Doc Holliday was a native of Georgia, and take him all in all he was possessed of the most daredevil and reckless bravery of any of his associates. He feared not man or devil and acted with such insane disregard of danger that it was generally believed he really courted death."[20]

Curiously, it was one who had known him, had even been called "friend" by him, who restored a darker hue to Doc Holliday's legend. In 1907, Bat Masterson authored a series of articles about men he had known titled "Famous Gunfighters of the Western Frontier" for *Human*

Life Magazine, which was edited by Bat's friend Alfred Henry Lewis. One of the subjects was Doc Holliday. Masterson wrote:

> Holliday had a mean disposition and an ungovernable temper, and under the influence of liquor was a most dangerous man. . . . Physically, Doc Holliday was a weakling who could not have whipped a healthy fifteen-year-old boy in a go-as-you-please fist fight, and no one knew this better than himself, and the knowledge of this fact was perhaps why he was so ready to resort to a weapon of some kind whenever he got himself into difficulty. He was hot-headed and impetuous and very much given to both drinking and quarrelling, and among men who did not fear him, was very much disliked.[21]

Masterson noted that Doc was unable to keep himself out of trouble: "He would no sooner be out of one scrape before he was in another, and the strange part of it is he was more often in the right than in the wrong, which has rarely ever been the case with a man who is continually getting himself into trouble." He gave a detailed account of the "indiscriminate killing of some negroes in the little Georgia village [that] was what first caused him to leave his home," then described his peregrinations in the West. Of his time in Dodge, Masterson wrote, "During his year's stay at Dodge . . . he did not have a quarrel with anyone, and, although regarded as a sort of grouch, he was not disliked by those with whom he had become acquainted." Even though "he showed no disposition to quarrel or shoot while in Dodge," Masterson believed that his trouble "was pretty much of his own seeking."

Bat fixed the image of Doc Holliday as the friend of Wyatt Earp with this statement: "His whole heart and soul were wrapped up in Wyatt Earp and he was always ready to stake his life in defense of any cause in which Wyatt was interested. . . . Damon did no more for Pythias than Holliday did for Wyatt Earp." Masterson concluded, "I have always believed that much of Holliday's trouble was caused by drink and for that reason held him to blame in many instances. While I assisted him substantially on several occasions, it was not because I liked him any too well, but on account of my friendship for Wyatt Earp, who did." Bat's article did little to enhance Doc's image, but it affirmed as a staple part of the legend the perception of Doc Holliday as Wyatt Earp's boon companion.

Interestingly, the popular writer Alfred Henry Lewis presented a somewhat different view of the relationship between Masterson and Holliday. In one story, he pictured the two of them sitting at a table discussing the trouble Doc was in following his arrest in Denver:

"It's tough lines, Bat," said Mr. Holiday [*sic*], as he poured himself a drink. "I've never done anything worse than down a man—always a warrior, at that—and now to have to stand up a party, even when it ain't on the level, comes plenty hard."

"But it's the only way, Doc," returned Mr. Masterson. . . . "It's the only trail," reiterated Mr. Masterson. "The message says that they start today from Tucson with the requisition papers. They'll be in Denver day after tomorrow. The only way to beat them is to have you under arrest. Our governor won't give up a man to Arizona who's wanted here at home. Those people from Tucson will get turned down. Meanwhile, you'll be on bail, and we can continue the case as long as they stay hankering around. That Arizona outfit can never take you in Colorado. This scheme will make you safe for life."

"And that won't be long," returned Mr. Holiday, "at the rate my lungs are lasting."

"On the whole," objected Mr. Holiday, following a statement of thought, "why not go back to Arizona and be tried? It's four to one they couldn't convict; and I've gone against worse odds than that ever since I was born."

"Man!" expostulated Mr. Masterson, "it would never come to trial. You wouldn't get as far as Albuquerque. Some of the gang would board the train and shoot you in the car seat—kill you, as one might say, upon the meet! It isn't as though you were to have a square deal. They'd get you on the train; get you with your guns off, too, you must remember, for you'd be under arrest, d' you see. Doc, you wouldn't last as long as a drink of whiskey."

Mr. Masterson spoke with earnestness. His brow was wise and wide, and his cool eye the home of counsel. It was these traits of cautious intelligence that gave Mr. Masterson station among his fellows as much as did that ready accuracy which belonged with his gun. Mr. Holiday knowing these things, yielded.

"What is your plan then?" said he.[22]

Here was Doc as a man with character, loath to allow fake charges to be brought against him even to save his life. There followed a flashback to review Doc's life in Lewis's inimitable style through Tombstone and into Colorado, until, at last, Bat sat at Doc's bedside when he was dying:

> "You must have used up a ton of lead, Doc," observed Mr. Masterson one afternoon, while in a mood of fine philosophy; "and considering your few years in the West, it's bordering on the marvelous. You simply shot your way out of one battle into another. How did you come to do it?"
>
> "It used to worry me," gasped Mr. Holiday, "to think that I must die, and I mixed up with everything that came along so as to forget myself. It occupied me and took my mind off my troubles."[23]

The *Valdosta Times* later reprinted the Lewis article, noting that Doc was "an old Valdosta boy" and observing, "He was a dentist by profession and was a victim of consumption. He went to Colorado for his health at a time when that section was under the heel of desperadoes and outlaws. He was against the lawless element and set about to purify the atmosphere, facing all sorts of dangers and killing numerous men who defied the law. He later died of the dread disease which caused him to go west. The story of his career reads like romance."[24] So, the portrait of Doc Holliday as a tragic consumptive embittered by life's turns and yet driven by loyalty and a sense of honor to make right choices became the standard view.

It was not the only view, however. The departure of the Earps from Cochise County in 1882, and the subsequent withdrawal of most of the Earps' old allies when the Tombstone boom played out, left the Cow-Boy view of the Earp-Clanton troubles as the dominant one in the area. In it, the Earps were remembered as killers and stage robbers.

In this Cow-Boy view of the Earps as criminal masters of Cochise County that emerged largely from Ike Clanton's testimony and editorial outbursts during the vendetta, Doc Holliday was the most vulnerable exhibit. Doc was the murderer of Bud Philpott, the cause of the street fight, and the coldest-blooded killer in Tombstone. This Doc Holliday had no redeeming personality traits. He was ruthless, immoral, and uncontrollable. And Doc's character made the Earps bad men. Even some of the Earps' friends, notably Bob Paul, were cited as believing that Doc was "the fourth man" in the Benson stage robbery and the man who killed Bud Philpott.[25]

In 1896, in the aftermath of the Sharkey-Fitzsimmons fight during which Wyatt Earp, who refereed the bout, was accused of throwing the fight, the *San Francisco Daily Call* published an article by Charles H. Hopkins, who had been in Tombstone, that portayed the Earps as ruthless outlaws who were eventually driven from Cochise County. In the feature, Hopkins added yet another twist to the story of Doc Holliday:

> Doc Holliday, who has grown famous as the Wells-Fargo shotgun messenger, was a member of the Earp crowd. Everybody has read about how Holliday stopped stage-robbing in Arizona. Well, he did stop it to a certain extent—that is to say, nobody could rob a stage who was Holliday's enemy. The Earps stood in with Holliday and his crowd of Wells-Fargo messengers, and every time we would hear of a stage that carried a lot of money or bullion being held up Wyatt Earp would collect a posse of his gang and start out to run the robbers down. If they could manage to catch any of the "rustlers" of the opposition crowd they would hang them without ceremony, come back to the town and explain how they tracked the road agents down.[26]

Over the years, articles by Alfred Henry Lewis (before his association with Bat Masterson changed his mind), Charles Michelson, John Scanlon, and others brought this image to the public view. Will H. Robinson, in a history of Arizona published in 1919, said that Doc Holliday "hung out a dentist sign, had gambling for a vocation and manslaughter for an avocation." Still, for the most part the pro–Cow-Boy old-timers' view of the Earps as bad men was largely confined to Arizona until the publication of William MacLeod Raine's *Famous Sheriffs and Western Outlaws* and, more important, William M. Breakenridge's *Helldorado: Bringing the Law to the Mesquite*.[27]

These books gave voice to the Cow-Boy perspective on a broader scale, although neither took much time to characterize Doc Holliday. Both portrayed him as a bad man. Breakenridge called him "a two-gun man and noted as a killer," but his most notable contribution to the legend of Doc Holliday was tampering with a *Nugget* article concerning the escape of Luther King from jail after the Benson stage robbery to include the statement "He was an important witness against Holliday," which was not in the original. For the most part, the old-timers seemed content to describe Doc simply by reference to his misdeeds. He was cowardly, ruthless, dishonest at cards, and a backshooter. Wyatt

Earp was their true target, and Doc was useful only to the extent he could be used against Wyatt.[28]

The persistent "anti-Earp" view rankled Wyatt Earp and eventually convinced him that he had to set the record straight. But Earp was also difficult. He wanted the story told, but on his terms, and he had Sadie around to watch over his reputation as well. Some time around 1920 Forestine Cooper Hooker wrote "Arizona Vendetta," which may have been an early effort to tell Wyatt's story the way that he wanted it told. It almost certainly had input from Earp, but if it was a collaboration, Hooker was one of the first to encounter just how difficult Wyatt was to please. Despite her connection to the family of Henry C. Hooker, the Arizona rancher who had supported the Earps, with whom Earp had remained friendly, he would not permit it to be published. It was an interesting effort, nonetheless, although her discussion of Doc was limited to his actions in support of Wyatt.[29]

At some point thereafter, Wyatt began to tell his story to a young friend, John H. Flood Jr., in hopes that, at last, he could tell the story his way. It was an exercise in naivete on both their parts. Despite revisions and the assistance of William S. Hart, the result was unpublishable. Wyatt did include Doc in his story, devoting a chapter to Doc saving his life, which concluded with a revealing, if out of place, sentence: "And poor Bat Masterson, and the world, wonder long, long years at the loyalty of Wyatt Earp for the stranger who proved his friend."[30] Thereafter, Doc was on hand as Wyatt's friend, although he handled some of the more controversial topics related to Doc gingerly or not at all. The Flood effort would have noteworthy consequences, however.

Perhaps the most revealing commentary on Doc's role in Wyatt's life, especially at Tombstone, came in a 1925 court case over the estate of Lotta Crabtree, the famous nineteenth-century actress who had lived in Tombstone for a time.[31] During the course of Wyatt's testimony, the attorneys asked him specifically about Doc:

Q: With you was allied Doc Holliday?

A: Yes.

Q: He was somewhat of a notorious character in those days?

A: Well, no. I couldn't say that he was notorious outside of this other faction trying to make him notorious. Of course he killed a man or two before he went there.

Q: Didn't he have the reputation of being a holder-up of stages?

A: I never heard of it until I left.

Q: With the Behans were allied the Clandons [*sic*]?

A: Yes. And the Behan side whenever they got a chance to hurt me over Holliday's shoulders they would do it. They would make a lot of talk about Doc Holliday.

Q: Because he was allied with you?

A: He never had no trouble in Tombstone outside of being in this street fight with me. Then on one occasion [*sic*] he got into some trouble with part of the combination that was against me, Joyce, and his partner, and he shot Joyce in the hand and the other fellow in the foot and of course that made them pretty sore against Holliday. But they knew that I was Holliday's friend and they tried to injure me every way they could.

Later in his testimony, Earp drove home what he regarded as the central point of his relationship with Doc at Tombstone in comments about his decision to run for sheriff:

[A]nd if I do say it myself I was a pretty strong man for the position. He [Behan] knew that he had to do me some way and he done everything in the world that he could against me. He stood in with this tough element, the cow boys and stage robbers and others, because they were pretty strong and he wanted their vote. Whenever they would get a chance to shoot anything at me over Holliday's shoulders they would do it. As they made Holliday a bad man. An awful bad man, which was wrong. He was a man that would fight if he had to.[32]

Pretty clearly, then, Wyatt saw Doc as a liability to his reputation and defending Doc an essential part of defending himself. During that same time period, Walter Noble Burns, a well-known Chicago journalist, published *The Saga of Billy the Kid*. Afterward, Burns turned his attention to Tombstone. In July 1926, while he was in Los Angeles, he approached Wyatt Earp about writing his biography and spoke with Flood about taking over his manuscript. Wyatt declined because he still hoped to salvage Flood's effort.

Earp did, however, offer to help Burns with a book about Doc. Later, Burns wrote Earp requesting information about Doc's involvement in the Benson stage robbery and about other associates of Wyatt's. Earp repeated his willingness to help with a book about Doc, although curiously adding, "I would much rather not have my name mentioned to [*sic*] freely. I am getting tired of it all, as there have been so many lies written about me in so many magazines in the last few years that it makes a man feel like fighting. I know you mean to do the right thing by me, but I would ask of you please to say as little as possible about me."[33]

In the letter, he focused his comments on Doc almost exclusively on the Benson stage robbery, concluding, "Doc was not in the Benson stage hold up. And he never did such a thing as hold ups in his life. He was his own worst enemy. Comes from a very respectful family in the South, gratuated [*sic*] as a dentist." Ironically, within days, Flood wrote Burns indicating that he was recommending that Earp reconsider collaborating with him. By then, Burns was nearing completion of *Tombstone: An Iliad of the Southwest*. Once he found out about Burns's book, Earp felt betrayed that Burns had written a book that focused on his life rather than Doc's. He tried to prevent its publication even though Burns provided a stunning portrait of Wyatt Earp as "the Lion of Tombstone."[34]

Burns's view of Doc Holliday was also compelling. "He was a rather tall, extremely slender, ash-blond, gray eyed fellow, immaculate in attire, fastidious in his habits, temperamental, hot tempered and cold blooded, querulous and sometimes a little quarrelsome, a wit as well as a desperado," Burns wrote. He went on:

> He was a consumptive, and the malady had left his face emaciated and very white and given it a look of refinement that might have passed for spirituality. One might have been tempted to suspect that this quiet, pale man with the fine gray eyes was a poet or a scholar who pored over erudite volumes under midnight lamps. But except for a few elegies done with finished elegance with his six-shooter, the doctor never displayed any poetic or literary leanings.
>
> He was, after a kind, a cynical philosopher, and his passing observations were spiced with a dry, acrid humour. Life seemed a bitter joke to him. He was reconciled to tuberculosis, he said, because it had left him so thin that it took might good shooting to hit him. He was still ready to bet, however, that in the home-stretch drive, a bullet would nose out consumption at the wire.

Burns claimed that Doc was an "excellent shot" with only Buckskin Frank Leslie his equal in Tombstone. "No scruples of any kind handicapped the doctor in his busy life," Burns said. "Though square with his friends, who would have trusted him with their last dollar, his honesty had various shades and nuances. If honest was convenient, he was honest; otherwise, he used a cold deck." He added, "His courage was his one outstanding virtue. He was afraid of nothing. Despite his delicate appearance and his physical weakness, there was something in the calm cold look of him which warned of danger." Here was the apotheosis of the Holliday legend appended to a review of Doc's life before Tombstone and signed with Wyatt's signature: "He was one of the finest, cleanest men in the world, though, of course, he was a little handy with his gun and had to kill a few fellows."[35]

Burns also appears to have been the first to say that Doc's final words were "This is funny." He added that "with his sense of humour strong to the last, the doctor doubtless considered it a choice joke that, after all his desperate adventures and narrow escapes, he should be dying in bed." It *was* funny for the reason Burns stated, and more, but the quote, for all that, has never been documented and seems highly improbable as Doc Holliday's last words, however appropriate they might be.

Not even Stuart N. Lake's *Wyatt Earp: Frontier Marshal*, published two years after Wyatt Earp died in 1929—and the work that finally had Earp's support in the writing of it—added significantly to the "good bad man" of Tombstone. In fact, if anything, Lake tried to temper Burns's view of Holliday. Lake said flatly that "Doc Holliday was a hot-headed, ill-tempered, trouble-hunting, and, withal, cold-blooded desperado."[36] Doubtless, Lake's view of Holliday was influenced by two old allies of Wyatt's, Fred Dodge, who plainly detested Doc, and John P. Clum, who said in 1929 after reading Wyatt's article from the *San Francisco Examiner*, August 2, 1896, for the first time, "I never approved of Holliday and this story makes it more difficult to defend Wyatt." He added flatly, "I will not appear as a supporter of Holliday."[37]

Lake had Bat Masterson attribute to Doc three redeeming traits: courage, loyalty to friends, and affection for Wyatt Earp. Bat allegedly said about Doc's feelings for Wyatt:

> The depth of this sentiment was shown not only by Doc's demonstrated willingness to stake his life for Wyatt without second thought; it was even more clearly established by the fact that, despite his almost uncontrollable temper and his maniacal love of a fight, Doc Holliday could avoid trouble when there was a possibility that some encounter might prove embarrassing to Wyatt. On more than one occasion Doc actually backed down before men whom he easily could

have killed, simply because gunplay at the time would have reacted unfavorably against Wyatt. To appreciate that fully, you had to know Holliday.[38]

Lake's Wyatt repeated the comparison of Doc to Buckskin Frank Leslie, then added, "But Leslie lacked Doc's fatalistic courage, a courage induced, I suppose, by the nature of Holliday's disease and the realization that he hadn't long to live, anyway. That fatalism, coupled with his marvelous speed and accuracy, gave Holliday the edge over any out-and-out killer I ever knew." Lake, in words attributed to Earp, claimed that Doc drank two to three quarts of liquor a day, yet never staggered or appeared to be intoxicated. "Under ordinary circumstances he might be irritable to the point of shakiness," Earp supposedly said, "only in a game or when a fight impended was there anything steely about his nerves."

Wyatt Earp: Frontier Marshal received excellent reviews as an extraordinary biography of an extraordinary man, but in southeastern Arizona it prompted a different response. Over the next several years, several Arizona old-timers, including Judge James C. Hancock, Anton Mazzanovich, Joseph F. Chisholm, Melvin Jones, and others raised their voices in protest against the view presented in Lake's book. These old-timers represented a revival of the Cow-Boy view with a fresh antipathy toward Wyatt Earp. Much, if not most of it, was folk history based on rumor and the poststreet fight campaign to discredit the Earps. The passage of time made the vendetta seem even more ruthless than it was and the obvious exaggerations of the Lake version of what happened gave a sense of credibility to their own mix of memory and rumor.[39]

Mazzanovich, an Arizona old-timer who wrote his own book, *Trailing Geronimo*, based on his experiences, but who played no direct role in the Tombstone story, wrote a series of articles for the *Bisbee Brewery Gulch Gazette*, beginning in November 1931. He observed, "No doubt a number of the old-timers will resent it. In fact it would have been better if the book had never been placed before an intelligent reading public." He added, "much has been written about Tombstone and Cochise County in the past and all stories are conflicting. Now Wyatt tells his story entirely different from all the rest that we have read. Some day perhaps some one will come out with the truth. To me the story [as told by Lake] is simply impossible." He specifically belittled the claims of Burns and Lake that they had interviewed old pioneers in preparing their books, concluding, "they sure missed a number of the old timers."[40]

Wyatt Earp: Frontier Marshal would help to polarize even further views of the Earp-Clanton troubles and help produce a controversy that continues to exist, but perhaps the most important consequence of Lake's book insofar as Doc Holliday's story was concerned came from Mary Katharine Cummings, an elderly woman at the Pioneers Home in Prescott, Arizona. Mary Katharine Cummings was none other than Kate Harony (aka Kate Elder, Kate Fisher, and Big Nose Kate), Doc's inamorata. She had lived in obscurity for decades since her separation from Doc at Tombstone, but Lake's book infuriated her, and she set about to have her say on the matter.

Mazzanovich, who claimed to have met Kate in Globe years before, was corresponding with Kate when *Wyatt Earp: Frontier Marshal* was published, and he sent her a copy, which resulted in Kate writing her recollections of her relationship with Doc. Her response to Mazzanovich formed the basis for articles published in the *Brewery Gulch Gazette* in April and June 1932. Mazzanovich apparently planned to publish her memoir in her own words in some other venue, although it was never published because of his death in 1938.[41]

At some point, Joseph Chisholm, another old-timer and writer associated with the *Brewery Gulch Gazette*, also developed an interest in Kate's story. Mazzanovich was uncooperative, but when he died, Chisholm obtained access to what Kate had written, after which he "visited her and had her verify the data contained in her correspondence with Tony." In the unpublished manuscript "Tombstone's Tale (The Truth of Helldorado)," Chisholm wrote:

> I have met Doc Holliday's widow in recent months and have since corresponded with her. She is a sweet-faced little woman whose keen intellect and droll humor when discussing her traducers would never lead one to believe that she is eighty-five years old. . . . It is inconceivable to one bred on the frontier that Earp because of personal resentment would so evilly misrepresent a woman in his declining years. Yet there it is in his so-called autobiography.[42]

Chisholm included the reminiscence written by Kate for Mazzanovich in his manuscript, declaring that "it required no editing for the lady is well-educated and intelligent," along with some additions from

Mary Katharine Cummings,
Doc's "Kate" of prior years.

his own contact with her. However, Kate apparently decided not to
allow Chisholm to use the material. She believed that her story would
sell for a lot of money, and when neither Mazzanovich nor Chisholm
offered to pay for her story or to help her find a publisher who would,
she balked. If Chisholm showed his manuscript to her, she might also
have been unhappy with Chisholm's depiction of Doc. Chisholm's
opinion seems to have changed about the "sweet-faced little woman"
after that, because in his book *Brewery Gulch*, which was not published
until twelve years after his death in 1937, he said Doc was "a vicious
killer if there ever was one in the Southwest," and described Kate as
"Doc's Lady Lou," identifying her with the character played by Mae
West in the 1933 film *She Done Him Wrong*, which had been so controversial that it led to greater government censorship of sex in the
movies in 1934. In the movie, Lady Lou was a singer and nightclub
owner with a vicious criminal boyfriend. She did not fear him, however, and, in fact, regularly enjoyed the company of other men. "She
was a buxom, comely baggage," Chisholm wrote of Kate, continuing
the Mae West analogy, adding, "She had plenty of nerve, that dance
hall girl."[43]

The story that Kate told to Mazzanovich and that was used by
Chisholm certainly put a different edge on the Holliday story. Essentially, she denied that Doc had a reputation as "the cold-blooded murderer that 'Wyatt Earp Frontier Marshal' portrays him" before he
went to Tombstone, and held that Wyatt Earp was responsible for all

of Doc's misfortunes thereafter. She believed that Doc "changed" once he was under Earp's influence. Kate's story provided new information, but it was also self-serving, designed not only to correct some misconceptions about Doc but also to portray herself in a more positive light and protect her own reputation.

In the fall of 1935, Mrs. W. J. Martin of Prescott, Arizona, contacted Arthur W. Bork, a family friend and a graduate student at the University of Arizona at the time. She asked his assistance in preserving the story of "the wife of Doc Holliday." She noted that "some history makers have discovered her and are trying to get her to tell them what she knows. She told them that I had her manuscript and was dealing about it. They try to get the information for nothing." Martin had a manuscript besides the account Kate had given to Mazzanovich. She told Bork, "I have been nearly four years getting her to finish it, and I want to sell it." She added that Chisholm was trying to get the story, and she wanted "to do something before he gets back here."[44]

On Thanksgiving Day, 1935, Bork and Martin interviewed Kate at the Pioneers Home in Prescott and acquired more details from her. Among other things, she told them that she had been born in Davenport, Iowa, November 7, 1850, that she had attended a convent in St. Louis, that she had married a dentist named Silas Melvin, who later died in Atlanta, Georgia, that she had married Doc at Valdosta on May 25, 1876, and that her maiden name was Mary Katharine Haroney. This information complemented, supplemented, and contradicted the materials that she had given to Mazzanovich. She also confirmed that the photograph of Doc in *Wyatt Earp: Frontier Marshal* was in fact Doc and had been taken by C. S. Fly. She said that she worked at a restaurant called the Globe in Globe and claimed to have gone to Colorado, where she took care of Doc until he died. She said his last words were, "Well, I'm going just as I told them,—the bugs would get me before the worms did."[45]

From 1935 to 1938, Bork attempted to get Kate's story published, but she insisted on being paid for it. When offered the opportunity to publish her account without payment, she refused. Bork recalled, "After unsuccessful efforts to interest the national magazines, we gave up." Later, in 1940, Kate wrote yet another account of her life with Doc to her niece, Lillian Raffert. This account made fewer claims and was more personal. She noted in closing, "there are quite a few that want me to write up things but as they don't want to give me any thing I don't write."

Neither of Doc's 1950s biographers had access to any of these accounts. The version prepared with Bork and Martin was finally published in *Arizona and the West* in 1977, in conjunction with material gathered from the Haroney family by Glenn G. Boyer.[46] The latter materials provided details about her childhood. This information was revealing and important. Unfortunately, after most of the family informants had passed away, Boyer claimed that Dr. Harony was the personal physician of the Austrian archduke Maximilian and accompanied him to Mexico during the ill-fated reign of Maximilian as emperor of Mexico. The Harony family had been settled in Davenport for more than a year before Maximilian even arrived in Mexico. Nevertheless, this tale opened the way to make Kate into an educated, multilingual aristocrat, adding more romance to Doc Holliday's story.[47]

Kate's relationship with Doc is one of the most perplexing parts of Doc's life as well as his legend. Despite popular images of a violent and abusive tryst and old-timer gossip about Kate's proclivities for sex acts frowned on even by her generation of Cyprian sisters, little survived to provide an "intimate portrait" of their life together. Doc left not a word about her, and Kate's accounts were self-serving and defensive. While they were emotional in the animosity they revealed against Wyatt Earp, they were surprisingly impersonal in describing her relationship with Doc. Kate's recollections were confused by fading memory, calculated to portray her in the best possible light, and yet filled with information that only someone close to Doc Holliday could possibly have known. It is this internal webbing of intimate knowledge that provides the most convincing evidence that Mary Katharine Cummings was in fact Kate Elder.[48]

She was a woman with a story to tell and much to hide. The accounts she wrote have to be sifted like river sand in a placer box to separate a great mass of debris from the nuggets of reality that do appear. And yet, there is a sense in which the very composition of emotion, subterfuge, and even outright lies in what she said reveal a fascinating set of insights into the nature of her relationship with Doc. Her recollection was unemotional and almost detached as far as her feelings for Doc were concerned. She defended him against charges that he was a killer and a drunkard, and she insisted that he treated her

well. She portrayed herself as loyal and solicitous. There was no romance in her story, however. Indeed, she expressed resentment toward
Doc, accusing him of gambling away her money and implying Doc's
complicity in shady dealings with her accusations of Wyatt Earp's involvement in stage robberies. She also found Doc weak in not standing up to Wyatt. In the end, one of the greatest difficulties she faced
was trying to defend Doc as a basically decent man, while insisting
that Wyatt Earp was a bad man involved in criminal activity. The contradictions in her writings reveal the difficulty she had with this issue.

The absence of any real sense of her affection for Doc is especially
underscored by the fawning romantic portrait of John Ringo she gave
to Chisholm. She fairly gushed over Ringo's appearance and manly
traits before concluding, "And he was noble for he never fought anyone except face to face. Every time I think of him my eyes fill with
tears."[49] There are no such terms of endearment over Doc anywhere
in her recollections. Indeed, her description of Ringo is the only place
in her writings where she evinces any emotion other than anger and
resentment. It is almost as if her defense of Doc as a "good man" was
essential to her own defense as a "good woman," whereas her sentimentality toward Ringo revealed her simply as a woman, without the
guile so painfully apparent in her defense of Doc.

Kate's accounts, especially what she wrote for Mazzanovich, provided important leads for tracing her relationship with Doc, as well as
Doc's movements. Still, she was careful not to detail her own colorful
past in Kansas and Texas before she and Doc came together for what
was a fairly stable relationship until Tombstone and Wyatt Earp came
between them. Kate's hatred of Wyatt Earp—and no other word can
explain her anger toward him—suggests a history between them that
cannot be explained away as mere resentment of his influence on Doc.
There is a harshness and an element of deceitfulness in Kate's accounts
that she could not hide. Even so, a bond did exist between Doc and
Kate that brought them back together time and again.

Kate claimed in her account to Mazzanovich that Doc sent for her
in his final days and that she went to Glenwood Springs, where they
were reconciled and she nursed him until his death. She made a similar statement to Bork, although it did not appear in the narrative he
helped her prepare, where she said simply that "[h]e went to Glenwood Spring [sic] where he was appointed Under Sheriff for two
terms. He died in service of his second term and is buried in one of

the Glenwood Spring cemeteries."[50] A reunion would have been appropriate, and it could have happened, but the contemporary record does not sustain a Glenwood Springs reconciliation. And given Kate's insistence that she was Mrs. John H. Holliday in her later accounts, if she had been at his side, it would have been more than a little odd that the only reference to a relative in the *Ute Chief* obituary would have been Mattie Holliday. How could the presence of a wife have escaped notice?

At the very least, Kate's story provided an important counterpoint to the view of her as the nasty whore described in the *Las Vegas Optic* in 1882 and the recollections of some old-timers. Bork always believed that her prime motive was "to give herself a good name," and that seems to be borne out by some of her writings. After she married George Cummings, a blacksmith, in 1888, she had done her best to hide her past. That marriage did not last, and Cummings committed suicide in 1915. Kate eventually began to work as a housekeeper for John J. Howard, a mining man in Dos Cabezas, Arizona, and moved in with him. Following Howard's death in 1930, she served as the executrix of his will. She sought admission to the Pioneers Home and had some difficulty getting in. At that time she claimed that she had come to Arizona in 1895. Her ancient hatred of Wyatt Earp was what brought her "out of hiding," so to speak, largely as the result of negative portrayals of her by Burns and Lake, both of which she attributed to Earp.[51]

Two stories illustrate what Kate faced. The first was a tale by an old-timer who claimed that he was present in a Bisbee saloon when Kate was killed. A drunk began shooting up the place, and everyone hit the floor. When the shooting was over, however, Kate did not get up. She was dead, and the locals could find no cause for her death. They sent for Doc Holliday, of course, who arrived shortly and examined her body. Doc discovered a tiny speck of blood on her buttocks, and after performing an autopsy he discovered that one of the drunk's bullets had made a direct hit on her rectum as she lay on the floor with her posterior slightly raised.[52]

The other story was told by Kate herself:

[H]ere is what happened in Globe one morning, A Merchant Mrs Baily brought a man in for breakfast after breafast [sic] hours, I waited on him because my girl was doing up the rooms, they got to talking about Tombstone, some how Doc & I were mentioned, he told Mrs Baily that Doc took me to New Mexico & killed me up in the mountains & that he helped to bury me, I said the poor woman. Mrs Baily & I laught [*sic*] but the poor man found out he made a fool of himself & never came back but it is laughable how some people will talk, I often laugh how often I have been dead & buried & turn up some place full of life.[53]

Kate's efforts to have her version told went unrewarded. Unfortunately, her story would remain obscure. Some of it would come to light in a piecemeal fashion with publication of Frank Waters's *The Earp Brothers of Tombstone: The Story of Mrs. Virgil Earp*, which purported to be the recollections of Allie Earp, Virgil's widow. Based on comparison with Waters's earlier unpublished manuscript "The Tombstone Travesty," the book included some of the materials from Mazzanovich and Chisholm, which, by then, had been acquired by Waters's close friend, the Earp researcher and collector John D. Gilchriese. In the book, Allie made statements that were not in "The Tombstone Travesty." Much of what was added came directly from Kate's remembrances.[54]

By the time Waters published his book in 1960, some changes were taking place in the popular view of Wyatt Earp and Doc Holliday. The first biography of Doc Holliday, written by John Myers Myers, was published in 1955.[55] It was a well-structured work that collected many of the stories about Doc and offered useful insights but suffered from too great a reliance on Stuart Lake. Patricia Jahns's biography, published two years after Myers's, was much less satisfying as a biography, but much more challenging to the legend of the "good bad man." Jahns questioned the authenticity of several of the standard events in Doc's life, including such episodes as the Ed Bailey killing, the Bud Ryan knifing, and the Mike Gordon shooting. She also questioned Doc's ability as a gun handler, and portrayed Wyatt Earp in a less than favorable light. Perhaps most dramatically, she emphasized the relationship between Doc and his cousin, Mattie, and suggested that it was a romantic one.[56] Throughout, her approach was novelistic; she filled in gaps by putting words into people's mouths and presuming to understand their thoughts.

Jahns's biography had the virtue of trying to present a more realistic view of Doc Holliday than the image that had survived virtually all challenges since the 1880s. Unwittingly, then, Jahns provided fodder for the debunkers who followed her. In Waters's book, and in the later

Wyatt Earp biography by Ed Bartholomew, Doc's image was diminished even more, so that he became little more than a cutthroat. Curiously, though, even in the worst depictions of him, he retained a genteel veneer. Bartholomew concluded that Doc was involved in stage robberies in New Mexico based on nothing more than the fact that one of the robbers spoke with a refined accent and vocabulary.[57]

In the "anti-Earp" literature that gained fresh credibility in the 1960s as part of a general revolt against Western gunfighters and outlaw heroes in general, Doc was increasingly portrayed as a quarrelsome and drunken troublemaker who was a lousy shot and a generally disreputable character. He was involved in the Benson stage robbery and the murder of Bud Philpott, and he was responsible for the street fight, which he started by gunning down the unarmed Tom McLaury without cause.

Of all the ideas that Jahns introduced, the one that produced the greatest interest and stirred the strongest feelings was the suggestion that Doc and Mattie were interested in each other romantically. Sister Mary Melanie died in 1939 after a long and distinguished career of service. The family rightly held her in high esteem and publicly disavowed any suggestion that she and Doc had been in love, but they never denied that she and Doc were close. "After Doc's death," one relative recalled, "she would talk of him and say that if people had only known him as she had, they would have seen a different man from the one of Western fame."[58]

At the time of her death, a trunk containing her belongings was turned over to her sister, Marie Mahoney. Apparently, before she died, Sister Mary Melanie had burned some of her letters from Doc, perhaps the most personal or the ones that revealed the darker side of John Henry, but the trunk still included a number of his letters. Carolyn Holliday Manley, a descendant of Robert Kennedy Holliday, recalled that "[m]y aunt Catharine says her daddy used to read those letters on a Sunday afternoon, and that they were wonderful, colorful letters describing the Old West." They were well written and full of historical detail, but they said little about his violent exploits and they certainly were not love letters. When Marie entered a nursing home, the trunk came into the possession of Carolyn's parents. Later, however, Marie left the nursing home and reclaimed her property. After that, she burned Doc's letters to Mattie to keep her sister's "personal life private."[59]

The story of a romantic attachment would not die. It was too appealing. Not even the family would completely deny the possibility. "The rumor was that they were in love," recalled Robert Lee Holliday, the grandson of Robert Alexander Holliday, Doc's cousin "Hub." Robert Lee added, "I don't know if he asked her to go out West with him, but I doubt it because of his tuberculosis."[60] Others in the family also remembered the rumors. Pat Jahns, Doc's biographer, recalled her exchange with Lillian McKey, the Valdosta relative who cautiously provided information to both Jahns and Myers: "The most that she ever wrote about Doc was in one letter where she wrote a whole paragraph about his relationship with Mattie Holliday," wrote Jahns. "This was followed several days later by an airmail letter denying the whole thing. It read very much as if she had told another family member about it and gotten a scolding. Very contrite."[61]

The reason was simple enough. Doc Holliday was an embarrassment to many in the family. Morgan DeLancey Magee, a great-grandson of John Stiles Holliday, remembered his grandmother, Mary Cowperwaite Fulton Holliday, saying, "No! 'Doc' Holliday is not a member of our family! In fact, that is not even his real name!"[62] Robert Lee Holliday added, "Much later in life I found out that Grandma Holliday thought Doc was a vagabond, gambler, and other unmentionable names, and disavowed any family relation with him. . . . It goes without saying that a respected Southern family would not admit any kinship to one of the Wild West's most notorious gamblers and gunfighters."[63]

Another factor in the family's attitude was Sister Mary Melanie's own reputation as a saintly woman, a reputation that made her a kind of legend in her own right. She visited Margaret's husband, John Marsh, daily while he was hospitalized in 1936 to 1937. Mattie's mother was the first cousin of Margaret Mitchell's grandmother, and Margaret Mitchell always insisted that Sister Mary Melanie was the inspiration for the saintly, self-sacrificing Melanie Hamilton in her novel *Gone with the Wind*. The inspiration is confirmed in striking fashion by comparison of Mitchell's word portrait of the young Melanie Hamilton with a family photograph of the young Mattie Holliday:

> She was a tiny, frailly built girl, who gave the appearance of a child masquerading in her mother's enormous hoop skirts—an illusion that was heightened by the shy, almost frightened look in her too large brown eyes. She had a cloud of curly dark hair which was so sternly repressed beneath its net that no vagrant tendrils escaped,

Sister Mary Melanie, Doc's beloved Mattie, in her last years. She had earned a reputation as a devoted and caring teacher and tender caregiver.

and this dark mass, with its long widow's peak, accentuated the heart shape of her face. Too wide across the cheek bones, too pointed at the chin, it was a sweet, timid face, but a plain face, and she had no feminine tricks of allure to make observers forget its plainness. She looked—and was—as simple as the earth, as good as bread, as transparent as water. But for all her plainness of feature and smallness of stature, there was a sedate dignity about her movements that was oddly touching and far older than her seventeen years.[64]

Gone with the Wind is filled with themes reminiscent of the lives of Doc and Mattie. First, one of the characters, Ellen Robillard, Scarlett O'Hara's mother, was in love with her first cousin, Philippe, who was forced to leave home and travel to New Orleans, where he was killed in a fight. Another character, Tony Fontaine, got into trouble and went to Texas. Scarlett's sister Carreen was in love with a young man who was killed at Gettysburg, and she devoted herself to a religious life afterward, eventually joining a convent. These are all set against the saintly behavior of Melanie Hamilton Wilkes and Scarlett's love for a man she cannot marry.

The author David O'Connell also notes that the choice of "Melanie" as Mattie's religious name had interesting implications. Before Vatican II, women who became nuns chose the name of a saint for the religious life. "Melanie" was a relatively rare choice in this respect. Two saints were named Melanie, one the granddaughter of the other. Melanie the Younger was a woman who fell in love with and married her first cousin, Pinian, who was himself later named a saint. After they had two children, both of whom died, Melanie and Pinian traveled to Jerusalem, where they both entered religious orders.

Of course, O'Connell also points out that Mattie may have chosen the name Mary Melanie because of the appearance of the Virgin Mary to a fifteen-year-old French peasant girl named Melanie Mathieu-Calvat, during which the Virgin Mary stressed the need for penance. The apparition at La Salette was widely acknowledged, and in 1879, just four years before Mattie joined the order, the pope recognized the site of the apparition as a basilica. This would offer a practical explanation of her choice of the name Mary Melanie with no mysterious connections to her cousin John Henry.

O'Connell suggests another, simpler explanation of their relationship, one especially consistent with Mattie's character. He notes that it was likely that John Henry did, in fact, at some point convert to Catholicism, as the local obituaries in Colorado said, because of Mattie's influence. He also believes that Mattie realized Doc needed her to be a steadying force in his life because of his illness or his demoralized lifestyle or both, which explains her ongoing correspondence with him after he left Georgia. He suggests that the relationship was platonic and that Mattie was simply "trying hard to keep her errant cousin on the right track." Mattie did not "carry 'love letters tied with a ribbon' with her when she dedicated her life to Christ." This is a plausible explanation of what happened, but the burning of the letters ensured that the possibility of unrequited love would remain a part of the legend of Doc Holliday.[65]

Henry Holliday left no comments about his son or his reputation as a Western gun player. Rather, he went on with his life in Valdosta, where he was active in both politics and business. He was involved in local politics, serving several terms as mayor, was credited with introducing pecan growing to southern Georgia, and lived a long, respectable life until his death on February 22, 1893.[66] In 1879, Henry wrote to his brother-in-law, A. W. McCoin, who lived in Laclede, Kansas, on behalf of a group of Lowndes County blacks who were interested in migrating to Kansas as a group. McCoin wrote a long response encouraging them to send a committee to investigate before moving to ensure that they would make the right choices. The former Freedman's Bureau agent still had the respect of the black community in Lowndes County.[67]

After Major's death, his widow continued to live in Valdosta, and on March 30, 1899, Rachel Martin Holliday married Joseph I. Gloer, a former Atlanta policeman. In 1905, they moved to Atlanta.[68] One of the later tales to add mystery to the Holliday legend was the report that in 1955 a box of junk found in the attic of a local home turned up in an antique shop in Waycross, Georgia. The box contained a wooden cross that appeared to be a grave marker and a bundle of letters post-marked Pensacola, Florida, written by John Henry Holliday. The owner of the shop dismissed the letters as forgeries because of the Pensacola postmarks and gave little thought to the possibility that they were actually written by Doc Holliday. The box and its contents had disap-peared before anyone made the connection between Waycross and Doc's stepmother, who had relatives there and could well have left materials there when she moved to Atlanta with her new husband. The cross would also fuel other speculation about Doc.[69]

All the contemporary sources said that Doc was buried in the new Linwood cemetery at Glenwood Springs. Over time, however, the grave marker disappeared and eventually the exact location of the grave was lost. In 1956, the city of Glenwood Springs decided to place a new headstone in the local cemetery for the benefit of visitors. Plac-ing the marker became a matter of local controversy. The city man-ager, A. E. Axtell, eventually placed the marker, insisting that it was on the site of Doc's grave. "Art Kendricks, before he died, took up and showed me the spot he was buried in," Axtell said. "Kendricks was mayor of Glenwood years ago and worked as a busboy at the old hotel when Doc stayed there."

Another old-time resident of Glenwood Springs, Wayne Burge, a local mortician, said, "Doc Holliday is buried in Glenwood Springs, but not on the Hill." Burge added, "I am aware of his true burial place but at this time, it is a residential area and it would not be feasible to bring it out to the public." And Charley Hopkins, another old-timer, said flatly, "I don't give a damn what any of those politicians say, he is buried right down on that corner [pointing to the corner of Ninth and Palmer]. . . . That's where he is buried because the guy that was stand-ing at the foot of the grave [George Manley] swore to it." Yet another story said that Doc's coffin washed away from its place in the Linwood cemetery down a gully and had to be reburied at a different site.[70]

The debate over where Doc was buried gained added significance and intensity in 1972, when Susan McKey Thomas, the granddaugh-ter of Doc's uncle William Harrison McKey, initiated an effort to have his body returned to Valdosta. Local authorities in Colorado resisted, and eventually state officials became involved; they made it plain that legal action would be required. Disappointed, Thomas did not pursue the matter further, but the controversy seemed to further exacerbate the question of Doc's burial site. Glenwood Springs leaders could use the argument that they could not return the body because they did not know exactly where it was. They even suggested the possibility of a lawsuit if they moved the wrong body.[71]

One of the most persistent stories over the years was that Doc's body had been buried in a "holding plot" at the foot of the hill because the ground at Linwood cemetery was frozen. This idea was finally discredited in 2005 because of evidence that in 1887, the town scavenger, Richard Hewson, was employed by the town council to remove bodies from the old town cemetery to Linwood. The very week that Doc died, Hewson was moving bodies from the old cemetery to the new cemetery on the hill. It would be unlikely then that Doc would be buried in a temporary grave. The contemporary sources had it right all along.[72]

Another variation on the story was that Doc's body was actually returned to Georgia at some point under instructions from Henry Holliday himself. The cross reported in the box found in Waycross would be explained by such a move. Curiously, Henry Holliday's grave has been lost as well, although the papers reported that he was buried in the cemetery at Valdosta. Bill Dunn, a researcher in Griffin, Georgia, believes that Doc and Henry are buried side by side in unmarked graves in Griffin, in a plot owned by close friends of the Holliday family. So far, no hard evidence has come to light to support such a claim, but the story does prove that legends rarely "rest in peace."[73]

Bruce Dettman, a capable and articulate student of both the Tombstone story and its manifestations in popular culture, coined the phrase "the Holliday mystique" to explain Doc Holliday's peculiar hold on the popular imagination. While Wyatt Earp's actions at Tombstone raised significant and troubling issues that transcend Tombstone and touch on important questions relating to justice and the law, Dettman suggests that Doc Holliday, not Wyatt Earp, explains the ongoing popularity of Tombstone as a subject of interest to movie audiences. He does not diminish Earp's central role in the story, nor does he play down the themes that are rightly at the center, but he hypothesizes that it has been the character of Doc Holliday, with his moral ambivalence and apparent fatalism, that has given the story its powerful appeal. Dettman writes that Doc, "with his questionable conduct, unlawful behavior, and nasty temperament, became a sounding board against which the ethically chiseled hero could not only showcase his high principles and steady resolve, but often . . . to sometimes seriously question them."[74]

Perhaps this is more a commentary on the portrayal of Wyatt Earp in film and fiction than on Doc's essential role, but Doc has consistently been the more compelling figure. This has been so because of the internal battle with which Doc struggled. The way in which he confronts himself as well as his enemies is more interesting than the self-confident, self-reliant, self-assured, and often self-righteous figure that Wyatt Earp inevitably presents. Earp's steady, serious, humorless character still wrestles with some of the most fundamental issues raised by the industrialization of America on the Western frontier, and, for that reason, his struggle with violence, justice, and law has power and importance. However, it is possible, Dettman suggests, that the legend of Wyatt Earp required Doc Holliday.[75]

The solitary defender of justice represented by Wyatt Earp was a more popular figure in the first half of the twentieth century. It ensured the success of *Wyatt Earp: Frontier Marshal*. But in the post–World War II era, with antiestablishment trends, revisionism, a more general cynicism, and greater attention to self-analysis, the solitary hero seemed naive and self-righteous. Before the end of World War II, Doc Holliday was almost always presented in the familiar B-Western sidekick role. Only in *The Arizonian* (1936), *Frontier Marshal* (1939), and *My Darling Clementine* (1946) did Doc have a more expanded role closer to the legendary fit. Not even the classic *Law and Order* (1932) really needed Doc, who bears no resemblance to the historical Doc Holliday. Oddly, one of the most compelling figures based on Doc Holliday was the character Hatfield in John Ford's *Stagecoach* (1939), who presented a deadly, polished Southern gentleman gambler in a role with no connection to the Tombstone story save John Wayne's name, Ringo.[76]

Beginning with the low-budget *Masterson of Kansas* (1954), Doc Holliday routinely stole films from Wyatt Earp, though rarely by design. Kirk Douglas's performance as Doc in *Gunfight at the O.K. Corral* (1956) completely overshadowed Burt Lancaster's puritanical Wyatt Earp. Even in the dark antiestablishment, antiwar *Doc* (1971), Wyatt Earp is a sniveling wimp without Doc, who is hardly admirable himself. In the pedestrian, Wyatt-centered *Wyatt Earp* (1994), the most interesting character is Doc Holliday. The most compelling scenes in the movie invariably involve him, and in a script obviously designed to showcase the moody, morose Wyatt Earp portrayed by Kevin Costner, Dennis Quaid as Doc still has the most memorable lines.[77]

In Kevin Jarre's *Tombstone* (1993), however, Doc Holliday, as portrayed by Val Kilmer, not only stole the movie from Kurt Russell's Wyatt Earp but also became a popular culture icon who crystalized the Doc Holliday legend. Cultured, cynical, fatalistic, and sardonic, Kilmer's morally challenged Doc seems resigned to his fate, yet he is drawn to Wyatt because of what he stands for. Doc is debauched but oddly principled. The ambiguity of his character makes him a more appealing hero for today's world than the vengeful Wyatt Earp, and yet draws him back to the imagery of the "good bad man" that predominated in accounts of Doc Holliday from the 1880s through Burns and Lake. It is the mystique that makes him so appealing.

Dettman offers interesting conclusions about the place of Doc Holliday in the Tombstone story:

> If then, after all these screen incarnations, the legend of Wyatt Earp did require the seeds of the troublesome dentist from Georgia to help harvest and cultivate it, then so did Doc who probably would have roamed the West until struck down by his disease as one of the West's more minor figures, need Wyatt's steadiness, patience, tenacity, moral rectitude and later gift for self-promotion, to assure his own Western immortality, fame, and Hollywood screen time. As they say, it was a good fit.[78]

Legends are not about life as it actually happened; rather, they are about what humanity values. Heroes do not always stand up well under the light of history, but they remind human beings of things they need and crave in their own lives, something deep and empowering that transcends who they actually are. Heroes are inevitably flawed, because it is not their deeds that make them heroes so much as their capacity to act in spite of their flaws. In the legendary interplay of Wyatt Earp and Doc Holliday can be seen some of the issues, great and small, that have troubled humankind across the centuries. In their story—in their weaknesses and in their strengths—generations of people see their own and find instruction and hope for themselves.

EPILOGUE

THE MEASURE OF A LEGEND

That "Doc" Holliday had his faults none will attempt to deny; but who among us has not, and who shall be the judge of these things?

— *Glenwood Springs Ute Chief*, November 12, 1887

ives evolve, experience shapes, and values change. John Henry Holliday was no exception to such laws of human conduct. He was—as all men are—more than the sum of the facts of his life. Were facts the measure, we would have too little to take the measure of him, because even now, great gaps exist in the factual base of Doc Holliday's life, and because so many of the "facts" are themselves in dispute. The legend that grew up around him is partially to blame for the confusion, and yet without the legend he might have been forgotten. The legend left him mysterious and compelling and fixed him in an imagery that, in all its variants—and they are surprisingly few—brooked no room for the transpositions wrought naturally by life's unplanned and unexpected vagaries.

Ironically, the facts and the legend cannot be separated successfully without destroying the truth, and those who seek "to set the record straight" run the risk of distorting reality as surely as those who uncritically accept the legend at face value. Unfortunately, extricating the man from the legend has proven a difficult and even misguided task. It is difficult because so much of his life was lived in relative obscurity with little opportunity or reason for documentation; it is misguided because for at least part of his life the legend directly affected who he was. Biographers must trace the evolution of a life through the

407

accumulation of its parts, but ultimately they must take a measure of the whole. In Doc Holliday's case, that cannot be done apart from the legend, because the legend was part of who he was.

By the time that Doc Holliday became a widely known public figure, he was already an anachronism. The heyday of the boom camp had passed. His profession as a gambler was even less respectable than it had been. Railroads and the age of exploitation were rapidly putting an end to the frontier age. However, it was then that he became notorious. The historian Richard White described the "decisive allure" that men like Doc had for the people of that age. He might well have been describing Wyatt Earp and Doc Holliday when he said that people made heroes of "strong men who defended themselves, righted their own wrongs, and took vengeance on their enemies despite the corruption of the existing order." Certain "manly virtues" won admiration even if they were embodied by men of less than noble character, so that a man like Doc had the respect even of many who disapproved his acts.[1]

He was measured, then, not merely by what he had done, but by attributes that he seemed to embody. And it did not matter whether the image was accurate. Men related to him based on what they *believed* about him or, perhaps, even needed from him. His reputation defined him. This was particularly true after Tombstone, so that he had a reputation and a kind of respect in Colorado that he had not known before. Doubtless, the nostalgic orientation of the time helped to fill in the gaps in his life with stories, both real and imagined, that made him more than he actually was, but that could not be blamed on him.

That he was a private man did not help. Even his friends, or those who called him friend, were ultimately as befuddled by him as strangers and those who had reasons to distrust or even to hate him. Even Wyatt Earp never seemed to really know Doc, and when Wyatt wrote about him later, he almost apologized for his friendship, which revealed more about Wyatt Earp's character than about Doc's. Wyatt was always too much concerned about what others thought; Doc never seemed to care. That was, at once, Doc's charm and his most frustrating quality. It was the thing that made men fear him and forced them to admire him.

Understanding Doc Holliday begins with his roots. He was a Southern gentleman, not a Southern aristocrat, but a gentleman nonetheless. He was taught manners and values that shaped who he was throughout his lifetime. He learned a code of honor that affected every area of his life. He spoke with that quiet courtesy that transcended class in the South. He was comfortable in the drawing room and on the dance floor. He was garrulous and charming. He valued family and friends. He understood that a man's word was his bond.

As he grew, Doc also acquired other "manly habits" common among Southern men. He learned to use firearms at an early age. Hunting, fishing, and horseback riding were as much a part of his education as reading, writing, arithmetic, and philosophy. The code he lived by taught him to stand up for himself and to defend himself, his family, and his friends from insult or injury. He was prepared to fight to protect his honor. The South of his day was not the Bible Belt, so that in spite of his mother's devoted religious teachings, the young John Henry learned to gamble—on cards, dice, horse racing, and cockfights—he learned to drink, he learned to fight, and he explored the mysteries of sex, all of which were regarded as normal in the "education" of Southern men.

His life was also shaped during a troubled time. He was born during the prelude to the Civil War, and he came of age in its aftermath. His life was nurtured on the animosities of that period, which added to his aggressiveness. He also experienced tensions at home. His mother was doting, his father distant. He was spoiled and used to having his way. Southern boys were given considerable freedom, but Doc grew protective of his mother as her health worsened and resentful toward his father. When his mother died, John Henry felt the loss deeper than anyone, and when his father remarried quickly, his resentment became rebellion. Initially, it focused on the issues of his time: Reconstruction and black soldiers and the very idea of occupation. It also flared in his relationships. He kept his anger hidden, for the most part, but it was there, and it came into the open in calculating, controlled ways, as exhibited in his remembered confrontation with a schoolmate.

He never entirely lost these traits. They likely caused some of his troubles in the West. They showed in his character as he developed. He was loyal to his friends. His friendship with Wyatt Earp was one proof of that, although not the only one. His sense of honor would allow no less than loyalty even when it caused him problems, as in the case of his friendship with William Leonard, the Tombstone stage robber.

He also expected loyalty from others, and there were times in his life when he was angered at the betrayal by friends.

He was courageous or a man without fear (not necessarily the same thing). This trait was not mere fatalism. It was not a part of him simply because he was dying. At times, he proved clearly that he wanted to live for as long as he could. No, it was bred into him to stand his ground, and he developed a bullheaded determination not to back away from a fight in the Western environment of gambling halls and saloons, where his reputation often depended on his resolve at the moment of conflict. At times, such as the Joyce incident and Tombstone and the Allen shooting in Leadville, he seemed foolhardy and desperate, but even if an episode ended badly, he did not back away from a fight.

To some he seemed cold blooded, but he was not a killer. His record never supported the claims of numerous homicides. His apparent willingness to kill was sufficient to build the reputation. Doubtless, he was skilled with firearms. Although he probably was not as proficient as Wyatt Earp claimed, even those who disliked him said that he was "noted for his coolness under fire as well as his skill as a dead shot."[2] In the street fight, Doc was cool, controlled, accurate, and deadly. In a few episodes, he seemed amateurish. Perhaps alcohol explained the difference. However, whether deadly accurate or grossly inaccurate, again, he was willing. He did not hesitate. His sense of honor would not allow it.

Doc drank too much. That seems clear. Whether his drinking problem developed from a debauched lifestyle or efforts to forget his lost dreams, or as a treatment for his tuberculosis is immaterial. How it affected him was always the subject of disagreement. Some claimed that he grew steadier the more he drank, but there were episodes in his life that are explained best as the consequence of too much alcohol. Some said that he was a mean drunk; others said he became more mellow. He may well have developed a high tolerance for alcohol, although a standard ration of two quarts a day is likely a tall tale.

Holliday lived in a netherworld. True enough, in the boom camps of the West gambling and saloonkeeping were "respectable" in the sense that they were essential to the economic and political life of the towns, but contrary to much of the popular literature on the West, the gambler's lifestyle did not enjoy the same level of respectability as other professions. It was, after all, the Victorian era, with all of its moralism and rigid standards of conduct. As the boom camps stabilized into more permanent communities, gambling and saloonkeeping were gradually pushed into their own districts if not eliminated entirely.[3] Doc understood this fact of life and accepted it. By Victorian standards, he was not a "good man," but accusations that he was a con man, capper, "top and bottom" man, or other tinhorn are largely the product of rumor mills and reform initiatives that assumed that all gamblers were crooked.

Doc fell into the gambler's life easily enough. He was likely introduced to the saloon world in Philadelphia, and he certainly experienced it in Atlanta in places like Lee Smith's various enterprises. It was not uncommon for business and professional men to frequent saloons in those days. He "deviated from the path of rectitude" in Dallas and gradually cut ties with the life he had known at faro tables, bars, and cribs. Self-pity, disillusionment, and bitterness were the hounds that drove him, and yet somehow the values of his youth never allowed him to reach the depravity he might have fallen into. Even his relationship with Kate Elder, while stormy, never became the abusive tryst that was later "remembered" by those with reasons to portray him as wicked.[4] His biggest battle was always with himself. That was why Mattie Holliday was so important to him; he needed her and what she stood for as anchors.

Despite the reminiscences of several who knew Doc, it is hard to find the glib and urbane wag the legend favors in portrayals of him. He could be genial and even funny, but he struggled to maintain a pleasant demeanor, which accounts for the contradictory views of him as sour and friendly. The few interviews that he gave do reveal a wry sense of humor. Nor is it surprising, given his condition, that his humor had a sardonic and caustic edge. He was not above spinning a yarn or two—another Southern tradition—for the benefit of the press. Telling a "windy" gave the press what it wanted, but his interviews—and all of them came after Tombstone—make clear that he thought of himself as an honorable man.[5]

"There is no doubt in my mind that Doc Holliday was loyal to his friends and a 'dead game sport'—whether he was playing poker, or pulling the trigger," John P. Clum wrote of Holliday in 1929. "I made a stage trip with him once from Tucson to Tombstone. He told me he came to Arizona, expecting to die from tuberculosis, and he intimated that this ailment often eliminated the joy of living and the fear of death, and that, while he would not deliberately provoke a gun fight, neither would he take the trouble to avoid it, as it might prove the boon that would end it all for him. You can understand that, in that frame of mind, he, doubtless, was a loyal friend and 'game' as a gambler, or in a gun fight, but *he was not a constructive citizen.*"

Clum's appraisal was a fair one. His recollection provides a plausible explanation for Doc's behavior in Tombstone by a man who disliked Holliday and blamed him for much of the trouble there. Clum was right, too, when he said that Holliday was not a "constructive citizen." By almost any standard, he was not a "good man." No one understood that better than he. Yet Doc was a man with admirable qualities, and his struggle with ancient core values that he himself questioned made his a tragic life, not merely a wasted one, and this perhaps explains why he remains such a compelling figure.[6]

There was an anger, amounting to an essence, in John Henry Holliday long before the doctor proclaimed him dying from a disease he already knew and understood and detested from experience. Blame it on the absence—or distance—of his father, the sickness and loss of his mother, the bloody times in which he reached puberty, or hopeless love. Whatever it was, it was there before he ever set foot outside of Georgia for the first time, and it made it unlikely that he could have lived his life peacefully as a partner in a Georgia dental practice, with or without consumption. Robert Alexander Holliday was what he should have been—respectable, successful, and prosperous. Doc could not have been those things. He was consumed by an inner fire that would not let him be.

What is most remarkable is the extent to which he kept his anger at bay. It was held in check by a code he could not expunge, no matter how much his cynicism told him that it was false and meaningless, until at last he recovered hope in a bloody exorcism that banished the rage and validated the code. He discovered meaning on the back trails of southeastern Arizona and, ironically, calmed the fury inside him in the violent exigency of vendetta. He found release in the meaning of an experience that restored his desire to live. Afterward, though, he was left with nothing but the emptiness of notoriety, and it drained away the power that had renewed his passion for life, until, at last, he lost the hope he had so recently found. Ironically, at the very moment he recovered the will to live, he lost all the reasons for wanting to live. Other men found in the image of him the very thing that he himself could not find. The legend failed only the man behind the legend.

This piecemeal and incomplete portrait does suggest several critical things about Doc Holliday. He was not a robber. Efforts to link him to the Benson stage robbery and the murder of Bud Philpott were always strained simply because these acts were so inconsistent with the rest of his life. Moreover, he would not have done such a thing because it would have jeopardized his friendship with Wyatt Earp. Doc's anger with Ike Clanton was due as much to Ike's willingness to betray his friends as to Ike's allegations against him and Wyatt. Similarly, his respect for Wyatt and his position in the community were enough to have prevented him from firing the first shot in the street fight. Once his friendship with Wyatt was sealed in Tombstone—and that likely came later than generally supposed—Doc honored it.

That did not mean that he was Wyatt Earp's lapdog, however. Wyatt did watch over him, but Doc had a mind of his own and went his own way most of the time. He was Wyatt's business partner in Tombstone. He respected Earp's position, and after the Joyce fiasco he tried to stay clear of trouble. He stood with his friend in the street fight, and he was loyal to Wyatt during the vendetta. Even Kate's bitterness over Wyatt's "hold" on Doc may well have had more to do with some previous animosity toward Wyatt than Doc's infatuation with Earp. During the Tombstone years, Holliday clearly moved about freely, in and out of Tombstone, following gambling opportunities, and once the vendetta posse was out of Arizona and Wyatt did not need him anymore, he once again went his own way.

Still, enough mystery, uncertainty, and controversy encompass John Henry Holliday's life that it would be foolhardy to claim that any statement about him is definitive. He was a complicated, troubled man, living in a difficult time, involved in events that were even then controversial. His life was eventually further obscured by his own notoriety long before he took the stage to Glenwood Springs and the end of the trail. He left impressions more than evidence.[7] Arguably, his story was not significant historically, but it was the stuff of high drama that continues to make him irresistible to novelists, screenwriters, and historians.

After all this time, nobody has truly dropped the loop on John Henry Holliday. Perhaps it is fitting that Black Jack, one of the characters of Alfred Henry Lewis, that spinner of tales from Doc's own time, should have the last word. Reflecting on Doc Holliday's life to Mr. Masterson over a drink following Doc's funeral, Black Jack declared, "We'll shorely miss him from our midst. An' when I think on his career, sort o' run over it hittin' the high places, I'm here to observe that Mr. Holliday was the vividest invalid an' the busiest, bar none, with which I ever crossed up. He certainly was an in-dee-fat-ig-a-ble sick man; an' that goes as it lays."[8]

It is hard to argue with that.

NOTES

Prologue: The Measure of a Man

1. *Glenwood Springs (Colorado) Ute Chief*, November 9, 1887.
2. *Denver Republican*, November 10, 1887.
3. *San Francisco Examiner*, August 2, 1896.
4. William Barclay Masterson, "Famous Gunfighters of the Western Frontier: Doc Holliday," *Human Life* (May 1907): 5.
5. *San Francisco Examiner*, May 27, 1882.
6. *Las Vegas Daily Optic*, July 20, 1881.
7. *Valdosta (Georgia) Daily Times*, February 11, 1888.
8. *Gunnison (Colorado) Daily News-Democrat*, June 18, 1882.
9. *San Francisco Examiner*, May 11, 1882.
10. *Denver Rocky Mountain News*, October 23, 1898.
11. *Tombstone (Arizona) Daily Epitaph*, July 29, 1882.
12. At the time of Holliday's death, the *Glenwood Springs Ute Chief* reported that Doc had corresponded with only one member of his family through the years and that that correspondence was apparently destroyed. In fact, he appears to have had at least sporadic correspondence with others, so it is still possible that some Holliday papers may be found.

1. Child of the Southern Frontier

1. Sylvia D. Lynch, *Aristocracy's Outlaw: The Doc Holliday Story* (New Tazewell, TN: Iris, 1994).
2. Kenneth Coleman, ed., *A History of Georgia* (Athens: University of Georgia Press, 1977), 126.
3. Grady McWhiney, *Cracker Culture: Celtic Ways in the Old South* (Tuscaloosa: University of Alabama Press, 1988).
4. John W. Caughey, *McGillivray of the Creeks* (Norman: University of Oklahoma Press, 1959), 3–57.
5. E. Merton Coulter, *Georgia: A Short History* (Athens: University of Georgia Press, 1947), 220.
6. The literature is extensive. One of the best summaries is also one of the older accounts reprinted from the *Bureau of American Ethnology Reports of the Smithsonian Institution:* James Mooney, *Historical Sketch of the Cherokee* (Chicago: Aldine, 1975), 110–124. Another valuable perspective is provided in Charles Warren, *The Supreme Court in United States History* (Boston: Little, Brown, 1922), 1:729–779.
7. Robert V. Remini, *Andrew Jackson and His Indian Wars* (New York: Viking, 2001), 254–271.
8. See Theda Perdue and Michael D. Greene, eds., *The Cherokee Removal: A Brief History with Documents* (New York: Palgrave Macmillan, 1995); Stan Hoig, *Night of the*

Cruel Moon: Cherokee Removal and the Trail of Tears (New York: Facts on File, 1996); John Ehle, *The Trail of Tears: The Rise and Fall of the Cherokee Nation* (New York: Doubleday, 1989).

9. For an interesting examination of the "Jacksonian character," see Edward Pessen, *Jacksonian America: Society, Personality, and Politics* (Homewood, IL: Dorsey, 1969), 5–38.

10. Martha Anne Holliday (Sister Mary Melanie), "Memoirs of the Holliday Family in Georgia," unpublished family papers, Catherine Holliday Neuhoff Collection; Henry Burroughs Holliday to Robert Alexander Holliday, May 7, 1884, Constance Knowles McKellar Collection; Karen Holliday Tanner, *Doc Holliday: A Family Portrait* (Norman: University of Oklahoma Press, 1998), 235–238.

11. Rachel Martin Holliday, Widow's Pension Claim File, Veteran's Bureau Records, Record Group 15, National Archives and Records Administration, Washington, DC.

12. Tanner, *Family Portrait*, 237.

13. Henry B. Holliday, Military Service Record, Captain Stell's Company, First Georgia Volunteers, United States Army Command, RG 393, NARA; Rachel Holliday, Widow's Pension Claim File, VBR, RG 15, NARA.

14. From an anonymous letter published in *Niles' Register*, July 24, 1838, quoted in Francis Paul Prucha, *The Sword of the Republic: The United States Army on the Frontier, 1783–1846* (New York: Macmillan, 1969), 166–167.

15. Mooney, *Historical Sketch*, 124.

16. Henry Holliday, MSR, USAC, RG 393, NARA; see also Albert Pendleton Jr. and Susan McKey Thomas, "Doc Holliday's Georgia Background," *Journal of Arizona History* 14 (Autumn 1973): 194–195.

17. Coulter, *Georgia*, 265.

18. Clement Eaton, *History of the Old South*, 2nd ed. (New York: Macmillan, 1966), 52–67, 388–415; Eugene D. Genovese, *The Slaveholders' Dilemma: Freedom and Progress in Southern Conservative Thought, 1820–1860* (Columbia: University of South Carolina Press, 1992); Mark M. Smith, *Debating Slavery: Economy and Society in the Antebellum American South* (New York: Cambridge University Press, 1998); William Kaufmann Scarborough, *Masters of the Big House: Elite Slaveholders of the Mid-Nineteenth Century South* (Baton Rouge: Louisiana State University Press, 2003); Edmund S. Morgan, *American Slavery, American Freedom* (New York: Norton, 2003).

19. W. J. Cash, *Mind of the South* (New York: Vintage, 1941), 3–60, challenged the "cavalier tradition" in a bold way, although others would later claim that it was already a straw man by the time he wrote. Perhaps, but it is still a part of popular history, and Cash's ideas have always stimulated controversy. Especially critical of his work was Eugene Genovese, *The World the Slaveholders Made: Two Essays in Interpretation* (New York: Vintage, 1969), 137–143, who reasserted the aristocratic pretensions of Southern slaveholders. C. Vann Woodward, *American Counterpoint: Slavery and Racism in the North-South Dialogue* (Boston: Little, Brown, 1971), 261–283, offered a balanced review of Cash. More recent literature suggests that the debate is not over, but Cash's point is especially relevant for the purposes of this work, and his critics merely underscore it. Bertram Wyatt-Brown, *Southern Honor: Ethics and Behavior in the Old South* (New York: Oxford University Press, 1982), passim, explores Southern notions of honor in depth, and McWhiney, *Cracker Culture*, is valuable to this general topic.

20. Cash, *Mind of the South*, 40.

21. Ibid., 30–49; Wyatt-Brown, *Southern Honor*, 88–114.

22. Wyatt-Brown, *Southern Honor*, 33–34, 89–92.

23. Sheldon Hackney, "Southern Violence," *American Historical Review* 74 (1969): 906–925; Dickson D. Bruce Jr., *Violence and Culture in the Antebellum South* (Austin: University of Texas Press, 1979); Edward L. Ayers, *Vengeance and Justice: Crime and Punishment*

in the 19th Century South (New York: Oxford University Press, 1984); Wyatt-Brown, *Southern Honor*, 368–369; McWhiney, *Cracker Culture*, 146–170.

24. Cash, *Mind of the South*, 44. Cash adds, "However careful they might be to walk softly, such men as these of the South were bound to come into conflict. And being what they were—simple, direct, and immensely personal—and their world being what it was—conflict with them could only mean immediate physical clashing, could only mean fisticuffs, the gouging ring, and knife and gun play."

25. Henry Holliday, MSR, USAC, RG 393, NARA.

26. Ibid.; Pendleton and Thomas, "Doc's Georgia Background," 202n.

27. Affidavit of witnesses, W. H. Powell and W. H. McKey, February 25, 1887, Mexican War Pensions, VA, RG 15, NARA.

28. License and Marriage Bond, Marriage Book C., p. 11; Minute Book A, pp. 62, 100, 132, Records of the Ordinary's Office, Spalding County, Georgia; Albert S. Pendleton Jr. and Susan McKey Thomas, *In Search of the Hollidays: The Story of Doc Holliday and His Holliday and McKey Families* (Valdosta, GA: Little River, 1973), 4, 13.

29. Pendleton and Thomas, *In Search of the Hollidays*, 13–14; Victoria Wilcox, "Mischievous Minor: From Lad to Lunger," *True West* 48 (November–December 2001): 19; Susan McKey Thomas Genealogical Notes. In 1838, Aaron Cloud constructed "Cloud's Tower," a 165-foot-high observation platform on Stone Mountain to attract attention to the area and to Andrew Johnson's hotel after the construction of a railroad west from Augusta. In 1849, the tower blew over in a windstorm and was replaced by a smaller edifice. David B. Freeman, *Carved in Stone: The History of Stone Mountain* (Macon, GA: Mercer University Press, 1997), 28–29.

30. Pendleton and Thomas, *In Search of the Hollidays*, 4; Deed Book A, pp. 52, 53, 56, 62, 457, 458, 615; Deed Book B, p. 167, Office of the Clerk of Superior Court, Spalding County, Georgia; Quimby Melton Jr., *History of Griffin* (Griffin, GA: Griffin Daily News, 1959), 43–50.

31. Alice Jane Holliday's obituary, written by Reverend N. B. Ousley for the *Valdosta South Georgia Watchman* in September 1866, clipping in the scrapbook of Anabelle Myddelton, a Valdosta school teacher, in the possession of Helen Hightower, Valdosta, Georgia.

32. Henry Burroughs Holliday Family Bible, Collections of the Christian Broadcasting Network, Virginia Beach, Virginia.

33. Ibid.

34. Ibid.; Baptismal Records, First Presbyterian Church, Griffin, Georgia; see also Wilcox, "Mischievous Minor," 19.

35. "Recollections of Mary Cowperwaite Fulton Holliday (Mrs. Robert Alexander Holliday, D.D.S.) Concerning John Henry Holliday, D.D.S., Collected and Transcribed by Carl Birger Olson between 1935 and 1940," typed manuscript, quoted in Tanner, *Family Portrait*, 13–14. This manuscript has been placed in the Karen Holliday Tanner Collection of Holliday family memorabilia and research materials at the Nita Stewart Haley Memorial Library and J. Evetts Haley History Center, Midland, Texas, which is under restriction for a period of ten years (from 1999) to allow Tanner to complete additional work on Holliday. As a result, the author has been unable to examine the Mary Fulton Holliday manuscript directly. However, letters from John T. Tanner to the author, January 1, 1999, and from Karen Holliday Tanner to the author, February 6, 1999, provided quotes from the document related to the cleft palate and other matters.

36. Tanner, *Family Portrait*, 15–16.

37. Fielding H. Garrison, *An Introduction to the History of Medicine*, 4th ed. (Philadelphia: Saunders, 1929), 505–506.

38. Joe Sam Robinson Jr. and D. W. Eastwood, "Publish or Perish—Crawford Long's Dilemma," *Southern Medical Journal* 65 (May 1972): 600–604. Welch is quoted in

Garrison, *Introduction to Medicine*, 505. See also F. K. Boland, *The First Anesthetic: The Story of Crawford Long* (Athens: University of Georgia Press, 1950), and Joseph Jacobs, *Some Personal Recollections and Private Correspondence of Dr. Crawford Williamson Long: Discoverer of Anaesthesia with Sulphuric Ether, Together with Documentary Proofs of His Priority in This Wonderful Discovery* (Atlanta: N.p., 1919), for the case supporting Long's claims.

39. In April 1852 (note date), Dr. Long presented a paper to the Georgia State Medical Society meeting in Savannah, in which he stated that he was "cautiously experimenting with ether as cases occurred." He stated, "Surgical operations are not of frequent occurrence in a country practice and especially in the practice of a young physician; yet I was fortunate enough to meet with two causes in which I could satisfactorily test the anesthetic power of ether." The cases involved "the extirpation of small tumors and the amputation of fingers and toes." No reference is made to cleft palate surgery, which would have been a major operation. Scrapbook, 105–109, File 1, Box 2, Crawford W. Long Collection, MS 49, University of Georgia Library, Athens, Georgia. See also Mrs. Frances Long Taylor to Dr. Garrett Quillian, August 20, 1921, describing Dr. Long's major operations between 1847 and 1877 in Boland, *First Anesthetic*, 73–75. Boland does say, "There must have been dozens of other cases." The Frances Long Taylor Papers, MS 1706, Box 2, File 2, UGA, contains a letterbook with references to other surgeries.

40. George Morris Dorrance, *The Operative Story of Cleft Palate* (Philadelphia: Saunders, 1933), 22–27. Dr. David Moline, an eminent dental surgeon and dental historian, in an interview with the author, July 29, 2004, pointed out that cleft palate surgery usually required several hours and was particularly difficult in the case of small children. Ether is an inhalation anesthesia. This meant that the surgeon would have to work in the airway while administering the anesthesia. Under the best of conditions this would have been an extremely risky and difficult operation in 1851 because of the small place where the surgery had to be done—in the case of an infant a very small place. It was not the kind of surgery two country doctors were likely to attempt, and, if they miraculously did so, it would have been major medical news and not something a physician, even then in the process of trying to gain recognition for his pioneering work in the use of ether as anesthesia as Long was, would have failed to publicize to the medical profession.

41. A. Vander Veer, "Cleft Palate," in *A Reference Handbook of the Medical Sciences*, edited by Albert H. Buck (New York: Wood, 1886), 2:180–184. Veer's comments on infant surgery are particularly interesting in light of the risks, complexity, and specialized tools involved. Dr. Moline, in an interview with the author, September 2, 2001, outlined the history of cleft palate surgery as well as its potential complications. He noted that surgery was usually attempted as early as possible because doctors believed that children would die without it, recuperative powers were greater, and speech impediments were less likely if surgery was done before speech patterns were begun.

42. M. F. Holliday manuscript, quoted in Tanner to the author, February 6, 1999; Tanner, *Family Portrait*, 16–18. A slight asymmetry in the lip is noticeable in Doc Holliday's dental school graduation photograph and is cited as evidence of a cleft palate.

43. Baptismal Record, First Presbyterian Church, Griffin, Georgia.

44. Tanner, *Family Portrait*, 17.

45. Coulter, *Georgia*, 309.

46. Northerners believed that slavery made white men cruel, violent, and lazy. Southerners believed that slavery acted as a leveler of white society by preventing the development of rigid social and economic class differences among whites.

47. Wiley Sword, *Southern Invincibility: A History of the Confederate Heart* (New York: St. Martin's Griffin, 1999), 8–28.

48. Quoted in Cash, *Mind of the South*, 73–74.

49. Pendleton and Thomas, *In Search of the Hollidays*, 13.

50. Tanner, *Family Portrait*, 26–27.

51. Marriage Certificate for Francisco E'Dalgo and Martha Freeman, June 12, 1854, Office of the Ordinary, Butts County, Georgia; Martha E'Dalgo, Confederate Widow's Pension File, Civil War Records Section, Georgia State Department of Archives and History, Atlanta, Georgia.

52. William Land McKey, Will and Related Documents, Will Book A, p. 26; Minute Book A, pp. 62, 100, 132; Docket Book A, p. 27; Guardianship Papers, p. 43, Record of the Office of the Ordinary, Spalding County, Georgia; *Griffin (Georgia) Independent South*, July 7, 1859.

53. Wyatt-Brown, *Southern Honor*, 140–148, 152–170.

54. Cash, *Mind of the South*, 72.

55. Sister Mary Melanie, "Family Memoirs."

56. Guardianship papers for Elisha Pritchard, p. 43, Office of the Ordinary, Spalding County, Georgia; Tanner; *Family Portrait*, 34.

57. Tanner, *Family Portrait*, 240.

58. James M. McPherson, *Battle Cry of Freedom: The Civil War Era* (New York: Oxford University Press, 1988), 195–196; James L. Huston, *The Panic of 1857 and the Coming of the Civil War* (Baton Rouge: Louisiana State University Press, 1987).

59. Melton, *History of Griffin*, 41–50.

60. Coulter, *Georgia*, 312–314.

61. Sister Mary Melanie, "Family Memoirs"; Wilcox, "Michievous Minor," 19; Patricia Jahns, *The Frontier World of Doc Holliday* (New York: Hastings House, 1957), 9–10.

62. Coulter, *Georgia*, 317–323.

63. Kenneth Coleman et al., *A History of Georgia* (Athens: University of Georgia Press, 1977), 187–188.

2. The World Turned Upside Down

1. Pleasant A. Stovall, *Robert Toombs: Statesman, Speaker, Soldier, Sage* (New York: Cassell, 1892); William Y. Thompson, *Robert Toombs of Georgia* (Baton Rouge: Louisiana State University, 1966); T. Conn Bryan, *Confederate Georgia* (Athens: University of Georgia Press, 1953), 14–18.

2. Jackie Kennedy, "Uncovering the Myth: Doc Holliday and His Griffin, GA, Home," *Georgia Backroads* 2 (Winter 2003), 37. Bill Dunn, a local historian, acquired a map of Camp Stephens drawn by Private Asbury H. Jackson, a Confederate soldier, that notes the location of Henry Holliday's second home in Spalding County.

3. Joseph E. Brown to Alexander H. Stephens, August 22, 1861, quoted in Ulrich Bonnell Phillips, ed., *The Correspondence of Robert Toombs, Alexander H. Stephens, and Howell Cobb* (New York: Da Capo, 1970), 574.

4. Robert Kennedy Holliday, John Stiles Holliday, James Taylor McKey, Thomas Sylvester McKey, William Harrison McKey, and Francisco E'Dalgo, Confederate Service Records, Civil War Records Section, Georgia State Department of Archives and History, Atlanta, Georgia.

5. Henry Burroughs Holliday, CSR, CWRS, GDAH; Patricia Jahns, *The Frontier World of Doc Holliday* (New York: Hastings House, 1957), 10–13.

6. Wiley Sword, *Southern Invincibility: A History of the Confederate Heart* (New York: St. Martin's Press, 1999), 64–65, notes the impact of the war on Southern women.

7. Karen Holliday Tanner, *Doc Holliday: A Family Portrait* (Norman: University of Oklahoma Press, 1998), 40–42; Jahns, *Frontier World*, 10–13. Especially useful for appraising the life of a child during the Civil War are James Marten, *The Children's Civil War* (Chapel Hill: University of North Carolina Press, 1998), passim, and Bertram Wyatt-Brown, *Southern Honor: Ethics and Behavior in the Old South* (New York: Oxford University Press, 1982), 133–162, 276–277.

8. Wyatt-Brown, *Southern Honor*, 51, 171, 241, 251–253.

9. Mark Caldwell, *The Last Crusade: The War on Consumption, 1862–1954* (New York: Atheneum, 1988), 17. Sheila M. Rothman, *Living in the Shadow of Death: Tuberculosis and the Social Experience of Illness in American History* (New York: Basic, 1994), 23–25, points out that decidedly different regimens were recommended for men and women with tuberculosis. While both sexes were considered "invalids," the treatment of women was consonant with their "domestic" roles. Rothman provides a detailed look at one New England woman's experience, pp. 77–127, which provides some insight into Alice Jane's experience as well.

10. Lillian McKey, "Record of Captain William Harrison McKey," unpublished manuscript prepared for the Valdosta Chapter of the United Daughters of the Confederacy, 1931–1935; William Harrison McKey, CSR, CWS, GDAH.

11. Henry B. Holliday, CSR, CWRS, GDAH; Compiled Military Service Record, Records of Confederate Soldiers Who Served in the Civil War, Record Group 109, National Archives and Records Administration, Washington, DC; Jahns, *Frontier World*, 10–13.

12. From the personal papers of Constance Knowles McKellar; Sister Mary Melanie, "Family Memoirs"; Victoria Wilcox, "Mischievous Minor: From Lad to Lunger," *True West* 48 (November–December 2001): 19.

13. James M. McPherson, *Battle Cry of Freedom: The Civil War Era* (New York: Oxford University Press, 1988), 671–674.

14. Peter Cozzens, *This Terrible Sound: The Battle of Chickamauga* (Urbana: University of Illinois Press, 1996), passim, presents the most detailed account of the events surrounding the battle of Chickamauga.

15. John B. Jones, quoted in McPherson, *Battle Cry of Freedom*, 681. For more detailed accounts, see Peter Cozzens, *The Shipwreck of Their Hopes: The Battles for Chattanooga* (Urbana: University of Illinois Press, 1994), and Jerry Korn, *The Fight for Chattanooga: Chickamauga to Missionary Ridge* (New York: Time-Life, 1985).

16. Mary Chesnut, quoted in McPherson, *Battle Cry of Freedom*, 681.

17. Deed Book C, pp. 641, 649, 651; Deed Book D, p. 218, Office of the Clerk of Superior Court, Spalding County, Georgia; Louis Schmeir, *Valdosta and Lowndes County: A Ray in the Sunbelt* (Northridge, CA: Windsor Publications, 1988), 22.

18. Jane Twitty Sheldon, *Pines and Pioneers: A History of Lowndes County, Georgia 1825–1900* (Atlanta, GA: Cherokee, 1976), 128–134.

19. *Valdosta South Georgia Times*, March 20, 1867.

20. Thannie Smith Wisenbaker, "First Impressions of Valdosta in 1865," 3, unpublished manuscript from the Mrs. Arthur Strom Collection, courtesy Susan McKey Thomas.

21. Deed Book B, p. 499, OCSP, Lowndes County, Georgia. The land was purchased on February 9, 1864, but it was not recorded until December 31, 1864. See also Albert S. Pendleton Jr. and Susan McKey Thomas, "Doc Holliday's Georgia Background," *Journal of Arizona History* 14 (Autumn 1973): 195–196.

22. William H. Nulty, *Confederate Florida: The Road to Olustee* (Tuscaloosa: University of Alabama Press, 1990); *The Battle of Olustee and the Olustee Battlefield Site* (Glen St. Mary's, FL: Olustee Battlefield Citizen Support Organization, n.d.).

23. Shelton, *Pines and Pioneers*, 148–149.

24. Tanner, *Family Portrait*, 45–46; Lee Kennett, *Marching through Georgia: The Story of Soldiers and Civilians during Sherman's Campaign* (New York: HarperCollins, 1995), 149.

25. McPherson, *Battle Cry of Freedom*, 747.

26. Sister Mary Melanie, "Family Memoirs," 2; Rita H. DeLorme, "Gunfighter 'Doc' Holliday, Sister M. Melanie Holliday, RSM; More Than a Pretty Love Story," *The Southern Cross*, December 9, 1999, reprinted in Rita H. DeLorme, *Memories and Milestones:*

Stories from the Archives (Savannah, GA: Monsignor Daniel J. Bourke Memorial Archives, Diocese of Savannah, 2001), 49.

27. Cobb to his wife, July 20, 1864, quoted in Phillips, *Correspondence*, 647.

28. McPherson, *Battle Cry of Freedom*, 774.

29. Aloysius Plaisance, O.S.B., "Emmeran Bliemel, O.S.B., Heroic Confederate Chaplain," *American Benedictine Review* 17 (1966): 209–216; Sister Mary Melanie, "Family Memoirs," 2.

30. Robert Kennedy Holliday to his wife, September 24, 1864, from the personal papers of Constance Knowles McKellar.

31. Sister Mary Melanie, "Family Memoirs," 2–3.

32. McPherson, *Battle Cry of Freedom*, 808.

33. Sister Mary Melanie, "Family Memoirs," 3; Burke Davis, *Sherman's March* (New York: Random House, 1980), 59–75; Kennett, *Marching through Georgia*, 258.

34. Deed Book B, p. 505, OCSP, Lowndes County, Georgia.

35. Lillian McKey, "Record of Thomas Sylvester McKey," unpublished manuscript prepared for the Valdosta Chapter of the United Daughters of the Confederacy; Thomas S. McKey, CSR, CWRS, GDAH.

36. Lilian McKey, "Personal and Family History," papers from the Martha Wiseman McKey Collection, Valdosta, Georgia, including an interview with W. A. "Zan" Griffith. John Myers Myers, *Doc Holliday* (Boston: Little, Brown, 1955), 14–15, emphasizes the boldness of this act, given the disorderly state of affairs, but notes, "It was alike typical of Doc that he was confident of being able to take care of himself, in the face of the circumstances, and that he returned with both horse and uncle in due time." Sylvia D. Lynch, *Aristocracy's Outlaw: The Doc Holliday Story* (New Tazewell, TN: Iris Press, 1994), 32, adds that "the incident is a dramatic foreshadowing of the character that would become John Holliday, the man."

37. William H. McKey, James McKey, Francisco E'Dalgo, John S. Holliday, George Holliday, Robert K. Holliday, CSRs, CWS, GDAH; Sister Mary Melanie, "Family Memoirs," 3; Lillian Henderson, comp., *Roster of the Confederate Soldiers of Georgia* (Hapeville, GA: Longrine and Porter, 1964), 1:659–660, 834, 2:268, 3:285, 509.

38. Alan Conway, *The Reconstruction of Georgia* (Minneapolis: University of Minnesota Press, 1966), 20.

39. Shelton, *Pines and Pioneers*, 150, 154–156; Records of the Assistant Commissioner for the State of Georgia, Bureau of Refugees, Freedmen, and Abandoned Lands, 1865–1869, RG 105, NARA; Elaine C. Everly, Old Military Branch, Military Archives Division, NARA, to the author, June 3, 1974; Paul A. Cimbala, *Under the Guardianship of the Nation: The Freedman's Bureau and the Reconstruction of Georgia, 1865–1870* (Athens: University of Georgia Press, 1997), 1–10.

40. Shelton, *Pines and Pioneers*, 151.

41. Wisenbaker, "First Impressions," 33–36.

42. Deed Book G, pp. 29, 30, 68–70 OCSP, Hamilton County, Florida; *Valdosta (Georgia) Daily Times*, March 4, 1932.

43. Schmier, *Valdosta*, 25.

44. Wisenbaker, "First Impressions," 37.

45. Wisenbaker, "First Impressions," 53–54; Shelton, *Pines and Pioneers*, 164–166; Lewis Beauregard Pendleton, *Echo of Drums* (New York: Schoen Printing, 1938), 180; Constance Pendleton, ed., *Confederate Memoirs: Early Life and Family History William Frederick Pendleton, Mary Lawson Young Pendleton* (Bryn Athyn, PA: N.p., 1958), 85.

46. The files of the Lowndes County Historical Society include a clipping from "The South's Last Boys in Gray," concerning Henry Taylor Dowling, who was from Lowndes County. Included is a letter from Dr. Grady E. Black, January 9, 1976. Black grew up in

Valdosta and recalled, "Another interesting fact is that he [Dowling] and my grandmother were well acquainted with the western gunfighter, 'Doc' Holliday. . . . As a child I remember hearing stories about his being at parties and my grandmother dancing with Doc Holliday." Entry 646, Register of Civilian Agents on Duty in Georgia, 1865–1867, Records Bureau of Refugees, Freedmen, and Abandoned Lands, RG 105, NARA; Schmeir, *Valdosta*, 25.

47. Undated clipping in the scrapbook of Annabelle Myddleton (believed to have been taken from the *Valdosta Watchman*, an early newspaper). Helen Hightower Collection, reprinted in Albert S. Pendleton and Susan McKey Thomas, *In Search of the Hollidays: The Story of Doc Holliday and His Holliday and McKey Families* (Valdosta, GA: Little River, 1973), 11. Myddleton was a teacher who arrived about 1865 and taught from her home. Wisenbaker, "First Impressions," 40.

48. Rev. N. B. Ousley, General Affidavit, February 6, 1894, Rachel Holliday, Widow's Pension File, Veteran's Bureau records, RG 15, NARA, affirms the date of marriage as December 18, 1866. Pendleton and Thomas, "Doc's Georgia Background," 203n, indicate that the courthouse records of this marriage were destroyed by fire. See also Martin Register, "In Search of Doc Holliday in Valdosta, GA," *Georgia Backroads* 2 (Spring 2003): 48.

49. *Valdosta Daily Times*, August 29, 1931;   Wyatt-Brown, *Southern Honor*, 164.

50. *Valdosta Daily Times*, December 31, 1898 (taken from the *Macon Telegraph*).

51. *Thomas S. McKey v. H. B. Holliday*, Guardian, Equity, January 23, 1873, Deed Book F, p. 33, OCSC, Spalding County, contains "a true extract from the minutes of the Court of Lowndes County, Georgia this 2nd day of February, 1870." Deed Book F, p. 94, dated March 28, 1873, contains the decision of the jury in Lowndes County, dated May 20, 1863, setting up the requirement for the petition dividing the Iron Front building.

52. Wisenbaker, "First Impressions."

53. Schmier, *Valdosta*, 25.

54. Entry 646, RCADG, 1865–1867, RBRFAL, RG 105, NARA.

55. The reorganization of the Freedman's Bureau is covered in detail in Cimbala, *Under the Guardianship of the Nation*. See also E. Merton Coulter, *Georgia: A Short History* (Athens: University of Georgia Press, 1947), 364–368, for a general description of the general changes ushered in by the Reconstruction. Elaine C. Everly, Old Military Branch, NARA, to the author, June 3, 1974, reported that Henry Holliday's career as agent was "rather uneventful." A visit to the National Archives and examination of both bureau records (RG 105) and military records for Georgia (RG 393) confirmed that Holliday was efficient and worked to assist freedmen, including complaints against white citizens, working to secure a church for freedmen, and interceding on behalf of a freedman who was, in his opinion, too severely punished for an offense. Holliday to headquarters, February 2, April 17, May 3, May 11, 1867, Register of Letters Received, Records of the Third Military District, Georgia, United States Army Commands, RG 393, NARA; Shelton, *Pines and Pioneers*, 158.

56. Conway, *Reconstruction of Georgia*, 156–161.

57. *Valdosta South Georgia Times*, April 8, 1868; Wisenbaker, "First Impressions," 54. The *Quitman (Georgia) Banner*, April 10, 1868, even suggested that the Republicans were themselves responsible, saying, "The negroes fled precipitately in every direction upon learning the discovery, but the leaders appeared perfectly unconcerned. It is the opinion of the majority of the citizens here that it was placed there designedly for political purposes. It was unquestionably a fine stroke for party capital, but they took every possible care for their safety by placing the smallest possible quantity of powder in the keg." See also the *Savannah (Georgia) News and Herald*, April 7, 10, 1868.

58. *South Georgia Times*, April 8, 1868.

59. Shelton, *Pines and Pioneers*, 160–161; *Savannah News and Herald*, April 7, 10, 1868. On April 10, the *News and Herald*, while condemning the incident, added, "The idea

that the young men of Valdosta would attempt with a handful of powder to blow up such a mass of villainy, ignorance, and vagabondism as must have composed Booby's auditory, is perfectly absurd—especially when it is considered that the Guy Fawkes of the enterprise in exploding the powder to which no train or fuse was set, must necessarily have blown himself up with the rest. However fearless and self sacrificing the projector of such a plot might be, it is utterly preposterous to suppose that any white man would be willing to be blown to Ballahack or anywhere else in such company."

60. *South Georgia Times*, April 15, 1868; *Savannah News and Herald*, April 15, 20, 1868; see also Shelton, *Pines and Pioneers*, 161–162.

61. *Savannah News and Herald*, May 9, 1868; *South Georgia Times*, May 13, 1868; Shelton, *Pines and Pioneers*, 162–163; Bench Docket, May Term, 1868, Lowndes County Superior Court, bearing the notation "May Term, 1873, Indictment missing—probably disposed of heretofore." Some of the critical military records appear to have been destroyed. See records, Third Military District, 1867–1868, LR, Box 6, RG 393, NARA. No additional information has been found on Henry Holliday. Only Henry Burroughs Holliday appears in the 1870 census for Lowndes County.

62. Wisenbaker, "First Impressions," 54, says that "several of the young men who were at the head of this movement left town but returned later on," and Zan Griffith, Doc's friend, said, "[H]e, along with several others, endeavored to blow up the courthouse when the Freedmen's Bureau had its headquarters there," quoted in Pendleton and Thomas, "Doc's Georgia Background," 192; *South Georgia Times*, May 20, 1868; Wilcox, "Mischievous Minor," 20. Tanner, *Family Portrait*, 60–61, places John Henry's trip to Jonesboro after the celebrated shooting at the Withlacoochee (discussed in chapter 2) rather than after the courthouse incident. For reasons explored in chapter 3, the courthouse episode seems a more likely cause.

63. Tanner, *Family Portrait*, 61.

64. James E. Sefton, *The United States Army and Reconstruction, 1865–1877* (Baton Rouge: Louisiana State University Press, 1967), 198–205.

65. April 17, 1869, Deed Book Q, pp. 393, 394, OCSC, Lowndes County, Georgia.

66. Helen S. Haines and Robert Thorburn, *75 Years of Dentistry: Diamond Jubilee Volume of the Florida State Dental Association* (Gainesville: University of Florida Press, 1960), 45–46; *Lake City (Florida) Citizen-Recorder*, May 1, 1903; Wisenbaker, "First Impressions," 50; Susan McKey Thomas to the author, November 24, 1974, author's files; "List of Matriculants, March 1, 1867," *Dental Times: A Quarterly Journal of Dental Science* (Spring 1867): 162.

67. George Holliday was married to Mary E. Wright on November 2, 1869. See *Atlanta Constitution*, December 21, 1915, and "Resolutions Passed in Honor of George Henry Holliday by the Board of Stewards of the First M. E. Church, Atlanta, Georgia, February 14, 1916," copy in the McKellar Collection. Tanner, *Family Portrait*, 60–61, says that, based on the M. F. Holliday manuscript, John Henry's uncle, Dr. John Stiles Holliday, had urged his nephew to go into dentistry during the time of his earlier Jonesboro stay.

68. J. Thomas Sharf and Thompson Westcott, *History of Philadelphia* (Philadelphia: L. H. Everts, 1884), 2:1662–1663; Milton B. Asbell, *A Century of Dentistry: A History of the University of Pennsylvania School of Dental Medicine, 1878–1978* (Philadelphia: University of Pennsylvania Press, 1977), 8; "Seventeenth Annual Announcement of the Pennsylvania College of Dental Surgery" (Philadelphia: Pennsylvania College of Dental Surgery, 1872), 2, 4, 5, 10, 11. The announcement may also be found in the *Dental Times* 8 (April 1872): 186–189. The detailed accounting of John Henry's curriculum is found in the *Dental Times* 8 (April 1872): 148–150.

69. John Henry's early biographers, Myers, *Doc Holliday*, 21, and Jahns, *Frontier World*, 31, stated that he attended dental school in Baltimore, and this was the standard view.

Joseph W. Looper, "John Henry Holliday, DDS: Georgia's Most Famous Dentist," *Journal of the American Dental Association* 87 (August 1973), 252, continued this view. However, the discovery of the photograph of young John Henry taken at the time of his graduation and bearing the name of a Philadelphia photographer raised the possibility that he attended school there. Dr. L. C. Holtzendorff, a dentist from Valdosta, Georgia, who had worked with Pendleton and Thomas during their research for *In Search of the Hollidays*, pursued the matter and first uncovered the Philadelphia connection. See Holtzendorff's letter to the editor, *Journal of the American Dental Association* 88 (January 1974): 30. It is supposed that the reason for the Baltimore connection is the report that Holliday sailed from Savannah to Baltimore en route to dental school. Later, other, more contemporary references to Philadelphia would be found in newspaper accounts of Holliday's life and career.

70. Tanner, *Family Portrait*, 63, 252n, reports that John Henry prepared a crown of pure swaged gold for a six-year-old girl that remained intact until the child died at the age of 102 in 1967. Dr. D. D. Allison confirmed her story with the Pierre Fouchard Academy in 1963, and later, on July 25, 1995, was interviewed by Tanner. The best evidence that John Henry practiced with Dr. Frink is found in the records of the Estate of Henry J. Morgan, Voucher 32, which show payment of $21 to John H. Holliday for filling six teeth and extracting three for Corinthia Morgan, on October 18, 1871, OCSC, p. 765. The *Valdosta Daily Times*, March 14, 1934, acknowledged Miss Morgan as one of the earliest settlers and an important source of information on early Valdosta. Unfortunately, she apparently recorded little of what she knew.

71. "Seventeenth Annual Announcement of the Pennsylvania College of Dental Surgery," 12; *Philadelphia Inquirer*, March 2, 1872; see also "Qualifications for Graduation," *Dental Times* 8 (January 1871): 150.

72. Conway, *Reconstruction of Georgia*, 201–202.

73. Wisenbaker, "First Impressions," 50; February 6, 1872, Deed Book C, pp. 654–655, OCSC, Lowndes County, Georgia.

74. Mary Katharine Harony Cummings, née Kate Elder, the woman with whom John Henry was involved during much of his Western career, wrote of John Henry, "After his graduation he remained in Philadelphia for a while, then went to St. Louis where he opened his office near the Planter's Hotel on Fourth Street." Typescript of Recollections of Mary Katharine Cummings as Given to Anton Mazzonovich, p. 1, original in the Kevin J. Mulkins Collection. John Henry had no office on Fourth, but August Jameson Fuches Jr. did. Dr. Fuches, John Henry's classmate, was from St. Louis. His thesis was on the same topic as John Henry's, diseases of the teeth. Fuches's preceptor was Dr. Homer Judd, who had his office at 819 Locust Street, St. Louis. The 1873 St. Louis City directory also indicates that Judd was the president of the Missouri Dental College. With this connection, the new Dr. Fuches immediately opened an office at 722 South Fourth Street. The Fourth Street reference in Kate's recollections is thus more than striking.

75. The first significant Hungarian immigration to Iowa came as the result of the 1848–1850 revolution, which attempted to separate Hungary from the Hapsburg empire. Laslo Ujhazi led a group of refugees to Decatur County in southern Iowa, where they acquired thousands of acres and formed New Buda. The colony did not last, but Hungarian immigrants continued to move into Iowa, with a sizable number settling in Davenport. See Bela Vassady, "A Colony of Hungarian Forty-eighters in Iowa," *The Annals of Iowa* 51 (Summer 1991): 26–52; Hildegard Binder Johnson, *German Forty-eighters in Davenport* (Iowa City: State Historical Society of Iowa, 1946). Michael Harony and his wife, Katharina Baldizar Harony and their children, including the daughter who would become Kate Elder, settled in Davenport in 1863; just when the family arrived in the United States is less clear. Mrs. Ernest L. Beckwith to Glenn G. Boyer, January 22, 1977, quoted in Glenn G. Boyer, "On the Trail of Big Nosed Kate," *Real West* 24 (March 1981): 17–18, and verified with Arthur W. Bork. See also Patrick A. Bowmaster, "A Fresh Look at 'Big Nose Kate,'"

Quarterly of the National Association for Outlaw and Lawman History 22 (July–September 1998): 12–24.

76. Papers relating to the Estate of Dr. Michael Harony, Case File No. 0453, County Court, Scott County, Iowa, contain the details of the guardianship of the Harony minor children under both Gustavus Susemihl and Otto Smith. Susemihl was married to Dr. Harony's half-sister, Amelia; Otto Smith was the family attorney.

77. Beckwith to Boyer, January 22, 1977, quoted in Boyer, "Big Nosed Kate," p. 17, stated emphatically that Kate said that she assumed the name Kate Fisher. The same information from the family was also provided to Arthur W. Bork, as outlined in Bork to Susan McKey Thomas, May 26, 1977, copy in the author's files. Kate Fisher was well known as the "best of 'Mazeppas'" in the late 1860s and early 1870s. *Mazeppa, or the Wild Horse of Tartary* was a popular and scandalous play at the time. See the *Brooklyn (New York) Eagle*, July 15, 1918.

78. In U.S. Census, 1870, St. Louis, Ward Five, p. 821, M593, Reel 814, NARA. Kate is listed as "about 23," which would be older than she actually was if reported accurately. She also lists her birthplace as "Baden" rather than Hungary, but this does not seem farfetched for a runaway with an accent in a community where Germans were plentiful.

79. Several different reminiscences by Kate exist. Cummings, Mazzanovich typescript, 1, is critical for the St. Louis period. Mazzanovich also prepared a series of columns based on her recollections for the *Bisbee (Arizona) Brewery Gulch Gazette*, April 15, 22, 29, June 3, 1932. The April 22 column "John H. (Doc) Holliday" and the June 3 column "Big Nosed Kate" are the most relevant to this portion of the story. Joe Chisholm's unpublished manuscript, "Tombstone's Tale (The Truth of Helldorado)," typescript in the Jack Burrows Collection, included much of the Mazzanovich material, but Chisholm added some information from his interviews with her. Arthur W. Bork also took down Kate's story, which was eventually published as Arthur W. Bork and Glenn G. Boyer, "The O.K. Corral Fight at Tombstone: A Footnote by Kate Elder," *Arizona and the West* 19 (Spring 1977): 75–84, but it did not mention the early years, nor did her letter to her niece, Lillie Raffert, March 18, 1940, copy in the author's file. The Raffert letter was published in Bob Boze Bell, *The Illustrated Life of Doc Holliday* (Phoenix, AZ: Tri Star–Boze Publications, 1994), 107–110.

80. In all her various accounts cited earlier, and in a few other fragments, Kate misremembered dates (not an uncommon failing in old-timer reminiscences). Her accounts are sometimes inaccurate and seem duplicitous at times, as if she wished to cover up parts of her past or vent decades-old anger, but, even with the confusion she reveals knowledge that could not be chance. In this case, for instance, she said that John Henry went home to claim his grandmother's inheritance, rather than his mother's, but the inheritance is a milestone hard to dismiss. See Cummings Mazzanovich typescript.

81. Tanner, *Family Portrait*, 67–72.

82. H. Herbert Johnson, ed., *Biographies of Past Presidents of the Georgia State Dental Society* (Atlanta: Georgia State Dental Society, 1926), 20; Georgia Dental Association, *History of Dentistry in Georgia* (Macon, GA: Southern Press, 1962), 23–26, 34–35, 37, 40.

83. Tanner, *Family Portrait*, 72–74. "John H. Haliday, Atlanta" was listed as practicing dentistry in Georgia before August 24, 1872, in the *Columbus Daily Sun*, April 2, 1873.

84. Deed Book F, p. 95, OCSC, Spalding County, Georgia.

85. Tanner, *Family Portrait*, 69.

3. Gone to Texas

1. *Atlanta Constitution*, January 4, 1873. Dr. Ford announced his return to the city in the *Constitution*, April 11, 1873. In May, he was elected president of the Georgia State Dental Society, and in his opening address, he announced that he had made the treatment of children's teeth a specialty, see Georgia Dental Association, *History of Dentistry in Georgia*

(Macon, GA: Southern Press, 1962), 47. He later moved his office from Whitehall to the corner of Broad and Alabama, *Atlanta Constitution*, June 1, 1873. That summer he went north to attend yet another convention and returned in September. *Atlanta Constitution*, September 28, 1873. But his health continued to deteriorate.

2. See also *Atlanta Constitution*, December 29, 1872.

3. Martha Anne Holliday (Sister Mary Melanie), "Memoirs of the Holliday Family in Georgia," unpublished manuscript, Catherine Holliday Neuhoff Collection, 3.

4. Mrs. Martha E'Dalgo, Affidavit, April 17, 1891, and supporting documents, Francisco E'Dalgo, Widow's Pension File, Confederate Service Records, Civil War Records Section, Georgia State Department of Archives and History, Atlanta, Georgia; Victoria Wilcox, "Mischievous Minor: From Lad to Lunger, *True West* 48 (November–December 2001): 21; Angeline Delegal to Susan McKey Thomas, January 10, 28, 1995. E'Dalgo's gravestone indicates that he was a Mason.

5. Deed Book F, pp. 95–96, Office of the Clerk of Superior Court, Spalding County, Georgia.

6. *Griffin (Georgia) News*, August 10, 1872.

7. *Griffin News*, August 4, 1872.

8. Judge L. P. Goodrich wrote in a 1940 article for the *Griffin News* that his father had told him that John Henry practiced dentistry in Griffin, copy of undated article provided to the author by Bill Dunn, and Quimby Melton Jr., *History of Griffin* (Griffin, GA: Griffin Daily News, 1959), 45, also says that he did. Jackie Kennedy, "Uncovering the Myth: Doc Holliday and His Griffin, GA Home," *Georgia Backroads* 2 (Winter 2003): 39, details the evidence of a dental office in the building. John Henry was certainly in Griffin in November when he registered his deed to his portion of the Iron Front Building, Deed Book F, p. 1, OCSC, Spalding County, Georgia. He was almost certainly not living with John Stiles Holliday at this point, because on December 20, 1872, he was registered at the National Hotel. *Atlanta Constitution*, December 21, 1872. He therefore had time to have practiced in Griffin briefly. However, when Henry conveyed the property held under guardianship to John Henry in September, he was listed as a resident of the "County of Fulton" and when John Henry registered at the National in December, he gave his address as "the city." If he did practice in Griffin, then he most likely did so between September and December 1872, or after he sold his property there in January 1873.

9. *Griffin News*, December 13, 1872.

10. *The State of Georgia v. Lee Smith*, Keeping a Gaming Table, April Term, 1872, Fulton County Superior Court. Lee Smith, age twenty-six, was keeping a saloon in Ward One when the census taker came in 1870. U.S. Census, 1870, p. 188, M593, Reel 151, National Archives and Records Administration, Washington, DC. His saloon was at 13 Peachtree, according to the 1870 *Atlanta City Directory*. A summary of Smith's employment is found in Gene Carlisle, *Why Doc Holliday Left Georgia* (Macon, GA: Carl Isle, 2004), 115–118; see also *Atlanta Constitution*, March 10, August 24, 1872; *Griffin News*, September 11, 1872.

11. Ann Fabian, *Card Sharps, Dream Books, and Bucket Shops: Gambling in 19th-Century America* (Ithaca, NY: Cornell University Press, 1990), 21.

12. Ibid. Jonathan Harrington Green, *An Exposure of the Arts and Miseries of Gambling, Designed Especially As a Warning to the Youthful and Inexperienced against the Evils of That Odious and Destructive Vice* (Philadelphia: N.p., 1847), 217–219, warned that a man "would act more rationally and correctly to burn his money than to bet it on faro." The problem, nineteenth-century observers noted, was that it was virtually impossible to find an honest faro game. Nevertheless, it remained very popular.

13. John R. Sanders, "Faro: Favorite Gambling Game of the Frontier," *Wild West* (October 1996).

14. *Atlanta Daily Sun*, May 28, 1872; *State v. Lee Smith*, Assault with Intent to Murder, Fulton County Superior Court; Carlisle, *Why Doc Left*, 116–117.

15. Carlisle, *Why Doc Left*, 117–118.

16. Karen Holliday Tanner, *Doc Holliday: A Family Portrait* (Norman: University of Oklahoma Press, 1998), 48–49, 58–60, 70–71, 88–89, 92, based on Sophie Walton Murphy, "Recollections of Sophie Walton, 1930–32, as told to Carl Birger Olson," typed manuscript, in the Karen Holliday Tanner Collection, Nita Stewart Haley Memorial Library and J. Evetts Haley History Center, Midland, Texas (restricted collection), says that Sophie Walton, a mulatto servant in the John Stiles Holliday household, taught the Holliday children, including John Henry after he moved into his uncle's household, to play cards. This is also detailed in Tanner to Susan McKey Thomas, July 17, 1994. Walton reportedly joined the Holliday household in 1864, after her owner, "Mr. Walton," could no longer care for her. She was eight years old at the time, which would make her five years younger than John Henry, and only sixteen when he moved into his uncle's house. Since she joined the family at eight, some question does arise as to where she learned the games she taught the boys. While she could have picked up the games and even shared them with the Holliday boys, John Henry, at twenty-one, was almost certainly a gambler by the time he arrived at John Stiles Holliday's home. Basic gambling games were a part of the education of boys in the South at the time. Also troubling is that Sophie Walton does not appear in the household of John Stiles Holliday in the U.S. census for 1870 or for 1880. "M[artha] A. Fuller," a black female servant, age twenty-five, and a twelve-year-old male mulatto servant named "Jno. Jones" are listed in the Holliday household in 1870, U.S. Census, 1870, Fourth Ward, Atlanta, Georgia, p. 96, M593, Reel 151, NARA; Martha Fuller and B. F. Charles, a seven-year-old black female appear in the 1880 census, U.S. Census for 1880, Fourth Ward, Atlanta, Georgia, T-9–148, p. 2. Much appreciated was Karen Tanner to the author, February 6, 18, 2004, for more information on the Walton recollections. For information on Robert A. Holliday, see "Nineteenth Annual Announcement of the Pennsylvania College of Dental Surgery" (Philadelphia: Pennsylvania College of Dental Surgery, 1874), 12; Tanner, *Family Portrait*, 75–77. Robert was older than John Henry and had worked in his father's grocery business.

17. *Atlanta Constitution*, November 10, 11, 1906; "History of the Atlanta Dental Supply Co.," from the personal papers of Constance Knowles McKellar, 9; *The Asodecoan, 1934* (Atlanta, GA: Senior Class of the Atlanta Southern Dental College, 1934), 4–6. He was credited with persuading the trustees of the Atlanta Medical College to establish the Atlanta Southern Dental College in 1887, the year that John Henry died. In 1894, he moved to New Orleans, where he operated a dental supply company. He was also instrumental in establishing the New Orleans College of Dentistry in 1899, which later became the dental department of the school of medicine at Tulane University. He returned to Atlanta in about 1904 and died in 1906.

18. *Valdosta (Georgia) Daily Times*, June 24, 1882.

19. Sheila M. Rothman, *Living in the Shadow of Death: Tuberculosis and the Social Experience of Illness in American History* (New York: Basic, 1994), 16.

20. *Griffin News*, December 1, 1872.

21. *Griffin News*, April 19, 1873.

22. "Ford," in *Biographies of Past Presidents of the Georgia State Dental Society*, edited by H. Herbert Johnson (Atlanta: Georgia State Dental Society, 1926), 20; Dr. Arthur C. Ford Collection, Atlanta Historical Society, Atlanta, Georgia.

23. Henry I. Bowditch, "Consumption in America," *Atlantic Monthly* (January–March 1869), reprinted in Barbara Gutmann Rosenkrantz, ed., *From Consumption to Tuberculosis: A Documentary History* (New York: Galand, 1994), 71; René J. Dubos and Jean Dubos, *The White Plague: Tuberculosis, Man, and Society* (New Brunswick, NJ: Rutgers University Press, 1987), 63–66; Mark Caldwell, *The Last Crusade: The War on Consumption, 1862–1954* (New York: Atheneum, 1988), 17.

24. John William Rogers, *The Lusty Texans of Dallas* (New York: Dutton, 1951).

25. John Abbott, "Robert Holliday: Restoring a Proud Family Name," *The Holliday House Gazette* (Winter 1998): 5–6; Rita H. DeLorme, "Gunfighter 'Doc' Holliday, Sister M. Melanie Holliday, RSM; More Than a Pretty Love Story," *The Southern Cross*, December 9, 1999, reprinted in Rita H. DeLorme, *Memories and Milestones: Stories from the Archives* (Savannah, GA: Monsignor Daniel J. Bark Memorial Archives, Diocese of Savannah, 2001), 50–51; *Atlanta Constitution*, July 2, 1994; Victoria Wilcox to the author, January 29, 1999; Teresa Green to the author, April 23, 2003; O'Connell, *Irish Roots of Gone with the Wind*, 82–85. Pat Jahns to Lillian McKey, February 17, 1951, copies from the private papers of Susan McKey Thomas, is a response to Miss McKey, which makes it clear just how protective the family was. Jahns also discusses this in a letter to Susan McKey Thomas, February 17, 1975. See also chapter 12.

26. Bertram Wyatt-Brown, *Southern Honor: Ethics and Behavior in the Old South* (New York: Oxford University Press, 1982), 217–218. In fact, cousinly marriages appear to have increased between 1861 and 1880 as an effort to concentrate wealth after suffering the pressures of war and Reconstruction. See also Wilcox, "Mischievous Minor," 20–21; Patricia Jahns, *The Frontier World of Doc Holliday* (New York: Hastings House, 1957), 24–25.

27. The best account of what happened to the letters is provided in an interview by Victoria Wilcox with Carolyn Holliday Manley of Decatur, Georgia, the Holliday relative who had the trunk containing the letters in her possession for a time and believed she would inherit the letters from Mattie's sister, Marie, in due course. But Mattie's sister retrieved the trunk and burned the letters "to keep her sister Mattie's personal life personal." Victoria Wilcox to the author, January 29, 1999.

28. Ronald Yeomans, telephone interview with the author, June 17, 2004, who was told by an uncle that his great-grandfather, born in 1873 or 1874, was John Henry's son. He was adopted under the name Jones. Yeomans also said that his uncle cautioned him not to "spread it around." Mary McVicar, who operates the museum on the site of Mannie Hyman's Saloon in Leadville, Colorado, reported that a young man came into her museum asking questions about Doc Holliday. He then showed her a family Bible that contained a sheet of onionskin paper on which was written the story of a woman from Georgia who went to Missouri, had a child (a girl), and returned to Georgia after placing the child with a couple who had no children, stipulating only that the child be named Alice Mary or Mary Alice. The father was said to be John Henry Holliday. When the child was about six, a rather handsome Southern-sounding gentleman stopped at the couple's home in Arkansas (where they had moved) and spoke with the child and walked her around the town on his horse, then left without ever returning. Mary McVicar to the author, June 28, 2004. In 1975, Susan McKey Thomas was also told that Doc fathered a daughter who grew up in California. Notes from the private papers of Susan McKey Thomas. Of the three stories, the Yeomans account is the most plausible, but none of them can be documented.

29. After the war, George Holliday had entered the grocery business with R. W. Tidwell in Atlanta. Later, John Stiles Holliday, after moving to Atlanta, joined this enterprise. R. W. Tidwell was either the son or nephew of Miles M. Tidwell, a Fayetteville attorney. Miles's daughter, Sarah, or "Sallie C." as she was listed in the 1870 census, was about nineteen when John Henry returned to Georgia. U.S. Census, 1870, Fayetteville, Georgia, p. 2, M593, Reel 149, NARA. Tanner quotes from "Recollections of Mary Cowperwaite Fulton Holliday (Mrs. Robert Alexander Holliday, DDS) Concerning John Henry Holliday, DDS, Collected and Transcribed by Carl Birger Olson between 1935 and 1940," typed manuscript, 6, as follows, "You asked about 'special' young ladies. I recall hearing only of one. She was one of the Tidwell girls, Sarah or Sallie. She was a niece, I believe, of Dr. Holliday's partner." Tanner believes, and it is plausible, that Sallie may have been R. W.'s sister. Karen Holliday Tanner to the author, February 6, 1999; see also John D. Tanner to the author, January 1, 1999.

30. Tanner, *Family Portrait*, 79–81, drawing from the recollections of M. C. F. Holliday and Sophie Walton.

31. Ibid., 80–81. This account is consistent with other accounts. Jahns, *Frontier World*, 40–42, details the itinerary from Atlanta to Dallas, using the *Atlanta Constitution*, July 15, 1871, and other biographers have followed suit.

32. *Bainbridge (Georgia) Semi-Weekly Democrat*, January 26, 1872, announced that "Maj. Holliday was elected Mayor of Valdosta last Saturday."

33. William Barclay Masterson, "Famous Gunfighters of the Western Frontier: Doc Holliday," *Human Life* (May 1907): 5.

34. Ibid. Masterson's account has the advantage of coming from Holliday. Whether Bat—or Holliday—embellished it is another question. For the record, Bat himself said, "While he never boasted about the killing of the negroes down in Georgia, he was nevertheless regarded by his new-made Texas acquaintances as a man with a record."

35. "Doc Holliday, as told by Mr. Moore, Nov. 1926," Files, Arizona Historical Society, Tucson, Arizona.

36. Joe Lineburger to the author, June 17, 2004. Lineburger says that his grandmother, whose great-aunt was Rachel Holliday, thought of Doc as a drunk and said that after the shooting "it got so hot locally he had to leave."

37. Mrs. J. K. (Clyde McKey) White, interview by Albert S. Pendleton Jr., September 21, 1972, quoted in Albert S. Pendleton Jr. and Susan McKey Thomas, *In Search of the Hollidays: The Story of Doc Holliday and His Holliday and McKey Families* (Valdosta, GA: Little River, 1973), 33.

38. *Valdosta Daily Times*, August 29, 1931; see also J. F. DeLacy to Robert N. Mullin, January 9, 1949, Stuart N. Lake Collection, Box 10, Huntington Library, San Marino, California. It is worth noting that if John Henry did kill someone, Tom McKey would have been an accessory, which would have given him another reason to minimize the incident. The Withlacoochee River was the boundary of the McKey property and the county line between Lowndes County and Brooks County. The only shooting that bears any resemblance to the incident in question was reported in the *Quitman (Georgia) Banner*, May 28, 1869 (Quitman was the county seat of Brooks County). The article stated that the body of a black man had been found on a "small creek about seven miles from Quitman." The body "was found to be literally riddled with buckshot, eleven of which had struck the unfortunate man in the body and arms." The man had apparently been killed while "striking for fish," but no clue was found as to the perpetrators. No further evidence has been found on the case, but if it was the fabled incident it occurred before the McKeys bought the property, and it certainly was not the occasion for John Henry's flight west.

39. Jack McKey to Victoria Wilcox, two undated letters and a drawing of "the Hell Bitch," as reconstructed from the scabbard. Jack McKey is Tom McKey's grandson.

40. Gary Cartwright, *Galveston: A History of the Island* (Austin: Texas Christian University Press, 1998), 118–129.

41. Lillian McKey, "Personal and Family History," papers from the Martha Wiseman McKey Collection, Valdosta, Georgia. Jonathan Leval McKey apparently settled in Texas about 1858. He and his wife had five children, although two died young. He joined the Third Texas Cavalry, commanded by Marcus H. Cansler, as a sergeant in June 1861, but quickly resigned in July for health reasons. He continued in service as a private until September. Cansler also resigned his commission in August 1861, and Charles H. Featherstone succeeded him. Afterward, McKey applied for compensation for "Services in Captain Featherstone's Company," in which enterprise Cansler had power of attorney. By 1870, the ravages of the war and reconstruction had seriously depleted his resources, but he eventually rebuilt his fortunes. His obituary from the *Brenham (Texas) Daily Banner* said: "John L. McKey has been a conspicuous figure in his country ever since the civil war. By close attention to business and the strictest economy, he amassed considerable wealth, and became, in

consequence, a factor of no mean proportions in the world of finance. Indeed there are few business men of long standing in this country who have not at some time during their business career realized the potency of his influence and means." Victoria Wilcox to Susan McKey Thomas, November 21, 1994; U.S. Census, 1870, Brenham, Subdivision Beat 3, Washington County, Texas, M593, Roll 1608, NARA; Confederate Service Records, Texas State Archives, Austin, Texas.

42. *Dallas Weekly Herald*, March 15, 1873, carried an excellent article on "The Social and Political Conditions" of Dallas County. Carl H. Moneyhon, *Texas after the Civil War: The Struggle of Reconstruction* (College Station: Texas A&M University Press, 2004), offers a useful analysis of the political climate of Texas at the time.

43. T. R. Fehrenbach, *Lone Star: A History of Texas and the Texans* (New York: Da Capo, 2000), 433–434; Rogers, *Lusty Texans of Dallas*; Darwin Payne, *Dallas: An Illustrated History* (Woodland Hills, CA: Windsor, 1982).

44. Thonnie Smith Wisenbaker, "First Impressions of Valdosta in 1865," 49, 55, unpublished manuscript from the Mrs. Arthur Strom Collection, courtesy Susan McKey Thomas; *Dallas City Directory, 1873*, 77; David O. Moline, DDS, to Susan McKey Thomas, July 15, 1995, including a copy of Dr. Moline's October 5, 1995, presentation to the Academy of the History of Dentistry, titled, "The Real True Story of Dr. John Holliday."

45. Moline, "The Real True Story"; Wilcox research notes; Susan McKey Thomas research notes. From 1840 to 1860, John Seegar, Dr. Seegar's father, ran a "respectable house of entertainment for travelers" on the post road that ran from Greenville, South Carolina, through Atlanta, to Mobile, Alabama, not far from the inn owned by John Henry's grandfather, which makes it likely that the two families knew each other. Dr. Seegar grew up in old Campbell County, next to Fayette County. He married Martha Rainwater on November 17, 1859, in Fulton County, *Georgia Marriages, 1699–1944*, myfamily.com, Provo, UT, 2004.

46. Moline, "The Real True Story." The only service record found is "James A. Segar," CSR, CWS, GDAH. This Segar served first as a private in Company B, Ninth Battalion, Georgia Volunteer Infantry, which was later absorbed along with the Third Battalion to form the Thirty-seventh Regiment, Georgia Volunteer Infantry. In the Thirty-seventh Regiment, he was part of Company E. James Segar was a seventeen-year-old farm laborer from the Minish district of Jackson County in 1860. U.S. Census, 1860, Jackson County, p. 198, M653, Reel 128, NARA. Tanner, *Family Portrait*, 84–86, says that John Seegar migrated to Texas before the war. This appears to be correct. The 1860 census shows "John A. Segar [*sic*]," erroneously listed as "M.D.," and his wife, Martha, at a hotel in Springville in Wood County, Texas. U.S. Census, 1860, Wood County, Texas, p. 11, M653, Reel 1308, NARA. This would seem to indicate that Seegar left for Texas soon after his marriage in November 1859.

47. J. A. Leegar [*sic*], "Galvanic Action from Amalgam Filling," *Dental Times* 9 (April 1872): 147. By November 1872, Dr. Seegar was well established in Dallas. Apparently, Seegar set up practice in Dallas in 1867. On November 23, he published an advertisement in *Norton's Union Intelligencer* as follows: "I am thankful for 5 years patronage [*sic*]. I now can be found one door east of the Keaton House, up stairs over Cochran's Drug Store, on Commerce Street. My office is well fitted up for the reception of ladies, very quiet & pleasant. My work is on exhibition both in the city & country. Broken gold plates taken at a fair valuation for work. All work warranted. Call & give me a trial. J. A. SEEGAR."

48. *Dallas Weekly Herald*, October 11, 1873.

49. *Gunnison (Colorado) Daily News-Democrat*, June 18, 1882. The records of the First Methodist Church are disorganized, and confirmation of his membership has not been possible so far. Cindy Booker, administrative assistant, First United Methodist Church of Dallas, to the author, August 5, 2004.

50. *Dallas Daily Commercial*, March 2, 1874. The firm of "Seegar & Holiday [*sic*]" is listed in *Lawson and Edmondson's Dallas City Directory and Reference Book for 1873–74*, 64, 96.

51. *State of Texas v. Dr. Holliday*, Cause No. 2236, Indicted for Gaming, Minutes, Fourteenth District Court, Dallas County, Texas, 1874–75, May 12, 1874, vol. 1, p. 209. On May 22, at the hearing, T. M. Myers posted $100 bond, which guaranteed that Doc would appear at his trial. He was being introduced to the practices of the law in frontier towns toward gambling. The antigambling sweeps were periodic and used more to raise money through fines than to end gambling. See also Tanner, *Family Portrait*, 91–93.

52. J. H. Holliday, Assessment Roll, Precinct No. 1, Office of County Tax Commissioner, Dallas County, TX, 20.

53. Jack McGuire, *Katy's Baby: The Story of Denison Texas* (Austin, TX: Nortex, 1991), 19–33; see also V. V. Masterson, *The Katy and the Great Southwest* (Norman: University of Oklahoma Press, 1952), 183–192.

54. Bob Young, "He Whipped Rowdy Denison into Shape," *Quarterly of the National Association and Center for Outlaw and Lawman History* 12 (Fall 1987): 13–16. Dora Neill Raymond, *Captain Lee Hall of Texas* (Norman: University of Oklahoma Press, 1940), is the standard work on Hall.

55. *Denison (Texas) Daily News*, June 18, 1873. By then, John Henry was already in trouble at Fort Griffin. On September 12, 1874, the *Dallas Weekly Herald* reported unclaimed letters for him at the Dallas post office.

56. *Denison (Texas) Daily News*, August 14, 1873; Masterson, *The Katy*, 200–207.

57. *Dallas Weekly Herald*, January 2, 1875. The *Austin Statesman*, January 3, 1875, reported, "The Herald does not even know the number of bar-rooms, keno and faro banks in Dallas. Who can tell!"

58. *Dallas Daily Commercial*, March 6, August 12, 14, 1874.

59. *State of Texas v. Charles Austin*, Cause No. 2636, Indicted for Carrying a Pistol, Minutes, Fourteenth District Court, Dallas County, p. 482; *State of Texas v. J. H. Holliday*, Cause No. 2643, Indicted for Assault to Murder, Minutes, Fourteenth District Court, Dallas County, pp. 486, 516. Charles Austin's Cause No. 2636 was dismissed on May 5, 1875, Minutes, Fourteenth District Court, Dallas County, vol. 1, p. 65.

60. *State of Texas v. Dr. Holliday*, Gaming, Fourteenth District Court, Dallas County, vol. 1, p. 5.

61. *Denison (Texas) Daily Cresset*, May 28, 1875.

62. Jahns, *Frontier World*, 52–60, presented the view that Holliday's first visit to Fort Griffin was a mere stop en route to Colorado by way of the stage roads that linked the frontier posts of Texas. After his troubles in Dallas, he decided to leave, she argues. "So he recollected all he'd heard of the boom towns of the west and picked Denver as the most promising for a gentleman of his talents and delicate state of health." Tanner, *Family Portrait*, 95–96, agrees. The biggest argument for this view is that Holliday himself said that he was in Denver in 1875 and 1876. Such a course seems unlikely for reasons that are clear in Jahns's own account, that the way west detailed by her became "lonelier and more dangerous as they progressed into Indian country." See also Roger Conger, *Frontier Forts of Texas* (Waco, TX: Texian, 1966), for an even greater sense of the distances, dangers, and discomforts involved in travel through central and western Texas. If John Henry wished to go to Denver, he could have taken the railroad north and then west by a route that would have been both more comfortable and less dangerous. More likely, then, John Henry was attracted by tales of the Fort Griffin boom itself.

63. J. R. Webb, "Henry Herron: Pioneer and Peace Officer during Fort Griffin Days," *West Texas Historical Association Yearbook* 20 (1944): 23. Herron, who was interviewed extensively by Webb, arrived in Fort Griffin at midsummer of 1875, a few weeks after Holliday.

64. Rufus Choate, Assistant Surgeon, "Medical History of the Post, Fort Griffin, Texas, 1867–1881," November 8, 1874, 23, Fort Griffin, Miscellaneous Post Records, Box 47, Records of the Adjutant General's Office, Record Group 94, NARA.

65. Ty Cashion, *A Texas Frontier: The Clear Fork Country and Fort Griffin, 1849– 1887* (Norman: University of Oklahoma Press, 1996), 164. Also available are Charles M. Robinson, *The Frontier World of Fort Griffin: The Life and Death of a Western Town* (Spokane, WA: Clark, 1992), and Carl Coke Rister, *Fort Griffin on the Texas Frontier* (Norman: University of Oklahoma Press, 1956). Cashion offers a revisionist approach to the violence of Fort Griffin, which is presented more explicitly in his "(Gun) Smoke Gets in Your Eyes: A Revisionist Look at 'Violent' Fort Griffin," *Southwestern Historical Quarterly* 98 (July 1995): 78–94.

66. James Kimmins Greer, *Bois d'Arc to Barb'd Wire: Ken Cary, Southwestern Frontier Born* (Dallas, TX: Dealy and Lowe, 1936), 329, quoted in Cashion, *Texas Frontier,* 192.

67. Jet Kenan to Etta Soule, September 15, 1945, Etta Soule Letters, Robert E. Nail Jr. Collection, Old Jail Art Center, Albany, Texas, quoted in Cashion, *Texas Frontier,* 191.

68. Don H. Biggers, *Shackelford County Sketches.* Edited by Joan Farmer (Albany, NY: Clear Fork, 1974), 39.

69. Ibid., 45.

70. R. K. DeArment, "'Hurricane Bill' Martin: Horse Thief," *True West* 38 (June 1991): 43–44; Edgar Rye, *The Quirt and the Spur: Vanishing Shadows of the Texas Frontier* (Austin, TX: Steck-Vaughn, 1967), 74–77.

71. Rye, *Quirt and Spur,* 74–76, provides the standard account, and other old-timers generally confirm it. For example, see Hervey E. Chesley, *Adventuring with the Old Timers: Trails Travelled—Tales Told* (Midland, TX: Nita Stewart Haley Memorial Library, 1979), 93.

72. Cashion, *Texas Frontier,* 190–191, provides a succinct account of the mood in Shackleford County at the time and argues that as the boom continued, local businessmen would persuade "officers of the court to wink at the 'victimless' crimes." The election of J. R. Fleming to the district court bench in 1876 completed the process, and thereafter, Fleming concentrated on controlling violence and "let the justices of the peace work with local people to set community standards." Unfortunately, Doc got caught in the initial crusade. See Cases 11–16, 34, Minutes of the District Court, Shackleford County, vol. A, 6-7-75 to 3-1-84, pp. 14–16. Holliday was actually arrested twice. The records show two cases, Case 13-4, *The State of Texas v. Lynch, Curly, Hurricane Bill, and Dock [sic] Holliday,* June 9, 1875, and Case 34-14, *The State of Texas v. Mike Lynch and Dock Holliday,* June 12, 1875. *Denver Republican,* May 22, 1882. Ed Bartholomew always insisted that Curly Bill rode with Hurricane Bill in his Kansas horse-stealing days.

73. Jahns, *Frontier World,* 57. She cites a document that has since disappeared from the records of Shackleford County. See also Tanner, *Family Portrait,* 46, 259– 260n. San Angelo was consistently referred to as "San Angela" in the press in 1875 and 1876. A. M. Hobby wrote on July 20, 1875, "San Angela, or Concho City, is a little town across the river [from Fort Concho], built chiefly of mud-brick (Mexican adobe) baked in the sun. It presents a miserable aspect, and looks like a fitting abode for wretchedness and poverty." It was not a place apt to hold Doc Holliday.

74. See Jahns, *Frontier World,* 57–89; Tanner, *Family Portrait,* 98–103; Ben T. Traywick, *John Henry (The "Doc" Holliday Story)* (Tombstone, AZ: Red Marie's Bookstore, 1996): 47–48.

75. John Charles Thompson, quoted in John Myers Myers, *Doc Holliday* (Boston: Little, Brown, 1955), 62. One problem with this report is that Holliday had no reputation as a killer for the simple reason that he had killed no one.

76. Jahns, *Frontier World,* 71–82, and Tanner, *Family Portrait,* 103, place Doc in Cheyenne and Deadwood until the spring of 1877. Myers, *Doc,* 62–64, places Holliday in Denver in the fall and winter of 1876.

77. Typescript of Recollections of Mary Katharine Cummings as Given to Anton Mazzanovich, 5–7, private collection of Kevin J. Mulkins; Cummings to Mazzanovich, undated transcript, 9–12, Robert N. Mullin Collection, Nita Stewart Haley Memorial Library and J. Evetts Haley History Center, Midland, Texas. See also Gary L. Roberts, "Bat Masterson and the Sweetwater Shootout," *Wild West* (October 2000): 42–50.

78. Arthur W. Bork, Notes of Interview with Mary Katharine Cummings, Thanksgiving 1935, copy in author's files, courtesy of Arthur W. Bork; Mrs. Ernest Beckwith to Bork, March 1, 1977, quoted in Arthur W. Bork and Glenn G. Boyer, "O.K. Corral Fight at Tombstone: A Footnote by Kate Elder," *Arizona and West* 19 (Spring 1977): 68. Silas H. Melvin, twenty-two years old, U.S. Census, 1870, St. Louis, Missouri, Central Township, p. 109, M593, Reel 808, NARA; Mary V. Bust, seventeen years old, U.S. Census, 1870, St. Louis, Missouri, St. Louis Township, p. 156, M593, Reel 809, NARA. Mary Bust was listed as the daughter of William and Malissa Bust. Her father was a steamboat pilot, and she was listed as "at school." St. Louis Marriage Records, vol. 15, p. 173. Mary Bust is listed as single and living with her parents in the U.S. Census, 1880, St. Louis, Missouri, p. 10, T9-725, NARA, although there is an age discrepancy showing her as only twenty-three. The *St. Louis City Directory* shows Silas H. Melvin selling tobacco and cigars at 410 Locust in 1873.

79. On June 3, 1874, Samuel Martin filed charges against Sallie Erp and Betsy Erp for establishing a brothel north of Douglas Avenue near the bridge over the Arkansas River. The case of *The State of Kansas v. Bessie Earp and Sallie Earp*, Case No. 814, came before the district court in September 1874 and was dismissed. Case Records of the District Court, Sedgwick County, Kansas, Wichita, and Proceedings of the District Court, September 1874 Term. Kate Elder was arrested for prostitution in June 1874, and the arrest of Kate Earb was reported in August 1874. Record of the Police Judge, Miscellaneous Papers, City of Wichita. Whether Kate Earp was Kate Elder is, of course, uncertain, but judging from the record, prostitutes associated with Bessie and Sallie were at times listed as Earp, including Eva Earp and Minnie Earp, besides Kate Earp. Ed Bartholomew, *Wyatt Earp: The Untold Story* (Toyahvale, TX: Frontier Book, 1963), 103, goes so far as to suggest that Kate Earp and Minnie Earp were actually Kate Elder and the woman who later became Hurricane Minnie Martin, suggesting that they left Wichita and went to Fort Griffin, Texas, together. Bartholomew, p. 102, was also the first to suggest the possibility of a relationship between Wyatt Earp and Kate before she renewed her acquaintance with Doc. However, recent research suggests that Sallie Earp may have been Sarah, or Sally, Haspel, a young prostitute Wyatt had known during his time at Peoria, Illinois. See three articles by Roger Jay, "'The Peoria Bummer': Wyatt Earp's Lost Year," *Wild West* (August 2003): 46–52, "Another Earp Arrest?" *NOLA Quarterly* 28 (October–December 2004): 19–23, and "Reign of the Rough-Scuff: Law and Lucre in Wichita," *Wild West* (October 2005): 22–28, 62. A review of the 1870 census for Kansas and Missouri indicates that the name "Elder" was fairly uncommon. Isaac S. Elder was marshal of Wichita in 1870. Nyle H. Miller and Joseph W. Snell, *Why the West Was Wild: A Contemporary Look at Some Highly Publicized Kansas Cowtown Personalities* (Topeka: Kansas State Historical Society, 1963), 645.

80. In both the *San Francisco Examiner*, August 2, 1896, and Stuart N. Lake, *Wyatt Earp: Frontier Marshal* (Boston: Houghton Mifflin, 1931), 198, 202, 223, 238, 265, Earp called her Kate Fisher. The *Wichita Beacon*, November 26, 1874, lists a letter for "Kate Fisher" under unclaimed mail, which would likely be after Kate left Wichita. It is plausible that someone who knew her as Kate Fisher before she assumed the name Kate Elder would have written her by that name. Kansas Census, 1875, Ford County, K-8, Kansas State Historical Society. Sherman quit Dodge before the end of 1875. He may have gone to Sweetwater, which seems likely, because he ran a saloon in Mobeetie (which replaced Sweetwater) in 1880. Bartholomew, *Untold Story*, 102. Kate probably accompanied Sherman, although she could have found work at either Charlie Norton's dance hall or the saloon owned by Harry Fleming and Billy Thompson there. See articles by Roberts, "Sweetwater Shootout," 45,

and "Corporal Melvin A. King: The Gunfighting Soldier of the Great American Myth," *Real West* (September 1987): 46.

81. Masterson, "Doc Holliday," 5.

82. *Dallas Weekly Herald*, March 11, 1876; Jacob Smith, Private, Company B, Tenth Cavalry, Fort Griffin, Texas, Final Papers, AGO, RG 94, NARA. The papers say simply that he was killed by "person unknown," following the post investigation. An alternative explanation was provided by the *Jacksboro (Texas) Frontier Echo*, March 10, 1876, which reported "[m]ore deviltry at Fort Griffin last Friday night [when] a couple of our Uncle Samuel's dusky warriors got into a quarrel about a damsel of color; blows followed hot words[,] and cold led [sic] finished the fight and life of one of the combatants." Notably, no soldier was arrested in the matter.

83. Masterson, "Doc Holliday," 5.

84. Fuches appeared at 422 S. Fourth Street. *St. Louis City Directory*, through 1876.

85. Bartholomew, *Untold Story*, 172, says that Kate went to "that haven during winter for so many Dodge girls, St. Louis." Bork notes, Thanksgiving 1935, provides the marriage date, although, in her effort to whitewash her story, Kate said they were married at Valdosta, Georgia.

86. Agnes Wright Spring, *The Cheyenne and Black Hills Stage and Express Routes* (Glendale, CA: Clark, 1949), 201–213; Tanner, *Family Portrait*, 262n.

87. Masterson, "Doc Holliday," 6, was very specific about "the summer of 1876," which is noteworthy because it was a centennial year and more likely to be remembered because of that, not to mention General George A. Custer's fall, which captured public attention in a dramatic way. Wilcox to the author, March 21, 2001. *Denver Republican*, June 22, 1887; Masterson, "Doc Holliday," 6. The *Denver City Directory, 1876*, lists John J. McKey living at Long John's Saloon at 507 Blake Street, near C. W. Babb's Variety House.

88. Regina Rapier, a great-niece of Mattie Holliday, related the story of the Pinkerton visit as passed down through the family to Victoria Wilcox, copy in author's files.

89. *Denver Republican*, June 22, 1887.

90. Masterson, "Doc Holliday," 6; *Denver City Directory, 1890* (Denver, CO: Ballenger and Richards, 1890).

91. *Denver Rocky Mountain News*, November 28, 30, December 1, 1876. Denver police records and police court records appear to have been lost.

92. Tanner, *Family Portrait*, 103–104. Interestingly, Henry Burroughs Holliday would later initiate contact with his brother-in-law, Arthur W. McCoin, on behalf of black citizens who were interested in migrating to Kansas. *Valdosta Daily Times*, September 27, 1879; *Galveston Daily News*, December 28, 1876, January 3, 5, 7, 1877. Three cases appear for *State of Texas v. Dr. Holliday* (no cause numbers), Minutes, Fourteenth District Court, Dallas County, Texas, January 8, 1877, vol. J, 80.

93. John C. Jacobs to J. Marvin Hunter, July 17, 1928, quoted in J. Marvin Hunter, *The Story of Lottie Deno: Her Life and Times* (Abilene, TX: Abilene Christian College, 1959), 58.

94. Tanner, *Family Portrait*, 105; *Galveston Daily News*, February 15, 1877.

95. Fourteenth District Court, Dallas County, Texas, May 8, 1877, vol. J, 80.

96. *Dallas Weekly Herald*, July 7, 1877; Tanner, *Family Portrait*, 106, 262–263n.

97. *Texas v. Henry Kahn*, Keeping a Gaming Table, File No. 23, April 30, 1877, District Court, Stephens County, Texas; *Texas v. H. Kahn and Geo. Clay*, File No. 96, Minutes of the District Court, 6-7-75 to 3-1-84, Shackleford County, Texas, p. 90. See *Dallas Weekly Herald*, March 27, 1875, for reference to the firm of E. M. Kahn & Brothers Clothing in Dallas. The Kahn Brothers Department Store was on the same block as John Henry's dental office. Henry Kahn was mentioned in the *List of Fugitives from Justice for the State of Texas and a Descriptive List of Escaped Convicts* (Austin, TX: State Printing Office, 1878), 167,

for the forgery charge in Shakleford County. The author has used *Fugitives from Justice: The Notebook of Texas Ranger Sergeant James B. Gillette* (Austin, TX: State House Press, 1997), which is a reproduction of Sergeant Gillette's personal copy of the *List* with his annotations and comments.

98. Tanner, *Family Portrait*, 106–198; *Fort Worth (Texas) Democrat*, July 21, 1877.

99. *Texas v. McCune* [and] *J. Holiday* [*sic*], Cause No. 3764, Minutes, Fourteenth District Court, Dallas County, Texas, September 14, 1877, vol. J, 466–467.

100. Beginning in January 1878, newspapers like the *Dallas Weekly Herald*, the *Galveston Daily News*, and the *Austin Statesman* almost daily reported violent episodes from Fort Griffin. For an especially balanced view of the deteriorating situation at Fort Griffin and the steps taken to change it, see Cashion, *Texas Frontier*, 188–233. Also useful is Robinson, *Fort Griffin*, 74–114. An essential work is Robert DeArment, *Bravo of the Brazos: John Larn of Fort Griffin, Texas* (Norman: University of Oklahoma Press, 2002), 65–143, who details the situation in Fort Griffin through the career of Sheriff John Larn, who was one of the organizers of the "Tin Hat" vigilance committee and ultimately its last victim. Also useful is Leon Clair Metz, *John Selman: Texas Gunfighter* (New York: Hastings House, 1966), 48–95.

101. *Galveston Daily News*, July 24, August 1, 9, 1877. Hunter, *Lottie Deno*, passim, contains most of the reminiscences about this legendary figure. Cynthia Ross, *Lottie Deno: Gambling Queen of Hearts* (Santa Fe, NM: Clear Light, 1994), passim, offers a useful but uncritical chronology. Rye, *Quirt and Spur*, 70, called her "a female monstrosity," and Cashion, *Texas Frontier*, 198, said that the "so-called 'lady gambler' inspired exaggerations and even outright fabrications." See also Robinson, *Fort Griffin*, 85–91.

102. W. Hubert Curry, *Sun Rising on the West: The Saga of Henry Clay and Elizabeth Smith* (Crosbyton, TX: Crosby County Pioneer Memorial, 1979), 133–134; 210–211.

103. Jacobs to Hunter, July 17, 1928, quoted in Hunter, *Lottie Deno*, 58. Alfred Henry Lewis, *Wolfville Nights* (New York: Grossett and Dunlap, 1902), tells a similar story about Doc in a fictional format, which is reprinted in Hunter, *Lottie Deno*, 49–57.

104. John Jacobs told the story in Hunter, *Lottie Deno*, 41.

105. *Daily Galveston News*, October 21, 1877. Another reason for a quieter Fort Griffin was suggested by the *Austin Statesman*, September 22, 1877: "They make no more to do about hanging men out at Fort Griffin that would naturally arise from the killing of so many bears. The vigilance committee pursued and hung three horse thieves to one tree three or four weeks ago, within a short distance of town, and the same committee lately started off on another lynching excursion."

106. Cummings, Mazzanovich typescript, 1–2. A review of Maverick County records revealed no legal troubles for Doc while in Eagle Pass. There were troubles there that fall and winter, however. See *Galveston Daily News*, October 21, 1877, and the *Austin Statesman*, December 8, 1877. Lee Hall replaced Leander H. McNelly as the captain of the Texas Rangers on that part of the border, and he made trouble for lawbreakers in Maverick County, including King Fisher. Fisher was arrested on November 19, 1877, and remained in jail until April 11, 1878, so that Doc missed the opportunity to meet him. O. C. Fisher, with J. C. Dykes, *King Fisher: His Life and Times* (Norman: University of Oklahoma Press, 1966), 92–98.

107. Lawrence Vivian, interview with the author, August 13, 1998. Charlie and Blue Vivian went west into the Eagle Pass area with the first ranging company. Blue Vivian sold his saloon to King Fisher in 1880. Fisher was married to Lawrence Vivian's great-great-great-aunt. The family passed down the story of Doc Holliday drinking and gambling at Old Blue's Saloon. Vivian first told the story of his family's connection to Doc in Eagle Pass to the author in the fall of 1997, not knowing about Kate Holliday's account.

108. Cummings, Mazzanovich typescript, 2.

109. Ibid.

110. Chesley, *Trails Travelled—Tales Told*, 97–98. Baldwin's partner was named Bob Fambro, and he reported him killed later at Shakespeare, New Mexico. The mention that Fambro and Doc were from the "same neighborhood" raises the question of whether he might have been the Robert Rambo arrested in connection with the courthouse incident in Valdosta, and he was doubtlessly the Bob Fambo stabbed by Billy Carroll, a bartender, during a quarrel in Shakespeare, New Mexico, as Baldwin said. Reportedly, he recalled his buffalo hunting days as he was dying. Ed Bartholomew, *Wyatt Earp: The Man and the Myth* (Toyahvale, TX: Frontier Book, 1964), 79–80. Six-year-old Robert E. Fambrough, the son of the merchant William P. Fambrough, was a resident of Griffin in Spalding County in 1860. U.S. Census, 1860, p. 20, Spalding County, Georgia, NARA. He was still in Griffin in 1870 attending school, though not living with his parents. U.S. Census, 1870, p. 49, Spalding County, Georgia. By 1880, he appears to have left Georgia, for he is not found in the 1880 census.

111. *San Francisco Examiner*, August 2, 1896.

112. Ibid.; see also Tanner, *Family Portrait*, 268–269n.

113. Cummings, Mazzanovich typescript, 4–5.

114. *Galveston Daily News*, April 3, 1878.

115. *Dodge City (Kansas) Times*, May 11, 1878, reported, "Mr. Wyatt Earp, who has during the past served with credit on the police arrived in this city from Texas last Wednesday. We predict that his services as an officer will be required this Summer." On May 14, the *Dodge City Ford County Globe* reported that he had been appointed assistant marshal. If Earp was correct in saying that Doc was already there when he returned, Doc must have arrived in late April or the first few days of May. He and Kate may even have accompanied the 12,000 head of cattle being driven north by Lytle, McDaniel & Company, and James Ellison and Company, which passed Fort Griffin in April. *Galveston Daily News*, April 19, 1878.

4. Cow Towns and Pueblos

1. Carolyn Manley to Karen Holliday Tanner, September 27, 1995. Courtesy Karen Holliday Tanner.

2. Ida Allen Rath, *The Rath Trail* (Wichita, KS: McCormick-Armstrong, 1961), 152–159; C. Robert Haywood, *Trails South: The Wagon Road Economy in the Dodge City–Panhandle Region* (Norman: University of Oklahoma Press, 1986), 128–134.

3. Gary L. Roberts, "From Tin Star to Hanging Tree: The Short Life and Violent Times of Billy Brooks," in *Prairie Scout*, vol. 3, edited by Joseph W. Snell et al. (Abilene: Kansas Corral of the Westerners, 1975), 17–42, provides the most complete summary of the violent birth of Dodge City.

4. Chris Penn, "Gunfire in Dodge City: The Night Ed Masterson Was Killed," *Wild West* (December 2004), 48–53; Roger Myers, "The Death of Edward John Masterson," *NOLA Journal* (April–June 2005): 36–47; Robert Palmquist, "Who Killed Jack Wagner?" *True West* (October 1993): 14–19.

5. Robert DeArment, *Bat Masterson* (Norman: University of Oklahoma, 1979), 86–140.

6. *Dodge City (Kansas) Times*, May 18, 1878.

7. *Dodge City Times*, May 4, 1878.

8. "Atrym" to the editor, June 2, 1878, *Rice County Gazette*, June 6, 1878.

9. "Atrym" to the editor, June 9, 1878, *Rice County Gazette*, June 13, 1878; *Dodge City Ford County Globe*, May 20, 1878.

10. Stanton D. Harn and Gary K. Helin, "Doc Holliday's Dental Chair," *Journal of the History of Dentistry* 47 (March 1999): 7–9; *Dodge City Times*, June 8, 1878. John Henry's connection to the Dodge House is also interesting because its owner, George B. Cox, was originally from Butts County, Georgia, the county next to Spalding County, where Doc spent his early years. Cox served in the Fourth Georgia Volunteer Infantry during the Civil War and traveled west afterward, settling in Dodge City in the fall of 1872. A. T. Andreas, *History of Kansas* (Chicago: A. T. Andreas, 1883), 2: 1561.

11. Robert M. Wright, *Dodge City: The Cowboy Capital* (Wichita, KS: Wichita Eagle Press, 1913), 249–251. Of course, the story is just a tale, although Wright said only "[o]ne we will call Doc Holliday, the other Creek," but it is interesting that Holliday was later associated with a man called Turkey Creek Jack Johnson at Tombstone.

12. Ibid.

13. Frank A. Dunn, "Celebrating a Holliday," *Oral Hygiene* (September 1933): 1338–1344.

14. Charles C. Lowther, *Dodge City, Kansas* (Philadelphia: Dorrance, 1940), 26–27.

15. William Barclay Masterson, "Famous Gunfighters of the Western Frontier: Doc Holliday," *Human Life* (May 1907): 5–6.

16. Masterson, "Doc Holliday," 6. Bat claimed that Kansas "was the only state in which he has lived in which he failed to either slay or bodily wound some person."

17. *Dodge City Times*, June 22, 1878.

18. *Dodge City Times*, June 22, 1878; "Atrym" to the editor, June 24, 1878; *Rice County Gazette*, June 27, 1878.

19. *Ford County Globe*, June 26, 1878.

20. *Ford County Globe*, June 18, 1878.

21. "Atrym" to the editor, July 14, 1878, *Rice County Gazette*, July 18, 1878, provides the most enlightening account of the killing. See Nyle H. Miller and Joseph W. Snell, *Why the West Was Wild: A Contemporary Look at Some Highly Publicized Kansas Cowtown Personalities* (Topeka: Kansas State Historical Society, 1963), 273–276, for the Dodge City accounts.

22. *City of Dodge City v. C. C. Peppard*, Pled Guilty, July 16, 1878, Notes from Docket, Police Judge, City of Dodge City, Kansas, July 5, 1878, to October 5, 1882, William S. Campbell (Stanley Vestal) Collection, Box 96, Western History Collection, University of Oklahoma, Norman, Oklahoma; C. Robert Haywood, "Comanche County Cowboy: A Case Study of a Kansas Rancher," *Kansas History* 4 (Autumn 1981): 166–190; Roger Myers to the author, July 25, 2002.

23. *City v. K. M. May, City v. Charles Reed*, Police Docket Notes. Reed was a fugitive from Texas wanted for murder, although Earp and other Dodge City authorities apparently did not know it. See *List of Fugitives from Justice for the State of Texas and a Descriptive List of Escaped Convicts* (Austin, TX: State Printing Office, 1878), 167.

24. *Dodge City Times*, July 27, 1878; Eddie Foy and Alvin F. Harlow, *Clowning through Life* (New York: Dutton, 1928), 112–114. The *National Police Gazette*, August 10, 1878, reported that "Wyatt Erpe [*sic*], a good fellow and brave officer," had an altercation with one of the drovers before the incident, but the local papers make no mention of it. Jesse Lincoln Driskill and his brother-in-law, William H. Day, were partners. His son, William Walter Driskill, and his grandsons, J. W. and W. W. (Tobe), would be active in the cattle industry for decades after the Civil War. Tobe would eventually be a cattleman in Wyoming, but in 1878 J. W. and Tobe managed a ranch near Dodge City. Jesse's in-laws, the Days, were involved as well. Hoy was from Illano County, Texas, and apparently was a drover with a small herd owned by William Day, a partner of the Driskills. The herd was driven north by Charles C. French and his brother, Harrison, connecting to the Driskill operation near Dodge before sale. The Driskill Family Papers, Texas State Archives, Austin, Texas; C. C. French, "When the Temperature Was 72 Degrees below Zero," in *The*

Trail Drivers of Texas, edited by J. Marvin Hunter and George W. Saunders (San Antonio, TX: Jackson, 1920), 741–743; Frank C. Rigler, "The Joel D. Hoy Story," *The Highlander* (January 25, 1973).

25. *Dodge City Times*, July 27, August 24, 1878; *Ford County Globe*, July 30, August 27, 1878. The *Globe* noted, on August 27, that "Messrs. Joe Day, Harrison and Charles French departed on Thursday night for their home in August in Texas. These gentlemen were companions of G. R. Hoy, who died on Wednesday last. . . . They returned to their homes feeling severely the absence of their companion whom they had just laid away." See also Casey Tefertiller, *Wyatt Earp: The Life behind the Legend* (New York: Wiley, 1997), 24–25.

26. "Dr. J. H. Holliday of Dodge City," *Holliday House Gazette* 2 (Fall 1997): 6–7; Victoria Wilcox, "A Pocket Dentist Office," *True West* 48 (November–December 2001): 45. In a telephone conversation with Dr. David O. Moline in August 2001, Dr. Moline advised the author that the kit was not a gold foil kit as originally reported, but an emergency kit containing a variety of tools.

27. Statement of Wyatt Earp, November 16, 1881, *Tombstone Daily Nugget* and *Tombstone Daily Epitaph*, November 17, 1881, *San Francisco Examiner*, August 2, 1896.

28. Stuart N. Lake, *Wyatt Earp: Frontier Marshal* (Boston: Houghton Mifflin, 1931), 213–215.

29. John Flood's notes of interview with Wyatt Earp, John D. Gilchreise Collection, undated typescript in author's files. Interestingly—and perhaps significantly—in this simple version, Doc Holliday shot no one. See also John H. Flood Jr., "Wyatt Earp, a Peace-officer of Tombstone," unpublished manuscript, 1927, 59–62, C. Lee Simmons Collection.

30. *Ford County Globe*, August 20, 1878. The drover involved was apparently James Kenedy, son of Texas rancher Mifflin Kenedy, and he was arrested by Marshal Charles Bassett. *City v. James Kennedy [sic]*, Police Docket Notes. In October 1878, Kenedy would later be pursued for the murder of Dora Hand. See Chuck Parsons, *James W. Kenedy, "Fiend in Human Form"* (London: English Westerners' Society, 2000), passim. The connection to Kenedy virtually eliminates the August incident as the episode involving Doc saving the life of Earp.

31. *Dodge City Times*, September 21, 1878; *Ford County Globe*, September 17, 24, 1878. For background, see Vernon R. Maddux, *In Dull Knife's Wake: The True Story of the Northern Cheyenne Exodus of 1878* (Norman, OK: Horse Creek, 2003), 19–18, and John H. Monnett, *Tell Them We Are Going Home: The Odyssey of the Northern Cheyennes* (Norman: University of Oklahoma Press, 2004), 44–103.

32. *Dodge City Times*, September 21, 1878.

33. Lake, *Frontier Marshal*, 209.

34. The *Ford County Globe* was not happy with local law enforcement and published several articles criticizing the officers' failure to control confidence men and pick pockets. See *Ford County Globe*, September 10, 14, 17, 1878. News that the Cheyennes were pushing through Ford County followed close by. The *Dodge City Times*, September 14, 1878, initially called the raid a hoax, but when the Cheyennes raided the Driskill camp at the mouth of Bluff Creek on September 16, the Driskill riders and other cattlemen in Dodge went after them early on the morning of September 17. *Ford County Globe*, September 17, 1878. They linked forces with Captain William C. Hemphill's company of cavalry and later engaged the Cheyennes in a sharp fight. Afterward, the officer chose not to pursue the Cheyennes further, believing their numbers to be too great, which generated some complaints from the cowboys. On Wednesday evening, September 18, the Driskill riders returned to Dodge. That was the day when the excitement over the raid reached fever pitch in Dodge, throwing "the people of Dodge into the wildest tremor." *Dodge City Times*, September 21, 1878. In the afternoon, the report of a fire west of Dodge sent a trainload of armed men to the rescue. They reached the scene, the farm of Harrison Beery, and man-

aged to save some of the haystacks and animals from the fire. Wyatt Earp was one of the principals in the effort. *Dodge City Times*, September 21. That evening, there was a quarrel between Al Manning, a bartender, and Jack Brown, a former policeman, in which a bystander was wounded by a gunshot. *Dodge City Times*, September 21, 1878; *Ford County Globe*, September 24, 1878. On September 19, 1878, Hemphill's troops arrived in Dodge. The incident described as a "disgraceful row" occurred that afternoon. Some believe that this was the occasion of Clay Allison's second visit to Dodge. See Roger Myers, "Western Lore: When Shootist Clay Allison Came to Dodge Hunting Trouble, He Found Wyatt Earp . . . Sort of," *Wild West* (December 2000): 60–64. Later in the evening the incident occurred that appears to have been the one in which Doc saved Wyatt Earp's life. It may have been a dispute between the drovers and the soldiers. The *Las Animas (Colorado) Leader*, September 20, made the incident seem a bit bloodier than the Dodge City papers, recording, "A shooting affray occurred here [Dodge City] last night between saloon keepers and cowboys in which one man was shot in the back, which is believed will prove fatal, another man came out with three fingers shot off, and the third man, a soldier, was rewarded for participation in the trouble by receiving a 36 calibre in the leg." Nothing of the sort was reported in the Dodge City papers. Ed Morrison, mentioned by Earp in his accounts, was in the area riding with the Days. See Ed Bartholomew, *Wyatt Earp: The Untold Story* (Toyahvale, TX: Frontier Book, 1963), 264–278. Near midnight, the same night, a bullwhacker named H. Gould, but called Skunk Curley, shot another man named Cogan and skipped town before he could be arrested. *Dodge City Times*, September 21, 1878. It was all of this activity that prompted the *Globe*'s observation on September 24, 1878, which was critical of the officers.

35. *Dodge City Times*, August 10, 1878.

36. *New York Sun*, June 3, 1886. This article was widely reprinted. For example, see *Denver Times*, June 15, 1886, *Valdosta Daily Times*, June 19, 1886, and *San Francisco Call*, June 20, 1886. Substantiation of the claim is far from definitive. Roger Myers to the author, July 14, 2002, and William R. Cox, *Luke Short and His Era* (New York: Doubleday, 1961), 63, prove helpful. Charles Wright was a common name. A Charles Wright was with the defenders of Adobe Walls in 1874 (most of whom were from Dodge City). Miller and Snell, *Why the West Was Wild*, 316. David Cruikshanks to Susan McKey Thomas, March 2, 1976, Susan McKey Thomas Collection, provided more detail, although documentation is sparse.

37. Arthur W. Bork and Glenn G. Boyer, "The O.K. Corral Fight at Tombstone: A Footnote by Kate Elder," *Arizona and the West* 19 (Spring 1977): 76; Masterson, "Doc Holliday," 5; Sheila M. Rothman, *Living in the Shadow of Death: Tuberculosis and the Social Experience of Illness in American History* (New York: Basic, 1994), 16.

38. Masterson, "Doc Holliday," 5; Flood notes of interview with Wyatt Earp, September 5, 1926, *Wyatt Earp, Tombstone and the West, from the Collection of John D. Gilchriese*, part 1 (San Francisco: Johns' Western Gallery, 2005), 71.

39. Bork and Boyer, "O.K. Corral Fight," 76; Chuck Hornung, interview by Mary Lail, Chuck Hornung Collection, copy in author's files.

40. Milton W. Callon, *Las Vegas: The Town That Wouldn't Gamble* (Las Vegas, NM: Las Vegas Daily Optic, 1962), 126–131.

41. *Las Vegas (New Mexico) Gazette*, September 14, 1878; *Territory of New Mexico v. W. S. Leonard*, Case No. 962, Assault with Intent to Murder, March 14, 1879, San Miguel County District Court Records, Las Vegas, New Mexico. *New Mexico v. W. S. Leonard*, Case No. 973, Carrying Deadly Weapons, March 15, 1879, SMCDCR, Las Vegas, New Mexico, New Mexico State Records Center and Archives, Santa Fe, New Mexico. Most accounts state that Doc's office and Leonard's store were in a two-story building on Bridge Street near the plaza. However, during the time that Leonard was in Las Vegas, there were

no two-story buildings on the National Road, and Bridge Street did not yet exist. Marcus Gottschalk to the author, October 2, 2004.

42. *New Mexico v. John H. Holliday*, Case No. 931, Keeping Gaming Table, March 8, 1879, SMCDCR, Las Vegas, New Mexico, NMSRCA.

43. Kate is quiet in her recollections about this separation, but there were contemporary accounts placing her in Santa Fe for a time. See *Las Vegas (New Mexico) Daily Optic*, July 20, 1881.

44. DeArment, *Masterson*, 148–154, and Floyd Benjamin Streeter, *Ben Thompson: Man with a Gun* (New York: Frederick Fell, 1957), 129–140, provide accounts of the "war" from the perspectives of two principals. For a more detailed account, see Robert G. Athearn, *Rebel of the Rockies: A History of the Denver and Rio Grande Western Railroad* (New Haven, CT: Yale University Press, 1962), 49–90.

45. Wright, *Cowboy Capitol*, 175.

46. Foy and Harlow, *Clowning through Life*, 102–104.

47. DeArment, *Masterson*, 149–150.

48. Ibid.

49. *Otero (New Mexico) Optic*, June 5, 1879.

50. Precinct 6, Colfax County Tax Assessment Rolls, 1891, quoted in Chuck Hornung, "Wyatt Earp and Doc Holliday: Their New Mexico Adventures," draft copy, 2005, with permission of the author.

51. *Otero Optic*, June 5, 1879; Bartholomew, *Untold Story*, 294–295; Ed Bartholomew, *Wyatt Earp: The Man and the Myth* (Toyahvale, TX: Frontier Book, 1964), 24–25.

52. *Otero Optic*, June 5, 1879.

53. Bartholomew, *Man and Myth*, 25; James E. Sherman and Barbara H. Sherman, *Ghost Towns and Mining Camps of New Mexico* (Norman: University of New Mexico Press, 1975), 166. Sam Baldwin provided an interesting description of Hurricane Bill. He said that Bill's sponsor in Otero was Ed Withers, a former Texas badman who ran a livery stable in Otero. Withers was killed, and Bill took off. Baldwin said that Bill later became marshal at Alamosa and died there. Hervey E. Chesley, *Adventuring with the Old Timers: Trails Travelled—Tales Told* (Midland, TX: Nita Stewart Haley Memorial Library, 1979), 93–94.

54. Tom Hilton, *Nevermore, Cimarron, Nevermore* (Fort Worth, TX: Western Heritage, 1970), 80.

55. *Ford County Globe*, June 10, 1878; DeArment, *Masterson*, 151–152. The night the Dodge City fighters left for Canon City another incident occurred that matched the description of the episode in which Doc saved Wyatt's life: "Last night the police undertook to disarm a squad of cow boys who had neglected to lay aside their six-shooters upon arriving in the city. The cow boys protested and war was declared. Several shots were fired, and one of the cow boys was wounded in the leg. The balance of the cow boys made their escape." *Ford County Globe*, June 10, 1879. Of course, Doc had left earlier in the day with the Santa Fe fighters, and the surrounding circumstances do not fit Earp's recollections.

56. Robert DeArment, "Tough Irish Lawman," *True West* 39 (June 1992): 26–33; Gary L. Roberts, "Thomas James Smith," in *The New Encyclopedia of the American West*, edited by Howard R. Lamar (New Haven, CT: Yale University Press, 1998), 1060–1061.

57. *Dodge City Times*, June 14, 1879; *Ford County Globe*, June 10, 1878; Victoria Wilcox to the author, August 28, 2001.

58. *Dodge City Times*, June 14, 1879; *Ford County Globe*, June 24, July 8, 1879; see also Roger Myers, "John Joshua Webb: From Lawman to Death Row," *Old West* 36 (Winter 1999): 21–22.

59. George D. Bolds, *Across the Cimarron* (New York: Crown, 1956), 71.

60. Transcript of Recollections of Mary Katharine Cummings as Given to Anton Mazzanovich, 5, Kevin J. Mulkins Collection.

61. John Myers Myers, *Doc Holliday* (Boston: Little, Brown, 1955), 112.

62. *Las Vegas Daily Optic*, June 19, 1879. For a brief survey of *Otero's* fate, see F. Stanley, *The Otero, New Mexico, Story* (Pantex, TX: N.p., 1962).

63. *Las Vegas Daily Optic*, August 7, 1908.

64. Howard Bryan, *Wildest of the West: True Tales of a Frontier Town on the Sante Fe Trail* (Sante Fe, NM: Clear Light, 1988), 98–101.

65. After returning from Dodge, Doc purchased property on Center Street from Thomas L. Preston and contracted with W. G. Ward, a track follower and builder, to construct a saloon. Jordan Webb, quite possibly another Santa Fe Railroad mercenary enlisted by John Joshua Webb, Doc's Dodge City acquaintance, apparently bought into the operation as well. The original purchase appears to have escaped documentation, but on October 8, 1879, Ward filed a claim of his contract in an effort to collect $137.50 outstanding on the debt. Such a contract is rare in the deed books and was occasioned by legal action against "Mr Hollyday commonlay called Doc Holyday [*sic*]." Because the contract shows the first payment of $45.00 on July 20, 1879, some researchers have assumed that July 20 was the date authorizing construction yet to be done and that the saloon was not operational on that date. See especially Karen Holliday Tanner, *Doc Holliday: A Family Portrait* (Norman: University of Oklahoma Press, 1998), 133. However, the contract explicitly states that the payment is for "work done," which means that the Center Street saloon was already open on July 20. Deed Record Book 11, San Miguel County, 449–450, Las Vegas, New Mexico. The author is indebted to Marcus C. Gottschalk, the leading authority on Las Vegas businesses, for helping to unravel this mystery. Gottschalk to the author, October 16, 2004. See especially, Marcus C. Gottschalk, *Pioneer Merchants of Las Vegas*, 2nd ed. (Las Vegas, NM: M. C. Gottschalk, 2004), 88.

66. Bartholomew, *Man and Myth*, 9–10; *Las Vegas Daily Gazette*, July 26, 1879; *Santa Fe New Mexican*, August 2, 1879.

67. *Las Cruces Thirty-Four*, July 30, 1879; *Las Vegas Daily Optic*, July 20, 1881.

68. *Las Vegas Daily Optic*, May 18, 1882.

69. *Las Vegas Daily Optic*, August 4, 1886, reprinted in the *Tucson Weekly Arizona Citizen*, August 14, 1886.

70. Bryan, *Wildest of West*, 108–113; Bartholomew, *Man and Myth*, 8–36; *Las Vegas Daily Optic*, July 20, 1881. Brown had earlier plied his trade as a gambler in Wichita and Dodge City, even then viewed as "one of the worst class of gamblers," said a Las Vegas correspondent to the *Chicago Times* in March 1880, quoted in Bryan, *Wildest of West*, 109.

71. *Las Vegas Daily Optic*, August 4, 1886.

72. *Territory v. James Pearson*, et al., Case No. 989, Permitting Gaming, August 12, 1879; *Territory v. James Pearson*, et al., Case No. 991, Aggravated Assault and Battery, August 12, 1879, SMCDCR, Las Vegas, New Mexico, NMSRCA.

73. A. M. Johnson and W. A. Requa to J. H. Holliday, July 30, 1879, Deed Record Book 12, San Miguel County, 182–185; *Territory of New Mexico v. H. G. Neill*, Case No. 1014, Keeping a Gaming Table, August 1, 1879; *Territory v. J. H. Holliday*, Case No. 990, Keeping a Gaming Table, August 12, 1879, SMCDCR, Las Vegas, New Mexico, NMSRCA.

74. *Las Vegas Daily Gazette*, August 7, 8, 10, 1879; Bryan, *Wildest of West*, 111–112; Bartholomew, *Man and Myth*, 12–13; Affidavit of John McPherson, August 9, 1879, with *Territory v. James Pearson*, Case No. 994, Murder, August 13, 1879, SMCDCR, Las Vegas, New Mexico, NMSRCA.

75. *Territory v. John Pearson*, Case No. 992, Carrying Deadly Weapons, August 12, 1879; *Territory v. Philip Pearson*, Case No. 993, Carrying Deadly Weapons, August 12, 1879; *Territory v. James Pearson*, Case No. 994, August 13, 1879; *Territory v. James Pearson*, Case No. 995, Carrying Deadly Weapons, August 13, 1879; *Territory v. J. H. Holliday*, Case

No. 996, Carrying Deadly Weapons, August 13, 1879, SMCDCR, Las Vegas, New Mexico, NMSRCA.

76.   Thomas L. Preston to Samuel N. Lacy, August 18, 1879, Deed Record Book 11, San Miguel County, 340–342; Thomas L. Preston and Lee (?) to B. O. Bertholf, September 1, 1879, Deed Record Book 11, San Miguel County, 342–344. The saloon property was later sold by Preston (without Lacy or Lee) to John Dougher, another liquor dealer from Old Town, on October 24, 1879, Deed Record Book 13, San Miguel County, 8–10. Preston moved to Soccoro shortly thereafter. Dougher thereafter sold the property on March 8, 1880, to Charles A. Rathbun, who converted it into the Chicago Boot and Shoe Store. Dougher to Rathbun, Deed Record Book 15, San Miguel County, 8–10. The building burned down in a New Town fire on September 18, 1880. See *Las Vegas Daily Optic*, September 20, 1880. Also critical is Marcus Gottschalk to the author, October 2, 2004.

77.   The *Las Vegas Daily Optic*, December 8, 1879, reported, "Jesse James was a guest at the Las Vegas Hot Springs from July 26th to 29th. Of course it was not generally known." The Hot Springs Hotel was called the Adobe Hotel at the time and was owned by W. Scott Moore. H. T. Wilson, *Historical Sketch of Las Vegas, New Mexico Territory* (Chicago: Hotel World, 1880), ii. James was a friend of Moore, who was from the same part of Missouri as Jesse. Dr. Henry F. Hoyt and Miguel A. "Gillie" Otero also claimed to have seen Jesse at the hot springs in separate accounts. See Bryan, *Wildest of West*, 100–102.

78.   *Las Vegas Daily Gazette*, August 24, 1879; *Santa Fe Weekly New Mexican*, August 23, August 30, 1879. Bartholomew, *Man and Myth*, 15–20, makes unfounded charges that Holliday was involved in the stage robberies based largely on the reference of one of the robbers to Governor William Arny as that "antediluvian gentleman." Apparently, in Bartholomew's view, Holliday was the only educated man in San Miguel County.

79.   *Las Vegas Daily Gazette*, September 26, 1879; *Ford County Globe*, September 30, 1879.

80.   *Ford County Globe*, September 9, 1879.

81.   Ibid.; Flood notes of interview with Wyatt Earp, September 5, 1926, *Gilchriese Collection Catalogue*, part 1, 71; *Ford County Globe*, September 30, 1879.

82.   *Las Vegas Daily Gazette*, September 12, 13, 1879. Webb was described as "one of the proprietors" of the former Holliday Saloon where he was arrested. *Las Vegas Daily Optic*, February 5, 1880. The *Optic*, February 17, 1881, announced that "Jordan Webb has returned to Las Vegas a free man, having been acquitted of complicity in the stage robbery. The conspiracy against him was somewhat annoying, but could not be made to stick." On February 24, 1881, the paper also reported that "[a] petition is circulating asking that Jordan J. Webb be appointed a policeman in East Las Vegas." Of the reunion of Doc and Wyatt and Jim and their wives, Kate wrote, "Doc ran across them at the Plaza, making the third time he had met Wyatt. He went to their camp with them just outside of town and they begged to join them on their trip to Arizona." Cummings, Mazzanovich typescript, 3.

83.   *Las Vegas Daily Gazette*, September 26, 1879.

84.   *Dodge City Times*, October 18, 1879; *Ford County Globe*, October 21, 28, 1879.

85.   Tefertiller, *Wyatt Earp*, 36; Flood notes of interview with Wyatt Earp, September 5, 1926, *Gilchriese Collection Catalogue*, part 1, 71; Cummings, Mazzanovich typescript, 3. Kate remembered: "When we left Las Vegas, New Mexico our party consisted of Wyatt Earp and his wife Mattie, my husband and myself, Jim Earp and his step-daughter. Doc and I rode in Wyatt Earp's wagon. We had to be on our guard while in New Mexico, because the Warm Springs Apaches were on the war path, led by their famous war chief, Victorio. We camped for two days close to the Zuni village near the Arizona line. . . . It was during our trip from Las Vegas to Prescott that Doc and Wyatt became such good friends, which meant the end of the happiness we had enjoyed ever since our marriage." Cummings, Mazzanovich typescript, 10.

86. W. G. Ward claim, October 7, 1879, Deed Record Book 11, San Miguel County, 449–450.

87. Johnson and Requa to Holliday, July 31, 1879, Deed Record Book 12, San Miguel County, 184. Kate claimed that while she and Doc were in Las Vegas, the police came to arrest him: "She said to him, 'I wonder if they want to get you.' She sat on the porch with a six gun and in her night gown and told them if they wanted anything to come and get it." The occasion of this incident is unclear. Arthur W. Bork, notes of interview with Mary Katharine Cummings, Thanksgiving 1935, copy in author's files, courtesy Arthur W. Bork.

88. *Prescott (Arizona) Daily Miner*, November 29, 1879.

89. *Prescott Daily Miner*, March 20, 1880.

90. Bork and Boyer, "O.K. Corral Fight," 76–77.

91. *Dodge City Times*, March 13, 1880; *Las Vegas Daily Optic*, January 26, February 7, 9, 1880; *Santa Fe New Mexican*, February 14, 1880; see also Frank Whitelaw's account in the *Las Vegas Daily Optic*, August 23, 1897, and Colin W. Rickards, *Mysterious Dave Mather* (Santa Fe, NM: Press of the Territorian, 1968), 7–8.

92. *Las Vegas Daily Optic*, January 26, 1880.

93. *Las Vegas Daily Gazette*, March 3, 1880.

94. *Las Vegas Daily Gazette*, March 3, 4, 1880; *Las Vegas Daily Optic*, February 28, 1880; *Ford County Globe*, March 9, 1880; *Territory of New Mexico v. J. J. Webb*, Case No. 1024, Murder, March 5, 1880, SMCDCR, Las Vegas, New Mexico, NMSRCA.

95. *Las Vegas Daily Gazette* March 2, 1880; *Las Vegas Daily Optic*, March 5, 1880; *Santa Fe New Mexican*, March 3, 1880; *Territory of New Mexico v. J. J. Webb*, Case No. 1026, Murder, March 8, 1880, SMCDCR, Las Vegas, New Mexico, NMSRCA.

96. *Las Vegas Daily Optic*, March 4, 1880; *Las Vegas Daily Gazette*, March 5, 1880; *Territory of New Mexico v. Hyman G. Neill*, Case No. 1027, Larceny, March 6, 1880, SMCDCR, Las Vegas, New Mexico, NMSRCA.

97. *Territory v. J. J. Webb*, Case No. 1029, Murder, March 12, 1880, SMCDCR, Las Vegas, New Mexico, NMSRCA; *Las Vegas Daily Optic*, March 11, 13, 1880; *Dodge City Times*, March 13, 1880; *Ford County Globe*, March 9, 16, 1880.

98. The *Las Vegas Daily Optic*, February 25, 1881, carried a detailed account of Webb's life. Myers, "John Joshua Webb," 25, provides a good summary of the outcome of the Webb case and of Webb's last days.

99. *Territory v. John H. Holliday*, Case No. 990, Keeping Gaming Table, August 12, 1879; *Territory v. John Holliday*, Case No. 996, Carrying Deadly Weapon, August 13, 1879, SMCDCR, Las Vegas, New Mexico, NMSRCA; Criminal Docket Book, San Miguel County, 79–80; Criminal Record Book of the District Court, San Miguel County, 527–528, 539; Civil Record Book A, District Court, San Miguel County, 121.

100. Miguel Antonio Otero, *My Life on the Frontier* (New York: Press of the Pioneers, 1935), 218.

101. Ibid., 216.

102. Ibid., 217–218.

103. C. W. Wright of Dodge City, Kansas, was listed as a recent arrival at the Mackley House in Las Vegas about the time that Doc left Las Vegas with Wyatt Earp in 1879. *Las Vegas Daily Gazette*, September 13, 1879. In the 1880 census, Wright was listed as a thirty-eight-year-old, single, white saloonkeeper, living in East Las Vegas, Precinct 29, p. 65. See the advertisement for his saloon in the *Las Vegas Daily Optic*, June 23, 1880. The *Leavenworth Daily Commercial*, July 26, 1874, lists Charles Wright as one of the defenders at Adobe Walls.

104. William R. Cox, *Luke Short and His Era* (New York: Doubleday, 1961), 179–182. At the time, the *Dallas News*, December 24, 1890, reported, "Wright has been regarded as a terrible man, while Short's reputation is that of a man of iron nerve."

105. F. Stanley, *The Duke City: The Story of Albuquerque, New Mexico, 1706–1956* (Pampa, TX: Pampa Print Shop, 1963), 36–37, 40–49. On June 2, 1880, the *Las Vegas Daily Optic* announced, "Holliday & Sanguinette, of Albuquerque, have leased the hotel de Kelly at Bernalillo and took charge today."

106. "J. H. Holladay" was listed as a dentist living with Richard Elliott and John J. Gosper in the same household. U.S. Census, Territory of Arizona, Yavapai County, Prescott, June 2, 3, 1880, 4; see also Tanner, *Family Portrait*, 141.

5. The Price of a Reputation

1. *Tucson (Arizona) Daily Citizen*, August 17, 1880; *Tucson (Arizona) Daily Star*, August 26, 27, September 2, 10, 12, 1880; *Tombstone (Arizona) Daily Epitaph*, August 24, September 15, 24, 1880. For a useful analysis of the sources, see Roger Jay, "The Gambler's War in Tombstone: Fact or Artifact?" *WOLA Journal* 14 (Spring 2005): 11–12. Also useful are Bob Alexander, *John H. Behan: Sacrificed Sheriff* (Silver City, NM: High-Lonesome, 2002), 58–59, and Casey Tefertiller, *Wyatt Earp: The Life behind the Legend* (New York: Wiley, 1997), 50–51.

2. Great Register of Pima County, District 17 (Tombstone), No. 1483, September 27, 1880. Oddly, Wyatt Earp, No. 3194, Morgan Earp, No. 3258, and James Earp, 3267, registered on the same day. Only Virgil had registered earlier, No. 2495, January 20, 1880.

3. Clara Spalding Brown to the editor, July 7, 1880, *San Diego Union*, July 14, 1880.

4. Clara Spalding Brown, "An Arizona Mining District," *The Californian* 4 (July–December 1881): 53–56; Brown to the editor, August 3, 1880, *San Diego Union*, August 10, 1880; *San Francisco Exchange*, September 28, 1880.

5. Two works provide essential background for any study of Tombstone: William B. Shillingberg, *Tombstone, A. T.: A History of Early Mining, Milling, and Mayhem* (Spokane, WA: Clark, 1999), and Lynn R. Bailey, *"Too Tough to Die": The Rise, Fall, and Resurrection of a Silver Camp, 1878 to 1990* (Tucson, AZ: Westernlore, 2004).

6. Brown to the editor, July 7, August 3, 1880, *San Diego Union*, July 14, August 10, 1880.

7. *Tombstone Daily Epitaph*, October 20, 1880.

8. For a good summary of the early days of the Earps in Tombstone, see Tefertiller, *Wyatt Earp*, 34–50.

9. *Dodge City Ford County Globe*, March 30, 1880.

10. Tefertiller, *Wyatt Earp*, 43–45.

11. Bailey, *"Too Tough to Die,"* 73–80, 97, 124–125. Boundaries for the red-light district were set by Ordinance No. 10, enacted April 18, 1881.

12. See Roger Jay, "The Gamblers' War in Tombstone," *Wild West* (October 2004): 38–45, 73; Jay, "Fact or Artifact?" 9–35.

13. Jay, "Fact or Artifact?" 9–10; Lynn R. Bailey and Don Chaput, *Cochise County Stalwarts: A Who's Who of the Territorial Years* (Tucson, AZ: Westernlore, 2000), 1:66, 206–207, 2:81, 168; Brown to the editor, August 3, 1880, *San Diego Union*, August 10, 1880.

14. The ownership of the Alhambra is somewhat confusing. It was apparently opened by Thomas H. Corrigan in 1880, and Dick Clark appears to have come to Tombstone to help him start up the operation before obtaining an interest in the Oriental's gambling concession. Mellgren took over as proprietor sometime in 1880, and Meagher joined him. See entries on Clark, Corrigan, Meagher, and Mellgren in Bailey and Chaput, *Cochise County Stalwarts*, 1:66, 75, 2:24–25.

15. Jay, "Fact or Artifact?" 12–13, reviews most of the sources about Tyler.

16. *Tombstone Daily Epitaph*, September 24, 1880.

17. *Tombstone Daily Epitaph*, October 12, 1880; *Tombstone Daily Nugget*, October 12, 1880.

18. *Territory of Arizona v. J. H. Holliday*, County Recorder's Office, Cochise County, Bisbee, Arizona; *Tombstone Daily Epitaph*, October 12, 16, 17, 23, 24, 1880. On October 23, the *Epitaph* reported, "During the past day or two inflammation set in on M. E. Joyce's wounded hand, and at one time it looked as though amputation would have to be resorted to in order to save [his] life. Yesterday, however, showed a change for the better, and the chances of saving the hand are much improved." In the end, the only thing that did not heal was the relationship between Joyce and Doc.

19. The exact arrival time of both Harris and Short is somewhat unclear. See Jay, "Fact or Artifact?" 25–26. The *Tucson Weekly Citizen*, February 27, 1881, said that Short had been working for Rickabaugh as a security guard for "some months." Harris left Dodge City in the fall of 1880, going first to San Francisco before moving to Tombstone. See *Dodge City Times*, October 9, 1880, January 1, 1881. Short has been usually depicted as one of the Dodge City crowd that included Harris, Masterson, and Earp, with Harris importing Short to Tombstone because of his personal knowledge of him. Curiously, no references to Short have been located in Dodge City until after he left Tombstone. That does not mean he could not have been there; many gamblers came and went with little notice, as Doc's own experience demonstrates. William R. Cox, *Luke Short and His Era* (New York: Doubleday, 1961), 44–65, has Short in Dodge in 1878 and 1879, except for excursions between cattle seasons. Wayne Short, *Luke Short: A Biography* (Tombstone, AZ: Devil's Thumb, 1996), 91, 139, says that Luke dealt for Harris and Beeson in the spring of 1878 and managed the gambling concession in the spring of 1879. By Luke's own account, he was located in Ogallalah, Nebraska, in 1878, until he worked with the army as a scout during the Indian troubles in Nebraska that year, after which he returned to Ogallalah before moving west to Leadville, Colorado, in 1879. Short says, "In June 1880 left Leadville and after a short time in Kansas City Mo went to Arizona and located in Tombstone in November 1880, remained in Arizionia [*sic*] till April 1881, when he went to Dodge City remained there during the summer of 1881, 2 & 3." Luke Short Dictation, Hubert Howe Bancroft Manuscript P-033, Bancroft Library, University of California, Berkeley, California. Significantly, William Barclay Masterson, "Famous Gunfighters of the Western Frontier: Luke Short," *Human Life* (April 1907): 9–10, also did not place him in Dodge City until after he left Tombstone. This raises the distinct possibility that Short and Harris arrived in Tombstone about the same time, but leaves unanswered the question of who actually hired Short and on whose advice.

20. The key sources are the *Tombstone Daily Epitaph*, October 28, 1880, the *Tucson Daily Citizen*, December 20, 1880, and the *Tucson (Arizona) Weekly Star*, November 4, December 22, 23, 25, 27, 1880. For analysis of the confrontation, see Steve Gatto, *Curly Bill: Tombstone's Most Famous Outlaw* (Lansing, MI: Protar House, 2003), 34–40, and Tefertiller, *Wyatt Earp*, 51–52; see also, Timothy W. Fattig, "'Let Him Beware Who Takes the Life of a Fellow Being': A Sketch of Frederick G. White, Tombstone's First Marshal," *NOLA Quarterly* 24 (April–June 2000): 5–11. There are numerous other accounts. See the notes of the works cited.

21. Fred Dodge, *Under Cover for Wells Fargo: The Unvarnished Recollections of Fred Dodge*. Edited by Carolyn Lake (Boston: Houghton Mifflin, 1969), 10. Also included in this work is Dodge's letter to Stuart N. Lake, October 28, 1928, in which he covered the Fred White shooting, see pp. 235–236. Robert J. Chandler, "Undercover for Wells Fargo: A Review Essay," *Journal of Arizona History* 41 (Spring 2000): 83–96, and Don Chaput, "Fred Dodge: Undercover Agent or Con Man," *NOLA Quarterly* 25 (January–March 2000): 10–15, have raised questions about Dodge's claims and suggested that he was a fraud, but the researchers Peter Brand and Robert F. Palmquist have uncovered primary sources that indicate that Fred Dodge was affiliated with Wells, Fargo as early as 1880. For example, see Application for "Special Ranger," February 1, 1900, with endorsement by G. A. Taft, Superintendent, Wells, Fargo & Co. Express, FB 401-130, Adjutant General's Records,

Texas State Library and Archives, Austin, Texas. In these documents, Dodge gives his occupation as "Special officer for Wells Fargo & Co." with "20 years" experience. A careful reading of Dodge's account suggests that the problem may lie in the unfortunate title of the book. His own account indicates that he initially operated as an informer rather than as an undercover agent. Later, he became an agent of Wells, Fargo. In 1882, Doc Holliday apparently claimed that he arrested Curly Bill. During an interview with the *Denver Republican*, May 22, 1882, Doc was quoted as saying, "Trouble first arose . . . by the killing of Marshal White by Curly Bill. Marshal White fell into my arms when he was shot and I arrested Curly Bill." He was under arrest at the time and needing to establish his reputation as a law and order supporter and may have exaggerated his role because of that, or, given his temperament, he may simply have enjoyed "pulling the legs" of reporters. In either case, while Doc was involved that night, he certainly did not catch the mortally wounded White or arrest him.

22. Tefertiller, *Wyatt Earp*, 51; Shillingberg, *Tombstone, A. T.*, 159–160; *Tombstone Daily Epitaph*, October 29, 31, 1880. Doc was part of the party that escorted Wyatt and Curly Bill as far as Benson, where Curly Bill was transferred to the train into Tucson.

23. *Tombstone Daily Epitaph*, October 29, November 1, 1880.

24. *Tombstone Daily Epitaph*, November 11, 1880; *Tombstone Daily Nugget*, November 2, 12, 1880; *Silver City, New Mexico, Grant County Herald*, November 13, 1880; see also Timothy W. Fattig, *Wyatt Earp: The Biography* (Honolulu, HI: Talei, 2002), 214–217.

25. The trial testimony was presented in the *Tucson Daily Citizen*, December 28, 1880; the judge's decision in the *Tucson Weekly Star*, December 28, 1880. Both are reprinted in Gatto, *Curly Bill*, 44–53.

26. Bailey, *"Too Tough to Die,"* 122–123. Bailey points out that the killing of Marshal White led to a public demand for changes in City Ordinance No. 9, which prohibited "carrying concealed weapons," to "prohibiting the carrying of deadly weapons in any way." He also notes that when Tombstone was granted a city charter on February 21, 1881, Tombstone abolished the old town marshal's office and created a police department with a chief of police and "such number of regular policemen" as required, supervised by a Board of Police Commissioners. Nashville Franklin Leslie was a mercurial character who had killed Mike Killeen the previous spring in a gunfight over Leslie's attention to Killeen's wife. Buckskin Frank, despite his shortcomings, including wife beating, was a close associate of Milt Joyce. See Bailey and Chaput, *Cochise County Stalwarts*, 2:6. He was officially appointed special deputy on November 29, 1880, with "power of arrest on the premises of the Oriental Saloon." Minute Book, Town Council, Village of Tombstone, 24; see also Alford E. Turner, ed., *The Earps Talk* (College Station, TX: Creative, 1980), 23n.

27. For discussion of the election dispute, see Tefertiller, *Wyatt Earp*, 53–54, and Shillingberg, *Tombstone, A. T.*, 162–168.

28. *Tombstone Daily Nugget*, November 12, 1880. Alexander, *Sacrificed Sheriff*, 67–68, argues that the circumstances suggest that Shibell asked for Earp's resignation.

29. *Tucson Daily Star*, November 14, 1880.

30. Shillingberg, *Tombstone, A. T.*, 166.

31. Ibid., 169–170; Tefertiller, *Wyatt Earp*, 54.

32. See Survey Field Notes for the First Northern Extension of the Mountain Maid Mining Claim, General Land Office, No. 6716, Mineral Certificate No. 78, Lot No. 62, November 10–16, 1880, and Record of Mines, County Recorder's Office, Book J, 432–433, Pima County, Arizona. The affidavit bearing Doc's signature is reproduced in Ben T. Traywick, *John Henry (The "Doc" Holliday Story)* (Tombstone, AZ: Red Marie's Bookstore, 1996), 93. See also Shillingberg, *Tombstone, A. T.*, 170– 171.

33. Tefertiller, *Wyatt Earp*, 55. A different perspective is offered by Alexander, *Sacrificed Sheriff*, 74–75. Wyatt Earp was never politically shrewd; Behan clearly was. Earp

might best be described as naive or at least inexperienced with party politics. His experience in Kansas, especially in Dodge, ill prepared him for the contentious politics of Arizona. There, city and county governments were both Republican, and although there were factions, they tended to work more cooperatively.

34. *Tombstone Daily Nugget*, December 8, 1880; George Whitwell Parsons, *The Private Journal of George W. Parsons* (Tombstone, AZ: Tombstone Epitaph, 1972), 107–108.

35. Gatto, *Curly Bill*, 57–63; Tefertiller, *Wyatt Earp*, 59–65.

36. The most balanced account of the Johnny-behind-the-Deuce affair is found in Tefertiller, *Wyatt Earp*, 56–59. Debate about the incident has centered on the role of Wyatt Earp, or, more fundamentally, if the crowd that gathered was a mob or a gaggle of curiosity seekers. The *Tucson Daily Citizen*, January 15, 1881, clearly demonstrates the intent of the crowd, noting, "Shortly after a mob collected and would undoubtedly have hung the prisoner but for the firmness of Marshal Sippy and the other officers." The *Citizen* did not mention Earp specifically, but, as Tefertiller demonstrates, he was clearly a major player in what happened. Parsons, *Journal*, 118.

37. Richard Brinsley Sheridan Clark was a remarkable character who retained a reputation for honesty as a gambler throughout his career. See Bailey and Chaput, *Cochise County Stalwarts*, 1:66. He, like Doc, was consumptive. See also C. L. Sonnichsen, *Billy King's Tombstone* (Tucson: University of Arizona Press, 1972), 117–141. For Leavy, see William B. Secrest, "Jim Levy: Top-Notch Gunfighter," *True West* 25 (August 1978): 24–26, 56–58; William Barclay Masterson, "Famous Gunfighters of the Western Frontier: Ben Thompson," *Human Life* (January 1907): 9; Joseph G. Rosa, *Gunfighter: Man or Myth?* (Norman: University of Oklahoma Press, 1969), 142–144.

38. Robert F. Palmquist, "Gambling on Water," *Arizona Territorial Justice Forum* (September 5, 2002): 12–18; the Wyatt Earp, Clark, and Holliday rights appear in Transcribed Millsites Book 1, pp. 150–153, County Recorder's Office, Cochise County, Bisbee, Arizona; Paul Cool, "The World of Sherman McMaster," *WOLA Journal* 7 (Autumn 1998): 10–22; Peter Brand, "Sherman W. McMaster(s): The El Paso Salt War, Texas Rangers, and Tombstone," *WOLA Journal* 8 (Winter 1999): 2–19.

39. Tefertiller, *Wyatt Earp*, 55–56, summarizes the sources well, but the author has followed Palmquist, "Gambling on Water," 15–16, in placing the episode in February 1881, rather than in late December 1880, as Tefertiller does, because it fits better with the existing primary sources and Wyatt Earp's known movements.

40. Tefertiller, *Wyatt Earp*, 56.

41. Testimony of John Behan, *Tombstone Daily Nugget* and *Tombstone Daily Epitaph*, November 2–5, 1881; John Flood's notes of interview with Wyatt Earp, September 5, 1926, 137–139, John D. Gilchreise Collection.

42. Bailey, *"Too Tough to Die,"* 96–97; Shillingberg, *Tombstone, A. T.*, 185–187; Tefertiller, *Wyatt Earp*, 67–69.

43. *Ford County Globe*, February 15, 1881. George T. Buffum, *Smith of Bear River* (New York: Grafton, 1906), 119–127, claimed that Masterson traveled to Tombstone with Judge William H. Stilwell and protected him from ruffians who were "offended" by his high silk hat. The *Arizona Weekly Citizen*, March 13, 1881, reported, "Masterson Bros., Jim Bruce, Charley Gill and Mr. Tipton have arrived from the Black Hills." The "Mr. Tipton" was Daniel G. Tipton, who would later be allied with the Earps and Doc Holliday.

44. *Santa Fe New Mexican*, March 2, 1881. For more on Storms, see Masterson, "Luke Short," 10, and Jay, "Fact or Artifact?" 26.

45. The best exposition of the Short-Storms affair is Robert F. Palmquist, "'Snuffing Out a Gambler': Short vs. Storms," *Wild West* (October 2004): 30–36. Other critical sources include the *Arizona Weekly Citizen*, February 27, 1881; the *Tucson Weekly Star*, March 3, 1881; Parsons, *Journal*, 128; John H. Flood Jr., "Wyatt Earp (a Peace Officer of Tombstone)," unpublished manuscript, 1927, 137–139, C. Lee Simmons Collection; and

Santa Fe New Mexican, March 2, 1881. Harry E. Gryden, a Dodge City attorney, friend of Harris, Short, Masterson, and Earp, and the local correspondent of the Associated Press, would report, doubtlessly based on his conversations with his friends, that Storms was hired by the Slopers. See *National Police Gazette*, July 23, 1883.

46. Parsons, *Journal*, 128; *Phoenix (Arizona) Herald*, March 4, 1881. The nature of the incident involving Dublin is unclear, but it may have started over the postmortem examination of Storms's body. Wyatt Earp testified at the Crabtree trial in 1925 that he was one of the men who carried Storms to his room at the San Jose House after he was shot. He said, "The doctor was going to hold a post mortem and they wanted me to stick around." Lotta Crabtree Probate Case, p. 295, Harvard Law Library, Harvard University, Cambridge, Massachusetts. The Lake notes in the Stuart N. Lake Collection, Huntington Library, San Marino, California, include the cryptic statement that "Dublin, Storms partner, tried to stop post mortem." See also Jay, "Fact or Artifact?" 26, for more about the possible identity of Dublin.

47. *Phoenix Herald*, March 4, 1881; *Las Vegas Daily Optic*, April 16, 1881. Ed Bartholomew, *Wyatt Earp: The Man and the Myth* (Toyahvale, TX: Frontier Book, 1964), 144–145, says McAllister was a gambler, not the Galeyville butcher.

48. Parsons, *Journal*, 130. He added, "Much bad blood today. Pistols pulled." Could this be one of the confrontations in the Earp literature that are undocumented? What is most troubling, in light of the standard accounts that make Earp a partner in the Oriental as early as January 1881 (see this discussion in Jay, "Fact or Artifact?" 16–20), is the absence of contemporary evidence linking Earp to the Oriental before the events in late February. There are references to Earp gambling at the Danner & Owens Saloon (run by his friend R. J. Winders), at Vogan's (where his brother James worked), and at the Eagle Brewery, but no direct references to the Oriental. Joyce later claimed that initially he was "a firm friend and supporter" of the Earps, "only going against them when John Behan, his warm personal friend, ran for Sheriff." *San Francisco Examiner*, November 30, 1889.

49. *Tombstone Daily Epitaph*, March 11, 1881. Kate joined Doc in Tombstone in early March. Typescript of Recollections of Mary Katharine Cummings as Given to Anton Mazzonovich, 2–3, Kevin J. Mulkins Collection.

50. Wyatt Earp to Walter Noble Burns, March 15, 1927, Walter Noble Burns Collection, Special Collections, University of Arizona Library, Tucson, Arizona. The physical description of Leonard comes from the reward poster released following the Benson stage robbery.

51. Ibid. Two other versions must be noted. First, the *Tucson Daily Star*, March 26, 1882, more than a year later, carried an extended review of the Earp–Cow-Boy troubles. In it, the *Star* claimed, "At about 8:30 that same evening [of the robbery attempt at Drew's Station], Doc Holliday rode up to a saloon in Charleston, ten miles from below the scene of the attempted robbery and inquired for Billy Clanton. On being told that he was not there, [Holliday] started for Tombstone, which was nine miles distant, and at about 10 o'clock rode up to a saloon on a back street in Tombstone and called for a big drink of whisky, which he drank at a gulp, without dismounting. His horse at the time was covered with foam. This all happened before the news of the murder reached Tombstone. At midnight the agent, and the Earp brothers, with Holliday, left town to meet Paul." Second, Wells, Fargo issued a statement in the March 23, 1882, issue of the *San Francisco Examiner* that said in part, "Doc Holiday [*sic*], although a man of dissipated habits and a gambler, has never been a thief and was never in any way connected with the attempted stage robbery when Philpot [*sic*], the stage driver was killed. For three quarters of an hour after the stage passed the Wells, two and a half miles from Tombstone, he was seen at the latter place, so drunk that he was helped upon his horse, and the robbery occurred thirteen miles from Tombstone, so it was utterly impossible for him to be there. Neither did he form a part of

agent Williams' and detective Paul's posse afterward." The juxtaposition of these two accounts provides clear contrasts in the timing of Holliday's movements, and the Wells, Fargo statement is critical in absolving Doc of participation, as the company was not in the habit of defending persons guilty of attempting to rob their gold shipments. Notably, the *Star*'s account, which was intended to implicate Holliday in the botched robbery attempt, had Doc arriving at a saloon in Tombstone "at about 10 o'clock." The robbery attempt occurred near ten o'clock, which means, if the *Star*'s report is accurate, that Doc could not have been involved.

52. Frederick R. Bechdolt to William M. Breakenridge, December 23, 1927, William M. Breakenridge Letters, Houghton Library, Harvard University, Cambridge, Massachusetts.

53. *Tombstone Daily Epitaph*, March 16, 17, 1881; *Tucson Daily Star*, March 17, 1881; *Sacramento (California) Daily Union*, March 17, 1881; Clara Spalding Brown to the editor, March 19, 1881, *San Diego Union*, March 26, 1881; *San Francisco Daily Exchange*, March 16, 1881; *San Francisco Examiner*, May 28, 1882; Parsons, *Journal*, 133; see also Coroner's Inquest, Elihu Philpott and Peter Roerig, March 1881, MS 150, F.326, Cochise County Records, Arizona Historical Society, Tucson, Arizona.

54. Ibid. Paul claimed that Bat Masterson was a passenger on the stage, according to the *Phoenix Arizona Republican*, June 26, 1892. See also "F" to the editor, March 16, 1881, *Phoenix Herald*, March 19, 1881. Kate would use the mention of rope beards to foster her claim that the Earps were somehow involved, stating, in one account (Mary Katharine Cummings, typescript of recollections prepared by Arthur W. Bork, unpublished manuscript, p. 3, copy in author's files, courtesy Arthur W. Bork) that Wyatt had opened a trunk, pulled out a fake beard, and asked her if she knew what it was. Frank Waters, *The Earp Brothers of Tombstone: The Story of Mrs. Virgil Earp* (New York: Clarkson N. Potter, 1960), 109, 130, has Allie Earp, Virgil's wife, mention the fake beards, but these references do not appear in his original work, "Tombstone Travesty," first version, 1936, Frank Waters Papers, Center for Southwest Research, University of New Mexico, Albuquerque, New Mexico. Although court records relating to Kate's specific accusations against Doc have disappeared, she was likely the source of the rope beards story. The *Tucson Star*, March 26, 1882, said, "In the meantime, Holliday had a quarrel with the woman he had been living with, and she denounced him before the authorities and swore that 'Doc' had a rope mask in his trunk for a month, before the killing of Philpot [*sic*], and that she knew that he was implicated in the murder." That is the earliest account linking Kate and the rope beard story.

55. *San Francisco Examiner*, May 28, 1882; *Tucson Weekly Star*, March 24, 1881; *Tucson Daily Citizen*, March 27, 1881; *Sacramento Daily Union*, March 22, 1881; *Phoenix Herald*, March 25, 1881.

56. Virgil Earp to Crawley P. Dake, March 21, 1881, quoted in Larry D. Ball, *The United States Marshals of New Mexico and Arizona Territories, 1846–1912* (Albuquerque: University of New Mexico Press, 1978), 118.

57. *Tombstone Daily Epitaph*, March 21, 24, 1881; *San Francisco Examiner*, May 28, 1882. Wyatt and Bat reached Tombstone on March 23, after their long walk.

58. Parsons, *Journal*, 134.

59. Cummings, Mazzanovich typescript, 11. On March 21, 1881, the *Tombstone Daily Epitaph* announced that "Kate Holliday [and] Mrs. King" had gone to Charleston by stage. The reason for the trip was not explained, but it was not the date she left for Globe.

60. From the beginning, the news reports said that the robbery involved four men (although rumors spread that there were more). Bill Leonard, Jim Crane, and Harry Head were still at large; Luther King was in custody. Hence, the reference to "the fourth" at Tombstone being followed is puzzling at best. It is true that some reports indicated that

King was implicated in the robbery but only as the holder of the horses. In fact, the *Tucson Daily Citizen* reported on March 27, 1881, that "a gentleman, just in from Willcox states that it is the general impression there that the supposed confederate in charge of Sheriff Behan [King] is not one of the parties concerned in the murder and attempted stage robbery, but that he is cognizant of their whereabouts and intentions, and is taken away to remove him from improper influence. It is also suspected that the officers are on a wrong scout, and the real culprits are now about the streets of Willcox unrecognized." In its report of the capture of King, the *Sacramento Daily Union*, March 22, 1881, suggested that possibly as many as nine men were involved and wrote, "Meanwhile it is certain that several men around town, among them *one who was a participant in the preliminary pursuit*, are under surveillance [italics added]." Some latter-day accounts included Doc in the original posse, but he was not mentioned in any of the contemporary documents, so this reference appears to have been about another person. The *Los Angeles Times*, March 24, 1881, identified the arrested man as "William Allen." A man of that name would be associated later with the outlaw element. See Tefertiller, *Wyatt Earp*, 103. Doc's friendship with Leonard made him vulnerable to rumor, but the certitude with which some writers have identified the fourth man as Doc is based on events that happened later and misrepresentations made by William M. Breakenridge in *Helldorado: Bringing Law to the Mesquite* (Boston: Houghton Mifflin, 1928), 212–213. Breakenridge confused the dates in the *Tombstone Daily Nugget* reports, then added a statement to a *Tucson Daily Star* article that did not appear in the original. He cites the article as March 24, but actually the article was published on March 31, which concerned King's escape. The sentence Breakenridge added said, "He was an important witness against Holliday." Robert F. Palmquist discovered the discrepancy. Palmquist to Tefertiller, August 7, 1995, copy in the author's files. See also Casey Tefertiller, "Resolving Earp Myths," *NOLA Quarterly* 21 (October–December 1997): 3–4.

61. William M. Breakenridge's handwritten statement, circa 1910, Special Collections, University of Arizona, Tucson, Arizona. The report of the movements of the suspect in the *Tucson Star* article on March 24 do not fit well with other accounts of Doc's movements, including Breakenridge's. The *Tucson Star*, March 26, 1882, provided further support for the idea that Doc was suspected in the days after the attempted holdup.

62. The reward poster was first reproduced in Tefertiller, *Wyatt Earp*, 209. Later, on August 25, 1881, the *Tucson Weekly Star* printed an article claiming that the robbery attempt was also part of a plot to assassinate Bob Paul and that he had avoided being killed only because he had swapped places with Bud Philpott and was driving at the time of the robbery attempt. See Tefertiller, *Wyatt Earp*, 87–88, 353n, for a discussion of the sources on this topic. This story lacks plausibility, if for the simple reason that it makes it hard to explain losing the traces when the first shots were fired or how Paul reacted so quickly. If it were true, it would make Doc's participation even less likely because it defies all logic to conclude that Holliday would be involved in a plot to kill Wyatt Earp's friend and ally.

63. *Tombstone Evening Gossip*, March 29, 1881. King was charged with "aiding and assisting to murder" in Judge A. O. Wallace's court. *Territory v. Luther King*, Justice of the Peace Court, Report of Criminal Business, List of Cases, F.386, CCR, AHS.

64. *Tombstone Evening Gossip*, March 29, 1881.

65. Ibid.

66. *San Francisco Examiner*, May 28, 1882.

67. *Tombstone Daily Nugget*, March 31, 1881.

68. Parsons, *Journal*, 136.

69. *Tucson Daily Citizen*, April 5, 1881.

70. *Tombstone Daily Epitaph*, March 30, 1881.

71. James B. Hume to Lida Munson, March (?) 1881, James B. Hume Collection, Bancroft Library, University of California, Berkeley, California.

72. *Tombstone Daily Epitaph*, March 30, 1881.

73. *Tucson Weekly Star*, April 8, 1881. The *Tombstone Daily Epitaph*, April 1, 1881, had already reported rumors of King's death but concluded that the rumors were false and "stories about King's death were started to throw the officers off the scent."

74. Brown to the editor, April 8, 1881, *San Diego Union*, April 14, 1881. See also *Tombstone Daily Epitaph*, April 4, 1881, for a detailed recounting of the expedition.

75. *Prescott (Arizona) Daily Miner*, April 6, 1881.

76. *San Francisco Examiner*, May 28, 1882. For a discussion of the importance of Harry Woods's appointment as undersheriff and its effect on the relationship between Behan and Earp, see Tefertiller, *Wyatt Earp*, 80–82; see also Alexander, *Sacrificed Sheriff*, 83.

77. Earp to Burns, March 15, 1927, Walter Noble Burns Collection.

78. *Territory of Arizona v. J. H. Holliday*, April 13, 1881, Docket Book, Justice's Court, City of Tombstone; *Tucson Daily Star*, April 28, 1881; Pink Simms to Noah H. Rose, April 4, 1935, quoted in Bartholomew, *Man and Myth*, 146–147. See also Karen Holliday Tanner, *Doc Holliday: A Family Portrait* (Norman: University of Oklahoma Press, 1998), 152.

79. *Ford County Globe*, April 19, 1881. This and other articles related to the fight at Dodge City appear in Nyle H. Miller and Joseph W. Snell, *Why the West Was Wild: A Contemporary Look at Some Highly Publicized Kansas Cowtown Personalities* (Topeka: Kansas State Historical Society, 1963), 410–413. The disposition of Luke Short's case and his departure from Tombstone is covered most authoritatively in Palmquist, "Short vs. Storms," 35–36. Most accounts have Rickabaugh offer Earp an interest in the Oriental in February 1881, about the time that Cochise County was created, and, in some, as a result of Earp's actions in the Johnny-behind-the-Deuce affair. See Jay, "Fact or Artifact?" 31–34, for a thorough review of the literature. The present account takes a different view based largely on the absence of contemporary evidence to support the early association. References do exist for Earp gambling at Danner & Owens Saloon, the Eagle Brewery, and Vogan's during the time when he is supposed to have been a partner in the Oriental. Furthermore, while Earp claims to have been an eyewitness to the Short-Storms shooting (see Flood, "Wyatt Earp," 130–133), he does not appear to have played any role until after the fight, at which time he was one of the men who carried Storms to the San Jose House. See Crabtree Testimony, 295. The Oriental appears to have been closed for the month of March, because the *Tombstone Daily Epitaph* announced on April 1, 1881, that the Oriental had reopened on March 29. Vizina and Cook would add a second story to the Oriental that spring, and Rickabaugh would open lavish rooms on the second floor on June 11, 1881, managed by "Mr. Freeze." See *Tombstone Daily Epitaph*, June 12, 15, 1881. Plausibly then, the departure of Masterson, Short, and Harris in April and May left Rickabaugh without security and anxious to find someone to fill the job. Turner, *Earps Talk*, 23, reports that gun expert Don Shumar of Tombstone had an 1881 business card for Rickabaugh & Company, listing as partners "W. Erp," Clark, and Rickabaugh, which almost certainly was printed after Harris left the partnership and returned to Dodge. From May 1881 forward, Earp is regularly connected to the Oriental in the sources, and, for these reasons, I offer the hypothesis that he became a partner later than generally supposed and at a point after the relationship between him and Milt Joyce had been strained, not only by his association with Holliday but also by his political differences with John Behan.

80. *Tucson Weekly Citizen*, May 29, 1881. This is potentially important because of Earp's claim that after his own confrontation with Tyler at the Oriental (an incident usually placed in mid-February), Tyler left town.

81. *Territory v. J. H. Holliday*, Case No. 23, Minutes of the District Court, Cachise [*sic*] County, 75, 77, William H. Stilwell Collection, Utah State Department of Archives, Salt Lake City, Utah. Other documents from the Criminal Register of Actions for Cochise County are reproduced in Traywick, *John Henry*, 109–111.

82. *Territory v. Holliday*, Minutes, pp. 75, 77, 78, 87; *Tombstone Daily Epitaph*, June 5, 1881.

83. Statement of Wyatt Earp, *Tombstone Daily Nugget* and *Tombstone Daily Epitaph*, November 17, 1881.

84. The telegram was presented in court by the Earps' defense attorney during the questioning of Ike Clanton at the Spicer hearing. See also the statement of Wyatt Earp, *Tombstone Daily Nugget* and *Tombstone Daily Epitaph*, November 17, 1881.

85. Testimony of Virgil Earp, *Tombstone Daily Nugget* and *Tombstone Daily Epitaph*, November 20 and 23, 1881.

86. Statement of Wyatt Earp, *Tombstone Daily Nugget* and *Tombstone Daily Epitaph*, November 17, 1881.

87. Tefertiller, *Wyatt Earp*, 85–86, summarizes the evidence.

88. *Tombstone Daily Epitaph*, June 9, 1881. The *Tombstone Daily Nugget*, June 9, 1881, identifies McCann as "Little Dan Burns." Burns was associated with the "top and bottom" gang at Benson. However, Fred Dodge wrote that McCann was his partner at Tombstone and said of him, "Dan was a good, and square Gambler and as soon as he got acquainted, he become very popular for he was a Man that you just had to like—Small of Stature, Irish, and witty—and a Game little fellow." Dodge said that he and McCann jointly ran a faro game. See Dodge, *Under Cover*, 25, 27–28.

89. *Tombstone Daily Epitaph*, June 21, 1881; *Mayor and Common Council of the City of Tombstone v. Wyatt Earp*, June 19, 1881, Recorder's Court, City of Tombstone.

90. *Tombstone Daily Epitaph*, June 12, 1881; *Mayor and Common Council of Tombstone v. M. E. Joyce*, June 11, 1881, Recorder's Court, City of Tombstone. Lake notes; Stuart N. Lake, *Wyatt Earp: Frontier Marshal* (Boston: Houghton Mifflin, 1931), 253– 254. What is missing in the Lake notes is any detail about the episode. One frustrating note is the single phrase "month or so," which seems to imply that the incident took place a month or so before the fire (which would place the incident closer to June 19 than to mid-February where Lake placed it). Philip J. Rasch notes, in reference to the *Epitaph* article, that the confrontation was between Wyatt and Doc (the two gamblers) and Milt Joyce (the other party), although he does not provide sources for his conclusion. Philip J. Rasch Collection, Box 2, AHS.

91. The details of the fire are covered in Bailey, *"Too Tough to Die,"* 98–99; Shillingberg, *Tombstone, A. T.*, 213–219; *Tombstone Daily Epitaph*, June 28, 1881. Joyce's losses were placed at $10,000, and Rickabaugh's at $5,000. The new Oriental would be a single story building but expanded to cover the entire lot. Gary L. Roberts, "The Leadville Years," *True West* 48 (November–December 2001): 67.

92. Tefertiller, *Wyatt Earp*, 81–82; Brown to the editor, August 23, 1881, *San Diego Union*, August 28, 1881. It should be noted that Mayor Clum kept up a steady barrage of attacks on Milt Joyce for his role on the Board of Supervisors and on Harry Woods, undersheriff and editor of the *Tombstone Daily Nugget*, through the spring and summer of 1881.

93. Bailey, *"Too Tough to Die,"* 126–127. Virgil Earp's bond as chief of police is found in MS 180, F.294, F.295, CCR, AHS.

94. *Tombstone Daily Nugget*, July 6, 1881. Although Kate got dates mixed, she claimed that Behan carried her before Justice of the Peace Wells Spicer, who questioned her at length about the Earps, Doc Holliday, and the Benson stage robbery. Cummings, Mazzanovich typescript, 12.

95. *Tombstone Daily Nugget*, July 6, 7, 9, 10, 1881; *Tombstone Daily Epitaph*, July 10, 1881; *Territory of Arizona v. J. H. Holliday*, Case No. 30, July 4, 1881, Murder, Justice's Court, Report of Wells Spicer, Justice of the Peace, September 30, 1881, Cochise County Board of Supervisors.

96. *Tombstone Daily Nugget*, July 7, 1881.

97. *Tombstone Daily Nugget*, July 9, 1881.

98. Joe Chisholm, "Tombstone's Tale (The Truth of Helldorado)," 66, unpublished manuscript, Jack Burrows Collection.

99. Ibid., 66–67.

100. Cummings, Mazzanovich typescript, 11.

101. Ibid., 13. Napa Nick, a well-known gambler in Tombstone, seems an unlikely choice as an assassin.

102. Arthur W. Bork and Glenn G. Boyer, "The O.K. Corral Fight at Tombstone: A Footnote by Kate Elder," *Arizona and the West* 19 (Spring 1977): 77–78; Cummings, "Bork Typescript," 4. The contrast between Kate's comments to Mazzanovich and her comments to Bork are so different that they are stunning. The Bork notes include the comment, "Mrs. Cummings always said, 'They never did find out who killed Bud Philpot [*sic*].'" Explaining the differences is difficult, except perhaps to suggest that her exchanges with Mazzanovich came shortly after she had read Lake's *Wyatt Earp: Frontier Marshal*, which clearly angered her. Her comments to Bork came later and seem more restrained (and defensive of Doc's reputation). She does not appear to have mellowed much in her attitude toward the Earps, however, adding the remark, "The cry was all over the camp that the hunters were hunting themselves," in reference to the posse that pursued the stage robbers. In context, it does not appear that she was accusing the Earps and Doc of stage robbery; she was simply reporting rumors. And that within itself is interesting because the contemporary sources do not appear to point the finger of suspicion at the Earps until after the O.K. Corral fight and the testimony of the Earps' enemies at the Spicer hearing. The basic—and most perplexing—question is which of her statements were more honest? Were her accounts to Mazzanovich exaggerated by her anger and her hatred for Wyatt, or were her accounts to Bork more of a coverup of her feelings about Doc's role in the affair? The best that can be said by way of answer is that Kate had no direct knowledge but did have suspicions.

103. *Tombstone Daily Nugget*, July 10, 1881.

104. *Sacramento Daily Union*, March 22, 1881; Wyatt Earp, Crabtree trial, 317.

105. Earp to Burns, March 15, 1927, Walter Noble Burns Collection.

106. Bechdolt to Breakenridge, December 23, 1927, Breakenridge Letters.

107. Writing to Mazzanovich, Kate made it plain that "[a]fter the stage hold-up Doc turned against me. I found out it was he who got Virgil Earp to lock me up in the hotel room. Wyatt and Virgil were doing all they could to get Doc to send me away, and no doubt would have carried their point if I had let them." Cummings, Mazzanovich typescript, 13. This, she claimed, was why she swore out a warrant against Doc. "In doing as I did I was taking a desperate chance, but I lost out." After that, she said, she went back to Globe. What is most striking about the situation, though, is that the contemporary accounts do not support the idea that the Earps were involved in the robbery. In July 1881, the Earps' reputation was generally good. Virgil had done an exceptional job as chief of police, and Wyatt was respected as well. The seed of their later troubles may well have been planted in their relationships with Joyce, Behan, and Ike Clanton, but the first public accusation of the Earps' complicity in the Benson stage robbery did not come until Ike Clanton's testimony at the Spicer hearing, following the street fight in October 1881. See Ike Clanton's testimony, quoted in Turner, *O.K. Corral Inquest*, especially 114–117. Almost all suspicion of the Earps was derivative of the accusations made in Clanton's testimony and related events, including press criticism in the early months of 1882 after Sam Purdy assumed editorship of the *Tombstone Daily Epitaph* and in old-timer reminiscences written years later by men like John Plesant Gray, J. C. Hancock, Joe Chisholm, and William M. Breakenridge. The theme was enlarged by the writers Frederic Bechdolt, Eugene Cunningham, William MacLeod Raine, Ed Bartholomew, and Frank Waters until it appeared that the stories were widely known and believed at the time of the robbery, which is simply not true. It is fair to say that in the emotion-charged atmosphere following the street fight in October 1881 many were prepared to believe the worst and did.

6. Friends and Enemies

1. Dodge claimed that he learned of Doc's role in the robbery from Johnny Barnes, who he claimed was also involved in the robbery attempt. Dodge said flatly, "Doc was a full fledged member of the holdup at the time Bud Philpot [*sic*] was killed and I know who killed him." Fred Dodge, *Under Cover for Wells Fargo: The Unvarnished Recollections of Fred Dodge.* Edited by Carolyn Lake (Boston: Houghton Mifflin, 1969), 24, 246. John Clum despised Doc without specifically naming him a culprit in the robbery. Bob Paul is said to have believed him guilty as well, based on the *Phoenix Republican* article of June 26, 1892, which states that "[t]he fourth and most notorious of these highwaymen was 'Doc Holliday.'" However, the article does not make it clear whether the third-person narrative accusing Doc of being one of the four robbers was the voice of Paul or of the reporter. See John Boessenecker, "Lawman Bob Paul's Doc and Wyatt Connection," *Wild West* (August 2003): 38-45, which reviews the Paul-Holliday connection and shows some ambivalence in attitude on the part of Paul toward Holliday, but presents no direct evidence that Paul believed Holliday to be a party to the Benson robbery attempt.

2. Fannie Kemble Wister, ed., *Owen Wister Out West: His Journals and Letters* (Chicago: University of Chicago Press, 1958), 220.

3. William B. Shillingberg, "The John D. Gilchriese Collection," *Wyatt Earp, Tombstone and the West from the Collection of John D. Gilchriese,* part 1 (San Francisco: Johns' Western Gallery, 2005), 5. See also Joe Chisholm, *Brewery Gulch: Frontier Days of Old Arizona, Last Outpost of the Great Southwest* (San Antonio: Naylor, 1949), 128–130, for a more melodramatic account in which young Billy was sent by Doc to Kate Elder with a message and was promised that if he would bring back an answer, Doc would give him a dollar. Instead of giving Billy a message, Kate said in no uncertain terms that she wanted nothing to do with Doc. Billy supposedly pleaded, "Just send him a piece of paper, Miss, if you only put your name on it . . . so's I kin get that dollar." Kate broke into laughter at that and sent Doc an "insulting answer to his note." Nona Neff Hixenbaugh, the daughter of Andrew S. Neff, a business partner and friend of Wyatt Earp, also remembered Doc's kindness to children, saying he "often patted her on the head." *Tombstone Daily Epitaph,* May 11, 1944.

4. *San Francisco Examiner,* May 28, 1882.

5. *San Francisco Examiner,* October 3, 1881.

6. *San Francisco Examiner,* May 28, 1882.

7. The best general discussions of the Cow-Boy problem are found in Larry D. Ball, *The United States Marshals of New Mexico and Arizona Territories, 1846–1912* (Albuquerque: University of New Mexico Press, 1978), 107–133, and Stephen Cresswell, *Mormons, Cowboys, Moonshiners, and Klansmen: Federal Law Enforcement in the South and West, 1870–1893* (Tuscaloosa: University of Alabama Press, 1991), 181–239, 290–298n.

8. Report of Special Agent R. M. Moore, January 31, 1880, p. 24, Special Agents Reports, U.S. Customs Service, Record Group 36, National Archives and Records Administration, Washington, DC.

9. Ben T. Traywick, *The Clantons of Tombstone* (Tombstone, AZ: Red Marie's Bookstore, 1997), provides a convenient summary of most of the available documents on the Clantons.

10. Paul Johnson, "Were the McLaurys Leaving Tombstone," *WOLA Journal* 7 (Autumn 1998): 2–6; Allen A. Erwin to the author, March 21, 1961; Casey Tefertiller, *Wyatt Earp: The Life behind the Legend* (New York: Wiley, 1997), 42–45.

11. William M. Breakenridge, *Helldorado: Bringing Law to the Mesquite* (Boston: Houghton Mifflin, 1928), 105.

12. *Phoenix (Arizona) Gazette,* November 28, 1897, reprinting the article from the *Washington Post.*

13. H. L. Williams, Special Agent, to William Windom, Secretary of the Treasury, June 27, 1881, W-93-1881, SAP, USCS, RG 36, NARA.

14. *San Francisco Examiner*, October 1, 1881.

15. Ibid.

16. Ringo has fascinated writers over time. Jack Burrows, *John Ringo: The Gunfighter Who Never Was* (Tucson: University of Arizona Press, 1987), argues that the Ringo story is largely a myth. Steve Gatto, in two works, *John Ringo: The Reputation of a Deadly Gunman* (Tucson, AZ: San Simon, 1995), and *Johnny Ringo* (Lansing, MI: Protar House, 2002), presents a summary of most of the known documents in a pro–Cow-Boy venue. David Johnson, *John Ringo* (Stillwater, OK: Barbed Wire, 1996), is a more traditional biography sympathetic to Ringo.

17. *San Francisco Examiner*, May 28, 1882.

18. *Tucson (Arizona) Daily Star*, February 17, April 16, 1881: *Prescott (Arizona) Daily Miner*, March 17, 1881, quoting the *Tombstone Gossip*. Moore to John Sherman, March 30, April 21, 30, May 1, December 1, 1880; Moore to A. K. Tingle, April 5, 1881, SAP, USCS, RG 36, NARA; Robert T. Lincoln to Attorney General, April 4, 1881; Attorney General to E. M. Pomroy, U.S. Attorney for Arizona, April 15, 29, 1881; Chief Clerk, Department of Justice, to Pomroy, April 15, 1881; Pomroy to Attorney General, April 21, 26, 1881; Crawley P. Dake to Attorney General, May 30, 1881; Attorney General to Dake, June 15, 1881, Records of the Department of Justice, RG 60, NARA.

19. *Tombstone Daily Epitaph*, March 18, 1881.

20. Jerome B. Collins to B. M. Jacobs, July 17, 1880, B. M. Jacobs File, Special Collections, University of Arizona, Tucson, Arizona. See also William A. Duffen, "'Jollification'—Arizona Style: A Description of Gunplay in 1880," *Arizona and the West* 1 (Spring 1959): 281–284.

21. *Silver City (New Mexico) Herald*, May 29, 1880.

22. *Tombstone Daily Epitaph*, August 8, 1880.

23. *San Francisco Daily Report*, November 2, 1881.

24. Moore to Windom, March 21, 1881; Moore to Tingle, April 6, 1881, M-69-1881, SAP, USCS, RG 36, NARA. In his April 6 report, Moore defined one area of concern: "There is a series of double ranches located along the Southern border of Arizona, as follows: Aquirre's one near Arivaca 65 miles S. W. of Tucson, and another 8 miles south of it, near Oro Blanco. Marsh and Driscoll's 30 or 40 miles below or south nearer Tucson; Then 50 miles East of M & D's come Vale Harvey & Co. and the Sanford Bros' each Co. having 2 ranches, one on Sonoita Crk. And the other on the Cienega; 50 or 60 miles East of these again on the San Pedro are the ranches of Land formerly the Slaughter and the Roberts ranches and finally 60 or 70 miles East of these in the Sulphur Springs valley are several other ranches. On these double ranches there are now from 1,000 to 6,000 head of cattle. It is easy to see how cattle could have been driven out of Mexico on to the border ranches, all distant from Tucson from 70 to 120 miles, there kept and rebranded, and thence driven north on to their fellow ranches where there were or would be called Arizona cattle."

25. For a review of the evidence, see Tefertiller, *Wyatt Earp*, 43–44; Steve Gatto, *The Real Earp: A Documentary Biography* (Silver City, NM: High-Lonesome, 2000), 33–35; Johnson, "McLaurys," 4–5.

26. *San Franciso Examiner*, May 28, 1882.

27. *Tucson Weekly Citizen*, February 13, 1881.

28. *Tucson (Arizona) Weekly Star*, February 17, March 10, 1881. This was in response to Governor Frémont's recommendation to create a volunteer company of one hundred men to patrol the back country; the *Star* thought this force too small. See George H. Kelly, *Legislative History of Arizona, 1864–1912* (Phoenix, AZ: Manufacturing Stationers, 1926), 98–101; see also Tefertiller, *Wyatt Earp*, 72–75.

29. *San Diego Union*, August 26, 1881.

30. L. Wollenburg to the editor, *Prescott Miner*, February 23, 1881.

31. *San Francisco Daily Report*, November 2, 1881.

32. *Tombstone Daily Nugget*, June 9, 1881; *Tucson Weekly Star*, June 16, 23, 1881.

33. *Denver Republican*, May 22, 1882.

34. Lynn R. Bailey, *"Too Tough to Die": The Rise, Fall, and Resurrection of a Silver Camp, 1878 to 1990* (Tucson, AZ: Westernlore, 2004), 126–127.

35. *Allen, et al., Owners of the Last Decision Mine v. Intervenor Mining Co.*, Marcus A. Smith and J. L. Lisle Account Books, 2:89, 98–106.

36. *Tombstone Daily Epitaph*, August 11, 1881; William B. Shillingberg, *Tombstone, A. T.: A History of Early Mining, Milling, and Mayhem* (Spokane, WA: Clark, 1999), 226; Ed Bartholomew, *Wyatt Earp: The Man and the Myth* (Toyahvale, TX: Frontier Book, 1964), 188–189.

37. *Silver City Grant County Herald and New Southwest*, July 30, 1881.

38. *Tucson Daily Star*, August 3, 1881; *Tombstone Daily Nugget*, August 3, 1881; Major General Orlando B. Willcox to U.S. Attorney General, attached to letter from U.S. Attorney General to Dake, August 10, 1881; J. W. Evans to Dake, August 4, 1881; Dake to Attorney General, August 5, 1881, DJ, RG 60, NARA.

39. *Tombstone Daily Epitaph*, August 5, 1881, reprinting the article from the *Tucson Daily Citizen*. Jose Otero to Frémont, August 6, 1881, including letters from Pedro Gutierrez to Otero, August 6, 1881, and Luis Torres to Frémont, August 6, 1881, enclosed with Dake to Attorney General, August 16, 1881, DJ, RG 60, NARA.

40. V. Morales to Wilcox, August 12, Records of the Department of the Secretary of the Interior, RG 48, NARA; *Tombstone Daily Epitaph*, August 13, 1881.

41. *Tombstone Daily Epitaph*, August 13, 14, 1881. Shillingberg, *Tombstone, A. T.*, 228–229, was the first scholar to use Mexican records, citing the file "Campana contra los Tejanos o Cow-boys," from the Biblioteca y Museo de Sonoro Archivo Historico, Hermosilla, Sonora, Mexico, which expands knowledge of the Cow-Boy problem from the Mexican perspective.

42. *Arizona Weekly Star*, August 25, 1881, reprinting the article from the *Tombstone Daily Nugget*, August 16, 1881.

43. *San Diego Union*, August 18, 1881, citing the article from the *Tombstone Daily Epitaph*, August 16, 1881, and the *San Diego Union*, August 20, 1881; citing an undated article from the *Tucson Arizona Weekly Star*. See also Greaves to S. M. Ashenfelter, August 17, 1881, *Silver City Grant County Herald and New Southwest*, August 20, 1881.

44. The critical accounts are the statements of Billy Byers, who survived the affair, published in the *Tucson Daily Star*, September 1, 1881, and John Plesant Gray, *When All Roads Led to Tombstone*, edited by W. Lane Rogers (Boise, ID: Tamarack Press, 1998), 54–56.

45. Kelton, AAG, to Adjutant General, August 22, 1881, Records of the Office of the Adjutant General, RG 94, NARA; see also *Sacramento Record-Union*, August 19, 1881.

46. *Tombstone Daily Nugget*, August 20, 1881.

47. Ibid.

48. Clara Spalding Brown to the editor, August 23, 1881, *San Diego Union*, August 28, 1881.

49. George Whitwell Parsons, *Private Journal of George W. Parsons* (Tombstone, AZ: Tombstone Epitaph, 1972), 170.

50. *San Francisco Daily Report*, August 23, 1881.

51. *San Diego Union*, August 20, 1881.

52. *Tombstone Daily Epitaph*, August 19, 1881.

53. Evans to Dake, August 5, 11, 1881, DJ, RG 60, NARA.

54. *Tombstone Daily Nugget*, September 7, 1881.

55. *Silver City Grant County Herald and New Southwest*, September 3, 1881.

56. Alward White to Abner Tibbetts, Collector of Customs, El Paso, Texas, September 28, 1881; White to H. L. Williams, September 28, 1881, USCS, RG 36, NARA.

57. Parsons, *Journal*, 170.

58. Gray, *All Roads*, 65. The *Tucson Daily Star*, September 1, 1881, offered a cogent analysis of what happened: "There is little room to doubt that the Mexicans who assailed the party killed, believed them to be cow-boys, who only a few days previous had made an attack on a small party of Mexicans in Sonora who were en route to Arizona. Be this as it may, the evidence is strong that at least some of the number killed were not to be classed as the best of citizens and were given to pilfering cattle." If the cattle were being driven east to west on the American side of the line, the twists and turns in the canyons would have brought them to within sight of the Mexican border at the point of the attack, which would have given the Mexicans reason to believe that the herd was being driven south to north.

59. The evidence is overwhelming that the Guadalupe Canyon affair was carried out by Mexican regulars. Byers, Earnshaw, and Gray all said that Mexicans were the attackers. A photograph of Old Man Clanton given to the Byers family bears the inscription on the reverse, "Mr. Clanton killed on Aug 13—81 by Mexicans with 4 other Americans in Guadalupe Canon [*sic*] New Mexico," and was signed by Ike and Fin Clanton. Another photograph of Will G. Lang similarly bears the inscription, "Will G. Lang Killed by Mexicans—Animas Valley New Mexico Aug 13, 1881 together with Gray, Cranton, Clanton, and Snow & Byers wounded." It is unlikely that Ike and Fin Clanton would have so inscribed a photograph of their father had they had any suspicion that the Earps were involved in their father's death. The first indication that the Earps and Doc were involved in the attack is found in the letter of William R. McLaury to his brother-in-law, David D. Appelgate, November 19, 1881, William R. McLaury Letters, New-York Historical Society, New York City, New York. McLaury told his brother-in-law concerning his brothers' deaths, "The cause of the murder was this[:] some time ago Holliday one of the murderers attempted to rob the express of Wells Fargo & Co. and in so doing shot and killed a stage driver and a passenger and the other parties engaged in the murder with him the Earp brothers were interested in the attempt at Exp. Robbery and young Clanton who was killed, a boy 18 years old knew the facts about the attempted robbery and had told his brother J. I. Clanton and Thos and Robt and they had got up facts intending to prosecute [*sic*] Holliday and the Earp Bros . . . had information of it. It is now known that two other men who knew of the murder in the attempted robbery have since then been killed in Mexico. The report was by 'Greasers' but at the time they were killed Holliday was out of town 'said to be visiting Georgia.' There will be an indictment agst Holliday and I think two of the Earps and one Williams fore the murders in the attempted robbery." The context of the letter indicates that McLaury had been given this information by locals. Since Ike Clanton is not known to have ever made any such claim, the most logical clue is provided by Jack Ganzhorn, *I've Killed Men* (New York: Devin, Adair, 1959), 27. Ganzhorn's book is a curiosity and has been generally discredited because Ganzhorn made claims that the facts of his life show to be false. However, his family was in the area, and he was in the position to have heard family stories. The story he provides concerning the Guadalupe Canyon affair has a coherence that makes it likely that his story came to him from his family. Ganzhorn claimed that Milt Joyce accused the Earps and Doc Holliday of involvement in the Benson stage robbery and that the death of Jim Crane enabled the Earps to "rest easy" because "[t]here was no man left alive to testify to their complicity in the Sandy Bob holdup and murder of Bud Philpot [*sic*]." Joyce also allegedly said that the Earps were out of town at the time of the Guadalupe Canyon affair hunting outlaws. Ganzhorn added, "Milt Joice's [*sic*] talk was made publicly in the barroom of the Oriental and was not challenged by any one of the Earp clan." Considering Joyce's troubles with Holliday and the Earps and his involvement in Kate's accusations against Doc in July, the story is not only

plausible but probable. The rumors were wrong, as the hard evidence shows, but they fed local suspicions among enemies of the Earps, although curiously none of the later critics of the Earps—Hancock, Gray, Breakenridge—made such claims. Wayne Montgomery, who claimed to have been the grandson of John Montgomery, "I Witnessed the O.K. Corral Fight," *True West* 18 (1971): 18–19, 60–64, and "quoting" from his grandfather's alleged diary, revived the story that the Earps killed Old Man Clanton and the others in Skeleton Canyon. He repeated the claim in Carl W. Breihan and Wayne Montgomery, *Forty Years on the Wild Frontier* (Greenwich, CT: Devin-Adair, 1985), 68–69. Montgomery was eventually exposed as a fraud, but the story had resurfaced. Glenn G. Boyer later picked up the idea of the Earps killing Old Man Clanton in "Welcome to Earp Country," *Arizona Highways* 58 (November 1982): 10, and developed it further in his *Wyatt Earp's Tombstone Vendetta* (Honolulu, HI: Talai, 1993), 111–121, in both cases in an abbreviated and limited fashion. Others followed his lead, including Ben T. Traywick, *John Henry (The "Doc" Holliday Story)* (Tombstone, AZ: Red Marie's Bookstore, 1996), 107–108, and Karen Holliday Tanner, *Doc Holliday: A Family Portrait* (Norman: University of Oklahoma Press, 1998), 155–157, 282–284n. The most elaborate presentation of the argument, although not necessarily the most convincing, is found in Michael M. Hickey, *John Ringo: The Final Hours—A Tale of the Old West* (Honolulu, HI: Talai, 1995), 377–452. Tanner presents the most complete summary of the circumstantial case, mentioning the McLaury letter and the claim of Dr. T. H. Smith of Valdosta, Georgia, that Doc returned home and stayed for several days with "the shade drawn and the doors closed." Quoted in the letter of Vera D. Hagen, President of the Lowndes County Historical Society, to Philip Rasch, January 15, 1972, Philip J. Rasch Collection, Box 2, Arizona Historical Society, Tucson, Arizona. (Smith's claim does not mention a particular time frame for the visit, and Tanner does note that no family sources indicate that Doc ever returned to Georgia.) Tanner also cites references that suggest Warren Earp was wounded in a fight and returned to his parents' home in Colton, California, to recover, including a letter said to have been written by Adelia Earp Edwards, the sister of the Earp brothers, that Warren was in California recovering from a gunshot wound received in a fight on the border when the October street fight occurred. This letter, said to have been in the Alford E. Turner Collection, was not found in the collection when it was acquired by C. Lee Simmons. Finally, Tanner cites the telegram of Marshal Dake to the Attorney General, August 5, 1881, DJ, RG 60, NARA, which indicated that a posse was in the field chasing outlaws and asserts that it was known to be "Earp-led," although that is by no means clear from the documents. In the end, the testimony of eyewitnesses and others close to the victims outweighs the rumors fostered by bitter enemies of the Earps like McLaury and Joyce and the pattern of circumstantial evidence offered by advocates of this conspiracy theory. Gatto, *Real Earp*, 97n, a writer generally critical of Wyatt Earp, concludes, "In recent years some authors have expressed the bizarre belief that the Guadalupe Canyon massacre was carried out by the Earps and a large posse under their command. The historical record shows beyond doubt that this scenario is *without merit* [italics added]." See also Casey Tefertiller, "Resolving Earp Myths," *NOLA Quarterly* 21 (October–December 1997): 5–8.

60. *Tombstone Daily Epitaph*, August 19, 1881.
61. *Tombstone Daily Epigraph*, August 16, 1881.
62. Ibid.
63. *Tombstone Daily Nugget*, September 10, 1881; *Tombstone Daily Epitaph*, September 10, 1881; Shillingberg, *Tombstone, A. T.*, 232–234; Peter Brand, "Sherman W. McMaster(s): The El Paso Salt War, Texas Rangers, and Tombstone," *WOLA Journal* 8 (Winter 1999): 8–12.
64. Gosper to Attorney General, September 30, 1881, DJ, RG 60, NARA.
65. *Tombstone Daily Nugget*, September 7, 16, 1881.
66. *San Francisco Daily Report*, September 20, 1881.

67. *Tombstone Daily Epitaph*, August 13, 1881.

68. *Tombstone Daily Epitaph*, September 10, 13, 1881; *Tombstone Daily Nugget*, September 13, 1881.

69. *Tombstone Daily Nugget*, October 27, 1881; *Tombstone Daily Epitaph*, October 27, 1881.

70. Testimony of Virgil Earp, quoted in Alford E. Turner, ed., *The O.K. Corral Inquest* (College Station, TX: Creative, 1981), 196.

71. Statement of Wyatt Earp, quoted in Turner, *O.K. Corral Inquest*, 158–159.

72. *San Diego Union*, August 26, 1881.

73. Ibid. On August 28, the *Tucson Daily Citizen* identified Morgan Earp as a member of the "top and bottom" gang. Although Morg spent time in Benson, he was not a part of the gang and had served as an officer in Benson. See *Las Vegas Daily Optic*, May 24, 1882; see also Bartholomew, *Man and Myth*, 219.

74. *San Francisco Daily Report*, September 13, 1881.

75. Parsons, *Journal*, 183–184.

76. *Tombstone Daily Epitaph*, October 13, 1881; *Tombstone Daily Nugget*, October 13, 1881.

77. *Tucson Weekly Star*, October 20, 1881; see also *Tombstone Daily Epitaph*, October 14, 1881; *Tombstone Daily Nugget*, October 14, 1884.

78. *Tombstone Daily Epitaph*, October 14, 1881; *Tucson Daily Star*, October 19, 1881; Testimony of Virgil Earp, quoted in Turner, *O.K. Corral Inquest*, 190.

79. Mary Katharine Cummings, typescript of recollections prepared by Anton Mazzanovich, 13–14, Kevin J. Mulkins Collection. On September 1, 1881, a cashier's check was drawn on the Pima County Bank for $25 made out to Kate Holliday, which is strong evidence that Kate and Doc were together at the time the festival opened. This important document was discovered by Bernice Cosulich, the Tucson historian, among the papers of George Amos of Tucson. A feature article in the *Tucson Arizona Daily Star*, December 13, 1953, included a reproduction of the check. The Amos Collection is now housed at the Arizona Historical Society at Tucson, but the check was not located by the Society's staff during the research for this book. The check is also reproduced in Ben T. Traywick, *John Henry (the "Doc" Holliday Story)* (Tombstone, AZ: Red Marie's Bookstore, 1996), 140, without attribution or commentary.

80. *Tucson Daily Citizen*, August 28, 1881.

81. Given the time frame, this would be near the end of the San Augustin festival or after it closed.

82. The *Tombstone Daily Nugget*, October 2, 1881, indicates that Doc left Tombstone on October 1.

83. Arthur W. Bork, notes of interview with Mary Katharine Cummings, Thanksgiving 1935, copy in author's files, courtesy Arthur W. Bork.

84. *Tombstone Daily Epitaph*, October 20, 1881. The article said that the "well known sporting man" returned home to find "the woman he was living with in company with another man, and suspecting improper intimacy between them, at once commenced beating and abusing the woman in a most brutal manner," after which he left town and had not been heard from at the time the article was printed. Timothy W. Fattig, *Wyatt Earp: The Biography* (Honolulu, HI: Talei, 2002), 349–350, concludes that the sporting man was Doc. According to Kate's account this was during the time that she and Doc were in Tucson. Kate told Bork that "she never feared him." In fact, she told him, "I went in to see once where he was with another woman. I had a big knife with me and said that I'd rip her open." He came away from her, Kate said, "because I wasn't afraid of him."

85. Cummings, Mazzanovich typescript, 14–15; *Tucson Weekly Star*, October 20, 1881.

86. Testimony of Virgil Earp, *Tombstone Daily Nugget* and *Tombstone Daily Epitaph*, November 20, 1881. Virgil said, "Wyatt Earp had been sworn in to act in my place while I

was in Tucson, and on my return his saloon [Oriental] was opened and I appointed him a 'Special,' to keep the peace, with power to make arrest."

87. Statement of Wyatt Earp, *Tombstone Daily Nugget* and *Tombstone Daily Epitaph*, November 17, 1881.

88. Cummings, Bork typescript, 6.

89. *Tombstone Daily Epitaph*, October 23, 25, 1881; *Tombstone Daily Nugget*, October 25, 1881.

90. *El Paso (Texas) Lone Star,* October 26, 29, 1881; see also Behan Financial Report, February 16, 1882, F.298, Cochise County Records, AHS.

91. Testimony of Ike Clanton, *Tombstone Daily Nugget*, November 13, 1881; Johnson, "McLaurys," 8–9; McLaury to Appelwhite, November 9, 1881, McLaury Letters.

92. In his testimony before the coroner's inquest, Ike said the confrontation took place at the Occidental lunch room; in his testimony at the Spicer hearing, he said that the incident took place at the Eagle Brewery Saloon, as well as at the Alhambra, where the confrontation actually occurred. *Tombstone Daily Nugget*, November 13, 1881. It is worth noting that Doc worked at the Alhambra, so that it is presumptuous to claim, as some have done, that Doc went into the Alhambra looking for trouble. Indeed, it could be argued that Ike going into a known haunt of Holliday's was the provocative act. A more likely scenario is that when he came into the saloon and spotted Clanton, Holliday approached him because of the conversation he had had with Wyatt.

93. Dodge, *Under Cover,* 26.

94. Testimony of Ike Clanton, *Tombstone Daily Nugget*, November 13, 1881.

95. Statement of Wyatt Earp, *Tombstone Daily Nugget* and *Tombstone Daily Epitaph*, November 17, 1881.

96. Testimony of Ike Clanton, *Tombstone Daily Nugget*, November 13, 1881.

97. Statement of Wyatt Earp, *Tombstone Daily Nugget* and *Tombstone Daily Epitaph*, November 17, 1881; *Tombstone Daily Epitaph*, October 27, 1881.

98. Statement of Wyatt Earp, *Tombstone Daily Nugget* and *Tombstone Daily Epitaph*, November 17, 1881.

99. Ibid.

100. Testimony of Virgil Earp, *Tombstone Daily Nugget* and *Tombstone Daily Epitaph*, November 20 and 23, 1881.

101. Ibid.

7. The Fremont Street Fiasco

1. Testimony of Ike Clanton and Ned Boyle, Doc. No. 94, the Wells Spicer Hearing, the original transcript of Document No. 94, in Justice's Court, Township No. 1, Cochise County, A. T., before Wells Spicer, J. P., *Territory of Arizona v. Morgan Earp et al., Defendants,* has been lost. During the Great Depression, the original document was edited as a Works Progress Administration project by Pat Hayhurst, who appears to have produced a less than accurate transcription of the document. He summarized material rather than presenting a verbatim transcript, and witnesses were not presented in correct order. Two typescripts of the document exist, while the original transcript was lost. Alford E. Turner, ed., *The O.K. Corral Inquest* (College Station, TX: Creative, 1981) is a published version of Hayhurst, but it contains differences from the Hayhurst typescripts as well as from the newspaper accounts. Both the *Tombstone (Arizona) Daily Epitaph* and the *Tombstone (Arizona) Daily Nugget* carried the testimony as well, although there are differences between them. To gain the best understanding of the testimony, it is necessary to compare the Hayhurst, the *Epitaph*, and the *Nugget*. For simplicity and ease of reference, I have used the newspaper accounts as the closest to the original documents. In some instances, I have

used the Hayhurst because the newspaper sources do not include some of the testimony. Pat Hayhurst, ed., "Transcript of Papers Related to Territory of Arizona vs. Morgan Earp, et al., Defendants," Arizona W.P.A. Project, copy in author's files, courtesy Robert N. Mullin.

2. Testimony of Julius Kelley, Doc. No. 94, *Tombstone Daily Nugget* and *Tombstone Daily Epitaph*, November 21, 1881.

3. Testimony of Virgil Earp, ibid., November 20, 1881.

4. Testimony of R. F. Hafford, ibid., November 2, 1881.

5. Arthur W. Bork and Glenn G. Boyer, eds., "The O.K. Corral Fight at Tombstone: A Footnote by Kate Elder," *Arizona and the West* 19 (August 1977): 80.

6. Testimony of Virgil Earp, Doc. No. 94, *Tombstone Daily Nugget* and *Tombstone Daily Epitaph*, November 20, 1881.

7. Statement of Wyatt Earp, ibid., November 17, 1881.

8. John P. Clum, "It All Happened at Tombstone," *Arizona and the West*, 1 (Autumn 1959): 233–234.

9. Testimony of Virgil Earp, Doc. No. 94, *Tombstone Daily Nugget* and *Tombstone Daily Epitaph*, November 20, 1881.

10. Statement of Wyatt Earp, ibid., November 17, 1881.

11. *Tombstone Daily Epitaph*, October 27, 1881.

12. Testimony of R. J. Campbell, Doc. No. 94, *Tombstone Daily Nugget* and *Tombstone Daily Epitaph*, November 24, 1881.

13. Testimony of A. Bauer, J. T. Batcher, and Thomas Keefe, ibid., November 11, 1881.

14. Statement of Wyatt Earp, ibid., November 17, 1881.

15. Testimony of Virgil Earp, ibid., November 20, 1881.

16. Testimony of William Allen, Doc. No. 94, Hayhurst transcript, 23. This characteristic still exists. A New Yorker moved south to manage a plant. When asked later by a friend how things were going, the new plant manager expressed concern. "I don't know whether I'm going to make it or not," he said. "You don't know who your enemies are down here. Everybody is so damned polite." Southern history is full of such stories.

17. Testimony of William Allen, Doc. No. 94, Hayhurst transcript.

18. Statement of Wyatt Earp, Doc. No. 94, *Tombstone Daily Nugget* and *Tombstone Daily Epitaph*, November 17, 1881.

19. Testimony of Virgil Earp, ibid., November 20, 1881.

20. Statement of Wyatt Earp, ibid., November 17, 1881; testimony of Ike Clanton, Doc. No. 94, Hayhurst transcript, 113–114.

21. Statement of Wyatt Earp, Doc. No. 94, *Tombstone Daily Nugget* and *Tombstone Daily Epitaph*, November 17, 1881.

22. Testimony of J. B. W. Gardiner, ibid., November 29, 1881.

23. Testimony of P. H. Fellehy, Doc. No. 48, *Tombstone Daily Nugget* and *Tombstone Daily Epitaph*, October 30, 1881; John H. Behan, Doc. No. 94, *Tombstone Daily Nugget* and *Tombstone Daily Epitaph*, November 3–6, 1881.

24. Testimony of Virgil Earp, Doc. No. 94, ibid., November 20, 1881.

25. Ibid.

26. Testimony of H. F. Sills and Virgil Earp, ibid., November 20, 23, 24, 1881. Sills was an important and impartial witness. See Jane Matson Lee and Mark Dworkin, "H. F. Sills: Mystery Man of the O.K. Corral Shootout," *WOLA Journal* 12, (Spring 2004): 4–21.

27. Testimony of West Fuller, Doc. No. 94, *Tombstone Daily Nugget* and *Tombstone Daily Epitaph*, November 8, 1881.

28. Testimony of P. H. Fellehy, Doc. No. 48, ibid., October 30, 1881; Stuart N. Lake notes in the Stuart N. Lake Collection, Huntington Library, San Marino, California; Forrestine C. Hooker, "An Arizona Vendetta (the Truth about Wyatt Earp—and Some Others),"

34–35, unpublished manuscript, circa 1920, Southwest Museum, Los Angeles, California; William B. Shillingberg, *Tombstone, A. T.: A History of Early Mining, Milling, and Mayhem* (Spokane, WA: Clark, 1999), 254.

29. John H. Flood Jr., "Wyatt Earp, a Peace-officer of Tombstone," 228, unpublished manuscript, 1927, C. Lee Simmons Collection.

30. Testimony of Virgil Earp, Doc. No. 94, *Tombstone Daily Nugget* and *Tombstone Daily Epitaph*, November 20, 23, 1881.

31. Ibid.

32. Statement of Wyatt Earp, ibid., November 17, 1881.

33. Testimony of James Kehoe, ibid., November 6, 1881.

34. Testimony of John Behan, Doc. No. 94, ibid., November 3–6, 1881.

35. Ibid.

36. Testimony of Ike Clanton, ibid., November 10–11, 13–15, 1881.

37. Testimony of R. F. Coleman and W. A. Cuddy, Doc. No. 48, *Tombstone Daily Nugget* and *Tombstone Daily Epitaph*, October 29, 30, 1881.

38. Testimony of Martha J. King, Doc. No. 94.

39. Testimony of John Behan, Doc. No. 48, *Tombstone Daily Nugget* and *Tombstone Daily Epitaph*, October 29, 1881.

40. Witnesses for the prosecution testified that at the point of confrontation someone in the Earp party said, "You sons-of-bitches have been looking for a fight and now you can have it!" Considering that the Earps had relaxed after their exchange with Sheriff Behan, it seems more likely that the epithet was the result of surprise that the Cow-Boys were still armed. The conclusion is speculative but reasonable in light of the circumstances.

41. In reconstructing the street fight, I have expanded on themes first developed in my article "The Fremont Street Fiasco; or, How to Start a Legend without Really Trying," *True West* 35 (July 1988): 14–20, in which I posited the thesis that the street fight was not premeditated by either side but was the consequence of a series of miscalculations. I have modified my stance since this article was first written, and I have relied heavily on the research of Jeff Morey, Casey Tefertiller, and Robert F. Palmquist. Morey's unpublished manuscript "The Gunfight, October 26, 1881" (copy in author's files) was extremely helpful, although Morey has refined some of his conclusions since that account was written. Morey, "Blaze Away," *True West* 48 (November–December 2001): 34–40, and Morey and Tefertiller, "O.K. Corral: A Fight Shrouded in Mystery," *Wild West* (October 2001): 38–44, 70, 72, are balanced and measured. Palmquist's unpublished "Tombstone Jurisprudence: The Earp-Holliday Hearing, 1881" (copy in author's files) was also helpful.

42. Statement of Wyatt Earp and testimony of Ike Clanton, Bill Claiborne, and Virgil Earp, Doc. No. 94, *Tombstone Daily Nugget* and *Tombstone Daily Epitaph*, November 2, 10, 11–17, 1881. The peculiar angle of the bullet that struck Morgan Earp caused Wyatt Earp to suspect that Tom McLaury may have fired a shot over his horse at Morgan or that William Allen fired the shot from across the street. Neither scenario can be confirmed. Mrs. J. C. Collier, whose family was visiting her brother-in-law, John Collier, the foreman at the Boston Mill, witnessed the shooting and noted that one of the Cow-Boys "used his horse as a barricade and shot under his neck," providing possible support for an armed Tom McLaury. She left Tombstone without testifying and told her story in a letter to the editor of the *Kansas City Star,* so she was never cross-examined in court. See the *Star* article reprinted in the *Tombstone Daily Epitaph*, December 30, 1881.

43. *Tombstone Daily Nugget*, October 27, 1881; testimony of Thomas Keefe, Bob Hatch, H. F. Sills, and Addie Borland, Doc. No. 94, *Tombstone Daily Nugget* and *Tombstone Daily Epitaph*, November 11–12, 18, 24, 29, 1881. Matthews described only the fatal wounds in his testimony; hence, he did not describe the shot to Billy Clanton's wrist or Doc's shot to Frank McLaury's chest. Wyatt claimed that Old Man Fuller told him that his son, West, had picked up Tom McLaury's pistol in "Wyatt Earp's Personal Diagram of the

Street Fight: Gunfight at the O.K. Corral, October 26, 1881, Tombstone, Arizona Territory," Wyatt Earp's Personal Diagrams of Prominent Historical Events (McLean, VA: United States Marshal's Foundation, 1989), and in Lake notes.

44. *Tombstone Daily Epitaph*, October 27, 1881; *Tombstone Daily Nugget*, October 27, 1881.

45. *Tombstone Daily Nugget*, October 27, 29, 1881.

46. Arthur W. Bork and Glenn G. Boyer, "The O.K. Corral Fight at Tombstone: A Footnote by Kate Elder," *Arizona and the West* 19 (Spring 1977): 80.

47. Testimony of W. S. Williams, Doc. No. 94, *Tombstone Daily Nugget* and *Tombstone Daily Epitaph*, November 29, 1881.

48. Testimony of John Behan and Virgil Earp, ibid., November 2–4, 20, 1881.

49. Frank Waters, "Tombstone's Travesty," 207, unpublished manuscript, 1934, Frank Waters Collection, University of New Mexico Library, Albuquerque, New Mexico.

50. *Tombstone Daily Epitaph*, October 27, 1881.

51. *Tombstone Daily Nugget*, October 27, 1881.

52. *San Francisco Daily Report*, October 27, 1881.

53. *San Francisco Exchange*, October 27, 1881.

54. *Tombstone Daily Epitaph*, October 28, 1881; *Tombstone Daily Nugget*, October 28, 1881.

55. Ibid.

56. Clara Spalding Brown to the editor, October 29, 1881, *San Diego Union*, November 3, 1881.

57. George Whitwell Parsons, *The Private Journal of George W. Parsons* (Tombstone, AZ: Tombstone Daily Epitaph, 1972): 189.

58. Testimony of John H. Behan, Doc. No. 48, *Tombstone Daily Nugget* and *Tombstone Daily Epitaph*, October 29, 1881.

59. Testimony of John Behan, Billy Claiborne, and Ike Clanton, ibid., October 29, 30, 1881.

60. *Tombstone Daily Nugget*, October 30, 1880.

61. Parsons, *Journal*, 190.

62. *Tombstone Daily Nugget*, October 30, 1881.

63. Minute Book A, Common Council, Village of Tombstone, October 29, 1881, p. 131.

64. *Tombstone Daily Nugget*, October 30, 1881.

65. Ibid. For further information on Woods's trip to El Paso, see the *El Paso (Texas) Lone Star*, October 26, 29, November 5, 1881.

66. *San Francisco Daily Report*, October 31, 1881.

67. *Tombstone Daily Nugget*, November 1, 1881.

68. Smith's role in the proceedings generally has been ignored. During the coroner's inquest, he was called as a witness (and potentially an important one since he had been seen speaking with Sheriff Behan and Frank McLaury just moments before the fight), but Coroner Matthews excused him without explanation. The reason was almost certainly that he was involved already with Ike Clanton in the prosecution of the Earps and Holliday. Ben Goodrich, the son of one of the founding fathers of Texas, a nephew of a defender of the Alamo, and a staunch advocate of Texans, was generally described as Ike Clanton's personal attorney in the case. The firm of Goodrich & Goodrich was already associated with Smith and would eventually become Goodrich & Smith. Alexander Campbell and James S. Robinson, other prosecuting attorneys, were also associated with Smith. The *Tombstone Daily Nugget*, November 1, 1881, identified the prosecution's legal counsel as "Messrs. Goodrich & Goodrich, Smith, Earll, Campbell & Robinson, Smith & Colby, J. M. Murphy, and District Attorney Price." All of this demonstrates that Smith was intimately involved with the case even though he did not take an active role in the court proceedings.

This is confirmed by the records of yet another law firm, Smith & Lisle, which show that Clanton paid the firm for services in the case. The entry in the record reads, "Nov. 1 [1881], Clanton, Ike, et al, fee for services in prosecution of Earp Bros & Holliday, charged with the murder of Wm Clanton & the McLowry [*sic*] boys, Dr//Cr $375.00 (Dr)," Marcus A. Smith–J. L. Lisle Account Books, 1877–1883, p. 86, MS 1192, Arizona Historical Society, Tucson, Arizona.

The date November 1, 1881, is particularly interesting because on that same date, John Behan took out a loan for $500 from the L. M. Jacobs Mercantile Company, which he would pay off December 30, 1881. Lionel M. Jacobs Collection, Vol. 122, Special Collections, University of Arizona, Tucson, Arizona. This doubtlessly explains why the defense during cross-examination at the Spicer hearing, on November 3, 1881, asked Behan how much he had contributed to the attorneys prosecuting the case, to which Behan responded, "I have not contributed a cent, nor have I promised to." Testimony of John H. Behan, Doc. No. 94, *Tombstone Daily Nugget* and *Tombstone Daily Epitaph*, November 4, 1881.

Interestingly, Behan and Billy Soule, his jailor, borrowed an additional $200 from Jacobs, on November 2. Two weeks later, on November 14, 1881, Ike Clanton and Behan returned to Jacobs and borrowed an additional $500 (which Clanton paid off on November 25, 1881). The circumstances make it possible that Behan acted as guarantor on a Clanton loan. In any event, Behan's involvement with Clanton in financial transactions during the hearing makes it hard to avoid the conclusion that John Behan was actively involved in the prosecution of the Earps in a personal way beyond his role as sheriff, which makes charges of bias against him more credible.

After he arrived in Tombstone, Will McLaury assumed at least some of the expenses in the case. He wrote to his sister, "[T]o prossecute [*sic*] these cases I have employed Alexander Campbell late of California and Ex Judge Robinson, your husband will know these men. As criminal lawyers they have no peers in this country. Also Goodrich & Goodrich of this place. At one time I did not know but I would prossecute myself. I wrote D. D. some of the circumstances everyone was intimidated and I had to go into court myself as an atty, but things are working well now I think." W. R. McLaury to Mrs. M. F. Appelgate, November 19, 1881, William R. McLaury Collection, New-York Historical Society, New York, New York.

John Roberts Adams, who was later hired by the family to expedite the settlement of the McLaury business in Cochise County, in a letter to Charles Appelgate, January 15, 1882, complained specifically about Smith and the Goodriches because they had refused to have anything more to do with the McLaury claims. Paul J. Johnson to the author, November 24, December 9, 2004. No references to McLaury appear in the Smith & Lisle account books, which suggests that McLaury dealt with the Goodrich firm. Steven A. Fazio, "Marcus Aurelius Smith: Arizona Delegate and Senator," in *Arizona and the West* 12 (Spring 1970): 24–25, says that Smith and the Goodrich brothers were in partnership by the end of 1881.

69. Steven Lubet, *Murder in Tombstone: The Forgotten Trial of Wyatt Earp* (New Haven, CT: Yale University Press, 2004), 79–82; Casey Tefertiller, *Wyatt Earp: The Life behind the Legend* (New York: Wiley, 1997), 130–131.

70. *Tucson (Arizona) Weekly Star*, November 3, 1881.

71. William R. McLaury to S. P. Greene, November 8, 1881; William R. McLaury to D. D. Appelgate, November 9, 1881, McLaury Papers; see also testimony of Martha J. King, Doc. No. 94.

72. *Tombstone Daily Nugget* and *Tombstone Daily Epitaph*, November 8, 1881; *San Francisco Chronicle*, November 8, 1881.

73. Testimony of West Fuller, Doc. No. 94, *Tombstone Daily Nugget* and *Tombstone Daily Epitaph*, November 6, 1881.

74. John J. Gosper to Samuel J. Kirkwood, Secretary of the Interior, November 29, 1881, *Lawlessness in Parts of Arizona* (Washington, DC: U.S. Government Printing Office, 1882); McLaury to Greene, November 8, 1881; McLaury to Appelgate, November 9, 1882, McLaury Papers.

75. Testimony of William F. Claibourne, Doc. No. 94, *Tombstone Daily Nugget* and *Tombstone Daily Epitaph*, November 9, 1881.

76. *Tucson Weekly Star*, November 3, 1881.

77. *San Francisco Examiner*, November 7, 1881.

78. McLaury to Greene, November 8, 1881, McLaury Papers.

79. Mary Katharine Cummings, typescript of recollections given to Anton Mazzanovich, Kevin J. Mulkins Collection.

80. Testimony of Ike Clanton, Doc. No. 94, *Tombstone Daily Nugget* and *Tombstone Daily Epitaph*, November 10–11, 1881.

81. *Tombstone Daily Nugget*, November 11, 1881.

82. Testimony of Ike Clanton, Doc. No. 94, *Tombstone Daily Nugget* and *Tombstone Daily Epitaph*, November 13–16, 1881.

83. Earp proceeded under section 133 of the Compiled Statutes of Arizona Territory. See Palmquist, "Tombstone Jurisprudence," 14–15; Lubet, *Murder in Tombstone*, 135–155.

84. Statement of Wyatt Earp, Doc. No. 94, *Tombstone Daily Nugget* and *Tombstone Daily Epitaph*, November 16, 1881.

85. Lubet, *Murder in Tombstone*, 156–164; Tefertiller, *Wyatt Earp*, 146–148.

86. Testimony of H. F. Sills, Doc. No. 94, *Tombstone Daily Nugget* and *Tombstone Daily Epitaph*, November 23–24, 1881.

87. *Tombstone Daily Nugget* and *Tombstone Daily Epitaph*, November 24, 1881.

88. Testimony of W. S. Williams, Doc. No. 94, *Tombstone Daily Nugget* and *Tombstone Daily Epitaph*, November 28, 1881.

89. Testimony of Addie Borland, ibid., November 29, 1881.

90. Testimony of J. H. Lucas, ibid., November 29, 1881.

91. Testimony of Ernest Storm, ibid., November 30, 1881.

92. Decision of Wells Spicer, Doc. No. 94, *Tombstone Daily Nugget* and *Tombstone Daily Epitaph*, December 1, 1881.

93. Ibid. For analysis of Spicer's decision, see Lubet, *Murder in Tombstone*, 179–202; Tefertiller, *Wyatt Earp*, 151–159; and Gary L. Roberts, "The Gunfight at the O.K. Corral: The Wells Spicer Decision," *Montana, the Magazine of Western History* 20 (Winter 1970): 63–74.

94. *Tombstone Daily Nugget*, December 1, 1881.

95. *San Francisco Examiner*, May 11, 1882. John P. Clum to George Kelly, August 30, 1929, reprinted in Ellis T. "Butch" Badon, "An Unexpected Nugget," *NOLA Quarterly* 25 (October–December 2001): 24–25.

96. McLaury to Appelgate, November 9, 1881, McLaury Papers.

8. Vengeance

1. *Valdosta (Georgia) Times*, June 24, 1882.

2. Thursday, December 1, 1881, George Whitwell Parsons, *The Private Journal of George W. Parsons* (Tombstone, AZ: Tombstone Daily Epitaph, 1972), 198.

3. *Tombstone (Arizona) Daily Nugget*, December 3, 1881.

4. William R. McLaury to D. D. Appelgate, November 9, 1881; McLaury to Mrs. M. F. Appelgate, November 17, December 9, 1881, William R. McLaury Papers, New-York Historical Society, New York, New York; *Tombstone Daily Nugget*, December 1, 1881. The *Nugget* had a point. W. A. Harwood, Marshall Williams, Sylvester B. Comstock, John

D. Kinnear, Oscar F. Thornton, Dave Calisher, Thomas R. Sorin, and Lewis W. Blinn were all identified with the pro-Earp business faction in Tombstone.

5. McLaury to Appelgate, December 9, 1881, McLaury Papers.

6. McLaury to Appelgate, November 17, 1881, McLaury Letters.

7. Mrs. J. C. Collier to editor, *Kansas City Star*, reprinted in the *Tombstone Epitaph*, December 30, 1881. "Millie" Collier was the sister-in-law of John Collier, who was superintendent of the Boston Mill in 1881. According to the *Tombstone Daily Epitaph*, January 21, 1937, Joseph C. Collier, his wife, and his two daughters came to Tombstone in 1881 because of Joseph Collier's health and the desire to be closer to his brother. Millie Collier and her daughter Josie were at the scene of the street fight. The author is indebted to Lynn Bailey and Woody Campbell for providing information about the Collier family.

8. William B. Shillingberg, *Tombstone, A. T.: A History of Early Mining, Milling, and Mayhem* (Spokane, WA: Clark, 1999), 283–284.

9. John J. Gosper to Crawley P. Dake, November 28, 1881, General Records of the Department of Justice, Record Group 60, National Archives and Records Administration, Washington, DC.

10. Dake to S. F. Phillips, Acting Attorney General, December 3, 1881, RG 60, NARA.

11. Gosper to President Chester A. Arthur, December 12, 1881, Department of Justice, Chronological President Files, RG 60, NARA; Larry D. Ball, *The United States Marshals of New Mexico and Arizona Territories, 1846–1912* (Albuquerque: University of New Mexico Press, 1978), 121–126; John P. Clum, *Apache Days and Tombstone Nights: John Clum's Autobiography, 1877–1887.* Edited by Neal B. Carmony (Silver City, NM: High-Lonesome, 1997), 62–64; Casey Tefertiller, *Wyatt Earp: The Life behind the Legend* (New York: Wiley, 1997), 163–164.

12. John P. Clum, "It All Happened at Tombstone," *Arizona Historical Review* 2 (October 1929): 55–62.

13. Tefertiller, *Wyatt Earp*, 165–166, provides a convenient and balanced summary of the sources.

14. Clum, "It All Happened at Tombstone," 56.

15. *Tombstone Daily Nugget*, as reprinted in the *Tucson (Arizona) Weekly Star*, December 22, 1881.

16. William M. Breakenridge, *Helldorado: Bringing the Law to the Mesquite* (Boston: Houghton Mifflin, 1928), 154–155.

17. *Tombstone Daily Nugget*, December 16, 1881.

18. Breakenridge, *Helldorado*, 155; see also Joe Chisholm, "Tombstone's Tale (the Truth of Helldorado," 98–99, unpublished manuscript, circa 1938, Jack Burrows Collection. Chisholm confused the chronology, but he made the interesting observation that "the Earps, cold-blooded Wyatt especially, had incited Holliday to kill a man (Joyce) they were afraid to go up against themselves. The manner in which Wyatt in his so-called autobiography (*Frontier Marshal*) sneers at the memory of Holliday would seem to lend credence to that surmise."

19. *Tombstone Daily Epitaph*, December 18, 1881.

20. *Tombstone Daily Nugget*, December 15, 1881.

21. *Tombstone Daily Epitaph*, December 18, 1881; see also Lynn R. Bailey, *A Tale of the "Unkilled": The Life, Times, and Writings of Wells W. Spicer* (Tucson, AZ: Westernlore, 1999), 127–130.

22. James Reilly to the editor, December 20, 1881, *Tombstone Daily Nugget*, December 21, 1881.

23. Ibid. Reilly's history of trouble with the Earps doubtlessly affected the public response to his comments.

24. "A Card" from E. F. Boyle, *Tombstone Weekly Epitaph*, December 26, 1881; see also Shillingberg, *Tombstone, A. T.*, 289, and Tefertiller, *Wyatt Earp*, 167–173.

25. *San Francisco Daily Exchange*, December 20, 1881.

26. Clara Spalding Brown to the editor, December 7, 1881, *San Diego Union*, December 13, 1881.

27. Shillingberg, *Tombstone, A.T.*, 290–291.

28. Breakenridge, *Helldorado*, 155–156.

29. *Tombstone Daily Epitaph*, December 30, 1881.

30. Forrestine C. Hooker, "An Arizona Vendetta (the Truth about Wyatt Earp—and Some Others)," 46, unpublished manuscript, circa 1920, Southwest Museum, Los Angeles, California.

31. *Tombstone Daily Nugget*, November 4, 1881; *Tombstone Daily Nugget*, reprinted in *Los Angeles Daily Herald*, November 16, 1881.

32. Dake to Phillips, December 3, 1881, Department of Justice, RG 60, NARA.

33. James D. Richardson, ed., *A Compilation of the Messages and Papers of the Presidents, 1789–1908*, X (New York: Bureau of National Literature, 1897–1915): 4688–9.

34. Entry for December 28, 1881, Parsons, *Journal*, 202.

35. Ibid., 202–203.

36. Ibid; see also Frank Waters, "Tombstone Travesty," unpublished manuscript, 1934, Frank Waters Collection, University of New Mexico Library, Albuquerque, New Mexico, where Allie Earp repeats this statement.

37. Entry for December 29, 1881, Parsons, *Journal*, 203.

38. *Phoenix (Arizona) Herald*, December 30, 1881; *Weekly Arizona Miner*, December 30, 1881.

39. *Phoenix Arizona Gazette*, December 30, 1881.

40. The full story of Wyatt Earp's posse has yet to be written. Important insights are provided in Peter Brand, "Sherman W. McMaster(s), the El Paso Salt War, Texas Rangers, and Tombstone," *WOLA Journal* 8 (Winter 1999): 2–191; Peter Brand, "Dan G. Tipton and the Earp Vendetta Posse," *Quarterly of the National Association for Outlaw and Lawman History* 24 (October–December 2000): 17–27; Peter Brand, "Wyatt Earp, Jack Johnson, and the Notorious Blunt Brothers," *Quarterly of the National Association for Outlaw and Lawman History*, 27 (October–December 2003): 36–47; Paul Cool, "The World of Sherman McMaster(s)," *WOLA Journal* 7 (Autumn 1998): 10–22; Paul Cool, "Escape of a Highwayman: The Riddle of Sherman McMaster," *WOLA Journal* 9 (Summer 2000): 2–13; Robert F. Palmquist, "Mining, Keno, and the Law: The Tombstone Careers of Bob Winders, Charley Smith, and Fred Dodge, 1879–1888," *Journal of Arizona History* 38 (Summer 1997): 138–148; Robert F. Palmquist, "He Was about Half Way Right: *Territory v. Blount*, 1881," *Journal of Arizona History* 40 (Winter 1999): 377–390; Fred Dodge, *Under Cover for Wells Fargo: The Unvarnished Recollections of Fred Dodge*, edited by Carolyn Lake (Boston: Houghton Mifflin, 1969), passim; Roy B. Young, *Cochise County Cowboy War: "A Cast of Characters"* (Apache, OK: Young, 1999), 128. At least three of the riders, McMaster, Johnson, and Vermillion, appear to have had some association with the Cow-Boys. They were all known as tough men who could be counted on in a fight. The *Tombstone Daily Nugget*, January 24, 1881, said of them: "[t]he Earp party is composed of desperate men who will each fight to the death, and it is stated that they have all been sworn in as Deputy United States Marshals, in which case they will have the color of law under which to act."

41. *Tombstone Daily Epitaph*, December 29, 1881.

42. *San Francisco Stock Report*, reprinted in *Arizona Sentinel (Yuma)*, January 14, 1882.

43. *Tombstone Daily Nugget*, January 1, 1882.

44. *Tombstone Daily Epitaph*, December 25, 1881; *Tombstone Daily Nugget*, January 1, 1882; see Tefertiller, *Wyatt Earp*, 176–179, and Shillingberg, *Tombstone, A. T.*, 290–296.

45. Shillingberg, *Tombstone, A. T.*, 295–296.

46. Tefertiller, *Wyatt Earp*, 179–182.

47. Leigh Chalmers, Examiner, Department of Justice, to A. H. Garland, Attorney General, September 3, 1885, Department of Justice, RG 60, NARA.

48. *Tombstone Daily Nugget*, January 7, 8, 1882; *Tombstone Daily Epitaph*, January 10, 11, 1882. The *Nugget* reported on February 8, 1882, that "Mr. L. Rickabaugh, late proprietor of the Oriental saloon, left by yesterday's coach for San Francisco." He traveled in Texas and Arizona, dabbling in various enterprises before returning to Tombstone in the autumn of 1884. In 1885, at Tucson, he was called out by a gambler named William H. Bennett. Rickabaugh shot Bennett in the leg. Bennett lost his leg, but Rickabaugh was discharged on grounds that he had shot in self-defense. *Tombstone Daily Record-Epitaph*, September 15, 16, 20, 23, 1885. He eventually returned to California, where he died in 1920. See Lynn R. Bailey and Don Chaput, *Cochise County Stalwarts: A Who's Who of the Territorial Years* (Tucson, AZ: Westernlore, 2000), 2:81.

49. Entry for January 17, 1882, Parsons, *Journal*, 206.

50. Walter Noble Burns, *Tombstone: The Iliad of the Southwest* (New York: Doubleday, 1927), 137–139, provides the most detailed account, having Ringo first challenge Wyatt Earp, who refused with the comment, "I'd be a fine simpleton—a peace officer and candidate for sheriff—to fight a duel with you in the street. Go and sleep it off." Earp then went into Bob Hatch's saloon, leaving Doc standing at the door, "a cold little smile on his cadaverous face," as "Ringo drew a handkerchief from the breast pocket of his coat and flipped a corner of it toward Holliday," eliciting the comment, "I'm your huckleberry, Ringo. . . . That's just my game," as Doc took the corner of the handkerchief. Burns said that Mayor Thomas intervened to prevent the fight. Of course, John Carr was mayor, not Thomas. Sarah Grace Bakarich, *Gunsmoke: The True Story of Old Tombstone* (Tombstone, AZ: Tombstone, 1954), 14, repeats essentially the same story, including Doc's signature line, "I'm your huckleberry." Breakenridge, *Helldorado*, 157–158. In Breakenridge's handwritten statement, circa 1910, in the Special Collections, University of Arizona, Tucson, 9, he has Ringo approach Holliday rather than Earp, "but his kind offer was not accepted and he turned his back on them and went back to his own side of the street while they all hurried into the nearest saloon and closed the door." John H. Flood Jr., "Wyatt Earp, a Peace-officer of Tombstone," 257–259, unpublished manuscript, 1927, C. Lee Simmons Collection, has Wyatt intervening with the comment, "Come on, enough of this!" as he grasps Doc by the elbow and leads him away. John Plesant Gray, *When All Roads Led to Tombstone: A Memoir*, edited by W. Lane Rogers (Boise, ID: Tamarack, 1998), 34, has Ringo challenge Wyatt, but notes, "Of course, Wyatt Earp was too wise to be caught in such a trap, but to the few scattering onlookers, it seemed a critical moment. Both men were of undoubted courage but the Earps knew it would not do to take up the challenge at that time." Gray mistakenly places the confrontation only days before Ringo's body was found and implies a connection.

51. George Parsons to Stuart N. Lake, October 25, 1928, Stuart N. Lake Collection, Letter Box 10, Huntington Library, San Marino, California.

52. *Tombstone Daily Nugget*, January 18, 1882, reprinted in *Tucson (Arizona) Weekly Citizen*, January 22, 1882. The *Tombstone Daily Epitaph*, January 18, 1882, noted that Chief of Police Flynn, "by his prompt action, gave unmistaken proof that he thoroughly understands his business and is fearless in its execution."

53. *Tombstone Daily Epitaph*, January 18, 1882. For further analysis, see Jack Burrows, *John Ringo: The Gunfighter Who Never Was* (Tucson: University of Arizona, 1987), 25–34, 62–65. Burrows notes, "No near-gunfight in the history of the Old West (not a single shot was fired) has been burdened with so many grossly inaccurate and personally intrusive accounts and interpretations of what happened or might have happened, or which reflect so much wishful thinking, as that storied encounter." Burrows concludes, "No hanky fluttered

between Johnny Ringo and Johnny Holliday and no one backed down." See also, Steve Gatto, *Johnny Ringo* (Lansing, MI: Protar House, 2002), 108–113; David Johnson, *John Ringo* (Stillwater, OK: Barbed Wire, 1996), 181–182. Gatto underscores the *Nugget's* emphasis that Ringo and Holliday "had been on bad terms for some time past" to make the confrontation more personal, and Timothy W. Fattig, *Wyatt Earp: The Biography* (Honolulu, HI: Talei, 2002), 472–474, argues that the quarrel concerned "Ringo's dalliances with Holliday mistress, Kate Elder."

54. *Tombstone Daily Epitaph*, November 16, 1881, and January 18, 1882.

55. Gatto, *Johnny Ringo*, 115–121. Note especially the endnotes, 218–219.

56. Chalmers to Garland, September 3, 1885, Department of Justice, RG 60, NARA.

57. Shillingberg, *Tombstone, A. T.*, 298–299.

58. *Tombstone Daily Nugget*, January 26, 1882.

59. *Tombstone Daily Nugget*, January 24, 26, 27, 1882.

60. Affidavit of James Earp, January 23, 1882, James Earp File, Arizona Historical Society, Tucson, Arizona.

61. Gatto, *Johnny Ringo*, 118–120.

62. Tefertiller, *Wyatt Earp*, 185–186.

63. *Tombstone Daily Nugget*, January 27, 1882.

64. *Tombstone Daily Nugget*, January 31, 1882; Tefertiller, *Wyatt Earp*, 187–189; Fattig, *The Biography*, 480–483.

65. *Tombstone Daily Epitaph*, February 3, 1882.

66. Lake to Stilwell, September 10, 1928, Lake Collection; Earp, "Wyatt Earp," 265. The frustration of the Earps and their allies was thus underscored by yet another failure of the court system to deal with the problems. One local wrote to the *Tucson Weekly Citizen*, "If by chance one or more of these robbers are arrested they have innumerable friends through whom they always do prove an alibi. Hence they obtain their liberty regardless of what may be the evidence against them. I venture to assert that a conviction of one of these festive cowboys will never be obtained in Cochise county as long as the present state of affairs exists."

67. Sheriff Behan's troubles are reviewed in Tefertiller, *Wyatt Earp*, 186–193. A more positive analysis of Behan is found in Bob Alexander, *John H. Behan: Sacrificed Sheriff* (Silver City, NM: High-Lonesome, 2002), 185–187. The most interesting commentaries, however, are the contemporary criticisms, including the editorials of Charles Reppy in the *Epitaph*, the letters of Clara Spalding Brown to the editor, January 29, March 10, 1882, *San Diego Union*, February 4, March 13, 1882, and the interview with James B. Hume published in the *National Police Gazette*, March 11, 1882. Hume said that Behan "is in with the cowboys and has got to be or his life would not be worth a farthing." Parsons, *Journal*, 211.

68. *Arizona Daily Star*, February 9, 1882.

69. Tefertiller, *Wyatt Earp*, 193.

70. Jay J. Wagoner, *Arizona Territory, 1863–1912: A Political History* (Tucson: University of Arizona Press, 1970), 194–198; Bailey and Chaput, *Cochise County Stalwarts*, 2:159–160; *Tombstone Daily Nugget*, February 8, 1882.

71. *Tombstone Daily Nugget* and *Tombstone Daily Epitaph*, February 2, 1882. The *Epitaph* called the gesture "a manly and generous one," while the *Nugget* predicted that it would "be hailed with satisfaction by a great majority of our law-abiding and order-loving citizens" and predicted "the inauguration of an era of confidence in the impartial enforcement of the laws, and consequent freedom from that feeling of disquietude and distrust which has of late prevailed throughout our county."

72. *Tombstone Daily Epitaph*, February 3, 1882; Bailey and Chaput, *Cochise County Stalwarts*, 1:197–199; see also *Tombstone Daily Nugget*, January 28, February 2, 1882.

73. *Tombstone Daily Nugget*, February 2, 1882.

74. Ike Clanton to Billy Byers, February 14, 1882, William Byers File, AHS.

75. *Territory of Arizona v. J. H. Holliday, Wyatt Earp, Morgan Earp, and Virgil Earp, Defendants*, Arrest Warrant, J. B. Smith, Justice of the Peace, Cochise County, February 9, 1882; Petition of Writ of Habeas Corpus, Wyatt Earp, Morgan Earp, and J. H. Holliday to J. H. Lucas, February 11, 15, 1882, reprinted in Alford E. Turner, ed., *The O.K. Corral Inquest* (College Station, TX: Creative, 1981), 230–245; *Tombstone Daily Epitaph*, February 11, 13, 15, 17, 1882; *Tombstone Daily Nugget*, February 9, 16, 19, 1882; Tefertiller, *Wyatt Earp*, 194–196; Hooker, "Arizona Vendetta," 42–46.

76. Entry for February 15, 1882, Parsons, *Journal*, 213.

77. Ex Parte J. H. Holliday, Wyatt Earp, and Morgan Earp, Habeas Corpus, to J. H. Lucas, reprinted in Turner, *Corral Inquest*, 238–239, 242–245.

78. *Tombstone Daily Nugget* and *Tombstone Daily Epitaph*, February 16, 1882; *Tucson Arizona Citizen*, February 19, 1882; entry for February 15, Parsons, *Journal*, 213; see also Brand, "Tipton and the Earp Vendetta Posse," 18–19.

79. *Tombstone Daily Nugget*, February 18, 1882. On February 28, the *Nugget* reprinted from the *Prescott (Arizona) Daily Democrat* an explanation of why: "We are informed by Marshal Dake that the resignations of the Earps, as United States Marshals, have not yet been accepted, owing to the fact that their accounts have not yet been straightened up. As soon as that is done they will step down and out." This explanation appears insufficient in light of the volume of correspondence and other documentation demonstrating Dake's active support of the Earps. See also Steve Gatto, *The Real Wyatt Earp: A Documentary Biography* (Silver City, NM: High-Lonesome, 2000), 163–164.

80. *Tombstone Daily Nugget*, February 14, 16, 1882.

81. Clara Spalding Brown to the editor, March 10, 1882; *San Diego Union*, March 13, 1882.

82. Deposition of Briggs Goodrich, Doc. No. 68, Coroner's Inquest, Morgan Earp, March 22, 1882, District Court of the First Judicial District, Cochise County, Arizona Historical Foundation, Arizona State University, Tempe, Arizona.

83. Ibid.

84. Waters, "Tombstone Travesty," 250–252.

85. *Tombstone Daily Epitaph*, March 20, 1881; testimony of Robert Hatch, D. G. Tipton, Dr. George E. Goodfellow, Sherman McMaster, Marietta Duarte Spence, Doc. No. 68, Coroner's Inquest, Morgan Earp; *Tombstone Daily Epitaph* and *Tombstone Daily Nugget*, March 23, 1882; Hooker, "Arizona Vendetta," 48–52; Earp, "Wyatt Earp," 270–276; Brown to the editor, March 26, *San Diego Union*, March 31, 1882.

86. This story appears to have originated with Glenn G. Boyer's *I Married Wyatt Earp: The Recollections of Josephine Sarah Marcus Earp* (Tucson: University of Arizona Press, 1976), 103, which purported to be the memoir of Josephine Earp. According to the account, when Doc learned of Morgan's death, "he went beserk." In actuality, this story appears to have been simply one more manufactured tale made up by Boyer. See Gary L. Roberts, "Trailing an American Mythmaker: History and Glenn G. Boyer's Tombstone Vendetta," *WOLA Journal* 6 (Spring 1998): 8–22, 49–53.

87. Entry for March 19, 1882, Parsons, *Journal*, 220.

88. Tefertiller, *Wyatt Earp*, 226–227; Shillingberg, *Tombstone, A. T.*, 311–312; Waters, "Tombstone Travesty," 253–260. Hooker, "Arizona Vendetta," 52a–53, has Wyatt telling the Cochise County grand jury that he knew who killed Morgan but refusing to give their names, with the comment, "No! I am going after them." He then told Virgil that he had to go home to Colton so that Wyatt would be free for the work he had to do.

89. *Denver Republican*, May 14, 1893.

90. Waters, "Tombstone Travesty," 257–258; Hooker, "Arizona Vendetta," 58.

91. George Hand, *Whiskey, Six-Gun, and Red-Light Ladies*, edited by Neal Carmony (Silver City, NM: High-Lonesome, 1994), 228.

92. The *Tucson Weekly Citizen*, April 12, 1882, printed the coroner's report on the death of Frank Stilwell. The True Bill in the case of *The Territory v. Doc Holliday, Wyatt Earp, Warren Earp, Sherman McMaster, and John Johnson* is found in the records of the Arizona Historical Foundation, Arizona State University, Tempe, Arizona. Fattig, *The Biography*, 859n, notes that Virgil later told a reporter (*San Francisco Examiner*, May 22, 1882) that Stilwell confessed to killing Morgan and named his partners in the crime, which prompted the *Tombstone Daily Epitaph*, June 3, 1882, to observe: "[W]e nevertheless cannot help expressing astonishment that a man with two pounds of buckshot in his stomach, four bullets in his heart, and his head mutilated by lead beyond recognition, could have had either time or inclination to make any statement whatever."

93. Wyatt Earp to Walter Noble Burns, March 15, 1927, Walter Noble Burns Collection, Special Collections, University of Arizona Library, Tucson, Arizona. Hooker, "Arizona Vendetta," 53–58, also suggests that only Doc was with him at Tucson. Hooker has "Deputy United States Marshal Ivans [*sic*]" meet Wyatt at "a watering hole east of Tucson" and warn him that Stilwell and "a half-breed" were in the area, noting, 54–55, "Tjis [*sic*] is the bunch that killed your brother. They rode across country from Tombstone and believe that you are leaving the Territory with Virgil. They plan to 'get' you both before you escape them. Look out when you reach Tucson." Fattig, *The Biography*, 512–517, follows this view. However, Earp, "Wyatt Earp," 278–279, has McMaster and Johnson accompanying Wyatt and Doc in escort of Virgil and meeting Evans when the party reached Tucson. Flood has Wyatt confront Stilwell alone. Nathan W. Waite, a passenger who joined the Earp party at Contention, testified at the hearing, "McMasters [*sic*] said that they would leave the train but afterwards changed their minds and came to Tucson to see Virgil and his wife on their way to California." Deputy Evans testified that Doc was the first person off the train, carrying two shotguns. He also testified that he warned Earp of Stilwell's presence. Ike Clanton testified that he saw McMaster, Johnson, and Warren with Wyatt and Doc outside the hotel where the Earp party had gone to eat. Details of the shooting were not provided in the testimony, so it is not clear how many of the Earp group were present. James Miller, a fireman on the westbound train, provided the most detail, reporting that he "saw a man running down the track on the east side of the engine and cross the track in front of it. Eight or ten minutes afterwards [I] saw four armed men pass on the west side of the engine and down to the left of the coaches standing on the side track. In about five minutes afterwards heard five or six shots fired in rapid succession. Saw but one man while they were shooting, but saw four men standing there when the train pulled out." On the strength of the wounds on Stilwell's body and the presence of Wyatt, Warren, Doc, McMaster, and Johnson at the depot, those men were identified as Stilwell's killers by the coroner's jury. Most likely, one of the Earp group remained with Virgil and Allie as guard while the shooting occurred, which would explain why Miller saw four men rather than five. *Tucson Weekly Citizen*, April 12, 1882; see also *Los Angeles Daily Herald*, March 22, 1882.

94. *Tucson (Arizona) Daily Star*, March 21, 22, 24, 1882.

95. Testimony of Marietta Duarte Spence, Doc. No. 68, Coroner's Inquest, Morgan Earp; see also the testimony as published in the *Tombstone Daily Nugget* and *Tombstone Daily Epitaph*, March 23, 1882.

96. Deposition of Briggs Goodrich, Doc. No. 68, Coroner's Inquest, Morgan Earp.

97. Entry for March 20, 1882, Parsons, *Journal*, 220–221. The *Los Angeles Daily Herald*, March 24, 1882, noted, "There is a very uneasy feeling among the cowboy element, as the Earps are rendered desperate by the attempted assassination of Virgil Earp and the cold-blooded murder of Morgan Earp."

98. *Tucson Weekly Citizen*, March 26, 1882. The *Tombstone Weekly Epitaph*, March 27, 1881, added "that there is positive evidence Stilwell was in Tombstone Saturday night at the time Morgan Earp was murdered and that he rode into Tucson on horseback on Sunday."

His fate, the *Epitaph* concluded, "verifies the saying that 'the way of the transgressor is hard.'" Clara Brown added, "Although only twenty-seven years of age, his career was not a beneficial one to his country, and his removal is no loss, however unlawful." Brown to the editor, March 26, 1882, *San Diego Union*, March 31, 1882; see also, Gray, *All Roads*, 41, who said that Behan refused to hold Stilwell because it was impossible for him to travel from Tombstone to Tucson in the time available, then added, "A long time afterward it came out that an old roan saddle horse could have told a different story had he the power of speech."

99. Tefertiller, *Wyatt Earp*, 231. Wyatt always insisted that Chris Bilicke greeted him with a handshake, a smile, and the comment, "Wyatt, Stillwell won't rob any more coaches now." See Hooker, "Arizona Vendetta," 61; Earp, "Wyatt Earp," 286; Stuart N. Lake notes in the Stuart N. Lake Collection, Huntington Library, San Marino, California.

100. Breakenridge, *Helldorado*, 174. The *Tombstone Daily Nugget*, March 22, 1882, generally supports Breakenridge's version, in having the members of the Earp party point their weapons at Sheriff Behan, although even it criticized Behan's delay in taking action. The *Tucson Daily Star*, March 22, 1882, offered similar criticism. A telegram from the *Star* on the evening of March 22 reported, "Tonight Sheriff Behan telegraphed Paul that he had attempted to make the arrest and was forcibly resisted by the party and a posse of their friends, and asked for assistance, and the Earp party had fled to the hills. Sheriff Paul left to-night on a special train for Tombstone to make the arrests. There is no doubt but that he will take them, but bloodshed is expected." *Los Angeles Daily Herald*, March 23, 1882.

101. Hooker, "Arizona Vendetta," 63; Lake notes. The *Tombstone Daily Epitaph*, March 22, 1882, presented the view that Wyatt brushed Behan aside without a confrontation, and Clara Brown added, "The party then went to a stable, mounted their horses, and left town. Behan claims that they resisted an arrest, but the bystanders claim that this was all that passed, and nothing was said about an arrest. He also asserts that every one of the party drew their guns on him, which is denied by the spectators. All were heavily armed, but no motion was made." Brown to the editor, March 26, 1882, *San Diego Union*, March 31, 1881.

102. Brown to the editor, March 26, 1882, *San Diego Union*, March 31, 1882.

103. Entry for March 21, 1882, Parsons, *Journal*, 221.

104. *Tombstone Daily Epitaph*, *Tombstone Daily Nugget*, *Tucson Daily Star*, *Tucson Daily Citizen*, March 22, 23, 1882. Parsons, *Journal*, 221, wrote on March 22, 1882, "Excitement again this morning. Sheriff went out with a posse supposably to arrest the Earp party, but they will never do it. The Cow-boy element is backing him strongly. John Ringo being one of the party. There is a prospect of a bad time and there are about three men who deserve to get it in the back of the neck. Terrible thing, this, for our town, but the sooner it is all over with the better. Went to church tonight. Took home Miss S." The *Epitaph*, March 23, confirmed that Ringo, Fin Clanton, and several other Cow-Boys were with Behan's posse. Clara Brown noted that "only a very daring man would be willing to face the Earps in their present mood, and it is reported that it was difficult to raise a posse." Brown to the editor, March 26, 1882, *San Diego Union*, March 31, 1882.

105. Proceedings of the Inquest upon the Body of Florentino Cruz appeared in the *Tombstone Daily Nugget*, March 25, 26, 1882. Useful secondary accounts appear in Tefertiller, *Wyatt Earp*, 234–235; Shillingberg, *Tombstone, A. T.*, 315–316; and Fattig, *The Biography*, 530–533.

106. Stuart N. Lake, *Wyatt Earp: Frontier Marshal* (Boston: Houghton Mifflin, 1931), 336; this comment also appears in the Lake notes concerning the episode. See also, Hooker, "Arizona Vendetta," 64–66; Earp, "Wyatt Earp," 290–294.

107. Entry for March 23, 1882, Parsons, *Journal*, 221. The *Tucson Weekly Star*, March 30, 1882, reported the arrest of Hank Swilling. The *Tombstone Daily Epitaph*, March 22, 1882, noted that Deputy Sheriff Frank Hereford had arrested "John Doe Freeze" (actually Frederick Bode) in connection with Morgan's murder, and the same issue carried a notice

that W. A. Freeze, "a quiet, nice gentleman, with hosts of friends and no eninies [*sic*] in Tombstone," was not the man implicated in the death of Morgan Earp.

108. J. A. Browder to the editor, March 29, 1882, *Tucson Daily Star*, March 31, 1882.

109. Brown to the editor, March 26, 1882, *San Diego Union*, March 31, 1882.

110. Breakenridge, *Helldorado*, 178.

111. *Tucson Daily Star*, March 28, 1882. A telegram from Tombstone confirmed the essence of these reports: "Sheriff Paul has returned from Tombstone. He says that he did not go in pursuit of the Earps because the posse selected by Sheriff Behan of Tombstone, were mostly hostile to the Earps and that a meeting meant bloodshed without any probability of arrest. Sheriff Paul says the Earps will come to Tucson and surrender to the authorities." *Los Angeles Daily Herald*, March 28, 1882; see also *Tombstone (Arizona) Commercial Advertiser*, March 25, 1882.

112. Brown to the editor, March 26, 1882, *San Diego Union*, March 31, 1882. The same view was expressed in an article from the *Tombstone Commercial Advertiser*, March 25, 1882, reprinted from the *Nugget*.

113. Entry for March 23, 1882, Parsons, *Journal*, 221.

114. *Tucson Daily Citizen*, March 25, 1882; *Tombstone Daily Epitaph*, March 24, 1882; *Tombstone Daily Nugget*, March 26, 1882; see also Brand, "Tipton and the Earp Vendetta Posse," 20.

115. *Tucson Daily Citizen*, March 25, 1882; *Phoenix Arizona Gazette*, March 24, 1882.

116. Entry for March 25, 1882, Parsons, *Journal*, 222. Dispatches from Tombstone indicated that Behan and a posse of twenty-four, including twelve "Charleston cowboys," left Contention on March 22 and that the group divided into two groups, one of which included Curly Bill. The dispatches correctly reported that the Earps were in the Whetstones pursued by the two groups. "We are expecting news of a fight any hour," was the report. *Tucson Weekly Citizen*, March 26, 1882. Gatto, *Real Wyatt Earp*, 179, argues that Curly Bill was not in Arizona based on Behan's bill for mileage for his deputies to El Paso (in search of defendants), dated February 17, 1882, in the case of *The Territory v. Curly Bill-Hicks et al.*, Financial Reports, Sheriff's Department, January–April 1882, Cochise County Records, MS 180, Box 8, f83, AHS. This expense was for the earlier trip to El Paso in December 1881 and is not a good indicator of Curly Bill's presence in 1882. Bill's name does not appear in Behan's report of expenses in his pursuit of the Earps, dated April 4, 1882, FRSD, January– April 1882, CCR, MS 180, Box 8, f83, AHS, where the names of the possemen appear, indicating the number of days served at the rate of $5 per day. Steve Gatto, *Curly Bill: Tombstone's Most Famous Outlaw* (Lansing, MI: Protar House, 2003), 160n, argues that since Brocius's name did not appear on the list, he did not serve. This is possible, of course, but even if he did serve, it is unlikely that his name would appear on the list simply because he was killed and there was no one to receive the funds. Furthermore, Behan disassociated himself from the party at the springs, saying it had "no connection with his posse." *Tombstone Daily Nugget*, March 26, 1882.

117. Hand, *Whiskey*, 9.

118. Tefertiller, *Wyatt Earp*, 238.

119. This account is distilled from contemporary newspaper coverage from the *Tombstone Daily Epitaph*, March 25, 27, 1882; *Tombstone Daily Nugget*, March 26, 1882; *Tucson Daily Star*, April 6, 1882; Hooker, "Arizona Vendetta," 67–70; Earp, "Wyatt Earp," 295–306; the Lake notes; Wyatt's account in the *Denver Republican*, May 14, 1893; the article ghostwritten for Wyatt, "How Wyatt Earp Routed a Gang of Arizona Outlaws," *San Francisco Examiner*, August 2, 1896, as well as miscellaneous other contemporary sources and reminiscences. Also useful were secondary analyses, including Tefertiller, *Wyatt Earp*, 237–239, Fattig, *The Biography*, 535–546, and Gatto, *Real Wyatt Earp*, 177–192.

120. Hooker, "Arizona Vendetta," 68; Earp, "Wyatt Earp," 303–304; *Denver Republican*, May 14, 1893.

121. Ibid.

122. *Denver Republican*, May 22, 1882.

123. *Tombstone Daily Epitaph*, March 25, 27, 1882; *Tombstone Daily Nugget*, March 26, 1882; Hooker, "Arizona Vendetta," 66–67.

124. Burns, *Tombstone*, 249; *Tombstone Daily Nugget*, March 31, April 1, 1882. The *Tucson Daily Star*, April 4, 1882, reported that the fight actually involved a group of prospectors who "repulsed" the Earp party. A dispatch published in the *Tucson Daily Star*, March 26, 1882, said, "There was a fight in the mountains between the Earps and some of the Sheriff's posse. Texas Jack's horse was killed and Wyatt Earp wounded. Nothing of Curly Bill being killed. Don't think it is so." In the same issue, another dispatch sent to Ike Clanton by John Chenowith advised Ike that one report said that four of the Earp party had been killed while another said that "one of the Earp party and Curly Bill are killed." Other reports were circulating as well. What does seem clear is that Behan had two groups in the field after the Earps, and the group encountered at Iron Springs was likely one of them.

125. An unidentified informant for the *Nugget* who claimed to have been en route to meet the Earps (doubtlessly either Kraker or Wright) told the journal that after the brief fight, "The Earp party retired behind an adjacent hill and halted. They were in a position commanding a view of the spring, and shortly after the fight saw a wagon come to the place and, as Wyatt believes, carry away the dead body of CurlyBill." *Tombstone Daily Nugget*, March 26, 1882. Hooker, "Arizona Vendetta" (on a page marked "Important" as an extra page inserted into the manuscript), 70½, related that "Thacker, himself, went to the place where he had been told Curly Bill had been buried and had the body dug up. Thacker identified Curly Bill's body, and then saw it reinterred. This was done by a Wells-Fargo [*sic*] detective to settle all doubts regarding paying reward offered for death of Curly Bill." Wyatt told essentially the same story to Frederick R. Bechdolt in 1927. See Bechdolt to William M. Breakenridge, December 23, 1927, William M. Breakenridge Letters, Houghton Library, Harvard University, Cambridge, Massachusetts; Fred Dodge to Stuart N. Lake, October 8, 1928; Dodge to Lake, September 15, 1929, Dodge, *Under Cover*, 234–235, 239. Dodge told Lake he was sure that Thacker did not have the body dug up. He seems to assume, however, that Thacker could not have investigated before body decomposition occurred. Thacker checked into the Cosmopolitan Hotel in Tombstone on March 21 (*Tombstone Daily Epitaph*, March 22, 1882) and was still in town a week later (*Tombstone Weekly Epitaph*, March 27, 1882), which means that he was in Tombstone at the time the fight occurred and could have visited the burial site within a matter of days after the killing and before decomposition would have made identification impossible. The *Tombstone Daily Epitaph*, March 8, 1951, published an article by Lillian M. S. McCoy in which she claimed to have a photograph of the dead Curly Bill. She said that she had been given the photo by James Wilkins, a traveling salesman for Folgers coffee. He claimed to have been present when the photo was made of the dead man sitting upright in a chair. The photo was not published with the article, and the story does not appear to have been pursued further. Curiously, she noted that the photo had been taken to provide "proof of his death."

126. Both quoted in Silver City's *Grant County Herald* and *New Southwest*, April 8, 1882. The literature arguing that Curly Bill was not killed at Iron Springs is extensive and based largely on reminiscences of old-timers. The best summary of the arguments and evidence that Curly Bill was not killed is found in Gatto, *Curly Bill*, 109–134.

127. *San Francisco Daily Exchange*, March 27, 1882.

128. *Tombstone Daily Nugget*, March 25, 31, April 4, 1882; *Tombstone Weekly Epitaph*, April 10, 1882; see also Fattig, *The Biography*, 546–547.

129. Judge Bryant L. Peel to the People of Tombstone, *Tombstone Daily Epitaph*, March 29, 1882, reprinted in *Los Angeles Daily Herald*, March 31, 1882; see also *Tombstone*

Daily Nugget, March 26, 29, 1882; *Tombstone Daily Epitaph*, March 28, 1882; *Tucson Daily Star*, March 31, 1882.

130. Entry for March 26, 1882, Parsons, *Journal*, 222.

131. *Tucson Weekly Citizen*, March 26, 1882.

132. *Tombstone Daily Nugget*, March 29, 1882; *Tucson Weekly Citizen*, April 9, 1882; *Los Angeles Daily Herald*, April 4, 1882; F. A. Trittle to President Chester A. Arthur, March 31, 1882, Department of Justice, Chronological President Files, RG 60, NARA; *Tombstone Daily Epitaph*, April 4, 1882; Bailey and Chaput, *Cochise County Stalwarts*, 1:198.

133. *San Diego Union*, April 30, 1882; *Tombstone Daily Epitaph*, March 29, April 1, 1882; *Tombstone Daily Nugget*, March 29, 30, 31, April 1, 1882; *Los Angeles Daily Times*, March 30, 1882; Breakenridge, *Helldorado*, 181–187.

134. Entry for March 30, 1882, Parsons, *Journal*, 223.

9. The Out Trail

1. Apart from the broader history of national development during the late nineteenth century, what happened in Arizona in 1880–1882 is difficult to understand. General works that provide the background include Rebecca Edwards, *New Spirits: Americans in the Gilded Age, 1865–1905* (New York: Oxford University Press, 2005); Ray Ginger, *Age of Excess: The United States from 1877 to 1914* (New York: Macmillan, 1965); Mark Wahlgren Summers, *Party Games: Getting, Keeping, and Using Power in Gilded Age Politics* (Chapel Hill: University of North Carolina Press, 2004); Alan Trachtenberg, *The Incorporation of America: Culture and Society in the Gilded Age* (New York: Hill and Wang, 1982); Robert H. Weibe, *The Search for Order* (New York: Hill and Wang, 1967); and Richard White, *"It's Your Misfortune and None of My Own": A New History of the American West* (Norman: University of Oklahoma Press, 1991). Richard Slotkin, *The Fatal Environment: The Myth of the Frontier in the Age of Industrialization, 1800–1890* (New York: Atheneum, 1985), is especially helpful for understanding the mind-set of the times. The relationship of violence to the changes taking place in the American West during the time are explored in Richard Maxwell Brown, *No Duty to Retreat: Violence and Values in American History and Society* (New York: Oxford University Press, 1991); David T. Courtwright, *Violent Land: Single Men and Social Disorder from the Frontier to the Inner City* (Cambridge, MA: Harvard University Press, 1996); Roger D. McGrath, *Gunfighters, Highwaymen, and Vigilantes: Violence on the Frontier* (Berkleley: University of California Press, 1984); and Clare V. McKanna Jr., *Homicide, Race, and Justice in the American West, 1880–1920* (Tucson: University of Arizona Press, 1996). I have provided my own perspective on the relationship of violence and frontier development in "Violence and the Frontier Tradition," in *Kansas and the West: Bicentennial Essays in Honor of Nyle H. Miller,* edited by Forrest R. Blackburn et al. (Topeka: Kansas State Historical Society, 1976), 96–111, and in the final chapter of *Death Comes for the Chief Justice: The Slough-Rynerson Quarrel and Political Violence in New Mexico* (Niwot: University Press of Colorado, 1990), 127–157. This brief bibliography is far from comprehensive. The works of Robert R. Dykstra, Joe B. Frantz, Patricia Nelson Limerick, Paula Mitchell Marks, Joseph G. Rosa, and Robert M. Utley, all of whom have addressed the broad issues of the nature of Western violence, should also be consulted.

2. *Tombstone (Arizona) Daily Epitaph*, March 27, 1882. The *Epitaph* reported, "The latest report about the Earps is that on Sunday morning they came into the lower part of town and took a breakfast especially ordered for the occasion after which they quietly rode away smoking the choicest of Havana cigars and with a copy of the Nugget in their pockets, feeling much refreshed in every respect." The same issue of the *Epitaph* reported that E. B. Gage, the Earps' staunch supporter and the man who had provided the funds that Kraker and Wright were carrying on the day of the Curly Bill fight, had left for Lowell, Massachusetts, after receiving a telegram that his mother had died. He was expected to be

away for at least six weeks. Charlie Smith rejoined the Earp posse when they left Tombstone. See also the entry for March 27, 1882, George Whitwell Parsons, *The Private Journal of George W. Parsons* (Tombstone, AZ: Tombstone Daily Epitaph, 1972), 222. Forrestine C. Hooker, "An Arizona Vendetta (the Truth about Wyatt Earp—and Some Others)," 70–70½, unpublished manuscript, circa 1920, Southwest Museum, Los Angeles, California, says that Texas Jack Vermillion went to Tombstone alone to find Smith and recover the money, but the contemporary sources suggest the scenario presented here. George Hand reported at the time that Sheriff Behan's posse "struck the trail of the Earp party a few miles below town [Contention], *returning toward Tombstone and followed it* [italics added]." George Hand, "Next Stop: Tombstone," in *George Hand's Contention Diary*, edited by Neal B. Carmony (Tucson, AZ: Trail to Yesterday Books, 1995), 13.

3. *Tucson (Arizona) Daily Star*, March 28, 29, 1882; *Sacramento Union*, March 28, 1882. On March 27, Chief of Police David Neagle reported that the Earp party had been seen fifteen miles north of Willcox by Deputy Sheriff Frank Hereford. Neagle believed that the Earps were en route to Tucson to surrender to Sheriff Bob Paul.

4. *Dos Cabezas Gold Note*, quoted in the *Tombstone Daily Epitaph*, April 4, 5, 1882; *Tombstone (Arizona) Weekly Epitaph*, April 10, 1882; Hooker, "Arizona Vendetta," 71; Timothy W. Fattig, *Wyatt Earp: The Biography* (Honolulu, HI: Talei, 2002), 549–551.

5. *Tombstone (Arizona) Daily Nugget* and *Tombstone Daily Epitaph*, March 28, 1882; *Tucson Daily Star*, March 29, 1882.

6. Hooker, "Arizona Vendetta," 72; see also John H. Flood Jr., *Wyatt Earp: A Peace-officer of Tombstone*, 312 (unpublished manuscript, 1927), C. Lee Simmons Collection. For information on Henry Hooker, see Lynn R. Bailey, *Henry Clay Hooker and the Sierra Bonita* (Tucson, AZ: Westernlore, 1998).

7. Hooker, "Arizona Vendetta," 73–74; Earp, "Wyatt Earp," 312–315.

8. Harry Woods presented Behan's view of the encounter in an article published in the *Tombstone Daily Nugget*, March 31, 1882, while Hooker's version was published in the *Tombstone Daily Epitaph*, April 14, 1882; see also Casey Tefertiller, *Wyatt Earp: The Life behind the Legend* (New York: Wiley, 1997), 242–244.

9. *Tombstone Daily Epitaph*, April 14, 1882.

10. William M. Breakenridge, handwritten statement, circa 1910, p. 12, Special Collections, University of Arizona Library, Tucson, Arizona. William M. Breakenridge, *Helldorado: Bringing the Law to the Mesquite* (Boston: Houghton Mifflin, 1928), 178–179, provides less detail. Breakenridge was correct that the Earp position was extremely well fortified. On March 29, 1882, the *Tombstone Daily Nugget* reported:

> A prominent citizen of Dos Cabezas, in town yesterday, informed a Nugget reporter that the Earp party are now encamped in a canyon in the Graham Mountains, not far from Hooker's ranch. They have chosen a position from which it would be extremely difficult to dislodge them and have announced their intention to remaining there, for some time at least. Our informant states that in a conversation with Wyatt Earp a few days since, the latter said if the Sheriff of Cochise county wanted him he could always find him at his camp. They are represented as being well supplied with money and food, which is furnished by friends of the fugitives.

Reprinted in the *Tucson Weekly Star*, April 1, 1882.

11. *Tombstone Daily Epitaph*, April 14, 1882.

12. Ibid. The *San Francisco Exchange* shared this view of Behan, noting, "The Sheriff has enlisted the cowboys under his banner, and he himself evidently has no stomach for the job." Reprinted in the *Tucson Daily Star*, March 28, 1882.

13. Hooker, "Arizona Vendetta," 77; *Tombstone Daily Epitaph*, March 28, 1882.

14. *National Police Gazette*, March 11, 1882.

15. *San Francisco Examiner*, March 23, 1882.

16. *Tombstone Daily Epitaph*, April 5, 1882; *Tombstone Daily Nugget*, April 6, 1882.

17. Stuart N. Lake notes, Stuart N. Lake Collection, Huntington Library, San Marino, California. Stuart N. Lake, *Wyatt Earp: Frontier Marshal* (Boston: Houghton Mifflin, 1931), 354–355, is more explicit, but must be taken with a grain of salt. In this case, however, his account has a certain plausibility. The *Tombstone Daily Epitaph*, April 12, 1882, reported the rumor "that members of the Earp party were in town last night spending several hours here. It is hardly probable that such was the case." This followed a rumor that a man "riding a horse supposed to be the one rode by Wyatt Earp when he left town" was stopped by officers. The rider told them that he had met Earp outside of town and traded horses with him. A posse was organized but found nothing. *Tombstone Daily Epitaph*, April 11, 1882. One report claimed that on the night of March 30 two men out searching for stock encountered a party of men, six or seven in number, asleep in a gulch near Tombstone with one man acting as sentinel. They asked him if he had seen stray horses. He said he had not and suggested that "the best thing they could do was to leave that vicinity as quickly as possible." The description provided of the sentinel fit "very well with that of Warren Earp." *Tombstone Daily Nugget*, April 1, 1882. This does not fit well with the known movements of the Earps.

18. Tefertiller, *Wyatt Earp*, 247; *Tucson Daily Star*, April 30, 1882.

19. *Tucson Daily Star*, March 30, 1882.

20. *San Diego Union*, March 28, 1882.

21. *Los Angeles Express*, reprinted in the *San Diego Union*, March 30, 1882.

22. *Los Angeles Daily Herald*, March 28, 1882.

23. Tefertiller, *Wyatt Earp*, 246; Reminiscences of Henry Morgan as told to Mrs. Geo. F. Kitt, 1930, Arizona Historical Society, Tucson, Arizona.

24. *Tombstone Daily Epitaph*, April 15, 1882; *Tombstone (Arizona) Weekly Epitaph*, April 17, 1882. Just when the establishment forces began to coalesce behind the Earps is unclear. Gosper and Dake were already working closely with business leaders in Tombstone even before Virgil was shot. After that incident, a growing sentiment existed in the business community for aggressive action, including vigilantism, if required. Dake's meeting with J. J. Valentine, James Hume's interview with the *National Police Gazette*, and John Thacker's active presence in Tombstone after March 21, when combined with Valentine's presence in Arizona early in April, not only made Wells, Fargo's growing discontent about the situation obvious but also demonstrated the company's active support of the Earps. In fact, the Wells, Fargo Cash Book for Tombstone, April 1882, shows that Thacker paid Wyatt Earp and his posse $150 in the matter of "Stilwell & Curly Bill," along with extra expenses for the months between January and April. Wells, Fargo's General Cash Books for January 1880 through September 1882 are housed in the Wells, Fargo & Company Bank, History Department, San Francisco, California, and I am grateful to Robert J. Chandler, curator and historian for the Wells Fargo Bank, who provided copies of the General Cash Book entries. Chandler's own article, "A Smoking Gun? Did Wells Fargo Pay Wyatt Earp to Kill Curly Bill and Frank Stilwell," *True West* 48 (July 2001): 42–43, first revealed this stunning evidence of Wells, Fargo's involvement in the so-called vendetta. I have used Chandler's explanation of symbols such as "a/c" based on his years of work with Wells, Fargo records.

25. *New Southwest and Grant County Herald*, April 22, 1882.

26. Chuck Hornung, "Wyatt Earp and Doc Holliday: Their New Mexico Adventures," 84–86, unpublished manuscript, 2004, copy in author's files.

27. Ibid., 88–90; *Albuquerque Evening Review* and *Albuquerque Daily Morning Journal*, April 16, 17, 18, 1882.

28. Lake notes; Earp, "Wyatt Earp," 326–327. McLain is most familiar as one of the members of the "Dodge City Peace Commission" that went to the aid of Luke Short in 1883. At that time, the *National Police Gazette*, July 21, 1883, provided this brief description of him: "M. F. McLean [sic] has an Arizona and Rio Grande record for wiping out Mexican

ruffians, and came from Lower California to see that his friend Luke Short could 'stay in town' to attend to his business. He is cool and clear-headed. The great ability which he displayed in managing a fight has obtained for him the sobriquet of 'The General.'"

29. Hornung, "New Mexico Adventures," 106–107. Interestingly, Governor Lionel Sheldon, J. J. Valentine of Wells, Fargo, and C. C. Wheeler, the general manager of the Atchison, Topeka, & Santa Fe Railroad, were all in Albuquerque between April 15 and April 17, 1882. After an unfortunate incident in Denver on April 12, 1882, in which Don Miguel Antonio Otero was conned by a character called Doc Baggs (see note 31 of this chapter), Otero returned to New Mexico and may have attended a meeting of the Santa Fe Railroad directors scheduled to meet in Santa Fe in mid-April before returning to Las Vegas on April 17 (see Las Vegas [New Mexico] Daily Optic, April 13, 1882). On April 20, 1882, the Optic reported that Don Miguel, his wife, and his son Page left Las Vegas for Denver to testify before the grand jury in the Baggs case. Sheldon's operations against the Cow-Boys have not been researched well, but some details are found in the microfilm edition of the Territorial Archives of New Mexico, State Records Center and Archives, Santa Fe, New Mexico. For detail on A. J. Fountain's campaign, see the attorney general's report on the 1882 campaign of militia activity against outlaws, roll 99.

30. In fact, in the undated draft of a letter apparently written by the younger Otero, he said, "Yes, I know Wyatt Earp. I knew him to be a gentleman and he held a reputation of being an excellent law officer. I knew the Earp brothers first in Kansas, but did not [see] much [of] them after that time. My father knew them best. I knew Doc Holliday at Las Vegas and told that adventure in My Life on the Frontier [Vol.] I." Otero to "My Dear Friend," undated, Chuck Hornung's private collection, and published in Chuck Hornung and Gary L. Roberts, "The Split," True West 48 (November– December 2001): 58–61. In 2001, Hornung purchased a deluxe edition of Miguel Antonio Otero's My Nine Years as Governor of New Mexico (Albuquerque: University of New Mexico Press, 1940) at a flea market in Albuquerque from a Hispanic man who told him that he was selling books originally owned by his grandmother. Hornung did not find the carbon until later that evening. The undated draft of the letter was identified as the work of Gillie Otero based on internal evidence in the letter itself as explained in the Hornung-Roberts article. The circumstances of the letter's discovery and some historical mistakes in both the letter and the hasty analysis of Hornung and Roberts prompted several researchers, most notably Scott Anderson and Woody Campbell, to question the authenticity of the letter.

Authenticity is only half the dilemma posed by the letter, however. Accuracy is the other. Authenticity revolves around the issue of whether the letter was written by Gillie Otero. After extensive dialogue with Anderson and Campbell, both highly capable researchers, Hornung and Roberts, while recognizing the possibility of a hoax, have concluded that the circumstances and internal evidence make a hoax unlikely and support the case for authenticity. The question of accuracy is another matter.

The problems posed by the letter in this respect are in no way unique; it is the one problem inherent in any reminiscence. Otero was writing about events that occurred nearly sixty years earlier, and some of the details in the letter include errors of the sort commonly found in recollections. Otero made mistakes and left things out—as he did in his published recollections. See Ramon F. Adams, Burs under the Saddle: A Second Look at Books and Histories of the West (Norman: University of Oklahoma Press, 1964), 395–402, for one critique of Otero's "memory." It is not surprising, then, to find some problems with detail in the letter.

Yet, even acknowledging some questionable statements, the letter does throw light on the Albuquerque sojourn of the Earps. What is most compelling is the extent to which the "Otero letter," as it has come to be called, supports the hypothesis previously developed by Roberts concerning the extent of the cabal of political and corporate support for Wyatt Earp during his so-called vendetta ride against the Cow-Boys. Hornung discusses the possible connection to the Earps (or at least to those supporting the Earps) in "New Mexico Adventures," 93–117. For sketches of both Oteros, father and son, see Howard R. Lamar, ed., *The New Encyclopedia of the American West* (New Haven, CT: Yale University Press, 1998), 836–837. More detail is found in Ralph Emerson Twitchell, *The Leading Facts of New Mexican History*, 5 vols. (Cedar Rapids, IA: Torch, 1911–1917). For context, see also Howard R. Lamar, *The Far Southwest, 1846–1912* (New Haven, CT: Yale University Press, 1966), and Robert W. Larson, *New Mexico's Quest for Statehood, 1846–1912* (Albuquerque: University of New Mexico Press, 1968). Especially valuable for the present study is the younger Otero's *My Life on the Frontier, 1864–1882* (New York: Press of the Pioneers, 1935), 216–218.

31. *Denver Republican*, April 15, 16, 18, 19, 1882; *Denver Daily News*, April 15, 18, 19, 1882; *Albuquerque Evening Review*, April 18, 28, 1882; *Las Vegas Daily Optic*, May 1, 1882. I am especially indebted to Scott Anderson and Woody Campbell for information and commentary on the Baggs affair. The *Las Vegas Daily Optic*, April 8, 1882, noted, "Gillie Otero is becoming a professional tourist. He gets off for Denver this evening." This report, combined with the research of Anderson and Campbell, demonstrates quite convincingly that Gillie Otero was in Denver on the weekend that the Earp party arrived in Albuquerque. This more than anything else has raised the concern of skeptics of the Otero letter, since Otero says that "I tired [tried] to help them in their quest to stay in New Mexico following the Tombstone trouble," and "Father sent me to see to the comfort of the Earp posse because his railroad supported the boys." In fact, the problem may be more apparent than real. On April 3, 1882, the *Albuquerque Evening Review* reported that "Gillie Otero is here. He managed to miss Page [his older brother]," at about the time that the Earps were planning their departure from Arizona; the *Las Vegas Daily Optic*, May 1, 1882, reported, "Gillie Otero is home from Denver, not with a man named Baggs." Otero's known movements support the hypothesis that Gillie made arrangements before leaving for Denver and had time to return to Albuquerque before the Earp party left for Colorado. In fact, in light of the Earps' eventually finding sanctuary in Colorado and Doc's comments to the Colorado press about prior arrangements being made, the presence of the Oteros in Denver during April means that the Oteros could have worked on the Earps' behalf while there as well. Further research needs to be done, but a narrow construction of the Otero letter is most likely a mistake.

32. *Albuquerque Evening Review*, April 18, 19, 1882. Albuquerque was an old city. The arrival of the railroad created (as it had in Las Vegas) a "New Town." Sam Blonger was appointed marshal by Armijo, subject to the approval of the "board of trade," the quasi government of New Town.

33. Hornung and Roberts, "The Split," 61, reported incorrectly that Henry Jaffa was the president of the board of trade when the Earp party arrived. In actuality, the chairman of the board of trade in 1882 was Colonel Molyneaux Bell. Jaffa had not yet become active in the New Town operations, and his Albuquerque branch store was located on the Old Town plaza and managed by Willie Prager, Jaffa's longtime partner, in 1882. Later, Jaffa would relocate to Second Street in New Town, and in 1885 he would be elected as Albuquerque's first mayor when New Town and Old Town consolidated into the single city. Mark Dworkin, "Henry Jaffa and Wyatt Earp: Wyatt Earp's Jewish Connection, a Portrait of Henry Jaffa, Albuquerque's First Mayor," *WOLA Journal* 13 (Fall 2004): 25–37, is uncertain just when Jaffa moved to Albuquerque to live, but he appears to have had a residence there in 1882, even if it was nothing more than an apartment at his Old Town store. Hornung, "New Mexico Adventures," 110–112, offers further information on Jaffa's activities and location in 1882. What makes the Jaffa connection even more interesting is his close friendship with Judge Columbus Moise, who had been Don Miguel Otero's private secretary.

Information relating to the Albuquerque bridge is also confusing. The standard works, F. Stanley, *The Duke City: The Story of Albuquerque, New Mexico, 1706–1956* (Pampa, TX: Pampa Print Shop, 1963), 48, and Marc Simmons, *Albuquerque: A Narrative History* (Albuquerque: University of New Mexico Press, 1982), 277–278, both indicate that construction of the Rio Grande bridge at Albuquerque was under way in the spring of 1882. The project was a private endeavor of the Albuquerque Bridge Company, with Franz Huning, a local businessman who owned a flour mill and contracted beef, as the primary investor. The effort was not the first bridge enterprise across the Rio Grande at Albuquerque—a railroad bridge existed in 1882—but the Huning bridge was intended to allow wagon and pedestrian traffic across the marshy approach to the river as well as the river itself. Hornung, "New Mexico Adventures," 128–129. The project stalled for lack of investors, and the *Albuquerque Evening Review*, April 19, 1882, indicated that the project was still stalled but that the company was seeking New York investors, during the very time that the Earps were in the city. What is not clear is whether any construction had already begun.

The final phase of construction on the bridge began in September 1882, and the local papers announced the completion of the bridge on November 1, 1882. *Albuquerque Evening Review*, August 15, November 1, 1882; *Albuquerque Morning Journal*, November 1, 2, 1882. Scott Johnson to Gary L. Roberts, May 25, 26, 27, 2005; Chuck Hornung to Gary L. Roberts, May 18, 27, 2005, provided invaluable assistance on this topic. A formal ribbon-cutting ceremony took place on December 12, 1882. What is clear is that the bridge was the topic of active discussion and concern while the Earps were in Albuquerque, and it is reasonable that Jaffa, a merchant interested in the future of the city, would have shown Earp at least the location of the bridge. However, Otero may well have misremembered the state of the bridge's progress at the time the Earps were in the city when he wrote his 1940 letter.

34. *Tombstone Daily Nugget*, May 10, 1882; *Tombstone Daily Epitaph*, May 10, 1882; *Albuquerque Evening Review*, May 13, 1882.

35. *Denver Republican*, May 22, 1882.

36. Dr. Arthur W. Bork, notes of interview with Mary Katharine Cummings, Thanksgiving, 1935, typescript provided to Roberts by Dr. Bork. Kate stated essentially the same information to Anton Mazzanovich in Typescript of Recollections of Mary Katharine Cummings as Given to Anton Mazzanovich, 16, Kevin J. Mulkins Collection. Kate consistently says that the argument took place in Gunnison, Colorado.

37. Breakenridge, *Helldorado*, 175–177. Steve Gatto, *Curly Bill: Tombstone's Most Famous Outlaw* (Lansing, MI: Protar House, 2003), 164n, cites the Helldorado file, from the Houghton Mifflin Collection, Houghton Library, Harvard University, Cambridge, Massachusetts, as revealing that Breakenridge was given the Arnold-Truly account by William Lutley, a Tombstone resident. So far, I have found no record of this story in print prior to the publication of *Helldorado*.

38. Earp to Lake, November 6, 1928, Lake Collection.

39. Otero to "Dear Old Friend," quoted in Hornung and Roberts, "The Split," 59.

40. William B. Shillingberg, *Tombstone, A. T.: A History of Early Mining, Milling, and Mayhem* (Spokane, WA: Clark, 1999), 236, says that Earp met Sadie in the late summer of 1881 (later than generally supposed), but their involvement at Tombstone (at whatever stage it was) was not generally known in 1940. For Doc's comments about Behan and his "girl," see *Denver Republican*, May 22, 1882.

41. *Tombstone Daily Epitaph*, May 20, 1882.

42. *Tucson Daily Star*, March 23, 24, 1882. These articles were followed in the *Tucson Weekly Star*, March 26, 1882, with a detailed account by "the San Francisco Tombstone correspondent [which] gives the story of the Feud from almost the beginning." These articles, especially the last, titled "The Vendetti," constituted a major rewriting of the Tomb-

stone story, which transformed what happened there into a personal feud and placed Doc Holliday in the role of primary provocateur. These stories enlarged on Ike Clanton's testimony at the Spicer hearing (while accepting most of its premises) and set the stage for a political attack on the Tritle administration in particular and on Republicans in general, which the *Star* would eventually accuse of taking "shelter under the Earpumbrella." *Tucson Daily Star*, June 1, 1882. What the *Star* did, in the process, was to give form to the anti-Earp interpretation of the Tombstone story down to the present day.

43. *San Diego Union*, April 30, 1882.

44. *Las Vegas Daily Optic*, May 24, 1882.

45. Tefertiller, *Wyatt Earp*, 251–252, discusses the impact of Purdy's arrival. Purdy may well have come to Tombstone to conduct the anti-Earp crusade. He remained in the role only briefly, giving up the editorship on July 29, 1882, and returning to Yuma. See Lynn R. Bailey and Don Chaput, *Cochise County Stalwarts: A Who's Who of the Territorial Years* (Tucson, AZ: Westernlore, 2000), 2:74.

46. See also *Tucson Daily Star*, May 21, 1882.

47. *Tombstone Weekly Commercial Advertiser*, April 22, 1882. For more information on Lyttleton Price, see Pamela Potter, "Western Lore: Tombstone Love Triangle," *Wild West* (December 2005): 60, 62–63. Apparently, Price was not well liked by either side. Fred Dodge, *Under Cover for Wells Fargo: The Unvarnished Recollections of Fred Dodge*, edited by Carolyn Lake (Boston: Houghton Mifflin, 1969), 40–42, called him "a man of no standing whatever—A moral Coward who was afraid to prosecute any bad man" and claimed further that "he was in Every way a very incompetent man" who was in the job for "what could be got out of it."

48. W. T. Sherman to B. H. Brewster, U.S. Attorney General, April 11, 1882, Records of the Department of Justice, Record Group 60, National Archives and Records Administration, Washington, DC.

49. Presidential Proclamation Respecting Disturbances in Arizona, Chester A. Arthur, May 3, 1882, Records of the Office of the Secretary of the Interior, RG 48, NARA. For a useful discussion of the proclamation, see Henry P. Walker, "Retire Peaceably to Your Homes: Arizona Faces Martial Law," *Journal of Arizona History* 10 (Winter 1968): 1–18.

50. *Tombstone Daily Epitaph*, May 5, 1882.

51. *San Diego Union*, May 7, 1882.

52. *Tucson Daily Star*, May 6, 1882.

53. *San Diego Union*, May 7, 1882.

54. *San Francisco Exchange*, May 6, 1882.

55. *Tucson Daily Citizen*, May 8, 1882.

56. Ibid. Based on its review of the papers' positions, the *Tucson Daily Citizen* concluded, "THEY EITHER LIED THEN OR THEY LIE NOW."

57. *San Diego Union*, May 10, 12, 1882; *Tombstone Daily Nugget*, May 11, 1882; *Phoenix Arizona Gazette*, May 18, 1882; *Tucson Daily Citizen*, May 16, 1882 (reprinted in the *San Diego Daily Union*, May 17, 1882).

58. J. H. Jackson to the editor, May 10, 1882, *Tombstone Daily Nugget*, May 11, 12, 1882.

59. *Tombstone Daily Epitaph*, June 1, 1882; *Tombstone Weekly Epitaph*, June 3, 1882.

60. Bryant L. Peel to the editor, May 9, 1882, *Tombstone Daily Nugget*, May 10, 1882.

61. *Virginia City (Nevada) Enterprise*, May 21, 1882, which included in its editorial on "The Situation in Arizona" a letter from Governor Tritle to the editor of the *Enterprise*, dated May 17, 1882. The *Enterprise's* editorial was reprinted in the *Prescott Arizona Democrat*, June 5, 1882. Many of the articles relating to the response to the presidential proclamation

cited here and more besides are found in Frederick A. Tritle Scrapbook, No. 3, File 3, MS 794, AHS.

62. Actually, Tipton's death was reported in three separate issues of the *Tombstone Daily Epitaph*, May 6, 8, 10, 1882; see also Ed Bartholomew, *Wyatt Earp: The Man and the Myth* (Toyahvale, TX: Frontier, 1964), 325–326, which quotes from the Texas Jack article, and *Las Vegas Daily Optic*, March 24, 25, 1882.

63. *Tombstone Daily Epitaph*, May 10, 1882; *Albuquerque Evening Review*, May 13, 1882. Finally, on May 19, 1882, the *Phoenix Daily Gazette* reported, "The statement going the rounds that Wyatt Earp had been killed in Arizona is not correct. His attorneys know nothing of the affair at least."

64. *Colton (California) Semi-Tropic*, quoted in *San Diego Union*, May 28, 1882; *New Southwest and Grant County Herald*, April 29, 1882.

65. *Albuquerque Evening Review*, May 13, 1882.

66. Ibid.; *Albuquerque Morning Journal*, May 14, 1882.

67. A few times in his life, Wyatt Earp claimed to have killed "Apache Hank" (Hank Swilling) besides Stilwell, Cruz, and Curly Bill. See *Denver Republican*, May 14, 1893, for example, and rumor named other victims as well. Sarah Grace Bakarich, *Gunsmoke: The True Story of Old Tombstone* (Tombstone, AZ: Tombstone, 1954), 65, reported, "After the killing of Morgan Earp, someone, gossip names Doc Holliday, killed a cowboy riding Curly Bill's horse as he passed beneath the rock outcropping called Robber's Roost on the Charleston Road." Bakarich stated that the horse was identified by Mayor Charles Thomas, adding, "The rider had been killed by a charge of buck-shot through the head. His identification was not definite but he was about the same size as Curly Bill." Such accounts are dubious. Swilling, for example, was apparently in jail for twenty days after his March 24, 1882, arrest and was later killed at Fronteras in Mexico. See Roy B. Young, *Cochise County Cowboy War: "A Cast of Characters"* (Apache, OK: Young, 1999), 122. It is fair to say, however, that the Cow-Boys scattered after the vendetta, some into New Mexico, Texas, and Mexico, and some into other parts of Arizona.

68. See Richard Maxwell Brown, "Law and Order on the American Frontier: The Western Civil War of Incorporation," in *Law for the Elephant, Law for the Beaver: Essays in the Legal History of the North American West*, edited by John McLaren et al. (Pasadena, CA: Ninth Judicial Circuit Historical Society, 1992), 74–89, and Roberts, *Death Comes for the Chief Justice*, 133–139. The balance between justice and order is also a major theme in Tefertiller, *Wyatt Earp*.

69. *Tucson Daily Citizen*, May 8, 1882.

70. *Tucson Daily Star*, March 30, 1882.

10. A Holliday in Denver

1. Robert K. DeArment, *Bat Masterson: The Man and the Legend* (Norman: University of Oklahoma Press, 1979), 218–224.

2. Peter Brand, "Daniel G. Tipton and the Earp Vendetta Posse," *Quarterly for the National Association for Outlaw and Lawman History* 24 (October–December 2000): 23–24.

3. *Trinidad (Colorado) News*, May 5, 1882; Casey Tefertiller, *Wyatt Earp: The Life behind the Legend* (New York: Wiley, 1997): 255.

4. *Trinidad News*, May 5, 1882.

5. *Pueblo (Colorado) Chieftain*, May 3, 4, 1882.

6. *Pueblo Chieftain*, May 6, 1882.

7. Ibid.

8. *Pueblo Chieftain*, May 17, 1882. On May 8, 1882, while Doc was in Pueblo, the old case against him in Arizona in the matter of his fight with Milt Joyce was dismissed

when Doc failed to appear. Case No. 23, *Territory of Arizona v. J. H. Holliday*, Minutes of the District Court, Cachise [*sic*] County, p. 453, William H. Stilwell Collection, Utah Department of Archives, Salt Lake City, Utah.

9. Robert K. DeArment, *Deadly Dozen: Twelve Forgotten Gunfighters of the Old West* (Norman: University of Oklahoma Press, 2003), 23–29, is the best summary of Desmond's career. Desmond's life had taken a turn for the worse in 1882 and would eventually cause him to leave Pueblo.

10. *Pueblo Chieftain*, May 17, 1882.

11. *Denver Republican*, May 22, 1882; *Gunnison (Colorado) Daily News-Democrat*, June 18, 1882.

12. *Pueblo Chieftain*, May 17, 1882; *Denver Daily Times*, May 16, 1882.

13. *Denver Daily Tribune*, May 26, 1882.

14. *Gunnison Daily News-Democrat*, June 18, 1882; *Denver Daily Tribune*, May 15, 1882 (showing "J. N. Vimont, Leadville" registered at the Windsor); *Corbett and Ballenger Leadville City Directory, 1882*, "JO. N., supt. Big Pitttsburgh [*sic*] Cons. Silver Mining Co., 211 Harrison av"; *Leadville City Record, 1882*, p. 47, "Big Pittsburg Consolidated Silver Mining Company—J. N. Vimont, Superintendent, Office, 211 Harrison avenue, Mine, East Fryer Hill"; Emma Walling to Susan McKey Thomas, July 5, 1995, copy in author's files.

15. *Denver Daily Rocky Mountain News*, May 16, 1882; *Denver Republican*, May 16, 1882; *Denver Daily Tribune*, May 16, 1882; *Pueblo Chieftain*, May 16, 1882.

16. *Denver Republican*, May 16, 1882.

17. *Denver Daily Tribune*, May 16, 1882. The reporter was apparently E. D. Cowen, who would later write about his experiences with Doc in an article for the *Denver Rocky Mountain News*, October 23, 1898.

18. *Denver Daily Tribune*, May 16, 1882.

19. Ibid.

20. *Denver Republican*, May 19, 1882.

21. *Denver Republican*, May 16, 1882.

22. Ibid.

23. *Denver Daily Rocky Mountain News*, May 16, 1882.

24. *Denver Republican*, May 16, 17, 19, 1882.

25. *Denver Daily Tribune*, May 17, 1882.

26. *Denver Daily Times*, May 17, 1882.

27. *Denver Daily Rocky Mountain News*, May 17, 1882.

28. *Denver Daily Times*, May 16, 1882.

29. *Pueblo Chieftain*, May 17, 1882.

30. *Denver Daily Tribune*, May 16, 1882.

31. *Denver Daily Rocky Mountain News*, May 17, 1882.

32. The *Denver Daily Tribune*, May 17, March 26, 1882, affirmed Holliday's relationship to Desmond, Lomery, and Cook. For Tritch's comments, see *Denver Daily Times*, May 17, 1882, and *Trinidad News*, May 20, 1882. On May 17, 1882, the *Tribune* also reported that the Cow-Boys in Arizona had threatened to kill Charles D. Reppy of the *Tombstone (Arizona) Daily Epitaph* and said that the "statement is corroborated by a letter from C. D. Reppy to his brother, Mr. George Reppy, of this city." The Reppy letter was also mentioned in the *Denver Daily Rocky Mountain News*, May 17, 1882, as follows: "Many of Holladay's [*sic*] statements are supported by a letter written by a Mr. Reppy, formerly editor of the Tombstone EPITAPH, to Mr. George Reppy, of Denver, and by other documents which Holladay has in his possession."

33. *Denver Daily Times*, May 17, 1882.

34. *Pueblo Chieftain*, May 17, 1882. Mallon's successful con of several former residents of Akron while he was in Pueblo would prove to be his first major mistake.

35. *Denver Republican*, May 16, 1882.

36. *Denver Daily Times*, May 17, 1882.

37. William Barclay Masterson, "Famous Gunfighters of the Western Frontier: Doc Holliday," *Human Life* (May 1907): 5; *Denver Daily Rocky Mountain News*, May 19, 1882; *Denver Daily Tribune*, May 19, 1882. The *Pueblo Chieftain*, May 20, 1882, claimed that the Denver papers distorted what happened in Denver and insisted that Marshal Jameson had had no trouble with Sheriff Spangler or his deputies. Jameson was popular in Pueblo, and on May 27 he was presented with a "handsome badge" in recognition of his services. See *Pueblo Chieftain*, May 28, 1882. No direct connection between Holliday and Jameson has been found before the Denver troubles, but even before the roles of Masterson and Jameson on behalf of Holliday became known, both the *Trinidad News* and the *Pueblo Chieftain* were outspoken in their support of Holliday. See *Trinidad News*, May 18, 20, 1882, and *Pueblo News*, May 17, 18, 1882, for examples. The *Chieftain*'s May 17, 1882, issue contained the first strong and informed defense of Doc in an article that also exposed Mallon as a con artist.

38. *Denver Daily Tribune*, May 19, 1882.

39. Ibid.; *Denver Daily Rocky Mountain News*, May 19, 1882.

40. *Denver Daily Tribune*, May 19, 1882.

41. *Denver Republican*, May 18, 1882.

42. *Pueblo Chieftain*, May 17, 18, 1882.

43. *Denver Daily Rocky Mountain News*, May 21, 1882.

44. *Denver Republican*, May 22, 1882.

45. *Tombstone Daily Epitaph*, May 17, 1882, reprinted in *Denver Republican*, May 22, 1882.

46. *Denver Republican*, May 22, 1882.

47. *Tucson Daily Star*, May 18, 1882; see also the *Tucson Daily Citizen*, May 18, 1882. For once the Tucson papers agreed. The *Prescott Arizona Democrat*, May 25, 1882, reprinted the *Star*'s article and agreed with the governor's decision.

48. *Denver Republican*, May 18, 1882.

49. *Tucson Daily Star*, May 18, 1882.

50. *Tombstone Daily Epitaph*, quoted in *Denver Republican*, May 22, 1882.

51. *Denver Daily Times*, May 17, 1882.

52. Ibid.

53. *Denver Daily Tribune*, May 20, 1882.

54. *Denver Republican*, May 20, 1880.

55. *Denver Daily Rocky Mountain News*, May 22, 1882.

56. *Denver Daily Tribune*, May 20, 1882.

57. *Denver Daily Times*, May 20, 1882.

58. *Denver Republican*, May 22, 1882. This reference to the Tombstone Cow-Boys being a part of the old "Fort Griffin gang" strongly suggested that Doc knew at least some of them before he went to Arizona.

59. Ibid.

60. *Denver Daily Rocky Mountain News*, May 22, 1882.

61. *Denver Daily Rocky Mountain News*, May 24, 1882.

62. *Denver Daily Rocky Mountain News*, May 25, 1882.

63. *Denver Republican*, May 26, 1882.

64. Ibid.

65. Ibid.

66. *Las Vegas (New Mexico) Daily Optic*, May 23, 1882.

67. *Albuquerque Evening Review*, quoted in Silver City's *New Southwest and Grant County Herald*, May 27, 1882.

68. *Denver Daily Rocky Mountain News*, May 26, 1882. That same day, Bob Paul wrote to his undersheriff in Tucson, "Holliday's friends are doing everything in their power to get him off, and will appear before the Governor and fight the requisition. He has three lawyers and all the sporting men in his favor. . . . There is more feeling over the Holliday affair here than there is in Tucson, and all in his favor, but I do not think I will have any trouble if he is turned over to me." Quoted in John Boessenecker, "Lawman Bob Paul's Doc and Wyatt Connection," *Wild West* (August 2003): 45.

69. *Las Vegas Daily Optic*, May 18, 29, 1882.

70. *Pueblo Chieftain*, May 18, 1882.

71. Fattig, *Wyatt Earp: The Biography*, 595, makes the case for Tabor's involvement, and it is reasonable, except for the political quarrel between the governor and him. Tabor had been elected lieutenant governor under Pitkin in 1878. In 1880, he was defeated by George B. Robinson, but Robinson died before he could take over the office, and Tabor took the highly questionable position that Robinson's death meant that he should continue in office, which he did until January 1883. The point of conflict between him and Governor Pitkin arose in the spring of 1882, when Senator Henry Teller resigned to become secretary of the interior. Both Tabor and Pitkin had designs on the office, but it fell to Pitkin to appoint someone to fill the seat temporarily until the Colorado legislature convened in November 1882. Tabor reasoned that if he secured the temporary post, the legislature would likely appoint him to the permanent position. Pitkin realized this as well, and so on April 11, 1882, he appointed George M. Chilcott of Pueblo instead, creating bitter feelings between Tabor and Pitkin. The Colorado press was filled with the story through April. This quarrel makes it unlikely that Tabor approached Pitkin on Doc's behalf, although he may well have taken a behind-the-scene role. I am grateful to Woody Campbell for providing the fruits of his research into the Tabor-Pitkin quarrel during the preparation of this book. Woody Campbell to Gary L. Roberts, April 7, 12, 2005. The *Las Vegas Daily Optic*, May 4, 1882, reported that Tabor was at Montezuma Springs in New Mexico for several days during which time he could have spoken with New Mexico authorities, but that is speculation.

72. *Tucson Daily Star*, May 26, 1882.

73. *Denver Daily Times*, May 30, 1882; *Denver Daily Rocky Mountain News*, October 23, 1898.

74. *Atlanta Constitution*, June 21, 1882; *Atlanta Post-Appeal*, July 8, 1882.

75. John H. Flood Jr.'s notes from an interview with Wyatt Earp, September 15, 1926, reproduced in Wyatt Earp, *Tombstone and the West: The Gilchriese Collections*, part 3 (San Francisco: Johns' Western Gallery, 2005), 5. Flood included part of this story without mentioning Crummy by name in "Wyatt Earp: A Peace-officer of Tombstone," 327–328 (manuscript written by John Henry Flood Jr., 1927), C. Lee Simmons Collection. Wyatt claimed in the Flood manuscript that Masterson had written to him two days before Crummy's visit, "Wyatt, I've done everything I can but I guess you'll have to go [to] the front. Don't lose any time, and see your friend." It may have been this message that prompted Crummy to go to Denver. Crummy almost certainly knew both Wyatt and Doc. He was in Tombstone in October 1880. He registered at the Grand Hotel, "G. W. Crummy, Lake City, Co.," the day after Doc's fight with Milt Joyce. *Tombstone Daily Epitaph*, October 12, 1880. His name apparently appears twice in the 1880 Colorado census; he is listed at Lake City, Hinsdale County, as "owner of mine," and at Silver Cliff, Custer County, as "saloonkeeper." If these two were, in fact, the same person, it was not unusual; double registration was common for people with businesses in more than one county. The Lake City enumeration shows him living with an older brother, J. W. Crummy. At any rate, Crummy and Pitkin had been business partners for at least two years when the Holliday case arose. Campbell to Roberts, January 22, 2005.

76. *Denver Daily Rocky Mountain News*, May 30, 1882; *Trinidad Daily News*, June 1, 1882; *Denver Daily Times*, May 31, 1882; *Denver Daily Tribune*, May 30, 1882. Tritle may well have sent defective papers deliberately. The *Tucson Daily Star*, June 1, 1882, proposed that Tritle had suggested to Pitkin: "'My dear brother, let this blow pass!' It passed."

77. *Denver Daily Rocky Mountain News*, May 30, 1882.

78. Ibid.; *Denver Daily Times*, May 31, 1882; *Denver Daily Tribune*, May 30, 1882.

79. *Denver Daily Tribune*, May, 30, 1882.

80. *Pueblo Chieftain*, June 1, 1882; *Denver Daily Rocky Mountain News*, June 1, 1882. The *Trinidad News*, June 2, 1882, reported, "Marshal Masterson who has been in Denver for some time past interesting himself in the release of Doc. Holliday, is home again." No evidence has come to light to suggest that Masterson was criticized in Trinidad for his interest in the case.

81. *Denver Daily Rocky Mountain News*, May 31, 1882.

82. *Tucson Daily Star*, June 2, 1882. The *Denver Daily Times*, May 31, 1882, noted, "The deputy sheriffs in Denver sympathize with Sheriff Paul because, by the governor's refusal to let Holladay [*sic*] go, they lose the reward they had hoped to pocket."

83. *Tucson Daily Star*, June 1, 1882.

84. *Tombstone Daily Epitaph*, May 31, 1882.

85. *Tucson Daily Star*, May 31, June 1, 1882. The *Denver Daily Times*, May 25, 1882, observed, "It is the general impression that the arrest of the Earp boys, the Arizona outlaws, is not desired for some reason or another. It is believed it would not be a difficult thing to get them if they were wanted."

86. *Gunnison Daily News-Democrat*, June 1, 1882.

87. *San Francisco Examiner*, May 27, 1882.

88. *Tucson Daily Star*, June 2, 1882.

89. *San Francisco Examiner*, May 27, 1882.

90. *Denver Daily Tribune*, May 26, 1882.

91. *Denver Daily Rocky Mountain News*, May 25, 1882.

92. *Denver Daily Times*, May 24, 1882.

93. *Denver Daily Times*, June 2, 1882; *Denver Daily Rocky Mountain News*, June 2, 1882; *Denver Daily Tribune*, June 2, 1882; *Gunnison Daily News-Democrat*, June 3, 1882.

94. Most of this information is from an unpublished manuscript, written by Peter Brand, "Perry Mallon—The Famous Man from Nowhere," which will be published after revision to include additional material. Brand, along with Jennifer Lewis and Jean Smith, who work with him as researchers, are doing important work on the so-called minor characters in the Tombstone story. Peter Brand to Gary L. Roberts, May 5, September 21, 22, 27, 2004, May 28, December 12, 2005; Ruth Rocco to Gary L. Roberts, May 5, 2004.

95. *Denver Republican*, June 2, 1882.

96. *Pueblo Chieftain*, June 1, 1882.

97. *Denver Republican*, June 2, 1882.

98. *Pueblo Chieftain*, June 6, 1882.

99. *Gunnison Daily News-Democrat*, June 18, 1882. The paper had reported, June 17, 1882, that Holliday had checked into the St. James Hotel on June 16.

100. *National Police Gazette*, September 2, 1882.

101. Judd Riley interview, Stuart N. Lake Collection, Box 11, Folder 41, Huntington Library, San Marino, California.

102. *Salida (Colorado) Mail*, July 8, 1882; *Lake City (Colorado) Silver World*, July 15, 1882.

103. Case No. 1851, *The People v. J. H. Holliday*, Larceny, July 11, 1882, District Court Records of Pueblo County, Colorado, Vol. 5, 354–355. The *Pueblo Chieftain*, July 19, 1882, reported that the case had been continued "on people's motion."

11. A Living—and Dying—Legend

1. *Atlanta Constitution*, June 21, 1882.

2. *Atlanta Post-Appeal*, July 8, 1882.

3. *Tombstone (Arizona) Daily Epitaph*, July 28, 1882.

4. *Denver Daily Rocky Mountain News*, June 14, 1882.

5. Describing Doc as the leader was commonplace in newspapers of the time.

6. Jack Burrows, *John Ringo: The Gunfighter Who Never Was* (Tucson: University of Arizona Press, 1987), is still the most satisfying biography of Ringo because of the author's careful and critical examination of the growth of the legend. David Johnson, *John Ringo* (Stillwater, OK: Barbed Wire, 1996), is the most detailed work factually. Steve Gatto has written two books about Ringo, *John Ringo: The Reputation of a Deadly Gunman* (Tucson: San Simon, 1995) and *Johnny Ringo* (Lansing, MI: Protar House, 2002), which contain some new material but focus primarily on the controversies about Ringo and demonstrate the vitality of the legend.

7. Wyatt Earp himself appears to have been the first to make this claim. Forrestine C. Hooker, "An Arizona Vendetta (The Truth about Wyatt Earp—and Some Others)," 77–78, unpublished manuscript, circa 1920, Southwest Museum, Los Angeles, California, and John Henry Flood Jr., "Wyatt Earp: A Peace-officer of Tombstone," 320–325 (unpublished manuscript, 1927), C. Lee Simmons Collection, were both based on interviews with Earp. The problem with these stories is that they have Earp killing Ringo on the way out of Arizona, when, in fact, Ringo's death came months later. Curiously, Earp made no such claim to Stuart N. Lake for his biography, *Wyatt Earp: Frontier Marshal* (Boston: Houghton Mifflin, 1931).

The first published account to say that Earp claimed to have killed Ringo appeared in Frank C. Lockwood, *Pioneer Days in Arizona* (New York: Macmillan, 1932), 283–285. The story was revived in 1964, in an article by Bob Thomas for the *Tucson (Arizona) Daily Star*, January 26, 1964, based on interviews with John D. Gilchriese, whose Wyatt Earp collection included the Flood manuscript and other early materials about the Tombstone troubles. The new variation on the story was that Earp went back into Arizona from Colorado on a secret expedition to kill Ringo. This version took a giant leap with the publication of the now discredited book Glenn G. Boyer, *I Married Wyatt Earp: The Recollections of Josephine Sarah Marcus Earp* (Tucson: University of Arizona Press, 1976), 108, followed by a series of Boyer articles culminating with his *Who Killed John Ringo* (Rodeo, NM: Historical Research Associates, 1997). Two Holliday biographies, Ben T. Traywick, *John Henry (The Doc Holliday Story)* (Tombstone, AZ: Red Marie's Bookstore, 1996), 193–207, and Karen Holliday Tanner, *Doc Holliday: A Family Portrait* (Norman: University of Oklahoma Press, 1998), 193–198, followed Boyer's line. All these accounts have Doc with Earp but not as the shooter. Yet, almost inevitably, Doc becomes the shooter in some screeds on the topic and a part of the plotline in movie versions of the story, most notably *Tombstone* (1993).

8. The *Gunnison (Colorado) Daily News-Democrat*, June 18, 1882, was the first major post-Denver article, but it was followed by many others. For example, see *Lake City (Colorado) Silver World*, July 15, 1882, and *Pueblo (Colorado) Chieftain*, November 26, 1882.

9. Don L. Griswold and Jean Harvey Griswold, *History of Leadville and Lake County, Colorado: From Mountain Solitude to Metropolis*, 2 vols. (Denver: Colorado State Historical Society and University Press of Colorado, 1996), is a meticulous account of early Leadville based on newspaper and other primary materials, some of which are no longer available, especially news accounts from the *Leadville (Colorado) Chronicle*, which are available nowhere else.

10. For a full description of life in Leadville in 1882, see Griswold and Griswold, *History of Leadville*, 1:933–1087.

11. Lewis Cass Carpenter, *Tourist's Guide to Leadville and the Carbonate Fields* (Denver: Denver Daily Tribune, 1879), quoted without page citation in Patricia Jahns, *The Frontier World of Doc Holliday* (New York: Hastings House, 1957): 261.

12. Sheila M. Rothman, *Shadow of Death: Tuberculosis and the Social Experience of Illness in American History* (New York: Basic, 1994), 179–180; Thomas Dormandy, *The White Death: A History of Tuberculosis* (New York: New York University Press, 2000), 129–137. Another important source for understanding the situation in the 1880s is Phyllis Allen Richmond, "American Attitudes towards the Germ Theory of Disease," *Journal of the History of Medicine and the Allied Sciences* 9 (October 1954): 428–454. Koch would receive the Nobel Prize for his discovery in 1905.

13. Rothman, *Shadow of Death*, 179–225, discusses the shifts in attitudes toward those with consumption during the last years of the nineteenth century.

14. Some confusion has existed about where Holliday lived in 1882. With the help of Roger Jay, Karen Holliday Tanner, and Mary McVicar in analyzing the city directories of the time, this seems to be the correct arrangement. Especially important was Roger Jay to Gary L. Roberts, January 30, 2002.

15. Roger Jay, "Spitting Lead in Leadville: Holliday's Last Stand," *Wild West* (December 2003): 38–45, 74; Gary L. Roberts, "The Leadville Years," *True West* 48 (November–December 2001): 66–71; Jahns, *Frontier World*, 261–264; and Tanner, *Family Portrait*, 201–203, combine to give a good feel for the environment in which Doc found himself.

16. *Leadville (Colorado) Daily Herald*, May 30, 1882.

17. Roger Jay, "The Lake County Independent Club, 1882," *Western Outlaw-Lawman History Association Journal* 11 (Winter 2003): 25–26.

18. Robert F. Palmquist, "He Was about Half Way Right: *Territory v. Blount*, 1881," *Journal of Arizona History* 40 (Winter 1999): 377–390; Peter Brand, "Wyatt Earp, Jack Johnson, and the Notorious Blount Brothers," *Quarterly of the National Association for Outlaw and Lawman History* 27 (October–December 2003): 36–47; Jay, "Lake County Independent Club," 28; and *Valdosta (Georgia) Daily Times*, February 11, 1888.

19. Jay, "Lake County Independent Club," 28. Jay has shared his research generously with Roberts and they both think it highly unlikely that Leadville's Neill was Hoodoo Brown.

20. *Leadville Daily Herald*, April 23, 1882.

21. Ibid.; see also Jay, "Lake County Independent Club," 28.

22. *Denver Daily Tribune*, June 3, 1882.

23. Holliday's association with the Earps in Arizona made him a Republican in the public mind at least, and his association with Republican interests in Colorado make this transformation clear.

24. Jay, "Lake County Independent Club," 27–28.

25. Ibid.

26. *Leadville Daily Herald*, October 21, 1882.

27. Griswold and Griswold, *History of Leadville*, 1:1056–1064.

28. *Pueblo Chieftain*, November 22, 26, 1882; G. D. No. 1851, *The People v. J. H. Holliday*, Larceny, November 25, 1882, Pueblo County District Court Records, Pueblo, Colorado, vol. 6, p. 38.

29. *Leadville (Colorado) Evening Chronicle*, December 6, 1882.

30. *Leadville Daily Herald*, December 23, 1882, reported that "G. H. Holliday" was fined $32 for drunkenness and carrying a concealed weapon. This was apparently Doc. Griswold and Griswold, *History of Leadville*, 1:1082.

31. *Leadville Evening Chronicle*, January 15, 1883.

32. G. D. No. 1851, *The People v. J. H. Holliday*, April 27, 1883, vol. 6, p. 141. Every indication is that this case was disposed of exactly as intended by its architects. Enough time was allowed to pass for it to slip from public consciousness.

33. *Denver Rocky Mountain News*, October 23, 1898; John Myers Myers, *Doc Holliday* (Boston: Little, Brown, 1955), 241.

34. *Dodge City (Kansas) Ford County Globe*, May 1, 1883; *Dodge City (Kansas) Times*, May 3, 1883. Nyle H. Miller and Joseph W. Snell, *Why the West Was Wild: A Contemporary Look at the Antics of Some Highly Publicized Kansas Cowtown Personalities* (Topeka: Kansas State Historical Society, 1963), 519–565, is the starting place for any study of what became known as the "Dodge City War." It presents the most critical documents relating to what happened. Robert K. DeArment, *Bat Masterson: The Man and the Legend* (Norman: University of Oklahoma, 1979), 252–266, is a useful secondary account. Casey Tefertiller, *Wyatt Earp: The Man behind the Myth* (New York: Wiley, 1997), 267–274, is also helpful. Roberts has also profited from discussions with William B. Shillingberg, a longtime student of Wyatt Earp's life, to understand the politically charged environment of Dodge City at the time.

35. These maneuverings are detailed from the contemporary press in Miller and Snell, *Why the West Was Wild*, 524–538.

36. *Silverton (Colorado) Democrat*, May 19, 1883; *La Plata (Colorado) Miner*, May 26, June 23, 1883; Mark Dworkin to Gary L. Roberts, July 29, August 3, 2005.

37. *Kansas City (Missouri) Journal*, May 15, 1883.

38. *Kansas City (Missouri) Evening Star*, May 15, 1883.

39. *Kansas City Evening Star*, May 16, 1883.

40. *San Francisco Examiner*, August 16, 1896.

41. *Topeka (Kansas) Daily Commonwealth*, June 2, 1883.

42. *Ford County Globe*, June 5, 1883. The *Globe* claimed that Mike Sutton "started for his cyclone building on Gospel Ridge, where he remained until a truce was arranged."

43. Ibid.

44. *Kansas City Evening Star*, June 7, 1883.

45. Miller and Snell, *Why the West Was Wild*, 561–563, provides the sources that complete the story.

46. William B. Shillingberg, "The John D. Gilchriese Collection: An Introduction," in *Wyatt Earp, Tombstone, and the West*, part 1 (San Francisco: John's Western Gallery, 2004), 9. Jack Burrows, who was present during the interview with Alice Earp Wells, related the same story to Gary L. Roberts, June 2, 2002. Burrows said that Alice was "infatuated with Doc" and described him as very affable and interested in her, in contrast to Wyatt, who was "very cold" and did not speak to her.

47. *Garden City (Kansas) Irrigator*, June 10, 1883. This was the same day that Wyatt and Bat left Dodge.

48. Reprinted in *Ford County Globe*, August 28, 1883.

49. *Leadville (Colorado) Carbonate Chronicle*, July 7, 1883.

50. From the *Leadville Evening Chronicle*, as reprinted in Griswold and Griswold, *History of Leadville*, 1:1216.

51. *Leadville Evening Chronicle*, September 10, 1883.

52. *Leadville Evening Chronicle*, September 11, 1881. Griswold and Griswold, *History of Leadville*, 1:1245–1246, provide further detail.

53. Griswold and Griswold, *History of Leadville*, 1:1246.

54. The incident at Hyman's occurred in October, but it was reported in the *Leadville Evening Chronicle*, December 8, 1883, at the time of trial. The Garvin-Gallagher incident was reported in the *Leadville Evening Chronicle*, October 23, 25, 1883.

55. Mattie entered the order October 1, 1883, took the habit February 4, 1884, and took first vows February 2, 1886. In 1886, she transferred from St. Vincent's Convent in Savannah to a teaching position at Immaculate Conception Convent in Atlanta. This information comes from an old ledger provided by Sister Jude Walsh, the archivist for St. Vincent's, and given to Roberts by Teresa Green, Eastover, South Carolina, March 26, April 23, 2003, and from records provided by Sister Mary Felicitus Powers, Sisters of Mercy Provincialate, Baltimore, Maryland, to Susan McKey Thomas, May 12, 1972. Also useful are Rita H. DeLorme, "Gunfighter 'Doc' Holliday, Sister M. Melanie Holliday, RSM: More Than a Pretty Love Story," *The Southern Cross* 79 (December 9, 1999): 3.

56. *Phoenix Weekly Herald*, November 15, 1883.

57. Rothman, *Shadow of Death*, 16; Tanner, *Family Portrait*, 205–206; Rene J. Dubos, *The White Plague: Tuberculosis, Man, and Society* (New Brunswick, NJ: Rutgers University Press, 1987), 63, says, "Accounts of the medical treatment of phthisis during the nineteenth century reveal that opiates were then used almost universally to quiet cough and diarrhea, and to ease mental anguish."

58. *Leadville Daily Herald*, January 18, 1884.

59. *Leadville Daily Herald*, December 27, 1883; see also Jay, "Lake County Independent Club," 26.

60. *Leadville Daily Herald*, August 26, 1884.

61. *Tucson Daily Citizen*, April 4, 1885. Notably, the paper mentioned that "Tyler was a Pacific and Holliday an easterner. There was an indistinguishable rivalry and animosity existing between the factions."

62. *Leadville (Colorado) Daily Democrat*, July 22, 1884.

63. *Leadville Daily Democrat*, August 20, 1884.

64. *Leadville Carbonate Chronicle*, July 24, 1884.

65. *Leadville Evening Chronicle*, August 20, 1884; *Leadville Carbonate Chronicle*, April 4, 1885.

66. *Leadville Evening Chronicle*, August 20, 1884.

67. The author is especially grateful to Robin Andrews, who is researching Tombstone's William Allen, and to Regina Andrus, who is researching Leadville's William Allen, for critical information that makes it clear that they were not the same man.

68. *Leadville Evening Chronicle*, August 20, 1884.

69. *Leadville Daily Herald*, August 26, 1884.

70. *Leadville Daily Democrat*, August 9, 1884.

71. *Leadville Evening Chronicle*, August 26, 1884.

72. Testimony of William Allen, Patrick Sweeney, and Frank Lomeister, *Leadville Daily Herald*, August 26, 1884.

73. Testimony of Ed Doude, Patrick Lorden, and James Ryan, ibid., August 26, 1884.

74. Testimony of Charles Robinson and J. H. Holliday, ibid., August 26, 1884.

75. Testimony of Lomeister, Sweeney, H. S. Faucett, Edmund Bradbury, and Holliday, ibid., August 26, 1884.

76. *Denver Daily Rocky Mountain News*, October 23, 1898.

77. Testimony of Holliday, *Leadville Daily Herald*, August 26, 1884.

78. Testimony of Patrick Lorden, ibid., August 26, 1884.

79. Testimony of Bradbury and Kellerman, ibid., August 26, 1884.

80. Testimony of Dr. F. F. D'Avignon, ibid., August 26, 1884.

81. *Leadville Daily Democrat*, August 20, 1884.

82. *Leadville Evening Chronicle*, August 20, 1884.

83. Ibid.

84. *Leadville Daily Democrat*, August 23, 1884.

85. Ibid.

86. *Leadville Daily Democrat*, August 21, 22, 1884.

87. *Leadville Daily Democrat*, August 22, 1884.

88. *Leadville Daily Democrat*, August 24, 1884; *Leadville Daily Herald*, August 26, 1884.

89. Testimony of Henry Kellerman, Sweeney, William Reynolds, Charles Robinson, Ryan, and Lorden, *Leadville Daily Herald*, August 26, 1884.

90. Testimony of Lomeister, ibid., August 26, 1884.

91. Testimony of Kellerman, ibid., August 26, 1884.

92. Testimony of Lomeister, ibid., August 26, 1884.

93. Testimony of Reynolds, ibid., August 26, 1884.

94. Testimony of Robinson, ibid., August 26, 1884.

95. Testimony of Ryan and Lorden, ibid., August 26, 1884.

96. Testimony of Mannie Hyman, ibid., August 26, 1884.

97. Testimony of J. H. Holliday, ibid., August 26, 1884.

98. Testimony of Cy Allen, ibid., August 26, 1884.

99. Ibid., August 26, 1884. In this account of the fight, Roberts used materials other than the testimony from the preliminary hearing cited, including newspaper accounts and testimony from the trial in March 1885, as described in Griswold and Griswold, *History of Leadville*, 2:1608–1611.

100. *Leadville Daily Democrat*, August 26, 1884.

101. *Leadville Evening Chronicle*, August 26, 1884; *Leadville Daily Herald*, August 27, 1884. The *Leadville Daily Democrat*, August 30, 1884, reported: "Two sureties have qualified on Doc Holliday's bond, and several more will be necessary before the court will approve it. These his friends have been unable thus far to procure, and the chances of his being released become a trifle more gloomy every day."

102. *Leadville Daily Democrat*, September 3, 1884.

103. Case No. 258, *The People of the State of Colorado v. John Holliday, alias Doc Holliday*, Records of the Criminal Court, Lake County, Colorado.

104. *Leadville Daily Democrat*, September 7, 1884.

105. *Leadville Daily Democrat*, September 9, 1884.

106. *Leadville Daily Democrat*, September 2, 3, 11, 1884.

107. *Yuma Arizona Sentinel*, September 13, 1884. The item was also picked up by other Arizona papers.

108. *Leadville Evening Chronicle*, October 27, 1884.

109. *Leadville Evening Chronicle*, October 28, 1884.

110. *Leadville Carbonate Chronicle*, March 22, 1885.

111. *Leadville Evening Chronicle*, December 19, 1884; *Leadville Daily Democrat*, December 16, 23, 1884.

112. *Leadville Daily Democrat*, December 20, 1884.

113. *Leadville Evening Chronicle*, February 28, 1885.

114. Griswold and Griswold, *History of Leadville*, 2:1587.

115. *Denver Daily Tribune-Republican*, March 28, 1885.

116. For the trial, Roberts relied chiefly on the *Leadville Carbonate Chronicle*, as presented in Griswold and Griswold, *History of Leadville*, 2:1608–1611, but the authors note, "Because of the tremendous amount of repetitious material published in the weekly *Carbonate Chronicle*, some deletions have been made in the account of the trial quoted." For this reason, and this reason alone, citations of testimony will be given from Griswold and Griswold rather than the newspaper itself.

117. Griswold and Griswold, *History of Leadville*, 2:1609–1610.

118. Ibid., 2:1610.

119. Ibid., 2:1610.

120. Ibid., 2:1611. Unfortunately, the *Leadville Carbonate Chronicle* summarized his testimony very briefly in contrast to a more detailed review of the testimony of most other witnesses.

121. Copies of the instructions to the jury as presented by the judge are found in Case No. 258, *Colorado v. Holliday*, Records of the Criminal Court.

122. Griswold and Griswold, *History of Leadville*, 2:1611.

123. Ibid., 2:1611. The defense's case rested on the principle that if Holliday believed that he had been threatened, he was justified in shooting Allen. The jury bought the argument.

124. *New Orleans Daily Picayune*, April 16, 1885, and *Valdosta Daily Times*, April 18, 1885, confirm Henry Holliday's attendance at the reunion of Mexican War veterans. Zan Griffith told Charles R. Dasher, an old-time Valdosta newspaperman, that he had gone with Major Holliday to take care of him and that he was present at the reunion of father and son. See Albert Pendleton Jr. and Susan McKey Thomas, "Doc Holliday's Georgia Background," *Journal of Arizona History* 14 (Autumn 1973): 202– 203. Even Pendleton and Thomas describe the story of a reunion as gossip. Susan McKey Thomas to Gary L. Roberts, August 24, 1994, relates the story of Kathryn H. Gardner, regarding Griffith's visits with Doc in the West as a young man of seventeen or eighteen. Griffith's obituary, *Valdosta Daily Times*, December 21, 1943, states, "As a young man he spent some time in Texas and Arizona. While there he was associated more or less intimately with the late 'Doc' Holliday." Griffith was living at the Valdes Hotel at the time, but he lost all of his belongings, including his correspondence with Doc and a saddle Doc had given him on one of his trips west, when the hotel burned in the 1920s. He left no record of his Western adventures. Albert S. Pendleton Jr. and Susan McKey Thomas, *In Search of the Hollidays: The Story of Doc Holliday and His Holliday and McKey Families* (Valdosta, GA: Little River, 1973), 34.

In my own conversation with Joe Davis, another Valdosta reporter, in 1961, he mentioned an elderly gentleman who had gone West as a boy and spent some time with Doc. He said that the man had shown him things that Doc had given Doc. J. P. Johnson of High Point, North Carolina, also recalled Griffith and his stories about Doc. Johnson to Albert S. Pendleton Jr., July 8, 1998. It is plausible that Griffith might have traveled with Major Holliday to New Orleans and possible, at least, that they could have met Doc there. Several facts argue against Doc being there, however. First, Doc was not flush with money at the time. Second, his health was deteriorating rapidly. Finally, as the Wyatt Earp biographer Casey Tefertiller argues, and Doc himself appeared to confirm at the time of the Allen shooting, because of the warrant issued for him in Arizona, he was afraid to leave Colorado for fear of another extradition attempt. The story is intriguing, but for now, Pendleton and Thomas, *In Search of the Hollidays*, 30, state the situation well: "A meeting might well have been arranged; but, of course, there is no known proof that such a meeting ever did take place."

125. Gene Carlisle, *Why Doc Holliday Left Georgia* (Macon, GA: Carl Isle, 2004), 150–154, takes the combination of events in New Orleans and the registration of one A. J. Holliday at the Hotel Royal on April 2, 1885, and makes a highly speculative argument that Doc was in New Orleans.

126. *Aspen (Colorado) Daily Times*, June 12, 1885.

127. Griswold and Griswold, *History of Leadville*, 2:1611.

128. Jay, "Holliday's Last Stand," 45, summarizes most of the known data.

129. *Leadville Herald-Democrat*, April 4, 1876; Griswold and Griswold, *History of Leadville*, 2:2223.

130. Clipping from a Cripple Creek, Colorado, newspaper, circa 1897, from a notebook in the possession of Regina Andrus, the great-granddaughter of Billy Allen.

131. Regina Andrus to Gary L. Roberts, August 15, 2001. City records indicate that while in Nome, Allen, who was acting as a deputy U.S. marshal, arrested Wyatt Earp on July 6, 1900. The case, *U.S. v. W. S. Erp* [*sic*], apparently concerned operating a saloon without a liquor license. Earp paid a fine of $50 and costs of $13.50 on July 7, 1900. He and his partner, Charles Hoxie, applied for and were granted the license later in the month. Copies of Nome City Records provided to Roberts by Tatyana Stepanova, Alaska State Archives, Juneau, Alaska, August 24, 2001.

132. Eugene Parsons to Stuart N. Lake, June 30, 1930, Stuart N. Lake Collection, Box 10, Huntington Library, San Marino, California; Tanner, *Family Portrait*, 213–214.

133. Lynn R. Bailey and Don Chaput, *Cochise County Stalwarts: A Who's Who of the Territorial Years* (Tucson, AZ: Westernlore, 2000), 1:206–210. Lynn R. Bailey, *The Valiants: The Tombstone Rangers and Apache War Frivolities* (Tucson, AZ: Westernlore, 1999), covers Joyce's life in more detail.

134. *San Francisco Examiner*, November 30, December 1, 1899.

135. *Aspen Daily Times*, May 5, 1885. Earp and his "wife," Josephine Sarah Marcus, arrived in Aspen from Texas and joined H. C. Hughes, who moved down from Montana, to open the Fashion Saloon. Earp had seen Dan G. Tipton in El Paso, where they had witnessed the gunfight at the Gem Saloon in which William Rayner had been killed. See Gary L. Roberts, "The Gem Saloon Shootout," *Wild West* (June 1992): 22–28. Reports that Holliday was also there are unfounded. Earp remained in Aspen through the summer and fall. He must have chuckled when he read in the local paper about Doc collecting a debt from Curly Mack at Leadville. He and Hughes apparently had a good operation; they hosted a dance there in August as reported in the *Aspen Daily Times*, August 12, 1885. It was from Aspen that Earp wrote to Arizona about his financial dealings with Marshal Dake in 1882, during the time that Leigh Chalmers, the Department of Justice's special investigator, was reviewing the financial affairs of former U.S. Marshal Crawley P. Dake. See Leigh Chalmers, Special Examiner, to A. H. Garland, U.S. Attorney General, September 8, 1885, Year File 2725-1885, Department of Justice, Record Group 60, National Archives and Records Service, Washington, DC. The *Aspen Daily Times*, September 19, 1885, reported that Curtis C. Bean, Arizona's first Republican delegate to the U.S. Congress in a decade, "spent Sunday in Aspen, on important business with Ex-Deputy U.S. Marshal Wyatt Earp."

On October 14, 1885, the *Times* reported that Earp assisted Arizona deputy U.S. Marshal E. M. Miles in the arrest of James Crothers, who was one of two men who had robbed a stage near Phoenix, Arizona, and stole money from the Wells, Fargo & Company box. Earp's connections in Arizona appear to have still been strong. Then on November 30, 1885, the *Times* reported that Earp and Hughes had left Aspen. So far, no evidence has come to light to show that Holliday visited Earp in Aspen while he was there.

136. Josephine Sarah Marcus Earp, Mabel Earp Cason, and Vinnolia Earp Ackerman, "She Married Wyatt Earp: The Recollections of Josephine Earp" unpublished manuscript, circa 1938, C. Lee Simmons Collection, Sonoita, Arizona.

137. Ibid.; *Denver Republican*, May 22, 1882.

138. Tanner, *Family Portrait*, 299n.

139. *Denver Tribune-Republican*, May 13, 1886; Jahns, *Frontier World*, 278– 279.

140. The Silverton article was widely published, appearing in the *Denver Daily Times*, June 15, 1886, *Valdosta Daily Times*, June 19, 1886, and *San Francisco Morning Call*, June 20, 1886, among others. Oddly, on May 26, 1886, the *Dallas Morning News* reported that a man named John Holliday, "who lives a few miles south of this city," was arrested on a "writ of lunacy." On June 2, 1886, the *Morning News* reported that "Dock [*sic*] Holliday was tried a second time on a writ of lunacy today before a jury and was a second time pronounced sane and released." This report is testimony to the reputation that the real Doc Holliday had by the time the Silverton article was published.

141. *Denver Tribune-Republican*, August 4, 1886; Jahns, *Frontier World*, 279.

142. *Denver Tribune-Republican*, August 4, 1886; Tanner, *Family Portrait*, 215–216.

143. *Denver Tribune-Republican*, August 4, 5, 1886.

144. Ibid., August 4, 1886.

145. Tanner, *Family Portrait*, 216.

146. Angela K. Parkison, *Hope and Hot Water, Glenwood Springs from 1878 to 1891* (Glenwood Springs, CO: Glenwood Springs Legacy, 2000), 93.

147. *Gunnison (Colorado) News-Champion*, July 17, 1930.

148. *Glenwood Springs (Colorado) Ute Chief*, November 12, 1887.

149. Parkison, *Hope and Hot Water*, 100–103, 106–109.

150. W. W. Crook to W. T. Moyers, May 23, 1943, Lake Collection, Box 10. Dr. Crook knew Doc in Leadville, and he claimed to have been in the bar at the time Doc shot Billy Allen, although he mistakenly said that Doc had killed Allen. Griswold and Griswold, *History of Leadville*, 1169–1170, 1266, 1372, 1542, 2151, affirm his presence in Leadville. See also Parkison, *Hope and Hot Water*, 111.

151. Eugene Parsons to Stuart N. Lake, July 25, 1930, Lake Collection, Box 10.

152. Parsons to Lake, June 30, 1930, reporting a conversation with a Glenwood Springs old-timer, Lake Collection, Box 10.

153. Rothman, *Shadow of Death*, 16; Parsons to Lake, June 30, 1930, Lake Collection, Box 10. Parsons was interviewing people who claimed to have known or at least seen Holliday in the early days.

154. Parkison, *Hope and Hot Water*, 109–110.

155. *Glenwood Springs (Colorado) Post*, August 23, 1985.

156. Typescript of Recollections of Mary Katharine Cummings as Given to Anton Mazzanovich, 16–17, Kevin J. Mulkins Collection. She made similar claims to Dr. Arthur W. Bork, Notes of Interview with Mary Katharine Cummings, Thanksgiving, 1935, typescript provided to Roberts by Dr. Bork. Tanner, *Family Portrait*, 216, based on information that came from the Harony family through Glenn G. Boyer, says that Kate's brother lived in Colorado at the time. In 2001–2002, further confirmation of her presence was provided with the publication of what appeared to be a reminiscence by Oregin Charles Smith, a friend of the Earps from Tombstone, which claimed that both Smith and Kate were present at Doc's death. This document was published in Karen Holliday Tanner and Clifton Brewer, "Doc Holliday's Last Days," *True West* 48 (November–December 2001): 75–79, and Karen Holliday Tanner, "The Last Days of Doc Holliday," *WOLA Journal* 10 (Winter 2002): 4–9. However, when a series of alleged "Charlie Smith letters" began to be published in the *Tombstone Tumbleweed* that clearly were not contemporary documents, the original source was reexamined with the result that it appeared that Tanner and others, including Roberts, had been misled. For a full discussion of the Charlie Smith story, see Gary L. Roberts, "The Charlie Smith Papers: Real or Fake?" *WOLA Journal* 12 (Spring 2004): 29–48. So far, no contemporary evidence has surfaced that would indicate that Kate or any other person from Holliday's past was with him at the time of his death. To the contrary, the contemporary accounts are emphatic that he died alone except for the charity of local caretakers. Given Victoria journalism's sentimentality, it seems highly unlikely that the press would have failed to mention the presence of a wife or old friend.

157. *Glenwood Springs Ute Chief*, November 12, 1887. Father Downey was responsible for several mining towns. Susan McKey Thomas has done extensive research on both Father Downey and Reverend Rudolph, which she shared with me. Both had long and successful careers in the service of their faiths, but apparently neither left any reflections on John Henry.

158. *Glenwood Springs Ute Chief*, November 12, 1887.

159. *Denver Evening Times*, November 10, 1887.

12. The Anatomy of a Western Legend

1. Lorenzo Walters, *Tombstone's Yesterday* (Tucson, AZ: Acme, 1928), 86–87.

2. This bombast, originally printed in the *Cincinnati (Ohio) Enquirer*, was called "the funniest part of the story" of Perry Mallon's arrest of Doc Holliday by the *Denver Republican*, June 2, 1882, a story that "round[s] off the hideous tale with a burst of laughter and turns what was nearly a tragedy into a roaring farce."

3. *New York Sun*, June 3, 1886. This article was widely reprinted as previously noted.

4. Such articles are not "reliable" in the sense of providing historical data, but they are important because they show the perception of contemporaries and the workings of the popular mind. Richard Slotkin, *The Fatal Environment: The Myth of the Frontier in the Age of Industrialization, 1800–1890* (New York: Atheneum, 1985), is essential for understanding effects of the frontier myth not only on the public mind but also on the actions of people. Slotkin's *Gunfighter Nation: The Myth of the Frontier in Twentieth-Century America* (New York: Atheneum, 1998), explores the continuing infatuation with the theme.

5. Richard White, "Outlaw Gangs of the Middle Border: American Social Bandits," *Western Historical Quarterly* 12 (1981): 387–408, while not specifically directed at Doc Holliday or other icons of the "gunfighter West," does offer keen insight into the "decisive allure" that nineteenth-century Americans (and their descendants for that matter) found "in strong men who defended themselves, righted their own wrongs, and took vengeance on their enemies despite the corruption of the existing order." Beyond White, an extensive literature exists that reinforces the points he makes and helps to explain the continuing popularity of frontier legends like Doc Holliday, Wyatt Earp, Billy the Kid, Wild Bill Hickok, and more, whether formatted as "hero worship," debunking, or "setting the record straight."

6. *Denver Republican*, November 10, 1887.

7. *Glenwood Springs (Colorado) Ute Chief*, November 12, 1887.

8. *Valdosta (Georgia) Daily Times*, January 28, 1888.

9. *Denver Field and Farm*, November 12, 1887.

10. Kent L. Steckmesser, *The Western Hero in History and Legend* (Norman: University of Oklahoma Press, 1965), 157–159, explores the multiplicity of images afforded to specific frontier "heroes" over time and summarizes the origin and growth of legends at 241–252. Ramon F. Adams, *A Fitting Death for Billy the Kid* (Norman: University of Oklahoma Press, 1960), is still an essential work for understanding the mythmaking process.

11. *Denver Republican*, December 25, 1887.

12. Ibid.

13. Ibid.

14. *Macon (Georgia) Telegraph*, reprinted in the *Valdosta Daily Times*, February 11, 1888.

15. Ibid.

16. *San Francisco Examiner*, August 16, 1896.

17. *Kansas City (Missouri) Journal*, reprinted in the *Phoenix Arizona Republican*, January 21, 1899. This is not the only place in the press in which Doc was described the arbiter of saloon fights, especially during the Dodge City War.

18. Ibid. Note the reference to Doc firing the first shot and how time had changed "daisy" to "dandy."

19. *Valdosta Daily Times*, December 31, 1898. Here is yet another example of the image of the "good bad man" that was so popular at the turn of the twentieth century. E. D. Cowen, Doc's friend from Denver and Leadville, in an article in the *Denver Rocky Mountain News* on October 23, 1898, about the "Happy Bad Men of the West," a detailed exposition of the theme, made sure to note, "The genesis of the bad man of the happy killing habit is not easily traced, and by this I don't mean the border ruffian or drunk-crazed

cowboy who killed for the same reason that certain human beings with symmetrical crani-ums commit burglary and other crimes." Rather, he wrote, "This unique character of American daring and the acutest sense of fair play, full of sentiments easily touched, but rarely spoken, incapable of abandoning a friend who had the law against him, and the bravest to execute the law when common sense dictated the justice of the decree.... Unerringly he was a home ruler, a local government man, with no fondness for far-away lawmakers, no confidence in their rectitude or wisdom, and a believer in the general cussedness of all human nature not embodied in his particular friends and relatives." The "type" he illustrated not only with Doc Holliday but with Wyatt Earp, Bat Masterson, and Billy Thompson as well.

20. *Washington Post*, February 16, 1906.

21. William Barclay Masterson, "Famous Gunfighters of the Western Frontier: Doc Holliday," *Human Life* (May 1907): 5–6.

22. Alfred Henry Lewis, *The Sunset Trail* (New York: Barnes, 1905), 339–358. Actu-ally, Lewis had a way of recycling stories. Apparently, this story appeared first in *Everybody's Magazine* in about 1904, before the publication of *Sunset Trail*. This seems to be confirmed by an article in the *Arizona Republican*, July 3, 1904. The *Valdosta Daily Times*, January 4, 1908, attributed the story to a recent issue of *Metropolitan Magazine*. What is most interest-ing, though, is the agreeable relationship that Lewis depicted between Holliday and Mas-terson, an image much at odds with the *Human Life* portrait, but believable based on Lewis's friendship with Masterson, the association of Masterson and Holliday at Dodge, and Masterson's role in blocking the extradition of Doc from Colorado in 1882.

23. Lewis, *Sunset Trail*, 356.

24. *Valdosta Daily Times*, January 4, 1908.

25. *Phoenix Arizona Republican*, June 26, 1892. Actually, the reference to Holliday being a participant in the robbery is not directly from Paul, and, in light of Paul's state-ments in Denver in 1882, something more is needed to confirm that Paul believed Holliday was involved. Fred Dodge to Stuart N. Lake, September 18, 1930, Carolyn Lake, ed., *Under Cover for Wells Fargo: The Unvarnished Recollections of Fred Dodge* (Boston: Houghton Mifflin, 1969), 246; and John P. Clum to George H. Kelly, August 23, 1929, reprinted in full in Ellis T. "Butch" Badon, "An Unexpected Nugget," *NOLA Quarterly* 25 (October–December 2001): 21–22.

26. *San Francisco Daily Call*, December 15, 1896. Casey Tefertiller, *Wyatt Earp: The Life behind the Legend* (New York: Wiley, 1997), 297, presents evidence that Hopkins had been in Tombstone and had been arrested in June 1881 for being drunk and disorderly by one of Virgil Earp's deputies.

27. Will H. Robinson, *The Story of Arizona* (Phoenix, AZ: Berryhill, 1919), William MacLeod Raine, *Famous Sheriffs and Western Outlaws* (New York: Doubleday, Doran, 1929); William M. Breakenridge, *Helldorado: Bringing the Law to the Mesquite* (Boston: Houghton Mifflin, 1928).

28. Casey Tefertiller, "Resolving Earp Myths," *NOLA Quarterly* 21 (October–December 1997): 3, is the first to point out Breakenridge's tampering with the *Nugget* account.

29. Forestine C. Hooker, "Arizona Vendetta (The Truth about Wyatt Earp—and Some Others)," unpublished manuscript, circa 1920, Southwest Museum, Los Angeles, California.

30. John H. Flood Jr., "Wyatt Earp: A Peace-officer of Tombstone," 62 (unpub-lished manuscript, 1927), C. Lee Simmons Collection.

31. Testimony of Wyatt Earp, Lotta Crabtree Probate Trial, pp. 315–316, William M. Breakenridge Collection, Harvard Law School Library, Harvard University, Cam-bridge, Massachusetts.

32. Ibid., 320.

33. Wyatt Earp to Walter Noble Burns, March 15, 1927, Walter Noble Burns Collection, Special Collections, University of Arizona Library, Tucson, Arizona.

34. See especially Earp to Burns, May 24, 1924, and Earp to Doubleday, Page & Company, May 24, 1927, Burns Collection.

35. Walter Noble Burns, *Tombstone: An Iliad of the Southwest* (New York: Doubleday, 1929), 52, 259.

36. Stuart N. Lake, *Wyatt Earp: Frontier Marshal* (Boston: Houghton Mifflin, 1931), 192–198.

37. Fred Dodge to Stuart N. Lake, September 18, 1930, Carolyn Lake, ed., *Under Cover for Wells Fargo: The Unvarnished Recollections of Fred Dodge* (Boston: Houghton Mifflin, 1969), 246, and John P. Clum to George H. Kelly, August 23, 1929, reprinted in full in Ellis T. "Butch" Badon, "An Unexpected Nugget," *NOLA Quarterly* 25 (October–December 2001): 21–22.

38. Lake, *Frontier Marshal*, 196. For Lake's account of Doc's death, derivative of Burns, see pp. 356–357.

39. The best sources for the reaction of Arizona pioneers who disapproved of Lake's portrayal of Wyatt Earp are the files of the Arizona Historical Society at Tucson. Here, both manuscript commentaries and Arizona newspaper clippings are filed for J. C. Hancock, Melvin Jones, and others. See also Adams, *Fitting Death*, 102–140, for an interesting analysis of "The Old-Timer [Who] Thinks He Remembers."

40. Anton Mazzanovich's series of articles on *Wyatt Earp: Frontier Marshal* ran in the *Bisbee (Arizona) Brewery Gulch Gazette*, November 13, 1931, February 19, March 11, April 15, 29, 1932. The quotes are from the November 13, 1931, article.

41. *Brewery Gulch Gazette*, April 22, June 3, 1932. Kate worked at the Cochise Hotel in Cochise, Arizona, as well as at Globe, so Mazzanovich could have crossed her path at either of those places.

42. Joe Chisholm, "Tombstone's Tale (The Truth of Helldorado)," 15½, unpublished manuscript, circa 1938, Jack Burrows Collection. He wrote, "Just before Tony Mazzanovich's death Doc Holliday's widow wrote the ex-cavalryman concerning the state of affairs in Tombstone in those days, and since then I have visited her and had her verify the data contained in her correspondence with Tony." Joe Chisholm, *Brewery Gulch: Frontier Days of Old Arizona—Last Outpost of the Great Southwest* (San Antonio, TX: Naylor, 1949), 123, 128–129. Eugene Cunningham, *Triggernometry: A Gallery of Gunfighters* (Caldwell, ID: Caxton Printers, 1941), 113, said of Kate, "She was a notorious character and the story I have heard, accounting for Holliday's infatuation for her, does not bear printing." Harry Sinclair Drago, *Wild, Woolly, and Wicked: The History of the Kansas Cow Towns and the Texas Cattle Trade* (New York: Potter, 1960), was also unkind: "She was coarse and crude and had a temper to shame a fishwife. Sisters of her scarlet profession accused her of indulging in sexual practices on which they frowned. It certainly couldn't have been her looks that made Doc provide her with bed and board for years." The sources for these accusations are far from clear.

43. Arthur W. Bork and Glenn G. Boyer, "The O.K. Corral Fight at Tombstone: A Footnote by Kate Elder," *Arizona and the West* (Spring 1977): 69–74.

44. Bork and Boyer, "O.K. Corral Fight," 70.

45. Dr. Arthur W. Bork, Notes of Interview with Mary Katharine Cummings, Thanksgiving, 1935, typescript provided to Gary L. Roberts by Dr. Bork.

46. Bork and Boyer, "O.K. Corral Fight," 65–84.

47. No reference to a connection to Maximilian appears in Bork and Boyer, "O.K. Corral Fight," or in Boyer's "On the Trail of Big Nosed Kate," *Real West* 24 (March 1981): 14–20, 50, but in his "Frontier 'Lost Person' Found," *True West* 39 (November 1992): 21,

the Maximilian story emerged. The story was picked up by several other writers, including Ben T. Traywick, *John Henry (The Doc Holliday Story)* (Tombstone, AZ: Red Marie's Bookstore, 1996), 54, despite the fact that the documentary record shows the Harony family in Iowa well before Maximilian went to Mexico. Patrick A. Bowmaster, "A Fresh Look at 'Big Nose Kate,'" *NOLA Quarterly* 22 (July–September 1998): 12–24, exposes the fallacy of this tale.

48. Several respected researchers in the field doubt that Mary Katharine Cummings was Kate Elder, and her reminiscences do contain puzzling errors. Once again, as in numerous other instances of old-timer reminiscences, researchers are faced with the question of authenticity and accuracy. In Kate's case, even some of her inaccurate statements oddly support the authenticity of her recollections.

49. Typescript of Recollections of Mary Katharine Cummings as Given to Anton Mazzanovich, inserted between pages 15 and 16, Kevin J. Mulkins Collection.

50. Ibid., 16–17; Bork Thanksgiving notes; Bork and Boyer, "O.K. Corral Fight," 81.

51. Bork and Boyer, "O.K. Corral Fight," 69.

52. This story appears to have been published first in *Guns Magazine* sometime in 1952. See John Myers Myers, *Doc Holliday* (Boston: Little, Brown, 1955), 253–254, who described the tale as "a legend which arouses admiration through its sheer and indelicate ingenuity."

53. Aunt Mary [Katharine Cummings] to My Dear Niece Lillie [Raffert], March 18, 1940, acquired from the family by Glenn G. Boyer (photocopy of original in Roberts's files) was published in Bob Boze Bell, *The Illustrated Life and Times of Doc Holliday* (Phoenix, AZ: Tri-Star-Boze, 1994), 107–110.

54. Frank Waters, "Tombstone Travesty (Original version)," 1934, Frank Waters Papers, Center for Southwest Research, University of New Mexico Library, Albuquerque, New Mexico, was deposited at the Arizona Historical Society largely because of Allie Earp's displeasure with it. Eventually, Waters retrieved it from the society, after a major rewrite that was published as Frank Waters, *The Earp Brothers of Tombstone: The Story of Mrs. Virgil Earp* (New York: Potter, 1960). In 1998, Jeffrey Wheat, an Earp researcher, found the manuscript in the Waters Papers at the University of New Mexico Library, which led to a comprehensive comparison of the manuscript with the book. A detailed examination of the "Tombstone Travesty vs. *The Earp Brothers of Tombstone*," which included Jeffrey Wheat, "The Waters Travesty," Casey Tefertiller, "What Was Not in Tombstone Travesty," and two articles by Gary L. Roberts, "Allie's Story: Mrs. Virgil Earp and the 'Tombstone Travesty'" and "The Real Tombstone Travesty: The Earp Controversy from Bechdolt to Boyer," appeared in *WOLA Journal* 8 (Fall 1999): 9–47, along with additional remarks by the editor Chuck Hornung. These articles document thoroughly how Waters integrated Kate's recollections into Allie's story when he wrote *The Earp Brothers of Tombstone*.

55. Myers, *Doc Holliday*.

56. Patricia Jahns, *The Frontier World of Doc Holliday* (New York: Hastings House, 1957). Especially interesting are letters from Myers and Jahns to Lillian McKey, the first cousin of Doc Holliday of Valdosta, Georgia, which today are in the possession of Susan McKey Thomas. "Miss Lillian" was very protective of the family name, but unfortunately she wrote her letters in longhand so that there are no copies of her letters to them. Susan McKey Thomas also corresponded with Pat Jahns, who recalled her exchange with Lillian McKey.

57. Ed Bartholomew, *Wyatt Earp: The Man and the Myth* (Toyahvale, TX: Frontier, 1964), 16.

58. John Abbott, "Robert Holliday: Restoring a Proud Family Name," *Holliday House Gazette* 3 (Winter 1998): 6.

59. *Atlanta Journal-Constitution*, July 3, 1994; Victoria Wilcox to Gary L. Roberts, January 29, 1999. Rita H. DeLorme, "Gunfighter 'Doc' Holliday, Sister M. Melanie Holliday, RSM: More Than a Pretty Love Story," *The Southern Cross* 79 (December 9, 1999): 3, says that Sister Melanie destroyed some of the correspondence herself and told "those close to her" that if she had not done so, "later historians might have looked upon him more favorably." Pat Jahns to Lillian McKey, February 17, 1951, wrote, "I should like to read those letters he wrote. They would prove better than anything where he was and what he was doing at the time of their correspondence." After John Myers Myers published his biography of Doc, Lillian McKey wrote him in an undated letter after reading the copy he sent her, disagreeing with his portrayal of John Henry. She concluded by stating, "Anyway, the tragedy is ended and let us hope the unfortunate man is at rest, after all his physical and mental sufferings." That doubtlessly was the feeling of most of the family. From Lillian McKey's correspondence, copies in Gary L. Roberts's files, courtesy Susan McKey Thomas.

60. Abbott, "Restoring a Proud Name," 6.

61. Pat Jahns to Susan McKey Thomas, February 17, 1975, copy in author's files.

62. Morgan De Lancey Magee, "A Lady Never Tells," *Holliday House Gazette* 1 (Fall 1996): 8.

63. Abbott, "Restoring a Proud Name," 6.

64. DeLorme, "More than a Love Story," 3.

65. David O'Connell, *The Irish Roots of Margaret Mitchell's Gone with the Wind* (Decatur, GA: Claves and Petry, 1996), 83–92.

66. *Valdosta Daily Times*, February 25, 1893; Susan McKey Thomas, "Henry Burroughs Holliday: 1819–1893, Lowndes County," unpublished manuscript, Roberts's collection. "Major" was a distinguished citizen of Valdosta for a number of years. He was politically active, having served as mayor for several terms. He also operated a nursery and is generally credited with introducing pecan growing to southern Georgia. For examples of his activities and service, see *Valdosta Daily Times*, January 13, September 15, 29, October 20, 1877, August 24, 1878, September 27, 1879, February 17, 1883, June 14, 1884, February 7, 14, 1885, April 18, 1885, December 27, 1890, January 17, March 7, 1891.

67. *Valdosta Daily Times*, September 27, 1879.

68. Albert S. Pendleton Jr. and Susan McKey Thomas, *In Search of the Hollidays: The Story of Doc Holliday and His Holliday and McKey Families* (Valdosta, GA: Little River, 1973), 55–58; *Atlanta Constitution*, February 24, 1914, October 20, 1921.

69. Victoria Wilcox, "Mischievous Minor: From Lad to Lunger," *True West* 48 (November–December 2001): 22.

70. *Glenwood Springs (Colorado) Sage-Reminder*, August 21, 1970.

71. J. R. Kirkpatrick, "Doc Holliday's Missing Grave," *True West* 37 (October 1990): 46–49. The family had an interest in Doc's grave as early as 1949, when J. F. DeLacy promised Lillian McKey he would try to find out more about Doc's burial site. DeLacy to Robert N. Mullin, January 9, 1949, Robert N. Mullin Collection, Nita Stewart Haley Memorial Library and J. Evetts Haley History Center, Midland, Texas. Pendleton and Thomas, *In Search of the Hollidays*, 52, reproduce a letter from May Knight of the Glenwood Springs Chamber of Commerce to Susan McKey Thomas, June 12, 1973, which consisted largely of an account by Art Kendricks, the employee at the Hotel Glenwood, who had helped Doc in his last days. He claimed to have personally placed a small wooden cross on the grave in the cemetery. See also *Valdosta Daily Times*, December 18, 1976; *Atlanta Journal*, June 22, 1978. Roberts has copies of the correspondence between Thomas and the Colorado authorities.

72. *Glenwood Springs Ute Chief*, November 19, 1887; City Council Minutes, April 25, June 20, November 7, 1887, Glenwood Springs City Council Records, Frontier Historical

Society, Glenwood Springs, Colorado; see also *Glenwood Springs (Colorado) Post-Independent*, April 19, 2005. Cindy Hines, Director of the Frontier Historical Society, in a letter to Gary L. Roberts, April 29, 2005, notes, "It makes no sense that Doc would be buried at the bottom of the hill because the ground was supposedly too frozen, if Hewson was moving bodies to the cemetery at the same time." These documents, combined with the contemporary accounts, would seem to settle the question of where he was buried.

73. Bill Dunn, "The Forgotten Graves," *Yesterday's Memories* (November 2000): 2–5; Jackie Kennedy, "Uncovering the Myth: Doc Holliday and His Griffin, GA, Home," *Georgia Backroads* 2 (Winter 2003): 40–41.

74. Bruce Dettman, "The Holliday Mystique," 1, unpublished manuscript, 2001, copy in Roberts's files, courtesy of Bruce Dettman.

75. Ibid., 1–3. Allen Barra, *Inventing Wyatt Earp: His Life and Many Legends* (New York: Carroll and Graf, 1998), 343–370, is a very good review of films that involve Wyatt Earp. He also recognizes the power of Holliday's presence on film and includes films not mentioned here.

76. Two articles by Shirley Ayn Linder, "When the Dealing's Done: John H. (Doc) Holliday and the Evolution of a Western Myth," *Journal of the West* 37 (April 1998): 53–60, and "Is There a Doctor in the House? The Legend of John H. (Doc) Holliday in the 20th Century," *True West* 48 (November–December 2001): 71, are also helpful.

77. Dettman, "Holiday Mystique," 2. Lawrence Kasdan, who directed *Wyatt Earp* (1994), wrote, "Whoever gets to play Doc in any of these stories gets the choice role. . . . That is the showy role. This is a guy who's dying when you meet him, who has given up all hope and therefore has no sense of responsibility and no worries about the future. He's given it all up and he has a kind of freedom."

78. Dettman, "Holliday Mystique," 3.

Epilogue: The Measure of a Legend

1. Richard White, "Outlaw Gangs of the Middle Border: American Social Bandits," *Western Historical Quarterly* 12 (1981): 403.

2. *Tucson (Arizona) Daily Star,* May 6, 1882.

3. Richard Slotkin, *The Fatal Environment: The Myth of the Frontier in the Age of Industrialization, 1800–1890* (New York: Atheneum, 1985), 284–290.

4. No substantive evidence has come to light that confirms that the relationship was abusive. Kate never accused Doc of physically abusing her.

5. See especially his interviews with the *Denver Republican*, May 22, 1882, the *Gunnison (Colorado) Daily News-Democrat,* June 18, 1882, and the *New York Sun,* June 3, 1886.

6. John P. Clum to George H. Kelly, August 23, 1929, printed in Ellis T. "Butch" Badon, "An Unexpected Nugget," *NOLA Quarterly* 25 (October–December 2001): 23–25.

7. Bruce Olds, *Bucking the Tiger: A Novel* (New York: Farrar, Straus, and Giroux, 2001), 369, notes, "To pursue Doc is to pilot largely in the dark."

8. Alfred Henry Lewis, *The Sunset Trail* (New York: Barnes, 1905), 357–358.

INDEX